Using Samba

Using Samba

SECOND EDITION

Using Samba

Jay Ts, Robert Eckstein,
and David Collier-Brown

Beijing · Cambridge · Farnham · Köln · Paris · Sebastopol · Taipei · Tokyo

Using Samba, Second Edition

by Jay Ts, Robert Eckstein, and David Collier-Brown

Published by O'Reilly & Associates, Inc., 1005 Gravenstein Highway North, Sebastopol, CA 95472.

O'Reilly & Associates books may be purchased for educational, business, or sales promotional use. Online editions are also available for most titles (*safari.oreilly.com*). For more information, contact our corporate/institutional sales department: (800) 998-9938 or *corporate@oreilly.com*.

Editor:	Andy Oram
Production Editor:	Darren Kelly
Cover Designer:	Edie Freedman
Interior Designer:	David Futato

Printing History:

January 2000:	First Edition.
February 2003:	Second Edition.

ISBN: 0-596-00256-4
[M]

[5/03]

Table of Contents

Preface

You are reading a book about Samba, a software suite that networks Windows, Unix, and other operating systems using Windows' native networking protocol. Samba allows Unix servers to offer Windows networking services by matching the filesystem and networking models of Unix to those of Windows. Samba acts as a bridge between the two systems, connecting the corresponding parts of their architectures and providing a translation wherever necessary.

Bridging the gap between systems as dissimilar as Windows and Unix is a complex task, which Samba handles surprisingly well. To be a good Samba administrator, your abilities must parallel Samba's. For starters, you need to know basic Unix system and network administration and have a good understanding of Windows filesystems and networking fundamentals. In addition, you need to learn how Samba fills in the "gray area" between Unix and Windows. Once you know how everything fits together, you'll find it easy to configure a Samba server to provide your network with reliable and high-performance computational resources.

Our job is to make all of that easier for you. We do this by starting out with a quick and yet comprehensive tour of Windows networking in Chapter 1, followed by tutorially-oriented Chapters 2 and 3, which tell you how to set up a minimal Samba server and configure Windows clients to work with it. Most likely, you will be surprised how quickly you can complete the required tasks.

We believe that a hands-on approach is the most effective, and you can use the Samba server you build in Chapters 2 and 3 as a test system for trying out examples that we show and describe throughout the book. You can jump around from chapter to chapter if you like, but if you continue sequentially from Chapter 4 onward, by the time you finish the book you will have a well-configured production Samba server ready for use. All you have to do is add the appropriate support for your intended purpose as we explain how to use each feature.

Audience for This Book

This book is primarily intended for Unix administrators who need to support Windows clients on their network, as well as anyone who needs to access the resources of a Windows network environment from a Unix client. While we assume you are familiar with basic Unix system administration, we do *not* assume you are a networking expert. We do our best along the way to help out with unusual definitions and terms.

Furthermore, we don't assume that you are an expert in Microsoft Windows. We carefully explain all the essential concepts related to Windows networking, and we go through the Windows side of the installation task in considerable detail, providing examples for both Windows 95/98/Me and Windows NT/2000/XP, which are significantly different. For the Unix side, we give examples that work with common Unix operating systems, such as Linux, Solaris, FreeBSD, and Mac OS X.

Organization

Here is a quick description of each chapter:

Chapter 1, *Learning the Samba*, introduces Samba and its capabilities, then describes the most important concepts of NetBIOS and SMB/CIFS networking. Finally, we give you a quick overview of the daemons and utilities that are included in the Samba distribution.

Chapter 2, *Installing Samba on a Unix System*, covers configuring, compiling, installing, setting up, and testing the Samba server on a Unix platform.

Chapter 3, *Configuring Windows Clients*, explains how to configure Microsoft Windows 95/98/Me and Windows NT/2000/XP clients to participate in an SMB network.

Chapter 4, *Windows NT Domains*, explains the ins and outs of Windows NT domains and how to configure Samba to work in a network set up as a Windows NT domain.

Chapter 5, *Unix Clients*, describes methods for accessing SMB shares on the network from Unix client systems.

Chapter 6, *The Samba Configuration File*, gets you up to speed on the structure of the Samba configuration file and shows you how to take control of file-sharing services.

Chapter 7, *Name Resolution and Browsing*, introduces name resolution, which is used to convert NetBIOS computer names into IP addresses, and browsing, the method used in SMB networking to find what resources are being shared on the network.

Chapter 8, *Advanced Disk Shares*, continues the discussion of file-sharing options, and covers more advanced functions such as permissions, access control lists, opportunistic locks, and setting up a Distributed filesystem tree.

Chapter 9, *Users and Security*, discusses how to set up Samba users, introduces you to Samba security, and shows you how to work with encrypted and nonencrypted passwords.

Chapter 10, *Printing*, discusses printer setup for sharing Unix printers on the SMB network, and allowing Unix workstations to access SMB shared printers.

Chapter 11, *Additional Samba Information,* bundles several miscellaneous topics associated with Samba, such as configuring Samba shares for programmers and internationalization issues.

Chapter 12, *Troubleshooting Samba,* details what to do if you have problems installing Samba. This comparatively large chapter is packed with troubleshooting hints and strategies for identifying what is going wrong.

Appendix A, *Example Configuration Files*, provides working examples of *smb.conf* files for use in configuring Samba for its more common applications. You can easily modify the examples for use in a wide variety of circumstances.

Appendix B, *Samba Configuration Option Quick Reference*, covers each option that can be used in the Samba configuration file.

Appendix C, *Summary of Samba Daemons and Commands*, is a quick reference that covers each server daemon and tool that make up the Samba suite.

Appendix D, *Downloading Samba with CVS*, explains how to download the latest development version of the Samba source code using CVS.

Appendix E, *Configure Options*, documents each option that can be used with the *configure* command before compiling the Samba source code.

Appendix F, *Running Samba on Mac OS X Server*, includes directions for sharing files and printers with the Server edition of Mac OS X.

Appendix G, *GNU Free Documentation License*, is the copyright license under which this book is published.

Conventions Used in This Book

The following font conventions are followed throughout this book:

Italic
> Filenames, file extensions, URLs, executable files, command options, and emphasis.

Constant width
> Samba configuration options, computer names, user and group names, hostnames, domain names, other code that appears in the text, and command-line information that should be typed verbatim on the screen.

Constant width bold
> Commands that are entered by the user and new configuration options that we wish to bring to the attention of the reader.

Constant width italic
> Replaceable content in code and command-line information.

 This designates a note, which is an important aside to the nearby text.

 This designates a warning related to the nearby text.

How to Contact Us

We have tested and verified the information in this book to the best of our ability, but you might find that features have changed (or even that we have made mistakes!). Please let us know about any errors you find, as well as your suggestions for future editions, by writing to:

> O'Reilly & Associates, Inc.
> 1005 Gravenstein Highway North
> Sebastopol, CA 95472
> (800) 998-9938 (in the United States or Canada)
> (707) 829-0515 (international/local)
> (707) 829-0104 (fax)

To ask technical questions or comment on the book, send email to:

> *bookquestions@oreilly.com*

We have a web page for this book where we list examples and any plans for future editions. You can access this information at:

> *http://www.oreilly.com/catalog/samba2*

You can also contact Jay Ts, the lead author of this edition, through his web site at:

> *http://www.jayts.com*

Acknowledgments

We thank Leon Towns-von Stauber for thoroughly researching the use of Samba on Mac OS X and writing material that appears in Chapters 2, 5, and 10, as well as the entire Appendix F. We also thank our technical reviewers Sam Johnston, Matthew Temple, Marty Leisner, and Don McCall.

Jay Ts

This book would have been extremely difficult to write if it hadn't been for the copy of VMware Workstation graciously provided by VMware, Inc. I want to thank Rik Farrow for his clarifying comments on security topics related to Samba and Windows, and both him and Rose Moon for their supportive friendship. Thanks also go to Mark Watson for his encouragement and advice on the topic of authoring technical books. Additionally, I'd like to express my appreciation to Andy Oram at O'Reilly for being a supportive, friendly, and easygoing editor, and for offering me terms that I could say yes to—something that a few other publishers didn't even approach. SuSE, Inc. generously provided a copy of SuSE Linux 8.1 Professional.

Robert Eckstein

I'd first like to recognize Dave Collier-Brown and Peter Kelly for all their help in the creation of this book. I'd also like to thank each technical reviewer who helped polish this book into shape on such short notice: Matthew Temple, Jeremy Allison, and of course Andrew Tridgell. Andrew and Jeremy deserve special recognition, not only for creating such a wonderful product, but also for providing a tireless amount of support in the final phase of this book—hats off to you, guys! A warm hug goes out to my wife Michelle, who once again put up with a husband loaded down with too much caffeine and a tight schedule. Thanks to Dave Sifry and the people at Linux-Care, San Francisco, for hosting me on such short notice for Andrew Tridgell's visit. And finally, a huge amount of thanks to our editor, Andy Oram, who (very) patiently helped guide this book through its many stages until we got it right.

David Collier-Brown

I'd particularly like to thank Joyce, who put up with me during the sometimes exciting development of the book. My thanks to Andy Oram, who was kind enough to provide the criticism that allowed me to contribute; the crew at ACE (Opcom) who humored the obvious madman in their midst; and Ian MacMillan, who voluntarily translated several of my early drafts from nerd to English. I would also like to give special thanks to Perry Donham, Drew Sullivan, and Jerry DeRoo for starting and sustaining this mad project. Finally, I'd like to thank Bob Eckstein for a final, sustained, and professional effort that lifted the whole book up to the level that Andy needed.

All

We would especially like to give thanks to Perry Donham and Peter Kelly for helping mold the first draft of this book. Although Perry was unable to contribute to subsequent drafts, his material was essential to getting this book off on the right foot. In addition, some of the browsing material came from text originally written by Dan Shearer for O'Reilly.

## CHAPTER 1

Learning the Samba

Samba is an extremely useful networking tool for anyone who has both Windows and Unix systems on his network. Running on a Unix system, it allows Windows to share files and printers on the Unix host, and it also allows Unix users to access resources shared by Windows systems.

Although it might seem natural to use a Windows server to serve files and printers to a network containing Windows clients, there are good reasons for preferring a Samba server for this duty. Samba is reliable software that runs on reliable Unix operating systems, resulting in fewer problems and a low cost of maintenance. Samba also offers better performance under heavy loads, outperforming Windows 2000 Server by a factor of 2 to 1 on identical PC hardware, according to published third-party benchmarks. When common, inexpensive PC hardware fails to meet the demands of a huge client load, the Samba server can easily be moved to a proprietary "big iron" Unix mainframe, which can outperform Windows running on a PC many times. If all that weren't enough, Samba has a very nice cost advantage: it's free. Not only is the software itself freely available, but also no client licenses are required, and it runs on high-quality, free operating systems such as Linux and FreeBSD.

After reading the previous paragraph, you might come to the conclusion that Samba is commonly used by large organizations with thousands of users on their networks—and you'd be right! But Samba's user base includes organizations all over the planet, of all types and sizes: from international corporations, to medium and small businesses, to individuals who run Samba on their Linux laptops. In the last case, a tool such as VMware is used to run Windows on the same computer, with Samba enabling the two operating systems to share files.

The types of users vary even more—Samba is used by corporations, banks and other financial institutions, government and military organizations, schools, public libraries, art galleries, families, and even authors! This book was developed on a Linux system running VMware and Windows 2000, with Adobe FrameMaker running on Windows and the document files served by Samba from the Linux filesystem.

Does all this whet your technological appetite? If so, we encourage you to keep reading, learn about Samba, and follow our examples to set up a Samba server of your own. In this and upcoming chapters, we will tell you exactly how to get started.

What Is Samba?

Samba is a suite of Unix applications that speak the Server Message Block (SMB) protocol. Microsoft Windows operating systems and the OS/2 operating system use SMB to perform client-server networking for file and printer sharing and associated operations. By supporting this protocol, Samba enables computers running Unix to get in on the action, communicating with the same networking protocol as Microsoft Windows and appearing as another Windows system on the network from the perspective of a Windows client. A Samba server offers the following services:

- Share one or more directory trees
- Share one or more Distributed filesystem (Dfs) trees
- Share printers installed on the server among Windows clients on the network
- Assist clients with network browsing
- Authenticate clients logging onto a Windows domain
- Provide or assist with Windows Internet Name Service (WINS) name-server resolution

The Samba suite also includes client tools that allow users on a Unix system to access folders and printers that Windows systems and Samba servers offer on the network.

Samba is the brainchild of Andrew Tridgell, who currently heads the Samba development team. Andrew started the project in 1991, while working with a Digital Equipment Corporation (DEC) software suite called Pathworks, created for connecting DEC VAX computers to computers made by other companies. Without knowing the significance of what he was doing, Andrew created a file-server program for an odd protocol that was part of Pathworks. That protocol later turned out to be SMB. A few years later, he expanded upon his custom-made SMB server and began distributing it as a product on the Internet under the name "SMB Server." However, Andrew couldn't keep that name—it already belonged to another company's product—so he tried the following Unix renaming approach:

```
$ grep -i '^s.*m.*b' /usr/dict/words
```

And the response was:

```
salmonberry
samba
sawtimber
scramble
```

Thus, the name "Samba" was born.

Today, the Samba suite revolves around a pair of Unix daemons that provide shared resources—called *shares* or *services*—to SMB clients on the network. These are:

smbd
> A daemon that handles file and printer sharing and provides authentication and authorization for SMB clients.

nmbd
> A daemon that supports NetBIOS Name Service and WINS, which is Microsoft's implementation of a NetBIOS Name Server (NBNS). It also assists with network browsing.

Samba is currently maintained and extended by a group of volunteers under the active supervision of Andrew Tridgell. Like the Linux operating system, Samba is distributed as open source software (*http://open-source.org*) by its authors and is distributed under the GNU General Public License (GPL). Since its inception, development of Samba has been sponsored in part by the Australian National University, where Andrew Tridgell earned his Ph.D. Since then, many other organizations have sponsored Samba developers, including LinuxCare, VA Linux Systems, Hewlett-Packard, and IBM. It is a true testament to Samba that both commercial and noncommercial entities are prepared to spend money to support an open source effort.

Microsoft has also contributed by offering its definition of the SMB protocol to the Internet Engineering Task Force (IETF) in 1996 as the Common Internet File System (CIFS). Although we prefer to use the term "SMB" in this book, you will also often find the protocol being referred to as "CIFS." This is especially true on Microsoft's web site.

What Can Samba Do for Me?

As explained earlier, Samba can help Windows and Unix computers coexist in the same network. However, there are some specific reasons why you might want to set up a Samba server on your network:

- You don't want to pay for—or can't afford—a full-fledged Windows server, yet you still need the functionality that one provides.
- The Client Access Licenses (CALs) that Microsoft requires for each Windows client to access a Windows server are unaffordable.
- You want to provide a common area for data or user directories to transition from a Windows server to a Unix one, or vice versa.
- You want to share printers among Windows and Unix workstations.
- You are supporting a group of computer users who have a mixture of Windows and Unix computers.
- You want to integrate Unix and Windows authentication, maintaining a single database of user accounts that works with both systems.

- You want to network Unix, Windows, Macintosh (OS X), and other systems using a single protocol.

Let's take a quick tour of Samba in action. Assume that we have the following basic network configuration: a Samba-enabled Unix system, to which we will assign the name toltec, and a pair of Windows clients, to which we will assign the names maya and aztec, all connected via a local area network (LAN). Let's also assume that toltec also has a local inkjet printer connected to it, lp, and a disk share named spirit—both of which it can offer to the other two computers. A graphic of this network is shown in Figure 1-1.

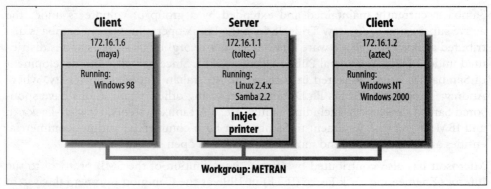

Figure 1-1. A simple network set up with a Samba server

In this network, each computer listed shares the same *workgroup*. A workgroup is a group name tag that identifies an arbitrary collection of computers and their resources on an SMB network. Several workgroups can be on the network at any time, but for our basic network example, we'll have only one: the METRAN workgroup.

Sharing a Disk Service

If everything is properly configured, we should be able to see the Samba server, toltec, through the Network Neighborhood of the maya Windows desktop. In fact, Figure 1-2 shows the Network Neighborhood of the maya computer, including toltec and each computer that resides in the METRAN workgroup. Note the Entire Network icon at the top of the list. As we just mentioned, more than one workgroup can be on an SMB network at any given time. If a user clicks the Entire Network icon, she will see a list of all the workgroups that currently exist on the network.

We can take a closer look at the toltec server by double-clicking its icon. This contacts toltec itself and requests a list of its *shares*—the file and printer resources—that the computer provides. In this case, a printer named lp, a home directory named jay, and a disk share named spirit are on the server, as shown in Figure 1-3. Note

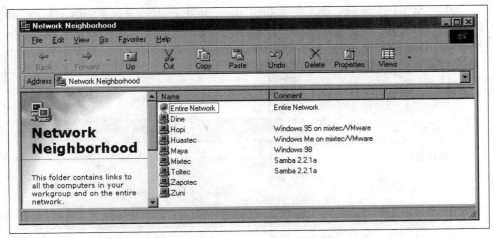

Figure 1-2. The Network Neighborhood directory

that the Windows display shows hostnames in mixed case (Toltec). Case is irrelevant in hostnames, so you might see toltec, Toltec, and TOLTEC in various displays or command output, but they all refer to a single system. Thanks to Samba, Windows 98 sees the Unix server as a valid SMB server and can access the spirit folder as if it were just another system folder.

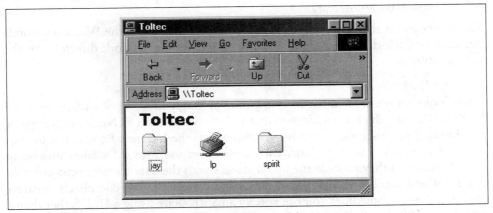

Figure 1-3. Shares available on the Toltec server as viewed from maya

One popular Windows feature is the ability to map a drive letter (such as E:, F:, or Z:) to a shared directory on the network using the Map Network Drive option in Windows Explorer.* Once you do so, your applications can access the folder across the network using the drive letter. You can store data on it, install and run programs from

---

* You can also right-click the shared resource in the Network Neighborhood and then select the Map Network Drive menu item.

it, and even password-protect it against unwanted visitors. See Figure 1-4 for an example of mapping a drive letter to a network directory.

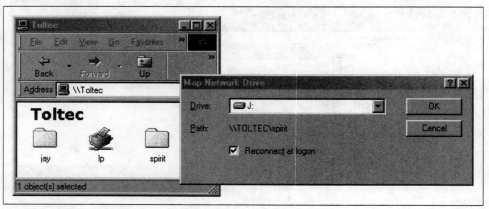

Figure 1-4. Mapping a network drive to a Windows drive letter

Take a look at the Path: entry in the dialog box of Figure 1-4. An equivalent way to represent a directory on a network computer is by using two backslashes, followed by the name of the networked computer, another backslash, and the networked directory of the computer, as shown here:

    \\network-computer\directory

This is known as the *Universal Naming Convention* (UNC) in the Windows world. For example, the dialog box in Figure 1-4 represents the network directory on the toltec server as:

    \\toltec\spirit

If this looks somewhat familiar to you, you're probably thinking of *uniform resource locators* (URLs), which are addresses that web browsers such as Netscape Navigator and Internet Explorer use to resolve systems across the Internet. Be sure not to confuse the two: URLs such as *http://www.oreilly.com* use forward slashes instead of backslashes, and they precede the initial slashes with the data transfer protocol (i.e., ftp, http) and a colon (:). In reality, URLs and UNCs are two completely separate things, although sometimes you can specify an SMB share using a URL rather than a UNC. As a URL, the *\\toltec\spirit* share would be specified as *smb://toltec/spirit*.

Once the network drive is set up, Windows and its programs behave as if the networked directory were a local disk. If you have any applications that support multiuser functionality on a network, you can install those programs on the network drive.* Figure 1-5 shows the resulting network drive as it would appear with other

---

* Be warned that many end-user license agreements forbid installing a program on a network so that multiple clients can access it. Check the legal agreements that accompany the product to be absolutely sure.

storage devices in the Windows 98 client. Note the pipeline attachment in the icon for the J: drive; this indicates that it is a network drive rather than a fixed drive.

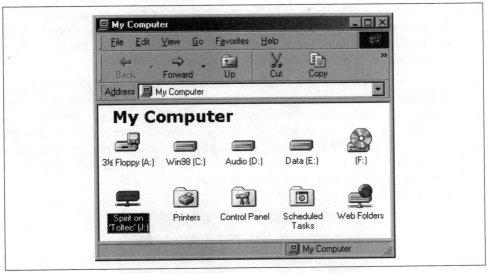

Figure 1-5. The Network directory mapped to the client drive letter J

My Network Places, found in Windows Me, 2000, and XP, works differently from Network Neighborhood. It is necessary to click a few more icons, but eventually we can get to the view of the toltec server as shown in Figure 1-6. This is from a Windows 2000 system. Setting up the network drive using the Map Network Drive option in Windows 2000 works similarly to other Windows versions.

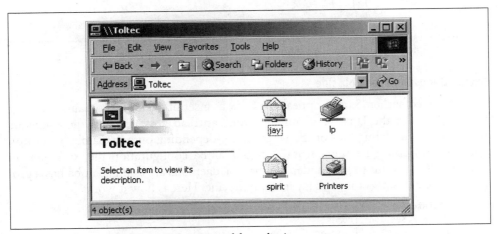

Figure 1-6. Shares available on Toltec (viewed from dine)

Sharing a Printer

You probably noticed that the printer lp appeared under the available shares for toltec in Figure 1-3. This indicates that the Unix server has a printer that can be shared by the various SMB clients in the workgroup. Data sent to the printer from any of the clients will be spooled on the Unix server and printed in the order in which it is received.

Setting up a Samba-enabled printer on the Windows side is even easier than setting up a disk share. By double-clicking the printer and identifying the manufacturer and model, you can install a driver for this printer on the Windows client. Windows can then properly format any information sent to the network printer and access it as if it were a local printer. On Windows 98, double-clicking the Printers icon in the Control Panel opens the Printers window shown in Figure 1-7. Again, note the pipeline attachment below the printer, which identifies it as being on a network.

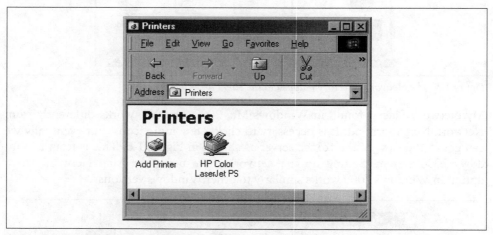

Figure 1-7. A network printer available on Toltec

Seeing things from the Unix side

As mentioned earlier, Samba appears in Unix as a set of daemon programs. You can view them with the Unix *ps* command; you can read any messages they generate through custom debug files or the Unix *syslog* (depending on how Samba is set up); and you can configure them from a single Samba configuration file: *smb.conf*. In addition, if you want to get an idea of what the daemons are doing, Samba has a program called *smbstatus* that will lay it all on the line. Here is how it works:

```
# smbstatus
Processing section "[homes]"
Processing section "[printers]"
Processing section "[spirit]"
```

```
Samba version 2.2.6
Service    uid   gid   pid     machine
-------------------------------------------
spirit     jay   jay   7735    maya    (172.16.1.6) Sun Aug 12 12:17:14 2002
spirit     jay   jay   7779    aztec   (172.16.1.2) Sun Aug 12 12:49:11 2002
jay        jay   jay   7735    maya    (172.16.1.6) Sun Aug 12 12:56:19 2002

Locked files:
Pid     DenyMode    R/W     Oplock     Name
-------------------------------------------------
7735    DENY_WRITE  RDONLY  NONE       /u/RegClean.exe   Sun Aug 12 13:01:22 2002

Share mode memory usage (bytes):
   1048368(99%) free + 136(0%) used + 72(0%) overhead = 1048576(100%) total
```

The Samba status from this output provides three sets of data, each divided into separate sections. The first section tells which systems have connected to the Samba server, identifying each client by its machine name (maya and aztec) and IP (Internet Protocol) address. The second section reports the name and status of the files that are currently in use on a share on the server, including the read/write status and any locks on the files. Finally, Samba reports the amount of memory it has currently allocated to the shares that it administers, including the amount actively used by the shares plus additional overhead. (Note that this is not the same as the total amount of memory that the *smbd* or *nmbd* processes are using.)

Don't worry if you don't understand these statistics; they will become easier to understand as you move through the book.

Getting Familiar with an SMB Network

Now that you have had a brief tour of Samba, let's take some time to get familiar with Samba's adopted environment: an SMB network. Networking with SMB is significantly different from working with common TCP/IP protocols such as FTP and Telnet because there are several new concepts to learn and a lot of information to cover. First, we will discuss the basic concepts behind an SMB network, followed by some Microsoft implementations of it, and finally we will show you where a Samba server can and cannot fit into the picture.

Understanding NetBIOS

To begin, let's step back in time. In 1984, IBM authored a simple application programming interface (API) for networking its computers, called the *Network Basic Input/Output System* (NetBIOS). The NetBIOS API provided a rudimentary design for an application to connect and share data with other computers.

It's helpful to think of the NetBIOS API as networking extensions to the standard BIOS API calls. The BIOS contains low-level code for performing filesystem operations on the local computer. NetBIOS originally had to exchange instructions with computers across IBM PC or Token Ring networks. It therefore required a low-level transport protocol to carry its requests from one computer to the next.

In late 1985, IBM released one such protocol, which it merged with the NetBIOS API to become the *NetBIOS Extended User Interface* (*NetBEUI*). NetBEUI was designed for small LANs, and it let each computer claim a name (up to 15 characters) that wasn't already in use on the network. By a "small LAN," we mean fewer than 255 nodes on the network—which was considered a generous number in 1985!

The NetBEUI protocol was very popular with networking applications, including those running under Windows for Workgroups. Later, implementations of NetBIOS over Novell's IPX networking protocols also emerged, which competed with NetBEUI. However, the networking protocols of choice for the burgeoning Internet community were TCP/IP and UDP/IP, and implementing the NetBIOS APIs over those protocols soon became a necessity.

Recall that TCP/IP uses numbers to represent computer addresses (192.168.220.100, for instance) while NetBIOS uses only names. This was a major issue when trying to mesh the two protocols together. In 1987, the IETF published standardization documents, titled RFC 1001 and 1002, that outlined how NetBIOS would work over a TCP/UDP network. This set of documents still governs each implementation that exists today, including those provided by Microsoft with its Windows operating systems, as well as the Samba suite.

Since then, the standard that this document governs has become known as *NetBIOS over TCP/IP*, or NBT for short.* The NBT standard (RFC 1001/1002) currently outlines a trio of services on a network:

- A name service
- Two communication services:
  —Datagrams
  —Sessions

The name service solves the name-to-address problem mentioned earlier; it allows each computer to declare a specific name on the network that can be translated to a machine-readable IP address, much like today's Domain Name System (DNS) on the Internet. The datagram and session services are both secondary communication protocols used to transmit data back and forth from NetBIOS computers across the network.

---

* You might also see the abbreviation NetBT, which is common in Microsoft literature.

Getting a Name

In the NetBIOS world, when each computer comes online, it wants to claim a name for itself; this is called *name registration*. However, no two computers in the same workgroup should be able to claim the same name; this would cause endless confusion for any computer that wanted to communicate with either of them. There are two different approaches to ensuring that this doesn't happen:

- Use an NBNS to keep track of which hosts have registered a NetBIOS name.
- Allow each computer on the network to defend its name in the event that another computer attempts to use it.

Figure 1-8 illustrates a (failed) name registration, with and without an NBNS.

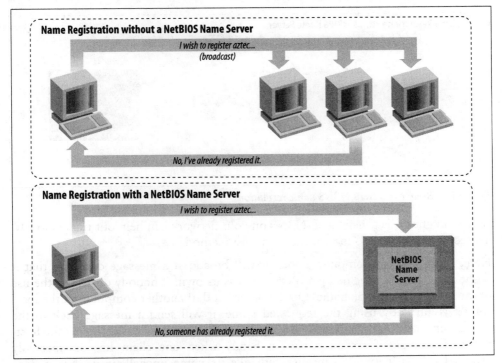

Figure 1-8. Broadcast versus NBNS name registration

As mentioned earlier, there must be a way to resolve a NetBIOS name to a specific IP address; this is known as *name resolution*. There are two different approaches with NBT here as well:

- Have each computer report back its IP address when it "hears" a broadcast request for its NetBIOS name.
- Use an NBNS to help resolve NetBIOS names to IP addresses.

Figure 1-9 illustrates the two types of name resolution.

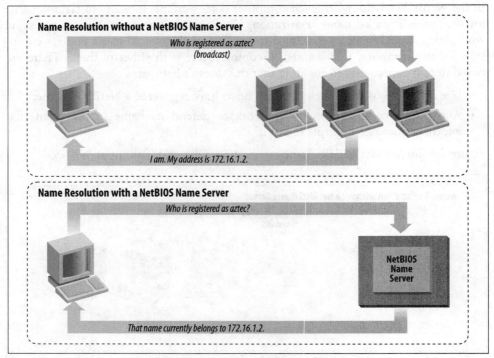

Figure 1-9. Broadcast versus NBNS name resolution

As you might expect, having an NBNS on your network can help out tremendously. To see exactly why, let's look at the broadcast method.

Here, when a client computer boots, it will broadcast a message declaring that it wishes to register a specified NetBIOS name as its own. If nobody objects to the use of the name, it keeps the name. On the other hand, if another computer on the local subnet is currently using the requested name, it will send a message back to the requesting client that the name is already taken. This is known as *defending* the hostname. This type of system comes in handy when one client has unexpectedly dropped off the network—another can take its name unchallenged—but it does incur an inordinate amount of traffic on the network for something as simple as name registration.

With an NBNS, the same thing occurs, except the communication is confined to the requesting computer and the NBNS. No broadcasting occurs when the computer wishes to register the name; the registration message is simply sent directly from the client to the NBNS, and the NBNS replies regardless of whether the name is already taken. This is known as *point-to-point communication*, and it is often beneficial on networks with more than one subnet. This is because routers are generally configured to block incoming packets that are broadcast to all computers in the subnet.

The same principles apply to name resolution. Without an NBNS, NetBIOS name resolution would also be done with a broadcast mechanism. All request packets would be sent to each computer in the network, with the hope that one computer that might be affected will respond directly back to the computer that asked. Using an NBNS and point-to-point communication for this purpose is far less taxing on the network than flooding the network with broadcasts for every name-resolution request.

It can be argued that broadcast packets do not cause significant problems in modern, high-bandwidth networks of hosts with fast CPUs, if only a small number of hosts are on the network, or the demand for bandwidth is low. There are certainly cases where this is true; however, our advice throughout this book is to avoid relying on broadcasts as much as possible. This is a good rule to follow for large, busy networks, and if you follow our advice when configuring a small network, your network will be able to grow without encountering problems later on that might be difficult to diagnose.

Node Types

How can you tell what strategy each client on your network will use when performing name registration and resolution? Each computer on an NBT network earns one of the following designations, depending on how it handles name registration and resolution: b-node, p-node, m-node, and h-node. The behaviors of each type of node are summarized in Table 1-1.

Table 1-1. NetBIOS node types

Role	Value
b-node	Uses broadcast registration and resolution only.
p-node	Uses point-to-point registration and resolution only.
m-node (mixed)	Uses broadcast for registration. If successful, it notifies the NBNS of the result. Uses broadcast for resolution; uses the NBNS if broadcast is unsuccessful.
h-node (hybrid)	Uses the NBNS for registration and resolution; uses broadcast if the NBNS is unresponsive or inoperative.

In the case of Windows clients, you will usually find them listed as h-nodes or hybrid nodes. The first three node types appear in RFC 1001/1002, and h-nodes were invented later by Microsoft, as a more fault-tolerant method.

You can find the node type of a Windows 95/98/Me computer by running the *winipcfg* command from the Start → Run dialog (or from an MS-DOS prompt) and clicking the More Info>> button. On Windows NT/2000/XP, you can use the ipconfig /all command in a command-prompt window. In either case, search for the line that says Node Type.

What's in a Name?

The names NetBIOS uses are quite different from the DNS hostnames you might be familiar with. First, NetBIOS names exist in a flat namespace. In other words, there are no hierarchical levels, such as in oreilly.com (two levels) or *ftp.samba.org* (three levels). NetBIOS names consist of a single unique string such as navaho or hopi within each workgroup or domain. Second, NetBIOS names are allowed to be only 15 characters and can consist only of standard alphanumeric characters (a–z, A–Z, 0–9) and the following:

    ! @ # $ % ^ & ( ) - ' { } . ~

Although you are allowed to use a period (.) in a NetBIOS name, we recommend against it because those names are not guaranteed to work in future versions of NBT.

It's not a coincidence that all valid DNS names are also valid NetBIOS names. In fact, the unqualified DNS name for a Samba server is often reused as its NetBIOS name. For example, if you had a system with a hostname of mixtec.ora.com, its NetBIOS name would likely be MIXTEC (followed by 9 spaces).

Resource names and types

With NetBIOS, a computer not only advertises its presence, but also tells others what types of services it offers. For example, mixtec can indicate that it's not just a workstation, but that it's also a file server and can receive Windows Messenger messages. This is done by adding a 16th byte to the end of the machine (resource) name, called the *resource type*, and registering the name multiple times, once for each service that it offers. See Figure 1-10.

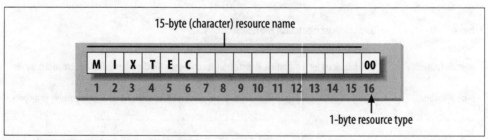

Figure 1-10. The structure of NetBIOS names

The 1-byte resource type indicates a unique service that the named computer provides. In this book, you will often see the resource type shown in angled brackets (<>) after the NetBIOS name, such as:

    MIXTEC<00>

You can see which names are registered for a particular NBT computer using the Windows command-line *nbtstat* utility. Because these services are unique (i.e., there cannot be more than one registered), you will see them listed as type UNIQUE in the output. For example, the following partial output describes the `toltec` server:

```
C:\>nbtstat -a toltec

          NetBIOS Remote Machine Name Table
     Name              Type        Status
     ---------------------------------------------
     TOLTEC            <00>  UNIQUE   Registered
     TOLTEC            <03>  UNIQUE   Registered
     TOLTEC            <20>  UNIQUE   Registered
     ...
```

This says the server has registered the NetBIOS name `toltec` as a machine (computer) name, as a recipient of messages from the Windows Messenger service, and as a file server. Some possible attributes a name can have are listed in Table 1-2.

Table 1-2. NetBIOS unique resource types

Named resource	Hexadecimal byte value
Standard Workstation Service	00
Messenger Service	03
RAS Server Service	06
Domain Master Browser Service (associated with primary domain controller)	1B
Master Browser name	1D
NetDDE Service	1F
Fileserver (including printer server)	20
RAS Client Service	21
Network Monitor Agent	BE
Network Monitor Utility	BF

Group names and types

SMB also uses the concept of groups, with which computers can register themselves. Earlier we mentioned that the computers in our example belonged to a *workgroup*, which is a partition of computers on the same network. For example, a business might very easily have an ACCOUNTING and a SALES workgroup, each with different servers and printers. In the Windows world, a workgroup and an SMB group are the same thing.

Continuing our *nbtstat* example, the `toltec` Samba server is also a member of the METRAN workgroup (the GROUP attribute hex 00) and will participate in elections for the browse master (GROUP attribute 1E). Here is the remainder of the *nbtstat* output:

```
        NetBIOS Remote Machine Name Table
    Name                    Type      Status
   --------------------------------------------------
    METRAN       <00>    GROUP       Registered
    METRAN       <1E>    GROUP       Registered
    ..__MSBROWSE__.<01>  GROUP       Registered
```

The possible group attributes a computer can have are illustrated in Table 1-3. More information is available in *Windows NT in a Nutshell* by Eric Pearce, also published by O'Reilly.

Table 1-3. NetBIOS group resource types

Named resource	Hexadecimal byte value
Standard Workstation group	00
Logon server	1C
Master Browser name	1D
Normal Group name (used in browser elections)	1E
Internet Group name (administrative)	20
<01><02>__MSBROWSE__<02>	01

The final entry, __MSBROWSE__, is used to announce a group to other master browsers. The nonprinting characters in the name show up as dots in an *nbtstat* printout. Don't worry if you don't understand all of the resource or group types. Some of them you will not need with Samba, and others you will pick up as you move through the rest of the chapter. The important thing to remember here is the logistics of the naming mechanism.

Scope ID

In the dark ages of SMB networking before NetBIOS groups were introduced, you could use a very primitive method to isolate groups of computers from the rest of the network. Each SMB packet contains a field called the *scope ID*, with the idea being that systems on the network could be configured to accept only packets with a scope ID matching that of their configuration. This feature was hardly ever used and unfortunately lingers in modern implementations. Some of the utilities included in the Samba distribution allow the scope ID to be set. Setting the scope ID in a network is likely to cause problems, and we are mentioning scope ID only so that you will not be confused by it when you later encounter it in various places.

Datagrams and Sessions

At this point, let's digress to discuss the responsibility of NBT: to provide connection services between two NetBIOS computers. NBT offers two services: the *session service* and the *datagram service*. Understanding how these two services work is not essential to using Samba, but it does give you an idea of how NBT works and how to troubleshoot Samba when it doesn't work.

The datagram service has no stable connection between computers. Packets of data are simply sent or broadcast from one computer to another, without regard to the order in which they arrive at the destination, or even if they arrive at all. The use of datagrams requires less processing overhead than sessions, although the reliability of the connection can suffer. Datagrams, therefore, are used for quickly sending nonvital blocks of data to one or more computers. The datagram service communicates using the simple primitives shown in Table 1-4.

Table 1-4. Datagram primitives

Primitive	Description
Send Datagram	Send datagram packet to computer or groups of computers.
Send Broadcast Datagram	Broadcast datagram to any computer waiting with a Receive Broadcast datagram.
Receive Datagram	Receive a datagram from a computer.
Receive Broadcast Datagram	Wait for a Broadcast datagram.

The session service is more complex. Sessions are a communication method that, in theory, offers the ability to detect problematic or inoperable connections between two NetBIOS applications. It helps to think of an NBT session as being similar to a telephone call, an analogy that obviously influenced the design of the CIFS standard.

Once the connection is made, it remains open throughout the duration of the conversation, each side knows who the caller and the called computer are, and each can communicate with the simple primitives shown in Table 1-5.

Table 1-5. Session primitives

Primitive	Description
Call	Initiate a session with a computer listening under a specified name.
Listen	Wait for a call from a known caller or any caller.
Hang-up	Exit a call.
Send	Send data to the other computer.
Receive	Receive data from the other computer.
Session Status	Get information on requested sessions.

Sessions are the backbone of resource sharing on an NBT network. They are typically used for establishing stable connections from client computers to disk or printer shares on a server. The client "calls" the server and starts trading information such as which files it wishes to open, which data it wishes to exchange, etc. These calls can last a long time—hours, even days—and all of this occurs within the context of a single connection. If there is an error, the session software (TCP) will retransmit until the data is received properly, unlike the "punt-and-pray" approach of the datagram service (UDP).

In truth, while sessions are supposed to handle problematic communications, they sometimes don't. If the connection is interrupted, session information that is open between the two computers might become invalid. If that happens, the only way to regain the session information is for the same two computers to call each other again and start over.

If you want more information on each service, we recommend you look at RFC 1001. However, there are two important things to remember here:

- Sessions always occur between two NetBIOS computers. If a session service is interrupted, the client is supposed to store sufficient state information for it to reestablish the connection. However, in practice, this often does not happen.

- Datagrams can be broadcast to multiple computers, but they are unreliable. In other words, there is no way for the source to know that the datagrams it sent have indeed arrived at their destinations.

An Introduction to the SMB Protocol

Now we're going to cover some low-level technical details and explore the elementals of the SMB protocol. You probably don't need to know much about this to implement a simple Samba network, and therefore you might want to skip or skim over this section and go on to the next one ("Windows Workgroups and Domains") on your first reading. However, assuming you are going to be responsible for long-term maintenance of a Samba network, it will help if you understand how it actually works. You will more easily be able to diagnose and correct any odd problems that pop up.

At a high level, the SMB protocol suite is relatively simple. It includes commands for all the file and print operations that you might perform on a local disk or printer, such as:

- Opening and closing files
- Creating and deleting files and directories
- Reading and writing files
- Searching for files
- Queueing and dequeueing files in a print spool

Each operation can be encoded into an SMB message and transmitted to and from a server. The original name "SMB" comes from the way in which the commands are formatted: they are versions of the standard DOS system-call data structures, or *Server Message Blocks*, redesigned for transmitting to another computer across a network.

SMB Format

Richard Sharpe of the Samba team defines SMB as a *request-response* protocol.[*] In effect, this means that a client sends an SMB request to a server and the server sends an SMB response back to the client. In only one rare circumstance does a server send a message that is not in response to a client.

An SMB message is not as complex as you might think. Let's take a closer look at the internal structure of such a message. It can be broken down into two parts: the *header*, which is a fixed size, and the *command string*, whose size can vary dramatically based on the contents of the message.

SMB header format

Table 1-6 shows the format of an SMB header. The COM field identifies the command being performed. SMB commands are not required to use all the fields in the SMB header. For example, when a client first attempts to connect to a server, it does not yet have a tree identifier (TID) value—one is assigned after it successfully connects—so a null TID is placed in its header field. Other fields can be padded with zeros when not used.

The SMB header fields are listed in Table 1-6.

Table 1-6. SMB header fields

Field	Size (bytes)	Description
0xFF 'SMB'	1	Protocol identifier
COM	1	Command code, from 0x00 to 0xFF
RCLS	1	Error class
REH	1	Reserved
ERR	2	Error code
REB	1	Reserved
RES	14	Reserved
TID	2	TID; a unique ID for a resource in use by the client
PID	2	Caller process ID
UID	2	User identifier
MID	2	Multiplex identifier; used to route requests inside a process

SMB command format

Immediately after the header is a variable number of bytes that constitute an SMB command or reply. Each command, such as Open File (COM field identifier:

---

[*] See *http://www.samba.org/cifs/docs/what-is-smb.html* for Richard's excellent summary of SMB.

SMBopen) or Get Print Queue (SMBsplretq), has its own set of parameters and data. Like the SMB header fields, not all of the command fields need to be filled, depending on the specific command. For example, the Get Server Attributes (SMBdskattr) command sets the WCT and BCC fields to zero. The fields of the command segment are shown in Table 1-7.

Table 1-7. SMB command contents

Field	Size (bytes)	Description
WCT	1	Word count
VWV	Variable	Parameter words (size given by WCT)
BCC	2	Parameter byte count
DATA	Variable	Data (size given by BCC)

Don't worry if you don't understand each field; they are not necessary for using Samba at an administrator level. However, they do come in handy when debugging system messages. We will show you some of the more common SMB messages that clients and servers send using a modified version of *tcpdump* later in this section. (If you prefer an SMB sniffer with a graphical interface, try Ethereal, which uses the GTK libraries; see *http://www.ethereal.com* for more information on this tool.)

 For more information on each command in the SMB protocol, see the *CIFS Technical Reference* at *http://www.snia.org/tech_activities/CIFS*.

SMB variations

The SMB protocol has been extended with new commands several times since its inception. Each new version is backward-compatible with the previous versions, so it is possible for a LAN to have clients and servers concurrently running different versions of the SMB protocol.

Table 1-8 outlines the major versions of the SMB protocol. Within each "dialect" of SMB are many sub-versions that include commands supporting particular releases of major operating systems. The ID string in column 2 is used by clients and servers to determine in which level of the protocol they will speak to each other.

Table 1-8. SMB protocol dialects

Protocol name	ID string	Used by
Core	PC NETWORK PROGRAM 1.0	
Core Plus	MICROSOFT NETWORKS 1.03	
LAN Manager 1.0	LANMAN1.0	
LAN Manager 2.0	LM1.2X002	
LAN Manager 2.1	LANMAN2.1	

Table 1-8. SMB protocol dialects (continued)

Protocol name	ID string	Used by
NT LAN Manager 1.0	NT LM 0.12	Windows NT 4.0
Samba's NT LM 0.12	Samba	Samba
Common Internet File System	CIFS 1.0	Windows 2000/XP

Samba implements the NT LM 0.12 specification for NT LAN Manager 1.0. It is backward-compatible with all the other SMB variants. The CIFS specification is, in reality, LAN Manager 0.12 with a few specific additions.

SMB Clients and Servers

As mentioned earlier, SMB is a client/server protocol. In the purest sense, this means that a client sends a request to a server, which acts on the request and returns a reply. However, the client/server roles can often be reversed, sometimes within the context of a single SMB session. For example, consider the two Windows 95/98/Me computers in Figure 1-11. The computer named maya shares a printer to the network, and the computer named toltec shares a disk directory. maya is in the client role when accessing toltec's network drive and in the server role when printing a job for toltec.

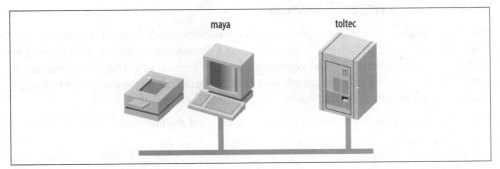

Figure 1-11. Two computers that both have resources to share

This brings out an important point in Samba terminology:

- A *server* is a computer with a resource to share.
- A *client* is a computer that wishes to use that resource.
- A computer can be a client, a server, or both, or it can be neither at any given time.

Microsoft Windows products have both the SMB client and server built into the operating system, and it is common to find Windows acting as a server, client, both, or neither at any given time in a production network. Although Samba has been developed primarily to function as a server, there are also ways that it and associated software can act as an SMB client. As with Windows, it is even possible to set up a Unix system to act as an SMB client and not as a server. See Chapter 5 for more details on this topic.

A Simple SMB Connection

The client and server must complete three steps to establish a connection to a resource:

1. Establish a NetBIOS session.
2. Negotiate the protocol variant.
3. Set session parameters, and make a tree connection to a resource.

We will examine each step through the eyes of a useful tool that we mentioned earlier: the modified *tcpdump* that is available from the Samba web site.

You can download the *tcpdump* program at *http://www.samba.org* in the *samba/ftp/tcpdump-smb* directory; the latest version as of this writing is 3.4-10. Use this program as you would use the standard *tcpdump* application, but add the -s 1500 switch to ensure that you get the whole packet and not just the first few bytes.

Establishing a NetBIOS Session

When a user first makes a request to access a network disk or send a print job to a remote printer, NetBIOS takes care of making a connection at the session layer. The result is a bidirectional channel between the client and server. The client and server need only two messages to establish this connection. This is shown in the following example session request and response, as captured by *tcpdump*.

First, the client sends a request to open a session, and *tcpdump* reports:

```
>>> NBT Packet
NBT Session Request
Flags=0x81000044
Destination=TOLTEC      NameType=0x20 (Server)
Source=MAYA            NameType=0x00 (Workstation)
```

Then the server responds, granting a session to the client:

```
>>> NBT Packet
NBT Session Granted
Flags=0x82000000
```

At this point, there is an open channel between the client and server.

Negotiating the Protocol Variant

Next, the client sends a message to the server to negotiate an SMB protocol. As mentioned earlier, the client sets its tree identifier (TID) field to zero, because it does not yet know what TID to use. A *tree identifier* is a number that represents a connection to a share on a server.

The command in the message is SMBnegprot, a request to negotiate a protocol variant that will be used for the entire session. Note that the client sends to the server a list of all the variants that it can speak, not vice versa:

```
>>> NBT Packet
NBT Session Packet
Flags=0x0
Length=154

SMB PACKET: SMBnegprot (REQUEST)
SMB Command   =  0x72
Error class   =  0x0
Error code    =  0
Flags1        =  0x0
Flags2        =  0x0
Tree ID       =  0
Proc ID       =  5315
UID           =  0
MID           =  257
Word Count    =  0
Dialect=PC NETWORK PROGRAM 1.0
Dialect=MICROSOFT NETWORKS 3.0
Dialect=DOS LM1.2X002
Dialect=DOS LANMAN2.1
Dialect=Windows for Workgroups 3.1a
Dialect=NT LM 0.12
```

The server responds to the SMBnegprot request with an index (with counting starting at 0) into the list of variants that the client offered, or with the value 0xFF if none of the protocol variants is acceptable:

```
>>> NBT Packet
NBT Session Packet
Flags=0x0
Length=84

SMB PACKET: SMBnegprot (REPLY)
SMB Command   =  0x72
Error class   =  0x0
Error code    =  0
Flags1        =  0x80
Flags2        =  0x1
Tree ID       =  0
Proc ID       =  5315
UID           =  0
MID           =  257
Word Count    =  17
NT1 Protocol
DialectIndex=5
[...]
```

In this example, the server responds with the value 5, which indicates that the NT LM 0.12 dialect will be used for the remainder of the session.

Set Session and Login Parameters

The next step is to transmit session and login parameters for the session, which you do using the SMBSesssetupX command. The parameters include the following:

- The account name and password (if there is one)
- The workgroup name
- The maximum size of data that can be transferred
- The number of pending requests that can be in the queue at a time

The resulting output from *tcpdump* is:

```
>>> NBT Packet
NBT Session Packet
Flags=0x0
Length=150

SMB PACKET: SMBsesssetupX (REQUEST)
SMB Command   = 0x73
Error class   = 0x0
Error code    = 0
Flags1        = 0x10
Flags2        = 0x0
Tree ID       = 0
Proc ID       = 5315
UID           = 1
MID           = 257
Word Count    = 13
Com2=0x75
Res1=0x0
Off2=120
MaxBuffer=2920
MaxMpx=50
VcNumber=0
SessionKey=0x1380
CaseInsensitivePasswordLength=24
CaseSensitivePasswordLength=0
Res=0x0
Capabilities=0x1
Pass1&Pass2&Account&Domain&OS&LanMan=
   JAY METRAN Windows 4.0 Windows 4.0

SMB PACKET: SMBtconX (REQUEST) (CHAINED)
smbvwv[]=
Com2=0xFF
Off2=0
Flags=0x2
PassLen=1
Passwd&Path&Device=
```

```
smb_bcc=23
smb_buf[]=\\TOLTEC\SPIRIT
```

In this example, the SMBsesssetupX Session Setup command allows for an additional SMB command to be piggybacked onto it (indicated by the letter X at the end of the command name). The hexadecimal code of the second command is given in the Com2 field. In this case the command is 0x75, which is the SMBtconX (Tree Connect and X) command. The SMBtconX message looks for the name of the resource in the *smb_buf* buffer. In this example, *smb_buf* contains the string \\TOLTEC\SPIRIT, which is the full pathname to a shared directory on toltec. Using the "and X" commands like this speeds up each transaction because the server doesn't have to wait on the client to make a second request.

Note that the TID is still zero. Finally, the server returns a TID to the client, indicating that the user has been authorized access and that the resource is ready to be used:

```
>>> NBT Packet
NBT Session Packet
Flags=0x0
Length=85

SMB PACKET: SMBsesssetupX (REPLY)
SMB Command   =   0x73
Error class   =   0x0
Error code    =   0
Flags1        =   0x80
Flags2        =   0x1
Tree ID       =   1
Proc ID       =   5315
UID           =   100
MID           =   257
Word Count    =   3
Com2=0x75
Off2=68
Action=0x1
[000] Unix Samba 2.2.6
[010] METRAN

SMB PACKET: SMBtconX (REPLY) (CHAINED)
smbvwv[]=
Com2=0xFF
Off2=0
smbbuf[]=
ServiceType=A:
```

The *ServiceType* field is set to "A" to indicate that this is a file service. Available service types are:

- "A" for a disk or file
- "LPT1" for a spooled output
- "COMM" for a direct-connect printer or modem
- "IPC" for a named pipe

Now that a TID has been assigned, the client can use it as a handle to perform any operation that it would use on a local disk drive. It can open files, read and write to them, delete them, create new files, search for filenames, and so on.

Windows Workgroups and Domains

Up to now, we've covered basic SMB technology, which is all you would need if you had nothing more advanced than MS-DOS clients on your network. We do assume you want to support Windows clients, especially the more recent versions, so next we'll describe the enhancements Microsoft has added to SMB networking—namely, Windows for Workgroups and Windows domains.

Windows Workgroups

Windows Workgroups are very similar to the SMB groups already described. You need to know just a few additional things.

Browsing

Browsing is the process of finding the other computers and shared resources in the Windows network. Note that there is no connection with a World Wide Web browser, apart from the general idea of "discovering what's there." On the other hand, browsing the Windows network is like the Web in that what's out there can change without warning.

Before browsing existed, users had to know the name of the computer they wanted to connect to on the network and then manually enter a UNC such as the following into an application or file manager to access resources:

```
\\toltec\spirit\
```

Browsing is much more convenient, making it possible to examine the contents of a network by using the point-and-click GUI interface of the Network Neighborhood (or My Network Places*) on a Windows client.

You will encounter two types of browsing in an SMB network:

- Browsing a list of computers and shared resources
- Browsing the shared resource of a specific computer

Let's look at the first one. On each LAN (or subnet) with a Windows workgroup or domain, one computer has the responsibility of maintaining a list of the computers

---

* This was originally called Network Neighborhood in Windows 95/98/NT, but Microsoft has changed the name to My Network Places in the more recent Windows Me/2000/XP. We will continue to call it Network Neighborhood, and if you're using a new version of Windows, be aware that My Network Places can act a little differently in some ways.

that are currently accessible through the network. This computer is called the *local master browser*, and the list that it maintains is called the *browse list*. Computers on a subnet use the browse list to cut down on the amount of network traffic generated while browsing. Instead of each computer dynamically polling to determine a list of the currently available computers, the computer can simply query the local master browser to obtain a complete, up-to-date list.

To browse the resources on a computer, a user must connect to the specific computer; this information cannot be obtained from the browse list. Browsing the list of resources on a computer can be done by double-clicking the computer's icon when it is presented in the Network Neighborhood. As you saw at the opening of the chapter, the computer will respond with a list of shared resources that can be accessed after the user is successfully authenticated.

Each server on a Windows workgroup is required to announce its presence to the local master browser after it has registered a NetBIOS name, and (theoretically) announce that it is leaving the workgroup when it is shut down. It is the local master browser's responsibility to record what the servers have announced.

 The Windows Network Neighborhood can behave oddly: until you select a particular computer to browse, the Network Neighborhood window might contain data that is not up-to-date. That means the Network Neighborhood window can be showing computers that have crashed or can be missing computers that haven't been noticed yet. Put succinctly, once you've selected a server and connected to it, you can be a lot more confident that the shares and printers really exist on the network.

Unlike the roles you've seen earlier, almost any Windows system (including Windows for Workgroups and Windows 95/98/Me or NT/2000/XP) can act as a local master browser. The local master browser can have one or more backup browsers on the local subnet that will take over in the event that the local master browser fails or becomes inaccessible. To ensure fluid operation, the local backup browsers will frequently synchronize their browse list with the local master browser.

Here is how to calculate the minimum number of backup browsers that will be allocated on a workgroup:

- If up to 32 Windows NT/2000/XP workstations are on the network, or up to 16 Windows 95/98/Me computers are on the network, the local master browser allocates one backup browser in addition to the local master browser.
- If the number of Windows NT/2000/XP workstations falls between 33 and 64, or the number of Windows 95/98/Me workstations falls between 17 and 32, the local master browser allocates two backup browsers.
- For each group of 32 NT/2000/XP workstations or 16 Windows 95/98/Me computers beyond this, the local master browser allocates another backup browser.

There is currently no upper limit on the number of backup browsers that can be allocated by the local master browser.

Browsing elections

Browsing is a critical aspect of any Windows workgroup. However, not everything runs perfectly on any network. For example, let's say that a computer running Windows on the desk of a small company's CEO is the local master browser—that is, until he switches it off while plugging in his massage chair. At this point the Windows NT Workstation in the spare parts department might agree to take over the job. However, that computer is currently running a large, poorly written program that has brought its processor to its knees. The moral: browsing has to be very tolerant of servers coming and going. Because nearly every Windows system can serve as a browser, there has to be a way of deciding at any time who will take on the job. This decision-making process is called an *election*.

An election algorithm is built into nearly all Windows operating systems such that they can each agree who is going to be a local master browser and who will be local backup browsers. An election can be forced at any time. For example, let's assume that the CEO has finished his massage and reboots his server. As the server comes online, it will announce its presence, and an election will take place to see if the PC in the spare parts department should still be the master browser.

When an election is performed, each computer broadcasts information about itself via datagrams. This information includes the following:

- The version of the election protocol used
- The operating system on the computer
- The amount of time the client has been on the network
- The hostname of the client

These values determine which operating system has seniority and will fulfill the role of the local master browser. (Chapter 7 describes the election process in more detail.) The architecture developed to achieve this is not elegant and has built-in security problems. While a browsing domain can be integrated with domain security, the election algorithm does not take into consideration which computers become browsers. Thus it is possible for any computer running a browser service to register itself as participating in the browsing election and (after winning) being able to change the browse list. Nevertheless, browsing is a key feature of Windows networking, and backward-compatibility requirements will ensure that it is in use for years to come.

Windows 95/98/Me authentication

Three types of passwords arise when Windows 95/98/Me is operating in a Windows workgroup:

- A Windows password
- A Windows Networking password
- A password for each shared resource that has been assigned password protection

The Windows password functions in a manner that might be a source of confusion for Unix system administrators. It is not there to prevent unauthorized users from using the computer. (If you don't believe that, try clicking the Cancel button on the password dialog box and see what happens!) Instead, the Windows password is used to gain access to a file that contains the Windows Networking and network resource passwords. There is one such file per registered user of the system, and they can be found in the *C:\Windows* directory with a name composed of the user's account name, followed by a *.pwl* extension. For example, if the user's account name is "sarah," the file will be *C:\Windows\sarah.pwl*. This file is encrypted using the Windows password as the encryption key.

 As a security measure, you might want to check for junk *.pwl* files on Windows 95/98/Me clients, which might have been created by mistakes users made while attempting to log on. A *.pwl* file is easily cracked and can contain valid passwords for Samba accounts and network shares.

The first time the network is accessed, Windows attempts to use the Windows password as the Windows Networking password. If this is successful, the user will not be prompted for two separate passwords, and subsequent logins to the Windows system will automatically result in logging on to the Windows network as well, making things much simpler for the user.

Shared network resources in the workgroup can also have passwords assigned to them to limit their accessibility. The first time a user attempts to access the resource, she is asked for its password, and a checkbox in the password dialog box gives the user the option to add the password to her password list. This is the default; if it is accepted, Windows will store the password in the user's *.pwl* file, and all further authentication to the resource will be handled automatically by Windows.

Samba's approach to workgroup authentication is a little different, which is a result of blending the Windows workgroup model with that of the Unix host upon which Samba runs. This will be discussed further in Chapter 9.

Windows NT Domains

The peer-to-peer networking model of workgroups functions fairly well as long as the number of computers on the network is small and there is a close-knit community of users. However, in larger networks the simplicity of workgroups becomes a limiting factor. Workgroups offer only the most basic level of security, and because each resource can have its own password, it is inconvenient (to say the least) for users to remember the password for each resource in a large network. Even if that were not a problem, many people find it frustrating to have to interrupt their creative workflow to enter a shared password into a dialog box every time another network resource is accessed.

To support the needs of larger networks, such as those found in departmental computing environments, Microsoft introduced domains with Windows NT 3.51. A *Windows NT domain* is essentially a workgroup of SMB computers that has one addition: a server acting as a domain controller (see Figure 1-12).

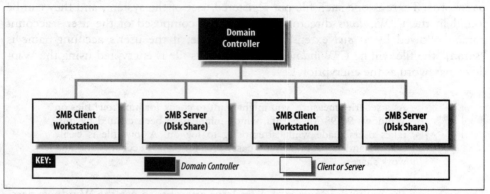

Figure 1-12. A simple Windows domain

Domain controllers

A *domain controller* in a Windows NT domain functions much like a Network Information Service (NIS) server in a Unix network, maintaining a domain-wide database of user and group information, as well as performing related services. The responsibilities of a domain controller are mainly centered around security, including *authentication*, the process of granting or denying a user access to the resources of the domain. This is typically done through the use of a username and password. The service that maintains the database on the domain controllers is called the Security Account Manager (SAM).

The Windows NT security model revolves around *security identifiers* (SIDs) and *access control lists* (ACLs). Security identifiers are used to represent objects in the domain, which include (but are not limited to) users, groups, computers, and processes. SIDs are commonly written in ASCII form as hyphen-separated fields, like this:

    S-1-5-21-1638239387-7675610646-9254035128-545

The part of the SID starting with the "S" and leading up to the rightmost hyphen identifies a domain. The number after the rightmost hyphen is called a *relative identifier* (RID) and is a unique number within the domain that identifies the user, group,

---

computer, or other object. The RID is the analog of a user ID (UID) or group ID (GID) on a Unix system or within an NIS domain.

ACLs supply the same function as "rwx" file permissions that are common in Unix systems. However, ACLs are more versatile. Unix file permissions only set permissions for the owner and group to which the file belongs, and "other," meaning everyone else. Windows NT/2000/XP ACLs allow permissions to be set individually for any number of arbitrary users and/or groups. ACLs are made up of one or more *access control entries* (ACEs), each of which contains an SID and the access rights associated with it.

ACL support has been added as a standard feature for some Unix variants and is available as an add-on for others. Samba supports mappings between Windows and Unix ACLs, and this will be covered in Chapter 8.

Primary and backup domain controllers

You've already read about master and backup browsers. Domain controllers are similar in that a domain has a *primary domain controller* (PDC) and can have one or more *backup domain controllers* (BDCs) as well. If the PDC fails or becomes inaccessible, its duties are automatically taken over by one of the BDCs. BDCs frequently synchronize their SAM data with the PDC so if the need arises, any one of them can immediately begin performing domain-controller services without impacting the clients. However, note that BDCs have read-only copies of the SAM database; they can update their data only by synchronizing with a PDC. A server in a Windows domain can use the SAM of any PDC or BDC to authenticate a user who attempts to access its resources and log on to the domain.

All recent versions of Windows can log on to a domain as clients to access the resources of the domain servers. The systems that are considered members of the domain are a more exclusive class, composed of the PDC and BDCs, as well as *domain member servers*, which are systems that have joined a domain as members, and are known to the domain controllers by having a computer account in the SAM database.

Authentication

When a user logs on to a Windows domain by typing in a username and password, a secure challenge and response protocol is invoked between the client computer and a domain controller to verify that the username and password are valid. Then the domain controller sends a SID back to the client, which uses it to create a Security Access Token (SAT) that is valid only for that system, to be used for further authentication. This access token has information about the user coded into it, including the username, the group, and the rights the user has within the domain. At this point, the user is logged on to the domain.

Subsequently, when the client attempts to access a shared resource within the domain, the client system enters into a secure challenge and response exchange with the server of the resource. The server then enters into another secure challenge and response conversation with a domain controller to check that the client is valid. (What actually happens is that the server uses information it gets from the client to pretend to be the client and authenticate itself with the domain controller. If the domain controller validates the credentials, it sends an SID back to the server, which uses the SID to create its own SAT for the client to enable access to its local resources on the client's behalf.) At this point, the client is authenticated for resources on the server and is allowed to access them. The server then uses the SID in the access token to determine what permissions the client has to use and modify the requested resource by comparing them to entries in the ACL of the resource.

Although this method of authentication might seem overly complicated, it allows clients to authenticate without having plain-text passwords travel through the network, and it is much more difficult to crack than the relatively weak workgroup security we described earlier.

Name service with WINS and DNS

The Windows Internet Name Service (WINS) is Microsoft's implementation of a NetBIOS name server (NBNS). As such, WINS inherits much of NetBIOS's characteristics. First, WINS is flat; you can have only simple machine names such as inca, mixtec, or navaho, and workgroups such as PERU, MEXICO, or USA. In addition, WINS is dynamic: when a client first comes online, it is required to report its hostname, its address, and its workgroup to the local WINS server. This WINS server will retain the information so long as the client periodically refreshes its WINS registration, which indicates that it's still connected to the network. Note that WINS servers are not workgroup- or domain-specific; they can contain information for multiple domains and/or workgroups, which might exist on more than one subnet.

Multiple WINS servers can be set to synchronize with each other. This allows entries for computers that come online and go offline in the network to propagate from one WINS server to another. While in theory this seems efficient, it can quickly become cumbersome if several WINS servers are covering a network. Because WINS services can cross multiple subnets (you'll either hardcode the address of a WINS server in each of your clients or obtain it via DHCP), it is often more efficient to have each Windows client, regardless of the number of Windows domains, point themselves to the same WINS server. That way, only one authoritative WINS server will have the correct information, instead of several WINS servers continually struggling to synchronize themselves with the most recent changes.

The currently active WINS server is known as the *primary WINS server*. You can also install a secondary WINS server, which will take over if the primary WINS server fails or becomes inaccessible. Both the primary and any other WINS servers will synchronize their address databases on a periodic basis.

In the Windows family of operating systems, only a server edition of Windows NT/2000 can act as a WINS server. Samba 2.2 can function as a primary WINS server, but cannot synchronize its database with other WINS servers. It therefore cannot act as a secondary WINS server or as a primary WINS server for a Windows secondary WINS server.

WINS handles name service by default, although Microsoft added DNS starting with Windows NT 4 Server. It is compatible with DNS that is standard on virtually every Unix system, and a Unix server (such as the Samba host) can also be used for DNS.

Trust relationships

One additional aspect of Windows NT domains not yet supported in Samba 2.2 is that it is possible to set up a *trust relationship* between domains, allowing clients within one domain to access the resources within another without the user having to go through additional authentication. The protocol that is followed is called *pass-through authentication,* in which the user's credentials are passed from the client system in the first domain to the server in the second domain, which consults a domain controller in the first (trusted) domain to check that the user is valid before granting access to the resource.

Note that in many aspects, the behaviors of a Windows workgroup and a Windows NT domain overlap. For example, the master and backup browsers in a domain are always the PDC and BDC, respectively. Let's update our Windows domain diagram to include both a local master and local backup browser. The result is shown in Figure 1-13.

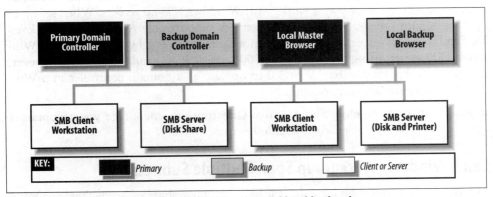

Figure 1-13. A Windows domain with a local master and local backup browser

The similarity between workgroups and NT domains is not accidental because the concept of Windows domains did not evolve until Windows NT 3.5 was introduced, and Windows domains were forced to remain backward-compatible with the workgroups present in Windows for Workgroups.

Samba can function as a primary domain controller for Windows 95/98/Me and Windows NT/2000/XP clients with the limitation that it can act as a PDC only, and not as a BDC.

Samba can also function as a *domain member server*, meaning that it has a computer account in the PDC's account database and is therefore recognized as being part of the domain. A domain member server does not authenticate users logging on to the domain, but still handles security functions (such as file permissions) for domain users accessing its resources.

Active Directory Domains

Starting with Windows 2000, Microsoft has introduced Active Directory, the next step beyond Windows NT domains. We won't go into much detail concerning Active Directory because it is a huge topic. Samba 2.2 doesn't support Active Directory at all, and support in Samba 3.0 is limited to acting as a client. For now, be aware that with Active Directory, the authentication model is centered around Lightweight Directory Access Protocol (LDAP), and name service is provided by DNS instead of WINS. Domains in Active Directory can be organized in a hierarchical tree structure, in which each domain controller operates as a peer, with no distinction between primary and backup controllers as in Windows NT domains.

Windows 2000/XP systems can be set up as simple workgroup or Windows NT domain clients (which will function with Samba). The server editions of Windows 2000 can be set up to run Active Directory and support Windows NT domains for backward compatibility (*mixed mode*). In this case, Samba 2.2 works with Windows 2000 servers in the same way it works with Windows NT 4.0 servers. When set up to operate in *native mode*, Windows 2000 servers support only Active Directory. Even so, Samba 2.2 can operate as a server in a domain hosted by a native-mode Windows 2000 server, using the Windows 2000 server's *PDC emulation mode*. However, it is not possible for Samba 2.2 or 3.0 to operate as a domain controller in a Windows 2000 Active Directory domain.

If you want to know more about Active Directory, we encourage you to obtain a copy of the O'Reilly book, *Windows 2000 Active Directory*.

Can a Windows Workgroup Span Multiple Subnets?

Yes, but most people who have done it have had their share of headaches. Spanning multiple subnets was not part of the initial design of Windows NT 3.5 or Windows for Workgroups. As a result, a Windows domain that spans two or more subnets is, in reality, the "gluing" together of two or more workgroups that share an identical name. The good news is that you can still use a PDC to control authentication across each subnet. The bad news is that things are not as simple with browsing.

As mentioned previously, each subnet must have its own local master browser. When a Windows domain spans multiple subnets, a system administrator will have to assign one of the computers as the *domain master browser*. The domain master browser will keep a browse list for the entire Windows domain. This browse list is created by periodically synchronizing the browse lists of each local master browser with the browse list of the domain master browser. After the synchronization, the local master browser and the domain master browser should contain identical entries. See Figure 1-14 for an illustration.

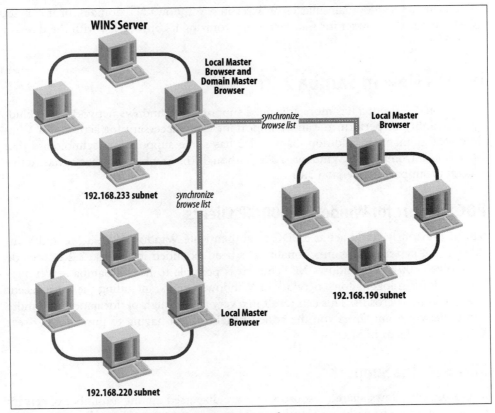

Figure 1-14. A workgroup that spans more than one subnet

Sound good? Well, it's not quite nirvana for the following reasons:

- If it exists, a PDC always plays the role of the domain master browser. By Microsoft design, the two always share the NetBIOS resource type <1B> and (unfortunately) cannot be separated.
- Windows 95/98/Me computers cannot become *or even contact* a domain master browser. This means that it is necessary to have at least one Windows NT/2000/XP system (or Samba server) on each subnet of a multisubnet workgroup.

Each subnet's local master browser continues to maintain the browse list for its subnet, for which it becomes authoritative. So if a computer wants to see a list of servers within its own subnet, the local master browser of that subnet will be queried. If a computer wants to see a list of servers outside the subnet, it can still go only as far as the local master browser. This works because at appointed intervals, the authoritative browse list of a subnet's local master browser is synchronized with the domain master browser, which is synchronized with the local master browser of the other subnets in the domain. This is called *browse list propagation*.

Samba can act as a domain master browser in a Windows NT domain, or it can act as a local master browser for a subnet, synchronizing its browse list with the domain master browser.

What's New in Samba 2.2?

In Version 2.2, Samba has more advanced support for Windows networking, including the ability to perform the more important tasks necessary for acting in a Windows NT domain. In addition, Samba 2.2 has some support for technologies that Microsoft introduced in Windows 2000, although the Samba team has saved Active Directory support for Version 3.0.

PDC Support for Windows 2000/XP Clients

Samba previously could act as a PDC to authenticate Windows 95/98/Me and Windows NT 4 systems. This functionality has been extended in Release 2.2 to include Windows 2000 and Windows XP. Thus, it is possible to have a Samba server supporting domain logons for a network of Windows clients, including the most recent releases from Microsoft. This can result in a very stable, high-performance, and more secure network, and gives you the added benefit of not having to purchase per-seat Windows CALs from Microsoft.

Microsoft Dfs Support

Microsoft Dfs allows shared resources that are dispersed among a number of servers in the network to be gathered together and appear to users as if they all exist in a single directory tree on one server. This method of organization makes life much simpler for users. Instead of having to browse around the network on a treasure hunt to locate the resource they want to use, they can go directly to the Dfs server and grab what they want. Samba 2.2 offers support for serving Dfs, so a Windows server is no longer needed for this purpose.

Windows NT/2000/XP Printing Support

Windows NT/2000/XP has a different Remote Procedure Call (RPC)–based printer interface than Windows 95/98/Me does. In Samba 2.2, the Windows NT/2000/XP interface is supported. Along with this, the Samba team has been adding support for automatically downloading the printer driver from the Samba server while adding a new printer to a Windows client.

ACLs

Samba now supports ACLs on its Unix host for Unix variants that support them. The list includes Solaris 2.6, 7, and 8, Irix, AIX, Linux (with either the ACL patch for the ext2/ext3 filesystem from *http://acl.bestbits.at* or when using the XFS filesystem), and FreeBSD (Version 5.0 and later). When using ACL support, Samba translates between Unix ACLs and Windows NT/2000/XP ACLs, making the Samba host look and act more like a Windows NT/2000/XP server from the point of view of Windows clients.

Support for Windows Client Administration Tools

Windows comes with tools that can be used from a client to manage shared resources remotely on a Windows server. Samba 2.2 allows these tools to operate on shares on the Samba server as well.

Integration with Winbind

Winbind is a facility that allows users whose account information is stored in a Windows domain database to authenticate on a Unix system. The result is a unified logon environment, in which a user account can be kept on either the Unix system or a Windows NT/2000 domain controller. This greatly facilitates account management because administrators no longer need to keep the two systems synchronized, and it is possible for users whose accounts are held in a Windows domain to authenticate when accessing Samba shares.

Unix CIFS Extensions

The Unix CIFS extensions were developed at Hewlett-Packard and introduced in Samba 2.2.4. They allow Samba servers to support Unix filesystem attributes, such as links and permissions, when sharing files with other Unix systems. This allows Samba to be used as an alternative to network file sharing (NFS) for Unix-to-Unix file sharing. An advantage of using Samba is that it authenticates individual users, whereas NFS authenticates only clients (based on their IP addresses, which is a poor security model). This gives Samba an edge in the area of security, along with its much greater configurability. See Chapter 5 for information on how to operate Unix systems as Samba clients.

And More...

As usual, the code has numerous improvements that do not show up at the administrative level in an immediate or obvious way. Samba now functions better on systems that employ PAM (Pluggable Authentication Modules), and there is new support for profiling. Samba's support for oplocks has been strengthened, offering better integration with NFS server-terminated leases (currently on Irix and Linux only) and in the local filesystem with SMB locks mapped to POSIX locks (which is dependent on each Unix variant's implementation of POSIX locks). And of course there have been the usual bug fixes.

What's New in Samba 3.0?

The main distinguishing feature of Samba 3.0 is that it includes support for Kerberos 5 authentication and LDAP, which are required to act as clients in an Active Directory domain. Another feature that appeared in Samba 3.0 is support for Unicode, which greatly simplifies supporting international languages.

In later Version 3 releases, the Samba team plans to develop support for WINS replication, allowing Samba to act as a secondary WINS server or as a primary WINS server with Windows or Samba secondary WINS servers. Also planned are support for acting as a Windows NT BDC and support for Windows NT domain trust relationships.

What Can Samba Do?

Now let's wrap up by showing where Samba can help out and where it is limited. Table 1-9 summarizes which roles Samba can and cannot play in a Windows NT or Active Directory domain or a Windows workgroup. Many of the Windows domain protocols are proprietary and have not been documented by Microsoft and therefore must be reverse-engineered by the Samba team before Samba can support them. As of Version 3.0, Samba cannot act as a backup in most roles and does not yet fully support Active Directory.

Table 1-9. Samba roles (as of Version 3.0)

Role	Can perform?
File server	Yes
Printer server	Yes
Microsoft Dfs server	Yes
Primary domain controller	Yes
Backup domain controller	No
Active Directory domain controller	No

Table 1-9. Samba roles (as of Version 3.0) (continued)

Role	Can perform?
Windows 95/98/Me authentication	Yes
Windows NT/2000/XP authentication	Yes
Local master browser	Yes
Local backup browser	Yes
Domain master browser	Yes
Primary WINS server	Yes
Secondary WINS server	No

An Overview of the Samba Distribution

As mentioned earlier, Samba actually contains several programs that serve different but related purposes. These programs are documented more fully in Appendix C. For now, we will introduce each of them briefly and describe how they work together.

The majority of the programs that come with Samba center on its two daemons. Let's take a refined look at the responsibilities of each daemon:

nmbd

> The *nmbd* daemon is a simple name server that supplies WINS functionality. This daemon listens for name-server requests and provides the appropriate IP addresses when called upon. It also provides browse lists for the Network Neighborhood and participates in browsing elections.

smbd

> The *smbd* daemon manages the shared resources between the Samba server and its clients. It provides file, print, and browse services to SMB clients across one or more networks and handles all notifications between the Samba server and the network clients. In addition, it is responsible for user authentication, resource locking, and data sharing through the SMB protocol.

New with Version 2.2, there is an additional daemon:

winbindd

> This daemon is used along with the name service switch to get information on users and groups from a Windows NT server and allows Samba to authorize users through a Windows NT/2000 server.

The Samba distribution also comes with a small set of Unix command-line tools:

findsmb

> A program that searches the local network for computers that respond to SMB protocol and prints information on them.

make_smbcodepage

A program used when working with Samba's internationalization features for telling Samba how to convert between upper- and lowercase in different character sets.

make_unicodemap

Another internationalization program used with Samba for compiling Unicode map files that Samba uses to translate DOS codepages or Unix character sets into 16-bit unicode.

net

A new program distributed with Samba 3.0 that can be used to perform remote administration of servers.

nmblookup

A program that provides NBT name lookups to find a computer's IP address when given its machine name.

pdbedit

A new program distributed with Samba 3.0 that is helpful for managing user accounts held in SAM databases.

rpcclient

A program that can be used to run MS-RPC functions on Windows clients.

smbcacls

A program that is used to set or show ACLs on Windows NT filesystems.

smbclient

An *ftp*-like Unix client that can be used to connect to SMB shares and operate on them. The *smbclient* command is discussed in detail in Chapter 5.

smbcontrol

A simple administrative utility that sends messages to *nmbd* or *smbd*.

smbgroupedit

A command that can be used to define mappings between Windows NT groups and Unix groups. It is new in Samba 3.0.

smbmnt

A helper utility used along with *smbmount*.

smbmount

A program that mounts an smbfs filesystem, allowing remote SMB shares to be mounted in the filesystem of the Samba host.

smbpasswd

A program that allows an administrator to change the passwords used by Samba.

smbsh

A tool that functions like a command shell to allow access to a remote SMB filesystem and allow Unix utilities to operate on it. This command is covered in Chapter 5.

smbspool
>   A print-spooling program used to send files to remote printers that are shared on the SMB network.

smbstatus
>   A program that reports the current network connections to the shares on a Samba server.

smbtar
>   A program similar to the Unix *tar* command, for backing up data in SMB shares.

smbumount
>   A program that works along with *smbmount* to unmount smbfs filesystems.

testparm
>   A simple program for checking the Samba configuration file.

testprns
>   A program that tests whether printers on the Samba host are recognized by the *smbd* daemon.

wbinfo
>   A utility used to query the *winbindd* daemon.

Each major release of Samba goes through an exposure test before it's announced. In addition, it is quickly updated afterward if problems or unwanted side effects are found. The latest stable distribution as of this writing is Samba 2.2.6, and this book focuses mainly on the functionality supported in Samba 2.2.6, as opposed to older versions of Samba.

How Can I Get Samba?

Source and binary distributions of Samba are available from mirror sites across the Internet. The primary web site for Samba is located at *http://www.samba.org/*. From there, you can select a mirror site that is geographically near you.

Most Linux and many Unix vendors provide binary packages. These can be more convenient to install and maintain than the Samba team's source or binary packages, due to the vendor's efforts to supply a package that matches its specific products.

CHAPTER 2
Installing Samba on a Unix System

Now that you know what Samba can do for you and your users, it's time to get your own network set up. Let's start with the installation of Samba. When dancing the samba, one learns by taking small steps. It's just the same when installing Samba; we need to teach it step by step. This chapter will help you start off on the right foot.

For illustrative purposes, we will be installing the 2.2.6 version of the Samba server on a Linux system running Version 2.4 of the kernel. However, the installation steps are essentially the same for all the platforms Samba supports.

Bundled Versions

Samba is in such popular use that many Unix distributions come with it already installed. If you choose to use a bundled version of Samba, you can breeze through most of this chapter, but you'll be stuck with the Samba version and compile-time options your vendor selected for you. That version of Samba can't be any newer than the operating system release, so you're likely to be pretty far behind the latest developments. On the other hand, you can be fairly sure that a bundled version has been installed properly, and perhaps it will take only a few simple modifications to your *smb.conf* file for you to be off and running. Samba is mature enough that you probably don't need the latest release to meet your basic needs, so you might be perfectly happy running a bundled version.

If you choose this option, be aware that your Samba files, including the very important *smb.conf,* might be in different places than they would be if you were to install from a binary or source distribution. For example, with the Red Hat, Debian, and Mandrake Linux distributions, *smb.conf* and some other Samba-related files are in the */etc/samba* directory.

If Samba is already installed on your system, you can check to see what version you have by using the command:

```
$ smbd -V
Version 2.2.6
```

(If this doesn't work, it might be because *smbd* is not in your shell's search path. If you have the *locate* or *whereis* command in your Unix variant, you can use it to locate the *smbd* executable.)

You might also be able to use a system-specific tool to query a software-package maintenance utility. On Red Hat Linux, you can use the *rpm* command to query the installed packages for Samba:

```
$ rpm -qa | grep samba
samba-client-2.0.8-1.7.1
samba-2.0.8-1.7.1
samba-common-2.0.8-1.7.1
```

This shows we have Samba 2.0.8, divided into three Red Hat Package Manager (RPM) packages, bundled with Red Hat 7.1. If your version of Samba is old, you might at the very least want to check with your vendor for an update.

Otherwise, if you're sure you are going to install from a binary or source distribution, you can remove the RPM packages as follows:

```
# rpm -e samba
# rpm -e samba-client
# rpm -e samba-common
```

If you are not using Red Hat Linux, consult your system's documentation to find the method that works for you.

Binary or Source?

Precompiled "binary" packages are also available for a large number of Unix platforms. These packages contain binaries for each Samba executable, as well as the standard Samba documentation. Note that while installing a binary distribution can save you a fair amount of time and trouble, you should keep a couple of issues in mind when deciding whether to use the binary or compile the source yourself:

- The binary packages can lag behind the latest version of the software by one or two (maybe more) minor releases, especially after a series of small changes and for less popular platforms. Compare the release notes for the source and binary packages to make sure there aren't any new features that you need on your platform.

- If you use a precompiled binary that is dynamically linked, you will need to ensure that you have the correct libraries required by the executables. If your system does not already have the required version of a library, you might have to install a new version. The *README* file or *makefile* that accompanies the binary distribution should list any special requirements.

  Many systems with shared libraries come with a nifty tool called *ldd*. This tool will tell you which libraries a specific binary requires and which libraries on the system satisfy that requirement. For example, checking the *smbd* program on our test machine gave us:

```
$ ldd smbd
        libdl.so.2 => /lib/libdl.so.2 (0x40026000)
        libnsl.so.1 => /lib/libnsl.so.1 (0x4002a000)
        libpam.so.0 => /lib/libpam.so.0 (0x40041000)
        libc.so.6 => /lib/libc.so.6 (0x40049000)
        /lib/ld-linux.so.2 => /lib/ld-linux.so.2 (0x40000000)
```

If there are any incompatibilities between Samba and specific libraries on your machine, the distribution-specific documentation should highlight them.

• If your precompiled binary is statically linked, it is still possible to have problems. There have been cases in which the statically linked C library calls in Samba programs have been out of sync with the operating-system kernel, even though this is "not supposed to happen."

• Keep in mind that each binary distribution carries preset values about the target platform, such as default directories and configuration option values. Again, check the documentation and the makefile included in the source directory to see which directives and variables were used when the binary was compiled. In some cases, these will not be appropriate for your situation.

A few configuration items can be reset with command-line options at runtime rather than at compile time. For example, if your binary tries to place any log, lock, or status files in the "wrong" place (for example, in */usr/local*), you can override this without recompiling.

One point worth mentioning is that the Samba source requires an ANSI C compiler. If you are on a legacy platform with a non-ANSI compiler, such as the *cc* compiler on SunOS Version 4, you'll have to install an ANSI-compliant compiler such as *gcc* before you do anything else.* If installing a compiler isn't something you want to wrestle with, you can start off with a binary package. However, for the most flexibility and compatibility on your system, we always recommend compiling from the latest stable or production source.

A typical installation will take about an hour to complete, including downloading the source files and compiling them, setting up the configuration files, and testing the server.

Here is an overview of the steps:

1. Download the source or binary files.
2. Read the installation documentation.
3. Configure a makefile.
4. Compile the server and utility programs.

---

* *gcc* binaries are available for almost every modern machine. See *http://www.gnu.org/* for a list of sites with *gcc* and other GNU software.

5. Install the server files.

6. Create a Samba configuration file.

7. Test the configuration file.

8. Start the Samba daemons.

9. Test the Samba daemons.

Downloading the Samba Distribution

If you would like to download the latest version of the Samba software, the primary web site is *http://www.samba.org*. Once connected to this page, you'll see links to several Samba mirror sites across the world, both for the standard Samba web pages and for sites devoted exclusively to downloading Samba. For the best performance, choose a site that is closest to your own geographic location.

The standard Samba web sites have Samba documentation and tutorials, mailing-list archives, and the latest Samba news, as well as source and binary distributions of Samba. The download sites (sometimes called *FTP sites*) have only the source and binary distributions. Unless you specifically want an older version of the Samba server or are going to install a binary distribution, download the latest source distribution from the closest mirror site. This distribution is always named:

```
samba-latest.tar.gz
```

which for the 2.2.6 release is an approximately 5MB file.

The source distribution has been archived with *tar* and then compressed with the GNU *gzip* program. To unpack it, move the file to the directory in which you want the Samba source directory to be located, then *cd* to that directory and run the command:

```
$ tar xvfz samba-latest.tar.gz
```

Or, if you do not have the GNU *tar* program (which also handles the unzipping):

```
$ gunzip samba-latest.tar.gz
$ tar xvf samba-latest.tar
```

In that latter case, you might need to install the GNU *gunzip* program first. While the *tar* command runs, it will print out a list of the files it installs.

Read the Documentation

This part might seem obvious, but at one time or other you probably uncompressed a package, blindly typed:

```
$ configure; make; make install
```

and walked away to get another cup of coffee. Do yourself a favor and be a little more careful this time.

In the top-level directory that you just installed, there is a file named *WHATSNEW.txt*, which contains the latest news about the release. If you are upgrading, you can find important information about bug fixes or configuration parameters that have been added or are no longer supported.

With both source and binary packages you'll find a large number of documents in the *docs* directory, in a variety of formats. One file is especially important:

```
docs/htmldocs/UNIX_INSTALL.html
```

This is the Samba Team's official instructions on installing Samba on a Unix system, which you might like to use as another perspective besides what we are telling you here.

In general, we expect you'll find to be most useful the files in the following directories:

docs/faq
> This is the Samba Frequently Asked Questions (FAQ) files.

docs/htmldocs
> This is the miscellaneous documentation in HTML format.

docs/textdocs
> Here is more documentation, in simple text format.

docs/manpages
> You don't need to worry about these yet; during the installation, the files will be installed so that you can use the *man* command to read them. But you can take a look in the directory to see which manpages are available.

Configuring Samba

Samba automatically configures itself prior to compilation. This reduces the likelihood of a machine-specific problem, but you might end up wishing for an option after Samba has been installed.

The source distribution of Samba 2.2 and above doesn't initially have a makefile. Instead, one is generated through a GNU *configure* script, which is located in the *samba-2.2.x/source/* directory. The *configure* script takes care of the machine-specific issues of building Samba.

> Before running the *configure* script, it is important that you become the root user on the system. Otherwise, you might get a warning such as:
>
> ```
> configure: warning: running as non-root will disable some
> tests
> ```
>
> You don't want any test to be disabled when the Samba makefile is being created; it would leave the potential for errors down the road when compiling or running Samba on your system.

When the *configure* script is run, it prints out messages telling what it is doing, and error messages might be mixed in. To make sure you see those very important error messages, we suggest you run *configure* with its standard output passed through some filter to capture the output and keep it from scrolling out of sight. One method is using the *more* command:

```
# ./configure | more
```

We will show you another in a moment.

Although you can run *configure* as previously with no options, you might want to add support for extra features by passing options on the command line. For example:

```
# ./configure --with-winbind
```

will configure the Samba makefile with support for winbind authentication. If you would like a complete list of options, type the following:

```
# ./configure --help
```

Each option enables or disables various features. You typically enable a feature by specifying the --with-*feature* option, which will cause the feature to be compiled and installed. Likewise, if you specify a --without-*feature* option, the feature will be disabled. A full list of configuration options is provided in Appendix E, but for now we want to point out three of them, which are features we cover later in this book:

--with-msdfs
> Include support for Microsoft Distributed filesystem (Dfs), which allows dispersed network resources to be clumped together into one easy-to-navigate directory tree. See Chapter 8.

--with-smbwrapper
> Include SMB wrapper support, which allows programs running on the Unix host to access SMB shared folders as if they were Unix filesystems. We recommend using this option. See Chapter 5.

--with-smbmount
> Include *smbmount* support, which allows SMB shared folders to be mounted in the Unix filesystem. At the time of this writing, support for this feature exists only for Linux. This is also covered in Chapter 5.

Each option is disabled by default, and none of the features is essential to Samba. However, you may want to include them in your configuration (as we will in our example) at least to be able to try out the options in later chapters.

In addition, Table 2-1 shows some other parameters that you can give the *configure* script if you wish to store parts of the Samba distribution in different places, perhaps to make use of multiple disks or partitions. Note that the defaults sometimes refer to a prefix specified earlier in the table.

Table 2-1. Additional configure options

Option	Meaning	Default
--prefix=*directory*	Install architecture-independent files at the base directory specified.	*/usr/local/samba*
--eprefix=*directory*	Install architecture-dependent files at the base directory specified.	*/usr/local/samba*
--bindir=*directory*	Install user executables in the directory specified.	*eprefix/bin*
--sbindir=*directory*	Install administrator executables in the directory specified.	*eprefix/bin*
--libexecdir=*directory*	Install program executables in the directory specified.	*eprefix/libexec*
--datadir=*directory*	Install read-only architecture-independent data in the directory specified.	*prefix/share*
--libdir=*directory*	Install program libraries in the directory specified.	*eprefix/lib*
--includedir=*directory*	Install package-include files in the directory specified.	*prefix/include*
--infodir=*directory*	Install additional information files in the directory specified.	*prefix/info*
--mandir=*directory*	Install manual pages in the directory specified.	*prefix/man*

Here is a sample execution of the *configure* script, which creates a Samba 2.2.6 makefile for the Linux platform. Note that you must run the configure script in the *source* directory and that we are showing you yet another way to capture the output of the script:

```
$ cd samba-2.2.6/source/
$ su
Password:
# ./configure --with-smbwrapper --with-smbmount \
--with-msdfs --with-syslog --with-utmp 2>&1 | tee config.my.log
loading cache ./config.cache
checking for gcc... (cached) gcc
checking whether the C compiler (gcc -O ) works... yes
checking whether the C compiler (gcc -O ) is a cross-compiler... no
checking whether we are using GNU C... (cached) yes
checking whether gcc accepts -g... (cached) yes
checking for a BSD-compatible install... (cached) /usr/bin/install -c

...(content omitted)...

checking configure summary
configure OK
creating ./config.status
creating include/stamp-h
creating Makefile
creating include/config.h
```

In general, any message from *configure* that doesn't begin with the words checking or creating is an error; it often helps to redirect the output of the configure script to a file so that you can quickly search for errors, as we did with the *tee* command earlier. If there was an error during configuration, more detailed information about it can be found in the *config.log* file, which is written to the local directory by the *configure* script, as well as in the *config.my.log* file, which we created by piping through the *tee* command. These files are very similar in both name and content, but be careful to check both of them for error messages before continuing!

If the configuration works, you'll see a `checking configure summary` message followed by a `configure OK` message and four or five file-creation messages. So far, so good.

Compiling and Installing Samba

At this point you should be ready to build the Samba executables. Compiling is also easy: in the *source* directory, type `make` on the command line. The *make* utility will produce a stream of explanatory and success messages, beginning with:

```
Using FLAGS = -O -Iinclude ...
```

This build includes compiles for both *smbd* and *nmbd* and ends in a linking command for *bin/nmblookup*. For example, here is a sample make of Samba Version 2.2.6 on a Linux server:

```
# make 2>&1 | tee make.log
Using FLAGS =  -O  -Iinclude -I./include -I./ubiqx -I./smbwrapper -D_LARGEFILE64
_SOURCE -D_FILE_OFFSET_BITS=64 -D_GNU_SOURCE  -DLOGFILEBASE="/usr/local/samba/va
r" -DCONFIGFILE="/usr/local/samba/lib/smb.conf" -DLMHOSTSFILE="/usr/local/samba/
lib/lmhosts"   -DSWATDIR="/usr/local/samba/swat" -DSBINDIR="/usr/local/samba/bin
" -DLOCKDIR="/usr/local/samba/var/locks" -DCODEPAGEDIR="/usr/local/samba/lib/cod
epages" -DDRIVERFILE="/usr/local/samba/lib/printers.def" -DBINDIR="/usr/local/sa
mba/bin"  -DHAVE_INCLUDES_H -DPASSWD_PROGRAM="/bin/passwd" -DSMB_PASSWD_FILE="/u
sr/local/samba/private/smbpasswd" -DTDB_PASSWD_FILE="/usr/local/samba/private/sm
bpasswd.tdb"
Using FLAGS32 =  -O  -Iinclude -I./include -I./ubiqx -I./smbwrapper -D_LARGEFILE
64_SOURCE -D_FILE_OFFSET_BITS=64 -D_GNU_SOURCE  -DLOGFILEBASE="/usr/local/samba/
var" -DCONFIGFILE="/usr/local/samba/lib/smb.conf" -DLMHOSTSFILE="/usr/local/samb
a/lib/lmhosts"   -DSWATDIR="/usr/local/samba/swat" -DSBINDIR="/usr/local/samba/b
in" -DLOCKDIR="/usr/local/samba/var/locks" -DCODEPAGEDIR="/usr/local/samba/lib/c
odepages" -DDRIVERFILE="/usr/local/samba/lib/printers.def" -DBINDIR="/usr/local/
samba/bin"  -DHAVE_INCLUDES_H -DPASSWD_PROGRAM="/bin/passwd" -DSMB_PASSWD_FILE="
/usr/local/samba/private/smbpasswd" -DTDB_PASSWD_FILE="/usr/local/samba/private/
smbpasswd.tdb"
Using LIBS = -ldl -lnsl -lpam
Compiling smbd/server.c
Compiling smbd/files.c
Compiling smbd/chgpasswd.c
Compiling smbd/connection.c
Compiling smbd/utmp.c
Compiling smbd/session.c
Compiling smbd/dfree.c
Compiling smbd/dir.c

...(content omitted)...
```

```
Compiling rpc_server/srv_srvsvc.c
Compiling rpc_server/srv_srvsvc_nt.c
Compiling rpc_server/srv_util.c
Compiling rpc_server/srv_wkssvc.c
Compiling rpc_server/srv_wkssvc_nt.c
Compiling rpc_server/srv_pipe.c
Compiling rpc_server/srv_dfs.c
Compiling rpc_server/srv_dfs_nt.c
Compiling rpc_server/srv_spoolss.c
Compiling rpc_server/srv_spoolss_nt.c
Compiling lib/util_getent.c
Compiling rpc_parse/parse_lsa.c
Compiling rpc_parse/parse_net.c
Compiling rpc_parse/parsen/smbmount
Compiling client/smbmnt.c
Linking bin/smbmnt
Compiling client/smbumount.c
Linking bin/smbumount
Compiling utils/nmblookup.c
Linking bin/nmblookup
```

If you encounter a problem when compiling, first check the Samba documentation to see if it is easily fixable. Another possibility is to search or post to the Samba mailing lists, which are given at the end of Chapter 12 and on the Samba home page. Most compilation issues are system-specific and almost always easy to overcome.

Now that the files have been compiled, you can install them into the directories you identified with the command:

```
# make install
```

If you happen to be upgrading, your old Samba files will be saved with the extension *.old,* and you can go back to that previous version with the command make revert. After doing a make install, you should copy the *.old* files (if they exist) to a new location or name. Otherwise, the next time you install Samba, the original *.old* will be overwritten without warning and you could lose your earlier version. If you configured Samba to use the default locations for files, the new files will be installed in the directories listed in Table 2-2. Remember that you need to perform the installation from an account that has write privileges on these target directories; this is typically the root account.

Table 2-2. Samba installation directories

Directory	Description
/usr/local/samba	Main tree
/usr/local/samba/bin	Binaries
/usr/local/samba/lib	*smb.conf, lmhosts,* configuration files, etc.
/usr/local/samba/man	Samba documentation
/usr/local/samba/private	Samba-encrypted password file

Table 2-2. Samba installation directories (continued)

Directory	Description
/usr/local/samba/swat	SWAT files
/usr/local/samba/var	Samba log files, lock files, browse list info, shared memory files, process ID files

Throughout the remainder of the book, we occasionally refer to the location of the main tree as */usr/local/samba*. In most configurations, this is the base directory of the installed Samba package; however, it can vary from system to system.

 Watch out if you've made */usr* a read-only partition. You will want to put the logs, locks, and password files somewhere else.

Here is the installation that we performed on our machine. You can see that we used */usr/local/samba* as the base directory for the distribution:

```
# make install 2>&1 | tee make-install.log
Using FLAGS =  -O  -Iinclude -I./include -I./ubiqx -I./smbwrapper -D_LARGEFILE64
_SOURCE -D_FILE_OFFSET_BITS=64 -D_GNU_SOURCE  -DLOGFILEBASE="/usr/local/samba/va
r" -DCONFIGFILE="/usr/local/samba/lib/smb.conf"
```

...(content omitted)...

```
The binaries are installed. You can restore the old binaries (if there
were any) using the command "make revert". You can uninstall the binaries
using the command "make uninstallbin" or "make uninstall" to uninstall
binaries, manpages and shell scripts.
```

...(content omitted)...

```
=======================================================================
The SWAT files have been installed. Remember to read the swat/README
for information on enabling and using SWAT.
=======================================================================
```

If the last message is about SWAT, you've successfully installed all the files. Congratulations! You now have Samba on your system!

Upgrading Your Installation

Eventually a new version of Samba will be released, and you will want to upgrade. This is simple; just repeat the same steps you used to install your current version. Download the source distribution from the Samba web site and install it, then run the ./configure, make, and make install commands as before. If you've forgotten which options you used with the *configure* script, take a look at the *source/config. status* file in your previous version's source distribution. The first few lines of this file show the options used the last time *configure* was run.

When you run the make install command to install your new version, the files of the previous version are replaced with the new ones, and then all you have to do is restart the Samba daemons to get your new version running. See the section later in this chapter called "Starting the Samba Daemons" for directions on how to do this.

Reconfiguring Samba

If you have already compiled Samba and wish to recompile the same source code with different *configure* options, you should run the following three commands in the *source* directory before rerunning the *configure* script:

```
# autoconf
# make clean
# rm config.cache
```

This ensures that you are starting with a clean slate and that your previous *configure* command does not leave any data around that can affect your new build. From here, you can rerun ./configure and then make and make install.

Setting Search Paths

You will probably want to run commands included in the Samba distribution without having to specify their full directory paths. For that to work, the directory in which the Samba executables are located, */usr/local/samba/bin* by default, must be added to your shell's PATH environment variable. This environment variable is usually set in one or more of the shell's startup files, which in the case of *bash* are */etc/profile* (systemwide) and the *.bash_profile* and *.bashrc* files in each user's home directory.

To be able to read the Samba manual pages using the *man* command, the directory where Samba's manual pages reside, */usr/local/samba/man* by default, must be in your MANPATH environment variable. On Red Hat Linux, this can be accomplished by adding the following two lines to */etc/man.config*:

```
MANPATH     /usr/local/samba/man
MANPATH_MAP /usr/local/samba/bin /usr/local/samba/man
```

Enabling SWAT

The Samba Web Administration Tool (SWAT) runs as a daemon under *inetd* or *xinetd* and provides a forms-based editor in your web browser for creating and modifying Samba's configuration file. For SWAT to work, entries must be added for it in the */etc/services* and */etc/inetd.conf* (or */etc/xinetd.d/swat*) configuration files. To add the entries, follow these two steps:

1. Check your */etc/services* file, and if it does not contain the following line, add it to the end of the file:

```
swat    901/tcp
```

2. Now for *inetd* or *xinetd*. These are "Internet super daemons" that handle starting daemons on demand, instead of letting them sit around in memory consuming system resources. Most systems use *inetd*, but *xinetd* is also used in some versions of Unix, notably the Red Hat Linux (Versions 7 and newer) that we use in our examples. You can use the *ps* command to see which of the two your system is running.

For *inetd*, add a line to the */etc/inetd.conf* file. (Check your *inetd.conf* manual page to see the exact format of the *inetd.conf* file if it differs from the following example.) Don't forget to change the path to the SWAT binary if you installed it in a different location from the default */usr/local/samba*:

```
swat    stream tcp nowait root  /usr/local/samba/bin/swat  swat
```

Then force *inetd* to reread its configuration file by sending it a SIGHUP (hangup) signal:

```
# /bin/kill -HUP -a inetd
```

Notice that we are using a version of the *kill* command that supports the *-a* option, so as to allow us to specify the process by name. On FreeBSD and Linux, you can use the *killall* command* as follows:

```
# killall -HUP inetd
```

If you are not running Linux or FreeBSD and your version of *kill* doesn't have the *-a* option, you will need to use the *ps* command to find the process ID and then supply that to *kill*:

```
# ps ax | grep inetd
  780 ?          S      0:00 inetd
 1981 pts/4      S      0:00 grep inetd
# kill -HUP 780
```

If your system is using *xinet*, add a file named *swat* in your */etc/xinetd.d* directory, containing the following:

```
# description: swat is the Samba Web Administration Tool, which
#        allows an administrator to configure Samba using a web
#        browser interface, with the URL http://localhost:901
service swat.
{
        socket_type             = stream
        wait                    = no
        protocol                = tcp
        only_from               = localhost
        user                    = root
        log_on_failure          += USERID
        server                  = /usr/local/samba/bin/swat
        port                    = 901
        disable                 = no
}
```

---

* Do not confuse this with the Solaris *killall* command, which performs part of the system shutdown sequence!

Then *xinetd* needs to be sent a signal* to make it reread its configuration files:

```
# /bin/kill -HUP -a xinetd
```

And that's pretty much it for the installation. Before you can start up Samba, however, you need to create a configuration file for it.

A Basic Samba Configuration File

The key to configuring Samba is its configuration file, *smb.conf*. This configuration file can be very simple or extremely complex, and the rest of this book is devoted to helping you get deeply personal with this file. For now, however, we'll show you how to set up a single file service, which will allow you to fire up the Samba daemons and see that everything is running as it should be. In later chapters, you will see how to configure Samba for more complicated and interesting tasks.

The installation process does not automatically create an *smb.conf* configuration file, although several example files are included in the Samba distribution. To test the server software, though, we'll use the following file, which you can create in a text editor. It should be named *smb.conf* and placed in the */usr/local/samba/lib* directory:†

```
[global]
    workgroup = METRAN
[test]
    comment = For testing only, please
    path = /usr/local/samba/tmp
    read only = no
    guest ok = yes
```

This brief configuration file tells the Samba server to offer the */usr/local/samba/tmp* directory on the server as an SMB share called *test*. The server also becomes part of the METRAN workgroup, of which each client must also be a part. If you have already chosen a name for your own workgroup, use the name of your workgroup instead of METRAN in the previous example. In case you are connecting your Samba system into an existing network and need to know the workgroup name, you can ask another system administrator or go to a Windows system in the workgroup and follow these instructions:

- Windows 95/98/Me/NT: open the Control Panel, then double-click the Network icon. Click the Identification tab, and look for the "Workgroup:" label.

---

* Depending on the version of *xinetd* you have and how it was compiled, you might need to send a USR1 or some other signal rather than the HUP signal. Check the manual page for *xinetd*(8) on your system for details.

† If you did not compile Samba, but instead downloaded a binary, check with the documentation for the package to find out where it expects the *smb.conf* file to be. Or, try running the *testparm* program and look for the location of *smb.conf* in the first line of output. If Samba came preinstalled with your Unix system, an *smb.conf* file is probably already somewhere on your system.

- Windows 2000: open the Control Panel and double-click the System icon. Click the Network Identification tab. The workgroup name will appear below the computer name.
- Windows XP: open the Control Panel in Classic View mode and double-click the System icon. Then click the Computer Name tab.

We'll use the [test] share in the next chapter to set up the Windows clients. For now, you can complete the setup by performing the following commands as root on your Unix server:

```
# mkdir /usr/local/samba/tmp
# chmod 777 /usr/local/samba/tmp
```

You might also want to put a file or two in the /usr/local/samba/tmp directory so that after your Windows systems are initially configured, you will have something to use to check that everything works.

We should point out that in terms of system security, this is the worst setup possible. For the moment, however, we only wish to test Samba, so we'll leave security out of the picture. In addition, we will encounter some encrypted password issues with Windows clients later on, so this setup will afford us the least amount of headaches.

Encrypted Passwords

If your Windows clients are using Windows 98 or Windows NT 4 Service Pack 3 or above (including Windows 2000 and Windows XP) and you are using a version of Samba earlier than 3.0, you must add the following entry to the [global] section of the Samba configuration file:

```
[global]
     encrypt passwords = yes
```

In addition, you must use the *smbpasswd* program (typically located in the directory /usr/local/samba/bin/) to enter the username/password combinations of the Samba users into Samba's encrypted password database. For example, if you wanted to allow Unix user steve to access shares from a client system, you would use this command:

```
# smbpasswd -a steve
New SMB password:
Retype new SMB password:
Added user steve.
```

When the first user is added, the program will output a message saying that the encrypted password database does not exist. Don't worry: it will then create the database for you. Make sure that the username/password combinations you add to the encrypted database match the usernames and passwords you intend to use on the Windows client side. You must run *smbpasswd* for each client user.

In Samba 3.0, passwords are encrypted by default, so the encrypt passwords = yes parameter in the configuration file is optional. However, you will still need to run the *smbpasswd* command to add users to the encrypted password file.

Using SWAT

Creating a configuration file with SWAT is even easier than writing a configuration file by hand. To invoke SWAT, use your web browser to connect to *http://localhost:901*, and log on as root with the root password, as shown in Figure 2-1.

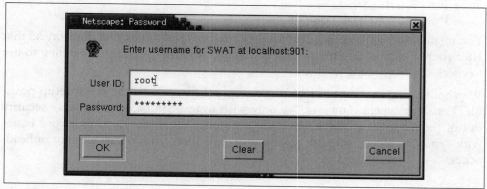

Figure 2-1. SWAT login

After logging in, click the GLOBALS button at the top of the screen. You should see the Global Variables page shown in Figure 2-2.

In this example, notice that SWAT retrieved the workgroup name from the *smb.conf* file that you created. (If it didn't, go back and perform that step correctly.) Make sure that the security field is set to USER.

If you are running Samba 2.2 and your Windows clients are at least Windows 98 or Windows NT 4 SP 3 or later versions, find encrypt passwords in the Security Options section and select yes.

The only other option you need to change from the menu is one determining which system on the LAN resolves NetBIOS addresses; this system is called the *WINS server*. At the very bottom of the page, set the wins support field to Yes, unless you already have a WINS server on your network. If you do, put the WINS server's IP address in the wins server field instead. Then return to the top of the screen, and press the Commit Changes button to write the changes out to the *smb.conf* file.

Next, click the SHARES icon. You should see a page similar to Figure 2-3. Select test (to the right of the Choose Share button), and click the Choose Share button. You will see the Share Parameters screen, as shown in Figure 2-3, with the comment and path fields filled in from your *smb.conf* file.

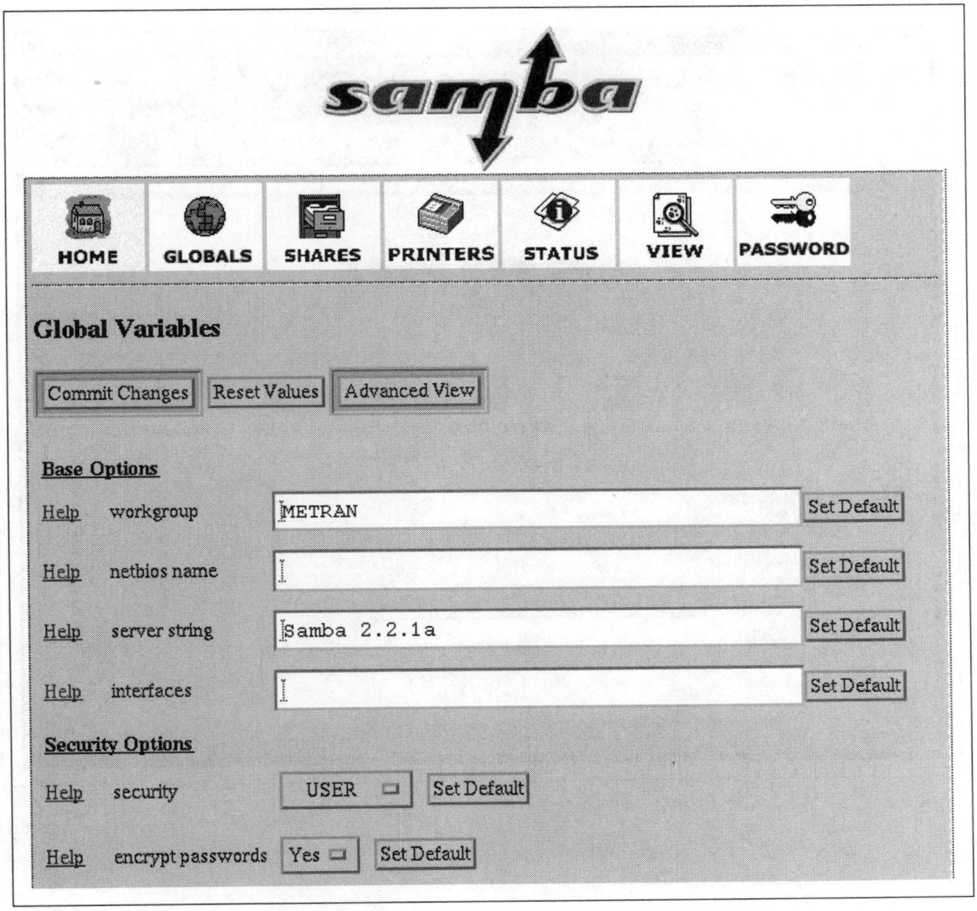

Figure 2-2. SWAT Global Variables page

If you specified that you want to use encrypted passwords on the GLOBALS page, click the PASSWORD button. Near the top of the screen, you will see the Server Password Management section. Enter your Unix username and password in the spaces, and click the Add New User button. This functions the same as the *smb-passwd* utility and creates an entry in the */usr/local/samba/private/smbpasswd* file to allow you to authenticate from a Windows client.

Now click the VIEW button at the top, and SWAT shows you the following *smb.conf* file:

```
# Samba config file created using SWAT
# from localhost (127.0.0.1)
# Date: 2002/09/05 04:56:43

# Global parameters
        workgroup = METRAN
```

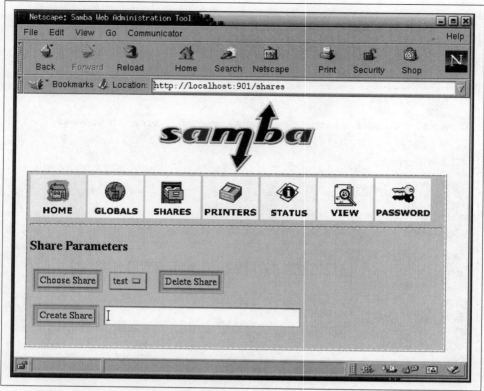

Figure 2-3. SWAT Share Parameters screen

```
        encrypt passwords = Yes
        wins support = Yes

[test]
        comment = For testing only!
        path = /usr/local/samba/tmp
        read only = No
```

Once this configuration file is completed, you can skip the next step because the output of SWAT is guaranteed to be syntactically correct.

Disabling Oplocks

The *smb.conf* file you have just created is certainly good enough for the purpose of initial setup and testing, and you can use it as a starting point from which to develop the configuration of your production Samba server. But before you get too far with that, we want to bring one thing to your attention.

If you are the type of administrator who is highly concerned about data integrity, you might want to make the following modification to your *smb.conf* file before continuing:

```
[global]
    oplocks = no
```

That is, use a text editor to add the line `oplocks = no` to the `[global]` section of your *smb.conf* file. With this example, as with other examples we will present throughout this book, you do not need to enter the `[global]` line again in your configuration file. We include it only to indicate in which section the parameter belongs.

The `oplocks = no` parameter disables opportunistic locking by clients. This will result in significantly poorer performance, but will help ensure that flaky Windows clients and/or unreliable network hardware will not lead to corrupted files on the Samba server.

We will cover opportunistic locking (oplocks) in more detail in the section "Locks and Oplocks" in Chapter 8, and recommend that you understand the ideas presented there before implementing a production Samba server that serves database files or other valuable data.

Testing the Configuration File

If you didn't use SWAT to create your configuration file, you should probably test it to ensure that it is syntactically correct. It might seem silly to run a test program against an eight-line configuration file, but it's good practice for the real ones that we'll be writing later on.

The test parser, *testparm*, examines an *smb.conf* file for syntax errors and reports any it finds along with a list of the services enabled on your machine. An example follows; you'll notice that in our haste to get the server running we mistyped `workgroup` as `workgrp` (the output is often lengthy, so we recommend capturing it with the *tee* command):

```
Load smb config files from smb.conf
Unknown parameter encountered: "workgrp"
Ignoring unknown parameter "workgrp"
Processing section "[test]"
Loaded services file OK.
Press Enter to see a dump of your service definitions
# Global parameters
[global]
    workgroup = WORKGROUP
    netbios name =
    netbios aliases =
    server string = Samba 2.2.6
    interfaces =
    bind interfaces only = No

...(content omitted)...

[test]
    comment = For testing only!
    path = /usr/local/samba/tmp
    read only = No
```

The interesting parts are at the top and bottom. The top of the output will flag any syntax errors that you might have made, and the bottom lists the services that the server thinks it should offer. A word of advice: make sure you and the server have the same expectations.

Firewall Configuration

As with any services that run on TCP/IP, the SMB networking services offered by Samba can be accessed from across the Internet unless your organization's firewall is properly configured. The following ports are used by Samba for SMB networking and SWAT:

Port 137
    Used for NetBIOS network browsing

Port 138
    Used for NetBIOS name service

Port 139
    Used for file and printer sharing and other operations

Port 445
    Used by Windows 2000/XP when NetBIOS over TCP/IP is disabled

Port 901
    Used by SWAT

At the minimum, your organization's Internet firewall should shut down all the ports in the list to traffic in both directions. Do not assume that preventing incoming connections is sufficient; there are cracks that trick Windows clients into sending data out of the local area network and into the Internet by SMB protocol, even from a local network that uses private IP addresses not forwarded by routers. If you want SMB traffic to travel across the Internet to remote sites, the best way is to use a virtual private network (VPN). See the O'Reilly book, *Virtual Private Networks*, for more information on this subject.

In addition, you might wish to configure a firewall on the Samba host system to keep SMB packets from traveling further than necessary within your organization's network. For example, port 901 can be shut down for remote accesses so that SWAT can be run only on the Samba host system. If you are using Samba to serve only a fraction of the client systems within your organization, consider allowing SMB packets (i.e., packets on ports 137–139 and 445) to go to or come from only those clients.

For more information on configuring firewalls, see the O'Reilly book *Building Internet Firewalls*.

Starting the Samba Daemons

Two Samba processes, *smbd* and *nmbd*, need to be running for Samba to work correctly. There are three ways to start them:

- Manually
- Automatically, during system boot
- From *inetd or xinetd*

Starting the Daemons Manually

If you're in a hurry, you can start the Samba daemons by hand. As root, simply enter the following commands:

```
# /usr/local/samba/bin/smbd -D
# /usr/local/samba/bin/nmbd -D
```

Samba will now be running on your system and is ready to accept connections. However, keep in mind that if either of the daemons exit for any reason (including system reboots), they will need to be restarted manually.

Automatic Startup

To have the Samba daemons started automatically when the system boots, you need to add the commands listed in the previous section to your standard Unix startup scripts. The exact method varies depending on the flavor of Unix you're using.

BSD Unix

With a BSD-style Unix, you need to append the following code to the *rc.local* file, which is typically found in the */etc* or */etc/rc.d* directories:

```
if [ -x /usr/local/samba/bin/smbd]; then
    echo "Starting smbd..."
    /usr/local/samba/bin/smbd -D
    echo "Starting nmbd..."
    /usr/local/samba/bin/nmbd -D
fi
```

This code is very simple: it checks to see if the *smbd* file exists and has execute permissions, and if it does, it starts up both of the Samba daemons on system boot.

System V Unix

With System V, things can get a little more complex. Depending on your Unix version, you might be able to get away with making a simple change to an *rc.local* file as with BSD Unix, but System V typically uses directories containing links to scripts that control daemons on the system. Hence, you need to instruct the system how to start and stop the Samba daemons. The first step to implement this is to modify the contents of the */etc/rc.d/init.d* directory by adding something similar to the following shell script, which for this example we will name *smb*:

```
#!/bin/sh

# Check that the Samba configuration file exists
[ -f /usr/local/samba/lib/smb.conf ] || exit 0

start()
{
        echo -n "Starting SMB services: "
        /usr/local/samba/bin/smbd -D
        ERROR=$?
        echo

        echo -n "Starting NMB services: "
        /usr/local/samba/bin/nmbd -D
        ERROR2=$?
        if [ $ERROR2 -ne 0 ]
        then
                ERROR=1
        fi
        echo

        return $ERROR
}

stop()
{
        echo -n "Shutting down SMB services: "
        /bin/kill -TERM -a smbd
        ERROR=$?
        echo

        echo -n "Shutting down NMB services: "
        /bin/kill -TERM -a nmbd
        ERROR2=$?
        if [ $ERROR2 -ne 0 ]
        then
                ERROR=1
        fi
        echo

        return $ERROR
}

case "$1" in
    start)
        start
        ;;
    stop)
        stop
        ;;
```

```
    *)
            echo "Usage: $0 {start|stop}"
            exit 1
    esac

    exit $?
```

With this script, you can start and stop *smbd* and *nmbd* like this:

```
# /etc/rc.d/init.d/smb start
Starting SMB services:
Starting NMB services:
# ps ax | grep mbd
  1268 ?         S        0:00 /usr/local/samba/bin/smbd -D
  1270 ?         S        0:00 /usr/local/samba/bin/nmbd -D
  1465 pts/2     S        0:00 grep mbd
# /etc/rc.d/init.d/smb stop
Shutting down SMB services:
Shutting down NMB services:
```

If you are having trouble writing a startup script for your system, check to see if there is a packaged release of Samba (available from your Unix vendor or the Samba FTP site). If so, you might be able to extract a startup script from it to use as a starting point. Typically, this script doesn't change much (if at all) from release to release, so using a script from an older Samba version should not be a problem. Another possibility is to check the *packaging* directory in the Samba source distribution. In that directory, there are subdirectories for many Unix versions in which you can find a startup script for those versions. Even if your version isn't included, you can probably find a startup script for a similar version to use as a starting point.

Finally, we need to add symbolic links to the *smb* script in the */etc/rc.d/rcX.d* directories:

```
# ln -s /etc/rc.d/init.d/smb /etc/rc.d/rc3.d/S35smb
# ln -s /etc/rc.d/init.d/smb /etc/rc.d/rc5.d/S35smb

# ln -s /etc/rc.d/init.d/smb /etc/rc.d/rc0.d/K35smb
# ln -s /etc/rc.d/init.d/smb /etc/rc.d/rc1.d/K35smb
# ln -s /etc/rc.d/init.d/smb /etc/rc.d/rc2.d/K35smb
# ln -s /etc/rc.d/init.d/smb /etc/rc.d/rc4.d/K35smb
# ln -s /etc/rc.d/init.d/smb /etc/rc.d/rc6.d/K35smb
```

The first two commands, with link names starting with an "S", cause Samba to be started when entering runlevels 3 or 5, which are the runlevels in which network file sharing (NFS) is normally enabled. The second group of commands, with link names starting with a "K", cause Samba to be shut down when entering any of the other runlevels (0, 1, 2, 4, or 6).

The links starting with "S" are used to start the daemons, and the links starting with "K" are used for killing them. When the runlevel is changed, the links starting with "K" in the corresponding directory (e.g., the *rc3.d* directory for runlevel 3) are executed, followed by the links starting with "S". If we wanted, we could have Samba restarted when switching between runlevels 3 and 5 by adding a *K35smb* link to each *rc3.d* and *rc5.d* directory.

The number after the K or S in the link names is used to set the order in which all the daemons with links in the directory are started or killed off. Get a long listing of the *rc3.d* or *rc5.d* directories to see how this is set up on your system. We use 35 to match the behavior of Red Hat's Samba RPM package. The important thing is to make sure when starting Samba that all services it requires are started before it. When shutting down, it is a good idea to shut down Samba before services it requires to avoid excess error messages in the log files, but the order is not as crucial.

Darwin and Mac OS X

An installation of Samba is bundled with the Darwin distribution, which is included in Mac OS X.* The Samba daemons are started during system boot by the script */System/Library/StartupItems/Samba/Samba*. To trigger the execution of this script, edit the file */etc/hostconfig* and change the SMBSERVER parameter to look like this:

```
SMBSERVER=-YES-
```

On Mac OS X, the graphical user interface (GUI) provides an alternative to using the command line. Launch the System Preferences application, and select Sharing (see Figure 2-4). Under the Services tab, turn on Windows File Sharing. This will make the aforementioned change to */etc/hostconfig* and immediately execute the startup item.

If you decide to install Samba yourself on Mac OS X, it's best not to stomp on the installation provided with the OS. Use the procedures detailed earlier in this chapter to install the software into */usr/local/samba* or some other area unaffected by OS upgrades. (Remember to set up users with *smbpasswd* if you're using encrypted passwords, as described earlier in this chapter. This step is handled automatically with entries in */var/db/samba/hash* if you're using the built-in server on Mac OS X.) Once you've got that working, you can edit the Samba startup item script to refer to your installation, like this:

```
#!/bin/sh
# Start Samba

. /etc/rc.common

if [ "${SMBSERVER:=-NO-}" = "-YES-" ]; then
    ConsoleMessage "Starting SMB server"

    if [ -f /usr/local/samba/lib/smb.conf ]; then
        /usr/local/samba/bin/smbd -D
```

* In this book, we cover Darwin Version 6.0 and OS X Version 10.2.

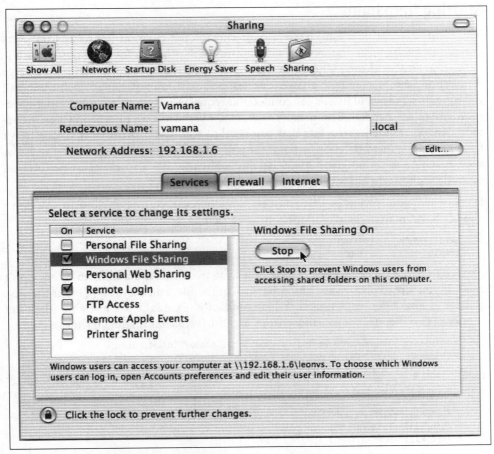

Figure 2-4. Mac OS X sharing preferences

```
          /usr/local/samba/bin/nmbd -D
    fi
fi
```

However, beware of OS updates, which can wipe out your changes. One solution is to make the script immutable, like this:

```
# chflags uchg /System/Library/StartupItems/Samba/Samba
```

Testing automatic startup

If you can afford a few minutes of downtime, reboot your system and again use the *ps* command to check that the *smbd* and *nmbd* daemons are running. And if you are managing a 24/7 server, we highly recommend that you find some downtime in which to reboot and perform this check. Otherwise, your next unscheduled downtime might surprise you with a mysterious absence of SMB networking services when the system comes up again!

Starting from inetd

The *inetd*[*] daemon is a Unix system's Internet "super daemon." It listens on ports defined in */etc/services* and executes the appropriate program for each port, which is defined in */etc/inetd.conf*. The advantage of this scheme is that you can have a large number of daemons ready to answer queries, but they don't all have to be running all the time. Instead, *inetd* listens for connection requests and starts the appropriate daemon when it is needed. The penalty is a small overhead cost of creating a new daemon process, as well as the fact that you need to edit two files rather than one to set things up. The *inetd* daemon is handy if you have only one or two Samba users or your machine is running too many daemons already. It's also easier to perform an upgrade without disturbing an existing connection.

If you wish to start from *inetd*, first open */etc/services* in your text editor. If you don't already have them defined, add the following two lines:

```
netbios-ssn      139/tcp
netbios-ns       137/udp
```

Next, edit */etc/inetd.conf*. Look for the following two lines and add them if they don't exist. If you already have smbd and nmbd lines in the file, edit them to point at the new *smbd* and *nmbd* you've installed. Your brand of Unix might use a slightly different syntax in this file; use the existing entries and the *inetd.conf* manual page as a guide:

```
netbios-ssn stream tcp nowait root /usr/local/samba/bin/smbd smbd
netbios-ns  dgram  udp wait   root /usr/local/samba/bin/nmbd nmbd
```

Finally, kill any *smbd* or *nmbd* processes and send the *inetd* process a hangup (HUP) signal to tell it to reread its configuration file:

```
# /bin/kill -TERM -a smbd
# /bin/kill -TERM -a nmbd
# /bin/kill -HUP -a inetd
```

After that, Samba should be up and running.

As we've pointed out before, Red Hat and perhaps other Unix vendors supply *xinetd* rather than *inetd*. If you need to use *xinetd*, you will need to supply a configuration file in the */etc/xinetd.d* directory.

Testing the Samba Daemons

We're nearly done with the Samba server setup. All that's left to do is to make sure everything is working as we think it should. A convenient way to do this is to use the

---

[*] With early releases of Samba 2.2, there were reports of intermittent errors when starting from *inetd*. We provide this information so that it will be available for later releases when the problem will hopefully have been identified and corrected.

smbclient program to examine what the server is offering to the network. If everything is set up properly, you should be able to do the following:

```
# /usr/local/samba/bin/smbclient -U% -L localhost
added interface ip=172.16.1.1 bcast=172.16.1.255 nmask=255.255.255.0
Domain=[METRAN] OS=[Unix] Server=[Samba 2.2.6]

        Sharename      Type      Comment
        ---------      ----      -------
        test           Disk      For testing only, please
        IPC$           IPC       IPC Service (Samba 2.2.6)
        ADMIN$         Disk      IPC Service (Samba 2.2.6)

        Server                   Comment
        ---------                -------
        TOLTEC                   Samba 2.2.6 on toltec

        Workgroup                Master
        ---------                -------
        METRAN                   TOLTEC
```

If there is a problem, don't panic! Try to start the daemons manually, and check the system output or the debug files at */usr/local/samba/var/log.smb* to see if you can determine what happened. If you think it might be a more serious problem, skip to Chapter 12 for help on troubleshooting the Samba daemons.

If it worked, congratulations! You now have successfully set up the Samba server with a disk share. It's a simple one, but we can use it to set up and test the Windows 95/98/Me and NT/2000/XP clients in the next chapter. Then we will start making it more interesting by adding services such as home directories, printers, and security, and by seeing how to integrate the server into a larger Windows domain.

## CHAPTER 3

Configuring Windows Clients

Configuring Windows to use your new Samba server is really quite simple. SMB is Microsoft's native language for resource sharing on a local area network, so much of the installation and setup on the Windows client side have been taken care of already.

Windows Networking Concepts

Windows is different from Unix in many ways, including how it supports networking. Before we get into the hands-on task of clicking our way through the dialog boxes to configure each version of Windows, we need to provide you with a common foundation of networking technologies and concepts that apply to the entire family of Windows operating systems.

For each Windows version, these are the main issues we will be dealing with:

- Making sure required networking components are installed and bound to the network adapter
- Configuring networking with a valid IP address, netmask and gateway, and WINS and DNS name servers
- Assigning workgroup and computer names
- Setting the username(s) and password(s)

In addition, some minor issues involving communication and coordination between Windows and Unix are different among Windows versions.

One can go crazy thinking about the ways in which Unix is different from Windows, or the ways in which members of the Windows family are different from each other in underlying technology, behavior, or appearance. For now let's just focus on their similarities and see if we can find some common ground.

Components

Unix systems historically have been monolithic in nature, requiring recompilation or relinking to create a kernel with a customized feature set. However, modern versions have the ability to load or unload device drivers or various other operating-system features as modules while the system is running, without even needing to reboot.

Windows allows for configuration by installing or uninstalling *components*. As far as networking goes, components can be one of three things:*

- Protocols
- Clients
- Services

Since Samba works using the TCP/IP protocol, of course we'll want to have that installed. In some cases, we also will want to find protocols to *uninstall*. For example, if Netware protocol (IPX/SPX) is not required on the network, it might as well be removed.

NetBEUI protocol should be removed if possible. Having NetBEUI running at the same time as NetBIOS over TCP/IP causes the system to look for services under two different protocols, only one of which is likely to be in use. When Windows is configured with one or more unused protocols, 30-second delays will result when Windows tries to communicate with the unused protocol. Eventually, it times out and tries another one, until it finds one that works. This fruitless searching results in terrible performance.

The other two items in the list, client and service components, are pretty much what you'd expect. Client components perform tasks related to connecting with network servers, and service components are for making the local system into a server of resources on the network. In Chapter 1 we told you that SMB systems can act as both clients and servers, offering resources on the network at the same time they request resources. In accordance with that, it is possible to install a component for SMB client services and, separately, a service component that allows file and printer shares on the local system to be accessible from other systems on the network.

Bindings

Once a networking component is installed, it must be *bound* to a hardware interface, or *adapter*, to be used on the network. At first this might seem like an odd complication; however, it is a conceptual model that allows the associations between hardware and software to be clearly displayed and easily modified through a graphical interface.

---

* We are intentionally omitting device drivers because they are hardware-specific, and we assume you are getting installation directions from the manufacturer.

We will want to make sure that your Windows client has both TCP/IP and the client component for SMB networking installed and also that it is bound to the network adapter that connects to our Samba network, which in most cases will be an Ethernet adapter.

IP Address

Just like any Unix system (or any other system that is using TCP/IP), your Windows systems will need an IP address. If you are using DHCP on your network, you can configure Windows to obtain its IP address automatically by using a DHCP server. Otherwise, you will need to assign a static IP address manually along with a netmask.*

If you are on a private network where you have the authority to assign your own IP addresses, you can select from addresses in one of three ranges:†

- 10.0.0.1 through 10.255.255.254
- 172.16.0.1 through 172.31.255.254
- 192.168.0.1 through 192.168.255.254

These address ranges are reserved for private networks not directly connected to the Internet. For more information on using these private network addresses, see RFC 1918.

If you're not maintaining your own separate network, see your system administrator for some available addresses on your network, as well as for the proper netmask to use.

You should also be prepared to enter the IP address of the default gateway for the network. In some networks, the default gateway is the system or router that connects the LAN to the Internet. In other cases, the default gateway connects a subnet into a larger departmental or enterprise network.

Name Resolution

Name resolution is the function of translating human-friendly hostnames, such as *hopi*, or fully qualified domain names (FQDNs), such as mixtec.metran.cx, into IP addresses, such as 172.16.1.11 or 172.16.1.7.

Unix systems can perform name resolution using an */etc/hosts* file at the minimum, and more commonly can also incorporate services such as DNS (Domain Name Sys-

---

* Make sure to use the same netmask as all other systems on the network. You can find the netmask in use by checking with Unix or Windows systems that have already been configured.

† Keep in mind that IP addresses ending in .0 are reserved for network addresses and that ones ending in .255 are for broadcast addresses. These should never be assigned to any system on the network.

tem) and NIS (Network Information Service). Thus, name resolution is not necessarily performed by one isolated part of the operating system or one daemon, but is a system that can have a number of dispersed parts (although the name service switch, with its */etc/nsswitch.conf* configuration file, helps to tie them together).

Although the specific implementation is different, name resolution in Windows is also performed by querying a number of resources, some of which are similar (or even identical) to their Unix counterparts.

Broadcast name resolution

On the other hand, there is one way in which Windows is not at all similar to Unix. If a Windows workstation is set up with no WINS name server, it will use the broadcast method of name resolution, as described in Chapter 1,* probably resulting in a very busy network. And even if you provide name servers for your Windows system to use, it might still resort to broadcast name resolution if it is unsuccessful at querying the name servers. For this reason, we recommend that you provide multiple reliable name servers for your Windows computers on the network.

If that weren't enough to get you interested in setting up WINS and DNS servers, broadcast name resolution is usually limited to working on the local subnet because routers are usually configured not to forward broadcast packets to other networks.

WINS

We've already told you about WINS in Chapter 1, and we don't have much more to say about it here. WINS can translate simple NetBIOS computer names such as *huastec* or *navajo* into IP addresses, as required on an SMB network. Of course, the interesting thing here is that Samba can act as a WINS server if you include the line:

```
wins support = yes
```

in your Samba server's *smb.conf* file. This can be a good thing, to be sure, and we highly recommend it. Not only will you have a reliable WINS server to reduce the number of broadcast packets, but you won't need to run Windows NT/2000/XP to get it.

 One caveat about using Samba as a WINS server is that Samba (up to Version 2.2, at least) cannot synchronize with other WINS servers. So if you specify a Samba server as your Windows system's WINS server, you must be careful not to specify any additional (i.e., secondary) WINS servers. If you do, you are likely to run into problems because the servers will not be able to synchronize their databases with each other. In Samba's defense, if you are using a Samba WINS server (running on a typically reliable Unix host), you will probably have little need for a secondary WINS server anyway.

---

* To be more explicit about this, the system will identify itself to the network as a b-node rather than an h-node.

LMHOSTS

All Windows versions support a backup method of name resolution, in the form of a
file called *LMHOSTS** that contains a lookup table of computer names and IP
addresses. This exists for "historical purposes," and is a rather awkward method of
name resolution because it requires the administrator (i.e., you!) to keep copies of
LMHOSTS up to date on every single Windows system on the network. To be fully
effective, *LMHOSTS* would have to be updated every time a new system were added
to (or removed from) the network. Of course, there might be ways to automate that
process, but a better option would be simply to run a WINS name server that is
intentionally designed to solve that specific problem.

There are perhaps a couple of reasons why you might want to bother with
LMHOSTS files. In rare situations, there might be no WINS server on the network.
Or maybe a WINS server exists, but it's unreliable. In both cases, if the Windows
system has a valid *LMHOSTS* file, it can help to avoid your network bogging down
from those dreaded broadcast name queries.

The format of the *LMHOSTS* file is simple and similar to the */etc/hosts* file with
which you might be familiar from running Unix systems. Here are the contents of a
sample *LMHOSTS* file:

```
172.16.1.1      toltec
172.16.1.2      aztec
172.16.1.3      mixtec
172.16.1.4      zapotec
172.16.1.5      huastec
172.16.1.6      maya
172.16.1.7      olmec
172.16.1.8      chichimec
172.16.1.11     hopi
172.16.1.12     zuni
172.16.1.13     dine
172.16.1.14     pima
172.16.1.15     apache
172.16.1.21     inca
172.16.1.22     qero
```

As you can see, the format is like that of */etc/hosts*, except that instead of an FQDN
(e.g., `toltec.metran.cx`), only a NetBIOS computer name (`toltec`) is given. One way
to create an *LMHOSTS* file for your Windows systems is to copy a */etc/hosts* file and
edit out the parts you don't need. This will work great if your network doesn't have a
DNS (or NIS) name server and the Unix system is dependent on */etc/hosts* for its own
name service. But if your Unix system is querying a DNS server (which is the most
frequent case on anything larger than the very smallest networks), you would be bet-

---

* We put the names of the *LMHOSTS* and *HOSTS* files in uppercase for additional clarity—to remind you that
we are referring to the files on Windows rather than on Unix, and because that's the way we see them in
other books on Windows. The case of the letters in the two names actually does not matter.

ter advised to look in the DNS server's configuration files for your source of computer names and IP addresses.

If you do not have administrative access to your network's DNS server, you might be able to use tools such as *nslookup*, *nmap*, and *dig* to query the server and obtain the information you need.

DNS

The DNS is responsible for translating human-readable, Internet-style hostnames such as `pima.metran.cx` or `sales.oreilly.com` into IP addresses.

On your first reading of this section, you might be wondering what a section on DNS is doing in a book about NetBIOS and SMB networking. Remember, we told you that Windows can use more than WINS (NetBIOS Name Service) in its strategy for performing name resolution. Because DNS is also able to supply IP addresses for simple hostnames (which are usually the same as NetBIOS computer names), it can be helpful to configure Windows to know about a DNS server on your network. This is slightly more important for newer Windows versions than older ones, and more so for Windows NT/2000/XP than for Windows 95/98/Me, because nowadays Microsoft is focusing more on TCP/IP as the standard protocol and DNS as the primary name service.

To find the address of your DNS server, look at the file */etc/resolv.conf* on your Samba server or any other Unix system on the local network that is using DNS. It looks like the following:

```
#resolv.conf
domain metran.cx
nameserver 127.0.0.1
nameserver 172.16.1.53
```

In this example, the first name server in the list is 127.0.0.1, which indicates that the Samba server is also a DNS server for this LAN.* In that case, you would use its network IP address (not 127.0.0.1, its localhost address) for your DNS server when configuring Windows. Otherwise, use the other addresses you find in the lines beginning with `nameserver`. Try to select ones on your own network. Any name servers listed in */etc/resolv.conf* should work, but you'll get better performance by using a server nearby.

All versions of Windows can be configured to know of multiple domain name servers, and you might wish to take advantage of this for increased reliability. If the first domain name server does not respond, Windows can try others in its list.

---

* The address 127.0.0.1 is known as the *localhost* address and always refers to itself. For example, if you type `ping 127.0.0.1` on a Unix server, you should always get a response, because you're pinging the host itself.

HOSTS

Similar to how the *LMHOSTS* file can be added to supplement WINS, the *HOSTS* file on a Windows system can be optionally added to supplement DNS name resolution. Most of our comments regarding *LMHOSTS* also apply here.

This time the format of the file is not just similar to that of */etc/hosts* found on Unix—the format is *exactly* the same. You can simply copy */etc/hosts* from your Samba server or other Unix system to the proper directory on your Windows system.

On Windows 95/98/Me, the *HOSTS* file goes in the Windows installation directory, which is usually *C:\Windows*. Note that a file called *hosts.sam* is already there, which is a sample *HOSTS* file provided by Microsoft.

On Windows NT/2000/XP, the *HOSTS* file goes in the *\system32\drivers\etc* directory under the Windows installation directory, which is usually *C:\WINNT*.

Passwords

Unix systems use username and password pairs to authenticate users either on a local system or in an NIS domain. Windows NT/2000/XP are very similar; a user supplies his username and password to log on to the local system or to a Windows domain.

When the SMB network is set up as a workgroup, things are different. There is no domain to log on to, although shares on the network can be password-protected. In this case, one password is associated with each password-protected share, rather than with individual users.

Samba's default user-level authentication in a workgroup is different from that of Windows. To access shares on the Samba host, users are required to supply a valid username and password for an account on the Samba host. This will be discussed in more detail in Chapter 9.

An unfortunate complication arises with passwords. In the first release of Windows 95 and in Windows NT 4.0 with Service Pack 2 (SP2) or less, as well as in all previous versions of Windows, passwords are allowed to be sent over the network in plain text. But in Windows 95 with the network redirector update,* Windows NT 4.0 SP3 or later, and all subsequent releases of Windows, a registry setting must be modified to enable plain-text passwords. These more modern versions of Windows prefer to send encrypted passwords, and if you are working with one of them (and don't want to have to modify the registry), you must have the line:

```
encrypt passwords = yes
```

in the [global] section of your *smb.conf* file. In addition, you must run the command:

```
# smbpasswd -a username
```

---

* This update is supplied in various update packages issued by Microsoft.

---

for each user on the Samba host to add their passwords to Samba's collection of encrypted passwords. We showed you how to do this in Chapter 2.

If your first attempt to access a Samba share results in a dialog box asking for a password for IPC$, as shown in Figure 3-1, it is probably because you neglected either or both of these two steps, and the Samba server did not recognize the encrypted password that the Windows system sent to it. Another possible dialog box that might come up is the one shown in Figure 3-2, which was presented by a Windows 2000 client.

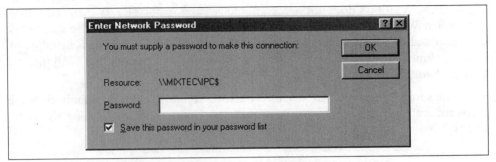

Figure 3-1. Windows 98 asking for IPC$ password

Figure 3-2. Windows 2000 logon error dialog

The rest of this chapter is divided into four sections. The first section covers setting up Windows 95/98/Me computers, and the rest of the sections cover Windows NT 4.0, Windows 2000, and Windows XP individually. Each section roughly parallels the order in which we've introduced networking concepts in this section. You need to read only the section that applies to the Windows version with which you are working, and once you have finished reading it, you can continue at the beginning of the next chapter where we will start covering more advanced Samba features and networking issues.

Keep in mind that we are continuing our example from Chapter 2, in which we are setting up a very simple prototype network using a workgroup that has very lax security. After you have the basics working, we recommend you continue with later chapters to learn how to implement both better security and a Samba domain.

Setting Up Windows 95/98/Me Computers

The Windows 95/98/Me operating systems are very similar to each other, and as far as this chapter is concerned, it is possible to treat them with a common set of directions.

Setting Up the Network

Samba uses TCP/IP to communicate with clients on the network, so you will need to make sure there is support for TCP/IP on each Windows client. Unlike Unix operating systems, Windows does not necessarily have support for TCP/IP installed. However, when Windows is installed on a computer with a network card or a network card is added to a system already running Windows, TCP/IP support is installed by default, along with the Client for Microsoft Networks, which supports SMB file and printer sharing.

To make sure both services are installed on your Windows system, double-click the Network icon in the Control Panel to open the Network dialog box, as shown in Figure 3-3.

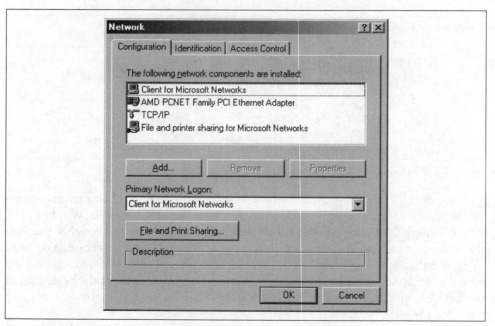

Figure 3-3. The Windows 95/98/Me Network dialog

You should see at least the Client for Microsoft Networks component installed on the system, and hopefully a networking device (preferably an Ethernet card) bound to the TCP/IP protocol. If there is only one networking hardware device, you'll see the TCP/IP protocol listed below the device to which it is bound, as shown in Figure 3-1.

You might also see "File and printer sharing for Microsoft Networks," which is used to make the system into a server. In addition, you might see NetBEUI or Novell Networking. Definitely remove NetBEUI unless you are sure you need it, and if you don't have any Novell servers on your network, you can remove Novell (IPX/SPX) as well. To remove a service, simply click its name and then click the Remove button.

Adding TCP/IP

If you don't see TCP/IP listed, you'll need to install the protocol.

You can add the protocol by inserting the Windows distribution CD-ROM in your CD-ROM drive and clicking the Add button below the component window. Indicate that you wish to add a protocol by selecting Protocol and clicking "Add..." on the following dialog box, which should look similar to Figure 3-4.

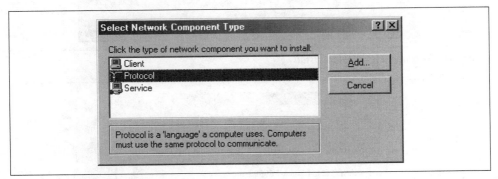

Figure 3-4. Selecting a component type

After that, select manufacturer Microsoft, then protocol TCP/IP, as shown in Figure 3-3, then click OK. After doing so, you will be returned to the network dialog. Click OK to close the dialog box, and Windows will install the necessary components from the CD-ROM and request that the system be rebooted. Go ahead and reboot the system, and you're set.

If Client for Microsoft Networks is not in the list, you can add it similarly. The only significant difference is that you are adding a client instead of a protocol, so make sure to select "Client" rather than "Protocol" when asked.

Configuring TCP/IP

If you have more than one networking device (for example, both an Ethernet card and a modem for dial-up networking), the protocol to hardware bindings will be indicated by arrows, as shown in Figure 3-5.

Select the TCP/IP protocol linked to the networking device that will be accessing the Samba network. If you have only one networking device, simply click the TCP/IP item. Now click the Properties button to open the TCP/IP Properties dialog. You should see something similar to Figure 3-6.

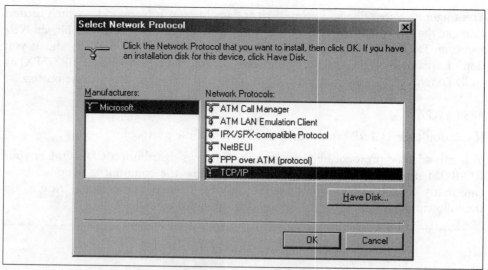

Figure 3-5. Selecting a protocol to install

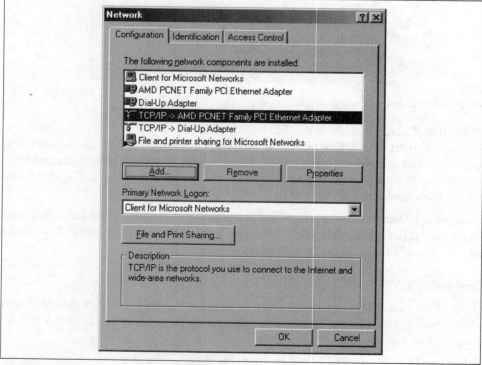

Figure 3-6. Selecting the correct TCP/IP protocol

IP Address tab

The IP Address tab is shown in Figure 3-7.

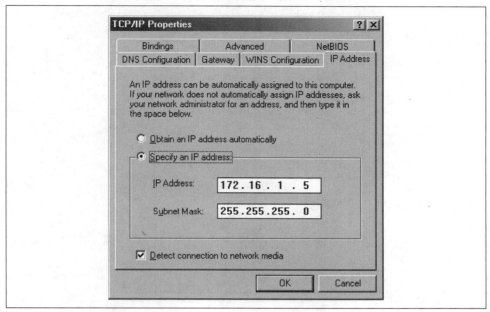

Figure 3-7. The IP Address tab

If you use DHCP on your network to provide IP addresses automatically to Windows systems, select the "Obtain an IP address automatically" radio button. Otherwise, click the "Specify an IP address" radio button and enter the client's address and subnet mask in the space provided. You or your network manager should have selected an address for the client on the same subnet (LAN) as the Samba server.

WINS Configuration tab

If you've enabled WINS on Samba or are choosing to make use of another WINS server on your network, you must tell Windows the server's address. After selecting the WINS Configuration tab, you will see the dialog box shown in Figure 3-8.

This is for Windows 98/Me; Windows 95 is just a little different, having separate spaces for the primary and backup WINS server IP addresses.

Select the "Enable WINS Resolution" radio button, and enter the WINS server's address in the space provided, then click the Add button. Do not enter anything in the Scope ID field.

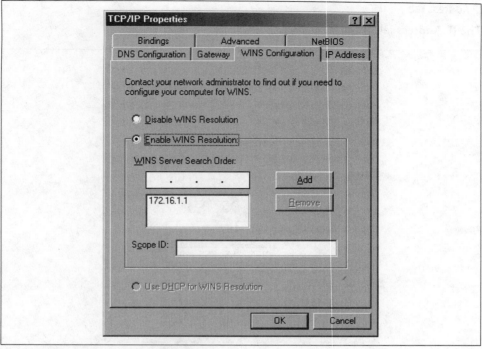

Figure 3-8. The WINS Configuration tab

A bug in Windows 95/98 sometimes causes the IP address of the WINS server to disappear after the OK button is clicked. This happens only when only a primary WINS server has been specified. The workaround is to fill in the fields for both primary and secondary WINS servers, using the same IP address for each.

DNS Configuration tab

Unless you are using DHCP, you will need to provide the IP address of one or more DNS servers. Click the DNS tab, then click the "Enable DNS" radio button, and type the IP address of one or more DNS servers into the appropriate field, shown in Figure 3-9, to add the server's address to the top DNS Server Search Order field.

Also, provide the hostname (which is the same as the NetBIOS computer name) of the Windows 95/98/Me computer and your Internet domain. (You will need to enter the computer name again later, along with the workgroup. Make sure to enter the same name each time.) You can safely ignore the Domain Suffix Search Order field for anything related to Samba.

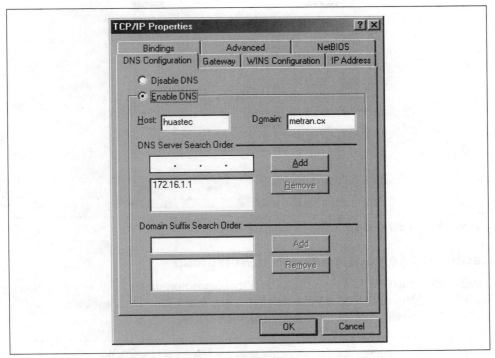

Figure 3-9. The DNS Configuration tab

LMHOSTS file

If you want to install an *LMHOSTS* file, it must be placed in your Windows installation directory (usually *C:\Windows*). In the same directory, Microsoft has provided a sample *LMHOSTS* file named *lmhosts.sam*, which you might want to look at for further information on the file's format.

NetBIOS tab

This tab appears in Windows 98/Me, but not in Windows 95. All you need to do here is make sure the checkbox is checked, enabling NetBIOS over TCP/IP. If TCP/IP is your only protocol installed (as we recommended earlier), the selection will be grayed out, with the box checked so that you couldn't uncheck it even if you wanted to.

Bindings tab

The final tab to look at is Bindings, as shown in Figure 3-10.

You should have a check beside Client for Microsoft Networks, indicating that it's using TCP/IP. If you have "File and printer sharing for Microsoft Networks" in the dialog, it should also be checked, as shown in Figure 3-10.

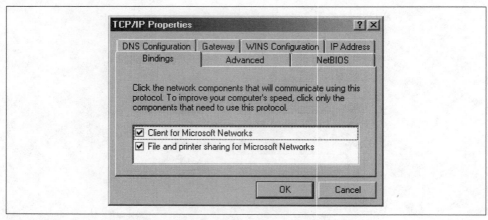

Figure 3-10. The Bindings tab

Setting the Computer Name and Workgroup

Finally, click the OK button in the TCP/IP configuration dialog, and you'll be taken back to the Network Configuration dialog. Then select the Identification tab, which will take you to the dialog box shown in Figure 3-11.

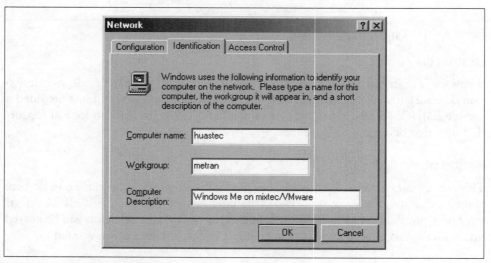

Figure 3-11. The Identification tab

This is where you set your system's NetBIOS name (which Microsoft likes to call "computer name"). Usually, it is best to make this the same as your DNS hostname, if you are going to have one for this system. For example, if the system's DNS name is huastec.metran.cx, give the computer a NetBIOS name of huastec on this tab.

You also set your workgroup name here. In our case, it's METRAN, but if you used a different one in Chapter 2, when creating the Samba configuration file, use that instead. Just don't call it WORKGROUP (the default workgroup name) or you'll be in the same workgroup as every misconfigured Windows computer on the planet!

You can also enter a comment string for this computer. See if you can come up with some way of describing it that will remind you of what and where it is when you see the comment in a list displayed on another computer. Everyone on the network will be able to see your comment, so be careful not to include any information that might be useful to crackers.

Finally, click the OK button and follow whatever instructions Windows provides. (You might have to insert your Windows distribution CD-ROM and/or reboot.)

Username and Password

You have probably already given Windows a username and password by now. However, to authenticate with the Samba server, your Windows username and password must match with a valid account on the Samba server.

It is simple to add a new user and password to a Windows 95/98/Me system. Just reboot or log out, and when you are prompted for a username and password, enter your Unix username and password. (If you are using encrypted passwords, you must run *smbpasswd* on the Unix host to enter them into Samba's password database, if you have not already done so.) You can use this method to add as many users as you want, so as to allow more than one user to use the Windows system to gain access to the Samba shares.

If you mistakenly entered the wrong password or your Unix password changes, you can change your password on the Windows system by going to the Control Panel and double-clicking the Passwords icon. This will bring up the Passwords Properties dialog. Click the Change Passwords tab, and you will see the dialog shown in Figure 3-12. Now click the "Change Windows Password..." button, which will bring up the Change Windows Password dialog box, shown in Figure 3-13. As indicated by the text entry fields in the dialog, enter your old password, and then the new password, and again to confirm it. Click the OK button and then the Close button on the Password Properties dialog box. Reboot or log out, and use your new password when you log in again.

Logging in for the first time

If you don't have a Change Passwords tab in the Passwords Properties window, it is because networking is not fully set up yet. Assuming you've followed all the directions given so far, you just need to reboot; when the system comes up, it will ask you to log in with a username and a password.

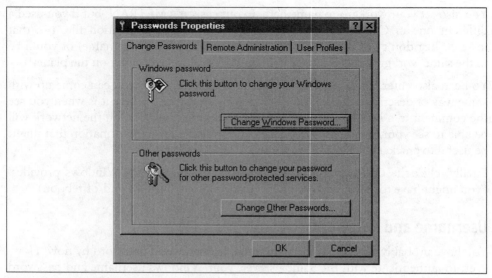

Figure 3-12. The Password Properties dialog

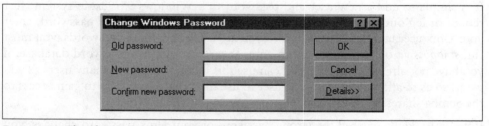

Figure 3-13. The Change Windows Password dialog

Now for the big moment. Your Samba server is running, and you have set up your Windows 95/98/Me client to communicate with it.

Accessing the Samba Server from Windows 95/98

Double-click the Network Neighborhood icon on the desktop. You should see your Samba server listed as a member of the workgroup, as shown in Figure 3-14.

Double-clicking the server name will show the resources that the server is offering to the network, as shown in Figure 3-15 (in this case, the *test* directory).

Accessing the Samba Server from Windows Me

Double-click the My Network Places icon on the desktop. You should see the test shared directory as shown in Figure 3-16.

Double-click the Entire Network icon, and you should see an icon for your work-group, as shown in Figure 3-17.

Figure 3-14. Windows 95/98 Network Neighborhood

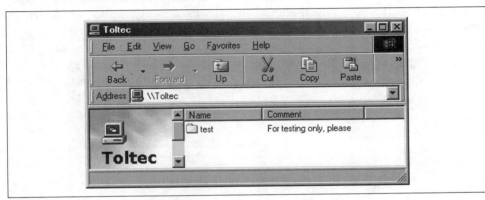

Figure 3-15. The test shared folder on the Toltec server

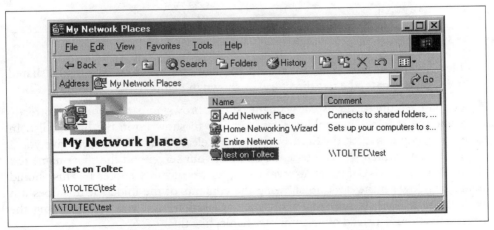

Figure 3-16. My Network Places on Windows Me

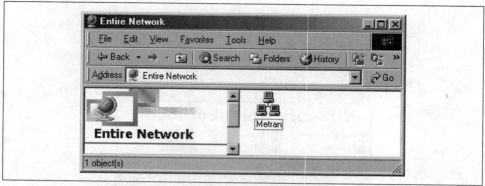

Figure 3-17. Entire Network window, showing the Metran workgroup

Double-clicking the workgroup icon will bring up a window showing every computer in the workgroup, which should include your Samba server, as shown in Figure 3-18.

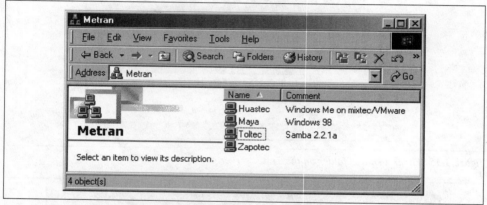

Figure 3-18. Computers in Metran workgroup

Double-click the Samba server's icon, and you will get a window showing its shared resources (in this case, the test directory) as shown in Figure 3-19.

If you don't see the server listed, it might be that browsing is not working correctly or maybe the server is just taking a few minutes to show up in the browse list. In either case, you can click the Start button, then select "Run...". This will give you a dialog box into which you can type the name of your server and the share name *test* in the Windows UNC format *server**test*, as we did in Chapter 1. This should open a window on the desktop showing the contents of the folder. If this does not work, there is likely a problem with name resolution, and you can try using the server's IP address instead of its computer name, like this:

    \\172.16.1.1\test

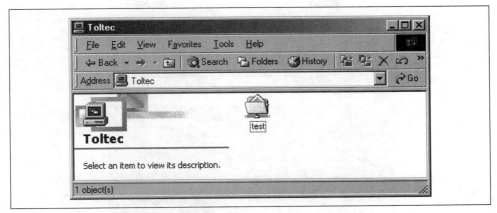

Figure 3-19. View of shares on the Toltec server

If things still aren't right, go directly to the section "The Fault Tree" in Chapter 12 to troubleshoot what is wrong with the network.

If it works, congratulations! Try copying files to and from the server using the Windows drag-and-drop functionality. You might be pleasantly surprised how seamlessly everything works.

Setting Up Windows NT 4.0 Computers

Configuring Windows NT is a little different than configuring Windows 95/98/Me. To use Samba with Windows NT, you will need both the Workstation service and the TCP/IP protocol. Both come standard with NT, but we'll work through installing and configuring them to make sure they are configured correctly.

Basic Configuration

This section presents the steps to follow for TCP/IP-related configuration on Windows NT to get it to cooperate with Samba. If you need more details on Windows NT network administration, refer to Craig Hunt and Robert Bruce Thompson's *Windows NT TCP/IP Network Administration* (O'Reilly), an excellent guide.

You should perform the following steps as the Administrator or another user in the Administrators group.

Installing the TCP/IP protocol

From the Control Panel, double-click the Network icon, click the Protocols tab in the Network dialog box, and look to see if you have the TCP/IP protocol installed, as shown in Figure 3-20.

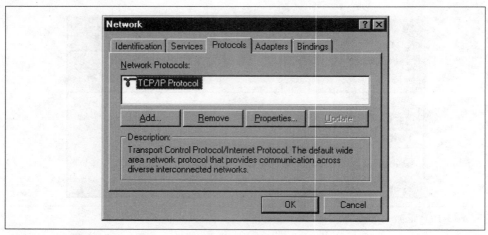

Figure 3-20. The Protocols tab

If the protocol is not installed, you need to add it. Click the Add button, which will display the Select Network Protocol dialog box shown in Figure 3-21. You should immediately see the TCP/IP protocol as one of the last protocols listed.

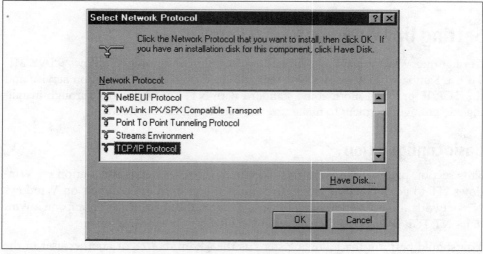

Figure 3-21. Select Network Protocol dialog box

Select TCP/IP as the protocol and confirm it. If possible, install only the TCP/IP protocol. If you see anything other than TCP/IP listed in the Protocols tab and it is not a protocol that you need, you can remove it. If you try to remove a protocol and get an error message saying that the protocol is being used by another service, you need to click the Services tab and remove that service before you can remove the protocol.

For example, to remove the NWLink IPX/SPX Compatible Transport protocol, you would need to remove the Client Service for Netware first.

Installing the Workstation service

After installing TCP/IP, click the Services tab in the Network dialog, and check that you have a Workstation service, as shown at the end of the list in Figure 3-22.*

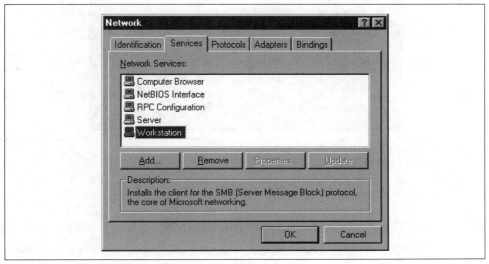

Figure 3-22. Network Services tab

This service is actually the Microsoft Networking Client, which allows the computer to access SMB services. The Workstation service is mandatory. The service is installed by default on both Windows NT Workstation 4.0 and NT Server 4.0. If it's not there, you can install it much like TCP/IP. In this case you need to click the Add button and then select Workstation Service, as shown in Figure 3-23.

Configuring TCP/IP

After you've installed the Workstation service, return to the Protocols tab and select the TCP/IP Protocol entry in the window. Then click the Properties button below the window. The Microsoft TCP/IP Protocol dialog will be displayed. There are five tabs in the dialog, and you will need to work with four of them:

- IP Address
- WINS Address

---

* Notice how in Windows NT, some clients are called "services"! In these directions, we will conform to Microsoft's terminology.

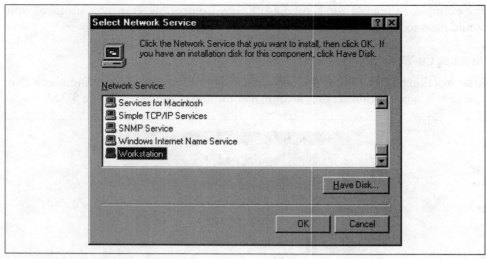

Figure 3-23. Select Network Service dialog box

- DNS
- Bindings

IP Address tab. The IP Address tab is shown in Figure 3-24.

Select the "Specify an IP address" radio button, and enter the computer's IP address and netmask in the space provided for the proper adapter (Ethernet card). You or your network manager should have selected an address for the client on the same subnet (LAN) as the Samba server. For example, if the server's address is 172.16.1.1 and its network mask is 255.255.255.0, you might use the address 172.16.1.13 (if it is available) for the NT workstation, along with the same netmask. If you use DHCP on your network, select the "Obtain an IP Address from a DHCP server" button instead.

The gateway field refers to a system typically known as a *router*. If you have routers connecting multiple networks, you should enter the IP address of the one on your subnet. In our example, the gateway happens to be the same system as the Samba server, but they do not by any means have to be the same.

WINS Address tab. Click the WINS Address tab, shown in Figure 3-25, and you can begin to enter information about name servers. Enter the address of your WINS server in the space labeled Primary WINS Server. If your Samba server is providing WINS service (in other words, you have the line wins support = yes in the *smb.conf* file of your Samba server), provide the Samba server's IP address here. Otherwise, provide the address of another WINS server on your network.

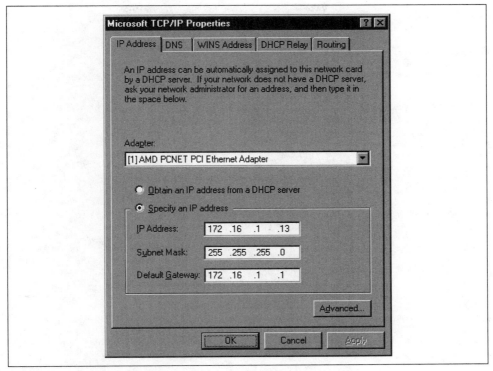

Figure 3-24. Microsoft TCP/IP Properties dialog for Windows NT

You probably noticed that there is a field here for the network adapter. This field must specify the Ethernet adapter on which you're running TCP/IP so that WINS will provide name service on the correct network. For example, if you have both a LAN and a dial-up adapter, make sure you have the LAN's network card specified here.

The checkboxes in the lower half of the dialog are for enabling two other methods of name resolution that Windows can incorporate into its name service. Samba doesn't require either of them, but you might want to enable them to increase the reliability or functionality of name service for your client. See Chapter 7 for further information on name resolution issues.

If you'd like to use a DNS server, select the Enable DNS for Windows Resolution checkbox. In addition, you will need to do some configuration to allow the Windows system to find the DNS server, unless you're using DHCP.

DNS tab. Click the tab for DNS, as shown in Figure 3-26. Enter the IP addresses for one or more DNS servers in the space provided. Also, enter the hostname (which should be the same as the NetBIOS computer name). You will enter this again later in another control panel, so make sure they match. Finally, enter the DNS domain on which this system resides. For example, if your workstation has a domain name such as *metran.cx*, enter it here. You can safely ignore the other options.

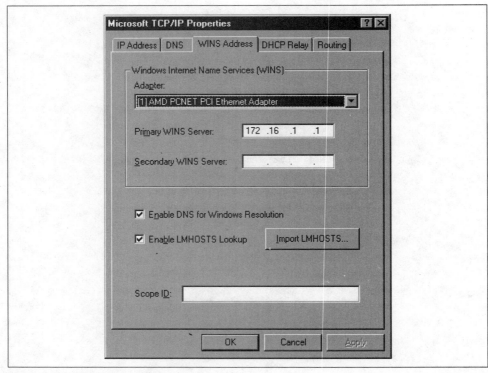

Figure 3-25. The WINS Address tab

The LMHOSTS file. If you want to install an *LMHOSTS* file, it must be placed in the directory *\system32\drivers\etc* under your Windows installation directory (usually *C:\WINNT*). The easy way to make sure it gets to the proper location is to use the Import LMHOSTS button on the WINS Address tab. (But if you want to do it over the network, you will have to do that after file sharing is configured!) Remember to click the Enable LMHOSTS Lookup checkbox on the WINS Address tab to enable this functionality.

When you are satisfied with your settings for IP Address, WINS Address, and DNS, click OK to return to the Network dialog box.

Bindings. Now click the Bindings tab, and check the bindings of network hardware, services, and protocols. Set the "Show Bindings for" field to "all services," and click all the + buttons in the tree. You should see a display similar to Figure 3-27, which shows that the NetBIOS, Server, and Workstation interface services are connected to the WINS client running TCP/IP protocol, and that the WINS client is bound to the Ethernet adapter of the local area network.

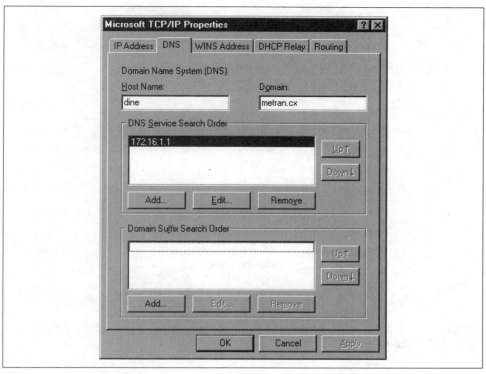

Figure 3-26. The DNS tab

You can safely leave the default values for the remainder of the tabs in the Network dialog box. Click the OK button to complete the configuration. Once the proper files are loaded (if any), you might need to reboot for your changes to take effect.

Computer Name and Workgroup

The next thing you need to do is to give the system a NetBIOS computer name. From the Control Panel, double-click the Network icon to open the Network dialog box. The first tab in this dialog box should be the Identification tab, as illustrated in Figure 3-28.

Here, you need to identify your computer with a name and change the default workgroup to the one you specified in the *smb.conf* file of your Samba server. Click the Change button below the two text fields. This will open an Identification Changes dialog box, where you can set the workgroup and the computer name, as shown in Figure 3-29.

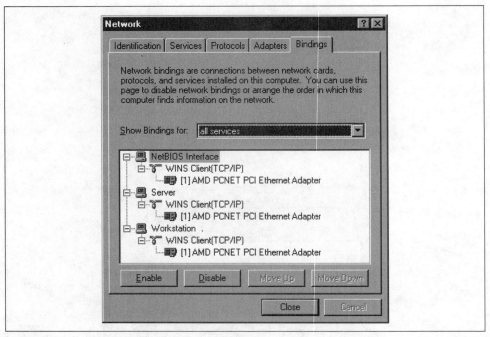

Figure 3-27. The Bindings tab

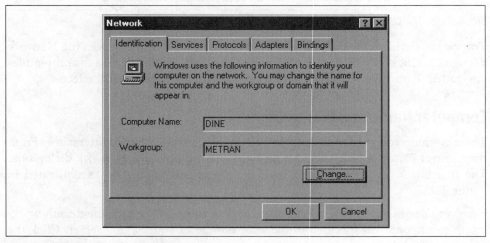

Figure 3-28. The Identification tab

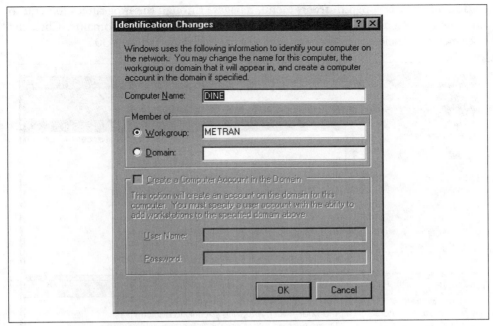

Figure 3-29. The Identification Changes dialog

You entered the computer name earlier as a DNS hostname while configuring TCP/IP, so be sure that the two names match. The name you set here is the NetBIOS name. You're allowed to make it different from the TCP/IP hostname, but doing so is usually not a good idea. Don't worry that Windows NT forces the computer name and the workgroup to be all capital letters; it's smart enough to figure out what you mean when it connects to the network.

Adding a User

In all the previous steps, you were logged into your Windows NT system as Administrator or another user in the Administrators group. To access resources on the Samba server, you will need to have a username and password that the Samba server recognizes as valid. Generally, the best way to do this is to add a user to your NT system, with the same username and password as a user on the Samba host system.

The directions in this section assume that your network is set up as a workgroup. If you have already set up your network as a domain, as we describe in Chapter 4, you do not need to follow the instructions here for adding a local user on the Windows NT client system. Simply log on to the domain from the client using a username and password in Samba's *smbpasswd* account database, and continue with the next section, "Connecting to the Samba Server."

To add a new user, open the Start menu, navigate through the Programs submenu to Administrative Tools (Common), and select User Manager for Domains. Click the User menu and select the first item, Add User..., shown in Figure 3-30.

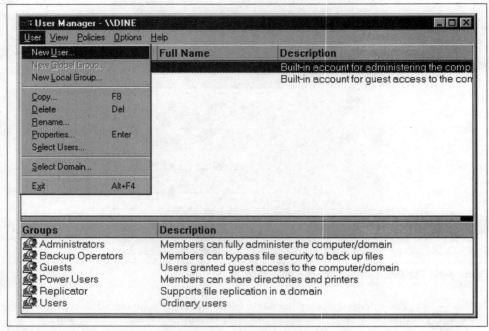

Figure 3-30. User Manager for Domains window

This brings up the New User dialog box shown in Figure 3-31.

Fill it out as shown, using the username and password that were added in the previous chapter, and make sure that only the checkbox labeled Password Never Expires is checked. (This is not the default!) Click the Add button to add the user, and then click the Close button. You should now see your new account added to the list in the User Manager dialog box.

Now open the Start menu, select Shut Down, and select the "Close all programs and log on as a different user?" radio button. Click the Yes button, then log in as the user you just added.

Connecting to the Samba Server

Now for the big moment. Your Samba server is running, and you have set up your NT client to communicate with it. Double-click the Network Neighborhood icon on the desktop, and you should see your Samba server listed as a member of the workgroup, as shown in Figure 3-32.

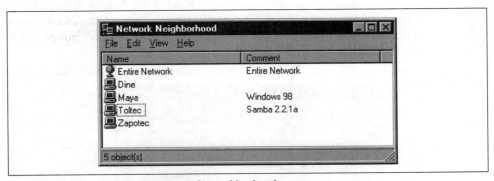

Figure 3-31. The New User dialog

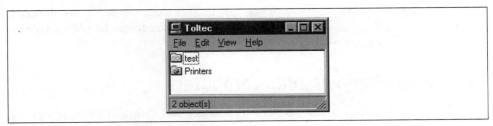

Figure 3-32. The Windows NT Network Neighborhood

Double-clicking the server name will show the resources that the server is offering to the network, as shown in Figure 3-33. In this case, the *test* directory and the default printer are offered to the Windows NT workstation.

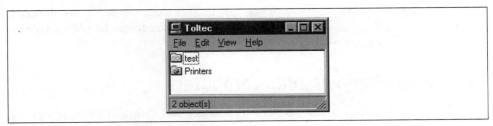

Figure 3-33. Shares offered by the Toltec server

If you don't see the server listed, don't panic. Select Run... from the Start menu. A dialog box appears that allows you to type the name of your server and its share directory in Windows format. For example, you would enter \\toltec\test, as shown in Figure 3-34, and use your server's hostname instead of "toltec".

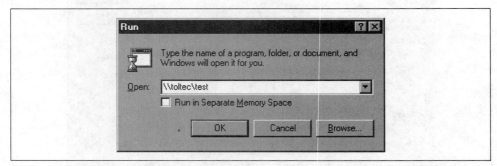

Figure 3-34. Opening a shared directory, using the server's NetBIOS name in the UNC

This will work even if browsing services are not set up right, which is a common problem. You can also work around a name-service problem by entering the server's IP Address (such as 172.16.1.1 in our example) instead of the Samba server's hostname, as shown in Figure 3-35. Go back and check your configuration, and if things still aren't right, go to the section "The Fault Tree" in Chapter 12 to troubleshoot what is wrong with the network.

Figure 3-35. Opening a shared directory, using the server's IP address in the UNC

If it works, congratulations! Try copying files to and from the server by dragging their icons to and from the folder on the Samba share. You might be pleasantly surprised how seamlessly everything works.

Setting Up Windows 2000 Computers

Although Windows 2000 is based on NT technology and is similar to Windows NT in many respects, configuring it for use with Samba is quite different.

You should perform the following steps as the Administrator or another user in the Administrators group.

Networking Components

Go to the Control Panel and double-click the Network and Dial-up Connections icon. You should see at least one Local Area Connection icon. If there is more than one, identify the one that corresponds to the network adapter that is connected to your Samba network. Right-click the Local Area Connection icon, and click the Properties button. (Or double-click the Local Area Connection icon, and then click the Properties button in the dialog box that comes up.) You should now be looking at the Local Area Connection Properties dialog box, as shown in Figure 3-36.

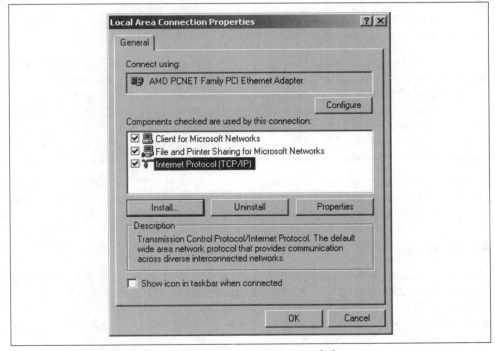

Figure 3-36. Windows 2000 Local Area Connection Properties dialog

First of all, you might want to click the Configure button under the field for the network adapter, to make sure you see the message "This device is working properly" in the Device status window. If there is a problem, make sure to correct it before continuing. You should also see the message "Use this device (enable)" in the Device usage field of the dialog box. Make sure to set it this way if it is not already. Click OK or Cancel to get back to the Local Area Connection Properties dialog box.

You should see at least the following two components:

- Client for Microsoft Networks
- Internet Protocol (TCP/IP)

If you do not see either Client for Microsoft Networks or Internet Protocol (TCP/IP) in your list, you will need to add them. For either, the method is to click the Install... button, click the type of component (Client or Protocol), and then click the Add... button. Next, click the component you want to add, and click the OK button. You should see the component added to the list with the others.

Some components should be removed if you see them in the list:

- NetBEUI Protocol
- NWLink NetBIOS
- NWLink IPX/SPX/NetBIOS Compatible Transport Protocol
- Client Service for Netware

If you see anything other than TCP/IP listed as a protocol, and it is not a protocol that you need, you can remove it. Uninstall NetBEUI, unless you are sure you need it, and the other three if you do not need to support Netware. If you try to remove a protocol and get an error message saying that the protocol is being used by another service, you need to remove that service before you can remove the protocol. For example, to remove the NWLink IPX/SPX Compatible Transport Protocol, you would need to remove the Client Service for Netware first.

To remove a component, click the component in the list, click the Uninstall button, and then click Yes in the dialog box that pops up. In some cases, Windows might need to reboot to put the change into effect.

Bindings

Next to each client, service, or protocol listed in the window in the Local Area Connections Properties dialog box, you will see a checkbox. Make sure the checkbox is checked for both Client for Microsoft Networks and Internet Protocol (TCP/IP). The check marks indicate the networking components are bound to the network adapter shown at the top of the dialog box.

Configuring TCP/IP

Now click Internet Protocol (TCP/IP), and then click Properties to open the Internet Protocol (TCP/IP) Properties dialog box, shown in Figure 3-37.

IP address

If you are using DHCP on your network to assign IP addresses dynamically, select the "Obtain IP address automatically" radio button. Otherwise, select the "Use the

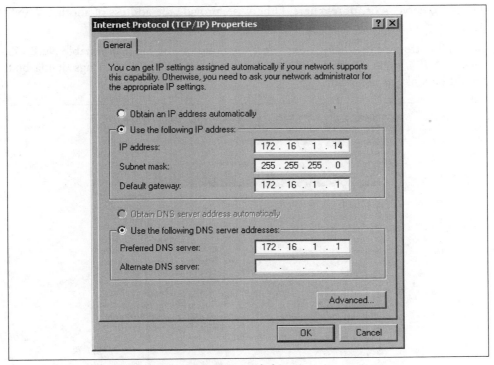

Figure 3-37. Internet Protocol (TCP/IP) Properties dialog

following address:" radio button, and fill in the computer's IP address and netmask in the spaces provided. You or your network manager should have selected an address for the client on the same subnet (LAN) as the Samba server. For example, if the server's address is 172.16.1.1 and its network mask is 255.255.255.0, you might use the address 172.16.1.14, if it is available, along with the same netmask. You can also fill in the IP address of the default gateway.

DNS server

In the lower part of the dialog box, click the "Use the following DNS server addresses:" radio button, and fill in the IP address of your DNS server.

Now click the Advanced... button to bring up the Advanced TCP/IP Settings dialog box, and then click the WINS tab.

WINS server

Enter the address of your WINS server in the space labeled "WINS addresses, in order of use:". If your Samba server is providing WINS service (in other words, you have the line wins service = yes in the *smb.conf* file of your Samba server), provide the Samba server's IP address here. Otherwise, provide the address of another WINS server on your network.

Near the bottom of the dialog box, select the radio button labeled "Enable NetBIOS over TCP/IP". Figure 3-38 shows what your Advanced TCP/IP Settings dialog box should look like at this point.

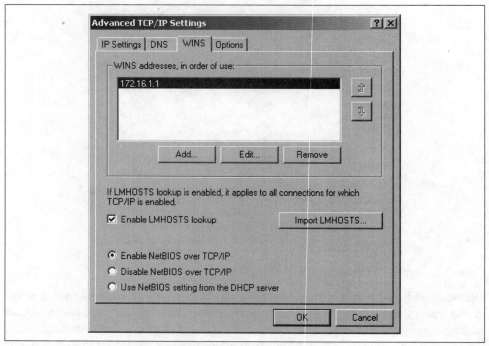

Figure 3-38. Advanced TCP/IP Settings dialog, showing WINS tab

The LMHOSTS file

If you want to install an *LMHOSTS* file, it must be placed in the *\system32\drivers\etc* directory under your Windows installation directory (usually *C:\WINNT*). The easy way to make sure it gets to the proper location is to use the Import LMHOSTS... button on the WINS Address tab. (But if you want to do it over the network, you will have to do that after file sharing is configured!) Remember to click the Enable LMHOSTS Lookup checkbox on the WINS Address tab to enable this functionality.

When you are satisfied with your settings for IP Address, WINS Address, and DNS, click the OK buttons in each open dialog box to complete the configuration. Windows might need to load some files from the Windows 2000 distribution CD-ROM, and you might need to reboot for your changes to take effect.

Computer and Workgroup Names

From the Control Panel, double-click the System icon to open the System Properties dialog box. Click the Network Identification tab, and your System Properties dialog box will look similar to Figure 3-39.

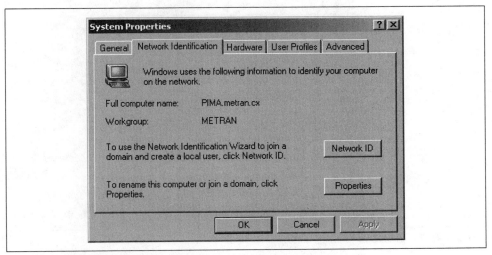

Figure 3-39. System Properties dialog, showing Network Identification tab

To give your system computer a name and a workgroup, click the Properties button, which will bring up the Identification Changes dialog box, as in Figure 3-40.

You need to identify your computer with a name and change the workgroup to the one you specified in the *smb.conf* file of your Samba server. Don't worry that Windows forces the computer name and the workgroup to be all capital letters; it's smart enough to figure out what you mean when it connects to the network.

Click the More... button to bring up the DNS Suffix and NetBIOS Computer Name dialog box, shown in Figure 3-41.

Enter the DNS domain name of this computer in the text field labeled Primary DNS Suffix for this computer:, and then click OK. You should now see the FQDN of this system underneath the label "Full computer name:". Click the OK button and then reboot when requested to put your configuration changes into effect. Once again, log in using your administrative account.

 There have been reports of authentication problems with Samba when a username on a Windows 2000 system is the same as its computer name.

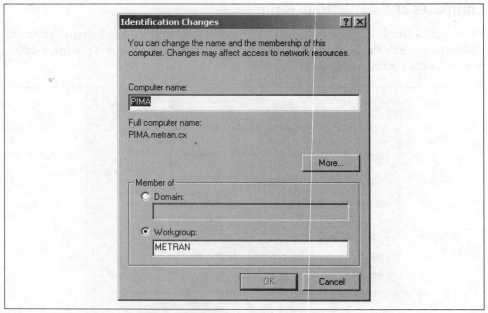

Figure 3-40. Identification Changes dialog

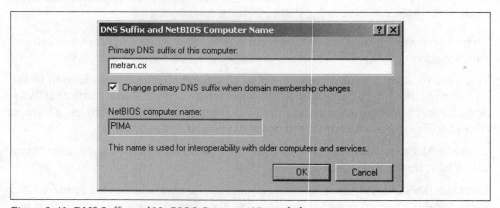

Figure 3-41. DNS Suffix and NetBIOS Computer Name dialog

Adding a Samba-Enabled User

So far, you have been logged into your Windows 2000 system as a user in the Administrators group. To access resources on the Samba server, you will need a username and password that the Samba server recognizes as valid. If your administrative account has such a username and password, you can use it, but you might want to access your system and the network from a nonadministrative user account instead.

The directions in this section assume that your network is set up as a workgroup. If you have already set up your network as a domain, as we describe in Chapter 4, you do not need to follow the instructions here for adding a local user on the Windows 2000 client system. Simply log on to the domain from the client using a username and password in Samba's *smbpasswd* account database, and continue with the next section, "Connecting to the Samba Server."

To add a new user, open the Control Panel, and double-click the Users and Passwords icon to open the Users and Passwords dialog box, shown in Figure 3-42.

Figure 3-42. Users and Passwords dialog

The first thing to do is make sure the checkbox labeled "Users must enter a user name and password to use this computer." is checked. Next, click the Add... button to bring up the first dialog box of the User Wizard, shown in Figure 3-43.

Fill out the fields, using the username of a valid user account on the Samba host, and then click the Next > button to enter and confirm the user's password. This password must be the same as the user's password on the Samba host. If you are using encrypted passwords, make sure this username and password are the same as what you used when you ran the *smbpasswd* program. Click the Next > button, which brings up the final dialog box, shown in Figure 3-44.

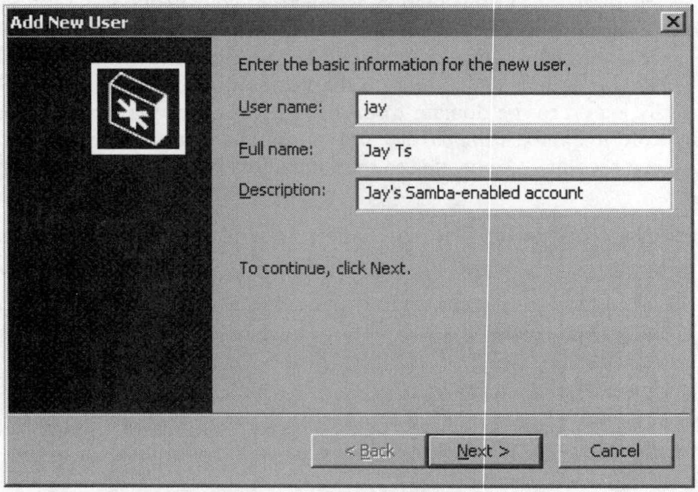

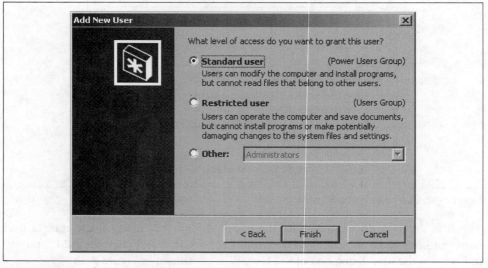

Figure 3-43. Adding a new user

Figure 3-44. Specifying a group for the new user

Pick a group for the user (the default Standard User should do), and click the Finish button. You should now see your new account added to the list in the Users and Passwords dialog box. Click the OK button to complete the process.

Now return to the Users and Passwords control panel window, click the Advanced tab, then click on the Advanced button. Click the Users folder in the left side of the Local Users and Groups window that appears, and then double-click the account you just added in the right side of the window. In the Properties window that opens, click the checkbox labeled Password never expires. You are done! Click the OK buttons in all the dialog boxes, and close all open windows.

Open the Start menu, select Shut Down, and select Log off *username* from the drop-down menu. Click the OK button, then log on with the username and password you just added.

Connecting to the Samba Server

Now for the big moment. Your Samba server is running, and you have set up your Windows 2000 client to communicate with it. Double-click the My Network Places icon on the desktop, and then double-click the Computers Near Me icon to browse the workgroup. You should see your Samba server listed as a member of the workgroup, as shown in Figure 3-45.

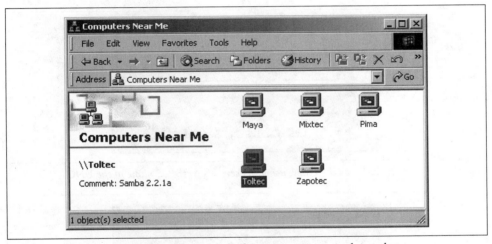

Figure 3-45. The Computers Near Me window, showing computers in the workgroup

Double-clicking the server name will show the resources that the server is offering to the network, as shown in Figure 3-46.

In this case, the *test* directory and the default printer are offered to the Windows 2000 workstation. If you don't see the server listed, don't panic. Select Run from the Start menu. A dialog box appears that allows you to type the name of your server and its share directory in Windows format. For example, you would enter *toltec*\ test, as shown in Figure 3-47, and use your server's hostname instead of "toltec".

This will work even if browsing services are not set up right, which is a common problem. You can also work around a name-service problem by entering the server's IP address (such as 172.16.1.1 in our example) instead of the Samba server's hostname, as shown in Figure 3-48.

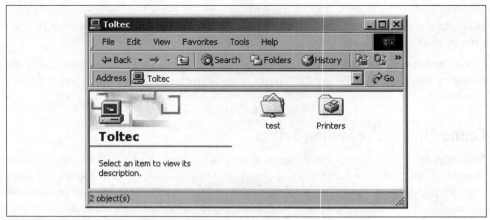

Figure 3-46. Shares offered by the Toltec server

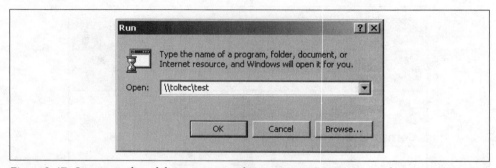

Figure 3-47. Opening a shared directory, using the server's NetBIOS name in the UNC

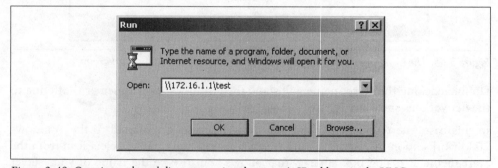

Figure 3-48. Opening a shared directory, using the server's IP address in the UNC

If things still aren't right, go directly to the section "The Fault Tree" in Chapter 12 to troubleshoot what is wrong with the network.

If it works, congratulations! Try copying files to and from the server. You will be pleasantly surprised how seamlessly everything works. Now that you've finished setting up the Samba server and its clients, you can proceed to the next chapter.

Setting Up Windows XP Computers

Although Windows XP is very similar to Windows 2000, it has a very different user interface, and there are a number of subtle differences. For example, getting to the Control Panel is different than in any previous version of Windows—one must click the Control Panel item from the Start menu (there is no Settings item in the Start menu in XP). By default, XP will display the Control Panel in Category View mode. If you see this, click the Switch to Classic View item in the upper-left corner of the window. All of our directions are for using the Control Panel in Classic View mode.

You should perform the following steps as the Administrator or another user in the Administrators group.

Networking Components

Go to the Control Panel and double-click the Network and Dial-up Connections icon. You should see at least one Local Area Connection icon. If there is more than one, identify the one that corresponds to the network adapter that is connected to your Samba network. Right-click the Local Area Connection icon and click the Properties button. (Or double-click the Local Area Connection icon and then click the Properties button in the dialog box that comes up.) You should now be looking at the Local Area Connection Properties dialog box, as shown in Figure 3-49.

First of all, you might want to click the Configure button under the field for the network adapter to make sure you see the message "This device is working properly" in the Device status window. If there is a problem, make sure to correct it before continuing. You should also see the message "Use this device (enable)" in the Device usage field of the dialog box. Make sure to set it this way if it is not already. Click OK or Cancel to close this dialog box, then reopen the Local Area Connection Properties dialog box.

You should see at least the following two components:

- Client for Microsoft Networks
- Internet Protocol (TCP/IP)

If you do not see either Client for Microsoft Networks or Internet Protocol (TCP/IP) in your list, you will need to add them. For either, the method is to click the Install... button, click the type of component (Client or Protocol), and then click the Add... button. Next, click the component you want to add, and click the OK button. You should see the component added to the list with the others.

If you see anything other than TCP/IP listed as a protocol, and it is not a protocol that you need, you can remove it. If NetBEUI appears in the list, uninstall it if you possibly can. Also uninstall any Netware-related components if you do not need to support Netware. If you try to remove a protocol and get an error message saying

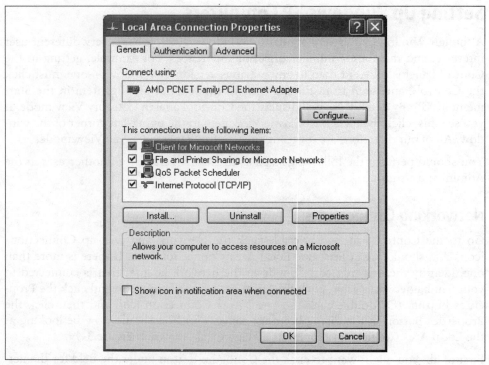

Figure 3-49. The Local Area Connection Properties dialog

that the protocol is being used by another service, you need to remove that service before you can remove the protocol. For example, to remove the NWLink IPX/SPX Compatible Transport Protocol, you would need to remove the Client Service for Netware first.

To remove a component, click the component in the list, click the Uninstall button, and then click Yes in the dialog box that pops up. In some cases, Windows might need to reboot to put the change into effect.

Bindings

Next to each client, service, or protocol listed in the window in the Local Area Connections Properties dialog box, you will see a checkbox. Make sure the checkbox is checked for both Client for Microsoft Networks and Internet Protocol (TCP/IP). The check marks indicate that the networking components are bound to the network adapter shown at the top of the dialog box.

Configuring TCP/IP

Now click Internet Protocol (TCP/IP) and then click Properties to open the Internet Protocol (TCP/IP) Properties dialog box, shown in Figure 3-50.

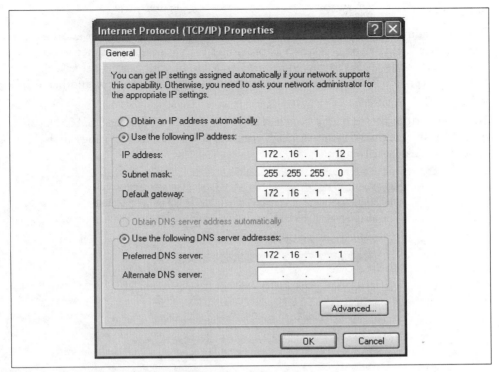

Figure 3-50. The Internet Protocol (TCP/IP) Properties dialog

IP address

If you are using DHCP on your network to assign IP addresses dynamically, select the "Obtain IP address automatically" radio button. Otherwise, select the "Use the following address:" radio button, and fill in the computer's IP address and netmask in the spaces provided. You or your network manager should have selected an address for the client on the same subnet (LAN) as the Samba server. For example, if the server's address is 172.16.1.1 and its network mask is 255.255.255.0, you might use the address 172.16.1.12 (if it is available) along with the same netmask. You can also fill in the IP address of the default gateway.

DNS server

In the lower part of the dialog box, click the "Use the following DNS server addresses:" radio button, and fill in the IP address of your DNS server.

Now click the Advanced... button to bring up the Advanced TCP/IP Settings dialog box, and then click the WINS tab.

WINS server

Enter the address of your WINS server in the space labeled "WINS addresses, in order of use:". If your Samba server is providing WINS service (in other words, you have the line wins support = yes in the *smb.conf* file of your Samba server), provide the Samba server's IP address here. Otherwise, provide the address of another WINS server on your network.

Near the bottom of the dialog box, select the radio button labeled Enable NetBIOS over TCP/IP. Figure 3-51 shows what your Advanced TCP/IP Settings dialog box should look like at this point.

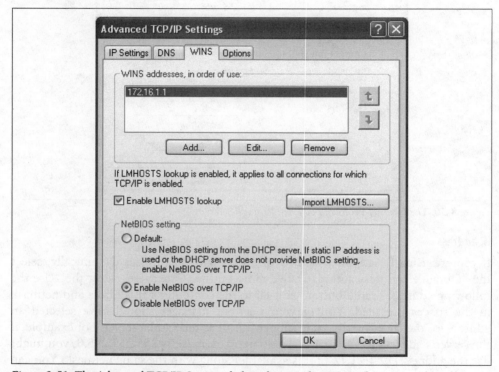

Figure 3-51. The Advanced TCP/IP Settings dialog, showing the WINS tab

The LMHOSTS file

If you want to install an *LMHOSTS* file, it must be placed in the *\system32\drivers\etc* directory under your Windows installation directory (usually *C:\WINNT*). The easy way to make sure it gets to the proper location is to use the Import LMHOSTS... button on the WINS Address tab. (But if you want to do it over the network, you will have to do that after file sharing is configured!) Remember to click the Enable LMHOSTS Lookup checkbox on the WINS Address tab to enable this functionality.

When you are satisfied with your settings for IP Address, WINS Address, and DNS, click the OK buttons in each open dialog box (and the Close button in the Local Area Connection Properties dialog box) to complete the configuration. Windows might need to load some files from the Windows XP distribution CD-ROM, and you might need to reboot for your changes to take effect.

Computer and Workgroup Names

From the Control Panel, double-click the System icon to open the System Properties dialog box. Click the Computer Name tab, and your System Properties dialog box will look similar to Figure 3-52.

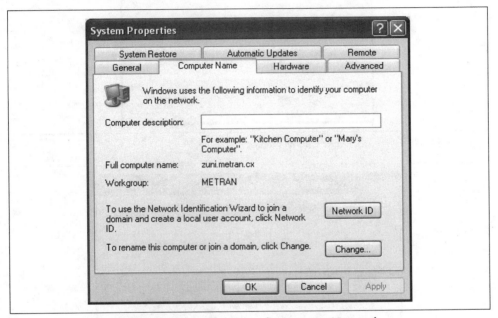

Figure 3-52. The System Properties dialog, showing the Computer Name tab

To give your system computer a name and a workgroup, click the Change... button, which will bring up the Computer Name Changes dialog box, as in Figure 3-53.

You need to identify your computer with a name and change the workgroup to the one you specified in the *smb.conf* file of your Samba server. Don't worry that Windows forces the workgroup to be all capital letters; it's smart enough to figure out what you mean when it connects to the network.

Click the More... button to bring up the DNS Suffix and NetBIOS Computer Name dialog box, shown in Figure 3-54.

Enter the DNS domain name of this computer in the text field labeled Primary DNS Suffix for this computer:, and then click OK. You should now see the FQDN of this

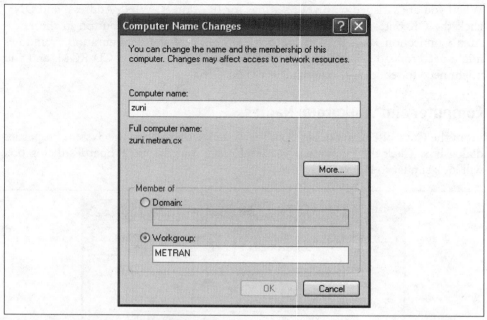

Figure 3-53. The Computer Name Changes dialog

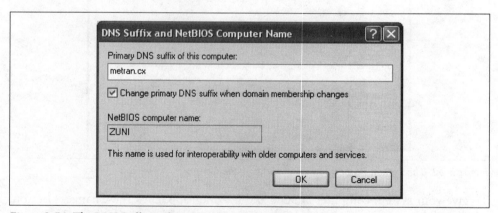

Figure 3-54. The DNS Suffix and NetBIOS Computer Name dialog

system underneath the label Full computer name: in the Computer Name Changes dialog box. Click the OK button and then reboot when requested to put your configuration changes into effect. Once again, log in using your administrative account.

 There have been reports of authentication problems with Samba when a username on a Windows XP system is the same as its computer name.

Adding a Samba-Enabled User

So far, you have been logged into your Windows XP system as a user in the Administrators group. To access resources on the Samba server, you will need to have a username and password that the Samba server recognizes as valid. If your administrative account has such a username and password, you can use it, but you might want to access your system and the network from a nonadministrative user account instead.

> The directions in this section assume that your network is set up as a workgroup. If you have already set up your network as a domain, as we describe in Chapter 4, you do not need to follow the instructions here for adding a local user on the Windows XP client system. Simply log on to the domain from the client using a username and password in Samba's *smbpasswd* account database, and continue with the next section, "Connecting to the Samba Server."

To add a new user, open the Control Panel, and double-click the Users Accounts icon to open the User Accounts window, shown in Figure 3-55.

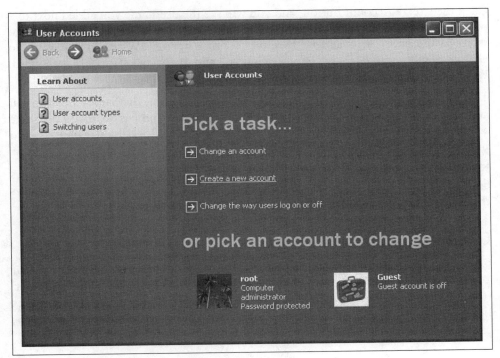

Figure 3-55. The User Accounts window

Click the Create a new account task, which will bring up the window shown in Figure 3-56. Enter the username, then click the Next > button.

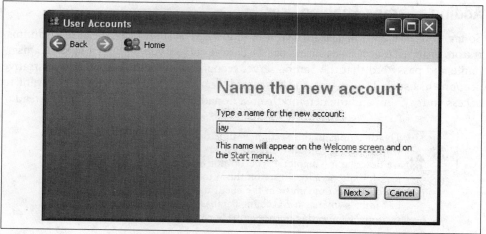

Figure 3-56. Entering the username

Click the radio button labeled "Limited", as shown in Figure 3-57.

Click the Create Account button, and you will see the username you added next to a picture at the bottom of the User Accounts window. We still need to assign a password to the account. Click the account to bring up the "What do you want to change about *username*'s account?" window, and then click Create a password. Enter the password, and enter it again to confirm it.

This password must be the same as the user's password on the Samba host. If you are using encrypted passwords, make sure this username and password are the same as what you used when you ran the *smbpasswd* program. Click the Create Password button, and you're done adding the account.

Now open the Start menu and click the Log Off button. In the Log Off Windows dialog box that pops up, again click the Log Off button. When Windows displays the login screen, click the user you just added, and type in the password to log in.

Connecting to the Samba Server

Now for the big moment. Your Samba server is running, and you have set up your Windows XP client to communicate with it. In the Start menu, select My Computer* to open the My Computer window. Click My Network Places, in the Other Places box in the left part of the window. You should see a folder icon for the *test* directory, as shown in Figure 3-58.

---

* If there is a My Network Places item in the Start menu at this point, you can save yourself a little time and just click that. If you don't see it, don't worry; it will appear automatically later.

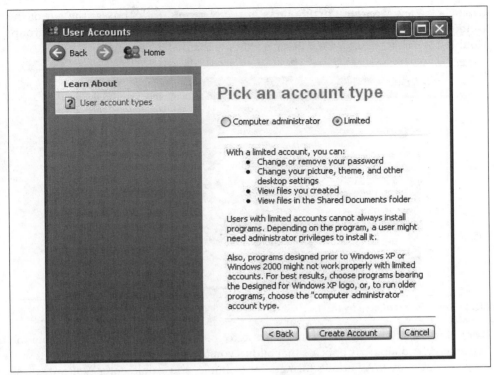

Figure 3-57. Setting the account type

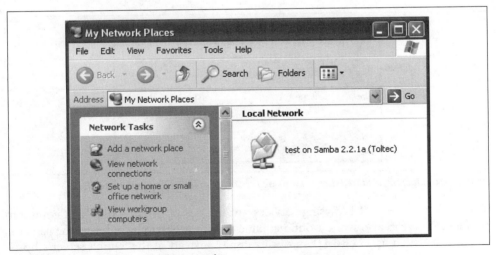

Figure 3-58. The My Network Places window

Now click View workgroup computers in the Network Tasks box at the left of the window. You should see your Samba server listed as a member of the workgroup. Double-click its icon, and you will see a window that looks like Figure 3-59.

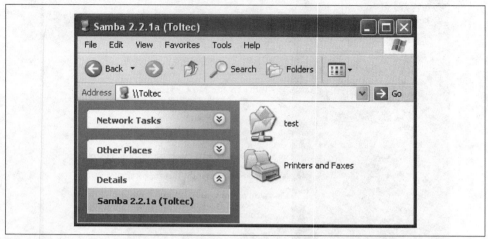

Figure 3-59. Shares offered by the Toltec server

If you don't see the server listed in the workgroup, don't panic. Select Run... from the Start menu. A dialog box appears that allows you to type the name of your server and its share directory in Windows format. For example, you would enter *toltec*\test, as shown in Figure 3-60, and use your server's hostname instead of "toltec".

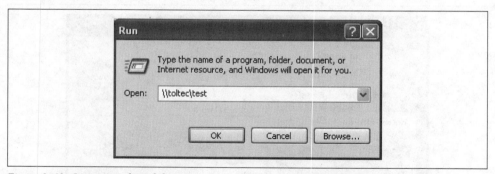

Figure 3-60. Opening a shared directory, using the server's NetBIOS name in the UNC

This will work even if browsing services are not set up right, which is a common problem. You can also work around a name-service problem by entering the server's IP Address (such as 172.16.1.1 in our example) instead of the Samba server's hostname, as shown in Figure 3-61.

If things still aren't right, go directly to the section "The Fault Tree" in Chapter 12 to troubleshoot what is wrong with the network.

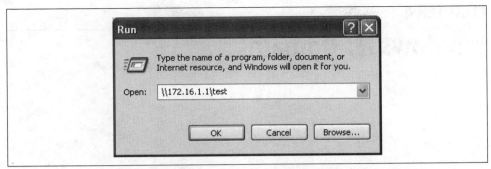

Figure 3-61. Opening a shared directory, using the server's IP address in the UNC

If it works, congratulations! Try copying files to and from the server by dragging their icons to and from the Samba server's *test* folder. You might be pleasantly surprised how seamlessly everything works.

CHAPTER 4
Windows NT Domains

In previous chapters, we've focused on workgroup networking to keep things simple and introduce you to networking with Samba in the most painless manner we could find. However, workgroup computing has its drawbacks, and for many computing environments, the greater security and single logon of the Windows NT domain make it worthwhile to spend the extra effort to implement a domain.

In addition to the domain features of that we discussed in Chapter 1, having a domain makes it possible to use *logon scripts* and *roaming profiles* (also called *roving profiles*). A logon script is a text file of commands that are run during startup, and a profile is a collection of information regarding the desktop environment, including the contents of the Start menu, icons that appear on the desktop, and other characteristics about the GUI environment that users are allowed to customize. A roaming profile can follow its owner from computer to computer, allowing her to have the same familiar interface appear wherever she logs on.

A Windows NT domain offers centralized control over the network. *Policies* can be set up by an administrator to define aspects of the users' environment and limit the amount of control they have over the network and their computers. It is also possible for administrators to perform remote administration of the domain controllers from any Windows NT/2000/XP workstation.

Samba 2.2 has the ability to act as a primary domain controller, supporting domain logons from Windows 95/98/Me/NT/2000/XP computers and allowing Windows NT/2000/XP* systems to join the domain as domain member servers. Samba can also join a domain as a member server, allowing the primary domain controller to be a Windows NT/2000 system or another Samba server.

---

* When we include Windows XP in discussions of Windows NT domains in this book, we are referring to Windows XP Professional and not to the Home edition. The reason for this is explained in the section on Windows XP later in this chapter.

Samba 2.2 does not support LDAP and Kerberos authentication of Active Directory, so it cannot act as a Windows 2000 Active Directory domain controller. However, Samba can be added to an Active Directory domain as a member server, with the Windows 2000 domain controllers running in either mixed or native mode. The Windows 2000 server (even if it is running in native mode) supports the Samba server by acting as a PDC emulator, using the Windows NT style of authentication rather than the Kerberos style.

If you're adding a Samba server to a network that has already been set up, you won't have to decide whether to use a workgroup or a domain; you will simply have to be compatible with what's already in place. If you do have a choice, we suggest you evaluate both workgroup and domain computing carefully before rolling out a big installation. You will have a lot of work to do if you later need to convert one to the other. One last thought on this matter is that Microsoft is developing Windows in the direction of increased use of domains and is intending that eventually Windows networks be composed solely of Active Directory domains. If you implement a Windows NT domain now, you'll be in a better position to transition to Active Directory later, after Samba has better support for it.

In this chapter, we cover various topics directly related to using Samba in a Windows NT domain, including:

- Configuring and using Samba as the primary domain controller
- Setting up Windows 95/98/Me systems to log on to the domain
- Implementing user-level security on Windows 95/98/Me
- Adding Windows NT/2000/XP systems to the domain
- Configuring logon scripts, roaming profiles, and system policies
- Adding a Samba server to a domain as a member server

Samba as the Primary Domain Controller

Samba 2.2 is able to handle the most desired functions of a primary domain controller in a Windows NT domain, handling domain logons and authentication for accessing shared resources, as well as supporting logon scripts, roaming profiles, and system policies.

You will need to use at least Samba 2.2 to ensure that PDC functionality for Windows NT/2000/XP clients is present. Prior to Samba 2.2, only limited user authentication for NT clients was present.

In this section, we will show you how to configure Samba as a PDC for use with Windows 95/98/Me and Windows NT/2000/XP clients. The two groups of Windows versions interact differently within domains, and in some cases are supported in slightly different ways. If you know you are going to be using only Windows 95/98/Me or Windows NT/2000/XP, you can set up Samba to support only that group. However, there isn't any harm in supporting both at the same time.

 If you would like more information on how to set up domains, see the file *Samba-PDC-HOWTO.html* in the *docs/htmldocs* directory of the Samba source distribution.

Samba must be the only domain controller for the domain. Make sure that a PDC isn't already active, and that there are no backup domain controllers. Samba 2.2 is not able to communicate with backup domain controllers, and having domain controllers in your domain with unsynchronized data would result in a very dysfunctional network.

 Although Samba 2.2 cannot function as, or work with, a Windows NT BDC, it is possible to set up another Samba server to act as a backup for a Samba PDC. For further information, see the file *Samba-BDC-HOWTO.html* in the *docs/htmldocs* directory of the Samba source distribution.

Configuring Samba to be a PDC is a matter of modifying the *smb.conf* file, creating some directories, and restarting the server.

Modifying smb.conf

First you will need to start with an *smb.conf* file that correctly configures Samba for workgroup computing, such as the one we created in Chapter 2, and insert the following lines into the [global] section:

```
[global]
        ; use the name of your Samba server instead of toltec
        ; and your own workgroup instead of METRAN
        netbios name = toltec
        workgroup = METRAN
        encrypt passwords = yes

        domain master = yes
        local master = yes
        preferred master = yes
        os level = 65

        security = user
        domain logons = yes

        ; logon path tells Samba where to put Windows NT/2000/XP roaming profiles
        logon path = \\%L\profiles\%u\%m
        logon script = logon.bat

        logon drive = H:
```

```
; logon home is used to specify home directory and
; Windows 95/98/Me roaming profile location
logon home = \\%L\%u\.win_profile\%m

time server = yes

; instead of jay, use the names of all users in the Windows NT/2000/XP
; Administrators group who log on to the domain
domain admin group = root jay

; the below works on Red Hat Linux - other OSs might need a different command
add user script = /usr/sbin/useradd -d /dev/null -g 100 -s /bin/false -M %u
```

And after the [global] section, add these three new shares:

```
[netlogon]
    path = /usr/local/samba/lib/netlogon
    writable = no
    browsable = no

[profiles]
    ; you might wish to use a different directory for your
    ; Windows NT/2000/XP roaming profiles
    path = /home/samba-ntprof
    browsable = no
    writable = yes
    create mask = 0600
    directory mask = 0700

[homes]
    read only = no
    browsable = no
    guest ok = no
    map archive = yes
```

Now for the explanation. If you are comparing this example to the configuration file presented in Chapter 2, you will notice that the first three parameter settings are similar. We start out in the [global] section by setting the NetBIOS name of the Samba server. We are using the default, which is the DNS hostname, but are being explicit because the NetBIOS name is used in UNCs that appear later in *smb.conf*. The next two lines, setting the workgroup name and choosing to use encrypted passwords, are identical to our *smb.conf* file from Chapter 2. However, things are now a little different: even though it still reads "workgroup", we are actually setting the name of the domain. For a workgroup, using encrypted passwords is optional; when using a domain, they are required.

The next four lines set up our Samba PDC to handle browsing services. The line domain master = yes causes Samba to be the domain master browser, which handles browsing services for the domain across multiple subnets if necessary. Although it looks very similar, local master = yes does not cause Samba to be the master browser on the subnet, but merely tells it to participate in browser elections and allow itself to win. (These two lines are yet more default settings that we include to be clear.)

The next two lines ensure that Samba wins the elections. Setting the preferred master parameter makes Samba force an election when it starts up. The os level parameter is set higher than that of any other system, which results in Samba winning that election. (At the time of this writing, an os level of 65 was sufficient to win over all versions of Windows—but make sure no other Samba server is set higher!) We make sure Samba is both the domain and local master browser because Windows NT/2000 PDCs always reserve the domain master browser role for themselves and because Windows clients require things to be that way to find the primary domain controller. It is possible to allow another computer on the network to win the role of local master browser, but having the same server act as both domain and local masters is simpler and more efficient.

The next two lines in the [global] section set up Samba to handle the actual domain logons. We set security = user so that Samba will require a username and password. This is actually the same as in the workgroup setup we covered in Chapters 1 and 2 because it is the default. The only reason we're including it explicitly is to avoid confusion: another valid setting is security = domain, but that is for having another (Windows or Samba) domain controller handle the logons and should never be found in the *smb.conf* of a Samba PDC. The next line, domain logons = yes, is what tells Samba we want this server to handle domain logons.

Defining a logon path is necessary for supporting roaming profiles for Windows NT/2000/XP clients. The UNC \\%L\profiles\%u refers to a share held on the Samba server where the profiles are kept. The variables %L and %u are replaced by Samba with the name of the server and the username of the logged on user, respectively. The section in *smb.conf* defining the [profiles] share contains the definition of exactly where the profiles are kept on the server. We'll get back to this topic a bit later in this chapter.

The logon script = logon.bat line specifies the name of an MS-DOS batch file that will be executed when the client logs on to the domain. The path specified here is relative to the [netlogon] share that is defined later in the *smb.conf* file.

The settings of logon drive and logon home have a couple of purposes. Setting logon drive = H: allows the home directory of the user to be connected to drive letter H on the client. The logon home parameter is set to the location of the home directory on the server, and again, %u is replaced at runtime by the logged on user's username. The home directory is used to store roaming profiles for Windows 95/98/Me clients. These parameters tie into the [homes] share that we are adding, as we will explain a bit later.

Setting time server = yes causes Samba to advertise itself as a time service for the network. This is optional.

The domain admin group parameter exists as a short-term measure in Samba 2.2 to give Samba a list of users who have administrative privileges in the domain. The list should contain any Samba users who log on from Windows NT/2000/XP systems and are members of the Administrators or Domain Admins groups, if roaming profiles are to work correctly.

The last parameter to add to the [global] section is add user script, and you will need it only if one or more of your clients is a Windows NT/2000/XP system. We will tell you more about this in the section "Adding Computer Accounts" later in this chapter.

The rest of the additions to *smb.conf* are the definitions for three shares. The [netlogon] share is necessary for Samba to handle domain logons because Windows clients need to connect to it during the logon process and will fail if the share does not exist. Other than that, the only function of [netlogon] is to be a repository for logon scripts and system-policy files, which we shall cover in detail later in this chapter. The path to a directory on the Samba server is given, and because the clients only read logon scripts and system-policy files from the share, the writable = no definition is used to make the share read-only. Users do not need to see the share, so we set browsable = no to make the share invisible.

The [profiles] share is needed for use with Windows NT/2000/XP roaming profiles. The path points to a directory on the Samba server where the profiles are kept, and in this case, the clients must be able to read and write the profile data. The create mask (read and write permitted for the owner only) and directory mask (read, write, and search permitted for the owner only) are set up such that a user's profile data can be read and written only by the user and not accessed or modified by anyone else.

The [homes] share is necessary for our definitions of logon drive and logon home to work. Samba uses the [homes] share to add the home directory of the user (found in */etc/passwd*) as a share. Instead of appearing as "homes", the share will be accessible on the client through a folder having the same name as the user's username. We will cover this topic in more detail in Chapter 9.

At this point, you might want to run *testparm* to check your *smb.conf* file.

Creating Directories on the Samba Server

The [netlogon] and [profiles] shares defined in our new *smb.conf* file reference directories on the Samba server, and it is necessary to create those directories with the proper permissions:

```
# mkdir /usr/local/samba/lib/netlogon
# chmod 775 /usr/local/samba/lib/netlogon
# mkdir /home/samba-ntprof
# chmod 777 /home/samba-ntprof
```

The directory names we use are just examples. You are free to choose your own.

Restarting the Samba Server

At this point, the only thing left to do is restart the Samba server, and the changes will be put into effect:

```
# /etc/rc.d/init.d/smb restart
```

(or use whatever method works on your system, as discussed in Chapter 2.) The server is now ready to accept domain logons.

Adding Computer Accounts

To interact in a domain, a Windows NT/2000/XP system must be a member of the domain. Domain membership is implemented using *computer accounts,* which are similar to user accounts and allow a domain controller to keep information with which to authenticate computers on the network. That is, the domain controller must be able to tell if requests that arrive from a computer are coming from a computer that it "knows" as being part of the domain. Each Windows NT/2000/XP system in the domain has a computer account in the domain controllers' database, which on a Windows NT/2000 hosted domain is the SAM database. Although Samba uses a different method (involving the *smbpasswd* file), it also treats computer accounts similarly to user accounts.

To create a computer account, an administrator configures a Windows NT/2000/XP system to be part of the domain. For Samba 2.2, the "domain administrator" is the root account on the Samba server, and you will need to run the command:

```
# smbpasswd -a root
```

to add the root user to Samba's password database. In this case, do not provide *smbpasswd* with the same password as the actual root account on the server. Create a different password to be used solely for creating computer accounts. This will reduce the possibility of compromising the root password.

When the computer account is created, two things must happen on the Samba server. An entry is added to the *smbpasswd* file, with a "username" that is the Net-BIOS name of the computer with a dollar sign ($) appended to it. This part is handled by the *smbpasswd* command, and you do not need to perform any additional action to implement it.

With Samba 2.2, an entry is also required in the */etc/passwd* file* to give the computer account a user ID (UID) on the Samba server. This account will never be used to log in to the Unix system, so it should not be given a valid home directory or login shell. To make this part work, you must set the add user script parameter in your

---

* The entry in */etc/passwd* might not be required in future Samba versions.

Samba configuration file, using a command that adds the entry in the proper manner. On our Red Hat Linux system, we set add user script to:

```
/usr/sbin/useradd -d /dev/null -g 100 -s /bin/false -M %u
```

This command adds an entry in /etc/passwd similar to the following:

```
aztec$:x:505:100::/dev/null:/bin/false
```

Again, notice that the username ends in a dollar sign. The user account shown has a "home directory" of /dev/null, a group ID (GID) of 100, and a "login shell" of /bin/false. The -M flag in our *useradd* command prevents it from creating the home directory. Samba replaces the %u variable in the *useradd* command with the NetBIOS name of the computer, including the trailing dollar sign. The basic idea here is to create an entry with a valid username and UID. These are the only parts that Samba uses. It is important that the UID be unique, not also used for other accounts—especially ones that are associated with Samba users.

If you are using some other variety of Unix, you will need to replace our *useradd* command with a command that performs the same function on your system. If a command such as *useradd* does not come with your system, you can write a shell script yourself that performs the same function. In any case, the command should add a password hash that does not correspond to any valid password. For example, in the /etc/shadow file of our Linux server, we find the following two lines:

```
jay:%1%zQ7j7ok8$D/IubyRAY5ovM3bTrpUCn1:11566:0:99999:7:::
zapotec$:!!:11625:0:99999:7:::
```

The first line is for jay's user account. The second field is the password hash—the long string between the first and second colons. The second line is for the computer account of zapotec, a domain member server. Its "username" ends with a dollar sign ($), and the second field in this case has been set to "!!", which is an arbitrary string not produced from any password. Therefore, there is no valid password for this account on the Linux host. Just about any ASCII string can be used instead of "!!". For example, you could use "DISABLED" instead.

 It is possible to create the entries for /etc/passwd and *smbpasswd* manually; however, we suggest this method be used very carefully, and only for initial testing, or as a last resort. The reason for this is to maintain security. After the computer account has been created on the server, the next Windows NT/2000/XP system on the network with a matching NetBIOS name to log on to the domain will be associated with this account. This allows crackers a window of opportunity to take over computer accounts for their own purposes.

Configuring Windows Clients for Domain Logons

The client-side configuration for Windows clients is really simple. All you have to do is switch from workgroup to domain networking by enabling domain logons, and in the case of Windows NT/2000/XP, also provide the root password you gave *smbpasswd* for creating computer accounts. This results in the Windows NT/2000/XP system becoming a member of the domain.

Windows 95/98/Me

To enable domain logons with Windows 95/98/Me, open the Control Panel and double-click the Network icon. Then click Client for Microsoft Networks, and click the Properties button. At this point, you should see a dialog box similar to Figure 4-1. Select the Logon to Windows Domain checkbox at the top of the dialog box, and enter the name of the domain as you have defined it with the `workgroup` parameter in the Samba configuration file. Then click OK, and reboot the machine when asked.

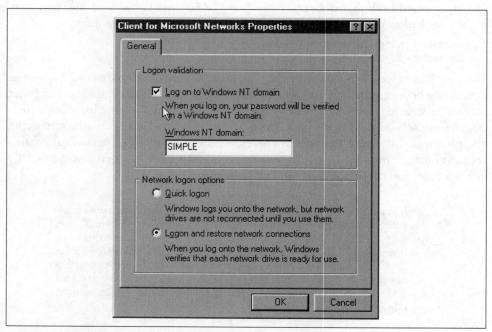

Figure 4-1. Configuring a Windows 95/98 client for domain logons

If Windows complains that you are already logged into the domain, you probably have an active connection to a share in the workgroup (such as a mapped network drive). Simply disconnect the resource temporarily by right-clicking its icon and choosing the Disconnect pop-up menu item.

When Windows reboots, you should see the standard logon dialog with an addition: a field for a domain. The domain name should already be filled in, so simply enter your password and click the OK button. At this point, Windows should consult the primary domain controller (Samba) to see if the password is correct. (You can check the log files if you want to see this in action.) If it worked, congratulations! You have properly configured Samba to act as a domain controller for Windows 95/98/Me machines, and your client is successfully connected.

User-Level Security for Windows 95/98/Me

Now that you have a primary domain controller to authenticate users, you can implement much better security for shares that reside on Windows 95/98/Me systems.* To enable this functionality, open the Control Panel, double-click the Network icon, and click the Access Control tab in the dialog box. The window should now look like Figure 4-2.

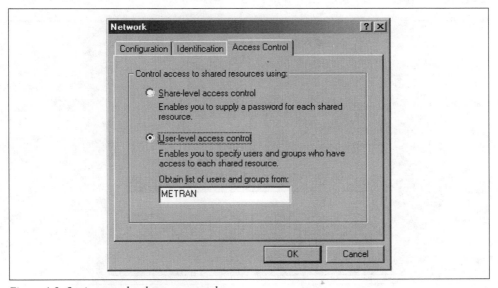

Figure 4-2. Setting user-level access control

---

* If you want to follow our example in this section, and your network doesn't have any Windows systems offering shares, see Chapter 5 for directions on how to create one. Make sure you understand how to set up shares before continuing with the directions presented here!

Click the User-level access control radio button, and type in the name of your domain in the text area. Click the OK button. If you get the dialog box shown in Figure 4-3, it means that shares are already on the system.

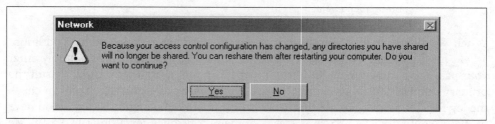

Figure 4-3. Error dialog while changing to user-level access control

In that case, you might want to cancel the operation and make a record of each of the computer's shares, making it easier to re-create them, and then redo this part. (To get a list of shares, open an MS-DOS prompt window and run the net view \\computer_name command.) Otherwise, you will get a message asking you to reboot to put the change in configuration into effect.

After rebooting, you can create shares with user-level access control. To do this, right-click the folder you wish to share, and select Sharing.... This will bring up the Shared Properties dialog box, shown in Figure 4-4.

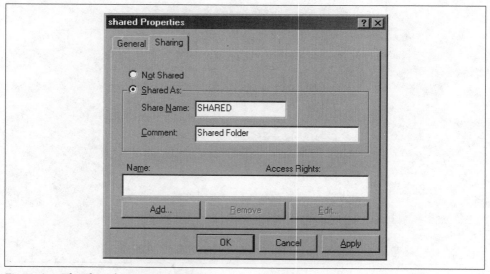

Figure 4-4. The Shared Properties dialog

Click the Shared As: radio button, and give the share a name and comment. Then click the Add... button, and you will see the Add Users dialog box, shown in Figure 4-5.

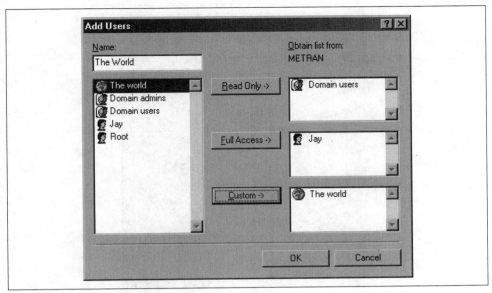

Figure 4-5. The Add Users dialog

What has happened is that Windows has contacted the primary domain controller (in this case, Samba) and requested a list of domain users and groups. You can now select a user or group and add it to one or more of the three lists on the righthand side of the window—for Read Only, Full Access, or Custom Control—by clicking the buttons in the middle of the window. When you are done, click the OK button. If you added any users or groups to the Custom Control list, you will be presented with the Change Access Rights dialog box, shown in Figure 4-6, in which you can specify the rights you wish to allow. Then click the OK button to close the dialog box.

You are now returned to the Shared Properties dialog box, where you will see the Name: and Access Rights: columns filled in with the permissions that you just created. Click the OK button to finalize the process. Remember, you will have to perform these actions on any folders that you had previously shared using share-level security.

Windows NT 4.0

To configure Windows NT for domain logons, log in to the computer as Administrator or another user in the Administrators group, open the Control Panel, and double-click the Network icon. If it isn't already selected, click on the Network Identification tab.

Click the Change... button, and you should see the dialog box shown in Figure 4-7. In this dialog box, you can choose to have the Windows NT client become a member of the domain by clicking the checkbox marked Domain: in the Member of box. Then type in the name of the domain to which you wish the client to log on; it should be the same as the one you specified using the workgroup parameter in the

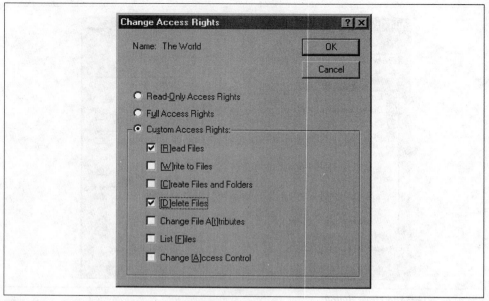

Figure 4-6. The Change Access Rights dialog

Samba configuration file. Click the checkbox marked Create a Computer Account in the Domain, and fill in "root" for the text area labeled User Name:. In the Password: text area, fill in the root password you gave *smbpasswd* for creating computer accounts.

> If Windows complains that you are already logged in, you probably have an active connection to a share in the workgroup (such as a mapped network drive). Disconnect the resource temporarily by right-clicking its icon and choosing the Disconnect pop-up menu item.

After you press the OK button, Windows should present you with a small dialog box welcoming you to the domain. Click the Close button in the Network dialog box, and reboot the computer as requested. When the system comes up again, the machine will automatically present you with a logon screen similar to the one for Windows 95/98/Me clients, except that the domain text area has a drop-down menu so that you can opt to log on to either the local system or the domain. Make sure your domain is selected, and log on to the domain using any Samba-enabled user account on the Samba server.

> Be sure to select the correct domain in the Windows NT logon dialog box. Once it is selected, it might take a moment for Windows NT to build the list of available domains.

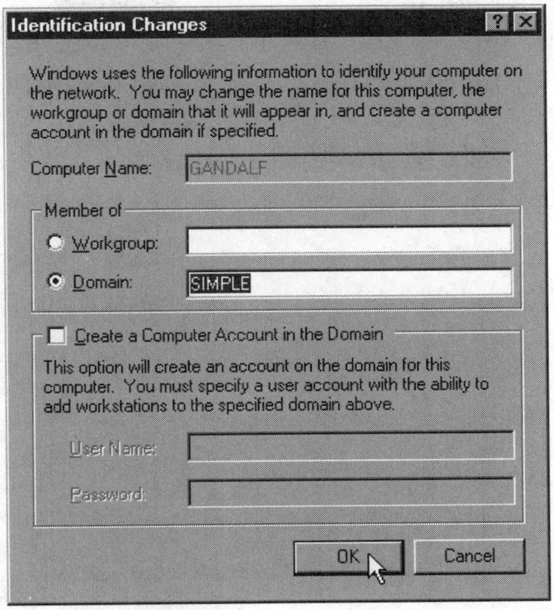

Figure 4-7. Configuring a Windows NT client for domain logons

After you enter the password, Windows NT should consult the primary domain controller (Samba) to see if the password is correct. Again, you can check the log files if you want to see this in action. If it worked, you have successfully configured Samba to act as a domain controller for Windows NT machines.

Windows 2000

To configure Windows 2000 for domain logons, log in to the computer as Administrator or another user in the Administrators group, open the Control Panel, and double-click the System icon to open the System Properties dialog box. Click the Network Identification tab, and then click the Properties button. You should now see the Identification Changes dialog box shown in Figure 4-8.

Click the radio button labeled "Domain:" and fill in the name of your domain in the text-entry area. Then click the OK button. This will bring up the Domain Username and Password dialog box. Enter "root" for the username. For the password, use the password that you gave to *smbpasswd* for the root account.

> If Windows complains that you are already logged in, you probably have an active connection to a share in the workgroup (such as a mapped network drive). Disconnect the resource temporarily by right-clicking its icon and choosing the Disconnect pop-up menu item.

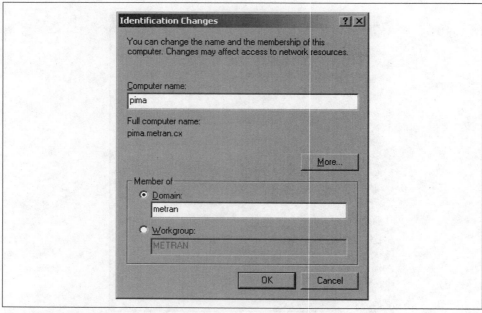

Figure 4-8. The Identification Changes dialog

After you press the OK button, Windows should present you with a small dialog box welcoming you to the domain. When you click the OK button in this dialog box, you will be told that you need to reboot the computer. Click the OK button in the System Properties dialog box, and reboot the computer as requested. When the system comes up again, the machine will automatically present you with a Log On to Windows dialog box similar to the one shown in Figure 4-9.

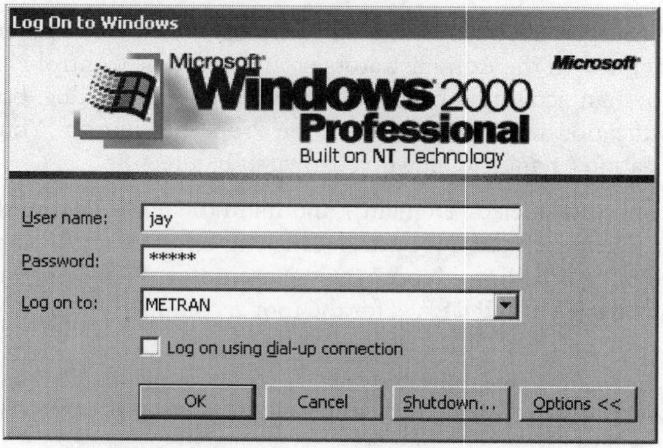

Figure 4-9. The Windows 2000 logon window

If you do not see the Log on to: drop-down menu, click the Options << button and it will appear. Select your domain, rather than the local computer, from the menu.

 Be sure to select the correct domain in the logon dialog box. Once it is selected, it might take a moment for Windows to build the list of available domains.

Enter the username and password of any Samba-enabled user in the User name: and Password: fields, and either press the Enter key or click the OK button. If it worked, your Windows session will start up with no error dialogs.

Windows XP Home

You have our condolences if you are trying to use the Home edition of Windows XP in a domain environment! Microsoft has omitted support for Windows NT domains from Windows XP Home, resulting in a product that is ill-suited for use in a domain-based network.

On the client side, Windows XP Home users cannot log on to a Windows NT domain. Although it is still possible to access domain resources, a username and password must be supplied each time the user connects to a resource, rather than the "single signon" of a domain logon. Domain features such as logon scripts and roaming profiles are not supported.

As a server, Windows XP Home cannot join a Windows NT domain as a domain member server. It can serve files and printers, but only using share-mode ("workgroup") security. It can't even use user-mode security, as Windows 95/98/Me can.

Considering these limitations, we do not recommend Windows XP Home for any kind of local area network computing.

Windows XP Professional

To configure Windows XP Professional for domain logons, log in to the computer as Administrator or another user in the Administrators group, open the Control Panel in Classic View, and double-click the System icon to open the System Properties dialog box. Click the Computer Name tab and then click the Change... button. You should now see the Computer Name Changes dialog box shown in Figure 4-10.

Click the radio button labeled "Domain:", and fill in the name of your domain in the text-entry area. Then click the OK button. This will bring up the Domain Username and Password dialog box. Enter "root" for the username. For the password, use the password that you gave to *smbpasswd* for the root account.

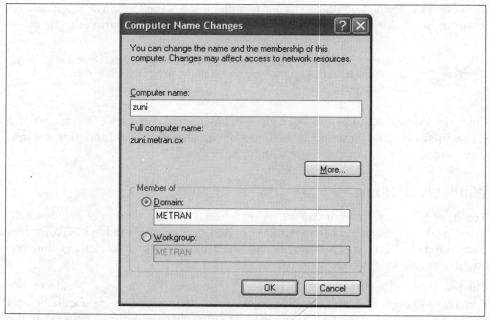

Figure 4-10. The Computer Name Changes dialog

 If Windows complains that you are already logged in, you probably have an active connection to a share in the workgroup (such as a mapped network drive). Disconnect the resource temporarily by right-clicking its icon and choosing the Disconnect pop-up menu item.

After you press the OK button, Windows should present you with a small dialog box welcoming you to the domain. When you click the OK button in this dialog box, you will be told that you need to reboot the computer to put the changes into effect. Click the OK buttons in the dialog boxes to close them, and reboot the computer as requested. When the system comes up again, the machine will automatically present you with a Log On to Windows dialog box similar to the one shown in Figure 4-11.

If you get a dialog box at this point that tells you the domain controller cannot be found, the solution is to change a registry setting as follows.

Open the Start Menu and click the Run... menu item. In the text area in the dialog box that opens, type in "regedit" and click the OK button to start the Registry Editor. You will be editing the registry, so follow the rest of the directions very carefully. Click the "+" button next to the HKEY_LOCAL_MACHINE folder, and in the contents that open up, click the "+" button next to the SYSTEM folder. Continue in the same manner to open CurrentControlSet, then Services, then Netlogon. (You will have to scroll down many times to find Netlogon in the list of services.) Then click the Parameters folder, and you will see items appear in the right side of the window.

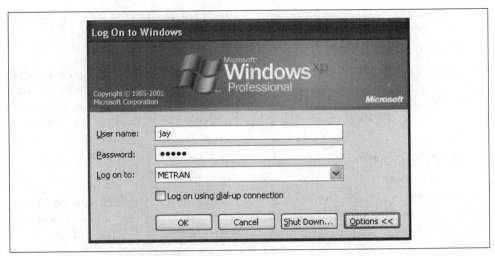

Figure 4-11. The Windows XP logon window

Double-click "requiresignorseal", and a dialog box will open. In the Value data: text area, change the "1" to a "0" (zero), and click the OK button, which modifies the registry both in memory and on disk. Now close the Registry Editor and log off and back on again.

If you do not see the Log on to: drop-down menu, click the Options << button and it will appear. Select your domain from the menu, rather than the local computer.

Be sure to select the correct domain in the logon dialog box. Once it is selected, it might take a moment for Windows to build the list of available domains.

Enter the username and password of any Samba-enabled user in the User name: and Password: fields, and either press the Enter key or click the OK button. If it worked, your Windows session will start up with no error dialogs.

Logon Scripts

After a Windows client connects with a domain controller (either to authenticate a user, in the case of Windows 95/98/Me, or to log on to the domain, in the case of Windows NT/2000/XP), the client downloads an MS-DOS batch file to run. The domain controller supplies the file assuming one has been made available for it. This batch file is the logon script and is useful in setting up an initial environment for the user.

In a Unix environment, the ability to run such a script might lead to a very complex initialization and deep customization. However, the Windows environment is mainly oriented to the GUI, and the command-line functions are more limited. Most commonly, the logon script is used to run a *net* command, such as *net use*, to connect a network drive letter, like this:

```
net use T: \\toltec\test
```

This command will make our [test] share (from Chapter 2) show up as the T: drive in My Computer. This will happen automatically, and T: will be available to the user at the beginning of her session, instead of requiring her to run the *net use* command or connect the T: drive using the Map Network Drive function of Windows Explorer.

Another useful command is:

```
net use H: /home
```

which connects the user's home directory to a drive letter (which can be H:, as shown here, or some other letter, as defined by logon drive). For this to work, you must have a [homes] share defined in your *smb.conf* file.

If you are using roaming profiles, you should definitely have:

```
net time \\toltec /set /yes
```

in your logon script. (As usual, replace "toltec" with the name of your Samba PDC.) This will make sure the clocks of the Windows clients are synchronized with the PDC, which is important for roaming profiles to work correctly.

Creating a Logon Script

In our *smb.conf* file, we have the line:

```
logon script = logon.bat
```

This defines the location and name of the logon script batch file on the Samba server. The path is relative to the [netlogon] share, defined later in the file like this:

```
[netlogon]
    path = /usr/local/samba/lib/netlogon
    writable = no
    browsable = no
```

With this example, the logon script is */user/local/samba/lib/netlogon/logon.bat*. We include the directives writable = no, to make sure network clients cannot change anything in the [netlogon] share, and also browsable = no, which keeps them from even seeing the share when they browse the contents of the server. Nothing in [netlogon] should ever be modified by nonadministrative users. Also, the permissions on the directory for [netlogon] should be set appropriately (no write permissions for "other" users), as we showed you earlier in this chapter.

Notice also that the extension of our logon script is *.bat*. Be careful about this—an extension of *.cmd* will work for Windows NT/2000/XP clients, but will result in errors for Windows 95/98/Me clients, which do not recognize *.cmd* as an extension for batch files.

Because the logon script will be executed on a Windows system, it must be in MS-DOS text-file format, with the end of line composed of a carriage return followed by a linefeed. The Unix convention is a *newline*, which is simply a linefeed character, so if you use a Unix text editor to create your logon script, you must somehow make it use the appropriate characters. With *vim* (a clone of the *vi* editor that is distributed with Red Hat Linux), the method is to create a new file and use the command:

```
:se ff=dos
```

to set the file format to MS-DOS style before typing in any text. With *emacs*, the same can be done using the command:

```
^X Enter f dos Enter
```

where ^X is a Control-X character and *Enter* is a press of the Enter key. Another method is to create a Unix-format file in any text editor and then convert it to MS-DOS format using the *unix2dos* program:

```
$ unix2dos unix_file >logon.bat
```

If your system does not have *unix2dos*, don't worry. You can implement it yourself with the following two-line Perl script:

```perl
#!/usr/bin/perl
open FILE, $ARGV[0];
while (<FILE>) { s/$/\r/; print }
```

Or, you can use Notepad on a Windows system to write your script and then drag the logon script over to a folder on the Samba server. In any case, you can check the format of your script using the *od* command, like this:

```
$ od -c logon.bat
```

You should see output resembling this:

```
0000000   n   e   t       u   s   e       T   :   \   \   t   o   l
0000020   t   e   c   \   t   e   s   t  \r  \n
0000032
```

The important detail here is that at the end of each line is a \r \n, which is a carriage return followed by a linefeed.

Our example logon script, containing a single *net use* command, was created and set up in a way that allows it to be run successfully on any Windows client, regardless of which Windows version is installed on the client and which user is authenticating or logging on to the domain. But what if we need to have different users, computers, or Windows versions running different logon scripts?

One method is to use variables inside the logon script that cause commands to be conditionally executed. For details on how to do this, you can consult a reference on batch-file programming for MS-DOS and Windows NT command language. One such reference is *Windows NT System Administration*, published by O'Reilly.

Windows batch-command language is very limited in functionality. Fortunately, Samba also supports a means by which customization can be handled. The *smb.conf* file contains variables that can be used to insert (at runtime) the name of the server (%L), the username of the person who is accessing the server's resources (%u), or the computer name of the client system (%m). To give an example, if we set up the path to the logon script as:

```
logon script = %u/logon.bat
```

we would then put a directory for each user in the [netlogon] share, with each directory named the same as the user's username, and in each directory we would put a customized *logon.bat* file. Then each user would have his own custom logon script. We will give you a better example of how to do this kind of thing in the next section, "Roaming Profiles."

 For more information on Samba configuration file variables, such as the %L, %u, and %m variables we just used, see Chapter 6 and Appendix B.

When modifying and testing your logon script, don't just log off of your Windows session and log back on to make your script run. Instead, restart (reboot) your system before logging back on. Because Windows often keeps the [netlogon] share open across logon sessions, the reboot ensures that Windows and Samba have completely released and reconnected the [netlogon] share, and the new version of the logon script is being run while logging on.

More information regarding logon scripts can be found in the O'Reilly book, *Managing Windows NT Logons*.

Roaming Profiles

One benefit of the centralized authentication of Windows NT domains is that a user can log on from more than just one computer. To help users feel more "at home" when logged on at a computer other than their usual one, Microsoft has added the ability for users' personal settings to "roam" from one computer to another.

All Windows versions can be configured individually for each user of the computer. Windows NT/2000/XP supports the ability to handle multiple user accounts, and Windows 95/98/Me can be configured for use by multiple users, keeping the configuration settings for each user separate. Each user can configure the computer's settings to her liking, and the system saves these settings as the user's *profile*, such that upon logging on to the system, the user is presented with her familiar desktop.

Some of the settings, such as folder options or the image used for the desktop background, are held in the registry. Others, including the documents and folders appearing on the desktop and the contents of the Start menu, are stored as folders and files in the filesystem.

When the profile is stored on the local system, it is called a *local profile*. On Windows NT, local profiles are stored in *C:\winnt\profiles*. On Windows 2000/XP, they can be found in *C:\Documents and Settings*. On Windows 95/98/Me, when configured for a single user (the default case), the local profile is scattered in places such as the registry and directories such as *C:\Windows\Desktop* and *C:\Windows\Start Menu*. When Windows 95/98/Me is configured for multiple users, the local profile of the preexisting user is moved to a folder in *C:\Windows\Profiles* that has the same name as the user, and any users that are subsequently added to the computer have their local profiles created in that directory as well. You can browse through the local profiles to see their structure—each has a registry file (*USER.DAT* for Windows 95/98/Me and *NTUSER.DAT* for Windows NT/2000/XP) and some folders that contain shortcuts and documents.

A roaming profile is a user profile that is stored on a server and "follows" its owner around the network so that when the user logs on to the domain from another computer, his profile is downloaded from the server and his familiar desktop appears on that computer as well.

 Samba can support roaming profiles, and it is a fairly simple matter to configure it for them. However, this is one feature that we recommend you *do not* use, at least until you are sure you understand roaming profiles well and are very confident that you can implement them with no harm incurred. If you want to (or are required to) implement roaming profiles for your Windows clients, we suggest you first set up a small domain with a Samba server and a few Windows clients exclusively for the purposes of research and testing. *Under no circumstances should you attempt to implement roaming profiles in a careless or frivolous manner.*

How Roaming Profiles work

We will start out by explaining to you how roaming profiles work when set up correctly. You will need a clear understanding of them to tell the difference between when they are working as they are designed and when they are not. In addition, roaming profiles can be a source of confusion for your users in many ways, and you should know how to detect when a problem with a client is related to roaming profile function or dysfunction.

 A definitive source of documentation on Windows NT roaming profiles is the Microsoft white paper *Implementing Policies and Profiles for Windows NT 4.0*, which can be found at *http://www.microsoft.com/ntserver/techresources/management/prof_policies.asp*.

During the domain logon process, the roaming profile is copied from the domain controller and used as a local profile during the user's logon session. When the user logs off the domain, the local profile is copied back to the domain controller and stored as the new roaming profile. When the local profile is changed, the server does not receive an update until the user logs off the domain or shuts down or reboots the client. The client does not send an update to the server during the logon session, and a client does not receive an update of a setting changed on another client during a logon session. When the user does log off, changes in the configuration settings in the local profile are sent to the server, and the updates of the roaming profile are available for the next logon session.

This simple behavior can lead to unexpected results when users are logged on to the domain on more than one client at a time. If a user makes a change to the configuration settings on one client and then logs off, the settings can result in the roaming profile being modified accordingly. But the next client that logs off might cause those changes to be overwritten, and if so, the settings from the first client will be lost. The behavior of different Windows versions varies with regard to this, and we've seen a wide variety of behaviors—not always in alignment with Microsoft's documentation or even working the same way on separate occasions. Sometimes Windows will refuse to overwrite a profile, perhaps giving an "access denied" error, and at other times it will seem to work while producing odd side effects. A common source of confusion is what happens if a file is added to or deleted from the desktop, which is by default configured to be part of the profile. A deleted file might later reappear, and it is even possible for a file to irrecoverably disappear without warning (on Windows 95/98). Or maybe a file that is added to the desktop on one client never gets added to the roaming profile and fails to propagate to other clients. This behavior is somewhat improved on Windows 2000/XP, which attempts to merge items into the profile that are added on concurrently logged-on clients.

One factor that comes into play is that Windows compares the timestamps of the local and roaming profiles and can refuse to overwrite a roaming profile if it is newer than the local profile on the client, or vice versa. For this reason, it is important to keep the clocks of the Windows clients and the Samba PDC synchronized. We have already shown you how to do this, using the *net time \\server /set /yes* command in the logon script.

Even when the server and clients are correctly configured, a number of things that can happen make things seem "broken." The most common occurrence is that some shortcuts on clients other than the one that created the roaming profile will not work. These shortcuts can exist on the desktop or as items in the Start menu. This behavior is a result of applications or files that exist on one computer but not others. Windows will display these shortcuts, but if they appear on the desktop, they will have a generic icon and will bring up an error message if a user double-clicks them.

Because profiles can and usually do include the contents of the desktop and other folders, it is possible for the roaming profile to grow to a huge size due to actions of a user, such as creating new files on the desktop or copying files there. By default, Internet Explorer keeps its disk cache in the *Temporary Internet Files* folder in the profile and has been known to populate this directory with thousands of files. This can result in a huge roaming profile that causes network congestion and very large delays while users are logging on to the domain. (A fix for this can be found in article Q185255 in the Microsoft Knowledge Base.)

One behavior we've seen a few times is that if, for some reason (e.g., a network error or misconfiguration), the roaming profile is not available during the logon process, Windows will use the local profile on the client instead. When this happens, the user might receive an unfamiliar profile, and all the benefits of roaming profiles are lost for that logon session.

Configuring Samba for Roaming Profiles

In an ideal world, different Windows versions would share the same roaming profile, allowing users to log on to the domain from any Windows client system, ranging from Windows 95 to Windows XP, and enjoy their familiar settings. It would even be possible to be logged on concurrently from multiple clients, and a change made to the profile on any of them would quickly propagate to all the others. Settings in a roaming profile made on a client that didn't apply to another would be handled sanely.

Unfortunately, this scenario does not work in reality, and it is important to maintain separate roaming profiles to prevent different Windows versions from using or modifying a roaming profile created by, and/or in use by, another version.

We do this by using configuration file variables to point to different profile directories. If you look at Table B-1 in Appendix B, which shows the variables that can be used, you might be tempted to use the %a variable, which is replaced by the name of the operating system the client is running. However, this does not work because all of Windows 95/98/Me will be seen as the same operating system, and likewise for Windows 2000/XP. So, we use %m to get the NetBIOS name of the client, and combine that with a symbolic link to point to the directory containing the profile for the Windows version that particular client is running.

Our additions to *smb.conf* that appeared earlier in this chapter included the two lines:

```
logon path = \\%L\profiles\%u\%m
logon home = \\%L\%u\.win_profile\%m
```

The first line specifies where the roaming profiles for Windows NT/2000/XP clients are kept, and the second line performs the same function for Windows 95/98/Me clients. In both cases, the location is specified as a UNC, but logon path (for Windows NT/2000/XP) is specified relative to the [profiles] share, while logon home (for Windows 95/98/Me) is specified relative to the user's home directory. This is done to comply with Samba's emulation of Windows NT/2000 PDC behavior.

The logon home UNC must begin by specifying the user's home directory, which in our previous example would be \\%L\%u. The variable %L expands to the NetBIOS name of the server (in this case, toltec), and %u expands to the name of the user. This must be done to allow the command:

```
C:\>net use h: /home
```

to function correctly to connect the user's home directory to drive letter H: on all Windows clients. (The drive letter used for this purpose is defined by logon drive.) We add the directory *.win_profile* to the UNC to put the Windows 95/98/Me roaming profile in a subdirectory of the user's home directory.

 Note that in both logon path and logon home, we absolutely avoid making the profile directory the same as the user's home directory, and the directory that contains the profile is not used for any other purpose. This is because when the roaming profile is updated, all directories and files in the roaming-profile directory that are not part of the roaming profile are deleted.

In the logon path line in *smb.conf*, we use %u to put the profiles directory in a subdirectory in the [profiles] share, such that each user gets her own directory that holds her roaming profiles.

We define the [profiles] share like this:

```
[profiles]
    writable = yes
    create mask = 0600
    directory mask = 0700
    browsable = no
    path = /home/samba-ntprof
```

The first four parameters in the previous share definition specify to allow roaming profiles to be written with the users' permissions, to create files with read and write permissions for the owner, and to create directories with read, write, and search permissions for the owner and no access allowed for other users. As with the [netlogon] share, we set browsable = no so that the share will not show up on the clients in Windows Explorer.

We've decided to put our Windows NT/2000/XP profiles in */home*, the default location of the home directories on Linux. This will make it simple to include the roaming profiles in backups of the home directories. You can use another directory if you like.

Notice that in both `logon path` and `logon home`, the directory we specify ends in `%m`, which Samba replaces with the NetBIOS name of the client. We are using the client's computer name to identify indirectly which version of Windows it is running.

Initially, the directories you specify to hold the roaming profiles will be empty and will become populated as clients log off for the first time. (Samba will even create the directories if they do not already exist.) At first, the directories will simply contain profiles that are identical to the clients' local profiles, and we highly recommend that you make a backup at this point before things get complicated. A listing of the roaming profile directory for user `iman`, after she has logged off from Windows 98 clients `mixtec` and `pueblo` and Windows Me clients `huastec` and `navajo`, might look something like the following:

```
$ ls -l /home/iman/.win_profile
total 4
drwx------   6 iman     iman         4096 Dec  8 18:09 huastec
drwx------   9 iman     iman         4096 Dec  7 03:47 mixtec
drwx------  11 iman     iman         4096 Dec  7 03:05 navajo
drwx------  11 iman     iman         4096 Dec  7 03:05 pueblo
```

If things were left like this, the clients would not share their roaming profiles, so next we change from using separate directories to having symbolic links point to common directories:

```
# mv mixtec Win98
# mv navajo WinMe
# rm huastec pueblo
# ln -s Win98 pueblo
# ln -s WinMe huastec
# chown iman:iman *
# ls -l /home/iman/.win_profile
total 6
lrwxrwxrwx   1 iman     iman            5 Nov 16 01:40 huastec -> WinMe
lrwxrwxrwx   1 iman     iman            5 Nov 16 01:40 mixtec -> Win98
lrwxrwxrwx   1 iman     iman            5 Nov 21 17:24 navajo -> WinMe
lrwxrwxrwx   1 iman     iman            5 Nov 23 01:16 pueblo -> Win98
drwx------   9 iman     iman         4096 Dec  7 03:47 Win98
drwx------  11 iman     iman         4096 Dec  7 03:05 WinMe
```

Now when `iman` logs on to the domain from either Windows 98 system, the client from which she is logging on will get the profile stored in the *Win98* directory (that started out as her local profile on `mixtec`). This works likewise for the Windows Me clients.

To show a more complete example, here is a listing of a fully operational Windows 95/98/Me profiles directory:

```
$ ls -l /home/jay/.win_profile
total 12
lrwxrwxrwx   1 jay      jay             9 Nov 16 22:14 aztec -> /home/jay
lrwxrwxrwx   1 jay      jay             5 Nov 16 01:40 hopi -> Win95
lrwxrwxrwx   1 jay      jay             5 Nov 16 01:40 huastec -> WinMe
```

```
lrwxrwxrwx   1 jay      jay             5 Nov 16 01:38 maya -> Win98
lrwxrwxrwx   1 jay      jay             5 Nov 16 01:40 mixtec -> Win98
lrwxrwxrwx   1 jay      jay             5 Nov 21 17:24 navajo -> WinMe
lrwxrwxrwx   1 jay      jay             5 Nov 23 01:16 pueblo -> Win98
lrwxrwxrwx   1 jay      jay             5 Nov 22 02:06 ute -> Win95
drwx------   6 jay      jay          4096 Dec  8 18:09 Win95
drwx------   9 jay      jay          4096 Dec  7 03:47 Win98
drwx------  11 jay      jay          4096 Dec  7 03:05 WinMe
lrwxrwxrwx   1 jay      jay             5 Nov 21 22:48 yaqui -> Win98
lrwxrwxrwx   1 jay      jay             9 Nov 16 22:14 zuni -> /home/jay
```

Again, the computer name of each client exists in this directory as a symbolic link that points to the directory containing the actual roaming profile. For example, maya, a client that runs Windows 98, has a symbolic link named *maya* to the *Win98* directory. A listing of *Win98* shows:

```
$ ls -l Win98
total 148
drwxr-xr-x   3 jay      jay          4096 Nov 23 01:30 Application Data
drwxr-xr-x   2 jay      jay          4096 Nov 23 01:30 Cookies
drwxr-xr-x   3 jay      jay          4096 Dec  7 03:47 Desktop
drwxr-xr-x   3 jay      jay          4096 Nov 23 01:30 History
drwxr-xr-x   2 jay      jay          4096 Nov 23 01:30 NetHood
drwxr-xr-x   2 jay      jay          4096 Dec  7 03:47 Recent
drwxr-xr-x   3 jay      jay          4096 Nov 23 01:30 Start Menu
-rw-r--r--   1 jay      jay        114720 Dec  7 03:46 USER.DAT
```

The contents of the *Win95* and *WinMe* directories appear similar and contain roaming profiles that work exactly as they should on their respective operating systems.

Notice in the previous listing that *aztec* and *zuni* are symbolic links to */home/jay*. We've cautioned you never to configure a roaming profile directory to be a user's home directory, but this is to handle something different. The clients aztec and zuni are Windows XP systems, which handle logon home differently than other versions of Windows. We have set logon home = \\%L\%u\.win profile, and all versions of Windows except for Windows XP strip off everything after \\%L\%u and correctly locate the home directory—in this case, */home/jay*. Windows XP uses the full UNC, so we simply add a symbolic link to redirect it to the correct directory to get the *net use H: /home* command to work as it should. The roaming profiles for Windows XP systems are not affected by this and are kept with the other roaming profiles in the Windows NT/2000/XP family, as shown in this listing:

```
$ ls -l /home/samba-ntprof/jay
total 16
lrwxrwxrwx   1 jay      jay             5 Nov 20 03:45 apache -> Win2K
lrwxrwxrwx   1 jay      jay             5 Nov 13 12:35 aztec -> WinXP
lrwxrwxrwx   1 jay      jay             5 Nov 13 12:34 dine -> WinNT
lrwxrwxrwx   1 jay      jay             5 Nov 24 03:44 inca -> Win2K
lrwxrwxrwx   1 jay      jay             5 Nov 13 12:34 pima -> Win2K
drwx------  13 jay      jay          4096 Dec  3 15:24 qero
drwx------  13 jay      jay          4096 Dec  1 20:31 Win2K
drwx------  12 jay      jay          4096 Nov 30 17:04 WinNT
```

```
drwx------   13 jay     jay         4096 Nov 20 01:23 WinXP
lrwxrwxrwx    1 jay     jay            5 Nov 20 06:09 yavapai -> WinXP
lrwxrwxrwx    1 jay     jay            5 Nov 13 12:34 zapotec -> Win2K
lrwxrwxrwx    1 jay     jay            5 Nov 13 12:35 zuni -> WinXP
```

As you can see, we are using a similar method for the Windows NT/2000/XP roaming profiles. In the listing, *qero* is not a symbolic link, but rather a directory that holds the roaming profile for qero, a Windows 2000 client that has recently been added. We had not created a symbolic link called *qero* before installing Windows 2000, so when jay logged off for the first time, Samba created a directory named *qero* and copied the roaming profile received from the client to the new directory. Because this is a separate directory from *Win2K*, which all other Windows 2000 clients are using to share their roaming profiles, the roaming profile for qero works like a local profile, except that it is stored on the primary domain controller.

This might seem like an odd thing to do, but it has some purpose. Sometimes you might wish to isolate a client in this manner, especially while the operating system is being installed and initially configured. Remember, if that client, with its default local profile, is logged off the domain, the local profile will be written to the roaming profile directory. If the client were using the shared roaming profile directory, the effect could be undesirable, to say the least. Using our method, the *qero* directory can later be renamed to make it into an archival backup, or it can just be deleted. Then a new symlink named *qero* can be created to point to the *Win2K* directory, and qero will share the roaming profile in *Win2K* with the other Windows 2000 clients.

An alternative method is simply to create the symbolic links before the clients are added to the network. After you become more comfortable with the way roaming profiles work, you might find this method to be simpler and quicker.

Again, we urge you to be careful about letting different versions of Windows share the same roaming profile. The method of configuring roaming profiles we've shown you here allows you to test a configuration for a few clients at a time without affecting your whole network of clients. For example, we could install a small number of Windows 2000 and Windows XP systems in the domain for testing purposes and then create symlinks for them that point to a directory called *Win2KXP* to find out if sharing roaming profiles between our Windows 2000 and Windows XP systems meets our expectations. The *Win2KXP* directory could be created as an empty directory, in which case it would have a roaming profile written to it by the first of the clients to log off. Or, *Win2KXP* could simply be a renamed roaming profile directory that was created by one of the clients when it was added to the domain.

Configuring Windows 95/98/Me for Roaming Profiles

For roaming profiles to work on Windows 95/98/Me clients, all you need to do is change one setting to allow each user to have a separate local profile. This has the side effect of enabling roaming profiles as well.

Open the Control Panel and double-click the Passwords icon to open the Passwords Properties dialog box. Click the User Profiles tab, and the dialog box will appear as shown in Figure 4-12.

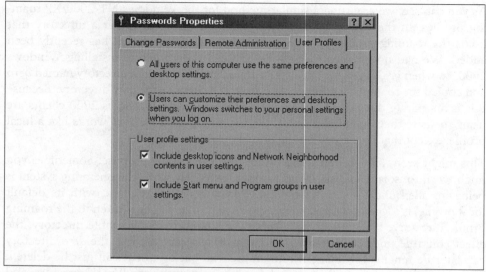

Figure 4-12. The Windows 98 Passwords Properties dialog

Click the button labeled "Users can customize their preferences and desktop settings." In the User profile settings box, you can check the options you prefer. When done, click the OK button and reboot as requested. During this first reboot, Windows will copy the local profile data to *C:\windows\profiles* but will not attempt to copy the roaming profile from the server. The next time the system is shut down, the local profile will be copied to the server, and when Windows reboots, it will copy the roaming profile from the server.

Configuring Windows NT/2000/XP for Roaming Profiles

Roaming profiles are enabled by default on Windows NT/2000/XP. In case you would like to check or modify your settings, follow these directions.

Make sure you are logged in to the local system as Administrator or another user in the Administrators group. Open the Control Panel and double-click the System icon. On Windows NT/2000, click the User Profiles tab, or on Windows XP, click the Advanced tab and then the Settings button in the User Profiles box. You should see the dialog box in Figure 4-13.

Notice in the figure that there are two entries for the username jay. The entry ZAPO-TEC\jay refers to the account on the local system, and METRAN\jay refers to the domain account. Recall that when a user logs on, a drop-down menu in the dialog

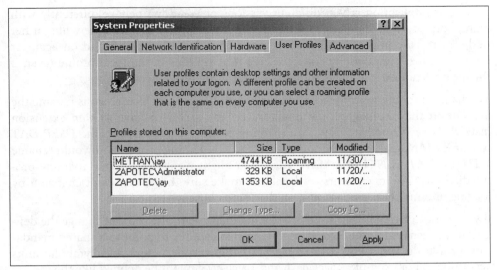

Figure 4-13. The Windows 2000 System Properties, User Profiles tab

box allows him to log on to a domain or log in to the local system. When jay logs in to the local machine, only the local profile is used. When logged on to the domain, the configuration shown will use the roaming profile. To switch a user's profile type for a domain logon account, click the account name to select it, then click the Change Type... button near the bottom of the dialog box. The Change Profile Type dialog box will appear. Click the radio button for either roaming or local profile, and then click the OK buttons for each dialog box.

Mandatory Profiles

With a simple modification, a roaming profile can be made into a mandatory profile, which has the quality of being unmodifiable by its owner. Mandatory profiles are used in some computing environments to simplify administration. The theory is that if users cannot modify their profiles, less can go wrong, and it is also possible to use the same standardized profile for all users.

In practice, some issues come up. Because the users can still modify the configuration settings in their local profile during their logon session, confusion can result the next time they log on to the domain and discover their changes have been "lost." If the user of a client reinstalls an application in a different place, the shortcuts to the program on the desktop, in the Start menu, or in a Quick Launch bar cannot be permanently deleted. They will reappear every time the user logs back on to the domain. Essentially, a mandatory profile is a roaming profile that always fails to update to the server upon logging off!

Another complication is that different versions of Windows behave differently with mandatory profiles. If a user who has a mandatory profile creates a new file on her desktop, the file might be missing the next time the user logs off and on again or reboots. Some Windows versions preserve desktop files in the local profile (even if the file does not exist in the mandatory profile), whereas others do not.

To change a roaming profile to a mandatory profile, all you have to do is rename the *.dat* file in the roaming profile directory on the server to have a *.man* extension instead. For a Windows 95/98/Me roaming profile, you would rename *USER.DAT* to *USER.MAN*, and for a Windows NT/2000/XP roaming profile, you would rename *NTUSER.DAT* to *NTUSER.MAN*. Also, you might want to make the roaming-profile directory and its contents read-only, to make sure that a user can't change it by logging into his Unix user account on the Samba host system.

If you want to have all your users share a mandatory profile, you can change the definitions of logon path and logon home in your *smb.conf* file to point to a shared mandatory profile on the server and adjust your directory structure and symbolic links accordingly. For example, logon path and logon home might be defined like this:

```
logon path = \\%L\profiles\%m
logon home = \\%L\%u\.win_profile\%m
```

Notice that we've removed the %u part of the path for logon path, and we would also change the directory structure on the server to do away with the separation of the profiles by username and have just one profile for each Windows NT/2000/XP version.

We cannot use the same treatment for logon home because it is also used to specify the home directory. In this case, we would change the symbolic links in each user's *.win_profile* directory to point to a common mandatory profile directory containing the mandatory profiles for each of Windows 95/98/Me. Again, check the ownership and permissions on the files in the directory, and modify them if necessary to make sure a user can't modify any files by logging into her Unix account on the Samba host system.

Logon Script and Roaming-Profile Options

Table 4-1 summarizes the options commonly used in association with Windows NT domain logon scripts and roaming profiles.

Table 4-1. Logon-script options

Option	Parameters	Function	Default	Scope
logon script	string (MS-DOS path)	Name of logon script batch file	None	Global
logon path	string (UNC server and share name)	Location of roaming profile	\\%N\%U\ profile	Global

Table 4-1. Logon-script options (continued)

Option	Parameters	Function	Default	Scope
logon drive	string (drive letter)	Specifies the logon drive for a home directory	Z:	Global
logon home	string (UNC server and share name)	Specifies a location for home directories for clients logging on to the domain	\\%N\%U	Global

logon script

This option specifies a Windows batch file that will be executed on the client after a user has logged on to the domain. Each logon script should be stored in the root directory of the [netlogon] share or a subdirectory. This option frequently uses the %U or %m variables (user or NetBIOS name) to point to an individual script. For example:

```
[global]
    logon script = %U.bat
```

will execute a script based on the username. If the user who is connecting is fred and the path of the [netlogon] share maps to the directory */export/samba/netlogon*, the script should be */export/samba/netlogon/fred.bat*. Because these scripts are downloaded to the client and executed on the Windows side, they must have MS-DOS-style newline characters rather than Unix newlines.

logon path

This option specifies the location where roaming profiles are kept. When the user logs on, a roaming profile will be downloaded from the server to the client and used as the local profile during the logon session. When the user logs off, the contents of the local profile will be uploaded back to the server until the next time the user connects.

It is often more secure to create a separate share exclusively for storing user profiles:

```
[global]
    logon path = \\hydra\profile\%U
```

For more information on this option, see the section "Roaming Profiles" earlier in this chapter.

logon drive

This option specifies the drive letter on a Windows NT/2000/XP client to which the home directory specified with the logon home option will be mapped. Note that this option will work with Windows NT/2000/XP clients only. For example:

```
[global]
    logon drive = I:
```

You should always use drive letters that will not conflict with fixed drives on the client machine. The default is Z:, which is a good choice because it is as far away from A:, C:, and D: as possible.

logon home

This option specifies the location of a user's home directory for use by the MS-DOS *net* commands. For example, to specify a home directory as a share on a Samba server, use the following:

```
[global]
    logon home = \\hydra\%U
```

Note that this works nicely with the [homes] service, although you can specify any directory you wish. Home directories can be mapped with a logon script using the following command:

```
C:\>net use i: /home
```

System Policies

A system policy can be used in a Windows NT domain as a remote administration tool for implementing a similar computing environment on all clients and limiting the abilities of users to change configuration settings on their systems or allowing them to run only a limited set of programs. One application of system policies is to use them along with mandatory profiles to implement a collection of computers for public use, such as in a library, school, or Internet cafe.

A system policy is a collection of registry settings that is stored in a file on the PDC and is automatically downloaded to the clients when users log on to the domain. The file containing the settings is created on a Windows system using the System Policy Editor. Because the format of the registry is different between Windows 95/98/Me and Windows NT/2000/XP, it is necessary to make sure that the file that is created is in the proper format. This is a very simple matter because when the System Policy Editor runs on Windows 95/98/Me, it will create a file in the format for Windows 95/98/Me, and if it is run on Windows NT/2000/XP, it will use the format needed by those versions. After the policy file is created with the System Policy Editor, it is stored on the primary domain controller and is automatically downloaded by the clients during the logon process, and the policies are applied to the client system.

On Windows NT 4.0 Server, you can run the System Policy Editor by logging in to the system as Administrator or another user in the Administrators group, opening the Start menu, and selecting Programs, then Administrative Tools, then System Policy Editor. On Windows 2000 Advanced Server, open the Start menu and click Run.... In the dialog box that comes up, type in C:\winnt\poledit.exe, and click the OK button.

If you are using a Windows version other than NT Server or Windows 2000 Advanced Server, you must install the System Policy Editor, and getting a copy of it can be a little tricky. If you are running Windows NT 4.0 Workstation or Windows 2000 Professional and have a Windows NT 4.0 Server installation CD-ROM, you can run the file \Clients\Svrtools\Winnt\Setup.bat from that CD to install the Client-based Network Administration Tools, which includes poledit.exe. Then open the Start menu, click Run..., type C:\winnt\system32\poledit.exe into the text area, and click the OK button.

If you are using Windows 95/98, insert a Windows 95 or Windows 98 distribution CD-ROM[*] into your CD-ROM drive, then open the Control Panel and double-click the Add/Remove Programs button. Click the Windows Setup tab, and then click the Have Disk... button. In the new dialog box that appears, click the Browse... button, then select the CD-ROM drive from the Drives drop-down menu. Then:

- If you are using a Windows 95 installation CD-ROM, double-click the admin, then apptools, then poledit folder icons.

- If you are using a Windows 98 installation CD-ROM, double-click the tools, then reskit, then netadmin, then poledit folder icons.

You should see "grouppol.inf" appear in the File name: text area on the left of the dialog box. Click the OK buttons in two dialog boxes, and you will be presented with a dialog box in which you should select both the Group Policies and System Policy Editor checkboxes. Then click the Install button. Close the remaining dialog box, and you can now run the System Policy Editor by opening the Start menu and selecting Programs, then Accessories, then System Tools, then System Policy Editor. Or click the Run... item in the Start Menu, and enter C:\Windows\Poledit.

When the System Policy Editor starts up, select New Policy from the File menu, and you will see a window similar to that in Figure 4-14.

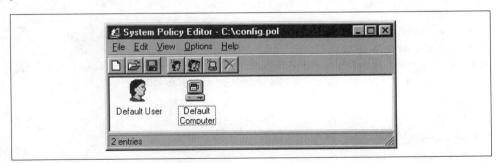

Figure 4-14. The System Policy Editor window

---

[*] The version of the System Policy Editor distributed with Windows 98 is an update of the version shipped with Windows 95. Use the version from the Windows 98 distribution if you can.

The next step is to make a selection from the File menu to add policies for users, groups, and computers. For each item you add, you will be asked for the username, or name of the group or computer, and a new icon will appear in the window. Double-clicking one of the icons will bring up the Properties dialog box, such as the one shown in Figure 4-15.

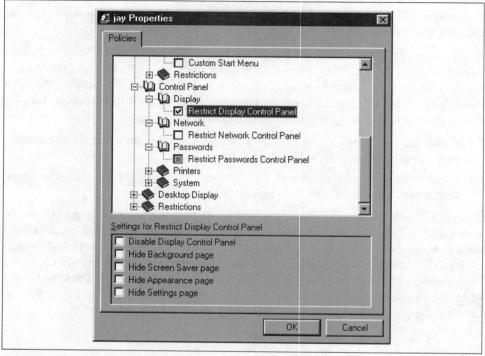

Figure 4-15. The Properties dialog of System Policy Editor

The upper window in the dialog shows the registry settings that can be modified as part of the system policy, and the lower window shows descriptive information or more settings pertaining to the one selected in the upper window. Notice in the figure that there are three checkboxes and that they are all in different states:

Checked
    Meaning that the registry setting is enabled in the policy
White (unchecked)
    Which clears the registry setting
Gray
    Which causes the registry setting on the client to be unmodified

Basically, if all the items are left gray (the default), the system policy will have no effect. The registry of the logged-on client will not be modified. However, if any of the items are either checked or unchecked (white), the registry on the client will be modified to enable the setting or clear it.

 In this section, we are giving you enough information on using the System Policy Editor to get you started—or, should we say, enough rope with which to hang yourself. Remember that a system policy, once put into action, will be modifying the registries of all clients who log on to the domain. The usual warnings about editing a Windows registry apply here with even greater importance. Consider how difficult (or even impossible) it will be for you to restore the registries on all those clients if anything happens to go wrong. *As with roaming profiles, casual or careless implementation of system policies can easily lead to domain-wide disaster.*

Creating a good system policy file is a complex topic, which we cannot cover in detail here. It would take a whole book, and yes, there happens to be an O'Reilly book on the subject, *Windows System Policy Editor*. Another definitive source of documentation on Windows NT system policies and the System Policy Editor is the Microsoft white paper *Implementing Policies and Profiles for Windows NT 4.0*, which can be found at *http://www.microsoft.com/ntserver/techresources/management/prof_policies.asp*.

Once you have created a policy, click the OK button and use the Save As... item from the File menu to save it. Use the filename *config.pol* for a Windows 95/98 system policy and *ntconfig.pol* for a policy that will be used on Windows NT/2000/XP clients. Finally, copy the *.pol* file to the directory used for the [netlogon] share on the Samba PDC. The *config.pol* and *ntconfig.pol* files must go in this directory—unlike roaming profiles and logon scripts, there is no way to specify the location of the system policy files in *smb.conf*. If you want to have different system policies for different users or computers, you must perform that part of the configuration within the System Policy Editor.

 If you have, or will have, any Windows Me clients on your network, be careful. Microsoft has stated that Windows Me does not support system policies. The odd thing about this is that it will download the policy from a *config.pol* file on the PDC, but there is no guarantee that the results will be what was intended. Check the effect of your system policy carefully on your Windows Me clients to make sure it is working how you want.

When a user logs on to the domain, her Windows client will download the *.pol* file from the server, and the settings in it (that is, the items either checked or cleared in the System Policy Editor) will override the client's settings.

If things "should work" but don't, try shutting down the Windows client and restarting, rather than just logging off and on again. Windows sometimes will hold the [netlogon] share open across logon sessions, and this can prevent the client from getting the updated *.pol* file from the server.

Samba as a Domain Member Server

Up to now, we've focused on configuring and using Samba as the primary domain controller. If you already have a domain controller on your network, either a Windows NT/2000 Server system or a Samba PDC, you can add a Samba server to the domain as a domain member server. This involves setting up the Samba server to have a computer account with the primary domain controller, in a similar way that Windows NT/2000/XP clients can have computer accounts on a Samba PDC. When a client accesses shares on the Samba domain member server, Samba will pass off the authentication to the domain controller rather than performing the task on the local system. If the PDC is a Windows server, any number of Windows BDCs might exist that can handle the authentication instead of the PDC.

The first step is to add the Samba server to the domain by creating a computer account for it on the primary domain controller. You can do this using the *smbpasswd* command, as follows:

```
# smbpasswd -j DOMAIN -r PDCNAME -Uadmin_acct%password
```

In this command, DOMAIN is replaced by the name of the domain the Samba host is joining, PDCNAME is replaced by the computer name of the primary domain controller, *admin_acct* is replaced by the username of an administrative account on the domain controller (either Administrator—or another user in the Administrators group—on Windows NT/2000, and root on Samba), and *password* is replaced with the password of that user. To give a more concrete example, on our domain that has a Windows NT 4 Server primary domain controller or a Windows 2000 Active Directory domain controller named SINAGUA, the command would be:

```
# smbpasswd -j METRAN -r SINAGUA -UAdministrator%hup8ter
```

and if the PDC is a Samba system, we would use the command:

```
# smbpasswd -j METRAN -r toltec -Uroot%jwun83jb
```

where jwun83jb is the password for the root user that is contained in the *smbpasswd* file, as we explained earlier in this chapter.

If you did it right, *smbpasswd* will respond with a message saying the domain has been joined. The security identifier[*] returned to Samba from the PDC is kept in the file */usr/local/samba/private/secrets.tdb*. The information in *secrets.tdb* is security-sen-

---

[*] This security identifier (SID) is part of an access token that allows the PDC to identify and authenticate the client.

sitive, so make sure to protect *secrets.tdb* in the same way you would treat Samba's password file.

The next step is to modify the *smb.conf* file. Assuming you are starting with a valid *smb.conf* file that correctly configures Samba to function in a workgroup, such as the one we used in Chapter 2, it is simply a matter of adding the following three lines to the [global] section:

```
workgroup = METRAN
security = domain
password server = *
```

The first line establishes the name of the domain (even though it says "workgroup"). Instead of METRAN, use the name of the domain you are joining. Setting security to "domain" causes Samba to hand off authentication to a domain controller, and the password server = * line tells Samba to find the domain controller for authentication (which could be the primary domain controller or a backup domain controller) by querying the WINS server or using broadcast packets if a WINS server is not available.

At this point, it would be prudent to run *testparm* to check that your *smb.conf* is free of errors. Then restart the Samba daemons.

If the PDC is a Windows NT system, you can use Server Manager to check that the Samba server has been added successfully. Open the Start menu, then select Programs, then Administrative Tools (Common), and then Server Manager. Server Manager starts up with a window that looks like Figure 4-16.

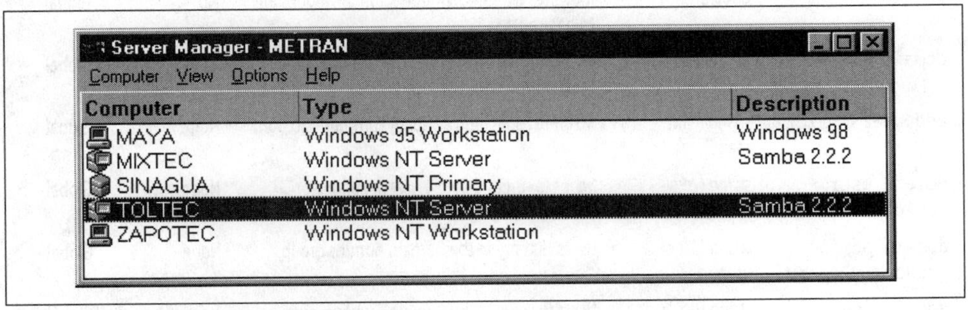

Figure 4-16. The Windows NT Server Manager window

As you can see, we've added both toltec and mixtec to a domain for which the Windows NT 4.0 Server system, sinagua, is the primary domain controller.

You can check your setup on Windows 2000 Advanced Server by opening the Start menu and selecting Programs, then Administrative Tools, then Active Directory Users and Computers. The window that opens up will look like Figure 4-17.

Click Computers in the left side of the window with the Tree tab. You should see your Samba system listed in the right pane of the window.

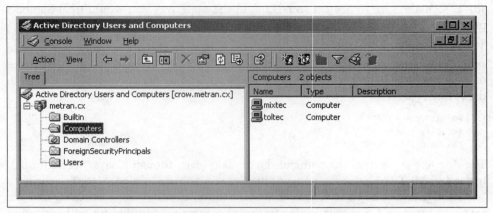

Figure 4-17. The Windows 2000 Active Directory Users and Computers window

Windows NT Domain Options

Table 4-2 shows the options that are commonly used in association with Samba on a Windows NT domain.

Table 4-2. Windows NT domain options

Option	Parameters	Function	Default	Scope
domain logons	boolean	Indicates whether Windows domain logons are to be used	No	Global
domain master	boolean	For telling Samba to take the role of domain master browser	Auto	Global
add user script	string (command)	Script to run to add a user or computer account	None	Global
delete user script	string (command)	Script to run to delete a user or computer account	None	Global
domain admin group	string (list of users)	Users that are in the Domain Admins group	None	Global
domain guest group	string (list of users)	Users that are in the Domain Guests group	None	Global
password server	string (list of computers)	List of domain controllers used for authentication when Samba is running as a domain member server	None	Global
machine password timeout	numeric (seconds)	Sets the renewal interval for NT domain machine passwords	604,800 (1 week)	Global

Here are detailed explanations of each Windows NT domain option listed in Table 4-2.

domain logons

This option configures Samba to accept domain logons as a primary domain controller. When a client successfully logs on to the domain, Samba will return a special token to the client that allows the client to access domain shares without consulting the PDC again for authentication. Note that the Samba machine must employ user-level security (security = user) and must be the PDC for this option to function. In addition, Windows machines will expect a [netlogon] share to exist on the Samba server.

domain master

In a Windows network, a local master browser handles browsing within a subnet. A Windows domain can be made up of a number of subnets, each of which has its own local master browser. The primary domain controller serves the function of domain master browser, collecting the browse lists from the local master browser of each subnet. Each local master browser queries the domain master browser and adds the information about other subnets to their own browse lists. When Samba is configured as a primary domain controller, it automatically sets domain master = yes, making itself the domain master browser.

Because Windows NT PDCs always claim the role of domain master browser, Samba should never be allowed to be domain master if there is a Windows PDC in the domain.

add user script

There are two ways in which add user script can be used. When the Samba server is set up as a primary domain controller, it can be assigned to a command that will run on the Samba server to add a Windows NT/2000/XP computer account to Samba's password database. When the user on the Windows system changes the computer's settings to join a domain, he is asked for the username and password of a user who has administrative rights on the domain controller. Samba authenticates this user and then runs the add user script with root permissions.

When Samba is configured as a domain member server, the add user script can be assigned to a command to add a user to the system. This allows Windows clients to add users that can access shares on the Samba system without requiring an administrator to create the account manually on the Samba host.

delete user script

There are times when users are automatically deleted from the domain, and the delete user script can be assigned to a command that removes a user from the Samba host as a Windows server would do. However, you might not want this to happen, because the Unix user might need the account for reasons other than use with Samba. Therefore, we recommend that you be very careful about using this option.

domain admin group

In a domain of Windows systems, it is possible for a server to get a list of the members of the Domain Admins group from a domain controller. Samba 2.2 does not have the ability to handle this, and the domain admin group parameter exists as a manual means of informing Samba who is in the group. The list should contain root (necessary for adding computer accounts) and any users on Windows NT/2000/XP clients in the domain who are in the Domain Admins group. These users must be recognized by the primary controller in order for them to perform some administrative duties such as adding users to the domain.

password server

In a Windows domain in which the domain controllers are a Windows primary domain controller, along with any number of Windows backup domain controllers, clients and domain member servers authenticate users by querying either the PDC or any of the BDCs. When Samba is configured as a domain member server, the password server parameter allows some control over how Samba finds a domain controller. Earlier versions of Samba could not use the same method that Windows systems use, and it was necessary to specify a list of systems to try. When you set password server = *, Samba 2.2 is able to find the domain controller in the same manner that Windows does, which helps to spread the requests over several backup domain controllers, minimizing the possibility of them becoming overloaded with authentication requests. We recommend that you use this method.

machine password timeout

The machine password timeout global option sets a retention period for Windows NT domain machine passwords. The default is currently set to the same time period that Windows NT 4.0 uses: 604,800 seconds (one week). Samba will periodically attempt to change the *machine account password*, which is a password used specifically by another server to report changes to it. This option specifies the number of seconds that Samba should wait before attempting to change that password. The timeout period can be changed to a single day by specifying the following:

```
[global]
    machine password timeout = 86400
```

 If you would like more information on how Windows NT uses domain usernames and groups, we recommend Eric Pearce's *Windows NT in a Nutshell*, published by O'Reilly.

## CHAPTER 5

Unix Clients

In Chapter 3 we showed you how to configure Windows systems to access shared resources on both Windows and Samba servers. This has probably opened up a whole new world of computing for you—one in which you have to run to a Windows system every time you want to copy a file between Unix and Windows! In this chapter, we will show you the "other side"—how to access SMB shares from your favorite Unix system.

You can access SMB resources from Unix in three ways, depending on your version of Unix. A program included with the Samba distribution called *smbclient* can be used to connect with a share on the network in a manner similar to using *ftp* when transferring files to or from an FTP site.

If your system is running Linux, you can use the smbfs filesystem to mount SMB shares right onto your Linux filesystem, just as you would mount a disk partition or NFS filesystem. The SMB shares can then be accessed and manipulated by all programs running on the Linux system: command shells, desktop GUI interfaces, and application software.

On some BSD-based systems, including Mac OS X, a pair of utilities named *smbutil* and *mount_smbfs* can be used to query SMB servers and mount shares.

For other Unix variants, *smbsh* can be run to enable common shell commands such as *cd*, *ls*, *mv*, *wc*, and *grep* to access and manipulate files and directories on SMB shares. This effectively extends the reach of the Unix shell and utilities beyond the Unix filesystem and into the SMB network.

All the Unix clients can access shares offered by either Windows systems or Samba servers. We have already shown you how to set up a share on a Samba server and could use that as an example to work with. But it's much more fun to use the Unix clients with shares served by Windows systems. So before we start covering the Unix clients in detail, we will take a quick detour and show you how to set up file shares on both Windows 95/98/Me and Windows NT/2000/XP systems.

Sharing Files on Windows 95/98/Me

When sharing files on Windows 95/98/Me, you can authenticate users in two different ways. Share-level security is the default and is easy to use. However, it is not as secure and can require users to type in passwords when connecting to shares. User-level security offers a better security model and can be used if you have either a Samba or Windows NT/2000 server on your network performing user authentication.

To configure the type of access control for your system, open the Control Panel, double-click the Network icon, then click the Access Control tab. You should see the dialog box shown in Figure 5-1.

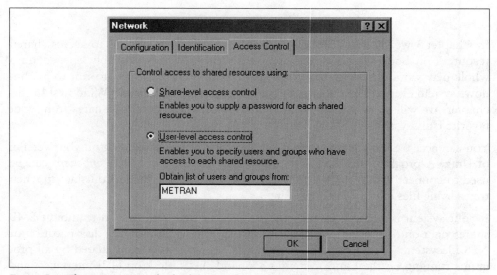

Figure 5-1. The Access Control tab of the Windows 98 Network Control Panel window

Click the "Share-level access control" or "User-level access control" radio button, depending on which you want to use. When using user-level access control, you will also need to fill in the name of your workgroup or Windows NT domain. Reboot as requested.

To share a folder, right-click the folder's icon and select Sharing.... This will open the Sharing tab of the folder's Properties dialog box. Click the "Shared As:" radio button, and fill in a name for the share (which defaults to the folder's name) and a description, which will be visible to client users. If you don't want the share to be visible in the Network Neighborhood view of other Windows clients, pick a name for the share that ends in a dollar sign ($).

Figure 5-2 shows what the Sharing tab of the folder's Properties dialog box will look like when using share-level security. The security settings are very simple. You can select a radio button for read-only access or full (read/write) access, or have the

---

user's permissions (either read-only or read/write) depend on which password they use. In accordance with which you select, you will be asked to assign either or both of the read-only and full-access passwords for the share.

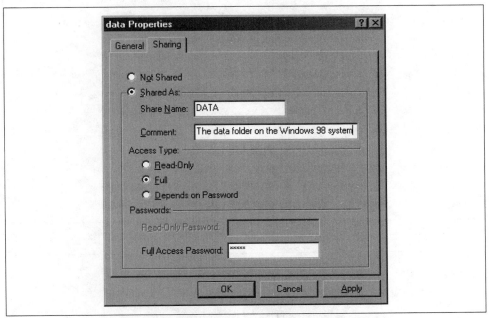

Figure 5-2. The Sharing tab of the folder's Properties dialog, with share-level security

If your system is configured with user-level security, the Sharing tab of the folder's Properties dialog box will look like Figure 5-3. As you can see, we've created a share named "DATA", and used the Add… button to create permissions that allow read-only access for all domain users and read/write (full access) for jay.

When you are done specifying your settings for the share, click on the OK button, and the share will become available to users on network clients. Unless you chose a share name ending in a dollar sign, you can see it in the Network Neighborhood or My Network Places of Windows clients on the network. You can also now use the Unix clients described in this chapter to connect to the share.

Sharing Files on Windows NT/2000/XP

To create a file share on Windows NT/2000/XP, you first must log in to the system as any member of the Administrators, Power Users, or Server Operators groups. Right-click the icon of a folder you wish to share, and click Sharing… in the pop-up menu. The Sharing tab of the folder's Properties dialog box will appear, as shown in Figure 5-4. Click the "Share this folder" radio button.

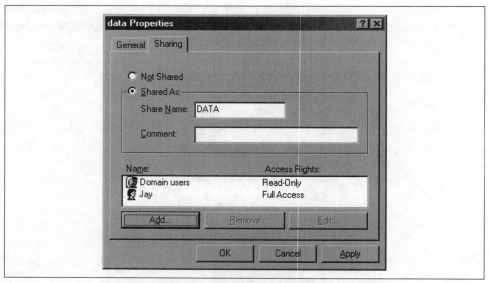

Figure 5-3. The Sharing tab of the folder Properties dialog, with user-level security

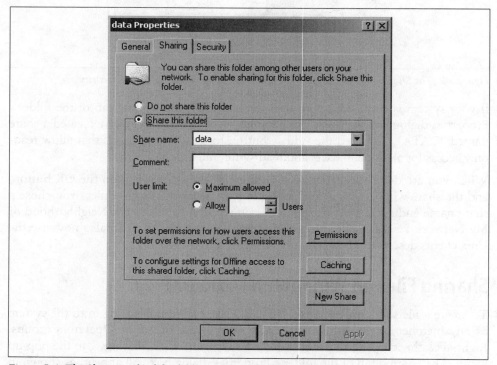

Figure 5-4. The Sharing tab of the folder's Properties dialog on Windows 2000

Share name: will default to the name of the folder, and you can change it if you want. One reason you might want to use a different name for the share is to make the share not appear in browse lists (as displayed by the Network Neighborhood, for example). This can be done by using a share name ending in a dollar sign ($). You can also add a description of the share in the Comment: text area. The description will appear to users of network clients and can help them understand the contents of the share.

By clicking the Permissions button, you can set permissions for the share on a user-by-user basis. This is equivalent to the user-level security of Windows 95/98/Me file sharing. On Windows NT/2000/XP, Microsoft recommends that share permissions be set to allow full access by everyone, with the permissions controlled on a file-by-file basis using filesystem access control lists (ACLs). The actual permissions given to network clients are a combination of the share permissions and file access permissions. To edit the ACL for the folder, click the Security tab. For more information on ACLs, see the section "Windows NT/2000/XP ACLs" in Chapter 8.

If you want, you can limit the number of users who can concurrently connect to the share using the "User limit:" radio button. The New Share button allows you to create multiple file shares for the same folder, each having its own name, comment, user limit, and other parameters.

When you are done, click the OK button, and the folder will be accessible from clients on the network.

smbclient

The Samba Team supplies *smbclient* as a basic part of the Samba suite. At first, it might seem to be a primitive interface to the SMB network, but *smbclient* is actually a versatile tool. It can be used for browsing shares on servers, testing configurations, debugging, accessing shared printers, backing up shared data, and automating administrative tasks in shell scripts. And unlike smbfs and *smbsh*, *smbclient* works on all Unix variants that support Samba.

In this chapter we'll focus mostly on running *smbclient* as an interactive shell, using its *ftp*-like commands to access shared directories on the network. Using *smbclient* to access printers and perform backups will be covered in Chapter 10.

A complete reference to *smbclient* is found in Appendix C.

Listing Services

The -L option can be used with *smbclient* to list the resources on a single computer. Assuming the Samba server is configured to take the role of the master browser, we can obtain a list of the computers in the domain or workgroup like this:

```
$ smbclient -L toltec
added interface ip=172.16.1.1 bcast=172.16.1.255 nmask=255.255.255.0
```

```
Password:
Domain=[METRAN] OS=[Unix] Server=[Samba 2.2.5]

        Sharename      Type       Comment
        ---------      ----       -------
        test           Disk       For testing only, please
        IPC$           IPC        IPC Service (Samba 2.2.5)
        ADMIN$         Disk       IPC Service (Samba 2.2.5)

        Server                    Comment
        ---------                 -------
        MAYA                      Windows 98
        MIXTEC                    Samba 2.2.5
        TOLTEC                    Samba 2.2.5
        ZAPOTEC

        Workgroup                 Master
        ---------                 -------
        METRAN                    TOLTEC
```

In the column labeled "Server", maya, mixtec, and zapotec are shown along with toltec, the Samba server. The services on toltec are listed under "Sharename". The IPC$ and ADMIN$ shares are standard Windows services that are used for network communication and administrative purposes, and *test* is the directory we added as a share in Chapter 2.

Now that we know the names of computers in the domain, we can list services on any of those computers. For example, here is how we would list the services offered by maya, a Windows 98 workstation:

```
$ smbclient -L maya
added interface ip=172.16.1.1 bcast=172.16.1.255 nmask=255.255.255.0
Password:


        Sharename      Type       Comment
        ---------      ----       -------
        PRINTER$       Disk
        HP             Printer    HP 932C on Maya
        D              Disk       D: on Maya
        E              Disk       E: on Maya

        ADMIN$         Disk
        IPC$           IPC        Remote Inter Process Communication

        Server                    Comment
        ---------                 -------

        Workgroup                 Master
        ---------                 -------
```

A shared printer is attached to maya, so we see the PRINTER$ administrative service, along with the HP share for the printer itself. Also on maya are the D and E shares,

---

which allow access across the network to maya's D: and E: drives. It is normal for the Server and Workgroup sections to be empty when listing services on a Windows client.

Authenticating with smbclient

As with any other SMB client, *smbclient* needs to supply a username and password if it is authenticating in a domain environment or if it is contacting a Samba server that is set up with user-level security. In a workgroup environment, it will at least need a password to use when connecting with a password-protected resource.

By default, *smbclient* uses the username of the user who runs it and then prompts for a password. If you are using *smbclient* a lot, you might tire of entering your password every time.

smbclient supports some alternate methods of entering a username and password. The password can be entered on the command line, like this:

```
$ smbclient //maya/e jayspassword
```

Or both the username and password can be supplied by using the *-U* option, including the username and password separated by a percent (%) character:

```
$ smbclient //maya/e -U kelly%kellyspassword
```

This method is useful if you are logged in to the system under an account that is not Samba-enabled or you are testing your configuration to see how it treats another user. With either method, you can avoid having to enter the username and/or password each time you run *smbclient* by creating an alias for the command or creating a shell function or shell script. For example, with the *bash* shell, it is possible to define a function like this:

```
smbcl( )
{
    smbclient $* -U jay%jayspassword
}
```

Adding the definition to the shell's startup script (which would be *~/.bash_profile* for *bash*) would result in the definition affecting all subsequent shell invocations.

Another method that can be used to supply both the username and password is to set the USER and PASSWD environment variables. Either set the USER environment variable using the *username%password* format, or set the USER environment variable to the username, and set PASSWD to the user's password.

It is also possible to create a credentials file containing the username on the first line and the password on the second line, like this:

```
username = jay
password = jayspassword
```

Then, *smbclient* is run using the *-A* option to specify the name of the file:

```
$ smbclient //maya/e -A ~/.smbpw
```

Of the methods we described in this section, the only one that is really secure is the default method of allowing *smbclient* to prompt for the password and typing in the password without echoing.

If security is a concern, you definitely should avoid providing your password on the command line because it is very easy for "shoulder surfers" to obtain, as well as anyone who looks through your shell's command history.

If you keep your Samba password in a credentials file, shell startup file, or shell script, make sure the file's permissions prohibit other users from reading or writing it. (Use an octal permissions mode of 0600.) Security experts never keep passwords in files owned by non-root users or accessible by anyone other than the superuser. As part of their security policy, some organizations do not permit passwords to be stored in files, so you might want to check first before using this method.

The authentication method that uses the USER and PASSWD environment variables isn't any more secure. Environment variables are usually set either on the command line or in one or more of the shell's startup files, so this method suffers from the same weaknesses we've just discussed. In addition, any program run by the user has access to the shell's environment variables, making a Trojan horse attack on the PASSWD variable really easy!

An Interactive smbclient Session

A common use for *smbclient* is to use it as an *ftp*-like shell to access SMB resources on the network. To begin a session, *smbclient* must be provided with the UNC of a resource (which you can find using the *-L* option) on the command line, like this:

```
$ smbclient //maya/e
added interface ip=172.16.1.3 bcast=172.16.1.255 nmask=255.255.255.0
Password:
smb: \>
```

Forward slashes are accepted by *smbclient* for the share's UNC, which makes entering the UNC on the command line easier. Backslashes can also be used, but they must be quoted or escaped, and it is somewhat more difficult to type '\\maya\e' or \\\\maya\\e. After connecting to the share, *smbclient* displays the smb: \> prompt, waiting for a command to be entered. Commands are similar to those with which you might be familiar in *ftp* and are also somewhat similar to Unix shell commands. To get a list of *smbclient* commands, use the *help* command:

```
smb: \> help
ls              dir             du              lcd             cd
pwd             get             mget            put             mput
rename          more            mask            del             open
rm              mkdir           md              rmdir           rd
prompt          recurse         translate       lowercase       print
printmode       queue           cancel          quit            q
```

```
exit          newer          archive          tar          blocksize
tarmode       setmode        help             ?            history
!
```

Some commands in the previous list are synonyms for other commands. For example, the *?* command is a synonym for *help*. You can give this command the name of another command as an argument to get a concise reminder of what the command does and how to use it:

```
smb: \> ? ls
HELP ls:
          <mask> list the contents of the current directory
```

The term <mask> refers to a file-matching pattern as commonly found in Unix shells and utilities. For example:

```
smb: \> ls *doc
  ms-ProfPol-wp.doc              A      131  Tue Dec 18 09:12:34 2002
  smbclient.doc                  A    33969  Mon Dec 10 20:22:24 2002
  smbmount.doc                   A     7759  Mon Dec 10 20:20:00 2002

            48590 blocks of size 524288. 40443 blocks available
```

lists all files ending in "doc" in the current directory on the remote system. In the listing, the leftmost column shows the filename. Moving left to right, we see the file's MS-DOS attributes, then its size, and the time it was last modified.

As with any other Unix utility, *smbclient* has a working directory on the local host. It also has another current directory on the remote SMB share. With *smbclient*, the *cd* command is used to move around on the remote system:

```
smb: \> cd trans
smb: \trans\>
```

Notice how the prompt changes to reflect the new current working directory. To change your current directory on the local system, use the *lcd* command:

```
smb: \trans\> lcd /u/snd
the local directory is now /u/snd
```

Most of *smbclient*'s commands are for performing operations on remote files and directories. There is no command for listing the contents of the local directory. However, *smbclient* allows a shell escape. Any command preceded by an exclamation point (!) is interpreted as a shell command and is run in a subshell on the local system. For example:

```
smb: \trans\> ! ls -l
total 16
drwxrwxr-x   2 jay      jay        4096 Jan 10 14:46 dr220-fet
drwxrwxr-x   2 jay      jay        4096 Sep 22 12:16 dr220-tube
-rw-rw-r--   1 jay      jay         131 Jan 10 02:22 readme.txt
drwxrwxr-x   7 jay      jay        4096 Jan 10 02:19 xll
```

lists the contents of *lu/snd*. By using *smbclient*'s commands to operate on the remote system—and shell-escaped commands to operate on the local system—it is possible to manipulate data on both systems without having to exit *smbclient* or open another shell window.

File transfer is performed using the *get* and *put* commands. The *get* command transfers a single file from the remote to the local system, and the *put* command copies a file from the local to the remote system. For example, the following command copies the file *readme.txt* to the SMB share:

```
smb: \trans\> put readme.txt
putting file readme.txt as \trans\readme.txt (127.9 kb/s) (average 10.7 kb/s)
```

 Unlike *ftp*, *smbclient* does not have *ascii* and *binary* commands to set the type of the file that is being transferred. Before transferring a text file from a Unix system to a Windows or Macintosh system, you might want to use the GNU *unix2dos* command to reformat newlines in the file to work with the carriage return linefeed (CRLF) standard:

```
$ unix2dos text_file >text_file.txt
```

and then transfer the CRLF-formatted version. After transferring a text file from a Windows or Macintosh system to Unix, you can use the GNU *dos2unix* command to perform the inverse operation:

```
$ dos2unix text_file.txt >text_file
```

To transfer more than one file with a single command, you can use the *mget* and *mput* commands, which accept a list of filenames in the command line. The list can be provided by typing in the filenames on the command line separated by spaces, or the group of files can be specified with a pattern as one would use in Unix shell commands. The command:

```
smb: \trans\> mget plain/*
```

copies all the files in the directory *plain* on the SMB share to the current directory on the local system. By default, *smbclient* prompts for each file, asking if you want to copy it:

```
smb: \trans\> mget plain/*
Get file tomm.wav? n
Get file toml.wav? n
Get file tomh.wav? n
Get file snare.wav? n
Get file rim.wav? n
Get file handclap.wav? n
Get file bassdrum.wav? n
```

If you are sure you want to copy all the files, you can turn off prompting with the *prompt* command, like this:

```
smb: \trans\> prompt
prompting is now off
```

By default, if you specify the name of a directory, *smbclient* will not copy the contents of the directory. To transfer the entire contents of directories listed in the *mput* or *mget* command, you must first use the *recurse* command:

```
smb: \trans\> recurse
directory recursion is now on
```

After setting things up with the *prompt* and *recurse* commands, we can copy a directory like this:

```
smb: \trans\> mget acc
getting file tomm.wav of size 55494 as tomm.wav (2580.6 kb/s) (average 2087.3 kb/s)
getting file toml.wav of size 57220 as toml.wav (2660.9 kb/s) (average 2167.6 kb/s)
getting file tomh.wav of size 55936 as tomh.wav (2601.2 kb/s) (average 2220.8 kb/s)
getting file snare.wav of size 22132 as snare.wav (1200.7 kb/s) (average 2123.7 kb/s)
getting file rim.wav of size 8314 as rim.wav (1623.8 kb/s) (average 2110.8 kb/s)
getting file handclap.wav of size 14180 as handclap.wav (1978.2 kb/s) (average 2106.2
kb/s)
getting file bassdrum.wav of size 6950 as bassdrum.wav (2262.3 kb/s) (average 2108.5
kb/s)
```

Directory recursion applies to all commands, so if an *ls* command is used while directory recursion is on, all files in the directory tree are listed. To turn directory recursion off again, simply re-enter the command. At the same time, you might also wish to toggle prompting back to its initial state:

```
smb: \trans\> recurse
directory recursion is now off
smb: \trans\> prompt
prompting is now on
```

There are other *smbclient* commands that you might find useful. The *mkdir* command can be used to create a directory; *rmdir* removes a directory; *rm* deletes a file; and *rename* changes a file's name. These behave very similarly to their Unix shell counterparts. Appendix C contains a complete reference to *smbclient* and its command set.

To exit *smbclient*, use the *exit* or *quit* command:

```
smb: \trans\> quit
```

Programming with smbclient

The *-c* option *of smbclient* allows a list of commands to be passed on the command line. To copy the file *maya\e\trans\readme.txt* to */u/snd/readme.txt*, we might use the command:

```
$ smbclient //maya/e -c "lcd /u/snd; cd trans; get readme.txt" -A ~/.smbpw
```

Everything that *smbclient* needs to know to perform the operation has been specified in the command. There is no interactive session, so a command such as this can be placed inside a shell script or a program in some other programming language.

By using *smbclient* in this manner, it is possible to create customized commands using shell functions, scripts or aliases. For example, suppose we wanted a command to print a short listing of files in a shared directory, showing just the names of the files. Using a *bash* function, we could define a command *smbls* as follows:

```
smbls( )
{
        share=`echo $1 | cut -d '/' -f '1-4'`
        dir=`echo $1 | cut -d '/' -f '5-'`
        smbclient $share -c "cd $dir; ls" -A ~/.smbpw | \
                        grep "^  " | cut -d ' ' -f 3 - | sort
}
```

After defining this function, we can use *smbls* like this:

```
$ smbls //maya/e
CD-images
lectures
ms-ProfPol-wp.doc
profile-map
readme.txt
RECYCLED
smbclient.doc
smbmount.doc
smbsh.txt
trans
$ smbls //maya/e/lectures
.
..
lecture1.mp3
lecture2.mp3
lecture3.mp3
lecture4.mp3
lecture5.mp3
lecture6.mp3
lecture7.mp3
lecture8.mp3
lecture9.mp3
```

Another use for *smbclient* in scripts is performing administrative tasks. Suppose a group of users on Windows clients are sharing a set of files as part of a project on which they are working. Instead of expecting them to coordinate making daily backups, we could write a script that copies the share to the Samba server and run the script nightly as a cron job. The directory on the Samba server could be shared as well, allowing any of the users to retrieve a backup file on their own, without having to bother an administrator.

Backups with smbclient

A major use of *smbclient* is to create and restore backups of SMB file shares. The backup files *smbclient* writes are in tar format, making them easy to work with and

---

portable among all Unix versions. Using *smbclient* on a Unix server to run network backups can result in a more centralized and easily managed solution for providing data integrity because both SMB shares and NFS filesystems can be backed up on the same system.

You can use *smbclient* to perform backups in two ways. When backing up an entire share, the simplest method is to use the *-Tc* option on the command line:

```
# smbclient //maya/e -A samba-domain-pw -Tc >maya-e.tar
```

This will create a tar archive of the *maya*\e share in the file *maya-e.tar*. By using the *-D* option, it is possible to back up a directory in the share, rather than the whole share:

```
# smbclient //maya/e -A samba-domain-pw -D trans -Tc >maya-e.tar
```

This causes *smbclient* to change its working directory to the *trans* directory of the *maya*\e share before starting the backup. It is also possible to use *smbclient*'s *tar* command in interactive mode, like this:

```
# smbclient //maya/e
added interface ip=172.16.1.3 bcast=172.16.1.255 nmask=255.255.255.0
Password:
smb: \> cd trans
smb: \trans\> tarmode full hidden system quiet
smb: \trans\> tar c maya-e-trans.tar
```

With the previous code, only the *trans* subdirectory in the *maya*\e share will be backed up, using the settings specified in the *tarmode* command. To have this type of backup run automatically from a script, use the *-c* option:

```
# smbclient //maya/e -A samba-domain-pw -c "cd trans; tarmode full hidden \
    system quiet; tar >maya-e-trans.tar"
```

Using either the *-T* command-line option or *smbclient*'s *tar* command, additional options can be supplied. It is necessary to specify either the *c* option to create a backup archive or the *x* option to extract (restore) one.[*] The other options can be appended to the option string and are explained in the section on *smbclient* in Appendix C. They allow you to create incremental backups, specify which files to include or exclude from the backup, and specify a few other miscellaneous settings. For example, suppose we wish to create an incremental backup of a share and reset the archive bit on the files to set things up for the next incremental backup. Instead of using the interactive commands:

```
smb: \> tarmode inc reset quiet
smb: \> tar c backup.tar
```

---

[*] An alternative to extracting the tar archive directly to the SMB share is to use the Unix system's *tar* command to extract it to a directory on the Unix server, then copy the desired file(s) to a shared directory. This allows a greater amount of control over the restoration process, as when correcting for an accidental file deletion or reverting a set of files to a previous condition.

we could either use the interactive command:

```
smb: \> tar cgaq backup.tar
```

or specify the *-Tcgaq* option on the *smbclient* command line.

Your best strategy for using *smbclient* for network backups depends on your local configuration. If you have only a few Windows systems sharing a small amount of data, you might create a script containing *smbclient -Tc* commands to back up each share to a separate tar file, placing the files in a directory that is included with regular backups of the Unix system. If you have huge SMB shares on your network, you might prefer to write the backup directly to a tape drive. You can do this with *smbclient* just as you would with a Unix *tar* command:

```
# smbclient //maya/d -A samba-domain-pw -Tc >/dev/tape
```

After you have become more familiar with *smbclient* and have an automated backup system in place, you might find that using Samba has dramatically decreased your anxiety regarding the integrity of your network's data. The authors of this book are experienced Unix system administrators, and we highly recommend having a backup strategy that has been carefully planned, implemented, and most importantly, *tested and known to work as it is supposed to*.

smbfs

On Linux, the smbfs filesystem can be used to mount SMB shares onto the Linux filesystem in a manner similar to mounting disk partitions on NFS filesystems. The result is so transparent that users on the Linux system might never be aware that they are accessing files through a Windows or Samba server. Files and directories appear as any other files or directories on the local Linux system, although there are a few differences in behavior relating to ownership and permissions.[*]

Although smbfs is based on the Samba code, it is not itself part of the Samba distribution. Instead, it is included with Linux as a standard part of the Linux filesystem support.

The *smbmount* and *smbmnt* programs are part of the Samba distribution and are needed on the client to mount smbfs filesystems. Samba must be compiled with the *--with-smbmount* configure option to make sure these programs are compiled. They refer to *smb.conf* for information they need regarding the local system and network configuration, so you will need a working *smb.conf* file on the system, even if it is not acting as a Samba server.

---

[*] Samba Versions 2.2.4 and later have support for Unix CIFS extensions developed by Hewlett-Packard, which add full support for Unix ownership, group, and permissions in smbfs filesystems when shared between two Samba systems. You will also need a recent version of smbfs in your Linux kernel.

Mounting an smbfs Filesystem

The *smbmount* command is used to mount an smbfs filesystem into the Linux filesystem. The basic usage is:

```
# smbmount Share-UNC mount-point -o options
```

Replace *Share-UNC* with the UNC for the SMB share, and *mount-point* with the full path to the directory in the Linux filesystem to use as the mount point. The *options* argument is used to set the exact manner in which the share is mounted. Let's look at an example of a *smbmount* command:

```
# smbmount //maya/e /smb/e \
    -o "credentials=/home/jay/.smbpw,uid=jay,gid=jay,fmask=664,dmask=775"
```

Here we are mounting share *maya**e* from a Windows 98 system on the mount point */smb/e* on the Linux system.

> If your Linux kernel doesn't include smbfs support, you will get the error message:
>
> ```
> ERROR: smbfs filesystem not supported by the kernel
> ```
>
> In this case, you must configure and compile a new kernel to include support for smbfs. When smbfs is installed, and an SMB share is mounted, you can run the command:
>
> ```
> $ cat /proc/filesystems
> ```
>
> and see a line that looks like:
>
> ```
> nodev    smbfs
> ```
>
> in the command's output.

The mount point must exist before *smbmount* is run and can be created using the *mkdir* command:

```
# mkdir /smb/e
```

The argument to the -o option might look a little complex. It is a comma-separated list of *key=value* pairs. The credentials key is set to the name of the credentials file, which is used to give *smbmount* a valid username and password with which to authenticate while connecting to the share. The format is identical to that used by *smbclient* (as explained in the previous section), so you can use the same credentials file for both clients. If you want, you can use the *key=value* pair username=*name%password* to specify the username and password directly in the *smbmount* command, although this is considerably less secure.

> The *smbmount* command accepts the same authentication methods as *smbclient*. The comments in the section on *smbclient* regarding supplying passwords on the command line—and keeping passwords in files and environment variables—also apply here.

The rest of the options tell *smbmount* how to translate between the SMB filesystem and the Unix filesystem, which differ in their handling of ownership and permissions. The *uid* and *gid* options specify the owner and group to be assigned to all directories and files in the mounted share.

The *fmask* and *dmask* options specify bitmasks for permissions of files and directories, respectively. These bitmasks are logically ANDed with whatever permissions are granted by the server to create the effective permissions on the client Unix system. On the server side, the permissions granted depend on the server's operating system. For a Windows 95/98/Me server using share-mode security, the MS-DOS read-only attribute can be set on individual files and directories and combined with the Full Access or Read Only permissions on the share as a whole. In user-level security mode, Windows 95/98/Me can have ACL-like permissions applied to the entire share, as discussed in Chapter 4. Windows NT/2000/XP support ACLs on individual files and directories, with Full Control, Change, or Read permissions that can be applied to the entire share. If the server is a Samba server, the permissions are whatever is defined by the Samba share and the local Unix system for the individual files and directories. In every case, the permissions applied to the share act to further limit access, beyond what is specified for the individual files and directories.

 You might think that the *fmask* and *dmask* permission masks can be used only to reduce the effective permissions on files and directories, but this is not always the case. For example, suppose that a file is being shared by a Windows 95/98/Me server using share-mode security and that some number of users have been given the Full Access password for the share. If the share is mounted with *smbmount* using an *fmask* of 666, read/write permissions are granted on the Unix system not only for the owner, but for everyone else on the Unix system as well!

After mounting the *maya**d* share to */smb/e*, here is what the contents of */smb/e* look like:

```
$ cd /smb/e ; ls -l
total 47
drwxrwxr-x  1 jay      jay           512 Jan  8 20:21 CD-images
drwxrwxr-x  1 jay      jay           512 Jan  6 21:50 lectures
-rw-rw-r--  1 jay      jay           131 Dec 18 09:12 ms-ProfPol-wp.doc
-rw-rw-r--  1 jay      jay            59 Dec 18 09:12 profile-map
-rw-rw-r--  1 jay      jay           131 Jan 15 05:01 readme.txt
drwxrwxr-x  1 jay      jay           512 Feb  4  2002 RECYCLED
-rw-rw-r--  1 jay      jay         33969 Dec 10 20:22 smbclient.doc
-rw-rw-r--  1 jay      jay          7759 Dec 10 20:20 smbmount.doc
-rw-rw-r--  1 jay      jay          1914 Dec 10 20:17 smbsh.txt
drwxrwxr-x  1 jay      jay           512 Jan 10 03:54 trans
```

For the most part, the files and directories contained in the mounted smbfs filesystem will work just like any others, except for limitations imposed by the nature of SMB networking. For example, not even the superuser can perform the operation:

```
# chown root lectures
chown: changing ownership of 'lectures': Operation not permitted
```

because SMB shares do not intrinsically support the idea of ownership. Some odd behaviors can result from this. For example, the command:

```
# chmod 777 readme.txt
```

does not produce an error message, although nothing has been changed. The file *readme.txt* still has permissions set to 664:

```
# ls -l readme.txt
-rw-rw-r--   1 jay     jay          131 Jan 15 05:01 readme.txt
```

Aside from little things such as these, the mounted smbfs filesystem can be used in conjunction with virtually any application, and you might be pleasantly surprised at how nicely it integrates with your Linux-based computing environment. You can even create symbolic links in the Unix filesystem, pointing to files and directories inside SMB shares. However, unless the server is a Samba server that supports Unix CIFS extensions, you will not be able to create a symbolic link inside the mounted smbfs filesystem.

Mounting smbfs Filesystems Automatically

As with other types of filesystems, an smbfs filesystem can be mounted automatically during system bootup by creating an entry for it in */etc/fstab*. The format for the entry is as follows:

```
Share-UNC mount-point  smbfs  options 0 0
```

Replace *Share-UNC* with the UNC of the share (using the forward slash format), and replace *mount-point* with the name of the directory in the Linux filesystem on which the share will be mounted. In place of *options*, simply use the string that you used with the *-o* flag in the *smbmount* command.

Once you have found the arguments to use with the *smbmount* command to mount the share the way you like it, it is a very simple matter to create the entry for */etc/fstab*. The *smbmount* command we used to mount the share *\\maya\e* on */smb/e* would translate to this */etc/fstab* entry:

```
//maya/e /smb/e  smbfs
credentials=/home/jay/.smbpw,uid=jay,gid=jay,fmask=664,dmask=775 0 0
```

(Please note that this should all go on one line.)

 If you make a mistake in modifying */etc/fstab*, your system might not reboot properly, and you might be forced to boot into single-user mode to fix the problem. Before you edit */etc/fstab*, be sure to make a backup copy of it, and be prepared to recover your system if anything goes wrong.

Once the entry has been added, the system will automatically mount the share when booting. Or, the system administrator can manually mount or unmount the share with commands such as these:

```
# mount /smb/e
# umount /smb/e
```

> It is possible to use *mount* and *umount* by giving them the UNC for the share using forward slashes, as in our */etc/fstab* entry. However, be careful about this. A share might be listed more than once in */etc/fstab* so that it can be mounted at more than one place in the Linux filesystem. If you use the UNC to specify the share you wish to mount or unmount, you might cause it to be mounted or unmounted at another mount point from the one you intended.

Common smbmount Options

Table 5-1 lists *key=value* pairs that can be used with the *-o* option of *smbmount* or in the options field of the */etc/fstab* entry for the smbfs filesystem. See the *smbmount* manual page for a complete list of options.

Table 5-1. smbmount options

Key	Value	Function
username	string	Provides the username, and optionally the password and workgroup, for authentication.
password	string	Provides the share or domain password, if it hasn't been supplied by another means.
credentials	string	Name of file containing the username and password.
uid	string or numeric	User ID to apply to all files and directories of the mounted share.
gid	string or numeric	Group ID to apply to all files and directories of the mounted share.
fmask	numeric	Permissions to apply to files. Default is based on current umask.
dmask	numeric	Permissions to apply to directories. Default is based on current umask.
debug	numeric	Debug level.
workgroup	string	Name of workgroup of remote server.
guest	(none)	Suppresses password prompt.
ro	(none)	Mount read-only.
rw	(none)	Mount read/write. This is the default.
ttl	numeric	Amount of time to cache the contents of directories. Defaults to 1000 ms .

smbsh

The *smbsh* program is part of the Samba suite and works on some, but not all, Unix variants.* Effectively, it adds a wrapper around the user's command shell, enabling it and common Unix utilities to work on files and directories in SMB shares, in addition to files and directories in the local Unix filesystem. From the user's perspective, the effect is that of a simulated mount of the SMB shares onto the Unix filesystem.

smbsh works by running the shell and programs run from it in an environment in which calls to the standard C library are redirected to the *smbwrapper* library, which has support for operating on SMB shares. This redirection can work only if the program being run is dynamically linked. Fortunately, modern Unix versions ship with most common utilities linked dynamically rather than statically.

 To determine whether a program is dynamically or statically linked, try using the *file* command.

To use *smbsh*, your Samba installation must be configured using the configure option `--with-smbwrapper`.

If you have a number of Unix systems with the same host operating system and architecture and don't want to bother with a full Samba installation, you can simply move the following files to the other systems:

```
/usr/local/samba/bin/smbsh
/usr/local/samba/bin/smbwrapper.so
/usr/local/samba/lib/smb.conf
```

Make sure that */usr/local/samba/bin* is in your shell's search path. The *smb.conf* file is needed only for *smbsh* to determine the workgroup or domain and does not need to be as elaborate as your Samba server's configuration file.

An Interactive Session with smbsh

To start *smbsh*, simply type in the *smbsh* command at the shell prompt. You will be prompted for a username and password with which to authenticate on the SMB network:

```
$ smbsh
Username: davecb
Password:
smbsh$
```

---

* At the time of this writing, *smbsh* does not work on HP/UX or Linux. However, Linux support might return in the future.

While working within the *smbsh* shell, you have a virtual */smb* directory. This does not actually exist in the Unix filesystem and is supported within *smbsh* only to help organize the SMB shares in a structure familiar to Unix users. You can list the contents of the */smb* virtual directory and get a list of workgroups in the local network, which are also presented as virtual directories:

```
smbsh$ cd /smb ; ls
ZOOL PLANK BACIL
```

You can change your working directory to one of the workgroup virtual directories, and listing one of them will show the computers in the workgroup:

```
smbsh$ cd ZOOL ; ls
ANTILLES        DODO            MILO            SEAL
ARGON           HANGGLIDE       OSTRICH         SPARTA
BALLET          INFUSION        PLAQUE          THEBES
CHABLIS         JAZ             PRAETORIAN      TJ
COBRA           KIKO            RAYOPCI         TRANCE
COUGUR          MACHINE-HEADPCI RUMYA           VIPERPCI
CRUSTY          MATHUMA         SCOT
```

Likewise, you can change your current directory to, and list the contents of, a computer virtual directory, and then you can see a listing of shares offered by that computer:

```
smbsh$ cd scot ; ls
ADMIN$      davecb      nc          np2s        pl
ace         dhcp-mrk03  np          nps         xp
cl          ep          np2         opcom
```

This is the lowest level of *smbsh*'s virtual directory system. Once you *cd* into a share, you are within the SMB share on the remote computer:

```
smbsh$ cd davecb ; ls
Mail                        mkanalysis_dirs.idx
SUNWexplo                   nfs.ps
Sent                        nsmail
allsun.html                 projects.txt
bin                         sumtimex
```

Once in a remote share, most of the Unix shell utilities will work, and you can operate on files and directories much as you would on any Unix system. You can even create symbolic links in the Unix filesystem pointing to files and directories in the SMB share. However, attempts to create symbolic links in the SMB share will fail unless the share is being served by Samba with support for Unix CIFS extensions.

smbutil and mount_smbfs

The *smbutil* and *mount_smbfs* programs provide SMB client functionality for FreeBSD, Darwin, and Mac OS X. Neither of the programs is part of the Samba distribution; however, we are including them to give you a little additional support in case you have BSD-related Unix systems on your network.

smbutil

The *smbutil* program provides functionality similar to some of the Samba suite's command-line utilities. It can be used to list the shares available on an SMB server or perform NetBIOS name lookups.

The first argument given to *smbutil* is one of a number of subcommands and is usually followed by arguments specific to the subcommand. For example, to list the resources offered by a server, use the *view* subcommand, and enter your server password when prompted:

```
% smbutil view //vamana
Password:
Share     Type     Comment
-----------------------------------------------------------------
public    disk
SS2500    printer  Stylus Scan 2500
IPC$      pipe     IPC Service (Samba 2.2.5)
ADMIN$    disk     IPC Service (Samba 2.2.5)
leonvs    disk     User Home Directories

5 shares listed from 5 available
```

If you wish to connect to the server with a username that differs from that on your client, you can specify it on the command line by preceding the name of the server with the username and using an at sign (@) as a separator:

```
% smbutil view //leonvs@vamana
```

You can also include the password after the username, using a colon (:) as a separator, to avoid being prompted for it:

```
% smbutil view //leonvs:leonspassword@vamana
```

Typing your password in the open like this is strongly discouraged. It's a little better if you use an encrypted password, which you can generate using *smbutil*'s *crypt* subcommand:

```
% smbutil crypt leonspassword
$$1625a5723293f0710e5faffcfc6
```

This can then be used in place of a clear-text password. However, the encryption is not particularly strong and will foil only the most casual inspection. As noted earlier, the only reasonably secure method of providing a password is to be prompted for it.

While starting up, *smbutil* reads the file *.nsmbrc* in the user's home directory. Also, the file */usr/local/etc/nsmb.conf* is read, and directives in that file override those in users' *~/.nsmbrc* files. This is to allow administrators to apply mandatory settings to all users. Directives can be placed in this file using the section and parameter format similar to that of the Samba configuration file. A list of common configuration parameters is given in Table 5-2.

For example, to keep your password in your *~/.nsmbrc* file, you can create an entry in the file such as the following:

```
[VAMANA:LEONVS]
     password=$$1625a5723293f0710e5faffcfc6
```

The section heading in brackets specifies the SMB server's NetBIOS name and the username to which the subsequent parameter settings apply. (The hostname and username should be supplied in uppercase characters.) Section headings can also consist of just a hostname or can contain a share name as a third element for specifying parameters applicable to a single share. Finally, if a [default] section is present, the settings in it apply to all connections.

The following example *.nsmbrc* shows some of the other parameters you might use:

```
[default]
     username=leonvs
     # NetBIOS name server
     nbns=192.168.1.3

[VAMANA]
     # server IP address
     addr=192.168.1.6
     workgroup=TEST

[VAMANA:LEONVS]
     password=$$1625a5723293f0710e5faffcfc6
```

Another thing you can do with *smbutil* is translate between IP addresses or DNS names and NetBIOS names. For example, the *status* subcommand takes an IP address or DNS hostname as an argument and returns the corresponding SMB server's NetBIOS name and workgroup:

```
% smbutil status 192.168.1.6
Workgroup: TEST
Server: VAMANA
```

The *lookup* subcommand returns the IP address associated with a given NetBIOS hostname. A NetBIOS name server can be optionally specified with the *-w* argument:

```
% smbutil lookup -w 192.168.1.3 VAMANA
Got response from 192.168.1.3
IP address of VAMANA: 192.168.1.6
```

mount_smbfs

The *mount_smbfs* program performs essentially the same function as *smbmount* on Linux. It mounts an SMB share on a directory in the local filesystem. The SMB share can then be accessed just like any other directory, subject to some behavioral differences noted earlier in the section "Mounting an smbfs Filesystem."

The command synopsis for *mount_smbfs* is:

```
mount_smbfs [options] Share-UNC mount-point
```

where *Share-UNC* is of the form:

```
//[workgroup;][username[:password]@]server[/share]
```

For example:

```
# mount_smbfs '//TEST;leonvs:$$1625a5723293f0710e5faffcfc6@vamana/leonvs' /
\Volumes/leonvs
```

The ownership and permissions of the mount point determine the default ownership and permissions for files and directories in the mounted share. These can be modified with command-line arguments, like this:

```
# mount_smbfs -u leonvs -g admin -f 0750 -d 0755 //leonvs@vamana/leonvs
\/Volumes/leonvs
```

In this example, the files and directories in the mounted share will be owned by the user leonvs and the group admin, with files and directories having permissions 750 and 755, respectively. (As usual, the permissions are specified in the octal format used by the Unix *chmod* command.)

The *mount_smbfs* command also makes use of settings in */usr/local/etc/nsmb.conf* and *~/.nsmbrc*, as described earlier. A list of common configuration parameters and command-line options is provided in Table 5-2.

Table 5-2. Common smbutil and mount_smbfs options

Command-line option	Configuration file parameter	Description
-I *hostname*	addr	Avoid NetBIOS name resolution and connect to the server using the specified DNS hostname or IP address.
-N	none	Do not prompt for a password.
-R *count*	retry_count	Number of times to retry connection before giving up.
-T *seconds*	timeout	Timeout, in seconds, per connection request.
-U *username*	username	Username to use for authentication. Defaults to Unix username.
-W *workgroup*	workgroup	Name of workgroup of remote server.
-d *mode*	none	Permissions to apply to directories in the mounted share. Defaults to the same as the file permissions, plus an execute (search) bit whenever the read bit is set.
-f *mode*	none	Permissions to apply to files in the mounted share. Defaults to the same as the permissions set on the directory used as the mount point.
-g *group*	none	Name or numeric GID to apply to all files and directories in the mounted share. Defaults to the group of the directory used as the mount point.
-n *long*	none	Disable support for long filenames. Restrict filenames to 8.3 naming standard.

Table 5-2. Common smbutil and mount_smbfs options (continued)

Command-line option	Configuration file parameter	Description
-u *username*	*none*	Username or numeric UID to apply as the owner of all files and directories in the mounted share. Defaults to the owner of the directory used as the mount point.
-w *hostname*	nbns	Hostname or IP address of the NetBIOS name server.
none	password	Password to use for authentication.

Mac OS X

In addition to *smbutil* and *mount_smbfs*, OS X includes a graphical interface to the functionality they provide. To use this interface, open the Go menu and select the Connect to Server… menu item. Instead of using a UNC, specify the share in the form of a Uniform Resource Identifier (URI) with a prefix of smb:// entered in the Address field, as shown in Figure 5-5.

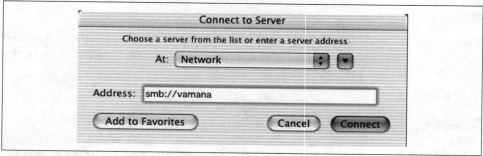

Figure 5-5. OS X Connect to Server dialog

You can specify a server, share, workgroup, username, and password (optionally encrypted with *smbutil crypt*) in the URI, in the same format as the UNC argument to *mount_smbfs*. If you don't specify a share name in the URI, you will be shown a window that lets you choose from a list of shares available to mount. See Figure 5-6.

Only guest-accessible shares will show up in the list until you've authenticated. After pressing the Authenticate button, you'll be prompted for a workgroup, username, and password, as shown in Figure 5-7. You'll also see this dialog if you provide a share name in the URI, but not a username and password.*

As usual for Mac OS X, shares are mounted under */Volumes*, but show up in the root of the Finder hierarchy.

---

* If you've previously stored your authentication information in a Keychain, you will instead be prompted for your Keychain password.

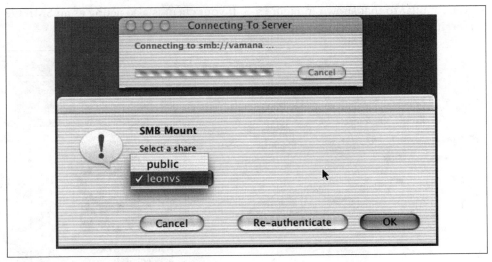

Figure 5-6. Selecting a share to mount

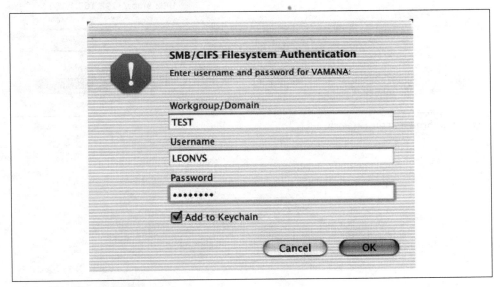

Figure 5-7. Client authentication

If you have a WINS server on your network, you can provide the server's IP address in the Directory Access application, or by using the wins server parameter in /etc/smb.conf.

If you don't know the name of a server to which you wish to connect, you can look for it in the browse list, using the graphical frontend to the *nmblookup* command provided with Samba. Click the downward-pointing arrow in the Connect to Server... dialog box to show a hierarchical, column-based view of available workgroups and

servers, similar to that shown in Figure 5-8. If your client is also acting as an SMB file
server, it won't show up in its own browse list.

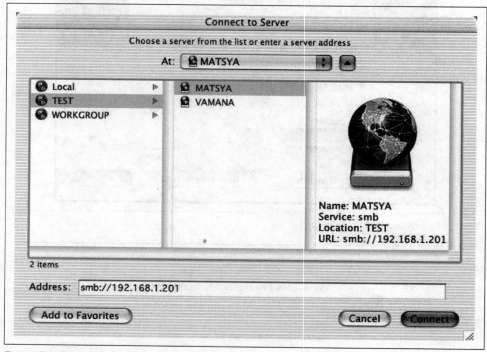

Figure 5-8. Browsing the network

## CHAPTER 6

The Samba Configuration File

In previous chapters, we showed you how to install Samba on a Unix server and set up Windows clients to use a simple disk share. This chapter will show you how Samba can assume more productive roles on your network.

Samba's daemons, *smbd* and *nmbd*, are controlled through a single ASCII file, *smb.conf*, that can contain over 300 unique options (also called parameters). Some of these options you will use and change frequently; others you might never use, depending on how much functionality you want Samba to offer its clients.

This chapter introduces the structure of the Samba configuration file and shows you how to use options to create and modify disk shares. Subsequent chapters will discuss browsing, how to configure users, security, printing, and other topics related to implementing Samba on your network.

The Samba Configuration File

The Samba configuration file, called *smb.conf* by default, uses the same format as Windows *.ini* files. If you have ever worked with a *.ini* file, you will find *smb.conf* easy to create and modify. Even if you haven't, you will find the format to be simple and easy to learn. Here is an example of a Samba configuration file:

```
[global]
    workgroup = METRAN
    encrypt passwords = yes
    wins support = yes
    log level = 1
    max log size = 1000
    read only = no
[homes]
    browsable = no
    map archive = yes
[printers]
    path = /var/tmp
    printable = yes
```

```
        min print space = 2000
    [test]
        browsable = yes
        read only = yes
        path = /usr/local/samba/tmp
```

This configuration file is based on the one we created in Chapter 2 and sets up a workgroup in which Samba authenticates users using encrypted passwords and the default user-level security method. Samba is providing WINS name server support. We've configured very basic event logging to use a log file not to exceed 1MB in size. The [homes] share has been added to allow Samba to create a disk share for the home directory of each user who has a standard Unix account on the server. In addition, each printer registered on the server will be publicly available, as will a single read-only share that maps to the */usr/local/samba/tmp* directory.

Configuration File Structure

Let's take another look at this configuration file, this time from a higher level:

```
    [global]
    ...
    [homes]
    ...
    [printers]
    ...
    [test]
    ...
```

The names inside the square brackets delineate unique *sections* of the *smb.conf* file; each section names the share (or service) to which the section refers. For example, the [test] and [homes] sections are unique disk shares; they contain options that map to specific directories on the Samba server. The [printers] share contains options that map to various printers on the server. All the sections defined in the *smb.conf* file, with the exception of the [global] section, will be available as a disk or printer share to clients connecting to the Samba server.

The remaining lines are individual configuration options for that share. These options will continue until a new section is encountered or until the end of the file is reached. Each configuration option follows a simple format:

    option = value

Options in the *smb.conf* file are set by assigning a value to them. We should warn you up front that some of the option names in Samba are poorly chosen. For example, read only is self-explanatory and is typical of many recent Samba options. The public option is an older option and is vague. It now has a less-confusing synonym guest ok (meaning it can be accessed by guests). Appendix B contains an alphabetical index of all the configuration options and their meanings.

Whitespace, quotes, and commas

An important item to remember about configuration options is that all whitespace within the *value* is significant. For example, consider the following option:

```
volume = The Big Bad Hard Drive Number 3543
```

Samba strips away the spaces up to the first T in The. These whitespaces are insignificant. The rest of the whitespaces are significant and will be recognized and preserved by Samba when reading in the file. Space is not significant in option names (such as read only), but we recommend you follow convention and keep spaces between the words of options.

If you feel safer including quotation marks at the beginning and end of a configuration option's value, you can do so. Samba will ignore these quotation marks when it encounters them. Never use quotation marks around an option name; Samba will treat this as an error.

Usually, you can use whitespaces or commas to separate a series of values in a list. These two options are equivalent:

```
netbios aliases = sales, accounting, payroll
netbios aliases = sales accounting payroll
```

In some cases, you must use one form of separation—sometimes spaces are required, and sometimes commas.

Capitalization

Capitalization is not important in the Samba configuration file except in locations where it would confuse the underlying operating system. For example, let's assume that you included the following option in a share that pointed to */export/samba/simple*:

```
PATH = /EXPORT/SAMBA/SIMPLE
```

Samba would have no problem with the path configuration option appearing entirely in capital letters. However, when it tries to connect to the given directory, it would be unsuccessful because the Unix filesystem *is* case-sensitive. Consequently, the path listed would not be found, and clients could not connect to the share.

Line continuation

You can continue a line in the Samba configuration file using the backslash, like this:

```
comment = The first share that has the primary copies \
          of the new Teamworks software product.
```

Because of the backslash, these two lines will be treated as one line by Samba. The second line begins at the first nonwhitespace character that Samba encounters; in this case, the o in of.

Comments

You can insert comments in the *smb.conf* configuration file by starting a line with either a hash (#) or a semicolon (;). For this purpose, both characters are equivalent. For example, the first three lines in the following example would be considered comments:

```
#  This is the printers section. We have given a minimum print
;  space of 2000 to prevent some errors that we've seen when
;  the spooler runs out of space.

[printers]
    public = yes
    min print space = 2000
```

Samba will ignore all comment lines in its configuration file; there are no limitations to what can be placed on a comment line after the initial hash mark or semicolon. Note that the line continuation character (\) will *not* be honored on a commented line. Like the rest of the line, it is ignored.

 Samba does not allow mixing of comment lines and parameters. Be careful not to put comments on the same line as anything else, such as:

```
    path = /d # server's data partition
```

Errors such as this, where the parameter value is defined with a string, can be tricky to notice. The *testparm* program won't complain, and the only clues you'll receive are that *testparm* reports the path parameter set to /d # server's data partition, and the failures that result when clients attempt to access the share.

Changes at runtime

You can modify the *smb.conf* configuration file and any of its options at any time while the Samba daemons are running. By default, Samba checks the configuration file every 60 seconds. If it finds any changes, they are immediately put into effect.

 Having Samba check the configuration file automatically can be convenient, but it also means that if you edit *smb.conf* directly, you might be immediately changing your network's configuration every time you save the file. If you're making anything more than a minor change, it may be wiser to copy *smb.conf* to a temporary file, edit that, run testparm *filename* to check it, and then copy the temporary file back to *smb.conf*. That way, you can be sure to put all your changes into effect at once, and only after you are confident that you have created the exact configuration you wish to implement.

If you don't want to wait for the configuration file to be reloaded automatically, you can force a reload either by sending a hangup signal to the *smbd* and *nmbd* processes or simply by restarting the daemons. Actually, it can be a good idea to restart the daemons because it forces the clients to disconnect and reconnect, ensuring that the new configuration is applied to all clients. We showed you how to restart the daemons in Chapter 2, and sending them a hangup (HUP) signal is very similar. On Linux, it can be done with the command:

```
# killall -HUP smbd nmbd
```

In this case, not all changes will be immediately recognized by clients. For example, changes to a share that is currently in use will not be registered until the client disconnects and reconnects to that share. In addition, server-specific parameters such as the workgroup or NetBIOS name of the server will not go into effect immediately either. (This behavior was implemented intentionally because it keeps active clients from being suddenly disconnected or encountering unexpected access problems while a session is open.)

Variables

Because a new copy of the *smbd* daemon is created for each connecting client, it is possible for each client to have its own customized configuration file. Samba allows a limited, yet useful, form of variable substitution in the configuration file to allow information about the Samba server and the client to be included in the configuration at the time the client connects. Inside the configuration file, a variable begins with a percent sign (%), followed by a single upper- or lowercase letter, and can be used only on the right side of a configuration option (i.e., after the equal sign). An example is:

```
[pub]
    path = /home/ftp/pub/%a
```

The %a stands for the client system's architecture and will be replaced as shown in Table 6-1.

Table 6-1. %a substitution

Client operating system ("architecture")	Replacement string
Windows for Workgroups	WfWg
Windows 95 and Windows 98	Win95
Windows NT	WinNT
Windows 2000 and Windows XP	Win2K
Samba	Samba
Any OS not listed earlier	UNKNOWN

In this example, Samba will assign a unique path for the [pub] share to client systems based on what operating system they are running. The paths that each client would see as its share differ according to the client's architecture:

```
/home/ftp/pub/WfwG
/home/ftp/pub/Win95
/home/ftp/pub/WinNT
/home/ftp/pub/Win2K
/home/ftp/pub/Samba
/home/ftp/pub/UNKNOWN
```

Using variables in this manner comes in handy if you wish to have different users run custom configurations based on their own unique characteristics or conditions. Samba has 20 variables, as shown in Table 6-2.

Table 6-2. Samba variables

Variable	Definition
Client variables	
%a	Client's architecture (see Table 6-1)
%I	Client's IP address (e.g., 172.16.1.2)
%m	Client's NetBIOS name
%M	Client's DNS name
User variables	
%u	Current Unix username
%U	Requested client username (not always used by Samba)
%H	Home directory of %u
%g	Primary group of %u
%G	Primary group of %U
Share variables	
%S	Current share's name
%P	Current share's root directory
%p	Automounter's path to the share's root directory, if different from %P
Server variables	
%d	Current server process ID
%h	Samba server's DNS hostname
%L	Samba server's NetBIOS name
%N	Home directory server, from the automount map
%v	Samba version
Miscellaneous variables	
%R	The SMB protocol level that was negotiated
%T	The current date and time
%$var	The value of environment variable var

Here's another example of using variables: let's say there are five clients on your network, but one client, maya, requires a slightly different [homes] configuration. With Samba, it's simple to handle this:

```
[homes]
    ...
        include = /usr/local/samba/lib/smb.conf.%m
    ...
```

The include option here causes a separate configuration file for each particular NetBIOS machine (%m) to be read in addition to the current file. If the hostname of the client system is maya, and if a *smb.conf.maya* file exists in the */usr/local/samba/lib* directory, Samba will insert that configuration file into the default one. If any configuration options are restated in *smb.conf.maya*, those values will override any options previously encountered in that share. Note that we say "previously." If any options are restated in the main configuration file after the include option, Samba will honor those restated values for the share in which they are defined.

If the file specified by the include parameter does not exist, Samba will not generate an error. In fact, it won't do anything at all. This allows you to create only one extra configuration file for maya when using this strategy, instead of one for each client that is on the network.

Client-specific configuration files can be used to customize particular clients. They also can be used to make debugging Samba easier. For example, if we have one client with a problem, we can use this approach to give it a private log file with a more verbose logging level. This allows us to see what Samba is doing without slowing down all the other clients or overflowing the disk with useless logs.

You can use the variables in Table 6-2 to give custom values to a variety of Samba options. We will highlight several of these options as we move through the next few chapters.

Special Sections

Now that we've gotten our feet wet with variables, there are a few special sections of the Samba configuration file that we should talk about. Again, don't worry if you do not understand every configuration option listed here; we'll go over each of them in the upcoming chapters.

The [global] Section

The [global] section appears in virtually every Samba configuration file, even though it is not mandatory. There are two purposes for the [global] section. Server-wide settings are defined here, and any options that apply to shares will be used as a default in all share definitions, unless overridden within the share definition.

To illustrate this, let's again look at the example at the beginning of the chapter:

```
[global]
    workgroup = METRAN
    encrypt passwords = yes
    wins support = yes
    log level = 1
    max log size = 1000
    read only = no
[homes]
    browsable = no
    map archive = yes
[printers]
    path = /var/tmp
    printable = yes
    min print space = 2000
[test]
    browsable = yes
    read only = yes
    path = /usr/local/samba/tmp
```

When a client connects to the [test] share, Samba first reads the [global] section and sets the option read only = no as the global default for each share it encounters throughout the configuration file. This includes the [homes] and [test] shares. When it reads the definition of the [test] share, it then finds the configuration option read only = yes and overrides the default from the [global] section with the value yes.

Any option that appears before the first marked section is assumed to be a global option. This means that the [global] section heading is not absolutely required; however, we suggest you always include it for clarity and to ensure future compatibility.

The [homes] Section

If a client attempts to connect to a share that doesn't appear in the *smb.conf* file, Samba will search for a [homes] share in the configuration file. If a [homes] share exists, the unresolved share name is assumed to be a Unix username. If that username appears in the password database on the Samba server, Samba assumes the client is a Unix user trying to connect to her home directory on the server.

For example, assume a client system is connecting to the Samba server toltec for the first time and tries to connect to a share named [alice]. There is no [alice] share defined in the *smb.conf* file, but there is a [homes], so Samba searches the password database file and finds an alice user account is present on the system. Samba then checks the password provided by the client against user alice's Unix password— either with the password database file if it's using nonencrypted passwords or with Samba's *smbpasswd* file if encrypted passwords are in use. If the passwords match, Samba knows it has guessed right: the user alice is trying to connect to her home

---

directory. Samba will then create a share called [alice] for her, with the share's path set to alice's home directory.

The process of using the [homes] section to create users (and dealing with their passwords) is discussed in more detail in Chapter 9.

The [printers] Section

The third special section is called [printers] and is similar to [homes]. If a client attempts to connect to a share that isn't in the *smb.conf* file and its name can't be found in the password file, Samba will check to see if it is a printer share. Samba does this by reading the printer capabilities file (usually */etc/printcap*) to see if the share name appears there.* If it does, Samba creates a share named after the printer.

This means that as with [homes], you don't have to maintain a share for each system printer in the *smb.conf* file. Instead, Samba honors the Unix printer registry if you ask it to, and it provides the registered printers to the client systems. However, there is a potential difficulty: if you have an account named fred and a printer named fred, Samba will always find the user account first, even if the client really needed to connect to the printer.

The process of setting up the [printers] share is discussed in more detail in Chapter 10.

Configuration Options

Options in the Samba configuration files fall into one of two categories: *global* options or *share* options. Each category dictates where an option can appear in the configuration file.

Global options
> Global options must appear in the [global] section and nowhere else. These are options that typically apply to the behavior of the Samba server itself and not to any of its shares.

Share options
> Share options can appear in share definitions, the [global] section, or both. If they appear in the [global] section, they will define a default behavior for all shares unless a share overrides the option with a value of its own.

---

* Depending on your system, this file might not be */etc/printcap*. You can use the *testparm* command that comes with Samba to dump the parameter definitions and determine the value of the printcap name configuration option. The value assigned to it is the default value chosen when Samba was configured and compiled, which should be correct.

In addition, configuration options can take three kinds of values. They are as follows:

Boolean
These are simply yes or no values, but can be represented by any of the following: yes, no, true, false, 1, or 0. The values are case-insensitive: YES is the same as yes.

Numeric
This is a decimal, hexadecimal, or octal number. The standard 0x*nn* syntax is used for hexadecimal and 0*nnn* for octal.

String
This is a string of case-sensitive characters, such as a filename or a username.

Configuration File Options

You can instruct Samba to include or replace configuration options as it is processing them. The options to do this are summarized in Table 6-3.

Table 6-3. Configuration file options

Option	Parameters	Function	Default	Scope
config file	string (name of file)	Sets the location of a configuration file to use instead of the current one	None	Global
include	string (name of file)	Specifies an additional set of configuration options to be included in the configuration file	None	Global
copy	string (name of share)	Allows you to clone the configuration options of another share in the current share	None	Share

config file

The global config file option specifies a replacement configuration file that will be loaded when the option is encountered. If the target file exists, the remainder of the current configuration file, as well as the options encountered so far, will be discarded, and Samba will configure itself entirely with the options in the new file. Variables can be used with the config file option, which is useful in the event that you want to use a special configuration file based on the NetBIOS machine name or user of the client that is connecting.

For example, the following line instructs Samba to use a configuration file specified by the NetBIOS name of the client connecting, if such a file exists. If it does, options specified in the original configuration file are ignored:

```
[global]
    config file = /usr/local/samba/lib/smb.conf.%m
```

If the configuration file specified does not exist, the option is ignored, and Samba will continue to configure itself based on the current file. This allows a default configuration file to serve most clients, while providing for exceptions with customized configuration files.

include

This option, discussed in greater detail earlier, copies the target file into the current configuration file at the point specified, as shown in Figure 6-1. This option also can be used with variables. You can use this option as follows:

```
[global]
    include = /usr/local/samba/lib/smb.conf.%m
```

If the configuration file specified does not exist, the option is ignored. Options in the include file override any option specified previously, but not options that are specified later. In Figure 6-1, all three options will override their previous values.

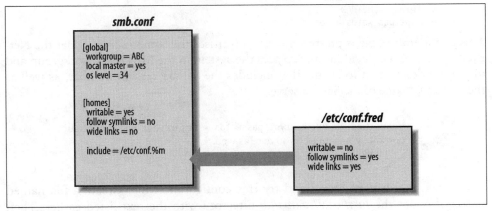

Figure 6-1. The include option in a Samba configuration file

The include option does not work with the variables %u (user), %P (current share's root directory), or %S (current share's name) because they are not set at the time the include parameter is processed.

copy

The copy configuration option allows you to clone the configuration options of the share name that you specify in the current share. The target share must appear earlier in the configuration file than the share that is performing the copy. For example:

```
[template]
    writable = yes
    browsable = yes
    valid users = andy, dave, jay
```

```
[data]
        path = /usr/local/samba
        copy = template
```

Note that any options in the share that invoked the copy directive will override those in the cloned share; it does not matter whether they appear before or after the copy directive.

Server Configuration

We will now start from scratch and build a configuration file for our Samba server. First we will introduce three basic configuration options that can appear in the [global] section of the *smb.conf* file:

```
[global]
        #  Server configuration parameters
        netbios name = toltec
        server string = Samba %v on %L
        workgroup = METRAN
        encrypt passwords = yes
```

This configuration file is pretty simple; it advertises the Samba server under the Net-BIOS name toltec. In addition, it places the system in the METRAN workgroup and displays a description to clients that includes the Samba version number, as well as the NetBIOS name of the Samba server.

 If you used the line encrypt passwords = yes in your earlier configuration file, you should do so here as well.

If you like, you can go ahead and try this configuration file. Create a file named *smb.conf* under the */usr/local/samba/lib* directory with the text listed earlier. Then restart the Samba server and use a Windows client to verify the results. Be sure that your Windows clients are in the METRAN workgroup as well. After double-clicking the Network Neighborhood on a Windows client, you should see a window similar to Figure 6-2. (In this figure, Mixtec is another Samba server, and Zapotec is a Windows client.)

You can verify the server string by listing the details of the Network Neighborhood window (select Details in the View menu). You should see a window similar to Figure 6-3.

If you were to click the *toltec* icon, a window should appear that shows the services that it provides. In this case, the window would be completely empty because there are no shares on the server yet.

Figure 6-2. Network Neighborhood showing Toltec, the Samba server

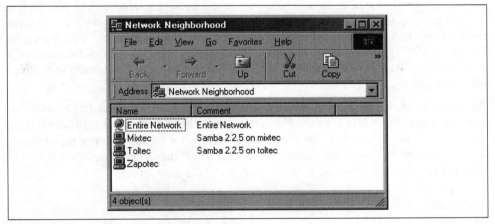

Figure 6-3. Network Neighborhood details listing

Server Configuration Options

Table 6-4 summarizes the server configuration options introduced previously. All three of these options are global in scope, so they must appear in the [global] section of the configuration file.

Table 6-4. Server configuration options

Option	Parameters	Function	Default	Scope
netbios name	string	NetBIOS name of the Samba server	Server's unqualified DNS hostname	Global
workgroup	string	NetBIOS group to which the server belongs	Defined at compile time	Global
server string	string	Descriptive string for the Samba server	Samba %v	Global

netbios name

The `netbios name` option allows you to set the NetBIOS name of the server. For example:

```
netbios name = YORKVM1
```

The default value for this configuration option is the server's hostname—that is, the first part of its fully qualified domain name. For example, a system with the DNS name `ruby.ora.com` would be given the NetBIOS name `RUBY` by default. While you can use this option to restate the system's NetBIOS name in the configuration file (as we did previously), it is more commonly used to assign the Samba server a NetBIOS name other than its current DNS name. Remember that the name given must follow the rules for valid NetBIOS machine names as outlined in Chapter 1.

Changing the NetBIOS name of the server is not recommended unless you have a good reason. One such reason might be if the hostname of the system is not unique because the LAN is divided over two or more DNS domains. For example, YORKVM1 is a good NetBIOS candidate for `vm1.york.example.com` to differentiate it from `vm1.falkirk.example.com`, which has the same hostname but resides in a different DNS domain.

Another use of this option is for relocating SMB services from a dead or retired system. For example, if `SALES` is the SMB server for the department and it suddenly dies, you could immediately reset `netbios name = SALES` on a backup Samba server that's taking over for it. Users won't have to change their drive mappings to a different server; new connections to `SALES` will simply go to the new server.

workgroup

The `workgroup` parameter sets the current workgroup (or domain) in which the Samba server will advertise itself. Clients that wish to access shares on the Samba server should be in the same NetBIOS group. Remember that workgroups are really just NetBIOS group names and must follow the standard NetBIOS naming conventions outlined in Chapter 1.

The default option for this parameter is set at compile time to `WORKGROUP`. Because this is the default workgroup name of every unconfigured Windows and Samba system, we recommend that you always set your workgroup name in the Samba configuration file. When choosing your workgroup name, try to avoid making it the same name as a server or user. This will avoid possible problems with WINS name resolution.

server string

The `server string` parameter defines a comment string that will appear next to the server name in both the Network Neighborhood (when shown with the Details view) and the comment entry of the Microsoft Windows printer manager.[*] You can use variables to provide information in the description. For example, our entry earlier was:

```
[global]
    server string = Samba %v on (%h)
```

The default for this option simply presents the current version of Samba and is equivalent to:

```
server string = Samba %v
```

Disk Share Configuration

We mentioned in the previous section that there were no disk shares on the toltec server. Let's continue building the configuration file and create an empty disk share called [data]. Here are the additions that will do it:

```
[data]
    path = /export/samba/data
    comment = Data Drive
    volume = Sample-Data-Drive
    writable = yes
```

The [data] share is typical for a Samba disk share. The share maps to the directory */export/samba/data* on the Samba server. We've also provided a comment that describes the share as a Data Drive, as well as a volume name for the share itself.

Samba's default is to create a read-only share. As a result, the writable option needs to be explicitly set for each disk share you wish to make writable.

We will also need to create the */export/samba/data* directory on the Samba server with the following commands:

```
# mkdir /export/samba/data
# chmod 777 /export/samba/data
```

Now, if we connect to the toltec server again by double-clicking its icon in the Windows Network Neighborhood, we will see a single share entitled data, as shown in Figure 6-4. This share has read/write access, so files can be copied to or from it.

Disk Share Configuration Options

The basic Samba configuration options for disk shares previously introduced are listed in Table 6-5.

---

[*] We are referring here to the window that opens when a printer icon in the Printers control panel is double-clicked.

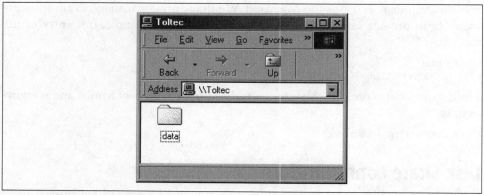

Figure 6-4. The initial data share on the Samba server

Table 6-5. Basic share configuration options

Option	Parameters	Function	Default	Scope
path (directory)	string (directory name)	Sets the Unix directory that will be provided for a disk share or used for spooling by a printer share.	/tmp	Share
comment	string	Sets the comment that appears with the share.	None	Share
volume	string	Sets the MS-DOS volume name for the share.	Share name	Share
read only	boolean	If yes, allows read-only access to a share.	yes	Share
writable (write ok or writeable)	boolean	If no, allows read-only access to a share. If yes, both reading and writing are allowed.	no	Share

path

This option, which has the synonym directory, indicates the pathname for the root of the shared directory or printer. You can choose any directory on the Samba server, so long as the owner of the Samba process that is connecting has read and write access to that directory. If the path is for a printing share, it should point to a temporary directory where files can be written on the server before being spooled to the target printer (*/tmp* and */var/spool* are popular choices). If this path is for a disk share, the contents of the folder representing the share name on the client will match the contents of the directory on the Samba server.

The directory specified as the value for path can be given as a relative path, in which case it will be relative to the directory specified by the root directory parameter. Because root directory defaults to root (/), it is generally a good idea to use absolute paths for the path parameter, unless root directory has been set to something other than the default.

comment

The comment option allows you to enter a comment that will be sent to the client when it attempts to browse the share. The user can see the comment by using the Details view on the share folder or with the *net view* command at an MS-DOS prompt. For example, here is how you might insert a comment for a share:

```
[network]
    comment = Network Drive
    path = /export/samba/network
```

Be sure not to confuse the comment option, which documents a Samba server's shares, with the server string option, which documents the server itself.

volume

This option allows you to specify the volume name of the share, which would otherwise default to the name of the share given in the *smb.conf* file.

Some software installation programs check the volume name of the distribution CD-ROM to make sure the correct CD-ROM is in the drive before attempting to install from it. If you copy the contents of the CD-ROM into a network share and wish to install from there, you can use this option to make sure the installation program sees the correct volume name:

```
[network]
    comment = Network Drive
    volume = ASVP-102-RTYUIKA
    path = /home/samba/network
```

read only, writable

The options read only and writable (also called writeable or write ok) are really two ways of saying the same thing, but they are approached from opposite ends. For example, you can set either of the following options in the [global] section or in an individual share:

```
read only = yes
writable = no
```

If either option is set as shown, data can be read from a share, but cannot be written to it. You might think you would need this option only if you were creating a read-only share. However, note that this read-only behavior is the *default* action for shares; if you want to be able to write data to a share, you must explicitly specify one of the following options in the configuration file for each share:

```
read only = no
writable = yes
```

If you specify more than one occurrence of either option, Samba will adhere to the last value it encounters for the share.

Networking Options with Samba

If you're running Samba on a multihomed system (on multiple subnets), you will need to configure Samba to use all the network interfaces. Another use for the options presented in this section is to implement better security by allowing or disallowing connections on the specified interfaces.

Let's assume that our Samba server can access both the subnets 192.168.220.* and 134.213.233.*. Here are our additions to the configuration file to add the networking configuration options:

```
[global]
    #  Networking configuration options
    hosts allow = 192.168.220. 134.213.233.
    hosts deny = 192.168.220.102
    interfaces = 192.168.220.100/255.255.255.0 \
                  134.213.233.110/255.255.255.0
    bind interfaces only = yes
```

Take a look at the hosts allow and hosts deny options. If these options sound familiar, you're probably thinking of the *hosts.allow* and *hosts.deny* files that are found in the */etc* directories of many Unix systems. The purpose of these options is identical to those files; they provide a means of security by allowing or denying the connections of other hosts based on their IP addresses. We could use the *hosts.allow* and *hosts.deny* files, but we are using this method instead because there might be services on the server that we want others to access without also giving them access to Samba's disk or printer shares.

With the hosts allow option, we've specified a 192.168.220 IP address, which is equivalent to saying: "All hosts on the 192.168.220 subnet." However, we've explicitly specified in a hosts deny line that 192.168.220.102 is not to be allowed access.

You might be wondering why 192.168.220.102 will be denied even though it is still in the subnet matched by the hosts allow option. It is important to understand how Samba sorts out the rules specified by hosts allow and hosts deny:

1. If no allow or deny options are defined anywhere in *smb.conf*, Samba will allow connections from any system.

2. If hosts allow or hosts deny options are defined in the [global] section of *smb.conf*, they will apply to all shares, even if either option is defined in one or more of the shares.

3. If only a hosts allow option is defined for a share, only the hosts listed will be allowed to use the share. All others will be denied.

4. If only a hosts deny option is defined for a share, any client which is not on the list will be able to use the share.

5. If both a hosts allow and hosts deny option are defined, a host must appear in the allow list and not appear in the deny list (in any form) to access the share. Otherwise, the host will not be allowed.

Take care that you don't explicitly allow a host to access a share, but then deny access to the entire subnet of which the host is part.

Let's look at another example of that final item. Consider the following options:

```
hosts allow = 111.222.
hosts deny = 111.222.333.
```

In this case, only the hosts that belong to the subnet 111.222.*.* will be allowed access to the Samba shares. However, if a client belongs to the 111.222.333.* subnet, it will be denied access, even though it still matches the qualifications outlined by hosts allow. The client must appear on the hosts allow list and *must not* appear on the hosts deny list to gain access to a Samba share.

The other two options that we've specified are interfaces and bind interface only. Let's look at the interfaces option first. Samba, by default, sends data only from the primary network interface, which in our example is the 192.168.220.100 subnet. If we would like it to send data to more than that one interface, we need to specify the complete list with the interfaces option. In the previous example, we've bound Samba to interface with both subnets (192.168.220 and 134.213.233) on which the system is operating by specifying the other network interface address: 134.213.233.100. If you have more than one interface on your computer, you should always set this option, as there is no guarantee that the primary interface that Samba chooses will be the right one.

Finally, the bind interfaces only option instructs the *nmbd* process not to accept any broadcast messages other than on the subnets specified with the interfaces option. This is different from the hosts allow and hosts deny options, which prevent clients from making connections to services, but not from receiving broadcast messages. Using the bind interfaces only option is a way to shut out all datagrams from foreign subnets. In addition, it instructs the *smbd* process to bind to only the interface list given by the *interfaces* option. This restricts the networks that Samba will serve.

Networking Options

The networking options we introduced earlier are summarized in Table 6-6.

Table 6-6. Networking configuration options

Option	Parameters	Function	Default	Scope
hosts allow (allow hosts)	string (list of hostnames)	Client systems that can connect to Samba.	None	Share
hosts deny (deny hosts)	string (list of hostnames)	Client systems that cannot connect to Samba.	None	Share

Table 6-6. Networking configuration options (continued)

Option	Parameters	Function	Default	Scope
interfaces	string (list of IP/ netmask combi- nations)	Network interfaces Samba will respond to. Allows cor- recting defaults.	System- dependent	Global
bind interfaces only	boolean	If set to yes, Samba will bind only to those interfaces spec- ified by the interfaces option.	no	Global

hosts allow

The hosts allow option (sometimes written as allow hosts) specifies the clients that have permission to access shares on the Samba server, written as a comma- or space-separated list of hostnames of systems or their IP addresses. You can gain quite a bit of security by simply placing your LAN's subnet address in this option.

You can specify any of the following formats for this option:

- Hostnames, such as ftp.example.com.
- IP addresses, such as 130.63.9.252.
- Domain names, which can be differentiated from individual hostnames because they start with a dot. For example, .ora.com represents all systems within the *ora.com* domain.
- Netgroups, which start with an at sign (@), such as @printerhosts. Netgroups are usually available only on systems running NIS or NIS+. If netgroups are sup-ported on your system, there should be a netgroups manual page that describes them in more detail.
- Subnets, which end with a dot. For example, 130.63.9. means all the systems whose IP addresses begin with 130.63.9.
- The keyword ALL, which allows any client access.
- The keyword EXCEPT followed by one or more names, IP addresses, domain names, netgroups, or subnets. For example, you could specify that Samba allow all hosts except those on the 192.168.110 subnet with hosts allow = ALL EXCEPT 192.168.110. (remember to include the trailing dot).

Using the ALL keyword by itself is almost always a bad idea because it means that crackers on any network can access your Samba server.

The hostname localhost, for the loopback address 127.0.0.1, is included in the hosts allow list by default and does not need to be listed explicitly unless you have speci-fied the bind interfaces only parameter. This address is required for Samba to work properly.

Other than that, there is no default value for the hosts allow configuration option. The default course of action in the event that neither the hosts allow or hosts deny option is specified in *smb.conf* is to allow access from all sources.

 If you specify hosts allow in the [global] section, that definition will override any hosts allow lines in the share definitions. This is the opposite of the usual behavior, which is for parameters set in share definitions to override default values set in the [global] section.

hosts deny

The hosts deny option (synonymous with deny hosts) specifies client systems that do not have permission to access a share, written as a comma- or space-separated list of hostnames or their IP addresses. Use the same format for specifying clients as the hosts allow option earlier. For example, to restrict access to the server from everywhere but example.com, you could write:

```
hosts deny = ALL EXCEPT .example.com
```

There is no default value for the hosts deny configuration option, although the default course of action in the event that neither option is specified is to allow access from all sources. Also, if you specify this option in the [global] section of the configuration file, it will override any hosts deny options defined in shares. If you wish to deny access to specific shares, omit both the hosts allow and hosts deny options from the [global] section of the configuration file.

 Never include the loopback address (localhost at IP address 127.0.0.1) in the hosts deny list. The *smbpasswd* program needs to connect through the loopback address to the Samba server as a client to change a user's encrypted password. If the loopback address is disabled, the locally generated packets requesting the change of the encrypted password will be discarded by Samba.

In addition, both local browsing propagation and some functions of SWAT require access to the Samba server through the loopback address and will not work correctly if this address is disabled.

interfaces

The interfaces option specifies the networks that you want the Samba server to recognize and respond to. This option is handy if you have a computer that resides on more than one network subnet. If this option is not set, Samba searches for the primary network interface of the server (typically the first Ethernet card) upon startup and configures itself to operate on only that subnet. If the server is configured for more than one subnet and you do not specify this option, Samba will only work on the first subnet it encounters. You must use this option to force Samba to serve the other subnets on your network.

The value of this option is one or more sets of IP address/netmask pairs, as in the following:

```
interfaces = 192.168.220.100/255.255.255.0 192.168.210.30/255.255.255.0
```

You can optionally specify a CIDR format bitmask, like this:

```
interfaces = 192.168.220.100/24 192.168.210.30/24
```

The number after the slash specifies the number of bits that will be set in the netmask. For example, the number 24 means that the first 24 (of 32) bits will be set in the bitmask, which is the same as specifying 255.255.255.0 as the netmask. Likewise, 16 would be equivalent to a netmask of 255.255.0.0, and 8 would be the same as a netmask of 255.0.0.0.

 This option might not work correctly if you are using DHCP.

bind interfaces only

The bind interfaces only option can be used to force the *smbd* and *nmbd* processes to respond only to those addresses specified by the interfaces option. The *nmbd* process normally binds to the all-addresses interface (0.0.0.0.) on ports 137 and 138, allowing it to receive broadcasts from anywhere. However, you can override this behavior with the following:

```
bind interfaces only = yes
```

This will cause Samba to ignore any packets (including broadcast packets) whose source address does not correspond to any of the network interfaces specified by the interfaces option. You should avoid using this option if you want to allow temporary network connections, such as those created through SLIP or PPP. It's very rare that this option is needed, and it should be used only by experts.

 If you set bind interfaces only to yes, add the local host address (127.0.01) to the "interfaces" list. Otherwise, *smbpasswd* will be unable to connect to the server using its default mode in order to change a password, local browse list propagation will fail, and some functions of swat will not work properly.

Virtual Servers

Virtual servers can be used to create the illusion of having multiple servers on the network, when in reality there is only one. The technique is simple to implement: a system simply registers more than one NetBIOS name in association with its IP address. There are tangible benefits to doing this.

For example, the accounting department might have an accounting server, and clients of it would see just the accounting disks and printers. The marketing department could have its own server, marketing, with its own reports, and so on. However, all the services would be provided by one medium-size Unix server (and one relaxed administrator) instead of having one small server per department.

Virtual Server Configuration Options

Samba will allow a server to use more than one NetBIOS name with the netbios aliases option. See Table 6-7.

Table 6-7. Virtual server configuration options

Option	Parameters	Function	Default	Scope
netbios aliases	string (list of Net-BIOS names)	Additional NetBIOS names to respond to, for use with multiple "virtual" Samba servers	None	Global

netbios aliases

The netbios aliases option can be used to give the Samba server more than one NetBIOS name. Each NetBIOS name listed as a value will be displayed in the Network Neighborhood of Windows clients. When a connection is requested to any of the servers, it will connect to the same Samba server.

This might come in handy, for example, if you're transferring three departments' data to a single Unix server with larger and faster disks and are retiring or reallocating the old Windows NT/2000 servers. If the three servers are called sales, accounting, and admin, you can have Samba represent all three servers with the following options:

```
[global]
    netbios aliases = sales accounting admin
    include = /usr/local/samba/lib/smb.conf.%L
```

See Figure 6-5 for what the Network Neighborhood would display from a client. When a client attempts to connect to Samba, it will specify the name of the server to which it's trying to connect, which is made available in the configuration file through the %L variable. If the requested server is sales, Samba will include the file */usr/local/samba/lib/smb.conf.sales*. This file might contain global and share declarations exclusively for the sales team, such as the following:

```
[global]
    workgroup = SALES
    hosts allow = 192.168.10.255

[sales2003]
    path = /usr/local/samba/sales/sales2003/
...
```

This particular example would set the workgroup to SALES as well and set the IP address to allow connections only from the SALES subnet (192.168.10). In addition, it would offer shares specific to the sales department.

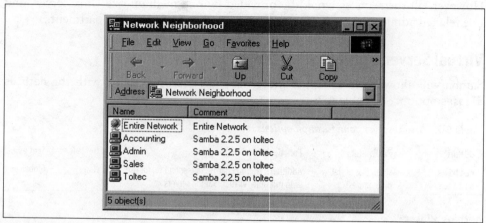

Figure 6-5. Using NetBIOS aliases for a Samba server

Logging Configuration Options

Occasionally, we need to find out what Samba is up to. This is especially true when Samba is performing an unexpected action or is not performing at all. To find out this information, we need to check Samba's log files to see exactly why it did what it did.

Samba log files can be as brief or verbose as you like. Here is an example of what a Samba log file looks like:

```
[2002/07/21 13:23:25, 3] smbd/service.c:close_cnum(514)
   maya (172.16.1.6) closed connection to service IPC$
[2002/07/21 13:23:25, 3] smbd/connection.c:yield_connection(40)
   Yielding connection to IPC$
[2002/07/21 13:23:25, 3] smbd/process.c:process_smb(615)
   Transaction 923 of length 49
[2002/07/21 13:23:25, 3] smbd/process.c:switch_message(448)
   switch message SMBread (pid 467)
[2002/07/21 13:23:25, 3] lib/doscalls.c:dos_ChDir(336)
   dos_ChDir to /home/samba
[2002/07/21 13:23:25, 3] smbd/reply.c:reply_read(2199)
   read fnum=4207 num=2820 nread=2820
[2002/07/21 13:23:25, 3] smbd/process.c:process_smb(615)
   Transaction 924 of length 55
[2002/07/21 13:23:25, 3] smbd/process.c:switch_message(448)
   switch message SMBreadbraw (pid 467)
[2002/07/21 13:23:25, 3] smbd/reply.c:reply_readbraw(2053)
   readbraw fnum=4207 start=130820 max=1276 min=0 nread=1276
```

```
[2002/07/21 13:23:25, 3] smbd/process.c:process_smb(615)
   Transaction 925 of length 55
[2002/07/21 13:23:25, 3] smbd/process.c:switch_message(448)
   switch message SMBreadbraw (pid 467)
```

Much of this information is of use only to Samba programmers. However, we will go over the meaning of some of these entries in more detail in Chapter 12.

Samba contains six options that allow users to describe how and where logging information should be written. Each of these are global options and cannot appear inside a share definition. Here is an example of some logging options that we are adding to our configuration file:

```
[global]
      log level = 2
      log file = /var/log/samba.log.%m
      max log size = 50
      debug timestamp = yes
```

Here, we've added a custom log file that reports information up to debug level 2. This is a relatively light debugging level. The logging level ranges from 1 to 10, where level 1 provides only a small amount of information and level 10 provides a plethora of low-level information. Levels 2 or 3 will provide us with useful debugging information without wasting disk space on our server. In practice, you should avoid using log levels greater than 3 unless you are working on the Samba source code.

The logging file is located in the */var/log* directory thanks to the log file configuration option. However, we can use variable substitution to create log files specifically for individual users or clients, such as with the %m variable in the following line:

```
log file = /usr/local/logs/samba.log.%m
```

Isolating the log messages can be invaluable in tracking down a network error if you know the problem is coming from a specific client system or user.

We've added a precaution to the log files: no one log file can exceed 50 KB in size, as specified by the max log size option. If a log file exceeds this size, the contents are moved to a file with the same name but with the suffix *.old* appended. If the *.old* file already exists, it is overwritten and its contents are lost. The original file is cleared, waiting to receive new logging information. This prevents the hard drive from being overwhelmed with Samba log files during the life of the Samba daemons.

We have decided to write the timestamps of the messages in the logs with the debug timestamp option, which is the default behavior. This will place a timestamp in each message written to the logging file. If we were not interested in this information, we could specify no for this option instead.

Using syslog

If you wish to use the system logger (syslog) in addition to or in place of the standard Samba logging file, Samba provides options for this as well. However, to use syslog, the first thing you will have to do is make sure that Samba was built with the `configure --with-syslog` option. See Chapter 2 for more information on configuring and compiling Samba. See Appendix E for more information about the `--with-syslog` option.

Once that is done, you will need to configure your */etc/syslog.conf* to accept logging information from Samba. If there is not already a `daemon.*` entry in the */etc/syslog.conf* file, add the following:

```
daemon.*            /var/log/daemon.log
```

This specifies that any logging information from system daemons will be stored in the */var/log/daemon.log* file. This is where the Samba information will be stored as well. From there, you can set a value for the `syslog` parameter in your Samba configuration file to specify which logging messages are to be sent to syslog. Only messages that have debug levels lower than the value of the `syslog` parameter will be sent to syslog. For example, setting the following:

```
syslog = 3
```

specifies that any logging messages with a level of 2 or below will be sent to both syslog and the Samba logging files. (The mappings to *syslog* priorities are described in the upcoming section "syslog.") To continue the example, let's assume that we have set the `log level` option to 4. Logging messages with levels of 2 and 1 will be sent to both syslog and the Samba logging files, and messages with a level of 3 or 4 will be sent to the Samba logging files, but not to syslog. If the `syslog` value exceeds the `log level` value, nothing will be sent to syslog.

If you want to specify that messages be sent only to syslog—and not to the standard Samba logging files—you can place this option in the configuration file:

```
syslog only = yes
```

If this is the case, any logging information above the number specified in the `syslog` option will be discarded, as with the `log level` option.

Logging Configuration Options

Table 6-8 lists each logging configuration option that Samba can use.

Table 6-8. Logging configuration options

Option	Parameters	Function	Default	Scope
log file	string (name of file)	Name of the log file that Samba is to use. Works with all variables.	Specified in Samba makefile	Global
log level (debug level)	numeric (0–10)	Amount of log/debug messages that are sent to the log file. 0 is none; 3 is considerable.	1	Global
max log size	numeric (size in KB)	Maximum size of log file.	5000	Global

Table 6-8. Logging configuration options (continued)

Option	Parameters	Function	Default	Scope
debug timestamp (timestamp logs)	boolean	If no, doesn't timestamp logs, making them easier to read during heavy debugging.	yes	Global
syslog	numeric (0–10)	Level of messages sent to *syslog*. Those levels below syslog level will be sent to the system logger.	1	Global
syslog only	boolean	If yes, uses *syslog* entirely and sends no output to the Samba log files.	no	Global

log file

By default, Samba writes log information to text files in the */usr/local/samba/var* directory. The log file option can be used to set the name of the log file to another location. For example, to put the Samba log information in */usr/local/logs/samba.log*, you could use the following:

```
[global]
    log file = /usr/local/logs/samba.log
```

You can use variable substitution to create log files specifically for individual users or clients.

You can override the default log file location using the *-l* command-line switch when either daemon is started. However, this does not override the log file option. If you do specify this parameter, initial logging information will be sent to the file specified after *-l* (or the default specified in the Samba makefile) until the daemons have processed the *smb.conf* file and know to redirect it to a new log file.

log level

The log level option sets the amount of data to be logged. Normally this is set to 0 or 1. However, if you have a specific problem, you might want to set it at 3, which provides the most useful debugging information you would need to track down a problem. Levels above 3 provide information that's primarily for the developers to use for chasing internal bugs, and it slows down the server considerably. Therefore, we recommend that for normal day-to-day operation, you avoid setting this option to anything above 3.

max log size

The max log size option sets the maximum size, in kilobytes, of the debugging log file that Samba keeps. When the log file exceeds this size, the current log file is renamed to add a *.old* extension (erasing any previous file with that name) and a new debugging log file is started with the original name. For example:

```
[global]
    log file = /usr/local/logs/samba.log.%m
    max log size = 1000
```

Here, if the size of any log file exceeds 1MB, Samba renames the log file *samba.log.machine-name.old*, and a new log file is generated. If there is already a file with the *.old* extension, Samba deletes it. We highly recommend setting this option in your configuration files because debug logging (even at lower levels) can quietly eat away at your available disk space. Using this option protects unwary administrators from suddenly discovering that most of the space on a disk or partition has been swallowed up by a single Samba log file.

debug timestamp or timestamp logs

If you happen to be debugging a network problem and you find that the timestamp information within the Samba log lines gets in the way, you can turn it off by giving either the timestamp logs or the synonymous debug timestamp option a value of no. For example, a regular Samba log file presents its output in the following form:

```
12/31/01 12:03:34 toltec (172.16.1.1) connect to server network as user jay
```

With a no value for this option, the output would appear without the timestamp:

```
toltec (172.16.1.1) connect to server network as user jay
```

syslog

The syslog option causes Samba log messages to be sent to the Unix system logger. The type of log information to be sent is specified as a numeric value. Like the log level option, it can be a number from 0 to 10. Logging information with a level less than the number specified will be sent to the system logger. Debug logs greater than or equal to the syslog level, but less than log level, will still be sent to the standard Samba log files. For example:

```
[global]
    log level = 3
    syslog = 1
```

With this, all logging information with a level of 0 would be sent to the standard Samba logs and the system logger, while information with levels 1, 2, and 3 would be sent only to the standard Samba logs. Levels above 3 are not logged at all. All messages sent to the system logger are mapped to a priority level that the syslogd daemon understands, as shown in Table 6-9. The default level is 1.

Table 6-9. syslog priority conversion

Log level	syslog priority
0	LOG_ERR
1	LOG_WARNING
2	LOG_NOTICE

Table 6-9. syslog priority conversion (continued)

Log level	syslog priority
3	LOG_INFO
4 and above	LOG_DEBUG

If you wish to use *syslog*, you will have to run configure --with-syslog when compiling Samba, and you will need to configure your *etc/syslog.conf* to suit. (See the section "Using syslog," earlier in this chapter.)

syslog only

The syslog only option tells Samba not to use its own logging files at all and to use only the system logger. To enable this, specify the following option in the global section of the Samba configuration file:

```
[global]
    syslog only = yes
```

CHAPTER 7
Name Resolution and Browsing

Name resolution is critical to Samba's operation because names are used to find the servers that share files or printers. *Browsing* takes the task of finding servers to a new level of sophistication by allowing a user to delve down into a hierarchy of networks, domains, hosts, and services offered by each server.

While name resolution and browsing are not difficult to configure, some complexity is introduced by the variety of available name-resolution systems. Historically, Unix and other TCP/IP users have moved from a flat hosts file to the Domain Name System, with the Network Information System being another popular choice. Meanwhile, Microsoft has moved from a broadcasting system to a simple, LAN-only name server called WINS and ultimately to DNS.

The reason for going over that history is that all previous systems of name resolution are still in use today! Finding a host is so crucial to networking that sites want robust (if limited) name-resolution systems to fall back on in case the main system fails. Browsing is also complicated by the frequent need to show hosts in other subnets. This chapter shows you how to configure your network to handle name resolution and browsing any way you want.

Some of the differences between Unix and Microsoft networking implementations are the result of fundamental design goals. Unix networking was originally designed largely to implement a relatively formal group of systems that were assumed to be small in number, well-maintained, and highly available, that have static IP addresses, and that wouldn't physically move around from place to place. Bringing a new server online was a labor-intensive task, but it did not have to be performed frequently. In contrast, Windows networking was originally developed as a peer-to-peer collection of small personal computers on a single subnet, having no centrally or hierarchically organized structure.

SMB networking is dynamic. Computers are allowed to leave the network at any time, sometimes without warning, and also to join or rejoin the network at any time. Furthermore, any user in a Windows network can add a new shared resource to the network or remove a resource that he had previously added. The change in the network's configuration is handled automatically by the rest of the network without requiring a system administrator to take any action.

Name Resolution

TCP/IP networks identify systems by IP addresses and always associate these addresses with more human-readable text names. In Microsoft's earliest networking implementations (for MS-DOS and Windows for Workgroups), the translation of names to network addresses was carried out in a manner that was very simple, yet very inefficient. When a system on the network needed an IP address corresponding to a name, it broadcasted the name to every other system on the network and waited for the system that owned the name to respond with its IP address.

The main problem with performing name resolution using broadcast packets is poor performance of the network as a whole, including CPU time consumed by each host on the network, which has to accept every broadcast packet and decide whether to respond to it. Also, broadcast packets usually aren't forwarded by routers, limiting name resolution to the local subnet. Microsoft's solution was to add WINS (Windows Internet Name Service) support to Windows NT so that the computers on the network can perform a direct query of the WINS server instead of using broadcast packets.

Modern Windows clients use a variety of methods for translating hostnames into IP addresses. The exact method varies depending on the version of Windows the client is running, how the client is configured (i.e., whether DNS server and/or WINS server IP addresses are provided), and whether the application software is accessing the network through Microsoft's Winsock or TCP/IP API. In general, Windows uses some combination of the following methods:

- Looking up the name in its cache of recently resolved names
- Querying DNS servers
- Using the DNS *Hosts* file
- Querying WINS servers
- Using the WINS *LMHOSTS* file
- Performing broadcast name resolution

The first method is pretty much self-explanatory. A hostname is checked against a cache of hostnames that have been recently resolved to IP addresses. This helps to save time and network bandwidth for resolving names that are used frequently.

When a Windows system is configured with the IP address of at least one DNS server, it can use DNS to resolve fully qualified domain names, such as those for sites on the Internet. The DNS servers can be either Windows NT/2000 or Unix systems.

You can learn more about DNS and DNS server configuration in the O'Reilly book *DNS and BIND*.

In this chapter, we focus mainly on name resolution using WINS, which is supported by Samba with the *nmbd* daemon.

WINS Clients and Server Interaction

There are two types of interaction between a WINS client and a server: the client keeps its own NetBIOS name* registered with the server and queries the server to get the IP address corresponding to the NetBIOS name of another system.

When a WINS client joins the network, it registers its NetBIOS name with the WINS server, which stores it along with the client's IP address in the WINS database. This entry is marked *active*. The client is then expected to renew the registration of its name periodically (typically, every four days) to inform the server that it is still using the name. This period is called the *time to live*, or TTL. When the client leaves the network by being shut down gracefully, it informs the server, and the server marks the client's entry in its database as *released*.

When a client leaves the network without telling the WINS server to release its name, the server waits until after it fails to receive the expected registration renewal from the client and then marks the entry as released.

In either case, the released name is available for use by other clients joining the network. It might persist in the released state in the WINS database, and if it is not reregistered, the entry will eventually be deleted.

More information on WINS can be found in the Microsoft white paper *Windows Internet Naming Service (WINS) Architecture and Capacity Planning*. It can be downloaded from the Microsoft web site at *http://www.microsoft.com*.

The lmhosts File

In Chapter 3 we showed you how to configure Windows systems to use the *LMHOSTS* file as an alternative to the WINS server for name resolution. Samba also can use an *LMHOSTS* file, which by default is */usr/local/samba/lib/lmhosts*. Samba's *lmhosts* is the same format as the Windows version. A simple *lmhosts* file might look like this:

```
172.16.1.1    toltec
172.16.1.6    maya
```

---

* As we explained in Chapter 1, a system can register under more than one NetBIOS name. We use the singular here only to keep our explanation simple.

The names on the right side of the entries are NetBIOS names, so you can assign resource types to them and add additional entries for computers:

```
172.16.1.1    toltec#20
172.16.1.1    metran#1b
172.16.1.6    maya#20
```

Here, we've made toltec the primary domain controller of the METRAN domain on the second line. This line starts with toltec's IP address, followed by the name metran and the resource type <1B>. The other lines are entries for toltec and maya as standard workstations.

If you wish to place an *lmhosts* file somewhere other than the default location, you will need to notify the *nmbd* process upon startup using the *-H* option, followed by the name of your *lmhosts* file, as follows:

```
# nmbd -H /etc/samba/lmhosts -D
```

Configuring Name Resolution for the Samba Suite

Various daemons and tools in the Samba suite need to perform name resolution. You can define the order in which the programs try each name-resolution method through the name resolve order parameter, like this:

```
[global]
    name resolve order = wins lmhosts hosts bcast
```

The string used to define the parameter can take up to four values:

lmhosts
> Uses the Samba server's local *lmhosts* file

hosts
> Uses the standard Unix name-resolution methods, which can be */etc/hosts*, DNS, NIS, or a combination, depending on how the local system is configured

wins
> Uses the WINS server

bcast
> Uses the broadcast method

The order in which they are specified is the order in which name resolution will be attempted. In our example, Samba will attempt to use its WINS server first for name resolution, followed by the *lmhosts* file on the local system. Next, the hosts value tells it to use Unix name-resolution methods. The word hosts can be misleading; it covers not only the */etc/hosts* file, but also the use of DNS or NIS (as configured on the Unix host). Finally, if those three do not work, it will perform a broadcast name resolution.

Setting Up Samba as a WINS Server

You can set up Samba as a WINS server by setting the wins support parameter in the configuration file, like this:

```
[global]
    wins support = yes
```

Believe it or not, that's all you need to do! The wins support option turns Samba into a WINS server. For most installations, Samba's default configuration is sufficient.

 Remember, Samba cannot communicate with Windows WINS servers. If you are using Samba as your WINS server, you must make sure not to allow any Windows systems or other Samba servers on your network to be configured as WINS servers. If you do, their WINS databases will not synchronize, resulting in inconsistent name resolution.

Configuring a DNS proxy

A Samba WINS server can check with the system's DNS server if a requested host cannot be found in its WINS database. With a typical Linux system, for example, you can find the IP address of the DNS server by searching the */etc/resolv.conf* file. In it, you might see an entry such as the following:

```
nameserver 127.0.0.1
nameserver 172.16.1.192
```

This tells us that the Linux system is configured to use a DNS server located at 172.16.1.192. (The 127.0.0.1 is the localhost address and is never a valid DNS server address.)

Now it is a simple matter of using the dns proxy option to tell Samba to use the DNS server:

```
[global]
    dns proxy = yes
```

 Although this allows Windows clients to resolve fully qualified Internet domain names through the Samba WINS server, it will work only for domain names that fit within the 15-character limitation of NetBIOS names. For this reason, we recommend you use dns proxy only to act as a supplement to your WINS server, rather than as a replacement for a DNS server.

Setting Up Samba to Use Another WINS Server

You can configure Samba to use a WINS server somewhere else on the network by simply providing it with the IP address of the WINS server. This is done with the global wins server configuration option, as shown here:

```
[global]
    wins server = 172.16.1.1
```

With this option enabled, Samba will direct all WINS requests to the server located at 172.16.1.1. Note that because the request is directed at a single machine, we don't have to worry about any of the problems inherent in broadcasting. However, Samba will not necessarily use the WINS server before other forms of name resolution. The order in which Samba attempts various name-resolution techniques is given with the name resolve order configuration option, which we discussed earlier.

The wins support and the wins server parameters are mutually exclusive; you cannot simultaneously offer Samba as the WINS server and use another system as the server! Typically, one Samba server is set up as the WINS server using wins support, and all other Samba servers are configured with the wins server parameter pointing to the Samba WINS server.

Configuring a WINS proxy

If you have a Samba server on a subnet that doesn't have a WINS server, and the Samba server has been configured with a WINS server on another subnet, you can tell the Samba server to forward any name-resolution requests with the wins proxy option:

```
[global]
    wins server = 172.16.200.12
    wins proxy = yes
```

Use this only in situations where the WINS server resides on another subnet. Otherwise, the broadcast will reach the WINS server regardless of any proxying.

Name-Resolution Configuration Options

Samba's name-resolution options are shown in Table 7-1.

Table 7-1. Name-resolution options

Option	Parameters	Function	Default	Scope
wins support	boolean	If set to yes, allows Samba to act as a WINS server	no	Global
wins server	string (IP address or DNS name)	Identifies a WINS server for Samba to use for name registration and resolution	None	Global
wins proxy	boolean	Allows Samba to act as a proxy to a WINS server on another subnet	no	Global
wins hook	string	Command to run when the WINS database changes	None	Global
dns proxy	boolean	If set to yes, allows a Samba WINS server to search DNS if it cannot find a name in WINS	no	Global

Table 7-1. Name-resolution options (continued)

Option	Parameters	Function	Default	Scope
name resolve order	string	The order of methods used to resolve Net-BIOS names	lmhosts hosts wins bcast	Global
max ttl	numeric	Maximum TTL in seconds for a requested NetBIOS name	259200 (3 days)	Global
max wins ttl	numeric	Maximum TTL in seconds for NetBIOS names given out by Samba as a WINS server	518400 (6 days)	Global
min wins ttl	numeric	Minimum TTL in seconds for NetBIOS names given out by Samba as a WINS server	21600 (6 hours)	Global

wins support

Samba will provide WINS name service to all machines in the network if you set the following in the [global] section of the *smb.conf* file:

```
[global]
    wins support = yes
```

The default value is no, which is typically used to allow a Windows NT/2000 server or another Samba server to be the WINS server. If you enable this option, remember that a Samba WINS server currently cannot exchange data with other WINS servers, so do not allow any other WINS servers on the network. When set to yes, this option is mutually exclusive with the wins server parameter.

wins server

Samba will use an existing WINS server on the network if you specify the wins server global option in your configuration file. The value of this option is either the IP address or DNS name (not NetBIOS name) of the WINS server. For example:

```
[global]
    wins server = 172.16.220.110
```

or:

```
[global]
    wins server = wins.metran.cx
```

For this option to work, the wins support option must be set to no (the default). Otherwise, Samba will report an error. You can specify only one WINS server using this option.

wins proxy

This option allows Samba to act as a proxy to another WINS server, and thus relay name registration and resolution requests from itself to the real WINS server, often outside the current subnet. The WINS server can be indicated through the wins server option. The proxy will then return the WINS response back to the client. You can enable this option by specifying the following in the [global] section:

```
[global]
    wins proxy = yes
```

wins hook

This option allows you to run a script or other program whenever the WINS database is modified. One application might be to set up another Samba server to act as a backup for another Samba WINS server. This is done by having the wins hook script call *rsync* to synchronize the WINS databases (*/usr/local/samba/var/locks/wins.dat*) on the two systems whenever an entry is added or deleted. The script would be specified in the Samba configuration file like this:

```
[global]
    wins hook = /usr/local/bin/sync_wins
```

dns proxy

If you want the DNS to be used if a NetBIOS name isn't found in WINS, you can set the following option:

```
[global]
    dns proxy = yes
```

This will permit *nmbd* to query the server's standard DNS. You might wish to deactivate this option if you do not have a permanent connection to your DNS server. This option should not be used in place of a DNS server on your network; it is intended for resolving NetBIOS names rather than fully qualified Internet domain names.

name resolve order

The global name resolve order option specifies the order of services that Samba will use in performing name resolution. The default order is to use the *lmhosts* file, followed by standard Unix name-resolution methods (some combination of */etc/hosts*, DNS, and NIS), then to query a WINS server, and finally to use broadcasting to determine the address of a NetBIOS name. You can override this option by specifying something like the following:

```
[global]
    name resolve order = lmhosts wins hosts bcast
```

This causes resolution to use the *lmhosts* file first, followed by a query to a WINS server, the */etc/hosts* file, and finally broadcasting. You need not use all four options. This option is covered in more detail in the section "Setting Up Samba as a WINS Server," earlier in this chapter.

max ttl

This option is used when Samba is not acting as a WINS server but is using another system on the network for its WINS server. It sets the maximum TTL for NetBIOS names registered by the Samba server with the WINS server. You should never need to alter this value.

max wins ttl

This option is used when Samba is providing WINS name service, and it sets the maximum TTL for NetBIOS names registered with Samba. You should never need to change this value from its default.

min wins ttl

This option is used when Samba is providing WINS name service, and it sets the minimum TTL for NetBIOS names registered with Samba. You should never need to alter this value from its default.

Browsing

Browsing was developed by Microsoft to help users find shared resources on the network. In a networked computing environment where users can add or remove shares at any time, it is important to have some automatic means of keeping track of the shared resources and allowing users to "browse" through them to find the ones they wish to use.

Before browsing was added to SMB networking, when anyone added a new share, the people with whom they wished to share the data or printer would have to be informed of the share's UNC, using some relatively low-tech method such as speaking to them in person or over the phone, or sending email. Already, this was very inconvenient in large organizations. To further complicate matters, the users working on client computers had to type in the share's UNC to connect to it. The only way to get around typing in the share's UNC every time it was used was to map a network drive to it, and with a large number of shares on the network, this could easily get out of hand.

Browsing in a Windows Network

To keep things simple, we will first describe network browsing in a network that contains only Windows systems and then show you how to add a Samba server.

The basic way browsing works is that one computer in the network takes on the role of the *master browser* (also called *local master browser*, *browse master*, or *browse server*) and keeps a list of all the computers on the local subnet that are acting as SMB servers. The list of computers is called the *browse list* and includes all Samba

---

servers, Windows NT/2000/XP systems, and any Windows 95/98/Me systems that have the "File and printer sharing for Microsoft Networks" networking component installed. The browse list also contains the names of all workgroups and domains. At this level, browsing is limited to the local subnet because the browsing protocol depends on broadcast packets, which are typically not forwarded to other subnets by routers.

A user at any Windows system can view the browse list by opening up the Network Neighborhood (or My Network Places), as we showed you in Chapter 1. Or, the *net view* command can be used from a Windows command prompt:

```
C:\>net view
Server Name              Remark


-------------------------------------------------------------------------------
\\MAYA                   Windows 98
\\MIXTEC                 Samba 2.2.5
\\OLMEC                  Windows XP Pro on Pentium/ASUS
\\TOLTEC                 Samba 2.2.5
\\YAQUI                  Windows 95 on mixtec/VMware
\\ZAPOTEC
The command completed successfully.
```

Then, *net view* can be used with a computer name as an argument to contact a server directly and list the resources it is sharing:

```
C:\>net view \\maya
Shared resources at \\maya

Windows 98

Share name   Type      Used as   Comment

-------------------------------------------------------------------------------
D            Disk
E            Disk
HP           Print
The command completed successfully.
```

The computers on the network involved in browsing are more than just the master browser and its clients. There are also backup browsers, which maintain copies of the browse list and respond to client requests for it. Backup browsers are therefore able to take over the role of master browser seamlessly in case it fails. The master browser usually doesn't serve the browse list directly to clients. Instead, its job is mainly to keep the master copy of the browse list up-to-date, and also periodically update the backup browsers. Clients are expected to get their copies of the browse list from backup browsers, selecting among them randomly to help to distribute the load on the backup browsers more evenly. Ideally, the interaction between any client and the master browser is limited to the client announcing when it joins or leaves the network (if it is a server) and requesting a list of backup browsers.

There can be more than one backup browser. A workgroup will have a backup browser if two or more computers are running Windows 95/98/Me or Windows NT Workstation (or another nonserver version of Windows NT/2000/XP) on the subnet. For every 32 additional computers, another backup browser is added.

In a Windows NT domain, the primary domain controller is always the local master browser, and if it fails, another Windows NT/2000 server (if one exists) will take over the role of local master browser. Other versions of Windows can function as backup browsers, but will never become a master browser if a Windows NT/2000 server is available.

In addition to acting as the local master browser, the primary domain controller also acts as the *domain master browser*, which ties subnets together and allows browse lists to be shared between master and backup browsers on separate subnets. This is how browsing is extended to function beyond the local subnet. Each subnet functions as a separate browsing entity, and the domain master browser synchronizes the master browsers of each subnet. In a Windows-only network, browsing cannot function across subnets unless a Windows NT/2000 PDC exists on the network. Samba can act as a domain master browser and can perform that task even in a workgroup network, which means that the Windows PDC is not required for this task. (It is also possible to use the remote browse sync parameter to configure a Samba server to synchronize its browse list with a Samba server on another subnet. In this case, each server must be acting as the local master browser of its subnet.)

Unless it is configured never to act as a browser, each computer on the subnet is considered a *potential browser* and can be ordered by the browse master to become a backup browser, or it can identify itself as a backup browser and accept the role on its own.

Browser Elections

When no master browser is running on the subnet, potential browsers choose a new master browser among themselves in a process called an *election*. An election is started by a computer in the subnet when it discovers that no master browser is currently running. If a master browser is shut down gracefully, it will broadcast an election request datagram, initiating an election by the remaining computers. If the master browser fails, the election can be started by a client computer that requests a list of backup browsers from the master browser or by a backup browser that requests to have its browse list updated from the master browser. In each case, the system fails to receive a reply from the master browser and initiates the election.

Browser elections are decided in multiple rounds of self-elimination. During each round, potential browsers broadcast election request datagrams containing their qualifications to notify other potential browsers that an election is happening and that if the recipient is more qualified, it should also broadcast a bid. When a potential browser receives an election request datagram from a more qualified opponent, it drops out, disqualifying itself from becoming the master browser. Otherwise, it responds with its own election request datagram. After a few rounds, only one potential browser is left in the election. After an additional four rounds of sending out an election request datagram and receiving no response, it becomes the master browser and sends a broadcast datagram announcing itself as the local master browser for the subnet. It then assigns runners-up in the election as backup browsers, as needed.

A potential browser's qualifications include the following:

- Whether it has recently lost an election
- The version of the election protocol it is running
- Its election criteria
- The amount of time the system has been up
- The computer's NetBIOS name

If the potential browser has lost an election recently, it immediately disqualifies itself. The version of the election protocol it is running is checked, but so far, all Windows systems (and Samba) use the same election protocol, so the check is not very meaningful. The election criteria are usually what determine which computer becomes the local master browser. There are two parts to the election criteria, shown in Tables 7-2 and 7-3.

Table 7-2. Operating-system values in an election

Operating system	Value
Windows NT/2000 Server, running as PDC	32
Windows NT/2000/XP, if not the PDC	16
Windows 95/98/Me	1
Windows for Workgroups	1

Table 7-3. Computer-role settings in an election

Role	Value
Domain master browser	128
WINS client	32
Preferred master	8
Running master	4
Recent backup browser	2
Backup browser	1

The operating-system type is compared first, and the system with the highest value wins. The values have been chosen to cause the primary domain controller, if there is one, to become the local master browser. Otherwise, a Windows NT/2000/XP system will win over a Windows for Workgroups or Windows 95/98/Me system.

When an operating-system type comparison results in a tie, the role of the computer is compared. A computer can have more than one of the values in Table 7-3, in which case the values are added.

A domain master browser has a role value of 128 to weight the election so heavily in its favor that it will also become the local master browser on its own subnet. Although the primary domain controller (which is always the domain master browser) will win the election based solely on its operating system value, sometimes there is no primary domain controller on the network, and the domain master browser would not otherwise be distinguished from other potential browsers.

Systems that are using a WINS server for name resolution are weighted heavily over ones that use broadcast name resolution with a role value of 32.

A *preferred master* is a computer that has been selected and configured manually by a system administrator to be favored as the choice master browser. When a preferred master starts up, it forces a browser election, even if an existing master browser is still active. A preferred master has a role value of 8, and the existing master browser gets a value of 4.

A backup browser that has recently been a master browser and still has an up-to-date browse list is given a role value of 2, and a potential browser that has been running as a backup browser gets a value of 1.

If comparing the operating-system type and role results in a tie, the computer that has been running the longest wins. In the unlikely event that the two have been up for the same amount of time, the computer that wins is the one with the NetBIOS name that sorts first alphabetically.

You can tell if a machine is a local master browser by using the Windows *nbtstat* command. Place the NetBIOS name of the machine you wish to check after the *-a* option:

```
C:\>nbtstat -a toltec

Local Area Connection:
Node IpAddress: [172.16.1.4] Scope Id: []

        NetBIOS Remote Machine Name Table

    Name               Type         Status
    ---------------------------------------------
    TOLTEC        <00>  UNIQUE       Registered
    TOLTEC        <03>  UNIQUE       Registered
    TOLTEC        <20>  UNIQUE       Registered
    .._MSBROWSE__.<01>  GROUP        Registered
    METRAN        <00>  GROUP        Registered
    METRAN        <1B>  UNIQUE       Registered
```

```
METRAN          <1C>  GROUP       Registered
METRAN          <1D>  UNIQUE      Registered
METRAN          <1E>  GROUP       Registered

MAC Address = 00-00-00-00-00-00
```

The resource entry that you're looking for is ..__MSBROWSE__.<01>. This indicates that the server is currently acting as the local master browser for the current subnet. If the machine is a Samba server, you can check the Samba *nmbd* log file for an entry such as:

```
nmbd/nmbd_become_lmb.c:become_local_master_stage2(406)
*****
Samba name server TOLTEC is now a local master browser for
workgroup METRAN on subnet 172.16.1.0
```

Or, you can use the *nmblookup* command with the -M option and the workgroup or domain name on any Samba server to find the IP address of the local master:

```
$ nmblookup -M metran
querying metran on 172.16.1.255
172.16.1.1 metran<1d>
```

Server Announcements

After the master browser election is decided, each server on the network announces itself to the network to allow the master and backup browsers to build their browse lists. At first, the server announcements happen every minute, but the interval is gradually stretched out to every 12 minutes. When a server is shut down gracefully, it sends an announcement that it is going offline to allow the master and backup browsers to remove it from the browse list. However, when a server goes offline by crashing or by some other failure, the master browser notices its disappearance only because it stops receiving server announcements. The master browser waits for three of the server's announcement periods before deciding that it is offline, which can take up to 36 minutes. Because backup browsers have their browse lists updated from the master browser once every 15 minutes, it can take up to 51 minutes for clients to be informed of a failed server.

For more detailed information on Microsoft's browsing protocols, consult the Microsoft documents *Browsing and Windows 95 Networking* and *CIFS/E Browser Protocol*. You can find these by searching for the titles on the Microsoft web site at *http://www.microsoft.com*.

More information on configuring Samba for browsing can be found in *BROWSING.txt* and *BROWSING-Config.txt* in the Samba distribution's *docs/textdocs* directory.

Configuring Samba for Browsing

Samba has full support for browsing and can participate as a master browser, a backup browser, a domain master browser, a potential browser, or just a server that doesn't participate in browsing elections. If you want to make sure your Samba server never becomes a master or backup browser, simply set:

```
[global]
    local master = no
```

Usually, you will want Samba to be available as a local master or at least a backup browser. In the simplest case, you don't need to do anything because Samba's default is to participate in browsing elections with its operating system value set to 20, which will beat any Windows system less than a Windows NT/2000 primary domain controller (see Table 7-2). The operating-system value Samba reports for itself in browser elections can be set using the os level parameter:

```
[global]
    os level = 33
```

The preceding value will allow Samba to beat even a Windows 2000 Advanced Server acting as a primary domain controller. As we show in the following section, though, forcing Samba to win this way is not recommended.

If you want to allow a Windows XP Professional system to be the master browser, you would need to set Samba lower:

```
[global]
    os level = 8
```

The maximum value for os level is 255 because it is handled as an 8-bit unsigned integer. Supposing we wanted to make absolutely sure our Samba server will be the local master browser at all times, we might say:

```
[global]
    local master = yes
    os level = 255
    preferred master = yes
```

The addition of the preferred master parameter causes Samba to start a browser election as soon as it starts up, and the os level of 255 allows it to beat any other system on the network. This includes other Samba servers, assuming they are configured properly! If another server is using a similar configuration file (with os level = 255 and preferred master = yes), the two will fight each other for the master browser role, winning elections based on minor criteria, such as uptime or their current role. To avoid this, other Samba servers should be set with a lower os level and not configured to be the preferred master.

Samba as the Domain Master Browser

Previously we mentioned that for a Windows workgroup or domain to extend into multiple subnets, one system would have to take the role of the domain master browser. The domain master browser propagates browse lists across each subnet in the workgroup. This works because each local master browser periodically synchronizes its browse list with the domain master browser. During this synchronization, the local master browser passes on the name of any server that the domain master browser does not have in its browse list, and vice versa. Each local master browser eventually holds the browse list for the entire domain.

There is no election to determine which machine assumes the role of the domain master browser. Instead, the administrator has to set it manually. By Microsoft design, however, the domain master browser and the PDC both register a resource type of <1B>, so the roles—and the machines—are inseparable.

If you have a Windows NT server on the network acting as a PDC, we recommend that you do not try to use Samba to become the domain master browser. The reverse is true as well: if Samba is taking on the responsibilities of a PDC, we recommend making it the domain master browser as well. Although it is possible to split the roles with Samba, this is not a good idea. Using two different machines to serve as the PDC and the domain master browser can cause random errors to occur in a Windows workgroup.

Samba can assume the role of a domain master browser for all subnets in the workgroup with the following options:

```
[global]
        domain master = yes
        preferred master = yes
        local master = yes
        os level = 255
```

The final three parameters ensure that the server is also the local master browser, which is vital for it to work properly as the domain master browser. You can verify that a Samba machine is in fact the domain master browser by checking the *nmbd* log file:

```
nmbd/nmbd_become_dmb.c:become_domain_master_stage2(118)
*****
Samba name server TOLTEC is now a domain master browser for
workgroup METRAN on subnet 172.16.1.0
```

Or you can use the *nmblookup* command that comes with the Samba distribution to query for a unique <1B> resource type in the workgroup:

```
# nmblookup METRAN#1B
Sending queries to 172.16.1.255
172.16.1.1 METRAN<1b>
```

Multiple subnets

You must remember three rules when creating a workgroup/domain that spans more than one subnet:

- You must have either a Windows NT/2000 or Samba server acting as a local master browser on each subnet in the workgroup/domain.

- You must have a Windows NT/2000 Server edition or a Samba server acting as a domain master browser somewhere in the workgroup/domain.

- A WINS server should be on the network, with each system on the network configured to use it for name resolution.

Samba has some additional features you can use if you don't have or want a domain master browser on your network and still need to have cross-subnet browsing. Consider the subnets shown in Figure 7-1.

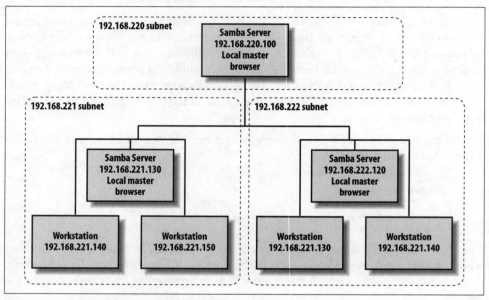

Figure 7-1. Multiple subnets with Samba servers

First, a Samba server that is a local master browser can use the remote announce configuration option to make sure that computers in different subnets are sent broadcast announcements about the server. This has the effect of ensuring that the Samba server appears in the browse lists of foreign subnets. To achieve this, however, the directed broadcasts must reach the local master browser on the other subnet. Be aware that many routers do not allow directed broadcasts by default; you might have to change this setting on the router for the directed broadcasts to get through to its subnet.

With the remote announce option, list the subnets and the workgroup that should receive the broadcast. For example, to ensure that machines in the 172.16.2 and 172.16.3 subnets and the METRAN workgroup are sent broadcast information from our Samba server, we could specify the following:

```
[global]
    remote announce = 172.16.2.255/METRAN \
        172.16.3.255/METRAN
```

Instead of supplying a broadcast address of the remote subnet, you are allowed to specify the exact address where broadcasts should be sent if the local master browser on the foreign subnet is guaranteed to always have the same IP address.

A Samba local master browser can synchronize its browse list directly with one or more Samba servers, each acting as a local master browser on a different subnet. This is another way to implement browsing across subnets. For example, let's assume that Samba is configured as a local master browser, and Samba local master browsers exist at 172.16.2.130 and 172.16.3.120. We can use the remote browse sync option to sync directly with the Samba servers, as follows:

```
[global]
        remote browse sync = 172.16.2.130 172.16.3.120
```

For this to work, the other Samba machines must also be local master browsers. You can also use directed broadcasts with this option if you do not know specific IP addresses of local master browsers.

Making a Share Invisible

You can keep a share from being in the browse list by using the browsable option. This Boolean option prevents a share from being seen in the Network Neighborhood or My Network Places. For example, to prevent the [data] share from being visible, we could write:

```
[data]
        path = /export/samba/userdata
        browsable = no
```

Although you typically don't want to do this to an ordinary disk share, the browsable option is useful in the event that you need to create a share with contents that you do not want others to see, such as a [netlogon] share for storing logon scripts for Windows domain control (see Chapter 4 for more information on logon scripts).

Another example is the [homes] share. This share is often marked nonbrowsable so that a share named [homes] won't appear when its machine's resources are browsed. However, if a user alice logs on and looks at the machine's shares, an [alice] share will appear under the machine.

What if we wanted to make sure alice's share appeared to everyone before she logs on? This could be done with the global auto services option. This option preloads shares into the browse list to ensure that they are always visible:

```
[global]
        auto services = alice
```

Browsing Options

Table 7-4 shows options that define how Samba handles browsing tasks.

Table 7-4. Browsing configuration options

Option	Parameters	Function	Default	Scope
announce as	string	Operating system that Samba will announce itself as.	NT Server	Global
announce version	numeric	Version of the operating system that Samba will announce itself as.	4.5	Global
browsable (browseable)	Boolean	Allows share to be displayed in list of machine resources.	yes	Share
browse list	Boolean	If yes, allows Samba to provide a browse list on this server.	yes	Global
auto services (preload)	string (share list)	List of shares that will always appear in the browse list.	None	Global
default service (default)	string (share name)	Name of a share (service) that will be provided if the client requests a share not listed in *smb.conf*.	None	Global
local master	Boolean	If yes, allows Samba to participate in browsing elections.	yes	Global
lm announce	yes, no, or auto	Enables or disables LAN Manager–style host announcements.	auto	Global
lm interval	numeric	Frequency in seconds that LAN Manager announcements will be made if activated.	60	Global
preferred master (prefered master)	Boolean	If yes, allows Samba to use the preferred master browser bit to attempt to become the local master browser.	no	Global
domain master	Boolean	If yes, allows Samba to become the domain browser master for the workgroup or domain.	no	Global
os level	numeric	Operating system level of Samba in an election for local master browser.	0	Global
remote browse sync	string (list of IP addresses)	Samba servers to synchronize browse lists with.	None	Global
remote announce	string (IP address/ workgroup pairs)	Subnets and workgroups to send directed broadcast packets to, allowing Samba to appear in their browse lists.	None	Global

announce as

This global configuration option specifies the type of operating system that Samba announces to other machines on the network. The default value for this option is NT Server, which causes Samba to masquerade as a Windows NT Server operating system. Other possible values are NT, NT Workstation, Win95, and WfW for a Windows for Workgroup operating system. You can override the default value with the following:

```
[global]
    announce as = Win95
```

We recommend against changing the default value of this configuration option.

---

announce version

This global option is frequently used with the announce as configuration option; it specifies the version of the operating system that Samba announces to other machines on the network. The default value of this option is 4.5, which places Samba above Windows NT Version 4.0, but below Windows 2000. You can specify a new value with a global entry such as the following:

```
[global]
    announce version = 4.3
```

We recommend against changing the default value of this configuration option.

browsable

The browsable option (also spelled browseable) indicates whether the share referenced should appear in the list of available resources for the system on which it resides. This option is always set to yes by default. If you wish to prevent the share from being seen in a client's browser, you can reset this option to no.

Note that this does not prevent someone from accessing the share using other means, such as specifying a UNC location (e.g., \\server\accounting) in Windows Explorer. It only prevents the share from being listed under the system's resources when being browsed.

browse list

You should never need to change this parameter from its default value of yes. If your Samba server is acting as a local master browser (i.e., it has won the browsing election), you can use the global browse list option to instruct Samba to provide or withhold its browse list to all clients. By default, Samba always provides a browse list. You can withhold this information by specifying the following:

```
[global]
    browse list = no
```

If you disable the browse list, clients cannot browse the names of other machines, their services, and other domains currently available on the network. Note that this won't make any particular machine inaccessible; if someone knows a valid machine name/address and a share on that machine, he can still connect to it explicitly using the Windows *net use* command or by mapping a drive letter to it using Windows Explorer. It simply prevents information in the browse list from being retrieved by any client that requests it.

auto services

The global auto services option, which is also called preload, ensures that the specified shares are always visible in the browse list. One common use for this option is to advertise specific user or printer shares that are created by the [homes] or [printers] shares, but are not otherwise browsable.

This option works best with disk shares. If you wish to force each of your system printers (i.e., those listed in the printer capabilities file) to appear in the browse list, we recommend using the load printers option instead.

Shares listed with the auto services option will not be displayed if the browse list option is set to no.

default service

The global default service option (sometimes called default) names a "last-ditch" share. The value is set to an existing share name without the enclosing brackets. When a client requests a nonexistent disk or printer share, Samba will attempt to connect the user to the share specified by this option instead. The option is specified as follows:

```
[global]
    default service = helpshare
```

When Samba redirects the requested, nonexistent service to the service specified by default service, the %S option takes on the value of the requested service, with any underscores (_) in the requested service replaced by forward slashes (/).

local master

This global option specifies whether Samba will attempt to become the local master browser for the subnet when it starts up. If this option is set to yes, Samba will participate in elections. However, setting this option by itself does not guarantee victory. (Other parameters, such as preferred master and os level, help Samba win browsing elections.) If this option is set to no, Samba will lose all browsing elections, regardless of which values are specified by the other configuration options. The default value is yes.

lm announce

The global lm announce option tells Samba's *nmbd* whether to send LAN Manager host announcements on behalf of the server. These host announcements might be required by older clients, such as IBM's OS/2 operating system. This announcement allows the server to be added to the browse lists of the client. If activated, Samba will announce itself repetitively at the number of seconds specified by the lm interval option.

You can specify the option as follows:

```
[global]
    lm announce = yes
```

This configuration option takes the standard Boolean values, yes and no, which enable or disable LAN Manager announcements, respectively. In addition, a third option, auto, causes *nmbd* to listen passively for LAN Manager announcements, but not to send any of its own initially. If LAN Manager announcements are detected for another machine on the network, *nmbd* will start sending its own LAN Manager announcements to ensure that it is visible. The default value is auto. You probably won't need to change this value from its default.

lm interval

This option, which is used in conjunction with lm announce, indicates the number of seconds *nmbd* will wait before repeatedly broadcasting LAN Manager–style announcements. LAN Manager announcements must be enabled for this option to work. The default value is 60 seconds. If you set this value to 0, Samba will not send any LAN Manager host announcements, regardless of the value of the lm announce option. You can reset the value of this option as follows:

```
[global]
    lm interval = 90
```

preferred master

The preferred master option requests that Samba set the preferred master bit when participating in an election. This gives the server a higher preferred status in the workgroup than other machines at the same operating-system level. If you are configuring your Samba machine to become the local master browser, it is wise to set the following value:

```
[global]
    preferred master = yes
```

Otherwise, you should leave it set to its default, no. If Samba is configured as a preferred master browser, it will force an election when it first comes online.

domain master

If Samba is the primary domain controller for your workgroup or NT domain, it should also be made the domain master browser. The domain master browser is a special machine that has the NetBIOS resource type <1B> and is used to propagate browse lists to and from each local master browser in individual subnets across the domain. To force Samba to become the domain master browser, set the following in the [global] section of the *smb.conf*:

```
[global]
    domain master = yes
```

If you have a Windows NT server on the network acting as a primary domain controller (PDC), we recommend that you do not use Samba to become the domain master browser. The reverse is true as well: if Samba is taking on the responsibilities of a

PDC, we recommend making it the domain master browser. Splitting the PDC and the domain master browser will cause unpredictable errors to occur on the network.

os level

The global os level option defines the operating-system value with which Samba will masquerade during a browser election. If you wish to have Samba win an election and become the master browser, set the os level higher than that of any other system on the subnet. The values are shown in Table 7-2. The default level is 20, which means that Samba will win elections against all versions of Windows, except Windows NT/2000 if it is operating as the PDC. If you wish Samba to win all elections, you can set its operating system value as follows:

```
[global]
    os level = 255
```

remote browse sync

The global remote browse sync option specifies that Samba should synchronize its browse lists with local master browsers in other subnets. However, the synchronization can occur only with other Samba servers and not with Windows computers. For example, if your Samba server were a master browser on the subnet 172.16.235, and Samba local master browsers existed on other subnets located at 172.16.234.92 and 172.16.236.2, you would specify the following:

```
[global]
    remote browse sync = 172.16.234.92 172.16.236.2
```

The Samba server would then directly contact the other machines on the address list and synchronize browse lists. You can also say:

```
[global]
    remote browse sync = 172.16.234.255 172.16.236.255
```

This forces Samba to broadcast queries to determine the IP addresses of the local master browser on each subnet, with which it will then synchronize browse lists. This works, however, only if your router doesn't block directed broadcast requests ending in 255.

remote announce

Samba servers are capable of providing browse lists to foreign subnets with the remote announce option. This is typically sent to the local master browser of the foreign subnet in question. However, if you do not know the address of the local master browser, you can do the following:

```
[global]
    remote announce = 172.16.234.255/ACCOUNTING \
                      172.16.236.255/ACCOUNTING
```

With this, Samba will broadcast host announcements to all machines on subnets 172.16.234 and 172.16.236, which will hopefully reach the local master browser of the subnet.

You can also specify exact IP addresses, if they are known, but this works only if the systems are guaranteed to maintain the role of master browser on their subnets. By appending a workgroup or domain name to the IP address, Samba announces that it is in that workgroup or domain. If this is left out, the workgroup set by the workgroup parameter is used.

## CHAPTER 8

Advanced Disk Shares

This chapter continues our discussion of configuring Samba from Chapter 6. We will cover some more advanced issues regarding the integration of Unix and Windows filesystems, including hidden files, Unix links, file permissions, name mangling, case sensitivity of filenames, file locking, opportunistic locking (oplocks), connection scripts, supporting Microsoft Dfs (Distributed filesystem) shares, and using NIS home directories.

Filesystem Differences

One of the biggest issues for which Samba has to correct is the difference between Unix and Microsoft filesystems. This includes items such as handling symbolic links, hidden files, and dot files. In addition, file permissions can also be a headache if not properly accounted for.

Hiding and Vetoing Files

Sometimes you need to ensure that a user cannot see or access a file at all. Other times, you don't want to keep users from accessing a file—you just want to hide it when they view the contents of the directory. On Windows systems, an attribute of files allows them to be hidden from a folder listing. With Unix, the traditional way of hiding files in a directory is to use a dot (.) as the first character in the filename. This prevents items such as configuration files from being seen when performing an ordinary *ls* command. Keeping a user from accessing a file at all, however, involves working with permissions on files and directories.

The first option we should discuss is the Boolean hide dot files. When it is set to yes, Samba reports files beginning with a period (.) as having their hidden attribute set. If the user has chosen to show all hidden files while browsing (e.g., using the Folder Options menu item under the View menu in Windows 98), he will still be able to see the files, although his icons will appear "ghosted," or slightly grayed-out. If the client is configured not to show hidden files, the files will not appear at all.

Instead of simply hiding files beginning with a dot, you can also specify a string pattern to Samba for files to hide, using the hide files option. For example, let's assume you specified the following in our example [data] share:

```
[data]
      hide files = /*.java/*README*/
```

Each entry for this option must begin, end, or be separated from another with a slash (/) character, even if only one pattern is listed. This convention allows spaces to appear in filenames. The slashes have nothing to do with Unix directories; they are instead acting as delimiters for the hide files values.

If you want to prevent users from seeing files completely, you can instead use the veto files option. This option, which takes the same syntax as the hide files option, specifies a list of files that should never be seen by the user. For example, let's change the [data] share to the following:

```
[data]
      veto files = /*.java/*README*/
```

The syntax of this option is identical to the hide files configuration option: each entry must begin, end, or be separated from another with a slash (/) character, even if only one pattern is listed. If you do so, files that match the pattern, such as *hello.java* and *README.txt*, will simply disappear from the directory, and the user cannot access them through SMB.

We need to address one other question. What happens if the user tries to delete a directory that contains vetoed files? This is where the delete veto files option comes in. If this Boolean option is set to yes, the user can delete both the regular files and the vetoed files in the directory, and the directory itself is removed. If the option is set to no, the user cannot delete the vetoed files, and consequently the directory is not deleted either. From the user's perspective, the directory appears empty, but cannot be removed.

The dont descend directive specifies a list of directories whose contents Samba should not make visible. Note that we say *contents*, not the directory itself. Users can enter a directory marked as such, but they are prohibited from descending the directory tree any farther—they always see an empty folder. For example, let's use this option with a more basic form of the share that we defined earlier in the chapter:

```
[data]
      dont descend = config defaults
```

In addition, let's assume that the */home/samba/data* directory has the following contents:

```
drwxr-xr-x   6 tom     users   1024 Jun 13 09:24 .
drwxr-xr-x   8 root    root    1024 Jun 10 17:53 ..
```

```
-rw-r--r--    2 tom      users      1024 Jun  9 11:43 README
drwxr-xr-x    3 tom      users      1024 Jun 13 09:28 config
drwxr-xr-x    3 tom      users      1024 Jun 13 09:28 defaults
drwxr-xr-x    3 tom      users      1024 Jun 13 09:28 market
```

If the user then connects to the share, she would see the directories in the share. However, the contents of the *config* and *defaults* directories would appear empty to her, even if other folders or files existed in them. In addition, users cannot write any data to the folder (which prevents them from creating a file or folder with the same name as one that is already there but invisible). If a user attempts to do so, she will receive an "Access Denied" message. The dont descend option is an administrative option—not a security option—and is not a substitute for good file permissions.

Links

When a client tries to open a symbolic link on a Samba server share, Samba attempts to follow the link to find the real file and let the client open it, as if the user were on a Unix machine. If you don't want to allow this, set the follow symlinks option like this:

```
[data]
      follow symlinks = no
```

You can test this by setting up and trying to access a symbolic link. Create a directory on the Unix server inside the share, acting as the user under which you will log in to Samba. Enter the following commands:

```
$ echo "This is a test" >hello.txt
$ ln -s hello.txt hello-link.txt
```

This results in the text file *hello.txt* and a symbolic link to it called *hello-link.txt*. Normally, if you double-click either one, you will receive a file that has the text "This is a test" inside of it. However, with the follow symlinks option set to no, you will receive an error dialog if you double-click *hello-link.txt*.

The wide links option, if set to no, prevents the client user from following symbolic links that point outside the shared directory tree. For example, let's assume that we modified the [data] share as follows:

```
[data]
      follow symlinks = yes
      wide links = no
```

As long as the follow symlinks option is disabled, Samba will refuse to follow any symbolic links outside the current share tree. If we create a file outside the share (for example, in someone's home directory) and then create a link to it in the share as follows:

```
ln -s ~tom/datafile ./datafile
```

the client cannot open the file in Tom's home directory.

Filesystem Options

Table 8-1 shows a breakdown of the options we discussed earlier. We recommend the defaults for most, except those listed in the following descriptions.

Table 8-1. Filesystem configuration options

Option	Parameters	Function	Default	Scope
dont descend	string (list of directories)	Indicates a list of directories whose contents Samba should make invisible to clients.	None	Share
follow symlinks	Boolean	If set to no, will not honor symbolic links.	yes	Share
getwd cache	Boolean	If set to yes, will use a cache for getwd() calls.	yes	Global
wide links	Boolean	If set to yes, will follow symbolic links outside the share.	yes	Share
hide dot files	Boolean	If set to yes, treats Unix hidden files as hidden files in Windows.	yes	Share
hide files	string (list of files)	List of file patterns to treat as hidden.	None	Share
veto files	string (list of files)	List of file patterns to never show.	None	Share
delete veto files	Boolean	If set to yes, will delete files matched by veto files when the directory they reside in is deleted.	no	Share

dont descend

The dont descend option can be used to specify various directories that should appear empty to the client. Note that the directory itself will still appear. However, Samba will not show any of the contents of the directory to the client user. This is not a good option to use as a security feature; it is really meant only as a convenience to keep users from casually browsing into directories that might have sensitive files. See our example earlier in this section.

follow symlinks

This option controls whether Samba will follow a symbolic link in the Unix operating system to the target or if it should return an error to the client user. If the option is set to yes, the target of the link will be interpreted as the file. If set to no, an error will be generated if the symbolic link is accessed.

getwd cache

This global option specifies whether Samba should use a local cache for the Unix *getwd()* (get current working directory) system call. You can override the default value of yes as follows:

```
[global]
    getwd cache = no
```

Setting this option to no can significantly increase the time it takes to resolve the working directory, especially if the wide links option is set to no. You should normally not need to alter this option.

wide links

This option specifies whether the client user can follow symbolic links that point outside the shared directory tree. This includes any files or directories at the other end of the link, as long as the permissions are correct for the user. The default value for this option is yes. Note that this option will not be honored if the follow symlinks options is set to no. Setting this option to no slows *smbd* considerably because it will have to check each link it encounters.

hide dot files

The hide dot files option hides any files on the server that begin with a dot (.) character to mimic the functionality behind several shell commands that are present on Unix systems. Like hide files, those files that begin with a dot have the DOS hidden attribute set, which doesn't guarantee that a client cannot view them. The default value for this option is yes.

hide files

The hide files option provides one or more directory or filename patterns to Samba. Any file matching this pattern will be treated as a hidden file from the perspective of the client. Note that this simply means that the DOS hidden attribute is set, which might or might not mean that the user can actually see it while browsing.

Each entry in the list must begin, end, or be separated from another entry with a slash (/) character, even if only one pattern is listed. This allows spaces to appear in the list. Asterisks can be used as a wildcard to represent zero or more characters. Questions marks can be used to represent exactly one character. For example:

```
hide files = /.jav*/README.???/
```

veto files

More stringent than the hidden files state is the state provided by the veto files configuration option. Samba won't even admit these files exist. You cannot list or open them from the client. This should not be used as a means of implementing security. It is actually a mechanism to keep PC programs from deleting special files, such as ones used to store the resource fork of a Macintosh file on a Unix filesystem. If both Windows and Macs are sharing the same files, this can prevent ill-advised power users from removing files the Mac users need.

The syntax of this option is identical to that of the hide files configuration option: each entry must begin, end, or be separated from another with a slash (/) character,

---

even if only one pattern is listed. Asterisks can be used as a wildcard to represent zero or more characters. Question marks can be used to represent exactly one character. For example:

```
veto files = /*config/*default?/
```

This option is primarily administrative and is not a substitute for good file permissions.

delete veto files

This option tells Samba to delete vetoed files when a user attempts to delete the directory in which they reside. The default value is no. This means that if a user tries to delete a directory that contains a vetoed file, the file (and the directory) will not be deleted. Instead, the directory remains and appears empty from the perspective of the user. If set to yes, the directory and the vetoed files will be deleted.

File Permissions and Attributes on MS-DOS and Unix

Originally, DOS was not intended to be a multiuser, networked operating system. Unix, on the other hand, was designed for multiple users from the start. Consequently, Samba must not only be aware of, but also provide special solutions for, inconsistencies and gaps in coverage between the two filesystems. One of the biggest gaps is how Unix and DOS handle permissions on files.

Let's take a look at how Unix assigns permissions. All Unix files have read, write, and execute bits for three classifications of users: owner, group, and world. These permissions can be seen at the extreme lefthand side when an *ls -al* command is issued in a Unix directory. For example:

```
-rwxr--r--   1 tom     users   2014 Apr 13 14:11 access.conf
```

Windows, on the other hand, has four principal bits that it uses with any file: read-only, system, hidden, and archive. You can view these bits by right-clicking the file and choosing the Properties menu item. You should see a dialog similar to Figure 8-1.*

The definition of each bit follows:

Read-only
    The file's contents can be read by a user but cannot be written to.

---

* The system checkbox will probably be grayed for your file. Don't worry about that—you should still be able to see when the box is checked and when it isn't.

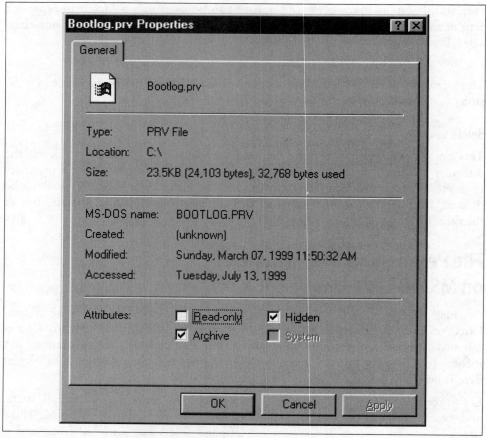

Figure 8-1. DOS and Windows file properties

System

    This file has a specific purpose required by the operating system.

Hidden

    This file has been marked to be invisible to the user, unless the operating system is explicitly set to show it.

Archive

    This file has been touched since the last DOS backup was performed on it.

Note that there is no bit to specify that a file is executable. DOS and Windows NT filesystems identify executable files by giving them the extensions *.exe*, *.com*, *.cmd*, or *.bat*.

Consequently, there is no use for any of the three Unix executable bits that are present on a file in a Samba disk share. DOS files, however, have their own attributes that need to be preserved when they are stored in a Unix environment: the archive, system, and hidden bits. Samba can preserve these bits by reusing the executable permission bits of the file on the Unix side—if it is instructed to do so. Mapping these bits, however, has an unfortunate side effect: if a Windows user stores a file in a Samba share, and you view it on Unix with the *ls -al* command, some of the executable bits won't mean what you'd expect them to.

Three Samba options decide whether the bits are mapped: map archive, map system, and map hidden. These options map the archive, system, and hidden attributes to the owner, group, and world execute bits of the file, respectively. You can add these options to the [data] share, setting each of their values as follows:

```
[data]
    map archive = yes
    map system = yes
    map hidden = yes
```

After that, try creating a file in the share under Unix—such as *hello.java*—and change the permissions of the file to 755. With these Samba options set, you should be able to check the permissions on the Windows side and see that each of the three values has been checked in the Properties dialog box. What about the read-only attribute? By default, Samba sets this whenever a file does not have the Unix owner write permission bit set. In other words, you can set this bit by changing the permissions of the file to 555.

The default value of the map archive option is yes, while the other two options have a default value of no. This is because many programs do not work properly if the archive bit is not stored correctly for DOS and Windows files. The system and hidden attributes, however, are not critical for a program's operation and are left to the discretion of the administrator.

Figure 8-2 summarizes the Unix permission bits and illustrates how Samba maps those bits to DOS attributes. Note that the group read/write and world read/write bits do not directly translate to a DOS attribute, but they still retain their original Unix definitions on the Samba server.

Creation Masks

File and directory creation masks are similar to umasks you have probably encountered while working with Unix systems. They are used to help define the permissions that will be assigned to a file or directory at the time it is created. Samba's masks work differently in that the bits that can be set are set in the creation mask, while in Unix umasks, the bits *cannot* be set are set in the umask. We think you will find Samba's method to be much more intuitive. Once in a while you might need to convert between a Unix umask and the equivalent Samba mask. It is simple: one is just the bitwise complement of the other. For example, an octal umask of 0022 has the same effect as a Samba mask of 0755.

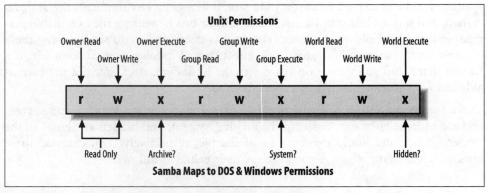

Figure 8-2. How Samba and Unix view the permissions of a file

Unix umasks are set on a user-by-user basis, usually while executing the GUI's or command-line shell's startup scripts. When users connect to a Samba share from a network client, these scripts are not executed, so Samba supplies the ability to set the creation masks for files and directories. By default, this is done on a share-by-share basis, although you can use the include parameter in the Samba configuration file (as explained in Chapter 6) to assign masks on a user-by-user basis, thus matching conventional Unix behavior.

To show how Samba's create masks work, suppose we have a Windows Me user connecting to his Unix home directory through Samba, and Samba is configured with create mask = 777 in the [homes] share. With this value, create mask will not affect the bits that are set on new files. If the user creates a file with Wordpad, it will appear in the Unix filesystem like this:

```
$ ls -l file.doc
-rwxrw-rw-   1 jay      jay               0 Sep 21 11:02 file.doc
```

Wordpad created the file with read/write permissions (i.e., the MS-DOS read-only attribute was not set), so Samba mapped the MS-DOS attributes to Unix read/write permissions for user, group, and other. The execute bit is set for the owner because by default, the map archive parameter is set to yes. The other execute bits are not set because map system and map hidden are set to no by default. You can customize this behavior as you see fit, and unless you do backups from MS-DOS or Windows systems, you might want to specify map archive = no to avoid Windows files from appearing as executables on the Unix system.

Now suppose we set create mask to have an effect. For example:

```
[homes]
    create mask = 664
```

This is equivalent to a Unix umask of 113. If the user creates the Wordpad document as before, it will show up as:

```
$ ls -l file.doc
-rw-rw-r--   1 jay      jay               0 Sep 22 16:38 file.doc
```

Comparing this to the previous example, notice that not only has the write permission for other disappeared as we expected, but so has the execute permission for owner. This happened because the value of create mask logically ANDs the owner's permissions with a 6, which has masked off the execute bit. The lesson here is that if you want to enable any of map archive, map system, or map hidden, you must be careful not to mask off the corresponding execute bit with your create mask.

The directory mask option works similarly, masking permissions for newly created directories. The following example will allow the permissions of a newly created directory to be, at most, 755:

```
[data]
    directory mask = 755
```

Also, you can force various bits with the force create mode and force directory mode options. These options will perform a logical OR against the file and directory creation masks, ensuring that those bits that are specified will always be set. You would typically set these options globally to ensure that group and world read/write permissions have been set appropriately for new files or directories in each share.

In the same spirit, if you wish to set explicitly the Unix user and group attributes of a file created on the Windows side, you can use the force user and force group options. For example:

```
[data]
    create mask = 744
    directory mask = 755
    force user = joe
    force group = accounting
```

These options assign the same Unix username and group to every client that connects to the share. However, this occurs *after* the client authenticates; it does not allow free access to a share. These options are frequently used for their side effects of assigning a specific user and group to each new file or directory that is created in a share. Use these options with discretion.

Finally, one of the capabilities of Unix that DOS lacks is the ability to delete a read-only file from a writable directory. In Unix, if a directory is writable, a read-only file in that directory can still be removed. This could permit you to delete files in any of your directories, even if the file was left by someone else.

DOS filesystems are not designed for multiple users, and so its designers decided that read-only means "protected against accidental change, including deletion," rather than "protected against some other user on a single-user machine." So the designers of DOS prohibited removal of a read-only file. Even today, Windows filesystems exhibit the same behavior.

Normally, this is harmless. Windows programs don't try to remove read-only files because they know it's a bad idea. However, a number of source-code control programs—which were first written for Unix—run on Windows and require the ability to delete read-only files. Samba permits this behavior with the delete readonly option. To enable this functionality, set the option to yes:

```
[data]
    delete readonly = yes
```

File and Directory Permission Options

The options for file and directory permissions are summarized in Table 8-2; each option is then described in detail.

Table 8-2. File and directory permission options

Option	Parameters	Function	Default	Scope
create mask (create mode)	numeric	Maximum permissions for files created by Samba.	0744	Share
directory mask (directory mode)	numeric	Maximum permissions for directories created by Samba.	0744	Share
force create mode	numeric	Forces the specified permissions (bitwise or) for directories created by Samba.	0000	Share
force directory mode	numeric	Forces the specified permissions (bitwise or) for directories created by Samba.	0000	Share
force group (group)	string (group name)	Effective group for a user accessing this share.	None	Share
force user	string (username)	Effective username for a user accessing this share.	None	Share
delete readonly	Boolean	Allows a user to delete a read-only file from a writable directory.	no	Share
map archive	Boolean	Preserve DOS archive attribute in user execute bit (0100).	yes	Share
map system	Boolean	Preserve DOS system attribute in group execute bit (0010).	no	Share
map hidden	Boolean	Preserve DOS hidden attribute in world execute bit (0001).	no	Share
inherit permissions	Boolean	If yes, permissions on new files and directories are inherited from parent directory.	no	Share

create mask

The argument for this option is an octal number indicating which permission flags can be set at file creation by a client in a share. The default is 0744, which means that the Unix owner can at most read, write, and optionally execute her own files, while members of the user's group and others can only read or execute them. If you need to change it for nonexecutable files, we recommend 0644, or rw-r--r--. Keep in mind that the execute bits can be used by the server to map certain DOS file attributes, as described earlier. If you're altering the create mask, those bits have to be part of the create mask as well.

directory mask

The argument for this option is an octal number indicating which permission flags can be set at directory creation by a client in a share. The default is 0744, which allows everyone on the Unix side to, at most, read and traverse the directories, but allows only you to modify them. We recommend the mask 0750, removing access by "the world."

force create mode

This option sets the permission bits that Samba will set when a file permission change is made. It's often used to force group permissions, as mentioned previously. It can also be used to preset any of the DOS attributes we mentioned: archive (0100), system (0010), or hidden (0001).

> When saving documents, many Windows applications rename their datafiles with a *.bak* extension and create new ones. When the files are in a Samba share, this changes their ownership and permissions so that members of the same Unix group can't edit them. Setting force create mode = 0660 will keep the new file editable by members of the group.

force directory mode

This option sets the permission bits that Samba will set when a directory permission change is made or a directory is created. It's often used to force group permissions, as mentioned previously. This option defaults to 0000 and can be used just like the force create mode to add group or other permissions if needed.

force group

This option, sometimes called group, assigns a static group ID that will be used on all connections to a share after the client has successfully authenticated. This assigns a specific group to each new file or directory created from an SMB client.

force user

The force user option assigns a static user ID that will be used on all connections to a share after the client has successfully authenticated. This assigns a specific user to each new file or directory created from an SMB client.

delete readonly

This option allows a user to delete a directory containing a read-only file. By default, DOS and Windows will not allow such an operation. You probably will want to leave this option turned off unless a program (for example, an RCS program) needs this capability; many Windows users would be appalled to find that they'd accidentally deleted a file that they had set as read-only.

map archive

The DOS archive bit is used to flag a file that has been changed since it was last archived (e.g., backed up with the DOS archive program). Setting the Samba option map archive = yes maps the DOS archive flag to the Unix execute-by-owner (0100) bit. It's best to leave this option on if your Windows users are doing their own backups or are using programs that require the archive bit. Unix lacks the notion of an archive bit entirely. Backup programs typically keep a file that lists what files were backed up on what date, so comparing file-modification dates serves the same purpose.

Setting this option to yes causes an occasional surprise on Unix when a user notices that a datafile is marked as executable, but rarely causes harm. If a user tries to run it, he will normally get a string of error messages as the shell tries to execute the first few lines as commands. The reverse is also possible; an executable Unix program looks like it hasn't been backed up recently on Windows. But again, this is rare and usually harmless.

For map archive to work properly, the execute bit for owner must not be masked off with the create mask parameter.

map system

The DOS system attribute indicates files that are required by the operating system and should not be deleted, renamed, or moved without special effort. Set this option only if you need to store Windows system files on the Unix fileserver. Executable Unix programs will appear to be nonremovable, special Windows files when viewed from Windows clients. This might prove mildly inconvenient if you want to move or remove one. For most sites, however, this is fairly harmless.

For map archive to work properly, the execute bit for group must not be masked off with the create mask parameter.

map hidden

DOS uses the hidden attribute to indicate that a file should not ordinarily be visible in directory listings. Unix doesn't have such a facility; it's up to individual programs (notably, the shell) to decide what to display and what not to display. Normally, you won't have any DOS files that need to be hidden, so the best thing to do is to leave this option turned off.

Setting this option to yes causes the server to map the hidden flag onto the executable-by-others bit (0001). This feature can produce a rather startling effect. Any Unix program that is executable by world seems to vanish when you look for it from a Windows client. If this option is not set, however, and a Windows user attempts to mark a file hidden on a Samba share, it will not work—Samba has no place to store the hidden attribute!

For map archive to work properly, the execute bit for other must not be masked off with the create mask parameter.

inherit permissions

When the inherit permissions option is set to yes, the create mask, directory mask, force create mode, and force directory mode are ignored. The normal behavior of setting the permissions on newly created files is overridden such that the new files and directories take on permissions from their parent directory. New directories will have exactly the same permissions as the parent, and new files will inherit the read and write bits from the parent directory, while the execute bits are determined as usual by the values of the map archive, map hidden, and map system parameters.

By default, this option is set to no.

Windows NT/2000/XP ACLs

Unix and Windows have different security models, and Windows NT/2000/XP has a security model that is different from Windows 95/98/Me. One area in which this is readily apparent is file protections. On Unix systems, the method used has traditionally been the 9-bit "user, group, other" system, in which read, write, and execute bits can be set separately for the owner of the file, the groups to which the owner belongs, and everyone else, respectively.

Windows 95/98/Me has a file-protection system that is essentially no protection at all. This family of operating systems was developed from MS-DOS, which was implemented as a non-networked, single-user system. Multiuser security simply was never added. One apparent exception to this is user-level security for shared files, which we will discuss in Chapter 9. Here, separate access permissions can be assigned to individual network client users or groups. However, user-level security on Windows 95/98/Me systems requires a Windows NT/2000 or Samba server to perform the actual authentication.

On Windows NT/2000/XP, user-level security is an extension of the native file security model, which involves access control lists (ACLs). This system is somewhat more extensive than the Unix security model, allowing the access rights on individual files to be set separately for any number of individual users and/or any number of arbitrary groups of users. Figures 8-3, 8-4, and 8-5 show the dialog boxes on a Windows 2000 system in which the ACL is set for a file. By right-clicking a file's icon and selecting Properties, then selecting the Security tab, we get to the dialog box shown in Figure 8-3. Here, we can set the basic permissions for a file, which are similar to Unix permissions, although not identical.

By clicking the Advanced tab, we can bring up the dialog box shown in Figure 8-4, which shows the list of access control entries (ACEs) in the ACL. In this dialog, ACEs can be added to or deleted from the ACL, or an existing ACE can be viewed

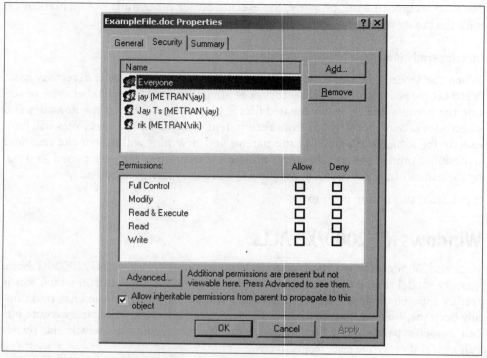

Figure 8-3. The Security tab of the file Properties dialog

and modified. Each ACE either allows or denies a set of permissions for a specific user or group.

Figure 8-5 shows the dialog box for adding an ACE. As you can see, there are more options for permissions in an ACL than with the permission bits on typical Unix systems. You can learn more about these settings in *Essential Windows NT System Administration*, published by O'Reilly.

In a networked environment where a Samba server is serving files to Windows NT/2000/XP clients, Samba has to map Unix permissions for files and directories to Windows NT/2000/XP access control lists. When a Windows NT/2000/XP client accesses a shared file or directory on a Samba server, Samba translates the object's ownership, group, and permissions into an ACL and returns them to the client.

Figure 8-6 shows the Properties dialog box for the file *shopping_list.doc* that resides on the Samba server.

From Unix, this file appears as:

```
$ ls -l shopping_list.doc
-rw-------   1 adilia   users       49 Mar 29 11:58 shopping_list.doc
```

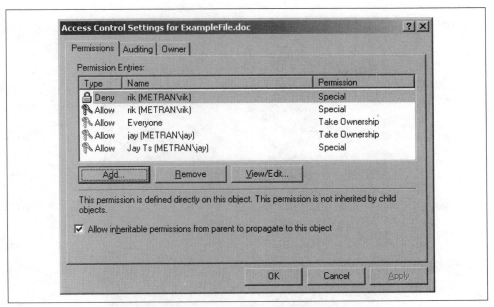

Figure 8-4. The Permissions tab of the Access Control Settings dialog

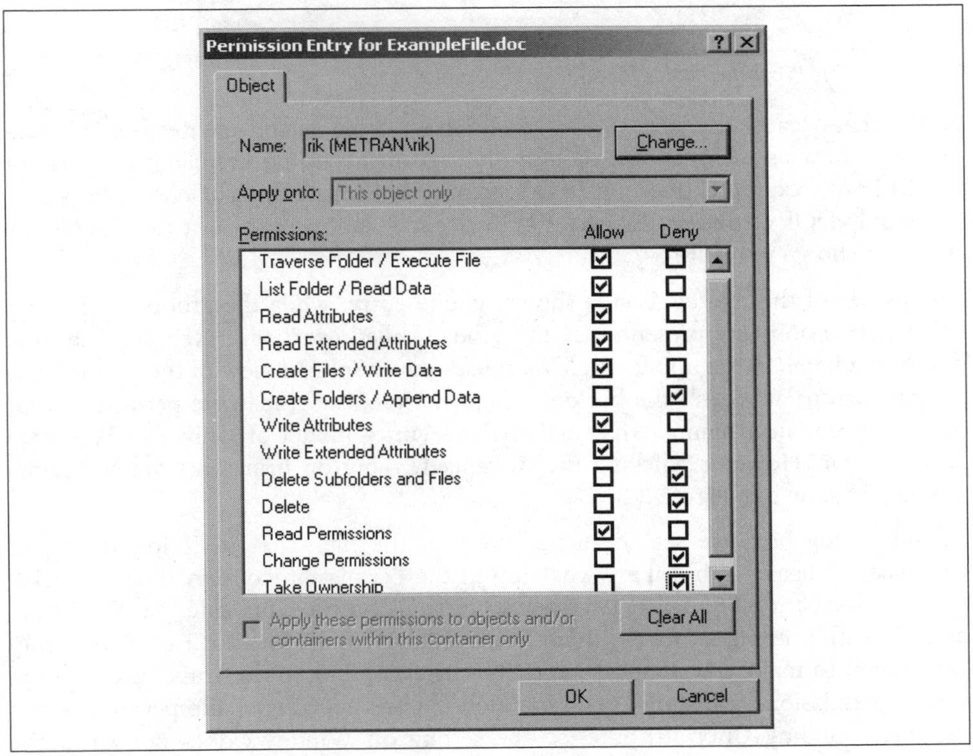

Figure 8-5. Permission Entry dialog, showing the settings of an ACE

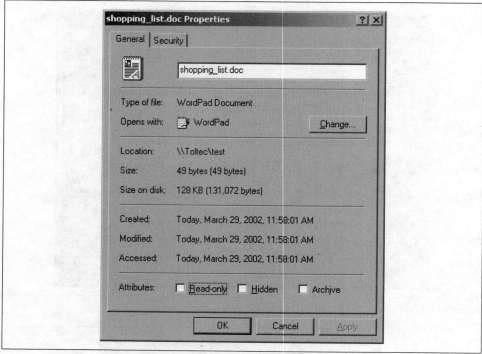

Figure 8-6. The Properties dialog for a file on the Samba server

Notice that because the file has read permissions for the owner, the Read-only check-box will show as cleared, even though the user on the Windows client (who is not adilia in this example) does not have read access permissions. The checkboxes here show only DOS attributes. By clicking the Security tab, we can start to examine the ACLs, as shown in Figure 8-7.

The owner of the file (adilia) is shown as one entry, while the group (users) and other permissions are presented as the groups called users and Everyone. Clicking one of the items in the upper windows causes the simplified view of the permissions in that item to appear in the bottom window. Here, the read/write permissions for adilia appear in a manner that makes the security model of Unix and Windows seem similar. However, clicking the Advanced... button brings up the additional dialog box shown in Figure 8-8.

In this dialog box, we see the actual ACL of the file. The ACEs for users and Everyone are listed with Take Ownership in the Permission column. This is a trick used by Samba for ACLs that have no permissions on the Unix side. On Windows, an ACL with nothing set results in no ACL at all, so Samba sets the Take Ownership permission to make sure that all the ACLs corresponding to the Unix "user, group, other" permissions will show up on Windows. The Take Ownership permission has no corresponding Unix attribute, so the setting on Windows does not affect the

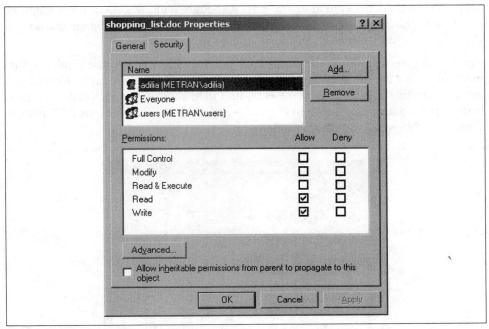

Figure 8-7. The Security tab of the Properties dialog for a file on the Samba server

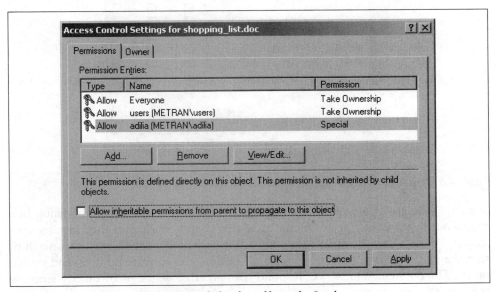

Figure 8-8. The Access Control Settings dialog for a file on the Samba server

actual file on the Unix system in any way. Although Windows client users might be misled into thinking they can take ownership of the file (that is, change the ownership of the file to themselves), an actual attempt to do so will fail.

The Permissions column for the adilia ACL is listed as Special because Samba reports permissions for the file that do not correspond to settings for which Windows has a more descriptive name. Clicking the entry and then clicking the View/Edit... button brings up the dialog box shown in Figure 8-9, in which the details of the ACL permissions can be viewed and perhaps modified.

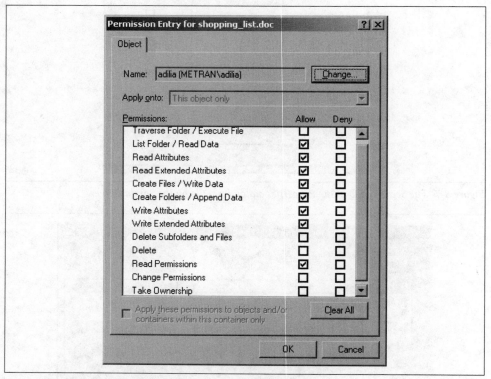

Figure 8-9. Permission Entry dialog for a file served by Samba

We say "perhaps" here because checking or unchecking boxes in this dialog box might not result in settings that Samba is able to map back into the Unix security model. When a user attempts to modify a setting (either permissions or ownership) that she does not have authority to change, or does not correspond to a valid setting on the Unix system, Samba will respond with an error dialog or by quietly ignoring the unmappable settings.

The ACLs for a directory are slightly different. Figure 8-10 shows the ACL view after clicking the Advanced button.

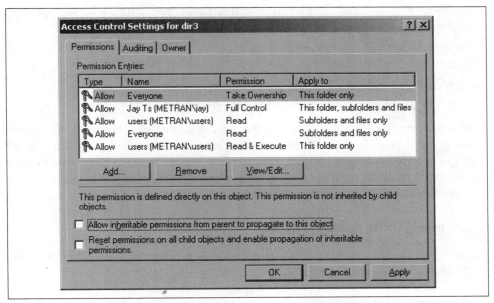

Figure 8-10. The Access Control Settings dialog for a directory on the Samba server

Here, there are two ACLs each for users and Everyone. One ACL specifies the permissions for the directory itself, and the other specifies permissions for the directory's contents. When changing settings in the View/Edit... dialog, there is an extra drop-down menu to apply the settings either to just the directory or to some combination of the directory and the files and directories it contains. If settings are applied to more than just the directory, Samba will match the behavior of a Windows server and change the permissions on the contents of the directory, as specified in the dialog.

Unix ACLs

In most cases, users of Windows clients will find the Unix security model to be sufficient. However, in some cases, people might want the Samba server to support the full Windows ACL security model. Even if they don't need the fine-grained control over file and directory permissions, they might find Samba's translation between ACLs and Unix permissions to be a source of confusion or frustration.

When the underlying Unix host operating system supports POSIX.1e ACLs, Samba provides much better support of Windows NT/2000/XP ACLs. Versions of Unix that offer the necessary support include the following:

- Solaris 2.6 and later
- SGI Irix
- Linux, with Andreas Grünbacher's kernel patch from *http://acl.bestbits.de* that adds ACL support to the Linux ext2 and ext3 filesystems
- Linux, with the XFS filesystem
- AIX
- FreeBSD 5.0 and later
- HP/UX 11.0 and later, with the JFS 3.3 filesystem layout Version 4

If you are fortunate enough to have a Unix host operating system with ACL support already provided, all you need to do is recompile Samba using the `--with-acl-support` configure option, as we described in Chapter 2. If you are running Linux and need to patch your kernel, things are much more complicated. We suggest you refer to the documentation that comes with the patch for details on using it.

Configuration Options for ACLs

Table 8-3 shows the Samba configuration options for working with Windows NT/ 2000/XP access control lists.

Table 8-3. ACL configuration options

Option	Parameters	Function	Default	Scope
nt acl support	Boolean	If yes, allows users on Windows NT/2000/XP clients to modify ACL settings	yes	Share
security mask	numeric	Bitmask that allows or denies permission settings on files	0777	Share
force security mode	numeric	Bits that are always set when modifying file permissions	0000	Share
directory security mask	numeric	Bitmask that allows or denies permission settings on directories	0777	Share
force directory security mode	numeric	Bits that are always set when modifying directory permissions	0000	Share

nt acl support

This parameter defaults to yes, which allows users on Windows NT/2000/XP clients to modify ACL settings for files on the Samba server. When set to no, files show up as owned by Everyone, with permissions appearing as "Full Control". However, *actual* ownership and permissions are enforced as whatever they are set to on the Samba server, and the user on the Windows client cannot view or modify them with the dialog boxes used for managing ACLs.

When enabled, support for Windows NT/2000/XP ACLs is limited to whatever ownerships and permissions can map into valid users and permissions on the Samba server. If the server supports ACLs (either "out of the box" or with an additional patch to enhance the filesystem), Samba's ACL support more closely matches that of a Windows NT/2000/XP server.

security mask

Using the security mask option, it is possible to define which file permissions users can modify from Windows NT/2000/XP clients. This is for files only and not directories, which are handled with the directory security mask option. The parameter is assigned a numeric value that is a Unix-style permissions mask. For bits in the mask that are set, the client can modify the corresponding bits in the files' permissions. If the bit is zero, the client cannot modify that permission. For example, if security mask is set as:

```
[data]
    security mask = 0777
```

the client can modify all the user/group/other permissions for the files in the share. This is the default. A value of 0 would deny clients from changing any of the permissions, and setting security mask as:

```
[data]
    security mask = 0666
```

would allow client users to modify the read and write permissions, but not the execute permissions.

Do not count on security mask for complete control because if the user can access the files on the Samba server through any other means (for example, by logging directly into the Unix host), he can modify the permissions using that method.

force security mode

The force security mode option can be used to define a set of permissions that are always set whenever the user on a Windows NT/2000/XP client modifies a file's permissions. (See the force directory security mode option for handling directories.)

Be careful to understand this properly. The mask given as the parameter's value is not necessarily equal to the resulting permissions on the file. The permissions that the client user attempts to modify are logically OR'd with the force security mode mask option, and any bits that are turned on will cause the file's corresponding permissions to be set. As an example, suppose force security mode is set in a share thusly:

```
[data]
    force security mode = 0440
```

(This sets the read bit for owner and group, but not other.) If a user on a Windows NT/2000/XP client modifies an ACL on a file in the [data] share and attempts to remove all read permissions, the read permission for other (Everyone) will be removed, but the read permission for the owner and group will remain. Note that this parameter cannot force a permission bit to be turned off.

As with the security mask option, if a user can access the files in the share through any means other than Samba, she can easily work around Samba's enforcement of this parameter.

The default value of force security mode is 0000, which allows users to remove any permission from files.

directory security mask

This option works exactly the same as the security mask option, except that it operates on directories rather than files. As with security mask, it has a default value of 0777, which allows Windows NT/2000/XP client users to modify all Unix permissions on directories in the share.

force directory security mode

This option works exactly the same as the force security mode option, except that it operates on directories rather than files. It also has a default value of 0000, which allows Windows NT/2000/XP client users to remove any permissions from directories in the share.

Name Mangling and Case

Back in the days of DOS and Windows 3.1, every filename was limited to eight uppercase characters, followed by a dot, and three more uppercase characters. This was known as the *8.3 format* and was a huge nuisance. Windows 95/98/Me, Windows NT/2000/XP, and Unix have since relaxed this problem by allowing longer, sometimes case-sensitive, filenames. Table 8-4 shows the current naming state of several popular operating systems.

Table 8-4. Operating system filename limitations

Operating system	File-naming rules
DOS 6.22 or below	Eight characters followed by a dot followed by a three-letter extension (8.3 format); case-insensitive
Windows 3.1 for Workgroups	Eight characters followed by a dot followed by a three-letter extension (8.3 format); case-insensitive
Windows 95/98/Me	255 characters; case-insensitive but case-preserving
Windows NT/2000/XP	255 characters; case-insensitive but case-preserving
Unix	255 characters; case-sensitive

Samba still has to remain backward-compatible with network clients that store files in just the 8.3 format, such as Windows for Workgroups. If a user creates a file on a share called *antidisestablishmentarianism.txt*, a Windows for Workgroups client cannot tell it apart from another file in the same directory called *antidisease.txt*. Like Windows 95/98/Me and Windows NT/2000/XP, Samba has to employ a special method for translating a long filename to an 8.3 filename in such a way that similar filenames will not cause collisions. This is called *name mangling*, and Samba deals with this in a manner that is similar, but not identical to, Windows 95 and its successors.

The Samba Mangling Operation

Here is how Samba mangles a long filename into an 8.3 filename:

- If the original filename does not begin with a dot, the first five characters before the dot (if there is one) are converted to uppercase. These characters are used as the first five characters of the 8.3 mangled filename.

- If the original filename begins with a dot, the dot is removed and then the previous step is performed on what is left.

- These characters are immediately followed by a special mangling character: by default, a tilde (~), although Samba allows you to change this character.

- The base of the long filename before the last period is hashed into a two-character code; parts of the name after the last dot can be used if necessary. This two-character code is appended to the filename after the mangling character.

- The first three characters after the last dot (if there is one) of the original filename are converted to uppercase and appended onto the mangled name as the extension. If the original filename began with a dot, three underscores (___) are used as the extension instead.

Here are some examples:

```
virtuosity.dat                          VIRTU~F1.DAT
.htaccess                               HTACC~U0.___
hello.java                              HELLO~1F.JAV
team.config.txt                         TEAMC~04.TXT
antidisestablishmentarianism.txt        ANTID~E3.TXT
antidisease.txt                         ANTID~9K.TXT
```

Using these rules will allow Windows for Workgroups to differentiate the two files on behalf of the poor individual who is forced to see the network through the eyes of that operating system. Note that the same long filename should always hash to the same mangled name with Samba; this doesn't always happen with Windows. The downside of this approach is that there can still be collisions; however, the chances are greatly reduced.

You generally want to use the mangling configuration options with only the oldest clients. We recommend doing this without disrupting other clients by adding an include directive to the *smb.conf* file:

```
[global]
    include = /usr/local/samba/lib/smb.conf.%a
```

This resolves to *smb.conf.WfWg* when a Windows for Workgroups client attaches. Now you can create a file */usr/local/samba/lib/smb.conf.WfWg*, which might contain these options:

```
[global]
    case sensitive = no
    default case = upper
    preserve case = no
    short preserve case = no
    mangle case = yes
    mangled names= yes
```

If you are not using Windows for Workgroups, you probably do not need to change any of these options from their defaults.

Representing and resolving filenames with Samba

Another item that we should point out is that there is a difference between how an operating system *represents* a file and how it *resolves* it. For example, you have likely run across a file on a Windows system called *README.TXT*. The file can be represented by the operating system entirely in uppercase letters. However, if you open an MS-DOS command prompt and enter the command:

```
C:\> notepad readme.txt
```

the all-caps file is loaded into the editing program, even though you typed the name in lowercase letters.

This is because the Windows 95/98/Me and Windows NT/2000/XP families of operating systems resolve filenames in a case-insensitive manner, even though the files are represented in a case-sensitive manner. Unix-based operating systems, on the other hand, always resolve files in a case-sensitive manner; if you try to edit *README.TXT* with the command:

```
$ vi readme.txt
```

you will likely be editing the empty buffer of a new file.

Here is how Samba handles case: if the preserve case is set to yes, Samba will always use the case provided by the operating system for representing (not resolving) filenames. If it is set to no, it will use the case specified by the default case option. The same is true for short preserve case. If this option is set to yes, Samba will use the default case of the operating system for representing 8.3 filenames; otherwise, it will use the case specified by the default case option. Finally, Samba will always resolve filenames in its shares based on the value of the case sensitive option.

Mangling Options

Samba allows more refined instructions on how it should perform name mangling, including those controlling the case sensitivity, the character inserted to form a mangled name, and the ability to map filenames manually from one format to another. These options are shown in Table 8-5.

Table 8-5. Name-mangling options

Option	Parameters	Function	Default	Scope
case sensitive (casesignames)	Boolean	If yes, treats filenames as case-sensitive (Windows doesn't).	no	Share
default case	string (upper or lower)	Case to assume as default (used only when preserve case is no).	Lower	Share
preserve case	Boolean	If yes, keep the case the client supplied (i.e., do not convert to default case).	yes	Share
short preserve case	Boolean	If yes, preserve case of 8.3-format names that the client provides.	yes	Share
mangled names	Boolean	Mangles long names into 8.3 DOS format.	yes	Share
mangle case	Boolean	Mangle a name if it is mixed case.	no	Share
mangling char	string (single character)	Gives mangling character.	~	Share
mangled stack	numeric	Number of mangled names to keep on the local mangling stack.	50	Global
mangled map	string (list of patterns)	Allows mapping of filenames from one format into another.	None	Share

case sensitive

This share-level option, which has the obtuse synonym casesignames, specifies whether Samba should preserve case when resolving filenames in a specific share. The default value for this option is no, which is how Windows handles file resolution. If clients are using an operating system that takes advantage of case-sensitive filenames, you can set this configuration option to yes as shown here:

```
[accounting]
    case sensitive = yes
```

Otherwise, we recommend that you leave this option set to its default.

default case

The default case option is used with preserve case. This specifies the default case (upper or lower) Samba uses to create a file on one of its shares on behalf of a client. The default case is lower, which means that newly created files will have lowercase names. If you need to, you can override this global option by specifying the following:

```
[global]
    default case = upper
```

If you specify this value, the names of newly created files are translated into uppercase and cannot be overridden in a program. We recommend that you use the default value unless you are dealing with a Windows for Workgroups or other 8.3 client, in which case it should be upper.

preserve case

This option specifies whether a file created by Samba on behalf of the client is created with the case provided by the client operating system or the case specified by the earlier default case configuration option. The default value is yes, which uses the case provided by the client operating system. If it is set to no, the value of the default case option (upper or lower) is used.

Note that this option does not handle 8.3 file requests sent from the client—see the upcoming short preserve case option. You might want to set this option to yes, for example, if applications that create files on the Samba server demand the file be all uppercase. If instead you want Samba to mimic the behavior of a Windows NT filesystem, you can leave this option set to its default, yes.

short preserve case

This option specifies whether an 8.3 filename created by Samba on behalf of the client is created with the default case of the client operating system or the case specified by the default case configuration option. The default value is yes, which uses the case provided by the client operating system. You can let Samba choose the case through the default case option by setting it as follows:

```
[global]
    short preserve case = no
```

If you want to force Samba to mimic the behavior of a Windows NT filesystem, you can leave this option set to its default, yes.

mangled names

This share-level option specifies whether Samba will mangle filenames for 8.3 clients. If the option is set to no, Samba will not mangle the names, and (depending on the client) they will either be invisible or appear truncated to those using 8.3 operating systems. The default value is yes. You can override it per share as follows:

```
[data]
    mangled names = no
```

mangle case

This option tells Samba whether it should mangle filenames that are not composed entirely of the case specified using the default case configuration option. The default for this option is no. If you set it to yes, you should be sure that all clients can handle the mangled filenames that result. You can override it per share as follows:

```
[data]
    mangle case = yes
```

We recommend that you leave this option alone unless you have a well-justified need to change it.

mangling char

This share-level option specifies the mangling character used when Samba mangles filenames into the 8.3 format. The default character used is a tilde (~). You can reset it to whatever character you wish. For instance:

```
[data]
    mangling char = #
```

mangled stack

Samba maintains a local stack of recently mangled 8.3 filenames; this stack can be used to reverse-map mangled filenames back to their original state. This is often needed by applications that create and save a file, close it, and need to modify it later. The default number of long filename/mangled filename pairs stored on this stack is 50. However, if you want to cut down on the amount of processor time used to mangle filenames, you can increase the size of the stack to whatever you wish, at the expense of memory and slightly slower file access:

```
[global]
    mangled stack = 100
```

mangled map

If the default behavior of name mangling is not sufficient, you can give Samba further instructions on how to behave using the mangled map option. This option allows you to specify mapping patterns that can be used in place of name mangling performed by Samba. For example:

```
[data]
    mangled map =(*.database *.db) (*.class *.cls)
```

Here, Samba is instructed to search each encountered file for characters that match the first pattern specified in the parenthesis and convert them to the modified second pattern in the parenthesis for display on an 8.3 client. This is useful in the event that name mangling converts the filename incorrectly or converts it to a format that the client cannot understand readily. Patterns are separated by whitespaces.

Locks and Oplocks

Concurrent writes to a single file are not desirable in any operating system. To prevent this, most operating systems use *locks* to guarantee that only one process can write to a file at a time. Operating systems traditionally lock entire files, although newer ones allow a range of bytes within a file to be locked. If another process attempts to write to a file (or section of one) that is already locked, it receives an error from the operating system and will have to wait until the lock is released.

Samba supports the standard DOS and NT filesystem (deny-mode) locking requests—which allow only one process to write to an entire file on a server at a given time—as well as byte-range locking. In addition, Samba supports a locking mechanism known in the Windows NT world as *opportunistic locking,* or *oplock* for short.

Opportunistic Locking

Opportunistic locking allows a client to notify the Samba server that it will not only be the exclusive writer of a file, but will also cache its changes to that file locally to speed up access by reducing network activity. This can result in a large performance gain—typically 30%—while at the same time reserving network bandwidth for other purposes.

Because exclusive access can be obtained using regular file locks, the value of opportunistic locks is not so much to lock the file as it is to cache it. In fact, a better name for opportunistic locking might be *opportunistic caching.*

When Samba knows that a file in one of its shares has been oplocked by a client, it marks its version as having an opportunistic lock and waits for the client to complete work on the file, at which point it expects the client to send its changes back to the Samba server for synchronization with the copy on the server.

If a second client requests access to that file before the first client has finished working on it, Samba sends an oplock break request to the first client. This tells the client to stop caching its changes and return the current state of the file to the server so that the interrupting client can use it as it sees fit. An opportunistic lock, however, is not a replacement for a standard deny-mode lock. It is not unheard of for the interrupting process to be granted an oplock break only to discover that the original process also has a deny-mode lock on a file as well. Figure 8-11 illustrates this opportunistic locking process.

In most cases, the extra performance resulting from the use of oplocks is highly desirable. However, allowing the client to cache data can be a big risk if either the client or network hardware are unreliable. Suppose a client opens a file for writing, creating an oplock on it. When another client also tries to open the file, an oplock break request is sent to the first client. If this request goes unfulfilled for any reason and the

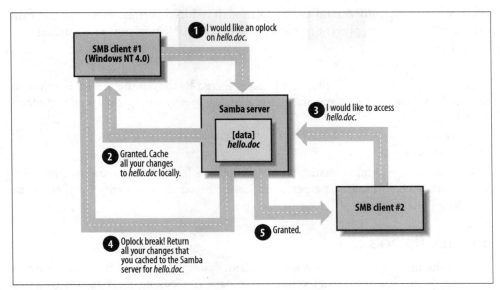

Figure 8-11. Opportunistic locking

second client starts writing to the file, the file can be easily corrupted as a result of the two processes writing to it concurrently. Unfortunately, this scenario is very real. Uncoordinated behavior such as this has been observed many times among Windows clients in SMB networks (with files served by Windows NT/2000 or Samba). Typically, the affected files are database files, which multiple clients open concurrently for writing.

A more concrete example of oplock failure occurs when database files are very large. If a client is allowed to oplock this kind of file, there can be a huge delay while the client copies the entire file from the server to cache it, even though it might need to update only one record. The situation goes from bad to worse when another client tries to open the oplocked file. The first client might need to write the entire file back to the server before the second client's file open request can succeed. This results in another huge delay (for both clients), which in practice often results in a failed open due to a timeout on the second client, perhaps along with a message warning of possible database corruption!

If you are having problems of this variety, you can turn off oplocks for the affected files by using the veto oplock files parameter:

```
[dbdata]
    veto oplock files = /*.dbm/
```

Use the value of the parameter (a list of filename-matching patterns separated by slash characters) to match all the files in the share that might be a source of trouble. The syntax of this parameter is similar to that of the veto files parameter.

If you want to be really careful and can live with reduced performance, you can turn off oplocks altogether, preventing the oplock break problem from ever occurring:

```
[global]
    oplocks = no
```

This disables oplocks for all files in all shares served by the Samba server. If you wish to disable oplocks in just a specific share, you can specify the oplocks = no parameter in just that share:

```
[database]
    oplocks = no
```

This example allows other shares, which might have less sensitive data, to attain better performance, while trading performance for better data integrity for files in the [database] share.

Unix and Oplocks

Most of the time, oplocks help Windows client systems cooperate to avoid overwriting each other's changes. Unix systems also have file-locking mechanisms to allow Unix processes to cooperate with each other. But if a file stored on a Samba system is accessed by both a Windows network client and a local Unix process—without an additional coordination between the two systems—the Unix process could easily ride roughshod over an oplock.

Some Unix systems have enhanced kernels that understand the Windows oplocks maintained by Samba. Currently the support exists only in SGI Irix and Linux.

If you leave oplocks enabled and your Unix system does not support kernel oplocks, you could end up with corrupted data when somebody runs a Unix process that reads or writes a file that Windows users also access. This is another case where the veto oplock files parameter can be used, assuming you can anticipate which Samba files are used by both Windows users and Unix users. For example, suppose the [usrfiles] share contains some ASCII text files with the *.txt* filename extension and OpenOffice word processor documents with the *.doc* filename extension, which Unix and Windows users both modify. We can use veto oplock files like this:

```
[usrfiles]
    veto oplock files = /*.txt/*.doc/
```

This will suppress the use of oplocks on *.txt* and *.doc* files, which will suppress client caching, while allowing the Windows and Unix programs to use regular file locking to prevent concurrent writes to the same file.

Locks and Oplocks Configuration Options

Samba's options for locks and oplocks are given in Table 8-6.

Table 8-6. Locks and oplocks configuration options

Option	Parameters	Function	Default	Scope
locking	Boolean	If yes, turns on byte-range locks.	yes	Share
strict locking	Boolean	If yes, denies access to an entire file if a byte-range lock exists in it.	no	Share
posix locking	Boolean	If yes, maps oplocks to POSIX locks on the local system.	yes	Share
oplocks	Boolean	If yes, turns on local caching of files on the client for this share.	yes	Share
kernel oplocks	Boolean	If yes, indicates that the kernel supports oplocks.	yes	Global
level2 oplocks	Boolean	If yes, allows oplocks to downgrade to read-only.	yes	Share
fake oplocks	Boolean	If yes, tells client the lock was obtained, but doesn't actually lock it.	no	Share
blocking locks	Boolean	Allows lock requestor to wait for the lock to be granted.	yes	Share
veto oplock files	string (list of file-names)	Does not oplock specified files.	None	Share
lock directory	string (fully qual-ified pathname)	Sets the location where various Samba files, including locks, are stored.	As specified in Samba makefile	Global

locking

The locking option can be used to tell Samba to engage or disengage server-side byte-range locks on behalf of the client. Samba implements byte-range locks on the server side with normal Unix advisory locks and consequently prevents other properly behaved Unix processes from overwriting a locked byte range.

This option can be specified per share as follows:

```
[accounting]
    locking = yes
```

If the locking option is set to yes, the requestor is delayed until the holder of either type of lock releases it (or crashes). If, however, the option is set to no, no byte-range locks are kept for the files, although requests to lock and unlock files will appear to succeed. The option is set to yes by default; however, you can turn this option off if you have read-only media.

strict locking

This option checks every file access for a byte-range lock on the range of bytes being accessed. This is typically not needed if a client adheres to all the locking mechanisms in place. This option is set to no by default; however, you can reset it per share as follows:

```
[accounting]
    strict locking = yes
```

If this option is set to yes, mandatory locks are enforced on any file with byte-range locks.

posix locking

On systems that support POSIX locking, Samba automatically maps oplocks to POSIX locks. This behavior can be disabled by setting posix locking = no. You should never need to change the default behavior, which is posix locking = yes.

oplocks

This option enables or disables support for oplocks on the client. The option is enabled by default. However, you can disable it with the following command:

```
[data]
    oplocks = no
```

If you are in an extremely unstable network environment or have many clients that cannot take advantage of opportunistic locking, it might be better to shut this Samba feature off. If the host operating system does not support kernel oplocks, oplocks should be disabled if users are accessing the same files from both Unix applications (such as *vi*) and SMB clients.

kernel oplocks

If a Unix application on the Samba host system (that is not part of the Samba suite) tries to open a file for writing that Samba has oplocked to a Windows client, it is likely to succeed (depending on the operating system), and both Samba and the client are never aware of it.

Some versions of Unix have support for oplocks in the kernel that can work along with Samba's oplocks. In this case, the Unix process trying to open the file is suspended while Samba directs the client to write its copy back. After that has happened, the operating system allows the open to complete. At the time of this writing, this feature is supported only by SGI Irix and Linux.

level2 oplocks

Windows NT/2000/XP clients can downgrade their read-write oplocks to read-only oplocks when another client opens the same file. This can result in significant improvements in performance on files that are written infrequently or not at all—especially executables—because all clients can then maintain a read-ahead cache for the file. By default, level2 oplocks is set to yes, and you probably won't need to change it.

Currently, Samba cannot support level 2 oplocks along with kernel oplocks and automatically disables level 2 oplocks when kernel oplocks are in use. (This might change in future releases as improved support for oplocks is added by the Samba developers.) If you are running Samba on a host system that supports kernel oplocks, you must set kernel oplocks = no to enable support for level 2 oplocks.

Disabling oplocks with oplocks = no also disables level 2 oplocks.

Samba can automatically detect its Unix host's support of kernel oplocks and will set the value of kernel oplocks automatically. You should never need to set this option in your Samba configuration file.

fake oplocks

When this option is set to yes, Samba pretends to allow oplocks rather than actually supporting them. If this option is enabled on a read-only share (such as a shared CD-ROM drive), all clients are told that the files are available for opportunistic locking and never warned of simultaneous access. As a result, Windows clients cache more of the file's data and obtain much better performance.

This option was added to Samba before opportunistic-locking support was available, and it is now generally considered better to use real oplocks. Do not ever enable fake oplocks on a read/write share.

blocking locks

Samba also supports *blocking locks*, a minor variant of range locks. Here, if the range of bytes is not available, the client specifies an amount of time that it's willing to wait. The server then caches the lock request, periodically checking to see if the file is available. If it is, it notifies the client; however, if time expires, Samba will tell the client that the request has failed. This strategy prevents the client from continually polling to see if the lock is available.

You can disable this option per share as follows:

```
[accounting]
    blocking locks = no
```

When set to yes, blocking locks are enforced on the file. If this option is set to no, Samba behaves as if normal locking mechanisms are in place on the file. The default is yes.

veto oplock files

You can provide a list of filenames that are never granted opportunistic locks with the veto oplock files option. This option can be set either globally or on a per-share basis. For example:

```
veto oplock files = /*.bat/*.htm/
```

The value of this option is a series of patterns. Each pattern entry must begin, end, or be separated from another with a slash (/) character, even if only one pattern is listed. Asterisks can be used as a wildcard to represent zero or more characters. Questions marks can be used to represent exactly one character.

We recommend that you disable oplocks on any files that are meant to be updated by Unix or are intended for simultaneous sharing by several processes.

lock directory

This option (sometimes called `lock dir`) specifies the location of a directory where Samba will store SMB deny-mode lock files. Samba stores other files in this directory as well, such as browse lists and its shared memory file. If WINS is enabled, the WINS database is written to this directory as well. The default for this option is specified in the Samba makefile; it is typically */usr/local/samba/var/locks*. You can override this location as follows:

```
[global]
    lock directory = /usr/local/samba/locks
```

You typically would not need to override this option, unless you want to move the lock files to a more standard location, such as */var/spool/locks*.

Connection Scripts

Samba supports a mechanism called *connection scripts*, by which commands can be executed on the server as clients connect to a share or later disconnect from it. By using configuration file variables along with some custom programming, you can create connection scripts that perform a wide range of functions. As a simple example, here is a "quick and dirty" way to monitor connections to shares on the Samba server in real time. First, the value of the preexec parameter is set as follows:

```
[global]
    preexec = /bin/echo %u at %m connected to //%L/%S on %T >>/tmp/smblog
```

This causes information about the user and the connection to be written to the file */tmp/smblog* whenever any client connects to any share. To watch clients connect, run the following command:

```
$ tail -f /tmp/smblog
jay at maya connected to //toltec/data on 2002/11/21 21:21:15
david at apache connected to //toltec/techs on 2002/11/21 21:21:57
sally at seminole connected to //toltec/payroll on 2002/11/21 21:22:16
martha at dine connected to //toltec/profiles on 2002/11/21 21:23:38
martha at dine connected to //toltec/netlogon on 2002/11/21 21:23:39
martha at dine connected to //toltec/martha on 2002/11/21 21:23:40
aaron at huastec connected to //toltec/netlogon on 2002/11/21 21:24:19
aaron at huastec connected to //toltec/aaron on 2002/11/21 21:24:20
```

With the *-f* option, the *tail* command monitors */tmp/smblog* and prints additional output as new data is appended to the file. Every time a new connection is made, an additional line is printed, showing the output of the preexec command. Notice the lines resulting from connections by user martha and aaron. User martha logged on to the domain from a Windows NT client, which accessed the [profiles] share to download her profile, then the [netlogon] share to read the logon script, and then her home directory (because her logon script contains a net use H: /home command) to connect her home directory to drive letter H. The connections from aaron are similar, except that he connected from a Windows 98 system, which does not use the [profiles] share. (See Chapter 4 for more information about domain logons.)

A more advanced use of connection scripts is to monitor the contents of users' home directories and/or other shared directories and perform checks ensuring that local administrative policies are followed. Checked items might include the following:

- Disk usage, on a per-share, per-directory, or per-file basis
- Types of files stored on the server
- Whether filenames follow naming guidelines
- Whether viruses have copied themselves to the Samba server

To handle this kind of task, a shell script or other program would be written to perform the checks and take appropriate actions, such as removing offending files. The root preexec parameter would be used to run the command as the root user, using configuration file variables to pass arguments. For example:

```
[homes]
    root preexec = admin_checks %S
    root preexec close = yes
```

In this example, a specially written administrative checking program (*admin_checks*) is used to monitor users' home directories on the Samba server. The %S variable is used to pass the name of the home directory to the script. The root preexec close parameter has been set to yes so that if *admin_checks* detects a serious violation of local policy, it can exit with a nonzero status, and the client is prevented from connecting.

Connection Script Options

Table 8-7 introduces some of the configuration options provided for setting up users.

Table 8-7. Connection script options

Option	Parameters	Function	Default	Scope
root preexec	string (Unix command)	Sets a Unix command to run as root, before connecting to the share.	None	Share
root preexec close	Boolean	If set to yes, nonzero exit status of root preexec command will disconnect.	no	Share
preexec (exec)	string (Unix command)	Sets a Unix command to run as the user before connecting to the share.	None	Share

Table 8-7. Connection script options (continued)

Option	Parameters	Function	Default	Scope
preexec close	Boolean	If set to yes, nonzero exit status of preexec command will disconnect.	no	Share
postexec	string (Unix command)	Sets a Unix command to run as the user after disconnecting from the share.	None	Share
root postexec	string (Unix command)	Sets a Unix command to run as root after disconnecting from the share.	None	Share

root preexec

This option specifies as its value a Unix command to be run *as the root user* before any connection to a share is completed. You should use this option specifically for performing actions that require root privilege.

To ensure security, users should never be able to modify the target of the root preexec command. In addition, unless you explicitly redirect it, any information the command sends to standard output will be discarded. If you intend to use any preexec or postexec script, you should ensure that it will run correctly before having Samba invoke it.

root preexec close

Sometimes you might want the share to disconnect if the root preexec script fails, giving the client an error rather than allowing it to connect. For example, if you are using root preexec to mount a CD-ROM or filesystem, it would make no sense to connect the client to it in the event that the mount fails. If you specify root preexec close = yes, the share will fail to connect if the root preexec script returns a nonzero exit status.

preexec

Sometimes just called exec, this option defines an ordinary unprivileged command run by Samba as the user specified by the variable %u. For example, a common use of this option is to perform logging, such as the following:

```
[homes]
    preexec = echo "%u connected from %m (%I)\" >>/tmp/.log
```

You must redirect the standard output of the command if you want to use it. Otherwise, it is discarded. This warning also applies to the command's standard error output. If you intend to use a preexec script, you should ensure that it will run correctly before having Samba invoke it.

preexec close

This is similar to root preexec close, except that it goes with the preexec option. By setting preexec close = yes, a preexec script that returns nonzero will cause the share to disconnect immediately.

postexec

Once the user disconnects from the share, the command specified with postexec is run as the user on the Samba server to do any necessary cleanup. This option is essentially the same as the preexec option. Again, remember that the command is run as the user represented by %u, and any information sent to standard output will be ignored.

root postexec

Following the postexec option, the root postexec command is run, if one has been specified. Again, this option specifies as its value a Unix command to be run *as the root user* before disconnecting from a share. You should use this option specifically for performing actions that require root privilege.

Microsoft Distributed Filesystems

In a large network where many shared folders are spread out over a large number of servers, it can be difficult for users to locate the resources they are trying to find. Browsing through Network Neighborhood or My Network Places can become an ordeal rather than a time-saving convenience. To mitigate this problem, Microsoft added an extension to file sharing called *Distributed filesystem* (Dfs). Using Dfs, it is possible to organize file shares on the network so that they appear to users as organized in a single directory tree on a single server, regardless of which servers on the network actually contain the resources. Instead of having to browse the entire network, users can go to the Dfs share and locate their data much more easily.

Dfs can also help administrators because it provides a level of indirection between the name of a shared folder and its actual location. The Dfs share contains references to resources on the network, and when a resource is accessed, the Dfs server hands the client off to the actual server of the resource. When moving resources to another computer, the reference to the resource in the Dfs share can be redirected to the new location in one step, with the change being entirely seamless for users.

To a limited extent, Dfs also can help improve performance for read-only shares because it provides load balancing. It is possible to set up a Dfs reference to point to identical shares on two or more servers. The Dfs server then divides requests between the servers, dividing the client load among them. However, this works well only for static, read-only data because no provision is included in Dfs for synchronization among the servers when changes are made on any of them.

Windows Dfs Clients

Modern versions of Windows come with client-side support for Dfs, and no extra configuration is required. Support is more limited for older versions, however. Windows for Workgroups cannot function as a Dfs client at all. Windows NT 4.0 must be upgraded to at least Service Pack 3 to act as a Dfs client, and the Dfs Client must be installed. Later service packs (such as Service Pack 6) include the Dfs Client. Windows 95 must also have the Dfs Client software installed to act as a Dfs client. Without the Dfs Client software, double-clicking a remote folder in a Dfs share will show an empty folder, and no error message will appear.

 To use the Dfs Client for Windows 95 or Windows NT, you must first download and install it. See the web page *http://microsoft.com/ntserver/nts/downloads/winfeatures/NTSDistrFile/default.asp* for a link to download the installation program and instructions on how to install the Dfs Client.

Configuring Samba for Dfs

To act as a Dfs server, Samba 2.2 must be compiled with the `--with-msdfs` configure option. (See Chapter 2 for instructions on configuring and compiling Samba.) Samba 3.0 includes Dfs support by default and does not need to be compiled with the `--with-msdfs` configure option.

Once a Dfs-enabled Samba server is running, there are just two steps to serving a Dfs share. First we will set up a Dfs root directory on the server, and then we will modify the *smb.conf* configuration file to enable the share.

Setting up the Dfs root

First we need to create a directory to act as the Dfs root:

```
# mkdir /usr/local/samba/dfs
```

This can be any directory, but it is important that it be owned by root and given the proper permissions:

```
# chown root:root /usr/local/samba/dfs
# chmod 755 /usr/local/samba/dfs
```

The Dfs directory tree can have subdirectories and files, just like any other shared directory. These will function just as they would in any other share, allowing clients to access the directories and files on the Samba server. The whole idea of Dfs, though, is to gather together shares on other servers by making references to them in the Dfs tree. The way this is implemented with Samba involves a clever use of symbolic links, which can be in the Dfs root directory or any subdirectory in the Dfs tree.

You are probably familiar with using symbolic links to create references to files that exist on the same system, and perhaps crossing a local filesystem boundary (which ordinary Unix links cannot do). But maybe you didn't know that symbolic links have a more general functionality. Although we can't display its contents directly, as we could with a text or binary file, a symbolic link "contains" an ASCII text string naming what the link points to. For example, take a look at the listing for these symbolic links:

```
$ ls -l wrdlnk alnk
lrwxrwxrwx    1 jay      jay             15 Mar 14 06:50 wrdlnk -> /usr/dict/words
lrwxrwxrwx    1 jay      jay              9 Mar 14 06:53 alnk -> dreamtime
```

As you can infer from the size of the *wrdlnk* link (15 bytes), the string */usr/dict/words* is encoded into it. The size of *alnk* (9 bytes) is smaller, corresponding to the shorter name of *dreamtime*.

Now let's create a link in our Dfs root for an SMB share:

```
# cd /usr/local/samba/dfs
# ln -s 'msdfs:maya\e' maya-e
# ls -l maya-e
lrwxrwxrwx    1 root     root            12 Mar 13 17:34 maya-e -> msdfs:maya\e
```

This link might appear as a "broken" link in a directory listing because it points to something that isn't a file on the local system. For example, the *file* command will report:

```
$ file maya-e
maya-e: broken symbolic link to msdfs:maya\e
```

However, *maya-e* is a valid reference to the *maya**e* share when used with Samba's Dfs support. When Samba encounters this file, it sees the leading `msdfs:` and interprets the rest as the name of a remote share. The client is then redirected to the remote share.

When creating links in the Dfs root directory, simply follow the same format, which in general is `msdfs:`*server**share*. Note that this is similar to a UNC appended onto the `msdfs:` string, except that in this case, the two backslashes preceding the server's name are omitted.

 The names for the symbolic links in Dfs shares must be in all lowercase.

In addition to regular network shares, you can use symbolic links of this type to reference Dfs shares on other Dfs servers. However, referencing printer shares does not work. Dfs is for sharing files only.

Load balancing

To set up a load-balancing Dfs share, create the symbolic link like this:

```
# ln -s 'msdfs:toltec\data,msdfs:mixtec\data' lb-data
```

That is, simply use a list of shares separated by commas as the reference. Remember, it is up to you to make sure the shared folders remain identical. Set up permissions on the servers to make the shares read-only to users.

The last thing we need to do is to modify the *smb.conf* file to define the Dfs root share and add Dfs support. The Dfs root is added as a share definition:

```
[dfs]
    path = /usr/local/samba/dfs
    msdfs root = yes
```

You can use any name you like for the share. The path is set to the Dfs root directory we just set up, and the parameter msdfs root = yes tells Samba that this share is a Dfs root.

To enable support for Dfs in the server, we need to add one line to the [global] section:

```
[global]
    host msdfs = yes
```

Restart the Samba daemons—or just wait a minute for them to reread the configuration file—and you will see the new share from Windows clients. If you have trouble accessing any of the remote shares in the Dfs share, recheck your symbolic links to make sure they were created correctly.

 If you previously had a share by the same name as your Dfs share, you might need to reboot Windows clients before they can access the share as a Dfs share.

Working with NIS

In networks where NIS and NFS are in use, it is common for users' home directories to be mounted over the network by NFS. If a Samba server being used to authenticate user logons is running on a system with NFS-mounted home directories shared with a [homes] share, the additional overhead can result in poor performance—about 30% of normal Samba speed.

Samba has the ability to work with NIS and NIS+ to find the server on which the home directories actually reside so that they can be shared directly from that server. For this to work, the server that holds the home directories must also have Samba running, with a [homes] share of its own.

NIS Configuration Options

Table 8-8 introduces the NIS configuration options specifically for setting up users.

Table 8-8. NIS options

Option	Parameters	Function	Default	Scope
nis homedir	Boolean	If yes, uses NIS instead of */etc/passwd* to look up the path of a user's home directory.	no	Global
homedir map	string (NIS map name)	Sets the NIS map to use to look up a user's home directory.	None	Global

nis homedir, homedir map

The nis homedir and homedir map options are for Samba servers on network sites where Unix home directories are provided using NFS, the automounter, and NIS.

The nis homedir option indicates that the home-directory server for the user needs to be looked up in NIS. The homedir map option tells Samba in which NIS map to look for the server that has the user's home directory. The server needs to be a Samba server so that the client can do an SMB connect to it, and the other Samba servers need to have NIS installed so that they can do the lookup.

For example, if user joe asks for a share called [joe], and the nis homedir option is set to yes, Samba will look in the file specified by homedir map for a home directory for joe. If it finds one, Samba will return the associated system name to the client. The client will then try to connect to that machine and get the share from there. Enabling NIS lookups looks like the following:

```
[globals]
     nis homedir = yes
     homedir map = amd.map
```

## CHAPTER 9

Users and Security

In this chapter, we cover the basic concepts of managing security in Samba so that you can set up your Samba server with a security policy suited to your network.

One of Samba's most complicated tasks lies in reconciling the security models of Unix and Windows systems. Samba must identify users by associating them with valid usernames and groups, authenticate them by checking their passwords, then control their access to resources by comparing their access rights to the permissions on files and directories. These are complex topics on their own, and it doesn't help that there are three different operating system types to deal with (Unix, Windows 95/98/Me, and Windows NT/2000/XP) and that Samba supports multiple methods of handling user authentication.

Users and Groups

Let's start out as simply as possible and add support for a single user. The easiest way to set up a client user is to create a Unix account (and home directory) for that individual on the server and notify Samba of the user's existence. You can do the latter by creating a disk share that maps to the user's home directory in the Samba configuration file and restricting access to that user with the valid users option. For example:

```
[dave]
        path = /home/dave
        comment = Dave's home directory
        writable = yes
        valid users = dave
```

The valid users option lists the users allowed to access the share. In this case, only the user dave is allowed to access the share. In some situations it is possible to specify that any user can access a disk share by using the guest ok parameter. Because we don't wish to allow guest access, that option is absent here. If you allow both authenticated users and guest users access to the same share, you can make some files accessible to guest users by assigning world-readable permissions to those files while restricting access to other files to particular users or groups.

When client users access a Samba share, they have to pass two levels of restriction. Unix permissions on files and directories apply as usual, and configuration parameters specified in the Samba configuration file apply as well. In other words, a client must first pass Samba's security mechanisms (e.g., authenticating with a valid username and password, passing the check for the valid users parameter and the read only parameter, etc.), as well as the normal Unix file and directory permissions of its Unix-side user, before it can gain read/write access to a share.

Remember that you can abbreviate the user's home directory by using the %H variable. In addition, you can use the Unix username variable %u and/or the client username variable %U in your options as well. For example:

```
[dave]
     comment = %U home directory
     writable = yes
     valid users = dave
     path = %H
```

With a single user accessing a home directory, access permissions are taken care of when the user account is created. The home directory is owned by the user, and permissions on it are set appropriately. However, if you're creating a shared directory for group access, you need to perform a few more steps. Let's take a stab at a group share for the accounting department in the *smb.conf* file:

```
[accounting]
     comment = Accounting Department Directory
     writable = yes
     valid users = @account
     path = /home/samba/accounting
     create mode = 0660
     directory mode = 0770
```

The first thing we did differently is to specify @account as the valid user instead of one or more individual usernames. This is shorthand for saying that the valid users are represented by the Unix group account. These users will need to be added to the group entry account in the system group file (*/etc/group* or equivalent) to be recognized as part of the group. Once they are, Samba will recognize those users as valid users for the share.

In addition, you need to create a shared directory that the members of the group can access and point to it with the path configuration option. Here are the Unix commands that create the shared directory for the accounting department (assuming */home/samba* already exists):

```
# mkdir /home/samba/accounting
# chgrp account /home/samba/accounting
# chmod 770 /home/samba/accounting
```

There are two other options in this *smb.conf* example, both of which we saw in the previous chapter. These options are create mode and directory mode. These options set the maximum file and directory permissions that a new file or directory can have. In this case, we have denied all world access to the contents of this share. (This is reinforced by the *chmod* command, shown earlier.)

Handling Multiple Individual Users

Let's return to user shares for a moment. If we have several users for whom to set up home directory shares, we probably want to use the special [homes] share that we introduced in Chapter 8. With the [homes] share, all we need to say is:

```
[homes]
    browsable = no
    writable = yes
```

The [homes] share is a special section of the Samba configuration file. If a user attempts to connect to an ordinary share that doesn't appear in the *smb.conf* file (such as specifying it with a UNC in Windows Explorer), Samba will search for a [homes] share. If one exists, the incoming share name is assumed to be a username and is queried as such in the password database (*/etc/passwd* or equivalent) file of the Samba server. If it appears, Samba assumes the client is a Unix user trying to connect to his home directory.

As an illustration, let's assume that sofia is attempting to connect to a share called [sofia] on the Samba server. There is no share by that name in the configuration file, but a [homes] share exists and user sofia is present in the password database, so Samba takes the following steps:

1. Samba creates a new disk share called [sofia] with the path specified in the [homes] section. If no path option is specified in [homes], Samba initializes it to her home directory.

2. Samba initializes the new share's options from the defaults in [globals], as well as any overriding options in [homes] with the exception of browsable.

3. Samba connects sofia's client to that share.

The [homes] share is a fast, painless way to create shares for your user community without having to duplicate the information from the password database file in the *smb.conf* file. It does have some peculiarities, however, that we need to point out:

- The [homes] section can represent any account on the machine, which isn't always desirable. For example, it can potentially create a share for root, bin, sys, uucp, and the like. You can set a global invalid users option to protect against this.

- The meaning of the browsable configuration option is different from other shares; it indicates only that a [homes] section won't show up in the local browse list, not that the [alice] share won't. When the [alice] section is created (after the initial connection), it will use the browsable value from the [globals] section for that share, not the value from [homes].

As we mentioned, there is no need for a path statement in [homes] if the users have Unix home directories in the server's */etc/passwd* file. You should ensure that a valid home directory does exist, however, as Samba will not automatically create a home directory for a user and will refuse a tree connect if the user's directory does not exist or is not accessible.

Controlling Access to Shares

Often you will need to restrict the users who can access a specific share for security reasons. This is very easy to do with Samba because it contains a wealth of options for creating practically any security configuration. Let's introduce a few configurations that you might want to use in your own Samba setup.

We've seen what happens when you specify valid users. However, you are also allowed to specify a list of invalid users—users who should never be allowed access to Samba or its shares. This is done with the invalid users option. We hinted at one frequent use of this option earlier: a global default with the [homes] section to ensure that various system users and superusers cannot be forged for access. For example:

```
[global]
    invalid users = root bin daemon adm sync shutdown \
                            halt mail news uucp operator
    auto services = dave peter bob

[homes]
    browsable = no
    writable = yes
```

The invalid users option, like valid users, can take group names, preceded by an at sign (@), as well as usernames. In the event that a user or group appears in both lists, the invalid users option takes precedence, and the user or group is denied access to the share.

At the other end of the spectrum, you can explicitly specify users who will be allowed superuser (root) access to a share with the admin users option. An example follows:

```
[sales]
        path = /home/sales
        comment = Sedona Real Estate Sales Data
        writable = yes
        valid users = sofie shelby adilia
        admin users = mike
```

This option takes both group names and usernames. In addition, you can specify NIS netgroups by preceding them with an @ as well; if the netgroup is not found, Samba will assume that you are referring to a standard Unix group.

Be careful if you assign administrative privileges to a share for an entire group. The Samba Team highly recommends you avoid using this option, as it essentially gives root access to the specified users or groups for that share.

If you wish to force read-only or read/write access on users who access a share, you can do so with the read list and write list options, respectively. These options can be used on a per-share basis to restrict a writable share or to grant write access to specific users in a read-only share, respectively. For example:

```
[sales]
        path = /home/sales
        comment = Sedona Real Estate Sales Data
        read only = yes
        write list = sofie shelby
```

The write list option cannot override Unix permissions. If you've created the share without giving the write-list user write permission on the Unix system, she will be denied write access regardless of the setting of write list.

Guest Access

As mentioned earlier, you can configure a share using guest ok = yes to allow access to guest users. This works only when using share-level security, which we will cover later in this chapter. When a user connects as a guest, authenticating with a username and password is unnecessary, but Samba still needs a way to map the connected client to a user on the local system. The guest account parameter can be used in the share to specify the Unix account that guest users should be assigned when connecting to the Samba server. The default value for this is set during compilation and is typically nobody, which works well with most Unix versions. However, on some systems the nobody account is not allowed to access some services (e.g., printing), and you might need to set the guest user to ftp or some other account instead.

If you wish to restrict access in a share only to guests—in other words, all clients connect as the guest account when accessing the share—you can use the guest only option in conjunction with the guest ok option, as shown in the following example:

```
[sales]
        path = /home/sales
        comment = Sedona Real Estate Sales Data
        writable = yes
        guest ok = yes
        guest account = ftp
        guest only = yes
```

Make sure you specify yes for both guest only and guest ok; otherwise, Samba will not use the guest account that you specify.

Access Control Options

Table 9-1 summarizes the options that you can use to control access to shares.

Table 9-1. Share-level access options

Option	Parameters	Function	Default	Scope
admin users	string (list of usernames)	Users who can perform operations as root	None	Share
valid users	string (list of usernames)	Users who can connect to a share	None	Share
invalid users	string (list of usernames)	Users who will be denied access to a share	None	Share
read list	string (list of usernames)	Users who have read-only access to a writable share	None	Share
write list	string (list of usernames)	Users who have read/write access to a read-only share	None	Share
max connections	numeric	Maximum number of connections for a share at a given time	0	Share
guest only (only guest)	Boolean	If yes, allows only guest access	no	Share
guest account	string (name of account)	Unix account that will be used for guest access	nobody	Share

admin users

This option specifies a list of users that perform file operations as if they were root. This means that they can modify or destroy any other user's files, regardless of the permissions. Any files that they create will have root ownership and will use the default group of the admin user. The admin users option allows PC users to act as administrators for particular shares. Be very careful when using this option, and make sure good password and other security policies are in place.

valid users, invalid users

These two options let you enumerate the users and groups who are granted or denied access to a particular share. You can enter a list of user and/or group names. If a name is prefixed by an at sign (@), it is interpreted as a group name—with NIS groups searched before Unix groups. If the name is prefixed by a plus sign (+), it is interpreted as the name of a Unix group, and NIS is not searched. If the name is prefixed by an ampersand (&), it is interpreted as an NIS group name rather than as a Unix group name. The plus sign and ampersand can be used together to specify whether NIS or Unix groups are searched first. For example:

```
[database]
    valid users = mary ellen sue &sales +marketing @dbadmin
    invalid users = gavin syd dana &techies +&helpdesk
```

In the valid users parameter, users mary, ellen, and sue are allowed access to the [database] share, as are the members of the Unix group marketing and NIS/Unix group dbadmin. The invalid users parameter denies access to the share by users gavin, syd, and dana, as well as members of the NIS group techies and Unix/NIS group helpdesk. In this last case, the list of Unix groups is searched first for the helpdesk group, and if it is not found there, the list of NIS groups is searched.

The important rule to remember with these options is that any name or group in the invalid users list will *always* be denied access, even if it is included (in any form) in the valid users list.

read list, write list

Like the valid users and invalid users options, this pair of options specifies which users have read-only access to a writable share and read/write access to a read-only share, respectively. The value of either options is a list of users. The read list parameter overrides any other Samba permissions granted—as well as Unix file permissions on the server system—to deny users write access. The write list parameter overrides other Samba permissions to grant write access, but cannot grant write access if the user lacks write permissions for the file on the Unix system. You can specify NIS or Unix group names by prefixing the name with an at sign (such as @users). Neither configuration option has a default value associated with it.

max connections

This option specifies the maximum number of client connections that a share can have at any given time. Any connections that are attempted after the maximum is reached will be rejected. The default value is 0, which is a special case that allows an unlimited number of connections. You can override it per share as follows:

```
[accounting]
    max connections = 30
```

This option is useful in the event that you need to limit the number of users who are accessing a licensed program or piece of data concurrently.

guest only

This share-level option (also called only guest) forces a connection to a share to be performed with the user specified by the guest account option. The share to which this is applied must explicitly specify guest ok = yes for this option to be recognized by Samba. The default value for this option is no.

guest account

This option specifies the name of the account to be used for guest access to shares in Samba. The default for this option varies from system to system, but it is often set to nobody. Some default user accounts have trouble connecting as guest users. If that occurs on your system, the Samba Team recommends using the ftp account as the guest user.

Username Options

Table 9-2 shows two additional options that Samba can use to correct for incompatibilities in usernames between Windows and Unix.

Table 9-2. Username options

Option	Parameters	Function	Default	Scope
username map	string (filename)	Sets the name of the username mapping file	None	Global
username level	numeric	Indicates the number of capital letters to use when trying to match a username	0	Global

username map

Client usernames on an SMB network can be relatively long (up to 255 characters), while usernames on a Unix network often cannot be longer than eight characters. This means that an individual user can have one username on a client and another (shorter) one on the Samba server. You can get past this issue by mapping a free-form client username to a Unix username of eight or fewer characters. It is placed in a standard text file, using a format that we'll describe shortly. You can then specify the pathname to Samba with the global username map option. Be sure to restrict access to this file; make the root user the file's owner and deny write access to others (with octal permissions of 744 or 644). Otherwise, an untrusted user with access to the file can easily map his client username to the root user of the Samba server.

You can specify this option as follows:

```
[global]
    username map = /usr/local/samba/private/usermap.txt
```

Each entry in the username map file should be listed as follows: the Unix username, followed by an equal sign (=), followed by one or more whitespace-separated SMB client usernames. Note that unless instructed otherwise (i.e., a guest connection), Samba will expect both the client and the server user to have the same password. You can also map NT groups to one or more specific Unix groups using the @ sign. Here are some examples:

```
jarwin = JosephArwin
manderso = MarkAnderson
users = @account
```

You can also use the asterisk to specify a wildcard that matches any free-form client username as an entry in the username map file:

```
nobody = *
```

Comments can be placed in the file by starting the line with a hash mark (#) or a semicolon (;).

Note that you can also use this file to redirect one Unix user to another user. Be careful, though, as Samba and your client might not notify the user that the mapping has been made and Samba might be expecting a different password.

username level

SMB clients (such as Windows) will often send usernames in SMB connection requests entirely in capital letters; in other words, client usernames are not necessarily case-sensitive. On a Unix server, however, usernames *are* case-sensitive: the user ANDY is different from the user andy. By default, Samba attacks this problem by doing the following:

1. Checking for a user account with the exact name sent by the client
2. Testing the username in all lowercase letters
3. Testing the username in lowercase letters with only the first letter capitalized

If you wish to have Samba attempt more combinations of upper- and lowercase letters, you can use the username level global configuration option. This option takes an integer value that specifies how many letters in the username should be capitalized when attempting to connect to a share. You can specify this option as follows:

```
[global]
    username level = 3
```

In this case, Samba attempts all possible permutations of usernames having three capital letters. The larger the number, the more computations Samba has to perform to match the username, and the longer the authentication will take.

Authentication of Clients

At this point, we should discuss how Samba authenticates users. Each user who attempts to connect to a share not allowing guest access must provide a password to make a successful connection. What Samba does with that password—and consequently the strategy Samba will use to handle user authentication—is the arena of the security configuration option. Samba currently supports four security levels on its network: *share*, *user*, *server*, and *domain*.

Share-level security
    Each share in the workgroup has one or more passwords associated with it. Anyone who knows a valid password for the share can access it.

User-level security
    Each share in the workgroup is configured to allow access from certain users. With each initial tree connection, the Samba server verifies users and their passwords to allow them access to the share.

Server-level security

> This is the same as user-level security, except that the Samba server uses another server to validate users and their passwords before granting access to the share.

Domain-level security

> Samba becomes a member of a Windows NT domain and uses one of the domain's domain controllers—either the PDC or a BDC—to perform authentication. Once authenticated, the user is given a special token that allows her access to any share with appropriate access rights. With this token, the domain controller will not have to revalidate the user's password each time she attempts to access another share within the domain. The domain controller can be a Windows NT/2000 PDC or BDC, or Samba acting as a Windows NT PDC.

Each security policy can be implemented with the global security option, as shown in Table 9-3.

Table 9-3. Security option

Option	Parameters	Function	Default	Scope
security	domain, server, share, or user	Indicates the type of security that the Samba server will use	user	Global

Share-Level Security

With share-level security, each share has one or more passwords associated with it, with the client being authenticated when first connecting to the share. This differs from the other modes of security in that there are no restrictions as to whom can access a share, as long as that individual knows the correct password. Shares often have multiple passwords. For example, one password might grant read-only access, while another might grant read/write access. Security is maintained as long as unauthorized users do not discover the password for a share to which they shouldn't have access.

OS/2 and Windows 95/98/Me both support share-level security on their resources. You can set up share-level security with Windows 95/98/Me by first enabling share-level security using the Access Control tab of the Network Control Panel dialog. Then select the "Share-level access control" radio button (which deselects the "User-level access control" radio button), as shown in Figure 9-1, and click the OK button. Reboot as requested.

Next, right-click a resource—such as a hard drive or a CD-ROM—and select the Properties menu item. This will bring up the Resource Properties dialog box. Select the Sharing tab at the top of the dialog box, and enable the resource as Shared As. From here, you can configure how the shared resource will appear to individual users, as well as assign whether the resource will appear as read-only, read/write, or a mix, depending on the password that is supplied.

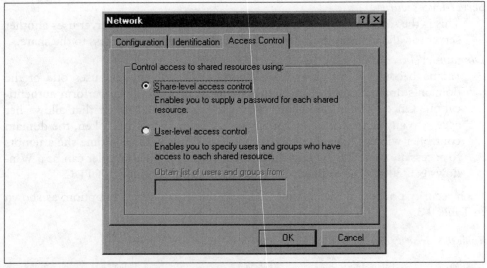

Figure 9-1. Selecting share-level security on a Windows 95/98/Me system

You might be thinking that this security model is not a good fit for Samba—and you would be right. In fact, if you set the security = share option in the Samba configuration file, Samba will still reuse the username/password combinations in the system password files to authenticate access. More precisely, Samba will take the following steps when a client requests a connection using share-level security:

1. When a connection is requested, Samba will accept the password and (if sent) the username of the client.

2. If the share is guest only, the user is immediately granted access to the share with the rights of the user specified by the guest account parameter; no password checking is performed.

3. For other shares, Samba appends the username to a list of users who are allowed access to the share. It then attempts to validate the password given in association with that username. If successful, Samba grants the user access to the share with the rights assigned to that user. The user will not need to authenticate again unless a revalidate = yes option has been set inside the share.

4. If the authentication is unsuccessful, Samba attempts to validate the password against the list of users previously compiled during attempted connections, as well as those specified under the share in the configuration file. If the password matches that of any username (as specified in the system password file, typically */etc/passwd*), the user is granted access to the share under that username.

5. However, if the share has a guest ok or public option set, the user will default to access with the rights of the user specified by the guest account option.

You can indicate in the configuration file which users should be initially placed on the share-level security user list by using the username configuration option, as shown here:

```
[global]
    security = share

[accounting1]
    path = /home/samba/accounting1
    guest ok = no
    writable = yes
    username = davecb, pkelly, andyo
```

Here, when a user attempts to connect to a share, Samba verifies the sent password against each user in its own list, in addition to the passwords of users davecb, pkelly, and andyo. If any of the passwords match, the connection is verified, and the user is allowed. Otherwise, connection to the specific share will fail.

Share-Level Security Options

Table 9-4 shows the options typically associated with *share-level security*.

Table 9-4. Share-level access options

Option	Parameters	Function	Default	Scope
only user	Boolean	If yes, usernames specified by username are the only ones allowed	no	Share
username (user or users)	string (list of usernames)	Users against which a client's password is tested	None	Share

only user

This Boolean option indicates whether Samba will allow connections to a share using share-level security based solely on the individuals specified in the username option, instead of those users compiled on Samba's internal list. The default value for this option is no. You can override it per share as follows:

```
[global]
    security = share
[data]
    username = andy, peter, valerie
    only user = yes
```

username

This option presents a list of usernames and/or group names against which Samba tests a connection password to allow access. It is typically used with clients that have share-level security to allow connections to a particular service based solely on a qualifying password—in this case, one that matches a password set up for a specific user:

```
[global]
    security = share
[data]
    username = andy, peter, terry
```

You can enter a list of usernames and/or group names. If a name is prefixed by an at sign (@), it is interpreted as a group name, with NIS groups searched before Unix groups. If the name is prefixed by a plus sign (+), it is interpreted as the name of a Unix group, and NIS is not searched. If the name is prefixed by an ampersand (&), it is interpreted as an NIS group name rather than a Unix group name. The plus sign and ampersand can be used together to specify whether NIS or Unix groups are searched first. When Samba encounters a group name in this option, it attempts to authenticate each user in the group until if finds one that succeeds. Beware that this can be very inefficient.

We recommend against using this option unless you are implementing a Samba server with share-level security.

User-Level Security

The default mode of security with Samba is *user-level security*. With this method, each share is assigned specific users that can access it. When a user requests a connection to a share, Samba authenticates by validating the given username and password with the authorized users in the configuration file and the passwords in the password database of the Samba server. As mentioned earlier in the chapter, one way to isolate which users are allowed access to a specific share is by using the valid users option for each share:

```
[global]
    security = user

[accounting1]
    writable = yes
    valid users = bob, joe, sandy
```

Each user listed can connect to the share if the password provided matches the password stored in the system password database on the server. Once the initial authentication succeeds, the client will not need to supply a password again to access that share unless the revalidate = yes option has been set.

Passwords can be sent to the Samba server in either an encrypted or a nonencrypted format. If you have both types of systems on your network, you should ensure that the passwords represented by each user are stored both in a traditional account database and Samba's encrypted password database. This way, authorized users can gain access to their shares from any type of client.* However, we recommend that you

---

* Having both encrypted and nonencrypted password clients on your network is one of the reasons why Samba allows you to include (or not include) various options in the Samba configuration file based on the client operating system or machine name variables.

move your system to encrypted passwords and abandon nonencrypted passwords if security is an issue. The "Passwords" section of this chapter explains how to use encrypted as well as nonencrypted passwords.

Server-Level Security

Server-level security is similar to user-level security. However, with server-level security, Samba delegates password authentication to another SMB password server—typically another Samba server or a Windows NT/2000 server acting as a PDC on the network. Note that Samba still maintains its list of shares and their configuration in its *smb.conf* file. When a client attempts to make a connection to a particular share, Samba validates that the user is indeed authorized to connect to the share. Samba then attempts to validate the password by passing the username and password to the SMB password server. If the password is accepted, a session is established with the client. See Figure 9-2 for an illustration of this setup.

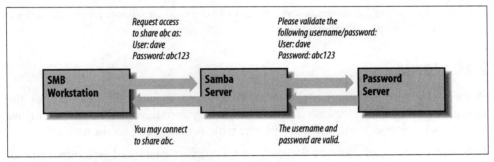

Figure 9-2. A typical system setup using server-level security

You can configure Samba to use a separate password server under server-level security with the use of the password server global configuration option, as follows:

```
[global]
    security = server
    password server = mixtec toltec
```

Note that you can specify more than one machine as the target of the password server; Samba moves down the list of servers in the event that its first choice is unreachable. The servers identified by the password server option are given as NetBIOS names, not their DNS names or equivalent IP addresses. Also, if any of the servers reject the given password, the connection automatically fails—Samba will not attempt another server.

One caveat: when using this option, you still need an account representing that user on the regular Samba server. This is because the Unix operating system needs a username to perform various I/O operations. The preferable method of handling this is to give the user an account on the Samba server but disable the account's password by replacing it in the system password file (e.g., */etc/passwd*) with an asterisk (*).

Domain-Level Security

With *domain-level security*, the Samba server acts as a member of a Windows domain. Recall from Chapter 1 that each domain has a primary domain controller, which can be a Windows NT/2000 or Samba server offering password authentication. The domain controller keeps track of users and passwords in its own database and authenticates each user when she first logs on and wishes to access another machine's shares.

As mentioned earlier in this chapter, Samba has a similar ability to offer user-level security, but that option is Unix-centric and assumes that the authentication occurs via Unix password files. If the Unix machine is part of an NIS or NIS+ domain, Samba authenticates users transparently against a shared password file in typical Unix fashion. Samba then provides access to the NIS or NIS+ domain from Windows. There is, of course, no relationship between the NIS concept of a domain and a Windows NT domain.

Configuring Samba for domain-level security is covered in Chapter 4 in the section "Samba as a Domain Member Server."

Passwords

Passwords are a thorny issue with Samba. So much so, in fact, that they are often the first major problem that users encounter when they install Samba. At this point, we need to delve deeper into Samba to discover what is happening on the network.

Passwords sent from individual clients can be either encrypted or nonencrypted. Encrypted passwords are, of course, more secure. A nonencrypted, plain-text password can be easily read with a packet-sniffing program, such as the modified *tcp-dump* program for Samba that we used in Chapter 1. Whether passwords are encrypted by default depends on the operating system that the client is using to connect to the Samba server. Table 9-5 lists which Windows operating systems encrypt their passwords and which send plain-text passwords by default.

Table 9-5. Windows operating systems with encrypted passwords

Operating system	Encrypted or plain text
Windows for Workgroups	Plain text
Windows 95	Plain text
Windows 95 with SMB Update	Encrypted
Windows 98	Encrypted
Windows Me	Encrypted
Windows NT 3.x	Plain text
Windows NT 4.0 before SP 3	Plain text

Table 9-5. Windows operating systems with encrypted passwords (continued)

Operating system	Encrypted or plain text
Windows NT 4.0 after SP 3	Encrypted
Windows 2000	Encrypted
Windows XP	Encrypted

Three different encryption methods are used. Windows 95/98/Me clients use a method inherited from Microsoft's LAN Manager network software. Windows NT/2000/XP systems use a newer system, called NT LAN Manager, or NTLM. A newer version of this (called NT LAN Manager Version 2, or NTLMv2) uses a different method for password hashing.

If encrypted passwords are supported, Samba stores the encrypted passwords in a file called *smbpasswd*. By default, this file is located in the *private* directory of the Samba distribution (typically */usr/local/samba/private*). At the same time, the client stores an encrypted version of a user's password on its own system. The plain-text password is never stored on either system. Each system encrypts the password automatically using a standard algorithm when the password is set or changed.

When a client requests a connection to an SMB server that supports encrypted passwords (such as Samba or Windows NT/2000/XP), the two computers undergo the following negotiations:

1. The client attempts to negotiate a protocol with the server.
2. The server responds with a protocol and indicates that it supports encrypted passwords. At this time, it sends back a randomly generated 8-byte challenge string.
3. The client uses the challenge string as a key to encrypt its already encrypted password using an algorithm predefined by the negotiated protocol. It then sends the result to the server.
4. The server does the same thing with the encrypted password stored in its database. If the results match, the passwords are equivalent, and the user is authenticated.

Note that even though the original passwords are not involved in the authentication process, you need to be very careful that the encrypted passwords located inside the *smbpasswd* file are guarded from unauthorized users. If they are compromised, an unauthorized user can break into the system by replaying the steps of the previous algorithm. The encrypted passwords are just as sensitive as the plain-text passwords—this is known as *plain-text-equivalent* data in the cryptography world. Of course, your local security policy should require that the clients safeguard their plain-text-equivalent passwords as well.

You can configure Samba to accept encrypted passwords with the following global additions to *smb.conf*. Note that we explicitly name the location of the Samba password file:

```
[global]
    security = user
    encrypt passwords = yes
    smb passwd file = /usr/local/samba/private/smbpasswd
```

Samba, however, will not accept any users until the *smbpasswd* file has been created and the users have been added to it with the *smbpasswd* command, as we showed you in Chapter 2.

Disabling Encrypted Passwords on the Client

While Unix authentication has been in use for decades—including the use of *telnet* and *rlogin* access across the Internet—it embodies well-known security risks. Plaintext passwords are sent over the Internet and can be retrieved from TCP packets by malicious snoopers. However, if you feel that your network is secure and you wish to use standard Unix */etc/passwd* authentication for all clients, you can do so, but you must disable encrypted passwords on those Windows clients that default to using them.

To do this, you must modify the Windows registry on each client system. The Samba distribution includes the *.reg* files you need for this, located in the source distribution's */docs/Registry* directory. Depending on the platform, you use one of the following files:

Win95_PlainPassword.reg
Win98_PlainPassword.reg
WinME_PlainPassword.reg
NT_PlainPassword.reg
Win2000_PlainPassword.reg

(For Windows XP, use the *.reg* file for Windows 2000.) You can perform the installation by copying the appropriate *.reg* file to a DOS floppy, inserting the floppy in the client's floppy drive, and running the *.reg* file from the Run menu item in the client's Start menu. (Or you can just double-click the file's icon.)

After you reboot the machine, the client will not encrypt its hashed passwords before sending them to the server. This means that the plain-text passwords can been seen in the TCP packets that are broadcast across the network. Again, we encourage you not to do this unless you are absolutely sure that your network is secure.

If passwords are not encrypted, use these two lines in your Samba configuration file:

```
[global]
    security = user
    encrypt passwords = no
```

The smbpasswd File

Samba stores its encrypted passwords in a file called *smbpasswd*, which by default resides in the */usr/local/samba/private* directory. The *smbpasswd* file should be guarded as closely as the Unix system's password file (either */etc/passwd* or */etc/shadow*). Only the root user should have read/write access to the *private* directory, and no other users should have access to it at all. In addition, the *smbpasswd* file should have all access denied to all users except for root. When things are set up for good security, long listings of the *private* directory and *smbpasswd* file look like the following:

```
# ls -ld /usr/local/samba/private
drwx------    2 root    root    4096 Nov 26 01:11 /usr/local/samba/private
# ls -l /usr/local/samba/private/smbpasswd
-rw-------    1 root    root    204 Nov 26 01:11 /usr/local/samba/private/smbpasswd
```

Before you can use encrypted passwords, you need to create an entry for each Unix user in the *smbpasswd* file. The structure of the file is somewhat similar to a Unix *passwd* file, but has different fields. Figure 9-3 illustrates the layout of the *smbpasswd* file; the entry shown is actually one line in the file.

Figure 9-3. Structure of the smbpasswd file entry (actually one line)

Normally, entries in the *smbpasswd* file are created automatically by the *smbpasswd* command. Still, you might like to know how to interpret data within the *smbpasswd* file, in case you'd like to see what accounts are stored in it or even modify it manually. Here is a breakdown of the individual fields:

Username
> This is the username of the account. It is taken directly from the system password file.

UID
> This is the user ID (UID) of the account. Like the username, it is taken directly from the system password file and must match the UID there.

LAN Manager Password Hash
> This is a 32-bit hexadecimal sequence that represents the password Windows 95/98/Me clients will use. It is derived by splitting the password into two 7-character strings, with all lowercase letters forced into uppercase. If fewer than 14

characters are in the password, the strings are padded with nulls. Then each 7-character string is converted to a 56-bit DES key and used to encrypt the constant string KGS!@#$%. The two 64-bit results are concatenated and stored as the password hash.

If there is currently no password for the user, the first 11 characters of the hash will consist of the sequence NO PASSWORD followed by X characters for the remainder. If the password has been disabled, it will consist of 32 X characters.

NT LAN Manager (NTLM) Password Hash
This is a 32-bit hexadecimal sequence that represents the password Windows NT/2000/XP clients will use. It is derived by hashing the user's password (represented as a 16-bit little-endian Unicode sequence) with an MD4 hash. The password is not converted to uppercase letters first.

Account Flags
This field consists of 11 characters between two braces ([ ]). Any of the following characters can appear in any order; the remaining characters should be spaces:

U   This account is a standard user account.

D   This account is currently disabled, and Samba should not allow any logins.

N   This account has no password associated with it.

W   This is a workstation trust account that can be used to configure Samba as a PDC when allowing Windows NT machines to join its domain.

Last Change Time
This code consists of the characters LCT- followed by a hexadecimal representation of the number of seconds since the epoch (midnight on January 1, 1970) that the entry was last changed.

Password Synchronization

Having a regular password (either in */etc/passwd* or */etc/shadow*) and an encrypted version of the same password (in the *smbpasswd* file) can be troublesome when you need to change both of them. Luckily, Samba affords you a limited ability to keep your passwords synchronized. Samba has a pair of configuration options to update a user's regular Unix password automatically when the encrypted password is changed on the system. The feature can be activated by specifying the unix password sync global configuration option:

```
[global]
    unix password sync = yes
```

With this option enabled, Samba attempts to change the user's regular password (as root) when the encrypted version is changed with *smbpasswd*. However, two other options have to be set correctly for this to work.

The easier of the two is passwd program. This option simply specifies the Unix command used to change a user's standard system password. It is set to /bin/passwd %u by default. With some Unix systems, this is sufficient, and you do not need to change anything. Others, such as Red Hat Linux, use */usr/bin/passwd* instead. In addition, you might want to change this to another program or script at some point in the future. For example, let's assume that you want to use a script called *changepass* to change a user's password. Recall that you can use the variable %u to represent the current Unix username. So the example becomes:

```
[global]
    unix password sync = yes
    passwd program = changepass %u
```

Note that this program is called as the root user when the unix password sync option is set to yes. This is because Samba does not necessarily have the old plain-text password of the user.

The harder option to configure is passwd chat. The passwd chat option works like a Unix chat script. It specifies a series of strings to send, as well as responses to expect from the program specified by the passwd program option. For example, this is what the default passwd chat looks like. The delimiters are the spaces between each grouping of characters:

```
passwd chat = *old*password* %o\n *new*password* %n\n *new*password* %n\n *changed*
```

The first grouping represents a response expected from the password-changing program. Note that it can contain wildcards (*), which help to generalize the chat programs to handle a variety of similar outputs. Here, *old*password* indicates that Samba is expecting any line from the password program containing the letters old followed by the letters password, without regard for what comes before, after, or between them. If Samba does not receive the expected response, the password change will fail.

The second grouping indicates what Samba should send back once the data in the first grouping has been matched. In this case, you see %o\n. This response is actually two items: the variable %o represents the old password, while the \n is a newline character. So, in effect, this will "type" the old password into the standard input of the password-changing program, and then "press" Enter.

Following that is another response grouping, followed by data that will be sent back to the password-changing program. (In fact, this response/send pattern continues indefinitely in any standard Unix *chat* script.) The script continues until the final pattern is matched.

You can help match the response strings sent from the password program with the characters listed in Table 9-6. In addition, you can use the characters listed in Table 9-7 to help formulate your response.

Table 9-6. Password chat response characters

Character	Definition
*	Zero or more occurrences of any character.
" "	Allows you to include matching strings that contain spaces. Asterisks are still considered wildcards even inside of quotes, and you can represent a null response with empty quotes.

Table 9-7. Password chat send characters

Character	Definition
%o	The user's old password
%n	The user's new password
\n	The linefeed character
\r	The carriage-return character
\t	The tab character
\s	A space

For example, you might want to change your password chat to the following entry. This handles scenarios in which you do not have to enter the old password. In addition, this also handles the new all tokens updated successfully string that Red Hat Linux sends:

```
passwd chat = *New password* %n\n *new password* %n\n *success*
```

Again, the default chat should be sufficient for many Unix systems. If it isn't, you can use the passwd chat debug global option to set up a new chat script for the password change program. The passwd chat debug option logs everything during a password chat. This option is a simple Boolean, as shown here:

```
[global]
    unix password sync = yes
    passwd chat debug = yes
    log level = 100
```

After you activate the password chat debug feature, all I/O received by Samba through the password chat can be sent to the *log.smbd* Samba log file with a debug level of 100, which is why we entered a new log level option as well. As this can often generate multitudes of error logs, it can be more efficient to use your own script—by setting the passwd program option—in place of */bin/passwd* to record what happens during the exchange. Be careful because the log file contains the passwords in plain text. Keeping files containing plain-text passwords can (or *should*) be against local security policy in your organization, and it also might raise serious legal issues. Make sure to protect your log files with strict file permissions and to delete them as soon as you've grabbed the information you need. If possible, use the passwd chat debug option only while your own password is being changed.

The operating system on which Samba is running might have strict requirements for valid passwords to make them more impervious to dictionary attacks and the like. Users should be made aware of these restrictions when changing their passwords.

Earlier we said that password synchronization is limited. This is because there is no reverse synchronization of the encrypted *smbpasswd* file when a standard Unix password is updated by a user. There are various strategies to get around this, including NIS and freely available implementations of the Pluggable Authentication Modules (PAM) standard, but none of them really solves all the problems.

More information regarding passwords can be found in the in the Samba source distribution file *docs/htmldocs/ENCRYPTION.html*.

Password Configuration Options

The options in Table 9-8 will help you work with passwords in Samba.

Table 9-8. Password configuration options

Option	Parameters	Function	Default	Scope
encrypt passwords	Boolean	If yes, enables encrypted passwords.	no	Global
unix password sync	Boolean	If yes, updates the standard Unix password database when a user changes his encrypted password.	no	Global
passwd chat	string (chat commands)	Sequence of commands sent to the password program.	See earlier section on this option	Global
passwd chat debug	Boolean	If yes, sends debug logs of the password-change process to the log files with a level of 100.	no	Global
passwd program	string (Unix command)	Program to be used to change passwords.	/bin/passwd %u	Global
password level	numeric	Number of capital-letter permutations to attempt when matching a client's password.	None	Global
update encrypted	Boolean	If yes, updates the encrypted password file when a client connects to a share with a plain-text password.	no	Global
null passwords	Boolean	If yes, allows access for users with null passwords.	no	Global
smb passwd file	string (filename)	Name of the encrypted password file.	/usr/local/ samba/private/ smbpasswd	Global
hosts equiv	string (filename)	Name of a file that contains hosts and users that can connect without using a password.	None	Global
use rhosts	string (filename)	Name of a *.rhosts* file that allows users to connect without using a password.	None	Global

encrypt passwords

The encrypt passwords global option switches Samba from using plain-text passwords to encrypted passwords for authentication. Encrypted passwords will be expected from clients if the option is set to yes:

```
encrypt passwords = yes
```

In Samba 2.2.x versions and with previous versions, encrypted passwords are disabled by default. This was changed in Samba 3.0 to make encrypted passwords enabled by default.

If you use encrypted passwords, you must have a valid *smbpasswd* file in place and populated with usernames that authenticate with encrypted passwords. (See the section "The smbpasswd File" earlier in this chapter.) In addition, Samba must know the location of the *smbpasswd* file; if it is not in the default location (typically */usr/local/samba/private/smbpasswd*), you can explicitly name it using the smb passwd file option.

If you wish, you can use update encrypted to force Samba to update the *smbpasswd* file with encrypted passwords each time a client connects using a nonencrypted password.

If you have a mixture of clients on your network, with some of them using encrypted passwords and others using plain-text passwords, you can use the include option to make Samba treat each client appropriately. To do this, create individual configuration files based on the client name (%m). These host-specific configuration files can contain an encrypted passwords = yes option that activates only when those clients are connecting to the server.

unix password sync

The unix password sync global option allows Samba to update the standard Unix password file when a user changes her encrypted password. The encrypted password is stored on a Samba server in the *smbpasswd* file, which is located by default in */usr/local/samba/private*. You can activate this feature as follows:

```
[global]
    unix password sync = yes
```

If this option is enabled, Samba changes the encrypted password and, in addition, attempts to change the standard Unix password by passing the username and new password to the program specified by the passwd program option (described earlier). Note that Samba does not necessarily have access to the plain-text password for this user, so the password changing program must be invoked as root.* If the Unix pass-

---

* This is because the Unix *passwd* program, which is the usual target for this operation, allows root to change a user's password without the security restriction that requests the old password of that user.

word change does not succeed, for whatever reason, the SMB password is not changed either.

passwd chat

This option specifies a series of send/response strings similar to a Unix chat script, which interface with the password-changing program on the Samba server. The "Password Synchronization" section earlier in this chapter covers this option in detail.

passwd chat debug

If set to yes, the passwd chat debug global option logs everything sent or received by Samba during a password chat. All the I/O received by Samba through the password chat is sent to the Samba logs with a debug level of 100; you must specify log level = 100 for the information to be recorded. The "Password Synchronization" section earlier in this chapter describes this option in more detail. Be aware that if you do set this option, the plain-text passwords will be visible in the debugging logs, which could be a security hazard if they are not properly secured. It is against the security policy of some organizations for system administrators to have access to users' passwords.

passwd program

The passwd program option specifies a program on the Unix Samba server that Samba can use to update the standard system password file when the encrypted password file is updated. This option defaults to the standard *passwd* program, usually located in the */bin* directory. The %u variable is typically used as the requesting user when the command is executed. The actual handling of input and output to this program during execution is handled through the passwd chat option. The "Password Synchronization" section earlier in this chapter covers this option in detail.

password level

With SMB, nonencrypted (or plain-text) passwords are sent with capital letters, just like the usernames mentioned previously. Many Unix users, however, choose passwords with both upper- and lowercase letters. Samba, by default, only attempts to match the password entirely in lowercase letters and not capitalizing the first letter.

Like username level, a password level option can be used to attempt various permutations of the password with capital letters. This option takes an integer value that specifies how many letters in the password should be capitalized when attempting to connect to a share. You can specify this option as follows:

```
[global]
    password level = 3
```

In this case, Samba then attempts all permutations of the password it can compute having three capital letters. The larger the number, the more computations Samba has to perform to match the password, and the longer a connection to a specific share might take.

update encrypted

For sites switching over to the encrypted password format, Samba provides an option that should help with the transition. The update encrypted option allows a site to ease into using encrypted passwords from plain-text passwords. You can activate this option as follows:

```
[global]
    update encrypted = yes
```

This instructs Samba to create an encrypted version of each user's Unix password in the *smbpasswd* file each time she connects to a share. When this option is enabled, you must have the encrypt passwords option set to no so that the client passes plain-text passwords to Samba to update the files. Once each user has connected at least once, you can set encrypted passwords = yes, allowing you to use only the encrypted passwords. The user must already have a valid entry in the *smbpasswd* file for this option to work.

null passwords

This global option tells Samba whether to allow access from users that have null passwords (encrypted or nonencrypted) set in their accounts. The default value is no. You can override it as follows:

```
null passwords = yes
```

We highly recommend against doing so because of the security risks this option can present to your system, including inadvertent access to system users (such as bin) in the system password file who have null passwords set.

smb passwd file

This global option identifies the location of the encrypted password database. By default, it is set to */usr/local/samba/private/smbpasswd*. You can override it as follows:

```
[global]
    smb passwd file = /etc/samba/smbpasswd
```

This location, for example, is common on many Red Hat distributions on which Samba has been installed using an RPM package.

hosts equiv

This global option specifies the name of a standard Unix *hosts.equiv* file that allows hosts or users to access shares without specifying a password. You can specify the location of such a file as follows:

```
[global]
    hosts equiv = /etc/hosts.equiv
```

The default value for this option does not specify any *hosts.equiv* file. Because using a *hosts.equiv* file is a huge security risk, we strongly recommend against using this option.

use rhosts

This global option specifies the name of a standard Unix user's *.rhosts* file that allows foreign hosts to access shares without specifying a password. You can specify the location of such a file as follows:

```
[global]
    use rhosts = /home/dave/.rhosts
```

The default value for this option does not specify any *.rhosts* file. Like the hosts equiv option discussed earlier, using such a file is a security risk. We highly recommend that you do not use this option unless you are confident in the security of your network.

Authentication with winbind

In Chapter 3, we showed you how to add Windows clients to a network in which user accounts were maintained on the Samba server. We added a user account to the Windows client using the same username and password as an account on the Unix system. This method works well in many computing environments. However, if a Samba server is added to a Windows network that already has a Windows NT/2000 primary domain controller, the PDC has a preexisting database of user accounts and group information that is used for authentication. It can be a big chore to transfer that database manually to the Unix server, and later maintain and synchronize the Unix and Windows databases.

In Chapter 4, we showed you how to add a Samba server as a domain member server to a network having a Windows NT/2000 primary domain controller. We set security = domain in the Samba configuration file to have the Samba server hand off authentication to the Windows PDC. Using that method, passwords are kept only on the PDC, but it is still necessary to set up user accounts on the Unix side to make sure each client has a valid Unix UID and group ID (GID). This is necessary for maintaining the file ownerships and permissions of the Unix security model. Whenever Samba performs an operation on the Unix filesystem on behalf of the Windows client, the user must have a valid UID and GID on the local Unix system.

A facility that has recently been added to Samba, winbind, allows the Windows PDC to handle not only authentication, but the user and group information as well. Winbind works by extending the Unix user and group databases beyond the standard /etc/passwd and /etc/group files such that users and groups on the Windows PDC also exist as valid users and groups on the Unix system. The extension applies to the entire Unix system and allows users who are members of a Windows domain to perform any action on the Unix system that a local user would, including logging in to the Unix system by *telnet* or even on the local system, using their domain usernames and passwords.

When winbind is in use, administration of user accounts can be done on the Windows PDC, without having to repeat the tasks on the Unix side. This includes password expiration and allowing users to change their passwords, which would otherwise not be practical. Aside from simplifying domain administration and being a great time saver, winbind lets Samba be used in computing environments where it otherwise might not be allowed.

Because this is a chapter on security, we want to point out that some issues might relate to allowing a Windows system to authenticate users accessing a Unix system! Whatever you might think of the relative merits of Unix and Windows security models (and even more importantly, their *implementations*), one thing is certain: adding winbind support to your Samba server greatly complicates the authentication system overall—and quite possibly allows more opportunities for crackers.

We present winbind in this chapter not as a means of improving security, but rather as a further example of Samba's ability to integrate itself into a modern Windows environment.

Installing winbind

Installing and configuring winbind is fairly complicated and involves the following steps:

1. Reconfigure, recompile, and reinstall Samba—to add support for winbind.
2. Configure the Unix name server switch.
3. Modify the Samba configuration file.
4. Start and test the *winbindd* daemon.
5. Configure the system to start and stop the *winbindd* daemon automatically.
6. Optionally, configure PAM for use with winbind.

At the time this book was written, winbind was supported only on Linux, so all of the following directions are specific to it. Other Unix flavors might be supported at a later time. In addition, we assume you have a Windows NT/2000 primary domain controller running on your network.

First, you will need to configure and compile Samba using the --with-winbind configure option. Directions for doing this are included in Chapter 2 in the section "Configuring Samba." As usual, run *make install* to reinstall the Samba binaries.

Configuring nsswitch

When Samba is compiled after being configured with the --with-winbind option, the compilation process produces a library called *libnss_winbind.so* in the *source/nsswitch* directory. This library needs to be copied to the */lib* directory:

```
# cp nsswitch/libnss_winbind.so /lib
```

Also, a symbolic link must be created for winbind to be fully functional:

```
# ln -s /lib/libnss_winbind.so /lib/libnss_winbind.so.2
```

The name of this symbolic link is correct for Samba 2.2.3 and Red Hat 7.1. The name might change—with a higher version number in the extension—in future releases. See the *winbindd* manual page for details.

Next, we need to modify */etc/nsswitch.conf* to make the lines for passwd and group look like this:

```
passwd:     files winbind
group:      files winbind
```

Then activate these changes by issuing the following command:

```
# /sbin/ldconfig
```

What we've just done is reconfigure the Linux name service switch, which allows name service and other tasks to be configured to use the traditional method (files in the */etc* directory) or an extension coded in a library, such as the *libnss_winbind.so* library we've just installed. We've specified in our configuration that Samba will search for user and group information first in the */etc/passwd* and */etc/group files*, and if they are not found there, in the winbind service.

Modifying smb.conf

To use winbind, we must have our Samba server added to the Windows NT domain as a domain member server (as we described in Chapter 4) and also add some parameters to the Samba configuration file to configure winbind. In addition to the options required to configure Samba as a domain member server, we need:

```
[global]
    winbind uid = 10000-20000
    winbind gid = 10000-20000
```

The winbind uid and winbind gid options tell winbind how to map between Windows relative identifiers (RIDs) and Unix UIDs and GIDs. Windows uses RIDs to identify users and groups within the domain, and to function, the Unix system must have a UID and GID associated with every user and group RID that is received from the Windows primary domain controller. The winbind uid and winbind gid parameters simply provide winbind with a range of UIDs and GIDs, respectively, that are allocated by the system administrator for Windows NT domain users and groups. You can use whatever range you want for each; just make sure the lowest number in the range does not conflict with any entries in your /etc/passwd or /etc/group files at any time, either now or in the future. It is important to be conservative about this. Once winbind adds an RID to UID/GID mapping to its database, it is very difficult to modify the mapping.

The file /usr/local/samba/locks/winbindd_idmap.tdb contains winbind's RID mapping file by default. We suggest you regard this file as extremely sensitive and make sure to guard it carefully against any kind of harm or loss. If you lose it, you will have to re-create it manually, which can be a very labor-intensive task.

Be careful when adding local users after domain users have started accessing the Samba server. The domain users will have entries created for them by winbind in /etc/passwd, with UIDs in the range you specify. If you are using a method of creating new accounts that automatically assigns UIDs, it might choose UIDs by adding 1 to the highest UID assigned thus far, which will be the most recent UID added by winbind. (This is the case on Red Hat Linux, with the *useradd* script, for example.) The UID for the new local user will be within the range allocated for winbind, which will have undesired effects. Make sure to add new local users using a method that assigns them UIDs in the proper range. For example, you can use the *-u* option of *useradd* to specify the UID to assign to the new user.

Restart the Samba daemons to put your changes to the configuration file into effect. If you have not already done so while adding your Samba server as a domain member server, you must issue the command:

```
# smbpasswd -j domain -r pdc -U Administrator
```

as we described in Chapter 4. At this point, you can start the *winbindd* daemon:

```
# winbindd
```

You might want to run a *ps ax* command to see that the *winbindd* daemon is running. Now, to make sure everything we've done up to this point works, we can use Samba's *wbinfo* command:

```
$ wbinfo -u
METRAN\Administrator
METRAN\bebe
```

```
METRAN\Guest
METRAN\jay
METRAN\linda
$ wbinfo -g
METRAN\Domain Admins
METRAN\Domain Guests
METRAN\Domain Users
```

The *-u* option queries the domain controller for a list of domain users, and the *-g* option asks for the list of groups. The output shows that the Samba host system can query the Windows PDC through winbind.

Another thing to check is the list of users and groups, using the *getent* command:

```
# getent passwd
root:x:0:0:root:/root:/bin/bash
bin:x:1:1:bin:/bin:
daemon:x:2:2:daemon:/sbin:
    ... deleted ...
jay:x:500:500:Jay Ts:/home/jay:/bin/bash
rik:x:501:501::/home/rik:/bin/bash
METRAN\Administrator:x:10000:10000::/home/METRAN/administrator:/bin/bash
METRAN\bebe:x:10001:10000:Bebe Larta:/home/METRAN/bebe:/bin/bash
METRAN\Guest:x:10002:10000::/home/METRAN/guest:/bin/bash
METRAN\jay:x:10003:10000:Jay Ts:/home/METRAN/jay:/bin/bash
METRAN\linda:x:10004:10000:Linda Lewis:/home/METRAN/linda:/bin/bash

# getent group
root:x:0:root
bin:x:1:root,bin,daemon
daemon:x:2:root,bin,daemon
    ... deleted ...
jay:x:500:
rik:x:501:
METRAN\Domain Admins:x:10001:METRAN\Administrator
METRAN\Domain Guests:x:10002:METRAN\Guest
METRAN\Domain Users:x:10000:METRAN\Administrator,METRAN\jay,METRAN\linda,METRAN\bebe
```

This shows that the Linux system is finding the domain users and groups through winbind, in addition to those in the */etc/passwd* and */etc/group* files. If this part doesn't work as shown earlier, with the domain users and groups listed after the local ones, check to make sure you made the symbolic link to *libnss_winbind.so* in */lib* correctly.

Now you can try connecting to a Samba share from a Windows system using a domain account. You can either log on to the domain from a Windows NT/2000/XP workstation or use *smbclient* with the *-U* option to specify a username.

If you get errors while attempting to log on to the domain, it is probably because you had previously configured the client system with a computer account on another domain controller. Commonly, you get a dialog box that says, "The domain *NAME* is not available." On a Windows 2000 system, the fix is to log in to the system as an administrative user and open the Control Panel, double-click the System icon, click the Network Identification tab, then click the Properties button. In the dialog that comes up, click the "Workgroup:" radio button and fill in the name of the workgroup (you can use the same name as the domain). Click the OK buttons in the dialogs, and reboot if requested.

This removes the computer account from the primary domain controller. Now log in again as the administrative user and repeat the previous directions, but change from the workgroup back to the domain. This creates a new computer account that "fits" the workstation to the new primary domain controller. If your network has backup domain controllers, it will take up to 15 minutes for the new computer account to propagate to the BDCs.

If you are using Windows NT/XP, the method is slightly different. For the exact procedure, see the section in Chapter 4 that is specific to your Windows version.

After logging in as a domain user, try creating a file or two in a Samba share. (You might need to change the permissions on the shared directory—say, to 777—to allow this access. This is very permissive, but after you finish reading this section, you will understand how to change ownership and permissions on the directory to restrict access to selected domain users.) After you've created files by one or more domain users, take a look at the directory's contents from a Linux shell. You will see something like this:

```
$ ls -l /u
-rwxrw-rw-   1 METRAN\b METRAN\D      0 Apr 13 00:00 bebes-file.doc
-rwxrw-rw-   1 METRAN\l METRAN\D      0 Apr 12 23:58 lindas-file.doc
drwxrwxr-x   6 jay      jay        4096 Jan 15 05:12 snd
$ ls -ln /u
total 4
-rwxrw-rw-   1 10001    10000         0 Apr 13 00:00 bebes-file.doc
-rwxrw-rw-   1 10004    10000         0 Apr 12 23:58 lindas-file.doc
drwxrwxr-x   6 500      500        4096 Jan 15 05:12 snd
```

We can even use the domain usernames and groups from the Linux shell:

```
# chown 'METRAN\linda:METRAN\Domain Users' /u
# ls -ldu /u
drwxrwxrwx   3 METRAN\l METRAN\D   4096 Apr 13 00:44 /u
# ls -ldn /u
drwxrwxrwx   3 10004    10000      4096 Apr 13 00:00 /u
```

Notice how the owner and group are listed as being those of the domain user and group. Unfortunately, the GNU *ls* command won't show the full names of the domain users and groups, but we can use the *-ln* listing to show the UIDs and GIDs and then translate with the *wbinfo* command:

```
$ wbinfo -s `wbinfo -U 10004`
METRAN\LINDA 1
$ wbinfo -s `wbinfo -G 10000`
METRAN\Domain Users 2
```

(It's a bit messy, but it works, and it shows that the winbind system is working!) At this point, you might want to modify your */etc/rc.d/init.d/smb* script to start and stop the *winbindd* daemon automatically along with the *smbd* and *nmbd* daemons. Starting with the script we presented in Chapter 2, we first add this code to the *start()* function:

```
echo -n $"Starting WINBIND services: "
/usr/local/samba/bin/winbindd
ERROR2=$?
if [ $ERROR2 -ne 0 ]
then
      ERROR=1
fi
echo
```

The previous code should be located after the code that starts *nmbd* and before the *return* statement.

 We start *winbindd* after *nmbd* because *winbindd* needs *nmbd* to be running to work properly.

In the stop() function, we add the following:

```
echo -n $"Shutting down WINBIND services: "
/bin/kill -TERM -a winbindd
ERROR2=$?
if [ $ERROR2 -ne 0 ]
then
      ERROR=1
fi
echo
```

Again, this code should be located after the code that stops *nmbd* and before the *return* statement.

Configuring PAM

Most popular Linux distributions use Pluggable Authentication Modules (PAM), a suite of shared libraries that provide a centralized source of authentication for applications running on the Unix system. PAM can be configured differently for each application (or service) that uses it, without needing to recompile the application. As a hypothetical example, if an organization's security policy mandated the use of passwords exactly 10 characters in length, a PAM module could be written to check the length of passwords submitted by users and reject any attempts to use a longer or shorter password. PAM would then be reconfigured to include the new module for services such as *ftp*, console login, and GUI login that call upon PAM to authenticate users.

If you are not already familiar with PAM, we suggest you read the documentation provided with the Linux PAM package before continuing. On most Linux systems, it is located in the */usr/share/doc* directory hierarchy. Another resource is the *Linux-PAM System Administrator's Guide*, which you can find on the Internet at *http://www.kernel.org/pub/linux/libs/pam*.

The rest of this section is about using the PAM module provided in the Samba distribution to enable Windows domain users to authenticate on the Linux system hosting Samba. Depending on which services you choose to configure, this allows Windows domain users to log in on a local console (or through *telnet*), log in to a GUI desktop on the Linux system, authenticate with an FTP server running on the Linux system, or use other services normally limited to users who have an account on the Linux system. The PAM module authenticates Windows domain users by querying winbind, which passes the authentication off to a Windows NT domain controller.

As an example, we will show how to allow Windows domain users to log in to a text console on the Linux system and get a command shell and home directory. The method used in our example can be applied (with variations) to other services.

All users who can log in to the Linux system need a shell and a home directory. Unix and Linux keep this user information in the password file (*/etc/passwd*), but information about Windows users isn't located there. Instead, in the Samba configuration file, we add the following to notify winbind what the shell and home directory for Windows domain users will be:

```
[global]
    template shell = /bin/bash
    template homedir = /home/%D/%U
```

The first line sets the `template shell` parameter, which tells winbind what shell to use for domain users that are logging in to the Unix host. The `template homedir` parameter specifies the location of users' home directories. The `%D` variable is replaced by the name of the domain in which the user's account resides, and `%U` is replaced by the user's username in that domain.

Before the domain users can successfully log in, their home directories must be created manually. To add a single account for `linda` in the METRAN domain, we would use these commands:

```
# mkdir /home/METRAN
# chmod 755 /home/METRAN
```

```
# mkdir /home/METRAN/linda
# chown 'METRAN\linda:METRAN\Domain Users' /home/METRAN/linda
# chmod 700 /home/METRAN/linda
```

One side effect of creating the home directories is that if the Samba server is configured with a [homes] share, the domain users can see and access their home directories through Samba's file sharing.

Next, we need to compile and install the PAM module in the Samba distribution. From the source directory in the Samba distribution, issue the following commands:

```
# make nsswitch/pam_winbind.so
# cp nsswitch/pam_winbind.so /lib/security
```

and check that it was copied over correctly:

```
# ls /lib/security/pam_winbind.so
/lib/security/pam_winbind.so
```

On Red Hat Linux, the PAM configuration files reside in */etc/pam.d*. Before making any modifications, we strongly advise making a backup of this directory:

```
# cp -pR /etc/pam.d /etc/pam.d.backup
```

The reason for this is that we will be modifying the Linux system's means of authenticating logins, and if our configuration goes awry, all users (including root) will be locked out of the system. In case the worst happens, we would reboot into single-user mode (by typing linux single at the LILO: prompt) or boot a rescue disk, and then we would issue these two commands:

```
# mv /etc/pam.d /etc/pam.d.bad
# mv /etc/pam.d.backup /etc/pam.d
```

Be very careful to make sure you can recover from any errors you make because when PAM encounters any configuration information it doesn't understand, its action is not to allow access. This means you must be sure to enter everything correctly! You might want to leave yourself logged in as root on a spare virtual terminal while you are modifying your PAM configuration to ensure yourself a means of easy recovery.

In the */etc/pam.d* directory, you will encounter a file for each service that uses PAM. We are interested only in the file corresponding to the login service, which is called *login*. It contains the following lines:

```
auth       required    /lib/security/pam_securetty.so
auth       required    /lib/security/pam_stack.so service=system-auth
auth       required    /lib/security/pam_nologin.so
account    required    /lib/security/pam_stack.so service=system-auth
password   required    /lib/security/pam_stack.so service=system-auth
session    required    /lib/security/pam_stack.so service=system-auth
session    optional    /lib/security/pam_console.so
```

The lines starting with auth are related to the function of authentication—that is, printing a password prompt, accepting the password, verifying that it is correct, and matching the user to a valid user and group ID. The line starting with account is for account management, which allows access to be controlled by other factors, such as what times during the day a user is allowed access. We are not concerned with the lines starting with password or session because winbind does not add to either of those functions.

The third column lists the PAM module, possibly with arguments, that is called in for the task. The *pam_stack.so* module has been added by Red Hat to act somewhat like a macro or a subroutine. It calls the file in the *pam.d* directory named by the service argument. In this case, the file */etc/pam.d/system-auth* contains a common set of lines that are used as a default for many services. Because we want to customize the login service for winbind, we first replace the *pam_stack.so* lines for auth and account with the auth and account lines from */etc/pam.d/system-auth*. This yields:

```
auth       required    /lib/security/pam_securetty.so
auth       required    /lib/security/pam_env.so
auth       sufficient  /lib/security/pam_unix.so likeauth nullok
auth       required    /lib/security/pam_deny.so
auth       required    /lib/security/pam_nologin.so
account    required    /lib/security/pam_unix.so
password   required    /lib/security/pam_stack.so service=system-auth
session    required    /lib/security/pam_stack.so service=system-auth
session    optional    /lib/security/pam_console.so
```

To add winbind support, we need to add a line in both the auth and account sections to call the *pam_winbind.so* module:

```
auth       required    /lib/security/pam_securetty.so
auth       required    /lib/security/pam_env.so
auth       sufficient  /lib/security/pam_winbind.so
auth       sufficient  /lib/security/pam_unix.so use_first_pass likeauth nullok
auth       required    /lib/security/pam_deny.so
auth       required    /lib/security/pam_nologin.so
account    sufficient  /lib/security/pam_winbind.so
account    required    /lib/security/pam_unix.so
password   required    /lib/security/pam_stack.so service=system-auth
session    required    /lib/security/pam_stack.so service=system-auth
session    optional    /lib/security/pam_console.so
```

The keywords required and sufficient in the second column are significant. The keyword required specifies that the result returned by the module (either to pass or fail the authentication) must be taken into account, whereas the keyword sufficient specifies that if the module successfully authenticates the user, no further lines need to be processed. By specifying sufficient for the *pam_winbind.so* module, we let winbind attempt to authenticate users, and if it succeeds, the PAM system returns to the application. If the *pam_winbind.so* module doesn't find the user or the password does not match, the PAM system continues with the next line, which performs authentication according to the usual Linux user authentication. This way, both domain users and local users can log in.

Notice that we also added the `use_first_pass` argument to the *pam_unix.so* module in the auth section. By default, both the *pam_winbind.so* and *pam_unix.so* modules print a password prompt and accept a password. In cases where users are logging in to the Linux system using their local accounts, this would require them to enter their password twice. The `user_first_pass` argument tells the *pam_unix.so* module to reuse the password that was given to the *pam_winbind.so* module, which results in users having to enter the password only once.

After modifying the *login* configuration file, switch to a spare virtual console and make sure you can still log in using a regular Linux account. If not, check your modifications carefully and try again until you get it right. Then log in using a domain user account from the Windows PDC database to check that the winbind authentication works. You will need to specify the username in *DOMAIN\user* format, like this:

```
login: METRAN\linda
Password:
```

More information on configuring winbind can be found in the Samba source distribution file *docs/htmldocs/winbind.html*, and in the *winbindd* manual page. If you would like to learn more about configuring PAM, we recommend the web page *http://www.kernel.org/pub/linux/libs/pam/* as a starting place. Some of the documentation for Linux PAM, including Red Hat's extensions, can also be found on Red Hat Linux in */usr/share/doc/pam-version*.

winbind Configuration Options

Table 9-9 summarizes some commonly used options that you can use to configure winbind.

Table 9-9. winbind options

Option	Parameters	Function	Default	Scope
winbind separator	string (single character)	Character to use as a separator in domain usernames and group names	Backslash (\\)	Global
winbind uid	string (numeric range)	Range of UIDs for RID-to-UID mapping	None	Global
winbind gid	string (numeric range)	Range of GIDs for RID-to-GID mapping	None	Global
winbind cache time	numeric	Number of seconds the *winbindd* daemon caches user and group data	15	Global
template homedir	string (directory name)	Directory to be used as the home directory of the logged-in domain user	/home/%D/%U	Global
template shell	string (command name)	The program to use as the logged-in domain user's shell	/bin/false	Global

winbind separator

On Windows systems, the backslash (\\) is commonly used as a separator in file names, UNCs, and the names of domain users and groups. For example, an account in the METRAN domain with a username of linda would be written as METRAN\linda. On Unix systems, the backslash is commonly used as a metacharacter for quoting, so the account would have to be specified as METRAN\\linda or 'METRAN\linda'. The winbind separator parameter allows another character to be used instead of the backslash character, making it much easier to type in domain user and group names. For example, with:

```
[global]
    winbind separator = +
```

the aforementioned account could be written simply as METRAN+linda on the Unix host, making it unnecessary to use additional backslashes or single quotes. Winbind then uses the same format for reporting domain user and group names.

winbind uid

As part of *winbindd*'s task of letting Windows NT domain users function as local users on the Unix host, *winbindd* supplies a Unix UID that is linked to the Windows RID of the domain user. The winbind uid parameter allows the Unix system administrator to allocate a range of UIDs for this purpose. It is very important that this range not overlap any UIDs used for other purposes on the Unix system, so we recommend you begin your range at a very high number, one much larger than the number of local users and NIS users that will ever exist. For example, winbind uid might be defined as:

```
[global]
    winbind uid = 10000-15000
```

on a system that would never have more than 9,999 local and NIS users, or for that matter, any other entries in */etc/passwd* that would use up another UID. Because the example allocates 5,000 UIDs to *winbindd*, the assumption is that there will never be more than 5,000 domain users accessing the Samba host.

If your method for adding new local users to the system assigns UIDs automatically, make sure it does not assign them within the range of UIDs allocated to winbind. This might happen if the algorithm used adds 1 to the highest UID assigned thus far.

There is no default for winbind uid, so you must specify it in your Samba configuration file for winbind to work.

winbind gid

This option works like winbind uid, except that it is for allocating a range of GIDs for use with *winbindd*. You might not need to allocate as many GIDs as UIDs because you probably have relatively few domain groups that need corresponding GIDs. (In many cases, users are all members of the Domain Users group, requiring only one GID.) However, it is best to play it safe, so make sure to allocate many more GIDs than you think you will need.

As with `winbind uid`, if you are using a method of adding new local users to your Unix host that automatically assigns GIDs, either make sure the method used doesn't conflict with winbind or set the GIDs manually.

There is no default for `winbind gid`, so you must specify it in your Samba configuration file for winbind to work.

winbind cache time

The *winbindd* daemon maintains a cache of user and group data that has been retrieved from the Windows PDC to reduce network queries and increase performance. The `winbind cache time` parameter allows the amount of time (in seconds) *winbindd* can use the cached data before querying the PDC to check for an update. By default, this interval is set to 15 seconds. This means that when any part of a user or group account on the PDC is modified, it can take up to 15 seconds for *winbindd* to update its own database.

template homedir

When the local Unix system is configured to allow domain users to log in, the user must be provided with a home directory for many programs, including command shells, to function properly. The `template homedir` option is used to set the name of the home directory. In the name of the directory, `%D` is replaced by the name of the Windows NT domain the user is in, and `%U` is replaced by his username. By default, `template homedir` is set to `/home/%D/%U`, which works fine for a network in which there might be more than one Windows NT domain, and it is possible for different people in different domains to have the same username. If you are sure you will never have more than one Windows NT domain on your network, or you have more than one domain but know for sure that unique users have identical usernames in each multiple domain, you might prefer to set `template homedir` like this:

```
[global]
    template homedir = /home/%U
```

template shell

This option specifies the program to use as the shell for domain users who are logged in to the Unix host. By default, it is set to */bin/false*, which effectively denies domain users to log in. If you wish to allow logins for domain users, set `template shell` to a valid command shell (or other program) that you want to act as the textual interface the domain users will receive when logged in. A common setting on Linux would be:

```
[global]
    template shell = /bin/bash
```

which would give users the Bash shell for their interactive login sessions.

CHAPTER 10
Printing

This chapter tackles the topic of setting up printers for use with Samba. Aside from the "coolness factor" of seeing documents from Windows word processing and graphics applications appearing in the output tray of the Unix printer, this facility can greatly increase the usefulness of your Samba server. In many organizations, using a Unix system as the print server has led to happier system administrators and users alike, due to the reduced frequency of problems.

Samba allows client machines to share printers connected to the Samba host system, and Samba can also send Unix documents to printers shared by Windows systems. In this chapter, we discuss how to get printers configured to work in either direction.

We focus in this chapter on getting Samba to serve up printers that are already functioning on the Unix host. We include just a few basics about setting up printers on Unix. Good references for this topic include *Network Printing*, *Essential System Administration*, and *Running Linux*, all by O'Reilly and Associates.

Sending Print Jobs to Samba

A printer shared by the Samba server shows up in the list of shares offered in the Network Neighborhood. If the printer is registered on the client machine and the client has the correct printer driver installed, the client can effortlessly send print jobs to a printer attached to a Samba server. Figure 10-1 shows a Samba printer as it appears in the Network Neighborhood of a Windows client.

To administer printers with Samba, you should understand the basic process by which printing takes place on a network. On the client system, the application software prints by utilizing the system's printer driver for the printer that will be creating the actual output. It is the printer driver software running on the client system that translates the application's high-level calls into a stream of binary data specific to the model of printer in use. In the case of a serial, parallel, or USB printer, the data is stored in a temporary file in the local system's printer queue and then sent through

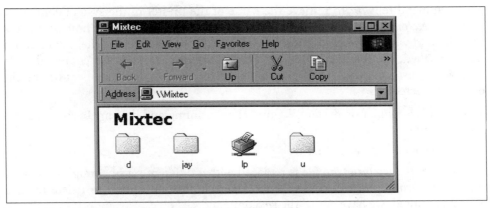

Figure 10-1. A Samba printer in the Network Neighborhood

the respective port directly to the printer. For a network printer, the file is sent over the network.

> Because the data has already been processed through a printer driver by the time it reaches the Samba host, make sure the printer on the Unix system is configured without any printer driver and that it will print whatever data it receives in raw form. If you already have the printer configured for use by Unix applications, you might need to set up another queue for it to print documents received from Windows clients correctly.

Sending a print job to a printer on a Samba server involves four steps:

1. Opening and authenticating a connection to the printer share
2. Copying the file over the network
3. Closing the connection
4. Printing and deleting the copy of the file

When a print job arrives at a Samba server, the print data is temporarily written to disk in the directory specified by the path option of the printer share. Samba then executes a Unix print command to send that datafile to the printer. The job is then printed as the authenticated user of the share. Note that this can be the guest user, depending on how the share is configured.

Print Commands

To print the document, you'll need to inform Samba of the command used to print and delete a file. On Linux, which uses a BSD-style printing system, a command that does this is:

```
lpr -r -Pprinter file
```

This command tells *lpr* to retrieve the name of the printer in the system configuration file (*/etc/printcap*) and interpret the rules it finds there to decide how to process the data and which physical device to send it to. Note that because the *-r* option has been specified, the file will be deleted after it has been printed. Of course, the file removed is just a copy stored on the Samba server; the original document on the client is unaffected.

The process is similar on System V Unix. Here, printing and deleting become a compound command:

```
lp -dprinter -s file; rm file
```

In this case, the */etc/printcap* file is replaced with a different set of configuration files residing in */usr/spool/lp*. Because the *lp* command has no option to delete the file after it is printed, we have added the *rm* command.

A Minimal Printing Setup

Let's start with a simple yet illustrative printing share. Assuming that you're on a Linux system and you have a printer called `netprinter` listed in the printer capabilities file, the following addition to your *smb.conf* file makes the printer accessible through the network:

```
[printer1]
    printable = yes
    print command = /usr/bin/lpr -P%p -r %s
    printer = netprinter
    printing = BSD
    path = /var/tmp
```

The variable `%s` in the `print command` option is replaced with the name of the file to be printed when Samba executes the command. There are four Samba configuration-file variables specifically for use with printing options. They are shown in Table 10-1.

Table 10-1. Printing variables

Variable	Definition
%s	The full pathname of the file on the Samba server to be printed
%f	The name of the file itself (without the preceding path) on the Samba server to be printed
%p	The name of the Unix printer to use
%j	The number of the print job (for use with lprm, lppause, and lpresume)

For other flavors of Unix, it is necessary to modify both the `printing` and `print command` options. For System V Unix, we would specify:

```
[printer1]
    printing = SYSV
    print command = lp -d%p -s %s; rm %s
```

With the printing = SYSV parameter, we notify Samba that the local printing system uses the System V Unix method. As mentioned earlier, the %p variable resolves to the name of the printer, while the %s variable resolves to the name of the file.

Clients might need to request the status of a print job sent to the Samba server. Because Samba sends print jobs to the Unix printing system for spooling, there might be a number of jobs in the queue at any given time. Consequently, Samba needs to communicate to the client not only the status of the current printing job, but also which documents are waiting to be printed on that printer. Samba also has to provide the client the ability to pause print jobs, resume print jobs, and remove print jobs from the printing queue. Samba provides options for each of these tasks. As you might expect, they borrow functionality from the following existing Unix commands:

- lpq
- lprm
- lppause
- lpresume

We cover these options in more detail later in this chapter. For the most part, Samba provides reasonable default values for them based on the value of the printing configuration option, so you can probably get by without having to formulate your own commands for them.

Here are a few important items to remember about printing shares:

- You must put printable = yes in all printer shares (even [printers]) so that Samba knows they are printer shares. If you forget, the shares will be unusable for printing and will instead be treated as disk shares.

- If you set the path configuration option in the printer section, any files sent to the printer(s) will be copied to the directory you specify instead of to the default location of /tmp. Because the amount of disk space allocated to /tmp can be relatively small in some Unix operating systems, many administrators prefer to use /var/tmp, /var/spool/tmp, or some other directory instead.

- If you set guest ok = yes in a printer share and Samba is configured for share-level security, anyone can send data to the printer as the guest account user.

Using one or more Samba machines as a print server gives you a great deal of flexibility on your LAN. You can easily partition your available printers, restricting some to members of one department, or you can maintain a bank of printers available to all. In addition, you can restrict a printer to a select few by adding the valid users option to its share definition:

```
[deskjet]
    printable = yes
    path = /var/spool/samba/print
    valid users = elizabeth cozy jack heather alexander lina emerald
```

All the other share accessibility options work for printing shares as well.

The [printers] Share

If a share named [printers] is in the configuration file, Samba will automatically read in your printer capabilities file and create a printing share for each printer that appears in the file. For example, if the Samba server had lp, pcl, and ps printers in its printer capabilities file, Samba would provide three printer shares with those names, each configured with the options in the [printers] share.

Recall that Samba obeys the following rules when a client requests a share that has not been created with an explicit share definition in the *smb.conf* file:

- If the share name matches a username in the system password file and a [homes] share exists, a new share is created with the name of the user and is initialized using the values given in the [homes] and [global] sections.

- Otherwise, if the name matches a printer in the system printer capabilities file and a [printers] share exists, a new share is created with the name of the printer and initialized using the values given in the [printers] section. (Variables in the [global] section do not apply here.)

- If neither of those succeeds, Samba looks for a default service share. If none is found, it returns an error.

This brings to light an important point: be careful that you do not give a printer the same name as a user. Otherwise, users end up connecting to a disk share when they might have wanted a printer share instead.

Here is an example [printers] share for a Linux system. Some of these options are already defaults; however, we have listed them anyway for illustrative purposes:

```
[printers]
        printable = yes
        printing = BSD
        printcap name = /etc/printcap
        print command = /usr/bin/lpr -P%p -r %s
        path = /var/spool/lpd/tmp
        min print space = 2000
```

Here, we've given Samba global options that specify the printing type (BSD), a print command to send data to the printer and later remove the temporary file, the location of our printer capabilities file, and a minimum disk space for printing of 2MB.

In addition, we've created a [printers] share for each system printer. Our temporary spooling directory is specified by the path option: */var/spool/lpd/tmp*. Each share is marked as printable—this is a necessary option, even in the [printers] section.

Testing the Configuration

After running *testparm* and restarting the Samba daemons, you can check to make sure everything is set up correctly by using *smbclient* to send a file to the printer. Connect to the printer using the command:

```
# smbclient /server/printshare
```

and then use the *print* command to print a file:

```
smb: /> print textfile
```

 If you connect to a print share served by a Windows 95/98/Me system configured to use user-mode security and cannot authenticate using what you know to be a correct username and password, try reconfiguring the Windows system to use share-mode security.

When you print something through the Samba server via *smbclient*, the following actions should occur:

- The job appears (briefly) in the Samba spool directory specified by the path.
- The job shows up in your print system's spool directory.
- The job disappears from the spool directory that Samba used.

If *smbclient* cannot print, you can reset the `print command` option to collect debugging information:

```
print command = echo "printed %s on %p" >>/tmp/printlog
```

A common problem with Samba printer configuration is forgetting to use the full pathnames for commands. Another frequent problem is not having the correct permissions on the spooling directory.* As usual, check your Samba log files and system log files for error messages. If you use BSD printing, you can change the `lp` keyword in the printer's printcap entry to something other than */dev/null*, allowing you to collect error messages from the printing system.

 More information on debugging printers is in the file *docs/textdocs/Printing.txt* in the Samba source distribution. The Unix print systems are covered in detail in Æleen Frisch's *Essential Systems Administration* (published by O'Reilly).

Enabling SMB Printer Sharing in Mac OS X

With Samba preinstalled with Mac OS X, sharing access to a printer among Windows clients is easy. First, of course, you should set up local access using the Print

---

* If you are using Linux, you can use the *checkpc* command to check for this type of error.

Center application (located in */Applications/Utilities*). Under the Printers menu, select Add Printer..., and make the appropriate selection from the pop-up menu. For example, if the printer is directly attached, select USB; if the printer is powered on, it should appear in the list. Choose the printer, and press the Add button.

Edit */etc/smb.conf*, uncommenting the [printers] share and making any additional configuration changes you feel are necessary. Finally, enable the Samba startup item as described in Chapter 2, either by checking Windows File Sharing in Sharing Preferences or by manually editing */etc/hostconfig*. Now your printer can be used by remote Windows clients.

On Mac OS X and some other BSD-based systems, you can test your configuration using *smbutil*. The following will send the file named *print_test_file* to the printer named *printshare* on the server *bsdserver*:

```
% smbutil print //bsdserver/printshare print_test_file
```

See Chapter 5 for more information on using *smbutil*.

Setting Up and Testing a Windows Client

Now that Samba is offering a workable printer, you can set up your access to it on a Windows client. Browse through the Samba server in the Network Neighborhood. It should now show each printer that is available. For example, in Figure 10-1, we saw a printer called lp.

Next, you need to have the Windows client recognize the printer. Double-click the printer icon to get started. If you try to select an uninstalled printer (as you just did), Windows will ask you if it should help configure it for the Windows system. Click the Yes or OK button, and the Printer Wizard will open.

If you are installing a printer on Windows 95/98/Me, the first thing the wizard will ask is whether you need to print from DOS. Let's assume you don't, so choose the "No" radio button and press the Next > button to get to the manufacturer/model window, as shown in Figure 10-2.

In this dialog box, you should see a large list of manufacturers and models for a huge number of printers. Select the manufacturer of your printer in the left side of the dialog box, and then the exact model of the printer in the list on the right side.

In some cases, you might not find your printer in the list, or the version of the printer driver included with Windows might be out of date. In cases such as these, consult the printer manufacturer's documentation on how to install the driver. Typically, you will click the Have Disk... button to install the driver from a CD-ROM or disk file.

If you don't see your printer on the list, but you know it's a PostScript printer, select Apple as the manufacturer and Apple LaserWriter as the model. This will give you the most basic PostScript printer setup—and arguably one of the most reliable. If

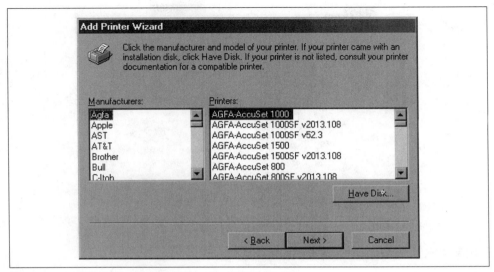

Figure 10-2. Setting the manufacturer and model of the printer

you already have PostScript printers attached, you will be asked about replacing or reusing the existing driver. Be aware that if you replace it with a new one, you might make your other printers fail. Therefore, we recommend you keep using your existing printer drivers as long as they're working properly.

Click the Next > or OK button. On Windows 95/98/Me, the Printer Wizard asks you to name the printer. On Windows NT/2000/XP, you need to right-click the printer's icon and select Properties to assign the printer a name. Figure 10-3 shows how we've named our printer to show that it's shared by the mixtec Samba server.

Finally, on Windows 95/98/Me the Printing Wizard asks if it should print a test page. Click the "Yes" radio button, then the Finish button, and you should be presented with the dialog box shown in Figure 10-4. On Windows NT/2000/XP, the printer test function is also accessed through the printer's Properties dialog box.

If the test printing was unsuccessful, click the No button and the Printing Wizard will walk you through some debugging steps for the client side of the process. If the test printing does work, the remote printer will now be available to all Windows applications through the File and Print menu items.

Printing to Windows Printers

If you have printers connected to systems running Windows 95/98/Me or Windows NT/2000/XP, the printers can also be accessed from your Unix system using tools that are part of the Samba distribution. First, it is necessary to create a printer share

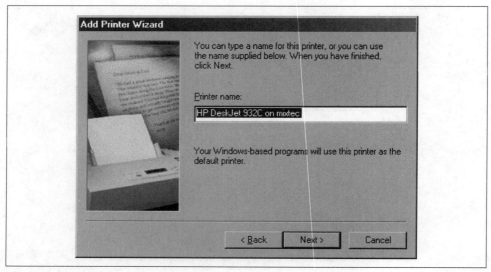

Figure 10-3. Setting the printer name

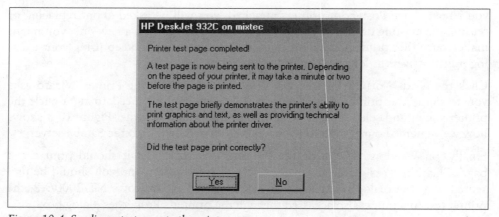

Figure 10-4. Sending a test page to the printer

on the Windows system. Then set up the printer on the Unix side by configuring a new printer and using a Samba printing program as the printer's filter.

Sharing Windows Printers

Sharing printers on Windows is not unlike sharing files. In fact, it is a little simpler. Open the Control Panel, then double-click the Printers icon to open the Printers window. Right-click the icon for the printer you want to share, and select Sharing.... This opens the dialog box shown in Figure 10-5 for a Windows 98 system, or Figure 10-6 on a Windows 2000 system. (The dialog box appears slightly different on other Windows versions, but functions almost identically.)

On Windows 95/98/Me systems, you may need to run file sharing in share-level (rather than user-level) access control mode to access a shared printer from Samba. To check or set this mode, go to Control Panel, then double-click on Network, then click on the Access Control tab. More detailed information on this can be found in Chapter 5.

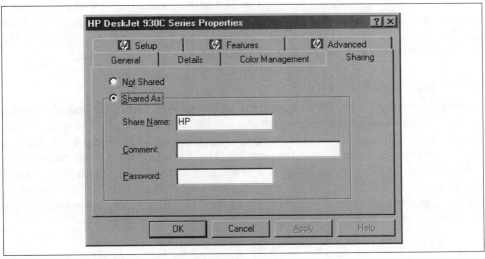

Figure 10-5. Sharing printers on Windows 98

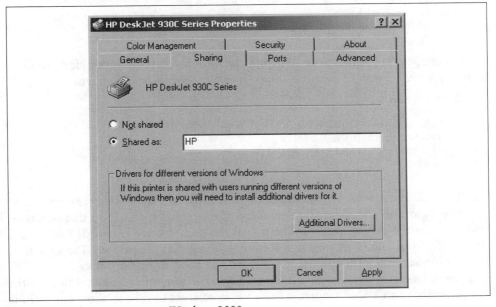

Figure 10-6. Sharing printers on Windows 2000

Click the "Shared as" radio button, then click the OK button. The printer is now accessible by other systems on the network.

Adding a Unix Printer

The Samba distribution comes with three programs that assist with printing on shared printers. The *smbprint* program works with systems that use the BSD printing system, *smbprint.sysv* works with systems that use System V printing, and *smbspool* works with systems that use the Common Unix Printing System (CUPS). In the following sections we show you how to install printers for each system.

BSD printers

The BSD printing system is used by many Unix variants, including Red Hat Linux. With BSD printing, all the printers on the system have an entry in the */etc/printcap* file, which is the database of printer capabilities used by the *lpd* line printer daemon and other programs that assist with printing. The Red Hat Linux implementation is a bit different in that */etc/printcap* is a machine-generated file, which is re-created every time the *lpd* daemon is restarted by the */etc/rc.d/init.d/lpd* script. Instead of editing */etc/printcap*, we will add an entry for our printer in */etc/printcap.local*, which the system automatically includes verbatim when creating */etc/printcap*.

> If you are using the version of Samba installed from an RPM file as on Red Hat Linux, you might be able to skip these directions and use the *printconf* tool, which has support for SMB printers. Unfortunately, this tool might not work correctly if you have installed Samba from the Samba source distribution.

Here is the entry we added to our */etc/printcap.local* file to support our Hewlett-Packard DeskJet 932C printer, which is shared by maya, a Windows 98 system:

```
lp|maya-hp932c:\
    :cm=HP 932C on maya:\
    :sd=/var/spool/lpd/maya:\
    :af=/var/spool/lpd/maya/acct:\
    :if=/usr/local/samba/bin/smbprint:\
    :mx=0:\
    :lp=/dev/null:
```

The first line creates names for the printer. We are calling it both maya-hp932c, to describe its location on the network and the type of printer, and lp so that programs will use it as the default printer. The rest of the lines specify keywords and values. The cm keyword allows us to assign a comment string to the printer. The sd and af keywords assign the printer's spool directory and accounting files, respectively. The if keyword assigns the print filter. We are using the *smbprint* command to send the output to the shared SMB printer. The mx keyword is set to zero to allow any size file to be printed, and lp is set to */dev/null* to discard error messages.

You can follow our model to create an entry for your own printer. If you want to go beyond the capabilities we used, refer to your system's *printcap(5)* manual page for a complete listing of keywords.

Go to your Samba source distribution's root directory, and install the *smbprint* program like this:

```
# cp examples/printing/smbprint /usr/local/samba/bin
```

We next create the printer's spool directory:

```
# cd /var/spool/lpd
# mkdir maya
# chown lp:lp maya
# chmod 700 maya
```

The *smbprint* program looks for a file named *.config* in the printer's spool directory, which contains information on how to connect to the printer share. We create this file and then fill in the required information:

```
# cd maya
# >.config
# chown lp:lp .config
# chmod 600 .config
```

Use your preferred text editor to edit the *.config* file, and enter three lines, like this:

```
server=maya
service=hp
password=""
```

This is for our shared printer having a UNC of *\\maya\hp*. When we created the printer share, we did not give it a password, so we use a null password here. If your printer share is on a Windows NT/2000/XP system, use your domain password.

Finally, restart the printer daemon:

```
# /etc/rc.d/init.d/lpd restart
```

You can now try printing something. Run the following command:

```
$ lpr textfile
```

If you have everything set up correctly, the file prints on the shared printer. If you get "stair stepping" of text, caused by the printer not returning to the left margin at the beginning of every line, modify the `if` keyword in your printcap entry to run *smbprint* with the *-t* option.

System V printers

Sending print jobs from a System V Unix system is a little easier than with the BSD system. Here, you need to edit the *smbprint.sysv* script in the *examples/printing* directory of the Samba distribution and do the following:

1. Change the server, service, and `password` parameters in the script to match the NetBIOS computer name, its shared printer service, and its password, respectively. For example, the following entries would be correct for the service in the previous example:

```
server = maya
service = hp
password = ""
```

2. Run the following commands, which create a reference for the new printer (which we are naming `hp_printer`) in the printer capabilities file:

```
# lpadmin -p hp_printer -v /dev/null -i ./smbprint.sysv
# enable hp_printer
# accept hp_printer
```

After you've done that, restart the Samba daemons and try printing to `hp_printer` using any standard Unix program.

CUPS printers

CUPS* uses a set of modules, called *backends*, to send print jobs to various destinations, such as local printers attached to parallel, serial, or Universal Serial Bus (USB) ports, or over the network using Unix line printer daemon (LPD) protocol, Internet Printing Protocol (IPP), AppleTalk Printer Access Protocol (PAP), and so on. The software package does not come with a backend for SMB; the Samba suite includes the *smbspool* utility for this purpose.

To enable printing to remote SMB printers using CUPS, create a symbolic link named *smb* in the CUPS backend directory pointing to *smbspool*. Depending on installation options, these could be in a number of places in the directory hierarchy, so be sure to check your system. Using a common default installation, the command would look like this:

```
# ln -s /usr/local/samba/bin/smbspool /usr/lib/cups/backend/smb
```

Issue a HUP signal to the CUPS daemon, *cupsd*, and check for the existence of SMB support with the *lpinfo -v* command. Its output should now include a line that says `network smb`.

To add a printer, use the CUPS web interface, accessible on the local system at *http://localhost:631/*, or use the *lpadmin* command:

```
# lpadmin -p hp932c -E -v smb://maya/hp932c -D "HP 932C on maya"
```

This creates and enables the new print spool called `hp932c`. The -*v* argument specifies the printer device, which in this case is accessed over the network using an SMB

---

* CUPS is open source software (*http://www.open-source.org*) developed by Easy Software Products. For more information, visit *http://www.cups.org*.

URI. If the printer is not guest-accessible, you'll need to provide a username and password in the URI. The full format is as follows:

```
smb://[username[:password]@][workgroup/]server/printshare
```

The *lpadmin* command makes changes to */etc/cups/printers.conf* and sends a HUP signal to the *cupsd* daemon, resulting in the creation of a local raw printer spool. In this example, print data is passed in raw format to the Windows system, which has the necessary printer drivers and printer description files to format the data appropriately. The *-D* option is used to give the printer a comment string.

Once you have the printer set up, it's time to test it out. CUPS understands both BSD-style and System V-style printing commands, so you can use whichever is more comfortable. Using the BSD *lpr* command, try something like:

```
$ lpr -P hp932c textfile
```

You should now be set up to use the printer from any application on the Unix system.

Samba Printing Options

Table 10-2 summarizes the Samba printing options.

Table 10-2. Printing configuration options

Option	Parameters	Function	Default	Scope
printing	bsd, sysv, cups, hpux, aix, qnx, plp, softq, or lprng	Printing system type of the Samba host	System-dependent	Share
printable (print ok)	boolean	Marks a share as a printing share	no	Share
printer (printer name)	string (Unix printer name)	Name for the printer that is shown to clients	System-dependent	Share
lpq cache time	numeric (time in seconds)	Amount of time in seconds that Samba will cache the printer queue status	10	Global
postscript	boolean	Treats all print jobs as PostScript by prefixing %! at the beginning of each file	no	Share
load printers	boolean	If yes, automatically loads each printer in the *printcap* file as printing shares	yes	Global
print command	string (shell command)	Unix command to perform printing	See below	Share
lpq command	string (shell command)	Unix command to return the status of the printing queue	See below	Share

Table 10-2. Printing configuration options (continued)

Option	Parameters	Function	Default	Scope
lprm command	string (shell command)	Unix command to remove a job from the printing queue	See below	Share
lppause command	string (shell command)	Unix command to pause a job on the printing queue	See below	Share
lpresume command	string (shell command)	Unix command to resume a paused job on the printing queue	See below	Share
printcap name (printcap)	string (filename)	Location of the printer capabilities file	System-dependent	Global
min print space	numeric (size in kilobytes)	Minimum amount of free disk space that must be present to print	0	Share
queuepause command	string (shell command)	Unix command to pause a queue	See below	Share
queueresume command	string (shell command)	Unix command to resume a queue	See below	Share

printing

The printing configuration option tells Samba which printing system to use. There are several different families of commands to control printing and print statusing. Samba supports seven different types, as shown in Table 10-3.

Table 10-3. Printing system types

Variable	Definition
BSD	Berkeley Unix system
SYSV	System V
CUPS	Common Unix Printing System
AIX	IBM's AIX operating system
HPUX	Hewlett-Packard Unix
QNX	QNX Realtime Operating System
LPRNG	LPR Next Generation
SOFTQ	SOFTQ system
PLP	Portable Line Printer

The value for this option must be one of these seven selections. For example:

```
printing = SYSV
```

The default value of this option is system-dependent and is configured when Samba is first compiled. For most systems, the *configure* script automatically detects the printing system to be used and configures it properly in the Samba makefile. However, if your system is a PLP, LPRNG, or QNX printing system, you need to specify this explicitly in the makefile or the printing share.

The most common system types are BSD, SYSV, and CUPS. Each printer on a BSD Unix server is described in the printer capabilities file—normally */etc/printcap*. See the section on the `printcap file` parameter for more information on this topic.

Setting the `printing` configuration option automatically sets at least three other printing options for the service in question: `print command`, `lpq command`, and `lprm command`. If you are running Samba on a system that doesn't support any of the printing styles listed in Table 10-3, simply set the commands for each of these manually.

printable

The `printable` option must be set to yes to flag a share as a printing service. If this option is not set, the share will be treated as a disk share instead. You can set the option as follows:

```
[printer1]
    printable = yes
```

printer

The option, also called `printer name`, specifies the name of the printer on the server to which the share points. This option has no default and should be set explicitly in the configuration file, even though Unix systems themselves often recognize a default name such as `lp` for a printer. For example:

```
[deskjet]
    printer = hpdkjet1
```

lpq cache time

The global `lpq cache time` option allows you to set the number of seconds for which Samba will remember the current printer status. After this time elapses, Samba will issue an *lpq* command (or whatever command you specify with the `lpq command` option) to get a more up-to-date status that it can report to users. This defaults to 10 seconds, but can be increased if your `lpq command` takes an unusually long time to run or you have lots of clients. A time setting of 0 disables caching of queue status. The following example resets the time to 30 seconds:

```
[deskjet]
    lpq cache time = 30
```

postscript

The `postscript` option forces the printer to treat all data sent to it as PostScript. It does this by prefixing the characters %! to the beginning of the first line of each job. It is normally used with PCs that insert a ^D (control-D or "end-of-file" mark) in front of the first line of a PostScript file. It will not, obviously, turn a non-PostScript printer into a PostScript one. The default value of this options is *no*. You can override it as follows:

```
[deskjet]
    postscript = yes
```

load printers

The load printers option tells Samba to create shares for all known printer names
and load those shares into the browse list. Samba will create and list a printer share
for each printer name in /etc/printcap (or the system equivalent). For example, if your
printcap file looks like this:[*]

```
lp:\
  :sd=/var/spool/lpd/lp:\         spool directory
  :mx#0:\                         maximum file size (none)
  :sh:\                           supress burst header (no)
  :lp=/dev/lp1:\                  device name for output
  :if=/var/spool/lpd/lp/filter:   text filter

laser:\
  :sd=/var/spool/lpd/laser:\      spool directory
  :mx#0:\                         maximum file size (none)
  :sh:\                           supress burst header (no)
  :lp=/dev/laser:\                device name for output
  :if=/var/spool/lpd/lp/filter:   text filter
```

the shares [lp] and [laser] are automatically created as valid print shares when
Samba is started. Both shares borrow the configuration options specified in the
[printers] section to configure themselves and are available in the browse list for the
Samba server. The default value for this option is yes. If you prefer to specify each
printer explicitly in your configuration file, use the following:

```
[global]
    load printers = no
```

print command, lpq command, lprm command, lppause command, lpresume command

These options tell Samba which Unix commands control and send data to the
printer. The Unix commands involved are: *lpr* (send to Line PRinter), *lpq* (List
Printer Queue), *lprm* (Line Printer ReMove), and optionally *lppause* and *lpresume*.
Samba provides an option named after each command, in case you need to override
any of the system defaults. For example, consider the following:

```
lpq command = /usr/ucb/lpq %p
```

This would set lpq command to use /usr/ucb/lpq. Similarly:

```
lprm command = /usr/local/bin/lprm -P%p %j
```

---

[*] We have placed annotated comments off to the right in case you've never dealt with this file before.

---

would set the Samba printer remove command to */usr/local/bin/lprm* and provide it the print job number using the %j variable.

The default values for each option are dependent on the value of the `printing` option. Table 10-4 shows the default commands for each printing option. The most popular printing system is BSD.

Table 10-4. Default commands for various printing options

Option	BSD, AIX, PLP, LPRNG	SYSV, HPUX	QNX	SOFTQ
print command	lpr -r -P%p %s	lp -c -d%p %s; rm %s	lp -r -P%p %s	lp -d%p -s %s; rm %s
lpq command	lpq -P%p	lpstat -o%p	lpq -P%p	lpstat -o%p
lprm command	lprm -P%p %j	cancel %p-%j	cancel %p-%j	cancel %p-%j
lppause command	lp -i %p-%j -H hold (SYSV only)	None	None	None
lpresume command	lp -i %p-%j -H resume (SYSV only)	None	None	qstat -s -j%j -r

It is usually unnecessary to reset these options in Samba, with the possible exception of the `print command`. This option might need to be set explicitly if your printing system doesn't have a *-r* (remove after printing) option on the printing command. For example:

```
print command = /usr/local/lpr -P%p %s; /bin/rm %s
```

With a bit of judicious programming, these *smb.conf* options can also be used for debugging:

```
print command = cat %s >>/tmp/printlog; lpr -r -P%p %s
```

Using the previous configuration, it is possible to verify that files are actually being delivered to the Samba server. If they are, their contents will show up in the file */tmp/printlog*.

After BSD, the next most popular kind of printing system is SYSV (or System V) printing, plus some SYSV variants for IBM's AIX and Hewlett-Packard's HP-UX. These systems do not have an */etc/printcap* file. Instead, the `printcap file` option can be set to an appropriate *lpstat* command for the system. This tells Samba to get a list of printers from the *lpstat* command. Alternatively, you can set the global configuration option `printcap name` to the name of a dummy *printcap* file you provide. In the latter case, the file must contain a series of lines such as:

```
lp|print1|My Printer 1
print2|My Printer 2
print3|My Printer 3
```

Each line names a printer followed by aliases for it. In this example, the first printer is called lp, print1, or My Printer 1, whichever the user prefers to use. The first name is used in place of %p in any command Samba executes for that printer.

Two additional printer types are also supported by Samba: LPRNG (LPR New Generation) and PLP (Public Line Printer). These are public domain and open source printing systems and are used by many sites to overcome problems with vendor-supplied software. Samba also supports the printing systems of the SOFTQ and QNX real-time operating systems.

printcap name

If the printcap name option (also called printcap) appears in a printing share, Samba uses the file specified as the system printer capabilities file (normally */etc/printcap*). However, you can reset it to a file consisting of only the printers you want to share over the network. The value must be the filename (with its complete path specified) of a printer capabilities file on the server:

```
[deskjet]
    printcap name = /usr/local/samba/lib/printcap
```

The CUPS printing system uses its own method of determining printer capabilities, rather than the standard *printcap* file. In this case, set printcap name as follows:

```
[global]
    printing = cups
    printcap name = cups
```

min print space

The min print space option sets the amount of space that must be available on the disk that contains the spool directory if printing is to be allowed. Setting it to zero (the default) turns the check off; setting it to any other number sets the amount of free space in kilobytes required. This option helps to avoid having print jobs fill up the remaining disk space on the server, which can cause other processes to fail:

```
[deskjet]
    min print space = 4000
```

queuepause command

This configuration option specifies a command that tells Samba how to pause an entire print queue, as opposed to a single job on the queue. The default value depends on the printing type chosen. You should not need to alter this option.

queueresume command

This configuration option specifies a command that tells Samba how to resume a paused print queue, as opposed to resuming a single job on the print queue. The default value depends on the printing type chosen. You should not need to alter this option.

## CHAPTER 11

Additional Samba Information

This chapter wraps up our coverage of the *smb.conf* configuration file with some miscellaneous options that can perform a variety of tasks. We talk briefly about options for time synchronization, internationalization, messages, and common Windows bugs. For the most part, you will use these options only in isolated circumstances.

Time Synchronization

In a network of computers, the systems on the network must agree on the current time and also on what time files have been modified. One example of the importance of synchronization is the roaming profiles we covered in Chapter 4. It is vital for all clients accessing a roaming profile to agree on what time it is and which client last modified the user's profile.

Time synchronization can also be very important to programmers. A useful group of settings consists of the following options:

```
[global]
    time server = yes
    dos filetimes = yes
    fake directory create times = yes
    dos filetime resolution = yes
    delete readonly = yes
```

If you set these options, Samba shares will provide compatibility of file-modification times that Visual C++, *nmake*, and other Microsoft programming tools require. Otherwise, PC *make* programs might think that all the files in a directory need to be recompiled every time. Obviously, this is not the behavior you want.

In Chapter 4, we showed you how to create a logon script that used the *net time* command to synchronize clients' clocks automatically when they log on to the domain. If your network is configured as a workgroup rather than a domain, you can still make use of *net time* by placing the command:

```
net time \\sambaserver /set /yes
```

in a startup script on each client that is run when the system boots. Samba always provides time service—regardless of whether it is running as a primary domain controller—or the time service configuration file parameter is set.

Assuming that domain users log on to the domain at least once per day and workgroup clients reboot frequently, the *net time* command can keep client systems' clocks fairly well synchronized. However, sometimes domain users stay logged on for longer periods, and workgroup clients can run for days between reboots. In the meantime, the systems' hardware clocks can wander enough to become a problem. It might be possible to work around this, depending on the version of Windows the client system is running. On Windows 98/Me, you can use the Task Scheduler to run the *net time* command at regular intervals. Likewise, on Windows 2000/XP you can use the MS-DOS *at* command. However, a better way to deal with this issue is to use Network Time Protocol, which we will discuss shortly.

Proper time synchronization is also important when operating in an Active Directory domain because Active Directory uses Kerberos authentication. When a Kerberos domain controller creates an authentication ticket for a client, the time is encoded into the challenge-and-response exchanges between the client and domain controller. If the client's clock disagrees with the server's clock, authentication can fail.

To provide proper time synchronization in Active Directory domains, Microsoft has adopted Network Time Protocol (NTP), using the name Windows Time Service for its implementation. For further information, the Microsoft white paper entitled *The Windows Time Service* can be downloaded from *http://www.microsoft.com*.

The nice thing about this is that NTP is the standard method for synchronizing Unix hosts on a network, so you can synchronize all your Unix systems (including the Samba server) and Windows systems with the following method:

1. Run NTP on the Unix systems in your network. For more information on using NTP, refer to *http://www.ntp.org*.

2. Use one of the Unix systems (such as the Samba host system) as an NTP server to serve Windows 2000/XP clients.

3. For other Windows clients, you might have to download an update from Microsoft to add Windows Time Service client support or use a third-party application such as the free analogX Atomic TimeSync (*http://www.analogx.com*). Or you can use the *net time* command to update the client's clock periodically, as discussed previously.

Time-Synchronization Options

To support roaming profiles, programmers accessing your Samba server, and other time-sensitive functions on your network, you'll want to be aware of the options listed in Table 11-1.

Table 11-1. Time-synchronization options

Option	Parameters	Function	Default	Scope
time server	Boolean	If yes, announces *nmbd* as an SMB time service to Windows clients	no	Global
time offset	numeric	Adds a specified number of minutes to the reported time	0	Global
dos filetimes	Boolean	Allows non-owners of a file to change its time if they can write to it	no	Share
dos filetime resolution	Boolean	Causes file times to be rounded to the next even second	no	Share
fake directory create times	Boolean	Sets directory times to avoid an MS *nmake* bug	no	Share

time server

Samba always operates as an SMB time server, matching the behavior of Windows systems. However, Samba's default is not to advertise itself as a time server to the network. When this option is set to yes, Samba advertises itself as an SMB time server:

```
[global]
    time service = yes
```

time offset

To deal with clients that don't properly process daylight savings time, Samba provides the time offset option. If set, it adds the specified number of minutes to the current time. This is handy if you're in Newfoundland and Windows doesn't know about the 30-minute time difference there:

```
[global]
    time offset = 30
```

dos filetimes

Traditionally, only the root user and the owner of a file can change its last-modified date on a Unix system. The share-level dos filetimes option allows the Samba server to mimic the characteristics of a DOS or Windows system: any user can change the last-modified date on a file in that share if she has write permission to it. To do this, Samba uses its root privileges to modify the timestamp on the file.

By default, this option is disabled. Setting this option to yes is often necessary to allow PC *make* programs to work properly. Without it, they cannot change the last-modified date themselves. This often results in the program thinking *all* files need recompiling when they really don't.

dos filetime resolution

The dos filetime resolution parameter is a share-level option. If set to yes, Samba rounds file times to the closest 2-second boundary. This option exists primarily to satisfy a quirk in Windows that prevents Visual C++ from correctly recognizing that a file has not changed. You can enable it as follows:

```
[data]
        dos filetime resolution = yes
```

We recommend using this option only if you are using Microsoft Visual C++ on a Samba share that supports opportunistic locking.

fake directory create times

The fake directory create times option exists to keep PC *make* programs sane. VFAT and NTFS filesystems record the creation date of a specific directory, while Unix does not. Without this option, Samba takes the earliest recorded date it has for the directory (often the last-modified date of a file) and returns it to the client. If this is not sufficient, set the following option under a share definition:

```
[data]
        fake directory create times = yes
```

If set, Samba will adjust the directory create time it reports to the hardcoded value January 1, 1980. This is primarily used to convince the Visual C++ *nmake* program that any object files in its build directories are indeed younger than the creation date of the directory itself and need to be recompiled.

Magic Scripts

Magic scripts are a method of running programs on Unix and redirecting the output back to the SMB client. These are essentially an experimental hack. However, some users and their programs still rely on these two options for their programs to function correctly. Magic scripts are not widely trusted, and their use is highly discouraged by the Samba Team.

Magic Script Options

Table 11-2 lists the options that deal with magic scripts on the Samba server.

Table 11-2. Magic script options

Option	Parameters	Function	Default	Scope
magic script	string (filename)	File to be executed by Samba, as the logged-on user, when closed	None	Share
magic output	string (filename)	File to log output from the magic file	*scriptname.out*	Share

magic script

If the `magic script` option is set to a filename and the client creates a file by that name in that share, Samba will run the file as soon as the user has opened and closed it. For example, let's assume that the following option was created in the share [accounting]:

```
[accounting]
    magic script = tally.sh
```

Samba continually monitors the files in that share. If one by the name of *tally.sh* is closed (after being opened) by a user, Samba will execute the contents of that file locally. The file will be passed to the shell to execute; it must therefore be a legal Unix shell script. This means that it must have newline characters as line endings instead of Windows CRLFs. In addition, you need to use the #! directive at the beginning of the file to indicate under which shell or interpreter the script should run, unless the script is for the default shell on your system.

magic output

This option specifies an output file to which the script specified by the `magic script` option will send output. You must specify a filename in a writable directory:

```
[accounting]
    magic script = tally.sh
    magic output = /var/log/magicoutput
```

If this option is omitted, the default output file is the name of the script (as stated in the `magic script` option) with the extension *.out* appended onto it.

Internationalization

Starting with Samba 3.0, Samba supports Unicode "on the wire," requiring no additional effort on your part to support filenames and other text containing characters in international character sets.

Internationalization Options

Samba 2.2.x has a limited ability to speak foreign tongues: if you need to support filenames containing characters that aren't in standard ASCII, some options that can help you are shown in Table 11-3.

Table 11-3. Internationalization options

Option	Parameters	Function	Default	Scope
client code page	Described in this section	Sets a code page to expect from clients	850	Global
character set	Described in this section	Translates code pages into alternate Unix character sets	None	Global

Table 11-3. Internationalization options (continued)

Option	Parameters	Function	Default	Scope
coding system	Described in this section	Translates code page 932 into an Asian character set	None	Global
valid chars	string (set of characters)	Adds individual characters to a code page	None	Global

client code page

The character sets on Windows platforms hark back to the original concept of a *code page*. These code pages are used by DOS and Windows clients to determine rules for mapping lowercase letters to uppercase letters. Samba can be instructed to use a variety of code pages through the use of the global client code page option to match the corresponding code page in use on the client. This option loads a code page definition file and can take the values specified in Table 11-4.

Table 11-4. Valid code pages with Samba 2.0

Code page	Definition
437	MS-DOS Latin (United States)
737	Windows 95 Greek
850	MS-DOS Latin 1 (Western European)
852	MS-DOS Latin 2 (Eastern European)
861	MS-DOS Icelandic
866	MS-DOS Cyrillic (Russian)
932	MS-DOS Japanese Shift-JIS
936	MS-DOS Simplified Chinese
949	MS-DOS Korean Hangul
950	MS-DOS Traditional Chinese

You can set the client code page as follows:

```
[global]
    client code page = 852
```

The default value of this option is 850, for MS-DOS Latin 1. You can use the *make_smbcodepage* tool that comes with Samba (by default in */usr/local/samba/bin*) to create your own SMB code pages, in the event that those listed earlier are not sufficient.

character set

The global character set option can be used to convert filenames offered through a DOS code page (see the previous section, "client code page") to equivalents that can be represented by Unix character sets other than those in the United States. For example, if you want to convert the Western European MS-DOS character set on the client to a Western European Unix character set on the server, you can use the following in your configuration file:

```
[global]
    client code page = 850
    character set = ISO8859-1
```

Note that you must include a client code page option to specify the character set from which you are converting. The valid character sets (and their matching code pages) that Samba accepts are listed in Table 11-5.

Table 11-5. Valid character sets

Character set	Matching code page	Definition
ISO8859-1	850	Western European Unix
ISO8859-2	852	Eastern European Unix
ISO8859-5	866	Russian Cyrillic Unix
ISO8859-7	737	Greek Unix
KOI8-R	866	Alternate Russian Cyrillic Unix

Normally, the character set option is disabled completely.

coding system

The coding system option is similar to the character set option. However, its purpose is to determine how to convert a Japanese Shift JIS code page into an appropriate Unix character set. To use this option, the client code page option described previously must be set to page 932. The valid coding systems that Samba accepts are listed in Table 11-6.

Table 11-6. Valid coding-system parameters

Character set	Definition
SJIS	Standard Shift JIS
JIS8	Eight-bit JIS codes
J8BB	Eight-bit JIS codes
J8BH	Eight-bit JIS codes
J8@B	Eight-bit JIS codes
J8@J	Eight-bit JIS codes
J8@H	Eight-bit JIS codes
JIS7	Seven-bit JIS codes
J7BB	Seven-bit JIS codes
J7BH	Seven-bit JIS codes
J7@B	Seven-bit JIS codes
J7@J	Seven-bit JIS codes

Table 11-6. Valid coding-system parameters (continued)

Character set	Definition
J7@H	Seven-bit JIS codes
JUNET	JUNET codes
JUBB	JUNET codes
JUBH	JUNET codes
JU@B	JUNET codes
JU@J	JUNET codes
JU@H	JUNET codes
EUC	EUC codes
HEX	Three-byte hexadecimal code
CAP	Three-byte hexadecimal code (Columbia AppleTalk Program)

valid chars

The valid chars option can be used to add individual characters to a code page. You can use this option as follows:

```
valid chars = Î
valid chars = 0450:0420 0x0A20:0x0A00
valid chars = A:a
```

Each character in the list specified should be separated by spaces. If there is a colon between two characters or a numerical equivalent, the data to the left of the colon is considered an uppercase character, while the data to the right is considered the lowercase character. You can represent characters both by literals (if you can type them) and by octal, hexadecimal, or decimal Unicode equivalents.

If you use this option, it must be listed after the client code page to which you wish to add the character.

Windows Messenger Service

One of the odd features of SMB protocol is its ability to send text messages between computers. Although both the name and functionality are similar to that of Windows Messenger, the two are not the same. Windows Messenger (also called MSN Messenger) is an Internet-oriented instant messenging service, while Windows Messenger Service is an older and simpler LAN-oriented service. Using the Windows Messenger Service, messages can be addressed to users, individual computers, or entire workgroups on the network.

The WinPopup tool (*Winpopup.exe*), shown in Figure 11-1, can be used on Windows 95/98/Me to send or receive messages. WinPopup is a handy tool for sending messages. However, to receive messages, it must already be running when the message is sent from the remote system.

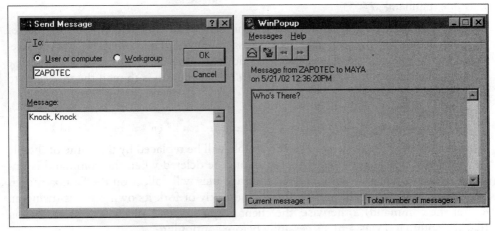

Figure 11-1. Sending a message from a Windows 95/98/Me system (left); receiving a message (right)

On Windows NT/2000/XP, the messenger service lets you receive messages without having an application already running; messages will automatically appear in a small dialog box on the screen when received, as shown in Figure 11-2.

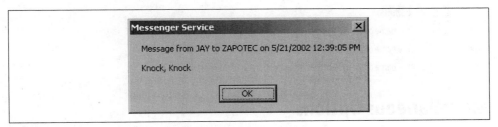

Figure 11-2. Receiving a message on a Windows 2000 system

To send messages, it is necessary to use the *net send* command from a command-prompt window, like this:

```
C:\> net send maya "Who's There?"
The message was successfully sent to MAYA.
```

Windows Messenger Service Configuration Option

Samba has a single option to handle Windows Messenger Service, `message command`, as shown in Table 11-7.

Table 11-7. Windows Messenger Service configuration option

Option	Parameter	Function	Default	Scope
message command	string (shell command)	Sets a command to run on Unix when a WinPopup message is received	None	Global

message command

Samba's message command option defines the command that will run on the server when a Windows Messenger Service message arrives. The command will be executed as the guest account user. What to do with messages is questionable because most Samba hosts run as unattended servers. One solution is to mail the messages to root like this:

```
[global]
    message command = /bin/mail -s "SMB Message From %f on %m" root <%s; rm %s
```

Note the use of variables here. The %s variable will be replaced by the name of the file in which the message resides. This file should be deleted when the command is finished with it; otherwise, a buildup of message files will collect on the Samba server. In addition, the command must either exit quickly or fork its own process (using an & after the command); otherwise, the client might suspend and wait for notification that the command was sent successfully before continuing.

In addition to the standard variables, Table 11-8 shows the three unique variables that you can use in a message command.

Table 11-8. message command variables

Variable	Definition
%s	The name of the file in which the message resides
%f	The name of the system that sent the message
%t	The name of the system that is the destination of the message

Miscellaneous Options

Many Samba options are available to deal with operating system issues on either Unix or Windows. In particular, some of these options are used for setting limits for clients' use of resources on the Unix server. The options shown in Table 11-9 deal with some of these issues.

Table 11-9. Miscellaneous options

Option	Parameters	Function	Default	Scope
deadtime	numeric (minutes)	Number of minutes of inactivity before a connection should be terminated.	0	Global
dfree command	string (command)	Used to specify a command that returns free disk space in a format recognized by Samba.	None	Global
fstype	NTFS, FAT, or Samba	Filesystem type reported by the server to the client.	NTFS	Global
keepalive	numeric (seconds)	Number of seconds between checks for an inoperative client.	300 (none)	Global

Table 11-9. Miscellaneous options (continued)

Option	Parameters	Function	Default	Scope
max disk size	numeric (MB)	Largest disk size to return to a client, some of which have limits. Does not affect actual operations on the disk.	0 (infinity)	Global
max mux	numeric	Maximum number of simultaneous SMB operations that clients can make.	50	Global
max open files	numeric	Limits number of open files to be below Unix limits.	10000	Global
max xmit	numeric	Specifies the maximum packet size that Samba will send.	65535 or 16644	Global
nt pipe support	Boolean	Turns off an NT/2000/XP support feature; for benchmarking or in case of an error.	yes	Global
nt smb support	Boolean	Turns off an NT/2000/XP support feature; for benchmarking or in case of an error.	yes	Global
ole locking compatibility	Boolean	Remaps out-of-range lock requests used on Windows to fit in allowable range on Unix. Turning it off causes Unix lock errors.	yes	Global
panic action	string	Command to run if Samba server fails; for debugging.	None	Global
set directory	Boolean	If yes, allows VMS clients to issue set dir commands.	no	Global
status	Boolean	If yes, allows Samba to monitor status for smbstatus command.	yes	Global
strict sync	Boolean	If no, ignores Windows application requests to perform a sync-to-disk.	no	Global
sync always	Boolean	If yes, forces all client writes to be committed to disk before returning from the call.	no	Global
strip dot	Boolean	If yes, strips trailing dots from Unix filenames.	no	Global
change notify timeout	numeric (seconds)	Interval between checks when a client asks to wait for a change in a specified directory.	60	Global
stat cache	Boolean	If yes, Samba will cache recent name mappings.	yes	Global
stat cache size	numeric	Number of entries in the stat cache.	50	Global

deadtime

This global option sets the number of minutes that Samba will wait for an inactive client before closing its session with the Samba server. A client is considered inactive when it has no open files and no data is being sent from it. The default value for this option is 0, which means that Samba never closes any connection, regardless of how long they have been inactive. This can lead to unnecessary consumption of the server's resources by inactive clients. We recommend that you override the default as follows:

```
[global]
    deadtime = 10
```

This tells Samba to terminate any inactive client sessions after 10 minutes. For most networks, setting this option as such will not inconvenience users because reconnections from the client are generally performed transparently to the user. See also the keepalive parameter.

dfree command

This global option is used on systems that incorrectly determine the free space left on the disk. So far, the only confirmed system that needs this option set is Ultrix. There is no default value for this option, which means that Samba already knows how to compute the free disk space on its own and the results are considered reliable. You can override it as follows:

```
[global]
    dfree command = /usr/local/bin/dfree
```

This option should point to a script that returns the total disk space in a block and the number of available blocks. The Samba documentation recommends the following as a usable script:

```
#!/bin/sh
df $1 | tail -1 | awk '{print $2" "$4}'
```

On System V machines, the following will work:

```
#!/bin/sh
/usr/bin/df $1 | tail -1 | awk '{print $3" "$5}'
```

fstype

This share-level option sets the type of filesystem that Samba reports when queried by the client. Three strings can be used as a value to this configuration option, as listed in Table 11-10.

Table 11-10. Filesystem types

Value	Definition
NTFS	Microsoft Windows NT filesystem
FAT	DOS FAT filesystem
Samba	Samba filesystem

The default value for this option is NTFS, which represents a Windows NT filesystem. There probably isn't a need to specify any other type of filesystem. However, if you need to, you can override the default value per share as follows:

```
[data]
    fstype = FAT
```

keepalive

This global option specifies the number of seconds that Samba waits between sending NetBIOS *keepalive packets*. These packets are used to ping a client to detect whether it is still alive and on the network. The default value for this option is 300 (5 minutes), which you can override as follows:

```
[global]
    keepalive = 600
```

The value of 600 (10 minutes) is good for networks populated by reliable clients. If your network contains relatively unreliable clients, you might prefer to set keepalive to a lower value, such as 30. If keepalive is set to 0, no NetBIOS keepalive packets will be sent. See also the deadtime parameter.

max disk size

This global option specifies an illusory limit, in megabytes, for each share that Samba is offering. It only affects how much disk space Samba reports the share as having and does not prevent more disk space from actually being available for use. You would typically set this option to prevent clients with older operating systems—or running buggy applications—from being confused by large disk spaces. For example, some older Windows applications become confused when they encounter a share larger than 1 gigabyte. To work around this problem, max disk size can be set as follows:

```
[global]
    max disk size = 1000
```

The default value for this option is 0, which means there is no upper limit.

max mux

This global option specifies the maximum number of concurrent SMB operations Samba allows. The default value for this option is 50. You can override it as follows:

```
[global]
    max mux = 100
```

max open files

This global option specifies the maximum number of open files that Samba should allow at any given time for all processes. This value must be equal to or less than the amount allowed by the operating system, which varies from system to system. The default value for this option is 10000. You can override it as follows:

```
[global]
    max open files = 8000
```

max xmit

This global option sets the maximum size of packets that Samba exchanges with a client. In rare cases, setting a smaller maximum packet size can increase performance, especially with Windows for Workgroups. In Samba versions up to 2.2.5, the default value for this option is 65535. In 2.2.7 and later versions, the default was changed to 16644 to match the behavior of Windows 2000 and improve support for Windows NT 4.0. You can override the default as follows:

```
[global]
    max xmit = 4096
```

nt pipe support

This global option is used by developers to allow or disallow Windows NT/2000/XP clients the ability to make connections to NT-specific SMB IPC$ pipes. As a user, you should never need to override the default:

```
[global]
    nt pipe support = yes
```

nt smb support

This global option is used by developers to negotiate NT-specific SMB options with Windows NT/2000/XP clients. The Samba Team has discovered that slightly better performance comes from setting this value to no. However, as a user, you should probably not override the default:

```
[global]
    nt smb support = yes
```

ole locking compatibility

This global option turns off Samba's internal byte-range locking manipulation in files, which gives compatibility with Object Linking and Embedding (OLE) applications that use high byte-range locks as a method of interprocess communication. The default value for this option is yes. If you trust your Unix locking mechanisms, you can override it as follows:

```
[global]
    ole locking compatibility = no
```

panic action

This global option specifies a command to execute in the event that Samba encounters a fatal error when loading or running. There is no default value for this option. You can specify an action as follows:

```
[global]
    panic action = /bin/csh -c
        'xedit <<: "Samba has shutdown unexpectedly";:'
```

set directory

This Boolean share-level option allows Digital Pathworks clients to use the *setdir* command to change directories on the server. If you are not using the Digital Pathworks client, you should not need to alter this option. The default value for this option is no. You can override it per share as follows:

```
[data]
    set directory = yes
```

status

This global option indicates whether Samba should log all active connections to a status file. This file is used only by the *smbstatus* command. If you have no intentions of using this command, you can set this option to no, which can result in a small increase of speed on the server. The default value for this option is yes. You can override it as follows:

```
[global]
    status = no
```

strict sync

This share-level option determines whether Samba honors all requests to perform a disk sync when requested to do so by a client. Many Windows clients request a disk sync when they are really just trying to flush data to their own open files. In this case, a disk sync is generally unnecessary on Unix due to its high reliability, and it mostly has the effect of substantially reducing the performance of the Samba host system. The default value for this option is no, which allows the superfluous disk sync requests to be ignored. You can override the default as follows:

```
[data]
    strict sync = yes
```

sync always

This share-level option decides whether every write to disk should be followed by a disk synchronization before the write call returns control to the client. Even if the value of this option is no, clients can request a disk synchronization; see the earlier strict sync option. The default value for this option is no. You can override it per share as follows:

```
[data]
    sync always = yes
```

strip dot

This global option determines whether to remove the trailing dot from Unix filenames that are formatted with a dot at the end. The default value for this option is no. You can override it per share as follows:

```
[global]
    strip dot = yes
```

change notify timeout

The change notify timeout global option emulates a Windows NT/2000 SMB feature called *change notification*. This allows a client to request that a Windows NT/2000 server periodically monitor a specific directory on a share for any changes. If changes occur, the server will notify the client.

Samba performs this function for its clients at an interval that defaults to 1 minute (60 seconds). Performing these checks too often can slow down the server considerably; however, you can use this option to specify an alternate time that Samba should wait between performing checks:

```
[global]
    change notify timeout = 30
```

stat cache

The stat cache global option turns on caching of recent case-insensitive name mappings. The default is yes. The Samba Team recommends that you never change this parameter.

stat cache size

The stat cache size global option sets the number of cache entries to be used for the stat cache option. The default here is 50. Again, the Samba Team recommends that you never change this parameter.

## CHAPTER 12

Troubleshooting Samba

Samba is extremely robust. Once you have everything set up the way you want, you'll probably forget that it is running. When trouble occurs, it's typically during installation or when you're trying to reconfigure the server. Fortunately, a wide variety of resources are available to diagnose these troubles. While we can't describe in detail the solution to every problem you might encounter, you should be able to get a good start at resolving the problem by following the advice given in this chapter.

The first section of this chapter lists the tool bag, a collection of tools available for troubleshooting Samba; the second section is a detailed how-to; the last section lists extra resources to track down particularly stubborn problems.

The Tool Box

Sometimes Unix seems to be made up of a grab bag of applications and tools. There are tools to troubleshoot tools. And of course, there are several ways to accomplish the same task. When trying to solve a problem related to Samba, a good plan of attack is to use the following:

- Samba logs
- Samba test utilities
- Unix utilities
- Fault tree
- Documentation and FAQs
- Samba newsgroups
- Searchable mailing list archives

Let's go over each of these one-by-one in the following sections.

Samba Logs

Your first line of attack should always be to check the log files. The Samba log files can help diagnose the vast majority of the problems faced by beginning- to intermediate-level Samba administrators. Samba is quite flexible when it comes to logging. You can set up the server to log as little or as much information as you want. Using substitution variables in the Samba configuration file allows you to isolate individual logs for each system, share, or combination thereof.

Logs are placed in */usr/local/samba/var/smbd.log* and */usr/local/samba/var/nmbd.log* by default. You can specify a log directory to use with the *-l* flag on the command line when starting the Samba daemons. For example:

```
# smbd -l /var/log/samba
# nmbd -l /var/log/samba
```

Alternatively, you can override the location and name using the log file configuration option in *smb.conf*. This option accepts all the substitution variables, so you could easily have the server keep a separate log for each connecting client system by specifying the following:

```
[global]
    log file = %m.log
```

Another useful trick is to have the server keep a log for each service (share) that is offered, especially if you suspect a particular share is causing trouble. To do this, use the %S variable, like this:

```
[global]
    log file = %S.log
```

Log levels

The level of logging that Samba uses can be set in the *smb.conf* file using the global log level or debug level option; they are equivalent. The logging level is an integer that can range from 0 to 10. At level 0, no logging is done. Higher values result in more voluminous logging. For example, let's assume that we will use a Windows client to browse a directory on a Samba server. For a small amount of log information, you can use log level = 1, which instructs Samba to show only cursory information, in this case only the connection itself:

```
05/25/02 22:02:11 server (192.168.236.86) connect to service public as user pcguest
(uid=503,gid=100) (pid 3377)
```

Higher debug levels produce more detailed information. Usually, you won't need more than level 3, which is fully adequate for most Samba administrators. Levels above 3 are used by the developers and dump enormous amounts of cryptic information.

Here is an example of output at levels 2 and 3 for the same operation. Don't worry if you don't understand the intricacies of an SMB connection; the point is simply to show you what types of information are shown at the different logging levels:

```
  /* Level 2 */
Got SIGHUP
Processing section "[homes]"
Processing section "[public]"
Processing section "[temp]"
Allowed connection from 192.168.236.86 (192.168.236.86) to IPC$
Allowed connection from 192.168.236.86 (192.168.236.86) to IPC/


  /* Level 3 */
05/25/02 22:15:09 Transaction 63 of length 67
switch message SMBtconX (pid 3377)
Allowed connection from 192.168.236.86 (192.168.236.86) to IPC$
ACCEPTED: guest account and guest ok
found free connection number 105
Connect path is /tmp
chdir to /tmp
chdir to /
05/25/02 22:15:09 server (192.168.236.86) connect to service IPC$ as user pcguest
(uid=503,gid=100) (pid 3377)
05/25/02 22:15:09 tconX service=ipc$ user=pcguest cnum=105
05/25/02 22:15:09 Transaction 64 of length 99
switch message SMBtrans (pid 3377)
chdir to /tmp
trans <\PIPE\LANMAN> data=0 params=19 setup=0
Got API command 0 of form <WrLeh> <B13BWz> (tdscnt=0,tpscnt=19,mdrcnt=4096,mprcnt=8)
Doing RNetShareEnum
RNetShareEnum gave 4 entries of 4 (1 4096 126 4096)
05/25/02 22:15:11 Transaction 65 of length 99
switch message SMBtrans (pid 3377)
chdir to /
chdir to /tmp
trans <\PIPE\LANMAN> data=0 params=19 setup=0
Got API command 0 of form <WrLeh> <B13BWz> (tdscnt=0,tpscnt=19,mdrcnt=4096,mprcnt=8)
Doing RNetShareEnum
RNetShareEnum gave 4 entries of 4 (1 4096 126 4096)
05/25/02 22:15:11 Transaction 66 of length 95
switch message SMBtrans2 (pid 3377)
chdir to /
chdir to /pcdisk/public
call_trans2findfirst: dirtype = 0, maxentries = 6, close_after_first=0, close_if_end
= 0 requires_resume_key = 0 level = 260, max_data_bytes = 2432
unix_clean_name [./DESKTOP.INI]
unix_clean_name [desktop.ini]
unix_clean_name [./]
creating new dirptr 1 for path ./, expect_close = 1
05/25/02 22:15:11 Transaction 67 of length 53
switch message SMBgetatr (pid 3377)
chdir to /
```

[... deleted ...]

We cut off this listing after the first packet because it runs on for many pages. However, be aware that log levels above 3 will quickly consume disk space with mega-

bytes of excruciating detail concerning Samba's internal operations. Log level 3 is extremely useful for following exactly what the server is doing, and most of the time it will be obvious where an error occurs by glancing through the log file.

Using a high log level (3 or above) will *seriously* slow down the Samba server. Remember that every log message generated causes a write to disk (an inherently slow operation) and log levels greater than 2 produce massive amounts of data. Essentially, you should turn on logging level 3 only when you're actively tracking a problem in the Samba server.

Activating and deactivating logging

To turn logging on and off, set the appropriate level in the [global] section of *smb.conf*. Then, you can either restart Samba or force the current daemon to reprocess the configuration file by sending it a hangup (HUP) signal. You also can send the *smbd* process a SIGUSR1 signal to increase its log level by one while it's running, like this:

```
# kill -SIGUSR1 1234
```

or a SIGUSR2 signal to decrease it by one:

```
# kill -SIGUSR2 1234
```

Logging by individual client systems or users

An effective way to diagnose problems without hampering other users is to assign different log levels for different systems in the [global] section of the *smb.conf* file. We can do this by building on the strategy we presented earlier:

```
[global]
    log level = 0
    log file = /usr/local/samba/var/log.%m
    include = /usr/local/samba/lib/smb.conf.%m
```

These options instruct Samba to use unique configuration and log files for each client that connects. Now all you have to do is create an *smb.conf* file for a specific client system with a log level = 3 entry in it (the others will pick up the default log level of 0) and use that log file to track down the problem.

Similarly, if only particular users are experiencing a problem—and it travels from system to system with them—you can isolate logging to a specific user by adding the following to the *smb.conf* file:

```
[global]
    log level = 0
    log file = /usr/local/samba/var/log.%u
    include = /usr/local/samba/lib/smb.conf.%u
```

Then you can create a unique *smb.conf* file for each user you wish to monitor (e.g., */usr/local/samba/lib/smb.conf.tim*). Files containing the configuration option log level = 3 and only those users will get more detailed logging.

Samba Test Utilities

A rigorous set of tests that exercise the major parts of Samba are described in various files in the */docs/textdocs* directory of the Samba distribution kit, starting with *DIAGNOSIS.txt*. The fault tree in this chapter is a more detailed version of the basic tests suggested by the Samba Team, but it covers only installation and reconfiguration diagnosis, such as *DIAGNOSIS.txt*. The other files in the */docs* subdirectories address specific problems and instruct you how to troubleshoot items not included in this book. If the fault tree doesn't suffice, be sure to look at *DIAGNOSIS.txt* and its friends.

Unix Utilities

Sometimes it's useful to use a tool outside the Samba suite to examine what's happening inside the server. Three diagnostic tools can be of particular help in debugging Samba troubles: *trace*, *tcpdump*, and *Ethereal*.

Using trace

The *trace* command masquerades under several different names, depending on the operating system you are using. On Linux it will be *strace*; on Solaris you'll use *truss*; SGI will have *padc* and *par*; and HP-UX will have *trace* or *tusc*. All have essentially the same function, which is to display each operating system function call as it is executed. This allows you to follow the execution of a program, such as the Samba server, and often pinpoints the exact call that is causing the difficulty.

One problem that *trace* can highlight is an incorrect version of a dynamically linked library. This can happen if you've downloaded prebuilt binaries of Samba. You'll typically see the offending call at the end of the *trace*, just before the program terminates.

A sample *strace* output for the Linux operating system follows. This is a small section of a larger file created during the opening of a directory on the Samba server. Each line lists a system call and includes its parameters and the return value. If there was an error, the error value (e.g., ENOENT) and its explanation are also shown. You can look up the parameter types and the errors that can occur in the appropriate *trace* manual page for the operating system you are using.

```
chdir("/pcdisk/public")                 = 0
stat("mini/desktop.ini", 0xbffff7ec)     = -1 ENOENT (No such file or directory)
stat("mini", {st_mode=S_IFDIR|0755, st_size=1024, ...}) = 0
stat("mini/desktop.ini", 0xbffff7ec)     = -1 ENOENT (No such file or directory)
open("mini", O_RDONLY)                   = 5
```

```
fcntl(5, F_SETFD, FD_CLOEXEC)              = 0
fstat(5, {st_mode=S_IFDIR|0755, st_size=1024, ...}) = 0
lseek(5, 0, SEEK_CUR)                      = 0
SYS_141(0x5, 0xbfffdbbc, 0xedc, 0xbfffdbbc, 0x80ba708) = 196
lseek(5, 0, SEEK_CUR)                      = 1024
SYS_141(0x5, 0xbfffdbbc, 0xedc, 0xbfffdbbc, 0x80ba708) = 0
close(5)                                   = 0
stat("mini/desktop.ini", 0xbffff86c)       = -1 ENOENT (No such file or directory)
write(3, "\0\0\0#\377SMB\10\1\0\2\0\200\1\0"..., 39) = 39
SYS_142(0xff, 0xbffffc3c, 0, 0, 0xbffffc08) = 1
read(3, "\0\0\0?", 4)                      = 4
read(3, "\377SMBu\0\0\0\0\0\0\0\0\0\0\0\0"..., 63) = 63
time(NULL)                                 = 896143871
```

This example shows several *stat() calls* failing to find the files they were expecting.
You don't have to be an expert to see that the file *desktop.ini* is missing from that
directory. In fact, many difficult problems can be identified by looking for obvious,
repeatable errors with *trace*. Often, you need not look further than the last message
before a crash.

Using tcpdump

The *tcpdump* program, as extended by Andrew Tridgell, allows you to monitor SMB
network traffic in real time. A variety of output formats are available, and you can filter the output to look at only a particular type of traffic. You can examine all conver-
sations between client and server, including SMB and NMB broadcast messages.
While its troubleshooting capabilities lie mainly at the OSI network layer, you can
still use its output to get a general idea of what the server and client are attempting to
do.

A sample *tcpdump* log follows. In this instance, the client has requested a directory
listing, and the server has responded appropriately, giving the directory names homes,
public, IPC$, and temp (we've added a few explanations on the right):

```
$ tcpdump -v -s 255 -i eth0 port not telnet
SMB PACKET: SMBtrans (REQUEST)                    Request packet
SMB Command      = 0x25                           Request was ls or dir

[000] 01 00 00 10                                 ....


>>> NBT Packet                                    Outer frame of SMB packet
NBT Session Packet
Flags=0x0
Length=226
[lines skipped]

SMB PACKET: SMBtrans (REPLY)                       Beginning of a reply to request
SMB Command      = 0x25                            Command was an ls or dir
Error class      = 0x0
Error code       = 0                               No errors
```

```
Flags1        =  0x80
Flags2        =  0x1
Tree ID       =  105
Proc ID       =  6075
UID           =  100
MID           =  30337
Word Count    =  10
TotParamCnt=8
TotDataCnt=163
Res1=0
ParamCnt=8
ParamOff=55
Res2=0
DataCnt=163
DataOff=63
Res3=0
Lsetup=0
Param Data: (8 bytes)
[000] 00 00 00 00 05 00 05 00                          ........

Data Data: (135 bytes)              Actual directory contents:
[000] 68 6F 6D 65 73 00 00 00  00 00 00 00 00 00 00 00  homes... ........
[010] 64 00 00 00 70 75 62 6C  69 63 00 00 00 00 00 00  d...publ ic......
[020] 00 00 00 00 75 00 00 00  74 65 6D 70 00 00 00 00  ....u... temp....
[030] 00 00 00 00 00 00 00 00  76 00 00 00 49 50 43 24  ........ v...IPC$
[040] 00 00 00 00 00 00 00 00  00 00 03 00 77 00 00 00  ........ ....w...
[050] 64 6F 6E 68 61 6D 00 00  00 00 00 00 00 00 00 00  donham.. ........
[060] 92 00 00 00 48 6F 6D 65  20 44 69 72 65 63 74 6F  ....Home Directo
[070] 72 69 65 73 00 00 00 49  50 43 20 53 65 72 76 69  ries...I PC Servi
[080] 63 65 20 28 53 61 6D                              ce (Sam
```

This is more of the same debugging session as we saw before with the *trace* command: the listing of a directory. The options we used were *-v* (verbose), *-i eth0* to tell *tcpdump* on which interface to listen (an Ethernet port), and *-s 255* to tell it to save the first 255 bytes of each packet instead of the default: the first 68. The option port not telnet is used to avoid screens of telnet traffic, because we were logged in to the server remotely. The *tcpdump* program actually has quite a number of options to filter just the traffic you want to look at. If you've used *snoop* or *etherdump*, it will look vaguely familiar.

You can download the modified *tcpdump* from the Samba FTP server, located at *ftp://samba.anu.edu.au/pub/samba/tcpdump-smb*. Other versions might not include support for the SMB protocol; if you don't see output such as that shown in the example, you'll need to use the SMB-enabled version.

Using Ethereal

Ethereal (*http://www.ethereal.com*) is a GUI-based utility that performs the same basic function as *tcpdump*. You might prefer Ethereal because it is much easier to use. Once you have Ethereal running, just do the following:

1. Select Start from the Capture menu.

2. Click the OK button in the dialog box that appears. This will bring up a dialog box showing how many packets Ethereal has seen. Perform the actions on the system(s) in your network to reproduce the problem you are analyzing.

3. Click the Stop button in the Ethereal dialog box to make it finish collecting data.

4. In the main Ethereal window, click any item in the upper window to view it in the lower window. In the lower window, click any of the boxes containing a plus sign (+) to expand the view.

Ethereal does a good job of translating the content of the packets it encounters into human-readable format, and you should have little trouble seeing what happened on the network during the capture period.

The Fault Tree

The fault tree presented in this section is for diagnosing and fixing problems that occur when you're installing and reconfiguring Samba. It's an expanded form of the trouble and diagnostic document *DIAGNOSIS.txt*, which is part of the Samba distribution.

Before you set out to troubleshoot any part of the Samba suite, you should know the following information:

- Your client IP address (we use 192.168.236.10)
- Your server IP address (we use 192.168.236.86)
- The netmask for your network (typically 255.255.255.0)
- Whether the systems are all on the same subnet (ours are)

For clarity, we've renamed the server in the following examples to server.example. com, and the client system to client.example.com.

How to Use the Fault Tree

Start the tests here, without skipping forward; it won't take long (about 5 minutes) and might actually save you time backtracking. Whenever a test succeeds, you will be given a name of a section to which you can safely skip.

Troubleshooting Low-Level IP

The first series of tests is that of the low-level services that Samba needs to run. The tests in this section verify that:

- The IP software works
- The Ethernet hardware works
- Basic name service is in place

Subsequent sections add TCP software, the Samba daemons *smbd* and *nmbd*, host-based access control, authentication and per-user access control, file services, and browsing. The tests are described in considerable detail to make them understandable by both technically oriented end users and experienced systems and network administrators.

Testing the networking software with ping

The first command to enter on both the server and the client is ping 127.0.0.1. This pings the loopback address and indicates whether any networking support is functioning. On Unix, you can use ping 127.0.0.1 with the statistics option and interrupt it after a few lines. On Sun workstations, the command is typically /usr/etc/ping -s 127.0.0.1; on Linux, just ping 127.0.0.1. On Windows clients, run ping 127.0.0.1 in an MS-DOS (command prompt) window, and it will stop by itself after four lines.

Here is an example on a Linux server:

```
$ ping 127.0.0.1
PING localhost: 56 data bytes 64 bytes from localhost (127.0.0.1):
icmp-seq=0. time=1. ms 64 bytes from localhost (127.0.0.1):
icmp-seq=1. time=0. ms 64 bytes from localhost (127.0.0.1):
icmp-seq=2. time=1. ms ^C
----127.0.0.1 PING Statistics----
3 packets transmitted, 3 packets received, 0% packet loss round-trip (ms)
min/avg/max = 0/0/1
```

If you get "ping: no answer from …" or "100% packet loss," you have no IP networking installed on the system. The address 127.0.0.1 is the internal loopback address and doesn't depend on the computer being physically connected to a network. If this test fails, you have a serious local problem. TCP/IP either isn't installed or is seriously misconfigured. See your operating system documentation if it's a Unix server. If it's a Windows client, follow the instructions in Chapter 3 to install networking support.

 If *you're* the network manager, some good references are Craig Hunt's *TCP/IP Network Administration*, Chapter 11, and Craig Hunt and Robert Bruce Thompson's *Windows NT TCP/IP Network Administration,* both published by O'Reilly.

Testing local name services with ping

Next, try to ping localhost on the Samba server. The localhost hostname is the conventional hostname for the 127.0.0.1 loopback interface, and it should resolve to that address. After typing ping localhost, you should see output similar to the following:

```
$ ping localhost
PING localhost: 56 data bytes  64 bytes from localhost (127.0.0.1):
icmp-seq=0. time=0. ms  64 bytes from localhost (127.0.0.1):
```

```
icmp-seq=1. time=0. ms  64 bytes from localhost (127.0.0.1):
icmp-seq=2. time=0. ms  ^C
```

If this succeeds, try the same test on the client. Otherwise:

- If you get "unknown host: localhost," there is a problem resolving the hostname *localhost* into a valid IP address. (This might be as simple as a missing entry in a local *hosts* file.) From here, skip down to the section "Troubleshooting Name Services" later in this chapter.

- If you get "ping: no answer," or "100% packet loss," but pinging 127.0.0.1 worked, name services is resolving to an address, but it isn't the correct one. Check the file or database (typically */etc/hosts* on a Unix system) that the name service is using to resolve addresses to ensure that the entry is correct.

Testing the networking hardware with ping

Next, ping the server's network IP address from itself. This should get you exactly the same results as pinging 127.0.0.1:

```
$ ping 192.168.236.86
PING 192.168.236.86: 56 data bytes 64 bytes from 192.168.236.86 (192.168.236.86):
icmp-seq=0. time=1. ms 64 bytes from 192.168.236.86 (192.168.236.86):
icmp-seq=1. time=0. ms 64 bytes from 192.168.236.86 (192.168.236.86):
icmp-seq=2. time=1. ms ^C
----192.168.236.86 PING Statistics----
3 packets transmitted, 3 packets received, 0% packet loss round-trip (ms)
min/avg/max = 0/0/1
```

If this works on the server, repeat it for the client. Otherwise:

- If ping *network_ip* fails on either the server or client, but ping 127.0.0.1 works on that system, you have a TCP/IP problem that is specific to the Ethernet network interface card on the computer. Check with the documentation for the network card or host operating system to determine how to configure it correctly. However, be aware that on some operating systems, the *ping* command appears to work even if the network is disconnected, so this test doesn't always diagnose all hardware problems.

Testing connections with ping

Now, ping the server by name (instead of its IP address)—once from the server and once from the client. This is the general test for working network hardware:

```
$ ping server
PING server.example.com: 56 data bytes 64 bytes from server.example.com (192.168.236.
86):
icmp-seq=0. time=1. ms 64 bytes from server.example.com (192.168.236.86):
icmp-seq=1. time=0. ms 64 bytes from server.example.com (192.168.236.86):
icmp-seq=2. time=1. ms ^C
----server.example.com PING Statistics----
3 packets transmitted, 3 packets received, 0% packet loss round-trip (ms)
min/avg/max = 0/0/1
```

If successful, this test tells us five things:

- The hostname (e.g., server) is being found by your local name server.
- The hostname has been expanded to the full name (e.g., server.example.com).
- Its address is being returned (192.168.236.86).
- The client has sent the Samba server four 56-byte UDP/IP packets.
- The Samba server has replied to all four packets.

If this test isn't successful, one of several things can be wrong with the network:

- First, if you get ping: no answer, or 100% packet loss, you're not connecting to the network, the other system isn't connecting, or one of the addresses is incorrect. Check the addresses that the *ping* command reports on each system, and ensure that they match the ones you set up initially.

  If not, there is at least one mismatched address between the two systems. Try entering the command arp -a, and see if there is an entry for the other system. (The *arp* command stands for the Address Resolution Protocol. The arp -a command lists all the addresses known on the local system.) Here are some things to try:

  —If you receive a message like 192.168.236.86 at (incomplete), the Ethernet address of 192.168.236.86 is unknown. This indicates a complete lack of connectivity, and you're likely having a problem at the very bottom of the TCP/IP protocol stack—the Ethernet interface layer. This is discussed in Chapters 5 and 6 of *TCP/IP Network Administration* (O'Reilly).

  —If you receive a response similar to server (192.168.236.86) at 8:0:20:12:7c: 94, the server has been reached at some time, or another system is answering on its behalf. However, this means that *ping* should have worked: you may have an intermittent networking or ARP problem.

  —If the IP address from ARP doesn't match the addresses you expected, investigate and correct the addresses manually.

- If each system can ping itself but not another, something is wrong on the network between them.

- If you get ping: network unreachable or ICMP Host Unreachable, you're not receiving an answer, and more than one network is probably involved.

  In principle, you shouldn't try to troubleshoot SMB clients and servers on different networks. Try to test a server and client that are on the same network:

  1. First, perform the tests for ping: no answer described earlier in this section. If this doesn't identify the problem, the remaining possibilities are the following: an address is wrong, your netmask is wrong, a network is down, or the packets have been stopped by a firewall.

  2. Check both the address and the netmasks on source and destination systems to see if something is obviously wrong. Assuming both systems really

are on the same network, they both should have the same netmasks, and *ping* should report the correct addresses. If the addresses are wrong, you'll need to correct them. If they are correct, the programs might be confused by an incorrect netmask. See the section "Netmasks," later in this chapter.

3. If the commands are still reporting that the network is unreachable and neither of the previous two conditions are in error, one network really might be unreachable from the other. This, too, is an issue for the network manager.

- If you get ICMP Administratively Prohibited, you've struck a firewall of some sort or a misconfigured router. You will need to speak to your network security officer.

- If you get ICMP Host redirect and *ping* reports packets getting through, this is generally harmless: you're simply being rerouted over the network.

- If you get a host redirect and no *ping* responses, you are being redirected, but no one is responding. Treat this just like the Network unreachable response, and check your addresses and netmasks.

- If you get ICMP Host Unreachable from gateway gateway name, ping packets are being routed to another network, but the other system isn't responding and the router is reporting the problem on its behalf. Again, treat this like a Network unreachable response, and start checking addresses and netmasks.

- If you get ping: unknown host hostname, your system's name is not known. This tends to indicate a name service problem, which didn't affect localhost. Have a look at "Troubleshooting Name Services," later in this chapter.

- If you get a partial success—with some pings failing but others succeeding—you have either an intermittent problem between the systems or an overloaded network. Ping a bit longer, and see if more than about three percent of the packets fail. If so, check it with your network manager: a problem might just be starting. However, if only a few fail, or if you happen to know some massive network program is running, don't worry unduly. The ICMP (and UDP) protocols used by *ping* are allowed to drop occasional packets.

- If you get a response such as smtsvr.antares.net is alive when you actually pinged client.example.com, either you're using someone else's address or the system has multiple names and addresses. If the address is wrong, the name service is clearly the culprit; you'll need to change the address in the name service database to refer to the correct system. This is discussed in "Troubleshooting Name Services," later in this chapter.

Servers are often *multihomed*—i.e., connected to more than one network, with different names on each net. If you are getting a response from an unexpected name on a multihomed server, look at the address and see if it's on your network (see the section "Netmasks," later in this chapter). If so, you should use that address, rather than one on a different network, for both performance and reliability reasons.

Servers can also have multiple names for a single Ethernet address, especially if they are web servers. This is harmless, albeit startling. You probably will want to use the official (and permanent) name, rather than an alias that might change.

- If everything works but the IP address reported is 127.0.0.1, you have a name service error. This typically occurs when an operating-system installation program generates an */etc/hosts* line similar to 127.0.0.1 localhost *hostname.domainname*. The localhost line should say 127.0.0.1 localhost or 127.0.0.1 localhost loghost. Correct it, lest it cause failures to negotiate who is the master browse list holder and who is the master browser. It can also cause (ambiguous) errors in later tests.

If this worked from the server, repeat it from the client.

Troubleshooting TCP

Now that you've tested IP, UDP, and a name service with *ping*, it's time to test TCP. Browsing and *ping* use ICMP and UDP; file and print services (shares) use TCP. Both depend on IP as a lower layer, and all four depend on name services. Testing TCP is most conveniently done using the FTP program.

Testing TCP with FTP

Try connecting via FTP, once from the server to itself, and once from the client to the server:

```
$ ftp server
Connected to server.example.com.
220 server.example.com FTP server (Version 6.2/OpenBSD/Linux-0.10) ready.
 Name (server:davecb):
331 Password required for davecb.
Password:
230 User davecb logged in.
 ftp> quit
221 Goodbye.
```

If this worked, skip to the next section, "Troubleshooting Server Daemons." Otherwise:

- If you received the message server: unknown host, name service has failed. Go back to the corresponding *ping* step, "Testing local name services with ping," and rerun those tests to see why name lookup failed.
- If you received ftp: connect: Connection refused, the system isn't running an FTP daemon. This is mildly unusual on Unix servers. Optionally, you might try this test by connecting to the system using *telnet* instead of *ftp*; the messages are very similar, and *telnet* uses TCP as well.
- If there was a long pause, and then ftp: connect: Connection timed out, the system isn't reachable. Return to the section "Testing connections with ping."

- If you received 530 Logon Incorrect, you connected successfully, but you've just found a different problem. You likely provided an incorrect username or password. Try again, making sure you use your username from the Unix server and type your password correctly.

Troubleshooting Server Daemons

Once you've confirmed that TCP networking is working properly, the next step is to make sure the daemons are running on the server. This takes three separate tests because no single one of the following will decisively prove that they're working correctly.

To be sure they're running, you need to find out whether the daemons:

1. Have started
2. Are registered or bound to a TCP/IP port by the operating system
3. Are actually paying attention

Tracking daemon startup

First, check the Samba logs. If you've started the daemons, the message smbd version number started should appear. If it doesn't, you need to restart the Samba daemons.

If the daemon reports that it has indeed started, look out for bind failed on port 139 socket_addr=0 (Address already in use). This means another daemon has been started on port 139 (*smbd*). Also, *nmbd* will report a similar failure if it cannot bind to port 137. Either you've started them twice, or the *inetd* server has tried to provide a daemon for you. If it's the latter, we'll diagnose that in a moment.

Looking for daemon processes with ps

Another way to make sure the daemons are running is to check their processes on the system. Use the *ps* command on the server with the "long" option for your system type (commonly ps ax or ps -ef), and see whether *smbd* and *nmbd* are already running. This often looks like the following:

```
$ ps ax
 PID TTY STAT TIME   COMMAND
   1 ?   S    0:03   init [2]
   2 ?   SW   0:00   (kflushd)
(...many lines of processes...)
 234 ?   S    0:14   nmbd -D3
 237 ?   S    0:11   smbd -D3
(...more lines, possibly including more smbd lines...)
```

This example illustrates that *smbd* and *nmbd* have already started as standalone daemons (the -D option) at log level 3.

Looking for daemons bound to ports

Next, the daemons have to be registered with the operating system so that they can get access to TCP/IP ports. The *netstat* command will tell you if this has been done. Run the command netstat -a on the server, and look for lines mentioning netbios, 137, or 139:

```
$ netstat -a
Active Internet connections (including servers)
Proto Recv-Q Send-Q  Local Address          Foreign Address         (state)
udp    0      0       *.137                  *.*
tcp    0      0       *.139                  *.*                     LISTEN
tcp    8370   8760    server.139             client.1439             ESTABLISHED
```

Among similar lines, there should be at least one UDP line for *.netbios- or *.137. This indicates that the *nmbd* server is registered and (we hope) is waiting to answer requests. There should also be at least one TCP line mentioning *.netbios- or *.139, and it will probably be in the LISTEN state. This means that *smbd* is up and listening for connections.

There might be other TCP lines indicating connections from *smbd* to clients, one for each client. These are usually in the ESTABLISHED state. If there are *smbd* lines in the ESTABLISHED state, *smbd* is definitely running. If there is only one line in the LISTEN state, we're not sure yet. If both of the lines are missing, a daemon has not succeeded in starting, so it's time to check the logs and then go back to Chapter 2.

If there is a line for each client, it might be coming either from a Samba daemon or from the master IP daemon, *inetd*. It's quite possible that your *inetd* startup file contains lines that start Samba daemons without your realizing it; for instance, the lines might have been placed there if you installed Samba as part of a Linux distribution. The daemons started by *inetd* prevent ours from running. This problem typically produces log messages such as bind failed on port 139 socket addr=0 (Address already in use).

Check your */etc/inetd.conf*; unless you're intentionally starting the daemons from there, netbios-ns (UDP port 137) or netbios-ssn (tcp port 139) servers should be mentioned there. If your system is providing an SMB daemon via *inetd*, lines such as the following will appear in the *inetd.conf* file:

```
netbios-ssn stream tcp nowait root /usr/local/samba/bin/smbd smbd
netbios-ns dgram udp wait root /usr/local/samba/bin/nmbd nmbd
```

If your system uses *xinetd* instead of *inetd*, see Chapter 2 for details concerning its configuration.

Checking smbd with telnet

Ironically, the easiest way to test that the *smbd* server is actually working is to send it a meaningless message and see if it is rejected. Try something such as the following:

```
$ echo "hello" | telnet localhost 139
Trying
Trying 192.168.236.86 ...
Connected to localhost. Escape character is '^]'.
Connection closed by foreign host.
```

This sends an erroneous but harmless message to *smbd*. If you get a Connected message followed by a Connection closed message, the test was a success. You have an *smbd* daemon listening on the port and rejecting improper connection messages. On the other hand, if you get telnet: connect: Connection refused, most likely no daemon is present. Check the logs and go back to Chapter 2.

Regrettably, there isn't an easy test for *nmbd*. If the *telnet* test and the *netstat* test both say that an *smbd* is running, there is a good chance that *netstat* will also be correct about *nmbd* running.

Testing daemons with testparm

Once you know there's a daemon, you should always run *testparm*, in hopes of getting something such as the following:

```
$ testparm
Load smb config files from /opt/samba/lib/smb.conf
Processing section "[homes]"
Processing section "[printers]" ...
Processing section "[tmp]"
Loaded services file OK. ...
```

The *testparm* program normally reports the processing of a series of sections and responds with Loaded services file OK if it succeeds. If not, it reports one or more of the following messages, which also appear in the logs as noted:

Allow/Deny connection from account (n) to service
> A *testparm*-only message produced if you have valid user or invalid user options set in your *smb.conf*. You will want to make sure that you are on the valid user list, and that root, bin, etc., are on the invalid user list. If you don't, you will not be able to connect, or users who shouldn't *will* be able to.

Warning: You have some share names that are longer than eight chars
> For anyone using Windows for Workgroups and older clients. They fail to connect to shares with long names, producing an overflow message that sounds confusingly like a memory overflow.

Warning: [name] service MUST be printable!
> A printer share lacks a printable = yes option.

No path in service name using [name]
> A file share doesn't know which directory to provide to the user, or a print share doesn't know which directory to use for spooling. If no path is specified, the service will try to run with a path of */tmp*, which might not be what you want.

Note: Servicename is flagged unavailable
> Just a reminder that you have used the available = no option in a share.

Can't find include file [name]
> A configuration file referred to by an include option did not exist. If you were including the file unconditionally, this is an error and probably a serious one: the share will not have the configuration you intended. If you were including it based on one of the % variables, such as %a (architecture), you will need to decide whether, for example, a missing Windows for Workgroups configuration file is a problem. It often isn't.

Can't copy service name, unable to copy to itself
> You tried to copy an *smb.conf* section into itself.

Unable to copy service—source not found: [name]
> Indicates a missing or misspelled section in a copy = option.

Ignoring unknown parameter name
> Typically indicates an obsolete, misspelled, or unsupported option.

Global parameter name found in service section
> Indicates that a global-only parameter has been used in an individual share. Samba ignores the parameter.

After the *testparm* test, repeat it with (exactly) three parameters: the name of your *smb.conf* file, the name of your client, and its IP address:

```
# testparm /usr/local/samba/lib/smb.conf client 192.168.236.10
```

This will run one more test that checks the hostname and address against hosts allow and hosts deny options and might produce the Allow connection from hostname to service and/or Deny connection from hostname to service messages for the client system. These messages indicate that you have hosts allow and/or hosts deny options in your *smb.conf*, and they prohibit access from the client system.

Troubleshooting SMB Connections

Now that you know the servers are up, you need to make sure they're running properly. We start by placing a simple *smb.conf* file in the */usr/local/samba/lib* directory.

A minimal smb.conf file

In the following tests, we assume you have a [temp] share suitable for testing, plus at least one account. An *smb.conf* file that includes just these is as follows:

```
[global]
    workgroup = EXAMPLE
    security = user
    browsable = yes
    local master = yes
[homes]
```

```
        guest ok = no
        browsable = no
[temp]
        path = /tmp
        public = yes
```

 The public = yes option in the [temp] share is just for testing. You probably don't want people without accounts storing things on your Samba server, so you should comment it out when you're done.

Testing locally with smbclient

The first test is to ensure that the server can list its own services (shares). Run the command smbclient -L localhost -U% to connect to the server from itself, and specify the guest user. You should see the following:

```
$ smbclient -L localhost -U%
Server time is Wed May 27 17:57:40 2002 Timezone is UTC-4.0
Server=[localhost]
User=[davecb]
Workgroup=[EXAMPLE]
Domain=[EXAMPLE]
    Sharename    Type     Comment
    ---------    -----    ----------
    temp         Disk
    IPC$         IPC      IPC Service (Samba 1.9.18)
    homes        Disk     Home directories
This machine does not have a browse list
```

If you received this output, move on to the next section, "Testing connections with smbclient." On the other hand, if you receive an error, check the following:

- If you get Get_hostbyname: unknown host localhost, either you've spelled its name wrong or there actually is a problem (which should have been seen back in "Testing local name services with ping"). In the latter case, move on to the section "Troubleshooting Name Services," later in this chapter.

- If you get Connect error: Connection refused, the server was found, but it wasn't running an *nmbd* daemon. Skip back to "Troubleshooting Server Daemons," earlier in this chapter, and retest the daemons.

- If you get the message Your server software is being unfriendly, the initial session request packet got a garbage response from the server. The server might have crashed or started improperly. The common causes of this can be discovered by scanning the logs for the following:

    —Invalid command-line parameters to *smbd*; see the *smbd* manual page.

    —A fatal problem with the *smb.conf* file that prevents the startup of *smbd*.
    Always check your changes with *testparm*, as was done in the section "Testing daemons with testparm," earlier in this chapter.

—Missing directories where Samba is supposed to keep its log and lock files.

—The presence of a server already on the port (139 for *smbd*, 137 for *nmbd*), preventing the daemon from starting.

- If you're using *inetd* (or *xinetd*) instead of standalone daemons, be sure to check your */etc/inetd.conf* (or *xinetd* configuration files) and */etc/services* entries against their manual pages for errors as well.

- If you get a Password: prompt, your guest account is not set up properly. The *-U%* option tells *smbclient* to do a "null login," which requires that the guest account be present but does not require it to have any privileges.

- If you get the message SMBtconX failed. ERRSRV—ERRaccess, you aren't permitted access to the server. This normally means you have a hosts allow option that doesn't include the server or a hosts deny option that does. Recheck with the command testparm smb.conf *your_hostname your_ip_address* (see the section "Testing daemons with testparm"), and correct any unintended prohibitions.

Testing connections with smbclient

Run the command smbclient *server*\temp to connect to the server's [temp] share and to see if you can connect to a file service. You should get the following response:

```
$ smbclient '\\server\temp'
Server time is Tue May  5 09:49:32 2002 Timezone is UTC-4.0 Password:
smb: \> quit
```

You might receive the following errors:

- If you get Get_Hostbyname: Unknown host name, Connect error: Connection refused, or Your server software is being unfriendly, see the previous section, "Testing locally with smbclient," for the diagnoses.

- If you get the message servertemp: Not enough '\' characters in service, you likely didn't quote the address, so Unix stripped off backslashes. You can also write the command:

```
smbclient \\\\server\\temp
```

or:

```
smbclient //server/temp
```

Now, provide your Unix account password to the Password: prompt. If you then get an smb: \> prompt, it worked. Enter quit and continue on to the next section, "Testing connections with net use." If you got SMBtconX failed. ERRSRV—ERRinvnetname, the problem can be any of the following:

- A wrong share name: you might have spelled it wrong, it might be too long, it might be in mixed case, or it might not be available. Check that it's what you expect with *testparm* (see the earlier section, "Testing daemons with testparm").

- A security = share parameter in your Samba configuration file, in which case you might have to add -U *your_account* to the *smbclient* command.

- An erroneous username.
- An erroneous password.
- An invalid users or valid users option in your *smb.conf* file that doesn't allow your account to connect. Recheck using testparm smb.conf *your_hostname your_ip_address* (see the earlier section, "Testing daemons with testparm").
- A valid hosts option that doesn't include the server, or an invalid hosts option that does. Also test this with *testparm*.
- A problem in authentication, such as if shadow passwords or the Password Authentication Module (PAM) is used on the server, but Samba is not compiled to use it. This is rare, but it occasionally happens when a SunOS 4 Samba binary (with no shadow passwords) is run without recompilation on a Solaris system (with shadow passwords).
- The encrypted passwords = yes option is in the configuration file, but no password for your account is in the *smbpasswd* file.
- You have a null password entry, either in Unix */etc/passwd* or in the *smbpasswd* file.
- You are connecting to [temp], and you do not have the guest ok = yes option in the [temp] section of the *smb.conf* file.
- You are connecting to [temp] before connecting to your home directory, and your guest account isn't set up correctly. If you can connect to your home directory and then connect to [temp], that's the problem. See Chapter 2 for more information on creating a basic Samba configuration file.

  A bad guest account will also prevent you from printing or browsing until after you've logged in to your home directory.

There is one more reason for this failure that has nothing at all to do with passwords: the path parameter in your *smb.conf* file might point somewhere that doesn't exist. This will not be diagnosed by *testparm*, and most SMB clients can't distinguish it from other types of bad user accounts. You will have to check it manually.

Once you have connected to [temp] successfully, repeat the test, this time logging in to your home directory (e.g., map network drive *server*\davecb). If you have to change anything to get that to work, retest [temp] again afterward.

Testing connections with net use

Run the command net use * *server*\temp on the Windows client to see if it can connect to the server. You should be prompted for a password, then receive the response The command was completed successfully.

If that worked, continue with the steps in the next section, "Testing connections with Windows Explorer." Otherwise:

- If you get `The specified shared directory cannot be found`, or `Cannot locate specified share name`, the directory name is either misspelled or not in the *smb.conf* file. This message can also warn of a name that is in mixed case, including spaces, or that is longer than eight characters.

- If you get `The computer name specified in the network path cannot be located` or `Cannot locate specified computer`, the directory name has been misspelled, the name service has failed, there is a networking problem, or the `hosts deny` option includes your host.

  —If it is not a spelling mistake, you need to double back at least to the section "Testing connections with smbclient" to investigate why it doesn't connect.

  —If *smbclient* does work, there is a name service problem with the client name service, and you need to go forward to the section "Testing the server with nmblookup" and see if you can look up both the client and server with *nmblookup*.

- If you get `The password is invalid for \server\username`, your locally cached copy on the client doesn't match the one on the server. You will be prompted for a replacement.

> Each Windows 95/98/Me client keeps a local *password* file, but it's really just a cached copy of the password it sends to Samba and NT/2000/XP servers to authenticate you. That's what is being prompted for here. You can still log on to a Windows system without a password (but not to NT/2000/XP).

If you provide your password and it still fails, your password is not being matched on the server, you have a `valid users` or `invalid users` list denying you permission, NetBEUI is interfering, or the encrypted password problem described in the next paragraph exists.

- If your client is Windows NT 4.0, NT 3.5 with Patch 3, Windows 95 with Patch 3, Windows 98, any of these with Internet Explorer 4.0, or any subsequent version of Windows, the system will default to Microsoft encryption for passwords. In general, if you have installed a major Microsoft product on any of the older Windows versions, you might have applied an update and turned on encrypted passwords. If the client is defaulting to encrypted passwords, you will need to specify `encrypt passwords = yes` in your Samba configuration file if you are using a version of Samba prior to Samba 3.0.

> Because of Internet Explorer's willingness to honor URLs such as *file://somehost/somefile* by making SMB connections, clients up to and including Windows 95 Patch Level 2 would happily send your password, in plain text, to SMB servers anywhere on the Internet. This was considered a bad idea, and Microsoft switched to using only encrypted passwords in the SMB protocol. All subsequent releases of Microsoft's products have included this correction.

- If you have a mixed-case password on Unix, the client is probably sending it in all one case. If changing your password to all one case works, this was the problem. Regrettably, all but the oldest clients support uppercase passwords, so Samba will try once with the password in uppercase and once in lowercase. If you wish to use mixed-case passwords, see the password level option in Chapter 9 for a workaround.

- You might have a valid users problem, as tested with *smbclient* (see the earlier section, "Testing connections with smbclient").

- You might have the NetBEUI protocol bound to the Microsoft client. This often produces long timeouts and erratic failures and is known to have caused failures to accept passwords in the past. Unless you absolutely need the NetBEUI protocol, remove it.

> The term "bind" is used here to mean connecting one piece of software to another. When configured correctly, the Microsoft SMB client is "bound to" TCP/IP in the bindings section of the TCP/IP properties panel under the Windows 95/98/Me Network icon in the Control Panel. TCP/IP in turn is bound to an Ethernet card. This is not the same sense of the word as binding an SMB daemon to a TCP/IP port.

Testing connections with Windows Explorer

Start Windows Explorer (not Internet Explorer), select Map Network Drive from the Tools menu, and specify the UNC for one of your shares on the Samba server to see if you can make Explorer connect to it. If so, you've succeeded and can skip to the next section, "Troubleshooting Browsing."

Windows Explorer is a rather poor diagnostic tool: it tells you that something's wrong, but rarely what it is. If you get a failure, you'll need to track it down with the Windows *net use* command, which has far superior error reporting:

- If you get The password for this connection that is in your password file is no longer correct, you might have any of the following:

  —Your locally cached copy on the client doesn't match the one on the server.

  —You didn't provide a username and password when logging on to the client. Some versions of Explorer will continue to send a null username and password, even if you provide a password.

  —You have misspelled the password.

  —You have an invalid users or valid users list denying permission.

  —Your client is defaulting to encrypted passwords, but Samba is configured with the encrypt passwords = no configuration file parameter.

  —You have a mixed-case password, which the client is supplying in all one case.

- If you get `The network name is either incorrect, or a network to which you do not have full access`, or `Cannot locate specified computer`, you might have any of the following:
    — Misspelled name

    — Malfunctioning service

    — Failed share

    — Networking problem

    — Bad path parameter in *smb.conf*

    — hosts deny line that excludes you

- If you get `You must supply a password to make this connection`, the password on the client is out of synchronization with the server, or this is the first time you've tried from this client system and the client hasn't cached it locally yet.

- If you get `Cannot locate specified share name`, you have a wrong share name or a syntax error in specifying it, a share name longer than eight characters, or one containing spaces or in mixed case.

Once you can reliably connect to the share, try again, this time using your home directory. If you have to change something to get home directories working, retest with the first share, and vice versa, as we showed in the earlier section, "Testing connections with net use." As always, if Explorer fails, drop back to that section and debug the connection there.

Troubleshooting Browsing

Finally, we come to browsing. We've left this for last, not because it is the most difficult, but because it's both optional and partially dependent on a protocol that doesn't guarantee delivery of a packet. Browsing is hard to diagnose if you don't already know that all the other services are running.

Browsing is purely optional: it's just a way to find the servers on your network and the shares that they provide. Unix has nothing of the sort and happily does without. Browsing also assumes all your systems are on a local area network (LAN) where broadcasts are allowable.

First, the browsing mechanism identifies a system using the unreliable UDP protocol; it then makes a normal (reliable) TCP/IP connection to list the shares the system provides.

Testing browsing with smbclient

We'll start with testing the reliable connection first. From the server, try listing its own shares using *smbclient* with a -L option and your server's name. You should get something resembling the following:

```
$ smbclient -L server
Added interface ip=192.168.236.86 bcast=192.168.236.255 nmask=255.255.255.0 Server
time is Tue Apr 28 09:57:28 2002 Timezone is UTC-4.0
Password:
Domain=[EXAMPLE] OS=[Unix] Server=[Samba 2.2.5]

        Sharename       Type        Comment
        ---------       ----        -------
        cdrom           Disk        CD-ROM
        c1              Printer     Color Printer 1
        davecb          Disk        Home Directories

        Server          Comment
        ---------       -------
        SERVER          Samba 2.2.5

        Workgroup       Master
        ---------       -------
        EXAMPLE         SERVER
```

- If you didn't get a Sharename list, the server is not allowing you to browse any shares. This should not be the case if you've tested any of the shares with Windows Explorer or the *net use* command. If you haven't done the smbclient -L localhost -U% test yet (see the earlier section, "Testing locally with smbclient"), do it now. An erroneous guest account can prevent the shares from being seen. Also, check the *smb.conf* file to make sure you do not have the option browsable = no anywhere in it: we suggest using a minimal *smb.conf* file (see the earlier section, "A minimal smb.conf file"). You need to have browsable enabled (which is the default) to see the share.

- If you didn't get a browse list, the server is not providing information about the systems on the network. At least one system on the net must support browse lists. Make sure you have local master = yes in the *smb.conf* file if you want Samba to be the local master browser.

- If you got a browse list but didn't get */tmp*, you probably have a *smb.conf* problem. Go back to "Testing daemons with testparm."

- If you didn't get a workgroup list with your workgroup name in it, it is possible that your workgroup is set incorrectly in the *smb.conf* file.

- If you didn't get a workgroup list at all, ensure that workgroup = EXAMPLE is present in the *smb.conf* file.

- If you get nothing, try once more with the options -I *ip_address* -n *netbios_name* -W *workgroup* -d3 with the NetBIOS and workgroup name in uppercase. (The -d3 option sets the log/debugging level to 3.) Then check the Samba logs for clues.

If you're still getting nothing, you shouldn't have gotten this far; double back to at least "Testing TCP with FTP," or perhaps "Testing connections with ping." On the other hand:

- If you get `SMBtconX failed. ERRSRV–ERRaccess`, you aren't permitted access to the server. This normally means you have a `hosts allow` option that doesn't include the server or a `hosts deny` option that does.
- If you get `Bad password`, you presumably have one of the following:
  — An incorrect `hosts allow` or `hosts deny` line
  — An incorrect `invalid users` or `valid users` line
  — A lowercase password and OS/2 or Windows for Workgroups clients
  — A missing or invalid guest account

  Check what your guest account is (see the earlier section, "Testing locally with smbclient"), change or comment out any `hosts allow`, `hosts deny`, `valid users`, or `invalid users` lines, and verify your *smb.conf* file with `testparm smb.conf` *your_hostname your_ip_address* (see the earlier section, "Testing daemons with testparm").
- If you get `Connection refused`, the *smbd* server is not running or has crashed. Check that it's up, running, and listening to the network with *netstat*. See the earlier section, "Troubleshooting Server Daemons."
- If you get `Get_Hostbyname: Unknown host name`, you've made a spelling error, there is a mismatch between the Unix and NetBIOS hostname, or there is a name service problem. Start name service debugging as discussed in the earlier section, "Testing connections with net use." If this works, suspect a name mismatch, and go to the later section, "Troubleshooting NetBIOS Names."
- If you get `Session request failed`, the server refused the connection. This usually indicates an internal error, such as insufficient memory to fork a process.
- If you get `Your server software is being unfriendly`, the initial session request packet received a garbage response from the server. The server might have crashed or started improperly. Go back to the section "Testing locally with smbclient," where the problem is first analyzed.
- If you suspect the server is not running, go back to the section "Looking for daemon processes with ps" to see why the server daemon isn't responding.

Testing the server with nmblookup

This will test the "advertising" system used for Windows name services and browsing. Advertising works by broadcasting one's presence or willingness to provide services. It is the part of browsing that uses an unreliable protocol (UDP) and works only on broadcast networks such as Ethernets. The *nmblookup* program broadcasts name queries for the hostname you provide and returns its IP address and the name of the system, much as *nslookup* does with DNS. Here, the *-d* (debug or log-level) and *-B* (broadcast address) options direct queries to specific systems.

First, we check the server from itself. Run *nmblookup* with a *-B* option of your server's name (to tell it to send the query to the Samba server) and a parameter of __SAMBA__ as the symbolic name to look up. You should get:

```
$ nmblookup -B server __SAMBA__
Added interface ip=192.168.236.86 bcast=192.168.236.255 nmask=255.255.255.0
Sending queries to 192.168.236.86 192.168.236.86 __SAMBA__
```

You should get the IP address of the server, followed by the name __SAMBA__, which means that the server has successfully advertised that it has a service called __SAMBA__, and therefore at least part of NetBIOS name service works.

- If you get Name_query failed to find name __SAMBA__, you might have specified the server name to the *-B* option, or *nmbd* is not running. The *-B* option actually takes a broadcast address: we're using a computer name to get a unicast address and to ask the server if it has claimed __SAMBA__. Try again with nmblookup -B *ip_address*, and if that fails too, *nmbd* isn't claiming the name. Go back briefly to the earlier section, "Testing daemons with testparm," to see if *nmbd* is running. If so, it might not be claiming names; this means that Samba is not providing the browsing service—a configuration problem. If that is the case, make sure that *smb.conf* doesn't contain the option browsing = no.

Testing the client with nmblookup

Next, check the IP address of the client from the server with *nmblookup* using the -B option for the client's name and a parameter of '*' meaning "anything," as shown here:

```
$ nmblookup -B client '*'
Sending queries to 192.168.236.10 192.168.236.10 *
Got a positive name query response from 192.168.236.10 (192.168.236.10)
```

You might get the following error:

- If you receive Name-query failed to find name *, you have made a spelling mistake, or the client software on the PC isn't installed, started, or bound to TCP/IP. Double back to Chapter 3 and ensure that you have a client installed that is listening to the network.

Repeat the command with the following options if you had any failures:

- If nmblookup -B *client_IP_address* succeeds but nmblookup -B *client_name* fails, there is a name service problem with the client's name; go to "Troubleshooting Name Services," later in this chapter.
- If nmblookup -B 127.0.0.1 '*' succeeds, but nmblookup -B *client_IP_address* fails, there is a hardware problem, and *ping* should have failed. See your network manager.

Testing the network with nmblookup

Run the command *nmblookup* again with a *-d2* option (for a debug level of 2) and a parameter of '*'. This time we are testing the ability of programs (such as *nmbd*) to use broadcast. It's essentially a connectivity test, done via a broadcast to the default broadcast address.

A number of NetBIOS over TCP/IP hosts on the network should respond with got a positive name query response messages. Samba might not catch all the responses in the short time it listens, so you won't always see all the SMB clients on the network. However, you should see most of them:

```
$ nmblookup -d 2 '*'
Added interface ip=192.168.236.86 bcast=192.168.236.255 nmask=255.255.255.0 Sending
queries to 192.168.236.255
Got a positive name query response from 192.168.236.191 (192.168.236.191)
Got a positive name query response from 192.168.236.228 (192.168.236.228)
Got a positive name query response from 192.168.236.75 (192.168.236.75)
Got a positive name query response from 192.168.236.79 (192.168.236.79)
Got a positive name query response from 192.168.236.206 (192.168.236.206)
Got a positive name query response from 192.168.236.207 (192.168.236.207)
Got a positive name query response from 192.168.236.217 (192.168.236.217)
Got a positive name query response from 192.168.236.72 (192.168.236.72) 192.168.236.
86 *
```

However:

- If this doesn't give at least the client address you previously tested, the default broadcast address is wrong. Try nmblookup -B 255.255.255.255 -d 2 '*', which is a last-ditch variant (using a broadcast address of all 1s). If this draws responses, the broadcast address you've been using before is wrong. Troubleshooting these is discussed in the "Broadcast addresses" section, later in this chapter.

- If the address 255.255.255.255 fails too, check your notes to see if your PC and server are on different subnets, as discovered in the earlier section, "Testing connections with ping." You should try to diagnose this step with a server and client on the same subnet, but if you can't, you can try specifying the remote subnet's broadcast address with -B. Finding that address is discussed in the section "Broadcast addresses," later in this chapter. The -B option will work if your router supports directed broadcasts; if it doesn't, you might be forced to test with a client on the same network.

As usual, you can check the Samba log files for additional clues.

Testing client browsing with net view

On the client, run the command *net view \\server* in an MS-DOS (command prompt) window to see if you can connect to the client and ask what shares it provides. You should get back a list of available shares on the server.

If this works, continue with the later section "Documentation and FAQs." Otherwise:

- If you get `Network name not found` for the name you just tested in the earlier section, "Testing the client with nmblookup," there is a problem with the client software itself. Double-check this by running *nmblookup* on the client; if it works and *net view* doesn't, the client is at fault.

- If *nmblookup* fails, there is a NetBIOS name service problem, as discussed in the later section, "Troubleshooting NetBIOS Names."

- If you get `You do not have the necessary access rights`, or `This server is not configured to list shared resources`, either your guest account is misconfigured (see the earlier section, "Testing locally with smbclient") or you have a `hosts allow` or `hosts deny` line that prohibits connections from your system. These problems should have been detected by the *smbclient* tests starting in the earlier section, "Testing browsing with smbclient."

- If you get `The specified computer is not receiving requests`, you have misspelled the name, the system is unreachable by broadcast (tested in the earlier section, "Testing the network with nmblookup"), or it's not running *nmbd*.

- If you get `Bad password error`, you're probably encountering the Microsoft-encrypted password problem, as discussed earlier in this chapter and in Chapter 9, with its corrections.

Browsing the server from the client

From the Windows Network Neighborhood (or My Network Places in newer releases), try to browse the server. Your Samba server should appear in the browse list of your local workgroup. You should be able to double-click the name of the server to get a list of shares.

- If you get an `Invalid password` error, it's most likely the encryption problem again.

- If you receive an `Unable to browse the network` error, one of the following has occurred:

  —You have looked too soon, before the broadcasts and updates have completed. Wait 30 seconds and try again.

  —There is a network problem you've not yet diagnosed.

  —There is no browse master. Add the configuration option `local master = yes` to your *smb.conf* file.

  —No shares are made browsable in the *smb.conf* file.

- If you receive the message `\\server is not accessible` then:

  — You have the encrypted password problem.

  — The system really isn't accessible.

  — The system doesn't support browsing.

If you've made it this far and the problem is not yet solved, either the problem is one we've not yet seen, or it is a problem related to a topic we have already covered, and further analysis is required. Name resolution is often related to difficulties with Samba, so we cover it in more detail in the next sections. If you know your problem is not related to name resolution, skip to the "Extra Resources" section at the end of the chapter.

Troubleshooting Name Services

This section looks at simple troubleshooting of all the name services you'll encounter, but only for the common problems that affect Samba.

There are several good references for troubleshooting particular name services: Paul Albitz and Cricket Liu's *DNS and Bind* (O'Reilly) covers the DNS, Hal Stern's *NFS and NIS* (O'Reilly) covers NIS ("Yellow pages"), while Windows Internet Name Service (WINS), *hosts/LMHOSTS* files, and NIS+ are best covered by their respective vendors' manuals.

The problems addressed in this section are as follows:

- Name services are identified.
- A hostname can't be looked up.
- The long (FQDN) form of a hostname works but the short form doesn't.
- The short form of the name works, but the long form doesn't.
- A long delay occurs before the expected result.

Identifying what's in use

First, see if both the server and the client are using DNS, WINS, NIS, or *hosts* files to look up IP addresses when you give them a name. Each kind of system has a different preference:

- Windows 95/98/Me tries WINS and the *LMHOSTS* file first, then broadcast, and finally DNS and *HOSTS* files.
- Windows NT/2000/XP tries WINS, then broadcast, then the *LMHOSTS* file, and finally *HOSTS* and DNS.
- Windows programs using the WINSOCK standard use the *HOSTS* file, DNS, WINS, and then broadcast. Don't assume that if a different program's name service works, the SMB client program's name service will!
- Samba daemons use *lmhosts*, WINS, the Unix system's name resolution, and then broadcast.
- Unix systems can be configured to use any combination of DNS, *HOSTS* files, NIS or NIS+, and *winbind*, generally in any order.

We recommend that the client systems be configured to use WINS and DNS, the Samba daemons to use WINS and DNS, and the Unix server to use DNS, *hosts* files, and perhaps NIS+. You'll have to look at your notes and the actual systems to see which is in use.

On the clients, the name services are all set in the TCP/IP Properties panel of the Networking Control Panel, as discussed in Chapter 3. You might need to check there to see what you've actually turned on. On the server, see if a */etc/resolv.conf* file exists. If it does, you're using DNS. You might be using the others as well, though. You'll need to check for NIS and combinations of services.

Check for a */etc/nsswitch.conf* file on Solaris and other System V Unix operating systems. If you have one, look for a line that begins with host: followed by one or more of files, bind, nis, or nis+. These are the name services to use, in order, with optional extra material in square brackets. The files keyword is for using *HOSTS* files, while bind (the Berkeley Internet Name Daemon) refers to using DNS.

If the client and server differ, the first thing to do is to get them in sync. Clients can use DNS, WINS, *HOSTS,* and *LMHOSTS* files, but not NIS or NIS+. Servers can use *HOSTS* and *LMHOSTS* files, DNS, NIS or NIS+, and *winbind*, but not WINS—even if your Samba server provides WINS services. If you can't get all the systems to use the same services, you'll have to check the server and the client carefully for the same data.

You can also make use of the -R (resolve order) option for *smbclient*. If you want to troubleshoot WINS, for example, you'd say:

```
$ smbclient -L server -R wins
```

The possible settings are hosts (which means whatever the Unix system is using, not just */etc/hosts* files), lmhosts, wins, and bcast (broadcast).

In the following sections, we use the term *long name* for a fully qualified domain name (FQDN), such as server.example.com, and the term *short name* for the host part of an FQDN, such as server.

Cannot look up hostnames

Try the following:

DNS

> Run nslookup *name*. If this fails, look for a *resolv.conf* error, a downed DNS server, or a short/long name problem (see the next section). Try the following:
>
> —Your */etc/resolv.conf* file should contain one or more nameserver lines, each with an IP address. These are the addresses of your DNS servers.
>
> —Ping each server address you find. If this fails for one, suspect the system. If it fails for each, suspect your network.

—Retry the lookup using the full domain name (e.g., `server.example.com`) if you tried the short name first, or the short name if you tried the long name first. If results differ, skip to the next section.

Broadcast/WINS

Broadcast/WINS does only short names such as `server`, and not long ones, such as `server.example.com`. Run `nmblookup -S server`. This reports everything broadcast has registered for the name. In our example, it looks like this:

```
$ nmblookup -S server
Looking up status of 192.168.236.86
received 10 names
        SERVER          <00> -         M <ACTIVE>
        SERVER          <03> -         M <ACTIVE>
        SERVER          <1f> -         M <ACTIVE>
        SERVER          <20> -         M <ACTIVE>
        .._MSBROWSE__.  <01> - <GROUP> M <ACTIVE>
        MYGROUP         <00> - <GROUP> M <ACTIVE>
        MYGROUP         <1b> -         M <ACTIVE>
        MYGROUP         <1c> - <GROUP> M <ACTIVE>
        MYGROUP         <1d> -         M <ACTIVE>
        MYGROUP         <1e> - <GROUP> M <ACTIVE>
```

The required entry is SERVER <00>, which identifies *server* as being this system's NetBIOS name. You should also see your workgroup mentioned one or more times. If these lines are missing, Broadcast/WINS cannot look up names and will need attention.

> The numbers in angle brackets in the previous output identify NetBIOS names as being workgroups, workstations, and file users of the messenger service, master browsers, domain master browsers, domain controllers, and a plethora of others. We primarily use <00> to identify system and workgroup names and <20> to identify systems as servers. The complete list is available at *http://support.microsoft.com/support/ kb/articles/q163/4/09.asp.*

NIS

Try `ypmatch name hosts`. If this fails, NIS is down. Find out the NIS server's name by running *ypwhich*, and ping the system to see if it's accessible.

NIS+

If you're running NIS+, try `nismatch name hosts`. If this fails, NIS is down. Find out the NIS+ server's name by running *niswhich*, and ping that system to see if it's accessible.

hosts and HOSTS files

Inspect the *HOSTS* file on the client (*C:\Windows\Hosts* on Windows 95/98/Me, and *C:\WINNT\system32\drivers\etc\hosts* on Windows NT/2000/XP). Each line should have an IP number and one or more names, the primary name first, then any optional aliases. An example follows:

```
127.0.0.1          localhost
192.168.236.1      dns.svc.example.com
192.168.236.10     client.example.com client
192.168.236.11     backup.example.com loghost
192.168.236.86     server.example.com server
192.168.236.254    router.svc.example.com
```

On Unix, localhost should always be 127.0.0.1, although it might be just an alias for a hostname on the PC. On the client, check that there are no #XXX directives at the ends of the lines; these are LAN Manager/NetBIOS directives and should appear only in *LMHOSTS* files.

LMHOSTS files

This file is a local source for LAN Manager (NetBIOS) names. It has a format similar to *hosts* files, but it does not support long-form domain names (e.g., server.example.com) and can have a number of optional #XXX directives following the NetBIOS names. There is usually an *lmhosts.sam* (for sample) file located in *C:\Windows* on Windows 95/98/Me, and in *C:\WINNT\system32\drivers\etc* on Windows NT/2000/XP, but it's not used unless it is renamed to *Lmhosts* in the same directory.

Long and short hostnames

Where the long (FQDN) form of a hostname works but the short name doesn't (for example, client.example.com works but client doesn't), consider the following:

DNS

This usually indicates that there is no default domain in which to look up the short names. Look for a default line in */etc/resolv.conf* on the Samba server with your domain in it, or look for a search line with one or more domains in it. One or the other might need to be present to make short names usable; which one depends on the vendor and version of the DNS resolver. Try adding domain *your_domain* to *resolv.conf*, and ask your network or DNS administrator what should be in the file.

Broadcast/WINS

Broadcast/WINS doesn't support long names; it won't suffer from this problem.

NIS

Try the command ypmatch *hostname* hosts. If you don't get a match, your tables don't include short names. Speak to your network manager; short names might be missing by accident or might be unsupported as a matter of policy. Some sites don't ever use (ambiguous) short names.

NIS+

Try nismatch *hostname* hosts, and treat failure exactly as with NIS.

hosts

If the short name is not in */etc/hosts*, consider adding it as an alias. Avoid, if you can, short names as primary names (the first one on a line). Have them as aliases if your system permits.

LMHOSTS

LAN Manager doesn't support long names, so it won't suffer from this problem.

On the other hand, if the short form of the name works and the long form doesn't, consider the following:

DNS

This is bizarre; see your network or DNS administrator, as this is probably a DNS setup error.

Broadcast/WINS

This is normal; Broadcast/WINS can't use the long form. Optionally, consider DNS. (Be aware that Microsoft has stated that it will eventually switch entirely to DNS, even though DNS does not provide name types such as <00>.)

NIS

If you can use *ypmatch* to look up the short form but not the long, consider adding the long form to the table as at least an alias.

NIS+

Same as NIS, except you use *nismatch* instead of *ypmatch* to look up names.

hosts and HOSTS

Add the long name as at least an alias, and preferably as the primary form. Also consider using DNS if it's practical.

LMHOSTS

This is normal. LAN Manager can't use the long form; consider switching to DNS or *hosts*.

Unusual delays

When there is a long delay before the expected result:

DNS

Test the same name with the *nslookup* command on the system that is slow (client or server). If *nslookup* is also slow, you have a DNS problem. If it's slower on a client, you might have too many protocols bound to the Ethernet card. Eliminate NetBEUI, which is infamously slow, and, optionally, Novell—assuming you don't need them. This is especially important on Windows 95, which is particularly sensitive to excess protocols.

Broadcast/WINS

Test the client using *nmblookup*; if it's faster, you probably have the protocols problem as mentioned in the previous item.

NIS

Try *ypmatch*; if it's slow, report the problem to your network manager.

NIS+

Try *nismatch*, similarly.

hosts and HOSTS

The *hosts* files, if of reasonable size, are always fast. You probably have the protocols problem mentioned previously under DNS.

lmhosts and LMHOSTS

This is not a name lookup problem; *LMHOSTS* files are as fast as *hosts* and *HOSTS* files.

Localhost issues

When a localhost isn't 127.0.0.1, try the following:

DNS

There is probably no record for localhost. A 127.0.0.1. Arrange to add one, as well as a reverse entry, 1.0.0.127.IN-ADDR.ARPA PTR 127.0.0.1.

Broadcast/WINS

Not applicable.

NIS

If localhost isn't in the table, add it.

NIS+

If localhost isn't in the table, add it.

hosts and HOSTS

Add a line that says 127.0.0.1 localhost.

LMHOSTS

Not applicable.

Troubleshooting Network Addresses

A number of common problems are caused by incorrect routing of Internet addresses or by the incorrect assignment of addresses. This section helps you determine what your addresses are.

Netmasks

Using the netmask, it is possible to determine which addresses can be reached directly (i.e., which are on the local network) and which addresses require forwarding packets through a router. If the netmask is wrong, the systems will make one of two mistakes. One is to route local packets via a router, which is an expensive waste of time—it might work reasonably fast, it might run slowly, or it might fail utterly. The second mistake is to fail to send packets from a remote system to the router, which will prevent them from being forwarded to the remote system.

The netmask is a number like an IP address, with one-bits for the network part of an address and zero-bits for the host portion. It is used as a bitmask to mask off parts of the address inside the TCP/IP code. If the mask is 255.255.0.0, the first 2 bytes are

---

the network part and the last 2 are the host part. More common is 255.255.255.0, in which the first 3 bytes are the network part and the last one is the host part.

For example, let's say your IP address is 192.168.0.10 and the Samba server is 192.168.236.86. If your netmask happens to be 255.255.255.0, the network part of the address is the first 3 bytes, and the host part is the last byte. In this case, the network parts are different, and the systems are on different networks:

Network part	Host part
192 168 000	10
192 168 235	86

If your netmask happens to be 255.255.0.0, the network part is just the first 2 bytes. In this case, the network parts match, and so the two systems are on the same network:

Network part	Host part
192 168	000 10
192 168	236 86

Make sure the netmask in use on each system matches the structure of your network. On every subnet, the netmask should be identical on each system.

Broadcast addresses

The broadcast address is a normal address, with the hosts part all one-bits. It means "all hosts on your network." You can compute it easily from your netmask and address: take the address and put one-bits in it for all the bits that are zero at the end of the netmask (the host part). The following table illustrates this:

	Network part	Host part
IP address	192 168 236	86
Netmask	255 255 255	000
Broadcast	192 168 236	255

In this example, the broadcast address on the 192.168.236 network is 192.168.236.255. There is also an old "universal" broadcast address, 255.255.255.255. Routers are prohibited from forwarding these, but most systems on your local network will respond to broadcasts to this address.

Network address ranges

A number of address ranges have been reserved for testing and for nonconnected networks; we use these for the examples in this book. If you don't have an address yet, feel free to use one of these to start. They include one class A network, 10.*.*.*, a range of class B network addresses, 172.16.*.* through 172.31.*.*, and 254 class C networks, 192.168.1.* through 192.168.254.*. The domain example.com is also reserved for unconnected networks, explanatory examples, and books.

If you're actually connecting to the Internet, you'll need to get an appropriate IP address and a domain name, probably through the same company that provides your connection.

Finding your network address

If you haven't recorded your IP address, you can learn it through the *ifconfig* command on Unix or the *ipconfig* command on Windows. (Check your manual pages for any options required by your brand of Unix. For example, `ifconfig -a` works on Solaris.) You should see output similar to the following:

```
$ ifconfig -a
le0: flags=63<UP,BROADCAST,NOTRAILERS,RUNNING >
        inet 192.168.236.11 netmask ffffff00 broadcast 192.168.236.255
lo0: flags=49<&lt>UP,LOOPBACK,RUNNING<&gt>
        inet 127.0.0.1 netmask ff000000
```

One of the interfaces will be loopback (in our examples, lo0), and the other will be the regular IP interface. The flags should show that the interface is running, and Ethernet interfaces will also say they support broadcasts (PPP interfaces don't). The other places to look for IP addresses are */etc/hosts* files, Windows *HOSTS* files, Windows *LMHOSTS* files, NIS, NIS+, and DNS.

Troubleshooting NetBIOS Names

Historically, SMB protocols have depended on the NetBIOS name system, also called the LAN Manager name system. This was a simple scheme where each system had a unique 20-character name and broadcast it on the LAN for everyone to know. With TCP/IP, we tend to use names such as client.example.com, stored in */etc/hosts* files through DNS or WINS.

The usual mapping of domain names such as server.example.com to NetBIOS names simply uses the server part as the NetBIOS name and converts it to uppercase. Alas, this doesn't always work, especially if you have a system with a 21-character name; not everyone uses the same NetBIOS and DNS names. For example, corpvm1 along with vm1.corp.com is not unusual.

A system with a different NetBIOS name and domain name is confusing when you're troubleshooting; we recommend that you try to avoid this wherever possible. NetBIOS names are discoverable with *smbclient*:

- If you can list shares on your Samba server with smbclient -L short_name, the short name is the NetBIOS name.

- If you get `Get_Hostbyname: Unknown host name`, there is probably a mismatch. Check in the *smb.conf* file to see if the NetBIOS name is explicitly set.

- Try to list shares again, specifying `-I` and the IP address of the Samba server (e.g., `smbclient -L server -I 192.168.236.86`). This overrides the name lookup and forces the packets to go to the IP address. If this works, there was a mismatch.

- Try with `-I` and the full domain name of the server (e.g., `smbclient -L server -I server.example.com`). This tests the lookup of the domain name, using whatever scheme the Samba server uses (e.g., DNS). If it fails, you have a name service problem. You should reread the earlier section, "Troubleshooting Name Services," after you finish troubleshooting the NetBIOS names.

- Try with the `-n` (NetBIOS name) option, giving it the name you expect to work (e.g., `smbclient -n server -L server-12`), but without overriding the IP address through `-I`. If this works, the name you specified with `-n` is the actual NetBIOS name of the server. If you receive `Get-Hostbyname: Unknown host SERVER`, it's not the right server yet.

- If nothing is working so far, repeat the tests specifying `-U` *username* and `-W` *workgroup*, with the username and workgroup in uppercase, to make sure you're not being derailed by a user or workgroup mismatch.

- If still nothing works and you had evidence of a name service problem, troubleshoot the name service (see the earlier section, "Troubleshooting Name Services") and then return to the NetBIOS name service.

Extra Resources

At some point during your work with Samba, you'll want to turn to online or printed resources for news, updates, and aid.

Documentation and FAQs

It's OK to read the documentation. Really. Nobody can see you, and we won't tell. In fact, Samba ships with a large set of documentation files, and it is well worth the effort to at least browse through them, either in the distribution directory on your computer under */docs* or online at the Samba web site: *http://www.samba.org*. The most current FAQ list, bug information, and distribution locations are located at the web site, with links to all the Samba manual pages and HOWTOs.

Samba Newsgroups

Usenet newsgroups have always been a great place to get advice on just about any topic. In the past few years, though, this vast pool of knowledge has developed something that has made it into an invaluable resource: a memory. Archival and search sites such as the one at Google (*http://groups.google.com/advanced_group_search*) have made sifting through years of valuable solutions as simple as a few mouse clicks.

The primary newsgroup for Samba is *comp.protocols.smb*. This should always be your first stop when there's a problem. More often than not, spending 5 minutes researching an error here will save hours of frustration while trying to debug something yourself.

When searching a newsgroup, try to be as specific as possible, but not too wordy. Searching on actual error messages is best. If you don't find an answer immediately in the newsgroup, resist the temptation to post a request for help until you've done a bit more work on the problem. You might find that the answer is in a FAQ or one of the many documentation files that ship with Samba, or a solution might become evident when you run one of Samba's diagnostic tools. If nothing works, post a request in *comp.protocols.smb*, and be as specific as possible about what you have tried and what you are seeing. Include any error messages that appear. It might be days before you receive help, so be patient and keep trying things while you wait.

 Once you post a request for help, keep poking at the problem yourself. Most of us have had the experience of posting a Usenet article containing hundreds of lines of intricate detail, only to solve the problem an hour later after the article has blazed its way across several continents. The rule of thumb goes something like this: the more folks who have read your request, the simpler the solution. Usually this means that once everyone in the Unix community has seen your article, the solution will be something simple such as, "Plug the power cord into the wall socket."

Samba Mailing Lists

The following are mailing lists for support with Samba. See the Samba home page, *http://www.samba.org/*, for information on subscribing and unsubscribing to these mailing lists:

samba@samba.org
> This is the primary mailing list for general questions and discussion regarding Samba.

samba-announce@samba.org
> This list is for receiving news regarding Samba, such as announcements of new releases.

samba-cvs@samba.org
> By subscribing to this list, you can automatically receive a message every time one of the Samba developers updates the Samba source code in the CVS repository. You might want to do this if you are waiting for a specific bug fix or feature to be applied. To avoid congesting your email inbox, we suggest using the digest feature, which consolidates messages into a smaller number of emails.

samba-docs@samba.org

> This list is for discussing Samba documentation.

samba-vms@samba.org

> This mailing list is for people who are running Samba on the VMS operating system.

samba-binaries@samba.org

> This is a list for developers to use when discussing precompiled Samba distributions.

samba-technical@samba.org

> This mailing list is for developer discussion of the Samba code.

Searchable versions of the Samba mailing list archives can be found at *http://marc. theaimsgroup.com.*

When posting messages to the Samba mailing lists, keep in mind that you are sending your message to a large audience. The notes in the previous section regarding Usenet postings also apply here. A well-formulated question or comment is more likely to be answered, and a poorly conceived message is *very* likely to be ignored!

Further Reading

Hunt, Craig. *TCP/IP Network Administration,* Third Edition. Sebastopol, CA: O'Reilly & Associates, 1997.

Hunt, Craig, and Robert Bruce Thompson. *Windows NT TCP/IP Network Administration.* Sebastopol, CA: O'Reilly & Associates, 1998.

Albitz, Paul, and Cricket Liu. *DNS and Bind,* Fourth Edition. Sebastopol, CA: O'Reilly & Associates, 1998.

Stern, Hal. *Managing NFS and NIS,* Second Edition. Sebastopol, CA: O'Reilly & Associates, 1991.

Example Configuration Files

Earlier in this book, we provided information on how to set parameters inside the Samba configuration file, but rarely have we shown an example of a complete file that can actually be used to run a server. In this appendix, we provide examples of complete configuration files for running Samba in the various modes we've discussed. Using one of these examples, you can run Samba as a workgroup authentication server, workgroup server, primary domain controller, or domain member server.

We have kept the examples simple so that they have the most universal application. They can be used as starting templates, which you can easily modify to fit your own needs, to get a Samba server up and running with minimal delay. The comments inside the files indicate what needs to be changed, and how, to work on a particular system on your network.

Samba in a Workgroup

If your network is configured as a workgroup, adding a Samba server is pretty simple. Samba even lets you add features, such as user-level security and WINS, that would normally require an expensive Windows NT/2000 Server.

Authentication and WINS Server

In a workgroup environment, Samba can be set up with share-level security and without offering WINS name service. This works and is simple, but we generally recommend that user-level security be enabled to allow Windows 95/98/Me systems to make use of it. Also, it only takes a single parameter to enable Samba as a WINS server, resulting in far better network efficiency. Here is the configuration file that does it:

```
[global]
    # replace "toltec" with your system's hostname

    netbios name = toltec
```

```
# replace "METRAN" with the name of your workgroup

workgroup = METRAN

security = user
encrypt passwords = yes

# Run a WINS server

wins support = yes

# The following three lines ensure that the Samba
# server will maintain the role of master browser.
# Make sure no other Samba server has its OS level
# set higher than it is here.

local master = yes
preferred master = yes
os level = 65

# Make home directories on the server available to users.

[homes]
    comment = %u's Home Directory
    browsable = no
    read only = no
    map archive = yes

# This is a shared directory, accessible by all
# users. Use your own share name and path.

[d]
    path = /d
    create mask = 0700
    read only = no
```

Generally, you will use a configuration file similar to this one when adding your first Samba server to the workgroup.

Workgroup Server

Things are a little different if another system—either a Samba server or Windows NT/2000 server—is already handling WINS and/or authentication. In this case, Samba is configured to use that server for WINS. Here is a configuration file that does this:

```
[global]
    # replace "mixtec" with your system's hostname

    netbios name = mixtec

    # replace "METRAN" with your workgroup name
```

```
    workgroup = METRAN

    security = user
    encrypt passwords = yes

    # Replace "172.16.1.1" with the IP address
    # of your WINS server. If there is none,
    # omit this line.

    wins server = 172.16.1.1

    # The OS level is set to 17 to allow
    # this system to win over all Windows
    # versions, but not the Samba server
    # that uses the configuration file
    # in the previous section.

    os level = 17

[homes]
    comment = %u's Home Directory
    browsable = no
    read only = no

# This is a shared directory, accessible by all
# users. Use your own share name and path.

[d]
    path = /d
    create mask = 0700
    read only = no
```

Once you have a server in your workgroup handling authentication and WINS, this is the configuration file to use when adding additional Samba servers to the workgroup.

Samba in a Windows NT Domain

When operating in a Windows NT domain, Samba can act either as a primary domain controller or as a domain member server.

Primary Domain Controller

Setting up Samba as a primary domain controller is more complicated than the other configurations. However, the extra difficulty is offset by having a more secure network and additional features such as logon scripts and roaming profiles. In the following configuration file, we also include support for a Microsoft Dfs share:

```
[global]
    # Replace "toltec" with the hostname of your system.
```

```
netbios name = toltec

# Replace "METRAN" with the name of your Windows NT domain.

workgroup = METRAN

# Run a WINS server

wins support = yes

# Always act as the local master browser
# and domain master browser.  Do not allow
# any other system to take over these roles!

domain master = yes
local master = yes
preferred master = yes
os level = 255

# Perform domain authentication.

security = user
encrypt passwords = yes
domain logons = yes

# The location of user profiles for Windows NT/2000/XP.

logon path = \\%L\profiles\%u\%m

# Users' Windows home directories and storage of Win95/98/Me roaming profiles.

logon drive = G:
logon home = \\toltec\%u\.win_profile\%m

# The following line is optional because
# Samba always offers NetBIOS time service.
# This causes it to also be advertised:

time server = yes

# The logon script used for all users,
# Relative to [netlogon] share directory.

logon script = logon.bat

# The group identifying administrative users.
# If you have domain users in the Domain Admins
# group, use them here instead of "jay".

domain admin group = root jay

# For adding machine accounts automatically.
# This example works on Linux. For other host
# operating systems, you might need a different
```

```
    # command.

    add user script = /usr/sbin/useradd -d /dev/null -g 100 -s /bin/false -M %u

    # Provide Microsoft Dfs support.

    host msdfs = yes

# The netlogon share is required for
# functioning as the primary domain controller.
# Make sure the directory used for the path exists.

[netlogon]
    path = /usr/local/samba/lib/netlogon
    writable = no
    browsable = no

# The profiles share is for storing
# Windows NT/2000/XP roaming profiles.
# Use your own path, and make sure
# the directory exists.

[profiles]
    path = /home/samba-ntprof
    writable = yes
    create mask = 0600
    directory mask = 0700
    browsable = no

[homes]
    comment = Home Directory
    browsable = no
    read only = no
    map archive = yes

# The Dfs share.
# Use your own path, making
# sure the directory exists.

[dfs]
    comment = Dfs share
    path = /usr/local/samba/dfs
    msdfs root = yes

# A shared directory, accessible by all domain users.
# Use your own share name and path.

[d]
    comment = %u's Home Directory
    path = /d
    create mask = 0700
    read only = no
```

See Chapter 4 for more information on configuring Samba as a primary domain controller, and see Chapter 8 for more information about setting up a Microsoft Dfs share.

Domain Member Server

In a domain that already has either a Samba PDC or Windows NT/2000 Server PDC, additional Samba servers can be added as domain member servers using the following configuration file:

```
[global]
    # Replace "mixtec" with the system's hostname.

    netbios name = mixtec

    # Replace "METRAN" with the name of your domain.

    workgroup = METRAN

    # Replace "172.16.1.1" with the
    # IP address of your WINS server.

    wins server = 172.16.1.1

    os level = 33

    security = domain
    encrypt passwords = yes
    password server = *

# Home directories.

[homes]
    comment = %u's Home Directory
    browsable = no
    read only = no
    map archive = yes

# This is an example printers
# share, which works for Linux.

[printers]
    printable = yes
    printing = BSD
    print command = /usr/bin/lpr -P%p %s
    path = /var/tmp
    min print space = 2000

# A shared directory, accessible by all domain users.
# Use your own share name and path.

[d]
    path = /d
    create mask = 0755
    read only = no
```

See Chapter 10 for more information on sharing printers with Samba.

Samba Configuration Option Quick Reference

The first section of this appendix lists each option that can be used in a Samba configuration file, which is usually named *smb.conf*. Most configuration files contain a global section of options that apply to all services (shares) and a separate section for various individual shares. If an option applies only to the global section, [global] appears to the right of its name in the following reference section.

Except where noted, when specifying elements of a list, the elements can be separated by spaces, tabs, commas, semicolons, escaped newlines, or escaped carriage returns.

Following this reference section is a glossary of value types, and a list of variables Samba recognizes.

Configuration File Options

abort shutdown script = command   [global]

| Allowable values: command | Default: NULL |

Specifies a command that stops the shutdown procedure started by shutdown script. The command will be run with the UID of the connected user. New in Samba 3.0.

add printer command = command   [global]

| Allowable values: command | Default: NULL |

Specifies a command that creates a new printer on the system hosting the Samba server. This command runs as root when the Windows NT/2000/XP Add Printer Wizard is run. The command will be passed a printer name, share name, port name, driver name, Windows NT/2000/XP driver location, and Windows 95/98/Me driver location, in that order. It will need to add the printer to the system and a share definition for the printer to *smb.conf*. See also add printer wizard, printing, and show add printer wizard.

add machine script = command [global]

Allowable values: command **Default:** NULL

Specifies a command that adds a computer to the Samba server's domain. New in Samba 3.0.

add share command = command [global]

Allowable values: command **Default:** NULL

Specifies a command that creates a new share on the Samba server. This command runs as root when a share is created using the Windows NT/2000/XP Server Manager. The client user must be logged on as the root user. The command will be passed the name of the Samba configuration file, the name of the share to be created, the full pathname of a directory on the Samba server (which must already exist), and a string to use as a comment for the share, in that order. The command must add a share definition for the share to *smb.conf*. See also add `printer command`, for adding a print share.

add user script = command [global]

Allowable values: command **Default:** NULL

Specifies a command that creates a new user on the system hosting the Samba server. This command runs as root when access to a Samba share is attempted by a Windows user who does not have an account on the hosting system, but does have an account maintained by a primary domain controller on a different system. The command should accept the name of the user as a single argument that matches the behavior of typical *adduser* commands. Samba honors the %u value (username) as the argument to the command. Requires security = server or security = domain. See also delete `user script`.

admin users = user list

Allowable values: user list **Default:** NULL

Specifies users who will be granted root permissions on the share by Samba.

ads server = value [global]

Allowable values: DNS hostname or IP address **Default:** NONE

Specifies the Active Directory server, used by Samba 3.0 for authenticating clients. Requires security = ads. New in Samba 3.0.

algorithmic rid base = number [global]

Allowable values: positive integer **Default:** 1000

Specifies the base value that Samba uses when calculating Windows domain security identifier equivalents to Unix UIDs. See also non `unix account range`. New in Samba 3.0.

allow hosts = host list

Allowable values: list of hosts or networks   **Default:** NULL

Specifies systems that can connect to the share or shares. If NULL, any system can access the share unless there is a hosts deny option. Synonym for hosts allow.

allow trusted domains = boolean   [global]

Allowable values: YES, NO   **Default:** YES

Allows access to users who lack accounts on the Samba server but have accounts in another, trusted domain. Requires security = server or security = domain.

announce as = value   [global]

Allowable values: NT, Win95, WfW   **Default:** NT

Has Samba announce itself as something other than an NT server. Discouraged because it interferes with serving browse lists.

announce version = value   [global]

Allowable values: two numbers separated by a dot character   **Default:** 4.5

Instructs Samba to announce itself as a different version SMB server. Discouraged.

auth methods = list   [global]

Allowable values: guest, sam, ntdomain   **Default:** NONE

Specifies what methods Samba tries in turn to authenticate users. New in Samba 3.0.

auto services = service list   [global]

Allowable values: service list   **Default:** NULL

Specifies a list of shares that always appear in browse lists. Also called preload.

available = boolean

Allowable values: YES, NO   **Default:** YES

If set to NO, denies access to a share. The share appears in the browse list, but attempts to access it will fail.

bind interfaces only = boolean   [global]

Allowable values: YES, NO   **Default:** NO

If set to YES, shares and browsing are provided only on interfaces in an interfaces list (see interfaces). If you set this option to YES, be sure to add 127.0.0.1 to the interfaces list to allow *smbpasswd* to connect to the local system to change passwords. This is a convenience option; it does not improve security.

block size = number

Allowable values: integer   **Default:** 1024

Sets the size of disk blocks as reported by *smbd* to the client. Obsolete starting with Samba 3.0.

blocking locks = boolean

Allowable values: YES, NO   **Default:** YES

If YES, honors byte range lock requests with time limits. Samba will queue the requests and retry them until the time period expires.

browsable = boolean

Allowable values: YES, NO   **Default:** YES

Allows a share to be announced in browse lists. Also called `browseable`.

browse list = boolean   **[global]**

Allowable values: YES, NO   **Default:** YES

If YES, serves the browse list to other systems on the network. Avoid changing.

browseable = boolean

Allowable values: YES, NO   **Default:** YES

Synonym for `browsable`.

case sensitive = boolean   **[global]**

Allowable values: YES, NO   **Default:** NO

If YES, uses the exact case the client supplied when trying to resolve a filename. If NO, matches either upper- or lowercase name. Avoid changing. Also called `casesignames`.

casesignames = boolean   **[global]**

Allowable values: YES, NO   **Default:** NO

Synonym for `case sensitive`.

change notify timeout = number   [global]

Allowable values: positive number   **Default:** 60

Sets the number of seconds between checks when a client asks for notification of changes in a directory. Avoid lowering.

change share command = command   [global]

Allowable values: command   **Default:** NULL

Specifies a command that modifies a share definition on the Samba server. This command runs as root when a share is created using the Windows NT/2000/XP Server Manager. The client user must be logged on as the root user. The command is passed the name of the Samba configuration file, the name of the share to be modified, the full pathname of a directory on the Samba server (which must already exist), and a string to use as a comment for the share, in that order. The command modifies the share definition for the share in *smb.conf*. See also add share command and delete share command.

character set = name

Allowable values: ISO8859-1, ISO8859-2, ISO8859-5, KOI8-R   **Default:** NULL

If set, translates from DOS code pages to the Western European (ISO8859-1), Eastern European (ISO8859-2), Russian Cyrillic (ISO8859-5), or Alternate Russian (KOI8-R) character set. The client code page option must be set to 850. Obsolete starting with Samba 3.0.

client code page = name

Allowable values: see Table 11-4 in Chapter 11   **Default:** 850 (MS-DOS Latin 1)

Sets the DOS code page explicitly, overriding any previous valid chars settings. Examples of values are 850 for Western European, 437 for the U.S. standard, and 932 for Japanese Shift-JIS. Obsolete starting with Samba 3.0.

code page directory = directory   [global]

Allowable values: full directory name   **Default:** */usr/local/samba/lib/codepages*

Specifies the directory that stores code pages. Obsolete starting with Samba 3.0.

coding system = value   [global]

Allowable values: euc, cap, hex, hexN, sjis, j8bb, j8bj, jis8, j8bh, j8@b, j8@j,   **Default:** NULL
j8@h, j7bb, j7bj, jis7, j7bh, j7@b, j7@j, j7@h, jubb, jubj, junet, jubh, ju@b, ju@j, ju@h

Sets the coding system used, notably for Kanji. This is employed for filenames and should correspond to the code page in use. The client code page option must be set to 932 (Japanese Shift-JIS). Obsolete starting with Samba 3.0.

comment = string

Allowable values: string   **Default:** NULL

Sets the comment corresponding to a share. The comment appears in places such as a *net view* listing or through the Network Neighborhood. See also the server string configuration option.

config file = filename   [global]

Allowable values: \filename   **Default:** NULL

Selects a new Samba configuration file to read instead of the current one. Used to relocate the configuration file or used with % variables to select custom configuration files for some users or systems.

copy = section name

Allowable values: existing section's name   **Default:** NULL

Copies the configuration of an already defined share into the share in which this option appears. Used with % variables to select custom configurations for systems, architectures, and users. Each option specified or copied takes precedence over earlier specifications of the option.

create mask = value

Allowable values: octal value from 0 to 0777   **Default:** 0744

Sets the maximum allowable permissions for new files (e.g., 0755). See also directory mask. To require certain permissions to be set, see force create mask and force directory mask. Also called create mode.

create mode = value

Allowable values: octal value from 0 to 0777   **Default:** 0744

Synonym for create mask.

csc policy = value

Allowable values: manual, documents, programs, or disable   **Default:** manual

Sets the client-side caching policy, telling them how to cache files offline if they are capable of doing so.

deadtime = number
[global]

Allowable values: number

Default: 0

Specifies the time in minutes before an unused connection will be terminated. Zero means never. Used to keep clients from tying up server resources for long periods of time. If used, clients must autoreconnect after the specified period of inactivity. See also keepalive.

debug hires timestamp = boolean
[global]

Allowable values: YES, NO

Default: NO

Changes the timestamps in log entries from seconds to microseconds. Useful for measuring performance.

debug pid = boolean
[global]

Allowable values: YES, NO

Default: NO

Adds the process ID of the Samba server to log lines, making it easier to debug a particular server. Requires debug timestamp = yes to work.

debug timestamp = boolean
[global]

Allowable values: YES, NO

Default: YES

Timestamps all log messages. Can be turned off when it's not useful (e.g., in debugging). Also called timestamp logs.

debug uid = boolean
[global]

Allowable values: YES, NO

Default: NO

Adds the real and effective user ID and group ID of the user being served to the logs, making it easier to debug one particular user.

debuglevel = number
[global]

Allowable values: number

Default: 0

Sets the logging level used. Values of 3 or more slow Samba noticeably. Also called log level. Recommended value is 1.

default = service name
[global]

Allowable values: share name

Default: NULL

Specifies the name of a service (share) to provide if someone requests a service he doesn't have permission to use or that doesn't exist. The path is set from the name the client specified, with any underscore (_) characters changed to slash (/) characters, allowing access to any directory on the Samba server. Use is discouraged. See also load printers. Also called default service.

default case = value

Allowable values: LOWER, UPPER   **Default:** LOWER

Sets the case in which to store new filenames. LOWER indicates lowercase, and UPPER indicates uppercase.

default devmode = boolean

Allowable values: YES, NO   **Default:** NO

Used with printer shares being accessed by Windows NT/2000/XP clients to set a default device mode for the printer. Can be problematic. Use with care.

default service = share name   [global]

Allowable values: share name   **Default:** NULL

Synonym for default.

delete printer command = command   [global]

Allowable values: command   **Default:** NULL

Specifies a command that removes a printer from the system hosting the Samba server and deletes its service definition from *smb.conf*. The command is passed a printer name as its only argument. See also add printer command, printing, and show add printer wizard.

delete readonly = boolean

Allowable values: NO, YES   **Default:** NO

If set to YES, allows delete requests to remove read-only files. This is not allowed in MS-DOS/Windows, but it is normal in Unix, which has separate directory permissions. Used with programs such as RCS.

delete share command = command

Allowable values: command   **Default:** NULL

Specifies a command that deletes a share from the Samba server. The command runs when a user logged in as the root user on a Windows NT/2000/XP system deletes a share using Server Manager. The command is passed the name of the Samba configuration file and the name of the share to be deleted. The command must remove the definition of the share from the configuration file. See also add share command and change share command.

delete user script = command [global]

Allowable values: full path to script   **Default:** NULL

Sets the command to run as root when a user connects who no longer has an account on the domain's PDC. Honors %u. Can be used to delete the user account automatically from the Samba server's host. Requires security = domain or security = user. Use with caution. See also add user script.

delete veto files = boolean

Allowable values: NO, YES   **Default:** NO

If set to YES, allows delete requests for a directory containing files or subdirectories the user can't see due to the veto files option. If set to NO, the directory is not deleted and still contains invisible files.

deny hosts = host list

Allowable values: hosts or networks   **Default:** NULL

Specifies a list of systems from which to refuse connections. Also called hosts deny.

dfree command = command [global]

Allowable values: command   **Default:** varies

Specifies a command to run on the server to return free disk space. Not needed unless the Samba host system's *dfree* command does not work properly.

directory = directory

Allowable values: Unix directory name   **Default:** varies

Sets the path to the directory provided by a file share or used by a printer share. If the option is omitted in the [homes] share, it is set automatically to the user's home directory; otherwise, it defaults to */tmp*. For a printer share, the directory is used to spool printer files. Honors the %u (user) and %m (machine) variables. Synonym for path.

directory mask = value

Allowable values: octal value from 0 to 0777   **Default:** 0755

Sets the maximum allowable permissions for newly created directories. To require that certain permissions be set, see the force create mask and force directory mask options. Also called directory mode.

directory mode = value

Allowable values: octal value from 0 to 0777   **Default:** 0755

Synonym for directory mask.

directory security mask = value

Allowable values: octal value from 0 to 0777   **Default:** same as directory mode

Controls which permission bits can be changed if a user edits the Unix permissions of directories on the Samba server from a Windows system. Any bit that is set in the mask can be changed by the user; any bit that is clear remains the same on the directory even if the user tries to change it. Requires nt acl support = YES.

disable spools = boolean   [global]

Allowable values: YES, NO   **Default:** NO

If set to YES, Windows NT/2000/XP systems will downgrade to Lanman-style printing. Prevents printer driver uploading and downloading from working. Use with care. See also use client driver.

dns proxy = boolean   [global]

Allowable values: YES, NO   **Default:** YES

If set to YES and if wins server = YES, looks up hostnames in DNS when they are not found using WINS.

domain admin group = user list   [global]

Allowable values: usernames and/or group names   **Default:** NULL

Specifies users who are in the Domain Admins group and have domain administrator authority when Samba is the PDC. See also domain guest group and domain logons. Useful in Samba 2.2 only. Obsolete in Samba 3.0.

domain guest group = user/group list   [global]

Allowable values: list of usernames and/or group names   **Default:** NULL

Specifies users who are in the Domain Guest group when Samba is the PDC. See also domain admin group and domain logons. Useful in Samba 2.2 only. Obsolete in Samba 3.0.

domain logons = boolean   [global]

Allowable values: YES, NO   **Default:** NO

Causes Samba to serve domain logons. This is one of the basic functions required when Samba is acting as the PDC.

domain master = boolean [global]

Allowable values: YES, NO **Default:** automatic

Makes Samba a domain master browser for its domain. When domain logons are enabled, domain master defaults to YES. Otherwise, it defaults to NO.

dont descend = list

Allowable values: list of directories **Default:** NULL

Prohibits a change directory or search in the directories specified. This is a browsing-convenience option; it doesn't provide any extra security.

dos filemode = boolean

Allowable values: YES, NO **Default:** NO

Allows anyone with write permissions to change permissions on a file, as allowed by MS-DOS.

dos filetime resolution = boolean

Allowable values: YES, NO **Default:** NO

Sets file times on Unix to match MS-DOS standards (rounding to the next even second). Recommended if using Visual C++ or a PC *make* program to avoid remaking the programs unnecessarily. Use with the dos filetimes option.

dos filetimes = boolean

Allowable values: YES, NO **Default:** NO

Allows nonowners to change file times if they can write to the files, matching the behavior of MS-DOS and Windows. See also dos filetime resolution.

encrypt passwords = boolean [global]

Allowable values: YES, NO **Default:** NO in Samba 2.2, YES in Samba 3.0

If enabled, Samba will use password encryption. Requires an *smbpasswd* file on the Samba server.

enhanced browsing = boolean [global]

Allowable values: YES, NO **Default:** YES

Automatically synchronizes browse lists with all domain master browsers known to the WINS server. Makes cross-subnet browsing more reliable, but also can cause empty workgroups to persist forever in browse lists.

enumports command = command   [global]

Allowable values: command   **Default:** NULL

Allows for a command to provide clients with customized MS-DOS/Windows port names
(e.g., PRN:) corresponding to printers. Samba's default behavior is to return Samba Printer
Port. The command must return a series of lines, with one port name per line.

exec = command

Allowable values: command   **Default:** NULL

Sets a command to run as the user before connecting to the share. Synonym for preexec.
See also the postexec, root preexec, and root postexec options.

fake directory create times = boolean

Allowable values: YES, NO   **Default:** NO

A bug fix for users of Microsoft *nmake*. If YES, Samba sets directory create times such that
nmake won't remake all files every time.

fake oplocks = boolean

Allowable values: YES, NO   **Default:** NO

If set, returns YES whenever a client asks if it can lock a file and cache it locally but does
not enforce the lock on the server. Results in performance improvement for read-only
shares. *Never use with read/write shares!* See also oplocks and veto oplock files.

follow symlinks = boolean

Allowable values: YES, NO   **Default:** YES

If set to YES, Samba follows symlinks in a file share(s). See the wide links option if you
want to restrict symlinks to just the current share.

force create mode = value

Allowable values: octal value from 0 to 0777   **Default:** 0

Takes effect when a user on a Windows client creates a file that resides on the Samba
server. This option ensures that bits set in this mask will always be set on the new file. Used
with the create mask configuration option.

force directory mode = value

Allowable values: octal value from 0 to 0777   **Default:** 0

Takes effect when a user on a Windows client creates a directory on the Samba server. This option ensures that bits set in the mask will be set on every newly created directory. Used with `directory mask`.

force directory security mode = value

Allowable values: octal value from 0 to 0777   **Default:** same as `force directory mode`

Takes effect when a user on a Windows client edits the Unix permissions of a directory on the Samba server. This option ensures that bits set in this mask will be set on the directory. Requires `nt acl support = YES`.

force group = value

Allowable values: a Unix group name   **Default:** NULL

Sets the effective group name assigned to all users accessing a share. Used to override a user's normal group memberships.

force security mode = value

Allowable values: octal value from 0 to 0777   **Default:** same as `force create mode`

Takes effect when a user on a Windows client edits the Unix permissions of a file on the Samba server. This option ensures that bits set in the mask will always be set on the file. Requires `nt acl support = YES`. See also `force directory security mode` for directories.

force unknown acl user = boolean

Allowable values: YES, NO   **Default:** NO

When set, unknown users or groups in Windows NT ACLs will be mapped to the user or group of the connected user. Obsolete starting with Samba 3.0.

force user = value

Allowable values: a single username   **Default:** NULL

Sets the effective username assigned to all users accessing a share. Discouraged.

fstype = string

Allowable values: NTFS, FAT, Samba   **Default:** NTFS

Sets the filesystem type reported to the client. Avoid changing.

getwd cache = boolean

[global]

Allowable values: YES, NO   **Default:** YES

Caches the current directory for performance. Recommended with the wide links option.

group = value

Allowable values: a Unix group name   **Default:** NULL

Synonym for force group.

guest account = value

Allowable values: a single username   **Default:** varies

Sets the name of the unprivileged Unix account to use for tasks such as printing and for accessing shares marked with guest ok. The default is specified at compile time and is usually set to nobody.

guest ok = boolean

Allowable values: YES, NO   **Default:** NO

If set to YES, doesn't need passwords for this share. Used with security = share. Synonym for public.

guest only = boolean

Allowable values: YES, NO   **Default:** NO

Forces users of a share to log on as the guest account. Requires guest ok or public to be YES. Also called only guest.

hide dot files = boolean

Allowable values: YES, NO   **Default:** YES

Treats files with names beginning with a dot as if they had the MS-DOS hidden attribute set. The files are either not displayed on a Windows client or appear grayed-out, depending on the settings on the client.

hide files = slash-separated list

Allowable values: patterns, separated by / characters   **Default:** NULL

Specifies a list of file or directory names on which to set the MS-DOS hidden attribute. Names can contain ? or * pattern characters and % variables. See also hide dot files and veto files.

hide local users = boolean
[global]

Allowable values: YES, NO   **Default:** NO

If set to YES, hides Unix-specific dummy accounts (`root`, `wheel`, `floppy`, etc.) from clients.

hide unreadable = boolean

Allowable values: YES, NO   **Default:** NO

If set to YES, hides all unreadable files.

homedir map = name
[global]

Allowable values: NIS map name   **Default:** NONE

Used with `nis homedir` to locate a user's Unix home directory from Sun NIS (not NIS+).

host msdfs = boolean
[global]

Allowable values: YES, NO   **Default:** NO

If set to YES and Samba was configured with the `--with-msdfs` option, provides Microsoft Distributed filesystem (Dfs) service, allowing Dfs-capable clients to browse Dfs trees on the Samba server. See also `msdfs root`.

hosts allow = host list

Allowable values: list of hosts or networks   **Default:** NULL

Specifies a list of systems that can access the share. If NULL, any system can access the share unless there is a `hosts deny` option. Synonym for `allow hosts`.

hosts deny = host list

Allowable values: list of hosts or networks   **Default:** NULL

Specifies a list of systems that cannot connect to the share. Synonym for `deny hosts`.

hosts equiv = filename
[global]

Allowable values: name of file   **Default:** NULL

Specifies the path to a file of trusted systems from which passwordless logons are allowed. Strongly discouraged because Windows NT/2000/XP users can always override the username—the only security in this scheme.

include = filename

Allowable values: name of file   **Default:** NULL

Includes the named file in *smb.conf* at the line where it appears. This option accepts most variables, but not %u (user), %P (current share's root directory), or %S (current share's name) because they are not set at the time the file is read.

inherit acls = boolean

Allowable values: YES, NO   **Default:** NO

If set, files and subdirectories are created with the same ACLs as their parent directories. Directories are given Unix permissions of 0777 (full permissions) ensuring that the ACL on the directory will govern the actual permissions given to clients. Requires POSIX ACL support to be provided on the Samba host system.

inherit permissions = boolean

Allowable values: YES, NO   **Default:** NO

If set, files and subdirectories are created with the same permissions as their parent directories. This allows Unix directory permissions to be propagated automatically to new files and subdirectories, especially in the [homes] share. This option overrides create mask, directory mask, force create mode, and force directory mode, but not map archive, map hidden, or map system. Samba never sets the setuid bit when creating a file or directory.

interfaces = interface list   [global]

Allowable values: interface list   **Default:** NULL (all interfaces except 127.0.0.1)

Sets the interfaces to which Samba will respond. The default is the system's primary interface only. Recommended on multihomed systems or to override erroneous addresses and netmasks. Allows interface names such as eth0, DNS names, address/netmask pairs, and broadcast/netmask pairs. See also bind interfaces only.

invalid users = user list

Allowable values: user list   **Default:** NULL

Specifies a list of users not permitted access to the share.

keepalive = number   [global]

Allowable values: number of seconds   **Default:** 300

Sets the number of seconds between checks for a crashed client. The value of 0 causes no checks to be performed. Setting keepalive = 3600 will turn on checks every hour. A value of 600 (every 10 minutes) is recommended if you want more frequent checks. See also socket options for another approach.

kernel oplocks = boolean [global]

Allowable values: YES, NO   **Default:** YES

Breaks the oplock when a local Unix process or NFS operation accesses an oplocked file, thus preventing corruption. This works only on operating systems that support kernel-based oplocks, such as Linux 2.4 and Irix. Avoid changing. See also oplocks and level2 oplocks.

lanman auth = boolean [global]

Allowable values: YES, NO   **Default:** YES

If set to YES, allows clients to use the (weak) LANMAN password hash used by Windows 95/98/Me. If set to NO, allows only the better NT1 hash used by Windows NT/2000/XP.

large readwrite = boolean [global]

Allowable values: YES, NO   **Default:** NO in Samba 2.2, YES in Samba 3.0

If set to YES, allows Windows 2000/XP to read and write 64KB at a time to improve performance. Requires Samba to be hosted by a 64-bit OS, such as Linux 2.4, Irix, or Solaris. Somewhat experimental.

ldap admin dn = string [global]

Allowable values: Distinguished Name   **Default:** NULL

Sets the Distinguished Name used by Samba when contacting the LDAP server. Requires Samba to be configured with the --with-ldapsam configuration option. Experimental option added in Samba 2.2.3 and obsolete in Samba 3.0.

ldap filter = string [global]

Allowable values: LDAP search filter   **Default:** `(&(uid=%u)(objectclass=sambaAccount))`

Sets the LDAP search filter. Requires that Samba be configured with the --with-ldapsam configuration option. Experimental option added in Samba 2.2.3 and obsolete in Samba 3.0.

ldap port = number [global]

Allowable values: positive integer   **Default:** In Samba 2.2, 636 if `ldap ssl = on`; otherwise 389

Sets the TCP port number for contacting the LDAP server. Requires that Samba be configured with the --with-ldapsam configuration option. Experimental option added in Samba 2.2.3 and obsolete starting with Samba 3.0. See also ldap ssl.

ldap server = value

Allowable values: fully qualified domain name

[global]

Default: localhost

Sets the domain name of the LDAP server. Requires that Samba be configured with the --with-ldapsam configuration option. Experimental option added in Samba 2.2.3 and obsolete starting with Samba 3.0.

ldap ssl = value

Allowable values: ON, OFF, START TLS

[global]

Default: ON

Sets whether Samba uses SSL to contact the LDAP server. ON and OFF turn SSL encryption on or off. The START TLS setting causes Samba to use LDAPv3 StartTLS extended operation. Requires that Samba be configured with the --with-ldapsam configuration option. Experimental option added in Samba 2.2.3 and obsolete in Samba 3.0.

ldap suffix = string

Allowable values: Distinguished Name

[global]

Default: NULL

Sets the base Distinguished Name to use for LDAP searches. Requires that Samba be configured with the --with-ldapsam configuration option. Experimental option added in Samba 2.2.3 and obsolete in Samba 3.0.

level2 oplocks = boolean

Allowable values: YES, NO

Default: YES

Allows files to be cached read-only on the client when multiple clients have opened the file. This allows executables to be cached locally, improving performance.

lm announce = value

Allowable values: AUTO, YES, NO

[global]

Default: AUTO

Produces OS/2 SMB broadcasts at an interval specified by the lm interval option. YES/NO turns them on/off unconditionally. AUTO causes the Samba server to wait for a LAN manager announcement from another client before sending one out. Required for OS/2 client browsing.

lm interval = number

Allowable values: number of seconds

[global]

Default: 60

Sets the time period, in seconds, between OS/2 SMB broadcast announcements.

load printers = boolean
[global]

Allowable values: YES, NO   **Default:** YES

Loads all printer names from the system's *printcap* file into the browse list. Uses configuration options from the [printers] section.

local master = boolean
[global]

Allowable values: YES, NO   **Default:** YES

Allows Samba to participate in elections for the local master browser. See also domain master and os level.

lock dir = directory
[global]

Allowable values: name of directory   **Default:** */usr/local/samba/var/locks*

Synonym for lock directory.

lock directory = directory
[global]

Allowable values: name of directory   **Default:** */usr/local/samba/var/locks*

Sets a directory in which to keep lock files. The directory must be writable by Samba and readable by everyone. Also called lock dir.

lock spin count = number
[global]

Allowable values: positive integer   **Default:** 2

Sets the number of attempts to attain a byte range lock. See also lock spin time.

lock spin time = number
[global]

Allowable values: number of microseconds   **Default:** 10

Sets the number of microseconds between attempts to attain a lock. See also lock spin count.

locking = boolean
[global]

Allowable values: YES, NO   **Default:** YES

Performs file locking. If set to NO, Samba accepts lock requests but won't actually lock resources. Turn off for read-only filesystems.

log file = filename
[global]

Allowable values: name of file   **Default:** varies

Sets the name and location of the log file. Allows all % variables.

log level = number [global]

Allowable values: number   **Default:** 0

Sets the logging level used. Values of 3 or more slow the system noticeably. Recommended value is 1. Synonym for debug level.

logon drive = value [global]

Allowable values: MS-DOS drive name   **Default:** Z:

Sets the drive to be used as a home directory for domain logons by Windows NT/2000/XP clients. See also logon home.

logon home = directory [global]

Allowable values: UNC of shared directory   **Default:** \\%N\%U

Sets the home directory of a Windows 95/98/Me or NT/2000/XP user. Allows NET USE H:/HOME from the command prompt if Samba is acting as a logon server. Append \profile or other directory to the value of this parameter if storing Windows 95/98/Me profiles in a subdirectory of the user's home directory. See logon path for Windows NT/2000/XP roaming profiles.

logon path = directory [global]

Allowable values: UNC of shared directory   **Default:** \\%N\%U\profile

Sets the path to the directory where Windows NT/2000/XP roaming profiles are stored. See also logon home for Windows 95/98/Me roaming profiles.

logon script = directory [global]

Allowable values: UNC of shared file   **Default:** NULL

Sets the pathname (relative to the [netlogon] share) of an MS-DOS/NT command to run on the client at logon time. Allows all % variables.

lppause command = command

Allowable values: command   **Default:** varies

Sets the command to pause a print job. Honors the %p (printer name) and %j (job number) variables.

lpq cache time = number [global]

Allowable values: number of seconds   **Default:** 10

Sets how long to keep print queue status cached, in seconds.

lpq command = command

Allowable values: command   **Default:** varies

Sets the command used to get printer status. Usually initialized to a default value by the printing option. Honors the %p (printer name) variable.

lpresume command = command

Allowable values: command   **Default:** varies

Sets the command to resume a paused print job. Honors the %p (printer name) and %j (job number) variables.

lprm command = command

Allowable values: command   **Default:** varies

Sets the command to delete a print job. Usually initialized to a default value by the printing option. Honors the %p (printer name) and %j (job number) variables.

machine password timeout = number

Allowable values: number of seconds   **Default:** 604800 (1 week)

Sets the period between (NT domain) computer account password changes.

magic output = filename

Allowable values: name of file   **Default:** *command.out*

Sets the output file for the magic scripts option. Default is the command name, followed by the *.out* extension.

magic script = filename

Allowable values: name of file   **Default:** NULL

Sets a filename for execution via a shell whenever the file is closed from the client, allowing clients to run commands on the server. The scripts will be deleted on completion, if permissions allow. Use is discouraged.

mangle case = boolean

Allowable values: YES, NO   **Default:** NO

Mangles a name if it is in mixed case.

mangled map = map list

Allowable values: list of to/from pairs   **Default:** NULL

Sets up a table of names to remap (e.g., *.html* to *.htm*).

mangled names = boolean

Allowable values: YES, NO   **Default:** YES

Sets Samba to abbreviate to the MS-DOS 8.3 style names that are too long or have unsupported characters.

mangled stack = number   [global]

Allowable values: number   **Default:** 50

Sets the size of the cache of recently mangled filenames.

mangling char = character

Allowable values: character   **Default:** ~

Sets the unique mangling character used in all mangled names.

mangling method = string   [global]

Allowable values: hash, hash2   **Default:** hash

Sets the algorithm used to mangle filenames. The hash2 method is a newer method introduced in Samba 2.2.x, and it creates different filenames than the hash method.

map archive = boolean

Allowable values: YES, NO   **Default:** YES

If YES, Samba sets the executable-by-user (0100) bit on Unix files if the MS-DOS archive attribute is set. If used, the create mask must contain the 0100 bit.

map hidden = boolean

Allowable values: YES, NO   **Default:** NO

If YES, Samba sets the executable-by-other (0001) bit on Unix files if the MS-DOS hidden attribute is set. If used, the create mask option must contain the 0001 bit.

map system = boolean

Allowable values: YES, NO   **Default:** NO

If YES, Samba sets the executable-by-group (0010) bit on Unix files if the MS-DOS system attribute is set. If used, the create mask must contain the 0010 bit.

---

map to guest = value   [global]

Allowable values: Never, Bad User, Bad Password   **Default:** Never

If set to Bad User, allows users without accounts on the Samba system to log in and be assigned the guest account. This option can be used as part of making public shares for anyone to use. If set to Bad Password, users who mistype their passwords will be logged in to the guest account instead of their own. Because no warning is given, the Bad Password value can be extremely confusing: we recommend against it. The default setting of Never prevents users without accounts from logging in.

max connections = number

Allowable values: number   **Default:** 0 (infinity)

Sets the maximum number of share connections allowed from each client system.

max disk size = number   [global]

Allowable values: size in MB   **Default:** 0 (no limit)

Sets the maximum disk size/free-space size (in megabytes) to return to the client. Some clients or applications can't understand large maximum disk sizes.

max log size = number   [global]

Allowable values: size in KB   **Default:** 5000

Sets the size (in kilobytes) at which Samba will start a new log file. The current log file will be renamed with a *.old* extension, replacing any existing file with that name.

max mux = number   [global]

Allowable values: number   **Default:** 50

Sets the number of simultaneous SMB operations that Samba clients can make. Avoid changing.

max open files = number   [global]

Allowable values: number   **Default:** 10000

Limits the number of files a Samba process will try to keep open at one time. Samba allows you to set this to less than the maximum imposed by the Unix host operating system. Avoid changing.

max print jobs = number

Allowable values: positive integer   **Default:** 1000

Limits the number of jobs that can be in the queue for this printer share at any one time. The printer will report out of space if the limit is exceeded. See also total print jobs.

max protocol = name   [global]

Allowable values: CORE, COREPLUS, LANMAN1, LANMAN2, NT1   **Default:** NT1

If set, limits the negotiation to the protocol specified, or older. See min protocol. Avoid using.

max smbd processes = number   [global]

Allowable values: integer   **Default:** 0 (no limit)

Limits the number of users who can connect to the server. Used to prevent degraded service under an overload, at the cost of refusing services entirely.

max ttl = number   [global]

Allowable values: number of seconds   **Default:** 259200 (3 days)

Sets the time to live (TTL) of NetBIOS names in the *nmbd* WINS cache. Avoid changing.

max wins ttl = number   [global]

Allowable values: number of seconds   **Default:** 518400 (6 days)

Limits the TTL, in seconds, of a NetBIOS name in the *nmbd* WINS cache. Avoid changing. See also min wins ttl.

max xmit = number   [global]

Allowable values: size in bytes   **Default:** 65535

Sets the maximum packet size negotiated by Samba. This is a tuning parameter for slow links and bugs in older clients. Values less than 2048 are discouraged.

message command = command   [global]

Allowable values: command   **Default:** NULL

Sets the command to run on the server when a WinPopup message arrives from a client. If it does not complete quickly, the command must end in & to allow immediate return. Honors all % variables except %u (user) and supports the extra variables %s (filename the message is in), %t (destination system), and %f (from).

min passwd length = number
[global]

Allowable values: integer   **Default:** 5

Synonym for min password length.

min password length = number
[global]

Allowable values: integer   **Default:** 5

Sets the shortest Unix password allowed by Samba when updating a user's password on its system. Also called min passwd length.

min print space = number

Allowable values: space in kilobytes   **Default:** 0 (unlimited)

Sets the minimum spool space required before accepting a print request.

min protocol = name
[global]

Allowable values: CORE, COREPLUS, LANMAN1, LANMAN2, NT1   **Default:** CORE

If set, prevents use of old (less secure) protocols. Using NT1 disables MS-DOS clients. See also lanman auth.

min wins ttl = number
[global]

Allowable values: number of seconds   **Default:** 21600 (6 hours)

Sets the minimum TTL, in seconds, of a NetBIOS name in the *nmbd* WINS cache. Avoid changing.

msdfs root = boolean

Allowable values: YES, NO   **Default:** NO

Makes the share a Dfs root. Requires the --with-msdfs configure option. Any symbolic links of the form msdfs:server\share will be seen as Dfs links. See also host msdfs.

name resolve order = list
[global]

Allowable values: lmhosts, wins, host, bcast   **Default:** lmhosts, host, wins, bcast

Sets the order of lookup when trying to get IP addresses from names. The host parameter carries out a regular name lookup using the server's normal sources: */etc/hosts*, DNS, NIS, or a combination of these.

netbios aliases = list [global]

Allowable values: list of NetBIOS names   **Default:** NULL

Adds additional NetBIOS names by which the Samba server will advertise itself.

netbios name = value

Allowable values: local hostname   **Default:** DNS name of system

Sets the NetBIOS name by which a Samba server is known, or the primary name if NetBIOS aliases exist. See also netbios aliases.

netbios scope = string [global]

Allowable values: string   **Default:** NULL

Sets the NetBIOS scope string, an early predecessor of workgroups. Samba will not communicate with a system with a different scope. This option is not recommended.

nis homedir = boolean [global]

Allowable values: YES, NO   **Default:** NO

If YES, the homedir map is used to look up the server hosting the user's home directory and return it to the client. The client will contact that system to connect to the share. This avoids mounting from a system that doesn't actually have the directory, which would cause the data to be transmitted twice. The system with the home directories must be an SMB server.

non unix account range = numeric range [global]

Allowable values: range of positive integers   **Default:** NONE

Specifies a range of Unix UIDs for Samba to use for user accounts and computer accounts that are maintained outside of */etc/passwd*. The UIDs in this range must not overlap those of regular Unix users in */etc/passwd*. See also algorithmic rid base. New in Samba 3.0.

nt acl support = boolean

Allowable values: YES, NO   **Default:** YES

Causes the Samba server to map Unix permissions to Windows NT ACLs.

nt pipe support = boolean [global]

Allowable values: YES, NO   **Default:** YES

Allows turning off of NT-specific pipe calls. This is a developer/benchmarking option and might be removed in the future. Avoid changing.

nt smb support = boolean   [global]

Allowable values: YES, NO   **Default:** YES

If YES, allows the use of NT-specific SMBs. This is a developer/benchmarking option that is obsolete in Samba 3.0. Avoid changing.

nt status support = boolean   [global]

Allowable values: YES, NO   **Default:** YES

If YES, allows the use of NT-specific status messages. This is a developer/benchmarking option and might be removed in the future. Avoid changing.

null passwords = boolean   [global]

Allowable values: YES, NO   **Default:** NO

If YES, allows access to accounts that have null passwords. Strongly discouraged.

obey pam restrictions = boolean   [global]

Allowable values: YES, NO   **Default:** NO

If set, Samba will adhere to the PAM's account and session restrictions. Requires --with-pam configuration option.

only guest = boolean

Allowable values: YES, NO   **Default:** NO

Forces users of a share to log on as the guest account. Synonym for guest only. Requires guest ok or public to be YES.

only user = boolean

Allowable values: YES, NO   **Default:** NO

Requires that users of the share be in the list specified by the user option.

oplock break wait time = number   [global]

Allowable values: number   **Default:** 0

This is an advanced tuning parameter and is recommended only for experts who know how Samba handles oplocks. This option might need to be set if a Windows system fails to release an oplock in response to a break request from the Samba server. Due to bugs on some Windows systems, they might fail to respond if Samba responds too quickly; the default on this option can be lengthened in such cases.

oplock contention limit = number

Allowable values: number of milliseconds   **Default:** 2

This is an advanced tuning parameter and is recommended only for experts who know how Samba handles oplocks. It causes Samba to refuse to grant an oplock if the number of clients contending for a file exceeds the specified value.

oplocks = boolean

Allowable values: YES, NO   **Default:** YES

If YES, supports local caching of oplocked files on the client. This option is recommended because it improves performance by about 30%. See also fake oplocks and veto oplock files.

os level = number   [global]

Allowable values: integer   **Default:** 20

Sets the candidacy of the server when electing a browse master. Used with the domain master or local master options. You can set a higher value than a competing operating system if you want Samba to win. Windows for Workgroups and Windows 95/98/Me use 1. Windows NT/2000/XP, when not acting as a PDC, use 16 and, when acting as a PDC, use 32. Warning: this can override non-Samba browse masters unexpectedly.

os2 driver map = filename   [global]

Allowable values: name of file   **Default:** NULL

Specifies a file containing mappings of Windows NT printer driver names to OS/2 printer driver names.

pam password change = boolean   [global]

Allowable values: YES, NO   **Default:** NO

If YES, and if Samba is configured with --with-pam, PAM is allowed to handle password changes from clients, instead of using the program defined by the passwd program parameter.

panic action = command   [global]

Allowable values: command   **Default:** NULL

Sets the command to run when Samba panics. Honors all % variables. For Samba developers and testers, /usr/bin/X11/xterm -display :0 -e gdb /samba/bin/smbd %d is a possible value.

passdb backend = list [global]

Allowable values: smbpasswd, smbpasswd_nua, tdbsam, tdbsam_nua, plugin   **Default:** smbpasswd

Specifies methods Samba uses to store and retrieve passwords when using a method other than the Unix system's */etc/passwd*. See also non unix account range. New in Samba 3.0.

passwd chat = string [global]

Allowable values: sequence of strings   **Default:** compiled-in value

Sets the chat strings used to change passwords on the server. Supports the variables %o (old password) and %n (new password) and allows the escapes \r, \n, \t, and \s (space) in the sequence. See also unix password sync, passwd program, passwd chat debug, and pam password change.

passwd chat debug = boolean [global]

Allowable values: YES, NO   **Default:** NO

Logs an entire password chat, including passwords passed, with a log level of 100. For debugging only. See also passwd chat, pam password change, and passwd program.

passwd program = command [global]

Allowable values: command   **Default:** */bin/passwd*

Sets the command used to change a user's password. Will be run as root. Supports %u (user). See also unix password sync.

password level = number [global]

Allowable values: number   **Default:** 0

Specifies the number of uppercase-letter permutations used to match passwords. A workaround for clients that change passwords to a single case before sending them to the Samba server. Causes repeated login attempts with mixed-case passwords, which can trigger account lockouts. Required for Windows 95/98/Me, plain-text passwords, and mixed-case passwords. Try to avoid using.

password server = list

Allowable values: list of NetBIOS names   **Default:** NULL

Specifies a list of SMB servers that validate passwords. Used with a Windows NT/2000 password server (PDC or BDC) and the security = server or security = domain configuration options. Caution: a Windows NT/2000 password server must allow logins from the Samba server. If set to *, Samba will look up the PDC by resolving the NetBIOS name WORKGROUP<1C>.

path = directory

Allowable values: name of directory   **Default:** varies

Sets the path to the directory provided by a file share or used by a printer share. If the option is omitted, it is set automatically in the [homes] share to the user's home directory; otherwise, defaults to */tmp*. Honors the %u (user) and %m (machine) variables.

pid directory = directory   [global]

Allowable values: name of directory   **Default:** */usr/local/samba/var/locks*

Sets the path to the directory where PID files are located.

posix locking = boolean

Allowable values: YES, NO   **Default:** YES

If set to YES, Samba will map file locks owned by SMB clients to POSIX locks. Avoid changing.

postexec = command

Allowable values: command   **Default:** NULL

Sets a command to run as the user after disconnecting from the share. See also the preexec, root preexec, and root postexec options.

postscript = boolean

Allowable values: YES, NO   **Default:** NO

Forces a printer to recognize a file as PostScript by inserting %! as the first line. Works only if the printer is actually PostScript-compatible.

preexec = command

Allowable values: command   **Default:** NULL

Sets a command to run as the user before connecting to the share. Synonym for exec. See also the postexec, root preexec, and root postexec options.

preexec close = boolean

Allowable values: YES, NO   **Default:** NO

If set, allows the preexec command to decide if the share can be accessed by the user. If the command returns a nonzero return code, the user is denied permission to connect.

preferred master = boolean   [global]

Allowable values: YES, NO   **Default:** auto

If YES, Samba is the preferred master browser. Causes Samba to call a browsing election when it comes online. See also os level.

prefered master = boolean   [global]

Allowable values: YES, NO   **Default:** auto

Synonym for preferred master.

preload = service list

Allowable values: list of shares   **Default:** NULL

Specifies a list of shares that always appears in browse lists. Synonym for auto services. See also load printers.

preserve case = boolean

Allowable values: YES, NO   **Default:** YES

Leaves filenames in the case sent by the client. If NO, it forces filenames to the case specified by the default case option. See also short preserve case.

printable = boolean

Allowable values: YES, NO   **Default:** NO

Sets a share to be a print share. Required for all printers. Synonym for print ok.

printcap name = filename   [global]

Allowable values: name of file   **Default:** /etc/printcap

Sets the path to the printer capabilities file used by the [printers] share. The default value changes to /etc/qconfig under AIX and lpstat on System V. Also called printcap.

print command = command

Allowable values: command   **Default:** varies

Sets the command used to send a spooled file to the printer. Usually initialized to a default value corresponding to the printing option. This option honors the %p (printer name), %s (spool file), and %f (spool file as a relative path) variables. The command must delete the spool file.

printer = name

Allowable values: printer name   **Default:** lp

Sets the name of the Unix printer used by the share. Also called `printer name`.

printer admin = user list

Allowable values: user list   **Default:** NULL

Specifies users who can administer a printer using the remote printer administration interface on a Windows system. The root user always has these privileges.

printer driver = name

Allowable values: exact printer driver string used by Windows   **Default:** NULL

Sets the string to pass to Windows when asked which driver to use to prepare files for a printer share. Note that the value is case-sensitive. Part of pre-2.2 printing system. Deprecated.

printer driver file = filename   [global]

Allowable values: name of file   **Default:** */usr/local/samba/printers/printers.def*

Sets the location of a *msprint.def* file. Usable by Windows 95/98/Me. Part of pre-2.2 printing system. Deprecated.

printer driver location = directory

Allowable values: UNC of shared directory   **Default:** *server**PRINTER$*

Sets the location of the driver for a particular printer. The value is the pathname of the share that stores the printer driver files. Part of pre-2.2 printing system. Deprecated.

printer name = name

Allowable values: name   **Default:** NULL

Synonym for `printer`.

printing = value

Allowable values: bsd, sysv, hpux, aix, qnx, plp, softq, lprng, cups   **Default:** bsd

Sets the printing style to a value other than that in which you've compiled. This sets initial values of at least `print command`, `lpq command`, and `lprm command`.

print ok = boolean

Allowable values: YES, NO | **Default:** NO

Synonym for `printable`.

private directory = directory   [global]

Allowable values: name of directory | **Default:** */usr/local/samba/private*

Specifies the directory used for storing security-sensitive files such as *smbpasswd* and *secrets.tdb*. New in Samba 3.0.

protocol = name   [global]

Allowable values: NT1, LANMAN2, LANMAN1, COREPLUS, CORE | **Default:** NT1

Synonym for `max protocol`.

public = boolean

Allowable values: YES, NO | **Default:** NO

If YES, passwords are not needed for this share. Also called `guest ok`.

queuepause command = command

Allowable values: full path to script | **Default:** varies

Sets the command used to pause a print queue. Usually initialized to a default value by the `printing` option.

queueresume command = command

Allowable values: full path to script | **Default:** varies

Sets the command used to resume a print queue. Usually initialized to a default value by the `printing` option.

read bmpx = boolean

Allowable values: YES, NO | **Default:** NO

If set to YES, supports the "Read Block Multiplex" message. Avoid changing.

read list = list

Allowable values: list of user and/or group names | **Default:** NULL

Specifies a list of users given read-only access to a writable share.

read only = boolean

Allowable values: YES, NO   **Default:** NO

Sets a share to read-only. Antonym of `writable`, `writeable`, and `write ok`.

read raw = boolean   [global]

Allowable values: YES, NO   **Default:** YES

Allows clients to read data using a 64K packet size. Recommended.

read size = number   [global]

Allowable values: positive integer   **Default:** 16384

Allows disk reads and writes to overlap network reads and writes. A tuning parameter. Do not set larger than the default.

realm = string   [global]

Allowable values: Kerberos realm name   **Default:** NONE

Specifies the realm name for Kerberos 5 authentication. Requires the `--with-krb5` configure option. New in Samba 3.0.

remote announce = remote list   [global]

Allowable values: list of remote addresses   **Default:** NULL

Adds workgroups to the list on which the Samba server will announce itself. Specified as an IP address and optional workgroup (for instance, 192.168.220.215/SIMPLE) with multiple entries separated by spaces. Addresses can be the specific address of the browse master on a subnet or on directed broadcasts (i.e., ###.###.###.255). The server will appear on those workgroups' browse lists. Does not require WINS.

remote browse sync = list   [global]

Allowable values: IP addresses   **Default:** NULL

Perform browse list synchronization with other Samba local master browsers. Addresses can be specific addresses or directed broadcasts (i.e., ###.###.###.255). The latter causes Samba to locate the local master browser on that subnet.

restrict anonymous = boolean   [global]

Allowable values: YES, NO   **Default:** NO

Denies access to users who do not supply a username. This is disabled by default because when the Samba server acts as the domain's PDC, the option can keep a client from revalidating its computer account when someone new logs in. Use of the option is recommended only when all clients are Windows NT/2000/XP systems.

root = directory [global]

Allowable values: name of directory   **Default:** NULL

Synonym for root directory.

root dir = directory [global]

Allowable values: name of directory   **Default:** NULL

Synonym for root directory.

root directory = directory [global]

Allowable values: name of directory   **Default:** /

Specifies a directory to *chroot()* before starting daemons. Prevents any access outside that directory tree. See also the wide links configuration option. Also called root and root dir.

root postexec = command

Allowable values: command   **Default:** NULL

Sets a command to run as root after disconnecting from the share. See also the preexec, postexec, and root preexec configuration options. Runs after the user's postexec command. Use with caution.

root preexec = command

Allowable values: command   **Default:** NULL

Sets a command to run as root before connecting to the share. See also the preexec, postexec, and root postexec configuration options. Runs before the user's preexec command. Use with caution.

root preexec close = boolean

Allowable values: YES, NO   **Default:** NO

If set, allows the root preexec command to decide if the share can be accessed by the user. If the command returns a nonzero return code, the user will be denied permission to connect.

security = value   [global]

Allowable values: share, user, server, domain   **Default:** user

Sets the client authentication method. If security = share, services are password-protected, available to everyone who knows the password. If security = user, users have accounts and passwords, and are required to authenticate with the server before accessing services. If security = server, users have accounts and passwords as with security = user, and a separate system authenticates them for Samba. If security = domain, Windows NT domain authentication is implemented using a Windows NT/2000 or other Samba server to validate accounts. See also the password server and encrypted passwords configuration options.

security mask = value

Allowable values: octal value from 0 to 0777   **Default:** 0777

Controls which permission bits can be changed if a user on a Windows NT/2000/XP system edits the Unix permissions of files on the Samba server using the Windows system's ACL editing dialog box. Any bit that is set in the mask can be changed by the user; any bit that is clear remains the same on the file even if the user tries to change it. Requires nt acl support = YES. Note that some rarely used bits map to the DOS system, hidden, and archive bits in the file attributes in a nonintuitive way.

server string = string   [global]

Allowable values: string   **Default:** Samba %v

Sets the name that corresponds to the Samba server in browse lists. Honors the %v (Samba version number) and %h (hostname) variables.

set directory = boolean

Allowable values: YES, NO   **Default:** NO

Allows the DEC Pathworks client to use the *set dir* command.

share modes = boolean

Allowable values: YES, NO   **Default:** YES

Directs Samba to support Windows-style whole-file (deny mode) locks. Do not change.

short preserve case = boolean

Allowable values: YES, NO   **Default:** YES

If set to YES, leaves mangled 8.3-style filenames in the case sent by the client. If NO, forces the case to that specified by the default case option. See also preserve case.

show add printer wizard = boolean [global]

Allowable values: YES, NO **Default:** YES

If set, tells clients that the Add Printer Wizard can be used to add a Samba printer from Windows NT/2000/XP clients. See also `add printer` command, `delete printer` comamnd, and `printer admin`.

shutdown script = command [global]

Allowable values: command **Default:** NONE

Specifies a command that initiates a system shutdown. The command is run with the UID of the connected user. The %m (message), %t (delay time), %r (reboot), and %f (force) options are supported. See also `abort shutdown script`. New in Samba 3.0.

smb passwd file = filename [global]

Allowable values: name of file **Default:** */usr/local/samba/private/smbpasswd*

Overrides the compiled-in path to the encrypted password file. See also `encrypted passwords` and `private dir`.

socket address = value [global]

Allowable values: IP address **Default:** NULL

Sets the address on which to listen for connections. Default is to listen to all addresses.

socket options = list [global]

Allowable values: socket option list **Default:** TCP_NODELAY

Sets OS-specific socket options. SO_KEEPALIVE makes TCP check clients every four hours to see if they are still accessible. TCP_NODELAY sends even tiny packets to keep delay low. Both are recommended wherever the operating system supports them.

source environment = filename [global]

Allowable values: name of file **Default:** NULL

Causes Samba to read a list of environment variables from a file upon startup. This can be useful when setting up Samba in a clustered environment. The filename can begin with a "|" (pipe) character, in which case it causes Samba to run the file as a command to obtain the variables.

The file must be owned by root and must not be world-writable. If the filename begins with a "|" character, it must point to a command that is neither world-writable nor resides in a world-writable directory.

The data should be in the form of lines such as SAMBA_NETBIOS_NAME=*myhostname*. This value will then be available in the *smb.conf* files as %$SAMBA_NETBIOS_NAME.

ssl = boolean   [global]

Allowable values: YES, NO   **Default:** NO

Makes Samba use SSL for data exchange with some or all hosts. Requires --with-ssl configure option.Obsolete starting with Samba 3.0.

ssl CA certDir = directory   [global]

Allowable values: name of directory   **Default:** */usr/local/ssl/certs*

Specifies a directory containing a file for each Certification Authority (CA) that the Samba server trusts so that Samba can verify client certificates. Part of SSL support. Requires --with-ssl configure option. Obsolete starting with Samba 3.0.

ssl CA certFile = filename   [global]

Allowable values: name of file   **Default:** */usr/local/ssl/certs/trustedCAs.pem*

Specifies a file that contains information for each CA that the Samba server trusts so that Samba can verify client certificates. Part of SSL support. Requires --with-ssl configure option. Obsolete starting with Samba 3.0.

ssl ciphers = list   [global]

Allowable values: list of ciphers   **Default:** NULL

Specifies which ciphers should be offered during SSL negotiation. Not recommended. Requires --with-ssl configure option. Obsolete starting with Samba 3.0.

ssl client cert = filename   [global]

Allowable values: name of file   **Default:** */usr/local/ssl/certs/smbclient.pem*

Specifies a file containing the server's SSL certificate, for use by *smbclient* if certificates are required in this environment. Requires --with-ssl configure option. Obsolete starting with Samba 3.0.

ssl client key = filename   [global]

Allowable values: name of file   **Default:** */usr/local/ssl/private/smbclient.pem*

Specifies a file containing the server's private SSL key, for use by *smbclient*. Requires --with-ssl configure option. Obsolete starting with Samba 3.0.

ssl compatibility = boolean

Allowable values: YES, NO

Default: NO

Determines whether SSLeay should be configured for bug compatibility with other SSL implementations. Not recommended. Requires `--with-ssl` configure option. Obsolete starting with Samba 3.0.

ssl hosts = host list

[global]

Allowable values: list of hosts or networks

Default: NULL

Requires that SSL be used with the hosts listed. By default, if the `ssl` option is set, the server requires SSL with all hosts. Requires `--with-ssl` configure option. Obsolete starting with Samba 3.0.

ssl hosts resign = host list

[global]

Allowable values: list of hosts or networks

Default: NULL

Suppresses the use of SSL with the hosts listed. By default, if the `ssl` option is set, the server requires SSL with all hosts. Requires `--with-ssl` configure option. Obsolete starting with Samba 3.0.

ssl require clientcert = boolean

[global]

Allowable values: YES, NO

Default: NO

Requires clients to use certificates when SSL is in use. This option is recommended if SSL is used. Requires `--with-ssl` configure option. Obsolete starting with Samba 3.0.

ssl require servercert = boolean

[global]

Allowable values: YES, NO

Default: NO

When SSL is in use, *smbclient* requires servers to use certificates. This option is recommended if SSL is used. Requires `--with-ssl` configure option. Obsolete starting with Samba 3.0.

ssl server cert = filename

[global]

Allowable values: name of file

Default: NULL

Specifies a file containing the server's SSL certificate. Requires `--with-ssl` configure option. Obsolete starting with Samba 3.0.

ssl server key = filename

[global]

Allowable values: name of file   **Default:** NULL

Specifies a file containing the server's private SSL key. If no file is specified and SSL is in use, the server looks up its key in its server certificate. Requires --with-ssl configure option. Obsolete starting with Samba 3.0.

ssl version = string

[global]

Allowable values: "ssl2", "ssl3", "ssl2or3", "tls1"   **Default:** "ssl2or3"

Defines which versions of the SSL protocol the server can use: Version 2 only ("ssl2"), Version 3 only ("ssl3"), Version 2 or 3 dynamically negotiated ("ssl2or3"), or Transport Layer Security ("tls1"). Requires --with-ssl configure option. Obsolete starting with Samba 3.0.

stat cache = boolean

[global]

Allowable values: YES, NO   **Default:** YES

Makes the Samba server cache client names for faster resolution. Should not be changed.

stat cache size = number

[global]

Allowable values: number   **Default:** 50

Determines the number of client names cached for faster resolution. Should not be changed.

status = boolean

[global]

Allowable values: YES, NO   **Default:** YES

If set to YES, logs connections to a file (or shared memory) accessible to *smbstatus*. Obsolete starting with Samba 3.0.

strict allocate = boolean

Allowable values: YES, NO   **Default:** NO

If set to YES, allocates all disk blocks when creating or extending the size of files, instead of using the normal sparse file allocation used on Unix. This slows the server, but results in behavior that matches that of Windows and helps Samba correctly report "out of quota" messages.

strict locking = boolean

Allowable values: YES, NO   **Default:** NO

If set to YES, checks locks on every access, not just on demand and at open time. Not recommended.

strict sync = boolean

Allowable values: YES, NO   **Default:** NO

If set to YES, Samba synchronizes to disk whenever the client sets the sync bit in a packet. If set to NO, Samba flushes data to disk whenever buffers fill. Defaults to NO because Windows 98 Explorer sets the bit (incorrectly) in all packets.

strip dot = boolean   [global]

Allowable values: YES, NO   **Default:** NO

Removes trailing dots from filenames. Dysfunctional in Samba 2.2; use `mangled map` instead.

sync always = boolean

Allowable values: YES, NO   **Default:** NO

If set to YES, Samba forces the data to disk through *fsync*(3) after every write. Avoid except to debug crashing servers.

syslog = number   [global]

Allowable values: number   **Default:** 1

Sets the level of Samba log messages to send to *syslog*. Higher is more verbose. The *syslog.conf* file must have suitable logging enabled.

syslog only = boolean   [global]

Allowable values: YES, NO   **Default:** NO

If set to YES, logs only to *syslog* instead of the standard Samba log files.

template homedir = path   [global]

Allowable values: full path to directory   **Default:** /home/%D/%U

Sets the home directory for Unix login sessions for users authenticated through winbind. %D will be replaced with user's domain name; %U by the username.

template shell = filename

Allowable values: full path to shell   **Default:** */bin/false*

Sets the shell for Unix login sessions for users authenticated through winbind. The default value prevents all Windows domain user logins.

time offset = number

[global]

Allowable values: number of minutes   **Default:** 0

Sets the number of minutes to add to the system time-zone calculation. Provided to fix a client daylight-savings bug. Not recommended.

time server = boolean

[global]

Allowable values: YES, NO   **Default:** NO

If set to YES, *nmbd* advertises itself as a provider of SMB time service to clients. This option only affects whether the time service is advertised. It does not enable or disable time service.

timestamp logs = boolean

[global]

Allowable values: YES, NO   **Default:** YES

Synonym for debug timestamp.

total print jobs = number

[global]

Allowable values: number   **Default:** 0 (no limit)

Limits total number of current print jobs on server. See also max print jobs.

unix extensions = boolean

[global]

Allowable values: YES, NO   **Default:** NO

If set to YES, supports CIFS Unix extensions, providing better filesystem support for Unix clients. Obsolete in Samba 3.0, which always offers support.

unix password sync = boolean

[global]

Allowable values: YES, NO   **Default:** NO

If set to YES, attempts to change the user's Unix password whenever the user changes her SMB password. Used to ease synchronization of Unix and Microsoft password databases. See also password program and passwd chat.

update encrypted = boolean [global]

Allowable values: YES, NO   **Default:** NO

Updates the encrypted password file when a user logs on with an unencrypted password. Provided to ease conversion from unencrypted to encrypted passwords.

use client driver = boolean [global]

Allowable values: YES, NO   **Default:** NO

Used for avoiding `Access Denied; Unable to connect` messages when connecting to a Samba printer from Windows NT/2000/XP clients. Necessary only when the client has a local printer driver for the Samba printer.

use mmap = boolean [global]

Allowable values: YES, NO   **Default:** varies

Tells Samba whether the *mmap()* system call works correctly on the Samba host. Default is automatically set correctly. Do not change.

use rhosts = boolean [global]

Allowable values: YES, NO   **Default:** NO

If set to YES, users' *~/.rhosts* files will be used to identify systems from which users can connect without providing a password. Discouraged. Obsolete in Samba 3.0.

use sendfile = boolean

Allowable values: YES, NO   **Default:** NO

If yes, Samba will perform some data transfers for exclusively oplocked files using the *sendfile()* system call, which results in significant performance improvements. This is available if Samba has been configured with the `--with-sendfile-support` option. This is an experimental option and is new in Samba 2.2.5.

user = user list

Allowable values: user list   **Default:** NULL

Synonym for username.

username = user list

Allowable values: user list   **Default:** NULL

Sets a list of users that are tried when logging on with share-level security in effect. Also called user or users. Discouraged. Use `NET USE \\`*server*`\`*share*`%`*user* from the client instead.

username level = number
[global]

Allowable values: number

Default: 0

Specifies the number of uppercase-letter permutations allowed to match Unix usernames. A workaround for Windows' single-case usernames. Use is discouraged.

username map = filename
[global]

Allowable values: name of file

Default: NULL

Names a file of Unix-to-Windows name pairs; used to map different spellings of account names and Windows usernames longer than eight characters.

users = user list

Allowable values: user list

Default: NULL

Synonym for username.

utmp = boolean
[global]

Allowable values: YES, NO

Default: NO

This is available if Samba has been configured with the --with-utmp option. If set, Samba adds *utmp/utmpx* records whenever a connection is made to a Samba server. Sites can use this option to record each connection to a Samba share as a system login.

utmp directory = directory
[global]

Allowable values: name of directory

Default: NULL

This is available if Samba has been configured with the --with-utmp option. If this option and utmp are set, Samba will look in the specified directory rather than the default system directory for *utmp/utmpx* files.

valid chars = list

Allowable values: list of numeric values

Default: NULL

Adds national characters to a character set map. See also client code page. Obsolete in Samba 3.0.

valid users = user list

Allowable values: user list

Default: NULL (allows everyone)

Specifies a list of users that can connect to a share. See also invalid users.

veto files = slash-separated list

Allowable values: slash-separated list of filenames   **Default:** NULL

Specifies a list of files that the client will not see when listing a directory's contents. See also delete veto files and hide files.

veto oplock files = slash-separated list

Allowable values: slash-separated list of filenames   **Default:** NULL

Specifies a list of files not to oplock (and cache on clients). See also oplocks and fake oplocks.

vfs object = filename

Allowable values: full path to shared library   **Default:** NULL

Specifies the shared library to use for Samba's Virtual File System (VFS). Requires the --with-vfs configure option.

vfs options = string

Allowable values: space-separated list of options   **Default:** NULL

Specifies parameters to the VFS. Requires the --with-vfs configure option. See vfs object.

volume = string

Allowable values: share name   **Default:** NULL

Sets the volume label of a disk share. Especially useful with shared CD-ROMs.

wide links = boolean

Allowable values: YES, NO   **Default:** YES

If set, Samba follows symlinks out of the disk share. See also the root dir and follow symlinks options.

winbind cache time = number   [global]

Allowable values: number of seconds   **Default:** 15

Sets the amount of time that the *winbindd* daemon caches user and group information.

winbind enum users = boolean   [global]

Allowable values: YES/NO   **Default:** YES

If set to NO, enumeration of users is suppressed by winbind. Discouraged.

winbind enum groups = boolean [global]

Allowable values: YES/NO   **Default:** YES

If set to NO, enumeration of groups is suppressed by winbind. Discouraged.

winbind gid = numeric range [global]

Allowable values: integer-integer   **Default:** NULL

Specifies the group ID range winbind uses for Windows NT domain users connecting to Samba.

winbind separator = character [global]

Allowable values: ASCII character   **Default:** \

Specifies the character winbind uses to separate a domain name and username.

winbind uid = numeric range [global]

Allowable values: integer-integer   **Default:** NULL

Specifies the user ID range winbind will use for Windows NT domain users connecting to Samba.

wins hook = command [global]

Allowable values: full path to script   **Default:** NULL

Specifies a command to run whenever the WINS server updates its database. Allows WINS to be synchronized with DNS or other services. The command is passed one of the arguments add, delete, or refresh, followed by the NetBIOS name, the name type (two hexadecimal digits), the TTL in seconds, and the IP addresses corresponding to the NetBIOS name. Requires wins service = YES.

wins proxy = boolean [global]

Allowable values: YES, NO   **Default:** NO

If set to YES, *nmbd* proxies resolution requests to WINS servers on behalf of old clients, which use broadcasts. The WINS server is typically on another subnet.

wins server = value [global]

Allowable values: hostname or IP address   **Default:** NULL

Sets the DNS name or IP address of the WINS server.

wins support = boolean

[global]

Allowable values: YES, NO **Default:** NO

If set to YES, activates the WINS service. The wins server option must not be set if wins support = YES.

workgroup = name

[global]

Allowable values: workgroup name **Default:** compiled-in

Sets the workgroup or domain to which the Samba server belongs. Overrides the compiled-in default of WORKGROUP. Choosing a name other than WORKGROUP is highly recommended.

writable = boolean

Allowable values: YES, NO **Default:** YES

Antonym for read only; writeable and write ok are synonyms.

writeable = boolean

Allowable values: YES, NO **Default:** YES

Antonym for read only; writable and write ok are synonyms.

write cache size = number

Allowable values: decimal number of bytes **Default:** 0 (disabled)

Allocates a write buffer of the specified size in which Samba accumulates data before a write to disk. This option can be used to ensure that each write has the optimal size for a given filesystem. It is typically used with RAID drives, which have a preferred write size, and with systems that have large memory and slow disks.

write list = user list

Allowable values: user list **Default:** NULL

Specifies a list of users that are given read/write access to a read-only share. See also read list.

write ok = boolean

Allowable values: YES, NO **Default:** YES

Synonym for writable.

write raw = boolean [global]

Allowable values: YES, NO **Default:** YES

Allows fast-streaming writes over TCP using 64KB buffers. Recommended.

Glossary of Configuration Value Types

boolean
> One of two values, either YES or NO.

character
> A single ASCII character.

command
> A Unix script or compiled program, with an absolute path specified for the executable and parameters.

directory
> An absolute path specification to a directory. For example:
>
>   /usr/local/samba/lib

filename
> An absolute path specification to a file. For example:
>
>   /etc/printcap

host list
> A list of hosts. Allows IP addresses, address masks, domain names, ALL, and EXCEPT.

interface list
> A list of interfaces, in either address/netmask or address/n-bits format. For example:
>
>   192.168.2.10/255.255.255.0, 192.168.2.10/24

map list
> A list of filename remapping strings such as (*.html *.htm).

name
> A single name of a type of object, as specified in the option's description.

number
> A positive integer.

numeric range
> Two numbers separated by a dash, specifying a minimum and a maximum value. For example:
>
>   100-250

remote list
> A list of subnet-broadcast-address/workgroup pairs. For example:
>
>   192.168.2.255/SERVERS 192.168.4.255/STAFF

service (share) list

>A list of service (share) names, without the enclosing parentheses.

slash-separated list

>A list of filenames, separated by "/" characters to allow embedded spaces. For example:

>>`/.*/My Documents/*.doc/`

string

>One line of arbitrary text.

user list

>A list of usernames and/or group names. *@group_name* includes whomever is in the NIS netgroup *group_name*, if one exists, or otherwise whomever is in the Unix group *group_name*. In addition, *+group_name* is a Unix group, *&group_name* is an NIS netgroup, and &+ and +& cause an ordered search of both Unix and NIS groups.

value

>A value of some miscellaneous type, as specified in the option's description.

Configuration File Variables

Table B-1 lists the Samba configuration file variables.

Table B-1. Configuration file variables

Name	Meaning
%a	Client's architecture (Samba, WfWg, WinNT, Win95, or UNKNOWN)
%d	Current server process's process ID
%D	User's Windows NT Domain
%f	Printer spool file as a relative path (printing only)
%f	User from which a message was sent (messages only)
%G	Primary group name of %U (requested username)
%g	Primary group name of %u (actual username)
%H	Home directory of %u (actual username)
%h	Samba server's (Internet) hostname
%I	Client's IP address
%j	Print job number (printing only)
%L	Samba server's NetBIOS name (virtual servers have multiple names)
%M	Client's (Internet) hostname
%m	Client's NetBIOS name
%N	Name of the NIS home directory server (without NIS, same as %L)
%n	New password (password change only)

Table B-1. Configuration file variables (continued)

Name	Meaning
%o	Old password (password change only)
%P	Current share's root directory (actual)
%p	Current share's root directory (in an NIS homedir map)
%p	Print filename (printing only)
%R	Protocol level in use (CORE, COREPLUS, LANMAN1, LANMAN2, or NT1)
%S	Current share's name
%s	Name of the file in which the message resides (messages only)
%s	Printer spool filename (printing only)
%T	Current date and time
%t	Destination system (messages only)
%U	Requested username for current share
%u	Current share's username
%v	Samba version
%$name	Value of environment variable name

Summary of Samba
Daemons and Commands

This appendix is a reference listing of command-line options and other information to help you use the programs that come with the Samba distribution.

Samba Daemons

The following sections provide information about the command-line parameters for *smbd*, *nmbd*, and *winbindd*.

smbd

The *smbd* program provides Samba's file and printer services, using one TCP/IP stream and one daemon per client. It is controlled from */usr/local/samba/lib/smb.conf*, the default configuration file, which can be overridden by command-line options.

The configuration file is automatically reevaluated every minute. If it has changed, most new options are immediately effective. You can force Samba to reload the configuration file immediately by sending a SIGHUP signal to *smbd*. Reloading the configuration file does not affect any clients that are already connected. To escape this condition, a client would need to disconnect and reconnect, or the server itself would have to be restarted, forcing all clients to reconnect.

Other Signals

To shut down an *smbd* process, send it the termination signal SIGTERM (15), which allows it to die gracefully, instead of a SIGKILL (9). With Samba versions prior to 2.2, the debugging level could be raised or lowered using SIGUSR1 or SIGUSR2. This is no longer supported. Use *smbcontrol* instead.

Command synopsis

```
smbd [options]
```

Options

-a

    Causes each new connection to the Samba server to append all logging messages to the log file. This option is the opposite of -o and is the default.

-D

    Runs the *smbd* program as a daemon. This is the recommended way to use *smbd*. It is also the default action when *smbd* is run from an interactive command line. In addition, *smbd* can be run from *inetd*.

-d *debug_level*

    Sets the debug (sometimes called logging) level. The level can range from 0 to 10. Specifying the value on the command line overrides the value specified in the *smb.conf* file. Debug level 0 logs only the most important messages; level 1 is normal; levels 3 and above are primarily for debugging and slow *smbd* considerably.

-h

    Prints usage information for the *smbd* command.

-i

    Runs *smbd* interactively, rather than as a daemon. This option is used to override the default daemon mode when *smbd* is run from the command line.

-l *log_directory*

    Sends the log messages to somewhere other than the location compiled into the executable or specified in the *smb.conf* file. The default is often */usr/local/samba/var/*, */usr/samba/var/*, or */var/log/*. The log file is placed in the specified directory and named *log.smbd*. If the directory does not exist, Samba's compiled-in default will be used.

-O *socket_options*

    Sets the TCP/IP socket options, using the same parameters as the socket options configuration option. Often used for performance tuning and testing.

-o

    Causes log files to be overwritten when opened (the opposite of -a). Using this option saves you from hunting for the right log entries if you are performing a series of tests and inspecting the log file each time.

-p *port_number*

    Sets the TCP/IP port number from which the server will accept requests. All Microsoft clients send to the default port of 139, except for Windows 2000/XP, which can use port 445 for SMB networking, without the NetBIOS protocol layer.

-P

    Causes *smbd* to run in "passive" mode, in which it just listens, and does not transmit any network traffic. This is useful only for debugging by developers.

-s *configuration_file*

    Specifies the location of the Samba configuration file. Although the file defaults to */usr/local/samba/lib/smb.conf*, you can override it on the command line. Typically used for debugging.

-v

    Prints the current version of Samba.

nmbd

The *nmbd* program is Samba's NetBIOS name service and browsing daemon. It replies to NetBIOS over TCP/IP (also called NetBT or NBT) name-service requests broadcast from SMB clients, and optionally to Microsoft's Windows Internet Name Service (WINS) requests. Both are versions of the name-to-address lookup required by SMB clients. The broadcast version uses UDP broadcast on the local subnet only, while WINS uses TCP, which can be routed. If running as a WINS server, *nmbd* keeps a current name and address database in the file */usr/local/samba/var/locks/wins.dat*.

An active *nmbd* daemon also responds to browsing protocol requests used by the Windows Network Neighborhood. This protocol provides a dynamic directory of servers, as well as the disks and printers that the servers are providing. As with WINS, this was initially done by making UDP broadcasts on the local subnet. With the addition of the local master browser to the network architecture, it is done by making TCP connections to a server. If *nmbd* is acting as a local master browser, it stores the browsing database in the file */usr/local/samba/var/locks/browse.dat*.

Some clients (especially older ones) cannot use the WINS protocol. To support these clients, *nmbd* can act as a WINS proxy, accepting broadcast requests from the non-WINS clients, contacting a WINS server on their behalf, and returning the WINS server's response to them.

Signals

Like *smbd*, the *nmbd* program responds to several Unix signals. Sending *nmbd* a SIGHUP signal causes it to dump the names it knows about to the */usr/local/samba/var/locks/namelist.debug* file. To shut down an *nmbd* process and allow it to die gracefully, send it a SIGTERM (15) signal, rather than a SIGKILL (9). With Samba versions prior to 2.2, the debugging level could be raised or lowered using SIGUSR1 or SIGUSR2. This is no longer supported. Use *smbcontrol* instead.

Command synopsis

```
nmbd [options]
```

Options

-a

Causes each new connection to the Samba server to append all logging messages to the log file. This option is the opposite of -o and is the default.

-d *debug_level*

Sets the debug (sometimes called logging) level. The level can range from 0 to 10. Specifying the value on the command line overrides the value specified in the *smb.conf* file. Debug level 0 logs only the most important messages; level 1 is normal; levels 3 and above are primarily for debugging and slow *nmbd* considerably.

-D

Instructs the *nmbd* program to run as a daemon. This is the recommended way to use *nmbd* and is the default when *nmbd* is run from an interactive shell. In addition, *nmbd* can be run from *inetd*.

-h

> Prints usage information for the *nmbd* command.

-H *lmhosts_file*

> Specifies the location of the *lmhosts* file for name resolution. This file is used only to resolve names for the local server, and not to answer queries from remote systems. The compiled-in default is commonly */usr/local/samba/lib/lmhosts*, */usr/samba/lib/lmhosts*, or */etc/lmhosts*.

-i

> Runs *nmbd* interactively, rather than as a daemon. This option is used to override the default daemon mode when *nmbd* is run from the command line.

-l *log_file*

> Sends the log messages to somewhere other than the location compiled into the executable or specified in the *smb.conf* file. The default is often */usr/local/samba/var/log.nmbd*, */usr/samba/var/log.nmbd*, or */var/log/log.nmbd*.

-n *NetBIOS_name*

> Allows you to override the NetBIOS name by which the daemon advertises itself. Specifying this option on the command line overrides the netbios name option in the Samba configuration file.

-O *socket_options*

> Sets the TCP/IP socket options, using the same parameters as the socket options configuration option. Often used for performance tuning and testing.

-o

> Causes log files to be overwritten when opened (the opposite of -a). This option saves you from hunting for the right log entries if you are performing a series of tests and inspecting the log file each time.

-p *port_number*

> Sets the UDP port number from which the server accepts requests. Currently, all Microsoft clients use only the default port, 137.

-s *configuration_file*

> Specifies the location of the Samba configuration file. Although the file defaults to */usr/local/samba/lib/smb.conf*, you can override it here on the command line. Typically used for debugging.

-v

> Prints the current version of Samba.

winbindd

The *winbindd* daemon is part of the winbind service and is used to allow Unix systems to obtain user and group information from a Windows NT/2000 server. Winbind maps Windows relative IDs (RIDs) to Unix UIDs and GIDs and allows accounts stored on the Windows server to be used for Unix authentication. Its purpose is to ease integration of Microsoft and Unix networks when a preexisting Windows domain controller is set up to handle user and computer accounts.

The daemon is accessed by users via the name service switch and PAM. The name service switch calls a library (*/lib/libnss_winbind.so*), which calls the daemon, which in turn calls the Windows NT/2000 server using Microsoft RPC. The PAM module for winbind can call the daemon similarly, allowing users whose accounts are stored on the Windows server to log in to the Unix system and run an interactive shell, FTP, or any other program that authenticates users through PAM.

The winbind subsystem is currently available only for the Linux operating system and a few other systems that use shared libraries, nsswitch and PAM.

Command synopsis

```
winbindd [options]
```

Options

-d *debuglevel*

Sets the debug (sometimes called logging) level. The level can range from 0 to 10. Specifying the value on the command line overrides the value specified in the *smb.conf* file. Debug level 0 logs only the most important messages; level 1 is normal; levels 3 and above are primarily for debugging.

-i

Runs *winbindd* interactively. This option is used to override the default, which is for winbindd to detach and run as a daemon.

Samba Distribution Programs

This section lists the command-line options and subcommands provided by each nondaemon program in the Samba distribution.

---

findsmb

This Perl script reports information about systems on the subnet that respond to SMB name-query requests. The report includes the IP address, NetBIOS name, workgroup/domain, and operating system of each system.

Command synopsis

```
findsmb [subnet_broadcast_address]
```

If a different subnet's broadcast address is provided, it will find SMB servers on that subnet. If no subnet broadcast address is supplied, *findsmb* will look on the local subnet.

The output from *findsmb* looks like this:

```
$ findsmb
                              *=DMB
                              +=LMB
    IP ADDR       NETBIOS NAME    WORKGROUP/OS/VERSION
    -----------------------------------------------------------------
```

```
172.16.1.1     TOLTEC     *[METRAN] [Unix] [Samba 2.2.6]
172.16.1.3     MIXTEC     +[METRAN] [Unix] [Samba 2.2.6]
172.16.1.4     ZAPOTEC     [METRAN] [Windows 5.0] [Windows 2000 LAN Manager]
172.16.1.5     HUASTEC    [      METRAN           ]
172.16.1.6     MAYA       [      METRAN           ]
172.16.1.7     OLMEC       [METRAN] [Windows 5.1] [Windows 2000 LAN Manager]
172.16.1.10    UTE        [      METRAN           ]
172.16.1.13    DINE        [METRAN] [Windows NT 4.0] [NT LAN Manager 4.0]
```

The system with an asterisk (*) in front of its workgroup name is the domain master browser for the workgroup/domain, and the system with a plus sign (+) preceding its workgroup name is the local master browser.

The *findsmb* command was introduced during the development of Samba 2.2 and is installed by default in Samba Versions 2.2.5 and later.

make_smbcodepage

This program is part of the internationalization features of Samba 2.2 and is obsolete in Samba 3.0, which supports Unicode automatically. The *make_smbcodepage* program compiles a binary codepage file from a text-format codepage definition. It can also perform the reverse operation, decompiling a binary codepage file into a text version. Examples of text-format codepage files can be found in the Samba distribution in the *source/codepages* directory. After Samba has been installed, examples of binary codepages can be found in the directory */usr/local/samba/lib/codepages*.

Command synopsis

```
make_smbcodepage c|d codepage_number input_file output_file
```

For the first argument, use c to compile a codepage and d to decompile a codepage file. The *codepage_number* argument is the number of the codepage being processed (e.g., 850). The *input_file* and *output_file* are the text- and binary-format codepages, with the types dependent on the operation (compiling or decompiling) that is being performed.

make_unicodemap

This program is part of the internationalization features of Samba 2.2 and is obsolete in Samba 3.0, which supports Unicode automatically. The *make_unicodemap* command compiles binary Unicode maps from text files, so Samba can display non-ASCII characters in file and directory names via the Unicode international alphabets. Examples of input mapping files can be found in the directory *source/codepages* in the Samba source distribution.

Command synopsis

```
make_unicodemap codepage_number inputfile outputfile
```

The input file is an ASCII map; the output file is a binary file loadable by Samba. The codepage is the number of the DOS codepage (e.g., 850) for the map.

net

The *net* command, new to Samba 3.0, is a program with a syntax similar to the MS-DOS/Windows command of the same name. It is used for performing various administrative functions related to Windows networking, which can be executed either locally or on a remote system.

Command synopsis

```
net [method] function [misc_options] [target_options]
```

The *function* argument is made up of one or more space-separated words. In Windows terminology, it is sometimes referred to as a function with options. Here we list every function in its complete form, including multiple words.

By default, the action is performed on the local system. The *target_options* argument can be used to specify a remote system (either by hostname or IP address), a domain, or a workgroup.

Depending on the function, the *method* argument can be optional, required, or disallowed. It specifies one of three methods for performing the operation specified by the rest of the command. It can be ads (Active Directory), rpc (Microsoft's DCE/RPC), or rap (Microsoft's original SMB remote procedure call). To determine which methods (if any) can be used with a function, the net help ads, net help rap, and net help rpc commands can be used to list the functions for each method.

Miscellaneous options

-d *level*

--debug=*level*
> Sets the debug (sometimes called logging) level. The level can range from 0 to 10.

-l

--long
> Specifies the long listing mode. This is provided for functions that print informational listings.

-n *name*

--myname=*name*
> Specifies the NetBIOS name for the client.

-p *port*

--port=*port*
> Specifies the port number to use.

-s *filename*

--conf=*filename*
> Specifies the name of the Samba configuration file, overriding the compiled-in default.

-U *username[%password]*

--user=*username[%password]*
> Specifies the username and, optionally, the password to use for functions that require authentication.

-W *name*

--myworkgroup=*name*

Specifies the name of the client's workgroup, overriding the definition of the workgroup parameter in the Samba configuration file.

Target options

-S *hostname*

Specifies the remote system using a hostname or NetBIOS name.

-I *ip_address*

Specifies the remote system using its IP address.

-w *workgroup*

Specifies the name of the target domain or workgroup.

Functions

abortshutdown

See the rpc abortshutdown function.

ads info

Prints information about the Active Directory server. The method (ads) must be specified to differentiate this function from the rpc info function.

ads join *OU*

Joins the local system to the Active Directory realm (organizational unit) specified by OU. The method (ads) must be specified to differentiate this function from the rpc join function.

ads leave

Removes the local system from the Active Directory realm.

ads password *username@REALM* -U*admin_username@REALM%admin_password*

Changes the Active Directory password for the user specified by *username@REALM*. The administrative account authentication information is specified with the -U option. The Active Directory realm must be supplied in all uppercase.

ads printer info *[printer] [server]*

Prints information on the specified printer on the specified server. The *printer* argument defaults to an asterisk (*), meaning all printers, and the *server* argument defaults to localhost.

ads printer publish *printer_name*

Publishes the specified printer in Active Directory.

ads printer remove *printer_name*

Removes the specified printer from Active Directory.

ads search *expr attrib*

Performs a raw Active Directory search, using the standard LDAP search expression and attributes specified by the *expr* and *attrib* arguments, respectively.

ads status

Prints details about the Active Directory computer account of the system.

change localhost pass

Changes the Active Directory password for the local system's computer trust account.

domain

Lists the domains or workgroups on the network.

file

Lists open files on the server.

file close *file_id*

Closes the specified file.

file info *file_id*

Prints information about the specified file, which must be open.

file user *username*

Lists all files opened on the server by the user specified by *username*.

group add *group_name*

Adds the specified group. This function accepts the miscellaneous option -C *comment* (which can also be specified as --comment=*string*) to set the descriptive comment for the group.

group delete *group_name*

Deletes the specified group.

groupmember add *group_name username*

Adds the user specified by *username* to the group specified by *group_name*.

groupmember delete *group_name username*

Deletes the user specified by *username* from the group specified by *group_name*.

groupmember list *group_name*

Lists the users who are members of the specified group.

help

Prints a help message for the *net* command.

help *method*

Prints a help message for *method*, which can be ads, rap, or rpc. This lists the functions that can use the method, along with a brief description.

help *function*

Prints a help message for the specified function, which can be more than one word.

info

Must be preceded by a method. See the ads info and rpc info functions.

join

Joins the computer to a Windows NT domain or Active Directory realm. If the method argument is not specified, a check is made to determine if Active Directory is in use, and if so, ads join is performed. Otherwise, rpc join is run. See also the ads join and rpc join functions.

leave

Must be preceded by a method. See the ads leave function.

lookup dc *[domain]*

Prints the IP address of the specified domain's domain controllers. The domain defaults to the value of the workgroup parameter in the Samba configuration file.

lookup host *hostname [type]*
> Prints the IP address of the specified host.

lookup kdc *[realm]*
> Prints the IP address of the specified realm's Kerberos domain controller. If *realm* is not specified, it defaults to the value of the realm parameter in the Samba configuration file.

lookup ldap *[domain]*
> Prints the IP address of the specified domain's LDAP server. If *domain* is not specified, it defaults to the value of the workgroup parameter in the Samba configuration file.

lookup master *[domain]*
> Prints the IP address of the master browser of the specified domain or workgroup. If *domain* is not specified, it defaults to the value of the workgroup parameter in the Samba configuration file.

password *username old_password new_password*
> Changes the password for the user specified by the *username* argument. The user's old and new passwords are provided in plain text as part of the command. Be careful regarding security issues. See also the ads password function.

printer info
> See the ads printer info function.

printer publish
> See the ads printer publish function.

printer remove
> See the ads printer remove function.

printq
> Prints information (including the job IDs) about printer queues on the server.

printq delete *queue_name*
> Deletes the specified printer queue. The -j *job_id* (which can also be specified as --jobid=*job_id*) option may be used to specify the job ID of the queue.

rpc abortshutdown
> Aborts the shutdown of a remote server.

rpc info
> Prints information about the server's domain. The method (rpc) must be specified to differentiate this function from the ads info function.

rpc join
> Joins a computer to a Windows NT domain. If the -U *username%password* option is included, the specified username and password will be used as the administrative account required for authenticating with the PDC. If the -U option is not included, this function can be used only to join the computer to the domain after the computer account has been created using the Server Manager. The method (rpc) must be specified to differentiate this function from the ads join function.

rpc shutdown
> Shuts down a server. This function accepts the -r, -f, -t, and -c miscellaneous options. The -r option (which can also be specified as --reboot) requests that the system reboot after shutting down. The -f option (which can also be specified as

--force) forces a shutdown. The -t *timeout* option (which can also be specified as
--timeout=*number*) specifies the number of seconds to wait before shutting down,
and the -c *comment* option (which can also be specified as --comment=*string*) can be
used to specify a message to the client user. On Windows, the comment appears
in the Message area in the System Shutdown dialog box.

rpc trustdom add *domain_name*
> Adds an account for the trust relationship with the specified Windows NT domain.

rpc trustdom establish *domain_name*
> Establishes a trust relationship with the specified Windows NT domain.

rpc trustdom revoke *domain_name*
> Revokes the trust relationship with the specified Windows NT domain.

search
> See the ads search function.

server
> Lists servers in the domain or workgroup, which defaults to the value of the workgroup
> parameter in the Samba configuration file.

session
> Lists clients with open sessions to the server.

session delete NetBIOS_*name*
> Closes the session to the server from the specified client. A synonym is session close.

session close
> A synonym for session delete.

share
> Lists the shares offered by the server. When a Windows 95/98/Me server is the target
> system, it might be necessary to specify the method as rap for this to work properly.

share add *share_name=server_path*
> Adds a share on the target server. The name of the share and the folder to be shared
> are specified by the *share_name=server_path* argument, with *server_path* the Windows
> directory name, with spaces and other special characters (if any) quoted and with the
> backslashes escaped (e.g., "data=C:\\Documents and Settings\\jay\\Desktop\\data").
> The -C *comment* option (which can also be specified as --comment=*string*) can be used
> to define a description for the share. The -M *number* option (which can also be specified
> as --maxusers=*number*) can be used to set the maximum number of users that can
> connect to the share. The method (rap or rpc) might need to be specified for this func-
> tion to work. The regular folder icon cannot change into a "shared folder" icon in
> Windows Explorer until the display is refreshed.

share delete *share_name*
> Deletes a share from the target server. The *share_name* argument is simply the name of
> the share on the target server, not a UNC. The method (rap or rpc) might need to be
> specified for this function to work. The "shared folder" icon in Windows Explorer
> cannot change back to the regular folder icon until the display is refreshed.

shutdown
> See the rpc shutdown function.

status

>See the ads status function.

time

>Displays the system time—in Unix *date* command format—on the target system.

time set

>Sets the local system's hardware clock using the time obtained from the operating system.

time system

>Sets the time on the local system using the time obtained from the remote system.

time zone

>Prints the time zone (in hours from GMT) in use on the system.

trustdom add

>See the rpc trustdom add function.

trustdom establish

>See the rpc trustdom establish function.

trustdom revoke

>See the rpc trustdom revoke function.

user

>Lists user accounts. The method can be specified as ads, rap, or rpc.

user add *username [password]*

>Adds a user account for the user specified by *username*. The -c *comment* option (which can also be specified as --comment=*string*) can be used to set a comment for the account. The -F *user_flags* option can be used to set flags (specified in numeric format) for the account. The method can be specified as ads, rap, or rpc.

user delete *username*

>Deletes the specified user's account. The method can be specified as ads, rap, or rpc.

user info *username*

>Lists the domain groups to which the specified user belongs. The method can be specified as ads, rap, or rpc.

nmblookup

The *nmblookup* program is a client program that allows command-line access to NetBIOS name service for resolving NetBIOS computer names into IP addresses. The program works by broadcasting its queries on the local subnet until a machine with the specified name responds. You can think of it as a Windows analog of *nslookup* or *dig*. This is useful for looking up regular computer names, as well as special-purpose names, such as __MSBROWSE__. If you wish to query for a particular type of NetBIOS name, add the NetBIOS type to the end of the name, using the format *netbios_name#<dd>*.

Command synopsis

    nmblookup [options] netbios_name

Options

-A

Interprets *netbios_name* as an IP address and does a node status query on it.

-B *broadcast_address*

Sends the query to the given broadcast address. The default is to send the query to the broadcast address of the primary network interface.

-d *debug_level*

Sets the debug (sometimes called logging) level. The level can range from 0 to 10. Debug level 0 logs only the most important messages. Level 1 is normal; levels 3 and above are primarily used by developers for debugging the *nmblookup* program itself and slow the program considerably.

-f

Prints the flags in the packet headers.

-h

Prints command-line usage information for the program.

-i *scope*

Sets a NetBIOS scope identifier. NetBIOS scope is a rarely used precursor to workgroups.

-M

Searches for a local master browser by looking up *netbios_name*<1d>. If *netbios_name* is specified as a dash (-), a lookup is done on the special name __MSBROWSE__.

-R

Sets the "recursion desired" bit in the packet. This causes the system that responds to try a WINS lookup and return the address and any other information the WINS server has saved.

-r

Uses the root port of 137. This option exists as a bug workaround for Windows 95. This option might require the user to be superuser.

-S

Performs a node status query once the name query has returned an IP address. This returns all the resource types that the system knows about, including their numeric attributes. For example:

```
$ nmblookup -S toltec
querying toltec on 172.16.1.255
172.16.1.1 toltec<00>
Looking up status of 172.16.1.1
        TOLTEC          <00> -          M <ACTIVE>
        TOLTEC          <03> -          M <ACTIVE>
        TOLTEC          <20> -          M <ACTIVE>
        .._MSBROWSE__. <01> - <GROUP> M <ACTIVE>
        METRAN          <00> - <GROUP> M <ACTIVE>
        METRAN          <1b> -          M <ACTIVE>
        METRAN          <1c> - <GROUP> M <ACTIVE>
        METRAN          <1d> -          M <ACTIVE>
        METRAN          <1e> - <GROUP> M <ACTIVE>
```

-s *configuration_file*
>   Specifies the location of the Samba configuration file. Although the file defaults to */usr/local/samba/lib/smb.conf*, you can override it here on the command line. Normally used for debugging.

-T
>   Translates IP addresses into resolved names.

-U *unicast_address*
>   Performs a unicast query to the specified address. Used with -R to query WINS servers.

Note that *nmblookup* has no option for setting the workgroup. You can get around this by putting workgroup = *workgroup_name* in a file and passing it to *nmblookup* with the -s option.

pdbedit

This program, new to Samba 3.0, can be used to manage accounts that are held in a SAM database. The implementation of the database can be any of the types supported by Samba, including the *smbpasswd* file, LDAP, NIS+ and the *tdb* database library. The user must be the superuser to use this tool.

Command synopsis

>   pdbedit *[options]*

Options

-a
>   Adds the user specified by the -u option to the SAM database. The command issues a prompt for the user's password.

-d *drive_letter*
>   Sets the Windows drive letter to which to map the user's home directory. The drive letter should be specified as a letter followed by a colon—e.g., H:.

-D *debug_level*
>   Sets the debug (sometimes called logging) level. The level can range from 0 to 10. Debug level 0 logs only the most important messages. Level 1 is normal, and levels 3 and above are primarily for debugging.

-e *pwdb_backend*
>   Exports the user account database to another format, written to the specified location. Used for migrating from one type of account database to another. The *pwdb_backend* argument is specified in the format of a database type, followed by a colon, then the location of the database. For example, to export the existing account database to an *smbpasswd* database in the file */usr/local/samba/private/smbpw*, *pwdb_backend* would be specified as smbpasswd:/usr/local/samba/private/smbpw. The allowable database types are smbpasswd, smbpasswd nua, tdbsam, tdbsam nua, ldapsam, ldapsam_nua, and plugin.

-f *full_name*
>   Sets the full name of the user specified with the -u option.

-h *unc*

    Sets the home directory path (as a UNC) for the user specified with the -u option.

-i *pwdb_backend*

    Specifies a password database backend from which to retrieve account information, overriding the one specified by the `passsdb backend` parameter in the Samba configuration file. This, along with the -e option, is useful for migrating user accounts from one type of account database to another. See the -e option regarding how to specify the *pwdb_backend* argument.

-l

    Lists the user accounts in the database. See also the -v option.

-m

    Indicates that the account is a computer account rather than a user account. Used only with the -a option when creating the account. In this case, the -u option specifies the computer name rather than a username.

-p *unc*

    Sets the directory in which the user's profile is kept. The directory is specified as a UNC.

-s *unc*

    Specifies the UNC of the user's logon script.

-u *username*

    Specifies the username of the account to add (with the -a option), delete (with the -x option), or modify.

-v

    Selects verbose mode when listing accounts with the -l option. The account fields will be printed.

-w

    Selects the `smbpasswd` listing mode, for use with the -l option, which prints information in the same format as it would appear in an *smbpasswd* file.

-x

    Deletes the user (specified with the -u option) from the account database.

---

rpcclient

This is a program for issuing administrative commands that are implemented using Microsoft RPCs. It provides access to the RPCs that Windows administrative GUIs use for system management. The *rpcclient* command is mainly for use by advanced users who understand the RPCs. More information on these can be found in Microsoft's Platform Software Development Kit (SDK), available for download from the Microsoft web site at *http://www.microsoft.com*.

You can run a single *rpcclient* command by using the -c `command string` option, or interactively with *rpcclient* prompting for commands.

Command Synopsis

rpcclient *server [options]*

Options

-A *filename*

Specifies a file from which to read the authentication values used in the connection. The format of the file is as follows:

```
username = value
password = value
domain   = value
```

This option is used to avoid password prompts or to have the password appear in plain text inside scripts. The permissions on the file should be very restrictive (0600, for example) to prevent access from unwanted users.

-c *command_string*

Executes a sequence of semicolon-separated commands. Commands are listed in the following section.

-d *debuglevel*

Sets the debug (sometimes called logging) level. The level can range from 0 to 10. Specifying the value on the command line overrides the value specified in the *smb.conf* file. Debug level 0 logs only the most important messages; level 1 is normal; levels 3 and above are primarily for debugging and slow the program considerably.

-h

Prints a summary of options.

-l *logbasename*

Sets the filename for log/debug files. The extension *.client* is appended to the filename.

-N

Does not prompt for a password. This is used when Samba is configured for share-mode security and a service with no password is being accessed.

-s *filename*

Specifies the location of the Samba configuration file, which by default is usually */usr/local/samba/lib/smb.conf*.

-U *username[%password]*

Sets the SMB username or username and password to use. Be careful when specifying the password with *%password*; this is a major security risk. If *%password* is not specified, the user will be prompted for the password, which will not be echoed. Normally the user is set from the USER or LOGNAME environment variable. The -U option by itself means to use the guest account. See also -A.

-W *domain*

Sets the domain, overriding the workgroup parameter in the Samba configuration file. If the domain is the server's NetBIOS name, it causes the client to log on using the server's local SAM database rather than the SAM of the domain.

rpcclient commands

Aside from a few miscellaneous commands, the *rpclient* commands fall into three groups: LSARPC, SAMR, and SPOOLSS. The function names mentioned in some of the commands are those documented in the Microsoft Platform SDK.

General commands

debuglevel *level*
> Sets the debugging level to *level*. With no argument, the current debugging level is printed.

help
> Prints help on the commands.

quit
> Exits *rpcclient*. A synonym is exit.

Local Security Authority Remote Procedure Calls (LSARPC) commands

enumprivs
> Lists the types of privileges known to this domain.

enumtrust
> Lists the domains trusted by this domain.

getdispname *priv_name*
> Prints information on the privilege named *priv_name*.

lookupsids *name*
> Finds a name that corresponds to a security identifier (SID).

lookupnames *sid*
> Finds the SID for one or more names.

lsaquery
> Queries the LSA object.

lsaenumsid
> Lists SIDs for the local LSA.

lsaquerysecobj
> Prints information on security objects for the LSA.

Security Access Manager RPC (SAMR) commands

createdomuser *username*
> Adds a new user in the domain.

deletedomuser *username*
> Removes a user from the domain.

enumalsgroups *type*
> Lists alias groups in the domain, along with their group RIDs. The *type* argument can be either builtin, to list Windows built-in groups such as Administrators and Power Users, or domain, to list groups in the domain. See also the *queryuseraliases* command.

enumdomgroups

Lists the groups in the domain, along with their group RIDs.

queryaliasmem *user_rid*

Prints information regarding alias membership. See also the *queryuseraliases* command.

querydispinfo

Prints out the account database. The information printed includes the RID, username, and full name of each user. The RID is printed in hexadecimal notation and can be used in this form for commands that take a RID as an argument.

querydominfo

Prints information regarding the domain. This includes the name of the domain, as well as the number of users, groups, and aliases.

querygroup *group_rid*

Given a group RID, prints the group name, description, number of members, and group description.

queryuser *user_rid*

Given a user RID, prints the corresponding username, full name, and other information pertaining to the user.

queryuseraliases *type user_rid*

Prints aliases for the user. The *type* argument can be either builtin or domain. Aliases are used with the Windows messaging service and act like usernames, but they can be attached to a computer rather than a user. This allows messages intended for a user to be sent to a computer on which the user is either not logged on, or logged on under another username.

queryusergroups *user_rid*

Prints information on each group inhabited by the user.

querygroupmem *group_rid*

Prints the RID and attributes for each member of the group.

samlookupnames *type username*

Looks up the *username* in the SAM database and prints its associated RID. The *type* argument can be either builtin, to look up built-in Windows usernames, or domain, to look up names in the domain.

samlookuprids *type rid*

Looks up *rid* in the SAM database and prints its associated group or username. The *type* argument can be either builtin, to look up built-in Windows usernames, or domain, to look up names in the domain. The RID argument can be given in either 0xDDD hexadecimal notation or decimal.

samquerysecobj

Prints information on security objects (such as ACLs) in the SAM database.

Windows NT/2000/XP Printing Services (SPOOLSS) commands

adddriver *arch config_file*

Adds a printer driver to the server. The driver files must already exist in the directory returned by *getdriverdir*. The *arch* argument can be one of Windows 4.0 for Windows

95/98/Me, or Windows NT x86, Windows NT PowerPC, Windows Alpha_AXP, and Windows NT R4000. Others might be introduced in the future.

The *config_file* should contain:

```
Long Printer Name:\
Driver File Name:\
Data File Name:\
Config File Name:\
Help File Name:\
NULL:\
Default Data Type:\
```

followed by a comma-separated list of files. Any empty fields should contain the string NULL.

addprinter *printername sharename drivername port*

Adds a printer on the remote server as *sharename*. The printer driver must already be installed on the server with *adddriver*, and the port must be a valid port name returned by *enumports*.

deldriver *drivername*

Deletes a printer driver (for all architectures) from the server's list of printer drivers.

enumports *[level]*

Prints information regarding the printer ports on the server. The *level* argument can be 1 or 2. Level 1 is the default and prints out only the Port Name. Information level 2 is the Port Name, Monitor Name, Description, and Port Type.

enumdrivers *[level]*

Lists all the printer drivers on the system. The *level* argument specifies the information level. Level 1 is the default and prints the Driver Name(s). Level 2 prints the Version, Driver Name, Architecture, Driver Path, Data File, and Config File. Level 3 prints the contents of Level 2, plus the Help File, one or more Dependent Files, Monitor Name, and Default Data Type.

enumprinters *[level]*

Lists all installed printers, regardless of whether they are shared. The *level* argument specifies the information level. Level 1 is the default, and prints Flags, Name, Description, and Comment. Level 2 prints the Server Name, Printer Name, Share Name, Port Name, Driver Name, Comment, Location, Separator File, Print Processor, Data Type, Parameters, Attributes, Priority, Default Priority, Start Time, Until Time, Status, Current Jobs, Average PPM (pages per minute), and a Security Descriptor.

getdriver *[level] printername*

Prints the printer driver information for the given printer. The *level* argument specifies the information level.

Level 1 is the default, and prints the Driver Name. Level 2 prints the Version, Driver Name, Architecture, Driver Path, Data File, and Config File. Level 3 prints the contents of level 2, plus the Help File, one or more Dependent Files, Monitor Name, and Default Data Type.

getdriverdir *arch*

Retrieves the share name and directory for storing printer driver files for a given architecture. Possible values for *arch* are "Windows 4.0" for Windows 95/98/Me, "Windows NT x86" for Windows NT on Intel, "Windows NT PowerPC" for Windows NT on PowerPC,

"Windows Alpha AXP" for Windows NT on Alpha, and "Windows NT R4000" for Windows NT on MIPS. Include the quote marks in the command.

getprinter *printername*

Prints the current printer information. The *level* argument specifies the information level.

openprinter *printername*

Attempts to open and close a specified printer and reports whether it was successful.

setdriver *printername drivername*

Unconditionally updates the printer driver used by an installed printer. Both the printer and printer driver must already be correctly installed on the print server.

setprinter *printername comment*

Assigns a comment string to a printer.

smbcacls

This program provides a way of modifying Windows NT ACLs on files and directories shared by the Samba server.

Command synopsis

    smbcacls //server/share filename [options]

Options

-A *acls*

Adds one or more ACLs to the file or directory. Any ACLs already existing for the file or directory are unchanged.

-M *acls*

Modifies the *mask* of the ACLs specified. Refer to the following section, "Specifying ACLs," for details.

-D *acls*

Deletes the specified ACLs.

-S *acls*

Sets the specified ACLs, deleting any ACLs previously set on the file or directory. The ACLs must contain at least a revision, type, owner, and group.

-U *username*

Sets the username used to connect to the specified service. The user is prompted for a password unless the argument is specified as *username%password*. (Specifying the password on the command line is a security risk.) If -U *domain\\username* is specified, the specified domain or workgroup will be used in place of the one specified in the *smb.conf* file.

-C *username*

Changes the owner of the file or directory. This is a shortcut for -M OWNER:*username*. The *username* argument can be given as a username or a SID in the form S-1-*N-N-D-D-D-R*.

-G *groupname*

Changes the group of the file or directory. This is a shortcut for -M GROUP:*groupname*. The *groupname* argument can be given as a group name or a SID in the form S-1-*N-N-D-D-D-R*.

-n

Causes all ACL information to be displayed in numeric format rather than in readable strings.

-h

Prints a help message.

Specifying ACLs

In the previous options, the same format is always used when specifying ACLs. An ACL is made up of one or more Access Control Entries (ACEs), separated by either commas or escaped newlines. An ACE can be one of the following:

```
REVISION:revision_number
OWNER:username_or_SID
GROUP:group_name_or_SID
ACL:name_or_SID:type/flags/mask
```

The *revision_number* should always be 1. The OWNER and GROUP entries can be used to set the owner and group for the file or directory. The names can be the textual ones or SIDs in the form S-1-*N-N-D-D-D-R*.

The ACL entry specifies what access rights to apply to the file or directory. The *name_or_SID* field specifies to which user or group the permissions apply and can be supplied either as a textual name or a SID. An ACE can be used to either allow or deny access. The *type* field is set to 1 to specify a permission to be allowed or 0 for specifying a permission to deny. The *mask* field is the name of the permission and is one of the following:

R   Read access.

W   Write access.

X   Execute permission.

D   Permission to delete.

P   Change permissions on the object.

O   Take ownership.

The following combined permissions can also be specified:

READ

Equivalent to RX permissions

CHANGE

Equivalent to RWXD permissions

FULL

Equivalent to RWXDPO permissions

The *flags* field is for specifying how objects in directories are to inherit their default permissions from their parent directory. For files, *flags* is normally set to 0. For directories, *flags* is usually set to either 9 or 2.

smbclient

The *smbclient* program is the "Swiss army knife" of the Samba suite. Initially developed as a testing tool, it has become a command shell capable of acting as a general-purpose Unix client, with a command set very similar to that of *ftp*. It offers the following set of functions:

- Interactive file transfer, similar to *ftp*
- Interactive printing to shared SMB printers
- Interactive tar format archiving
- Sending messages on the SMB network
- Batch mode tar format archiving
- "What services do you have?" querying
- Debugging

Command synopsis

```
smbclient //server/share [password] [options]
```

It is possible to run *smbclient* noninteractively, for use in scripts, by specifying the -c option along with a list of commands to execute. Otherwise, *smbclient* runs in interactive mode, prompting for commands such as this:

```
smb:\>
```

The backslash in the prompt is replaced by the current directory within the share as you change your working directory with *smbclient*'s *cd* command.

Options

-A *authfile*

Specifies a file from which to read the username and password used for the connection. The format of the file is as follows:

```
username = value
password = value
domain   = value
```

This is to avoid having the password prompted for or have it appear in plain text in scripts. The permissions on the file should be very restrictive (0600, for example) to prevent access by unwanted users.

-b *buffer_size*

Sets the size of the buffer used when transferring files. It defaults to 65520 bytes and can be changed as a tuning measure. Generally it should be quite large or set to match the size of the buffer on the remote system. It can be set smaller to work around Windows bugs: some Windows 98 systems work best with a buffer size of 1200.

-B *IP_addr*

Sets the broadcast address.

-c *command_string*

Passes a command string to the *smbclient* command interpreter. The argument consists of a semicolon-separated list of commands to be executed.

-d debug_level
> Sets the debug (logging) level, from 0 to 10, with A for all. Overrides the value in *smb.conf*. Debug level 0 logs only the most important messages; level 1 is normal; debug levels 3 and above are for debugging and slow *smbclient* considerably.

-D init_dir
> Upon starting up, causes *smbclient* to change its working directory to *init_dir* on the remote host.

-E
> Sends output from commands to *stderr* instead of *stdout*.

-h
> Prints the command-line help information (usage) for *smbclient*.

-I IP_address
> Sets the IP address of the server to which the client connects.

-i scope
> Sets a NetBIOS scope identifier.

-l log_file
> Sends the log messages to *log_file* rather than to the log file specified in the Samba configuration file or the compiled-in default.

-L server
> Lists services (shares) offered by the server. This can be used as a quick way to test an SMB server to see if it is working. If there is a name-service problem, use the -I option to specify the server.

-M NetBIOS_name
> Allows you to send messages using the Windows messaging protocol. Once a connection is established, you can type your message, pressing Ctrl-D to end. The -U and -I options can be used to control the "From" and "To" parts of the message.

-N
> Suppresses the password prompt. Useful when using share mode security and accessing a service that has no password.

-n NetBIOS_name
> Allows you to override the NetBIOS name by which *smbclient* will advertise itself.

-O socket_options
> Sets the TCP/IP socket options using the same parameters as the socket options configuration option. Often used for performance tuning and testing.

-p port_number
> Sets the port number with which *smbclient* will connect.

-R resolve_order
> Sets the resolve order of the name servers. This option is similar to the resolve order configuration option and can take any of the four parameters lmhosts, host, wins, and bcast, in any order. If more than one is specified, the argument is specified as a space-separated list. This option can be used to test name service by specifying only the name service to be tested.

-s filename
> Specifies the location of the Samba configuration file. Used for debugging.

-t *terminal_code*

Sets the terminal code for Asian languages.

-T *command_string tarfile*

Runs the tar archiver, which is *gtar* compatible. The tar file that is written to or read from is specified by *tarfile*. The two main commands are c (create) and x (extract), which can be followed by any of these:

a

Resets the archive attribute on files after they have been saved. See also the g option.

b *size*

Sets the block size for writing the tar file, in 512-byte units.

g

Backs up only files that have their archive bit set. See also the a option.

I *filename*

Includes files and directories. This is the default, so specifying this is redundant. To perform pattern matching, see also the r option.

N *filename*

Backs up only those files newer than *file*.

q

Suppresses diagnostics.

r

Performs regular expression matching, which can be used along with the I or E option to include or exclude files.

X *filename*

Excludes files and directories.

-U *username*

Sets the username and, optionally, the password used for authentication when connecting to the share.

-W *workgroup*

Specifies the workgroup/domain in which *smbclient* will claim to be a member.

smbclient commands

help *[smbclient_command]*

With no command specified, prints a list of available commands. If a command is specified as an argument, a brief help message will be printed for it.

! *[shell_command]*

Shell escape. With no command specified, runs a Unix shell. If a command is specified, runs the command in a Unix shell.

altname *filename*

Causes *smbclient* to request from the server and then print the old-style, 8.3-format filename for the specified file.

cancel *print_jobid [...]*
> Causes *smbclient* to request the server to cancel one or more print jobs, as specified by the numeric job IDs provided as arguments. See also the *queue* command, which prints job IDs.

chmod *filename octal_mode*
> Requests that the server change the Unix file permissions on *filename* to *octal_mode*, specified in octal numeric format. Works only if the server supports Unix CIFS extensions.

chown *filename UID GID*
> Requests that the server change the owner and group of the file specified by *filename* to those provided as decimal numeric arguments *UID* and *GID*. Works only if the server supports Unix CIFS extensions.

cd *[directory]*
> With no argument, prints the current working directory on the remote system. If a directory name is supplied as an argument, changes the working directory on the remote system to that specified.

del *filename*
> Requests that the server delete one or more files, as specified by the argument, from the current working directory. The argument can be a filename globbing pattern using the * and ? characters.

dir *[filename]*
> With no arguments, prints a list of files and directories in the working directory on the server. If an argument is provided, only files and directories whose names match the argument will be listed. The argument can be a filename globbing pattern using the * and ? characters.

exit
> Quits the *smbclient* program after terminating the SMB connection to the server.

get *remote_file [local_file]*
> Copies the file specified by *remote_file* from the server to the local system. If no *local_file* argument is specified, *smbclient* will name the local file the same as it is named on the server. If *local_file* is specified, it will be used as the name of the local copy. See also the *lowercase* command.

help *[command]*
> A synonym for the *?* command.

lcd *[directory]*
> If no argument is provided, prints the name of *smbclient*'s working directory on the local system. If a directory name is provided as an argument, changes *smbclient*'s working directory to the directory specified.

link *link_name filename*
> Requests that the server create a hard link to *filename* and name it *link_name*. This command works only if the server supports Unix CIFS extensions.

lowercase
> Toggles the boolean lowercasing setting. When this setting is on, names of files copied from the server with the *get* and *mget* commands will be changed to all lowercase. This is mainly used for accessing servers that report filenames in all uppercase only.

ls *[filename]*

> A synonym for *dir*.

mask *[globbing_pattern]*

> Sets the filename globbing pattern for use with the *mget* and *mput* commands when recursion is turned on. (When recursion is off, the setting has no effect.) Both *mget* and *mput* accept a globbing pattern as arguments; however, those patterns apply only to the current directory. This command specifies the pattern used for all subdirectories that are recursively traversed. The pattern stays in effect until it is changed with another *mask* command. To return the setting to its original default, specify a *globbing_pattern* of an asterisk (*), which matches all files. See also the *mget*, *mput*, and *recurse* commands.

mdir *directory*

> A synonym for the *mkdir* command.

mget *pattern*

> When recursion is turned off, copies files matching the file-globbing pattern, as specified by the argument, from the current working directory on the server to the local system. When recursion is on, the *pattern* argument is used to match directories in the current working directory, and the pattern specified by the *mask* command is used for matching files within each directory and all subdirectories. See also the *lowercase*, *mask*, and *recurse* commands.

print *filename*

> Prints the specified file. This requires that *smbclient* be connected to a print share. See also the *printmode* command.

printmode *mode*

> Sets the mode that is used by the *print* command. The mode can be either text, for printing text files such as the ASCII files commonly found on Unix, or graphics, for printing binary files.

prompt

> Toggles the prompting mode. When prompting is on (the default), the *mget* and *mput* commands will interactively prompt the user for permission to transfer each file. The user can answer either y (yes) or n (no), followed by a newline, to this prompt. When prompting is off, all the files will be transferred with no prompts issued.

put *local_file [remote_file]*

> Copies the file specified by *local_file* from the local to the remote system. If no *remote_file* argument is specified, *smbclient* will name the remote file the same as it is named on the local system. If *remote_file* is specified, it will be used as the name of the remote copy. See also the *lowercase* command.

queue

> Prints information on the print queue on the server. This requires that *smbclient* is connected to a print share.

quit

> A synonym for *exit*.

rd *directory*

> A synonym for *rmdir*.

recurse

> Toggles the recursion mode, which affects the *mget* and *mput* commands. When recursion is off (the default), the *mget* and *mput* commands will copy only files from the current working directory that match the file-globbing pattern specified as an argument to the command, and the pattern set by the *mask* command is ignored. When recursion is turned on, the *mget* and *mput* commands recursively traverse any directories that match the pattern specified as the argument to the command, and the pattern set by the *mask* command is used to match files in those directories.

rm *filename*

> A synonym for *del*.

rmdir *directory*

> Requests that the server remove the specified directory.

setmode *filename attributes*

> Requests that the server assign the specified MS-DOS file attributes on the specified file. The *attributes* argument has the format of a leading plus sign (+) or minus sign (-) either to set or to unset the attribute(s), respectively, followed by one or more of the characters r (read), s (system), h (hidden), or a (archive).

symlink *link_name filename*

> Requests that the server create a symbolic link named *link_name* to *filename*. This command works only if the server supports Unix CIFS extensions. The server will not create a link that refers to a file not in the share to which *smbclient* is connected.

tar *cmd_str*

> Performs an archiving operation using the tar format. This is the interactive form of the -T command-line operation, and the *cmd_str* argument is specified in the same manner. See also the *tarmode* command.

blocksize *size*

> Sets the block size, in units of 512 bytes, for files written by the *tar* command.

tarmode *mode ...*

> Specifies how the *tar* command performs its archiving, including how it handles the archive attribute on files. Multiple *mode* arguments can be provided, chosen from the following:
>
> full
>
> > All files will be included, regardless of whether their archive attribute is set. This is the default.
>
> inc
>
> > Only files that have the archive attribute set will be included in the backup.
>
> reset
>
> > The archive attribute will be unset by *tar* after the file is included in the archive.
>
> noreset
>
> > The archive attribute will be left unchanged. This is the default.
>
> system
>
> > Files with the system attribute set will be included in the archive. This is the default.

nosystem

> Files with the system attribute set will not be included in the archive.

hidden

> Files with the hidden attribute set will be included in the archive. This is the default.

nohidden

> Files with the hidden attribute set will not be included in the archive.

verbose

> As files are included in the archive (when creating the archive) or are read from the archive (when extracting it), the name of each file will be printed. This is the default.

noverbose

> This turns verbose mode off, causing *tar* to perform its work quietly.

quiet

> An antonym for the verbose mode. When quiet is on, verbose is off, and vice versa.

smbcontrol

The *smbcontrol* command sends control messages to running *smbd* or *nmbd* processes.

Command synopsis

```
smbcontrol -i [options]
```

or:

```
smbcontrol [options] process message-type [parameters]
```

Options

-i

> Runs *smbcontrol* interactively, executing commands until a blank line or "q" is read. The user must have superuser privileges.

-s *filename*

> Specifies the location of the Samba configuration file.

-d *debuglevel*

> Sets the debugging level for logging. The debug level can be set from 0 to 10.

Whether *smbcontrol* commands are issued in interactive mode or from the command line, the commands are in the same format. Each command has up to three parts:

process

> Specifies the process or group of processes to which to send the message. If *process* is smbd, all *smbd* processes will receive the message. If *process* is nmbd, only the main *nmbd* process (identified by Samba's *nmbd.pid* file) receives the message. If *process* is the numeric PID of a running process on the system, that process will receive the message.

message-type

> Specifies the type of message that is sent. For more information, see the section "smbcontrol message types" that follows.

parameters

Specifies additional parameters required by some messages.

smbcontrol message types

close-share *share_name*

Closes the connection to a share or shares. If *share_name* is specified as an asterisk (*), connections to all shares will be closed. To close a single connection, *share_name* is given as the name of a share, as specified in the Samba configuration file, not including the enclosing brackets. Warning: no message is printed if there is an error in specifying *share_name*.

debug *num*

Sets the debugging level. The *num* parameter specifies the level, which can be from 0 to 10.

debuglevel

Prints the current debugging level.

force-election

Can be used only with *nmbd*, telling it to force a master browser election.

ping *number*

Sends *number* of pings and reports when they receive a reply or timeout. Used for connectivity testing.

profile *mode*

Controls profiling statistics collection. If *mode* is on, profile statistics will be collected. If *mode* is off, collection of statistics is turned off. If *mode* is specified as count, only counting statistics are collected (and not timing statistics). If *mode* is flush, the data set is cleared (initialized).

profilelevel

Prints the current profiling level.

printer-notify *printer_name*

Sends a printer notify message to Windows NT/2000/XP for the specified printer. This message can be sent only to *smbd*. Warning: no message is printed if the *printer_name* parameter is specified incorrectly.

smbgroupedit

This command, new to Samba 3.0, sets up mappings between Unix groups and Windows NT/2000/XP groups and also allows a Unix group to become a domain group. This command must be run by the superuser.

Command synopsis

smbgroupedit *[options]*

Options

-a *Unix_group_name*

Adds a mapping for the specified Unix group. The -n option is used along with this option to specify the Windows NT group to which the Unix group is mapped.

-c *SID*

Changes a mapping between a Windows NT group and a Unix group. The Windows NT group is specified as a SID with this option, and the Unix group is specified with the -u option.

-d *description*

Specifies a comment for the mapping, which will be stored along with it.

-l

When used with the -v option, prints a long listing. This is the default. The information printed includes the name of the Windows NT group, its SID, its corresponding Unix group (if a mapping has been defined), the group type, the comment, and the privileges of the group.

-n *Windows_group_name*

Specifies the name of the Windows NT group. Used with the -a option.

-p *privilege*

Used along with the -a option to specify a Windows NT privilege to be given to the Unix group.

-s

When used with the -v option, prints a short listing. The information printed includes just the name of the Windows NT group, its SID, and, if a mapping has been defined, its corresponding Unix group. This option is useful for determining the SID of a group, for use with the -c option.

-t *TYPE*

Assigns a Windows group type to the group. *TYPE* is a single character, and is one of b (built-in), d (domain), or l (local).

-u *Unix_group_name*

Specifies the name of the Unix group to map to the Windows NT group. Used with the -c option.

-v

Prints a list of groups in the Windows NT domain in which the Samba server is operating. See also the -l and -s options.

-x *Unix_group_name*

Deletes the mapping for the Unix group specified.

smbmnt

This is a low-level helper program for mounting smbfs filesystems. It used by *smbmount* to do the privileged part of the mount operation on behalf of an ordinary user. Generally, users should not run this command directly.

Command synopsis

```
smbmnt mnt_point [options]
```

Options

-r

Mounts the filesystem as read-only.

-u *uid*

Specifies the UID to use for the owner of the files.

-g *gid*

Specifies the GID to use for the group of the files.

-f *mask*

Specifies the octal file mask.

-d *mask*

Specifies the octal directory mask.

-o *options*

Specifies the list of options that are passed to the smbfs module.

To allow users to mount SMB shares without help from an administrator, set the "set user ID" permission on the *smbmnt* executable. However, note that this can raise security issues.

---

smbmount

This program mounts an smbfs filesystem on a mount point in the Unix filesystem. It is typically called as *mount.smb* from *mount*, although it can also be run directly by users. After mounting the smbfs filesystem, *smbmount* continues to run as a daemon as long as the filesystem is mounted. It logs events in the file *log.smbmount* in the same directory as the other Samba log files (which is commonly */usr/local/samba/var* by default). The logging level is controlled by the debug level parameter in the Samba configuration file.

Command synopsis

        smbmount *service mount_point [-o options]*

The service argument specifies the SMB share to mount, given as a UNC. The *mount_point* argument specifies a directory to use as the mount point. The options to *smbmount* are specified as a comma-separated list of *key=value* pairs. The documented options are as follows. Others can be passed if the kernel supports them.

Options

username=*name*

Specifies the username to connect as. If this is not provided, the environment variable USER will be tried. The name can be specified as *username%password*, *user/workgroup*, or *user/workgroup%password*.

password=*string*

Specifies the SMB password. If no password is provided using this option, the *username* option, or the *credentials* option, the environment variable PASSWD is used. If that also does not exist, *smbmount* will prompt interactively for a password.

`credentials=`*`filename`*

> Specifies a file that contains a username and password in the following format:
>
> ```
> username = value
> password = value
> ```

`uid=`*`number`*

> Sets the Unix user ID to be used as the owner of all files in the mounted filesystem. It can be specified as a username or numeric UID. Defaults to the UID of the user running *smbmount*.

`gid=`*`number`*

> Sets the Unix group ID to be used as the group for all files in the mounted filesystem. It can be specified as a group name or a numeric GID. Defaults to the GID of the user running *smbmount*.

`port=`*`number`*

> Sets the TCP port number. This is 139, which is required by most Windows versions.

`fmask=`*`octal_mask`*

> Sets the Unix permissions of all files in the mounted filesystem. Defaults to the user's current umask.

`dmask=`*`octal_mask`*

> Sets the Unix permissions of all directories in the mounted filesystem. Defaults to the current umask.

`debug=`*`number`*

> Sets the debugging level.

`ip=`*`host`*

> Sets the destination hostname or IP address.

`netbiosname=`*`name`*

> Sets the computer name to connect as. This defaults to the hostname of the local system.

`workgroup=`*`name`*

> Sets the workgroup or domain.

`sockopt=`*`opts`*

> Sets TCP socket options.

`scope=`*`num`*

> Sets the NetBIOS scope.

`guest`

> Don't expect or prompt for a password.

`ro`

> Mounts the share read-only.

`rw`

> Mounts the share read-write.

`iocharset=`*`charset`*

> Sets the charset used by the Linux machine for codepage-to-charset translation. See also the *codepage* option.

---

codepage=*page*

> Sets the DOS code page. See also the *iocharset* option.

ttl=*milliseconds*

> Sets the time to live, in milliseconds, for entries in the directory cache. A higher value gives better performance on large directories and/or slower connections. The default is 1000ms. Try 10000ms (10 seconds) as a starting value if directory operations are visibly slow.

smbpasswd

The *smbpasswd* program provides the general function of managing encrypted passwords. How it works depends on whether it is run by the superuser or an ordinary user.

For the superuser, *smbpasswd* can be used to maintain Samba's *smbpasswd* file. It can add or delete users, change their passwords, and modify other attributes pertaining to the user that are held in the *smbpasswd* file.

When run by ordinary users, *smbpasswd* can be used only to change their encrypted passwords. In this mode of operation, *smbpasswd* acts as a client to the *smbd* daemon. The program will fail if *smbd* is not operating, if the hosts allow or hosts deny parameters in the Samba configuration file do not permit connections from localhost (IP address 127.0.0.1), or if the encrypted passwords option is set to no. It is also possible for *smbpasswd* to change a user's password when it is maintained on a remote system, including a Windows NT domain controller.

Command synopsis

When run by the superuser:

    smbpasswd [options] [username] [password]

In this case, the username of the user whose *smbpasswd* entry is to be modified is provided as the second argument.

Otherwise:

    smbpasswd [options] [password]

Superuser-only options

-a *username*

> Adds a user to the encrypted password file. The user must already exist in the system password file (*/etc/passwd*). If the user already exists in the *smbpasswd* file, the -a option changes the existing password.

-d *username*

> Disables a user in the encrypted password file. The user's entry in the file will remain, but will be marked with a flag disabling the user from authenticating.

-e *username*

> Enables a disabled user in the encrypted password file. This overrides the effect of the -d option.

-j *domain*

Joins the Samba server to a Windows NT domain as a domain member server. The *domain* argument is the NetBIOS name of the Windows NT domain that is being joined. See also the -r and -U options.

-m

Indicates that the account is a computer account in a Windows NT domain rather than a domain user account.

-n

Sets the user's password to a null password. For the user to authenticate, the parameter null passwords = yes must exist in the [global] section of the Samba configuration file.

-R *resolve_order_list*

Sets the resolve order of the name servers. This option is similar to the resolve order configuration option and can take any of the four parameters lmhosts, host, wins, and bcast, in any order. If more than one is specified, the argument is specified as a space-separated list.

-w *password*

For use when Samba has been compiled with the --with-ldapsam configure option. Specifies the password that goes with the value of the ldap admin dn Samba configuration file parameter.

-x *username*

Deletes the user from the *smbpasswd* file. This is a one-way operation, and all information associated with the entry is lost. To disable the account without deleting the user's entry in the file, see the -d option.

Other options

-c *filename*

Specifies the Samba configuration file, overriding the compiled-in default.

-D *debug_level*

Sets the debug (also called logging) level. The level can range from 0 to 10. Debug level 0 logs only the most important messages; level 1 is normal; levels 3 and above are primarily for debugging and slow the program considerably.

-h

Prints command-line usage information.

-L

Causes *smbpasswd* to run in local mode, in which ordinary users are allowed to use the superuser-only options. This requires that the *smbpasswd* file be made readable and writable by the user. This is for testing purposes.

-r *NetBIOS_name*

Specifies on which machine the password should change. If changing a Windows NT domain password, the remote system specified by *NetBIOS_name* must be the PDC for the domain. The user's username on the local system is used by default. See also the -U option for use when the user's Samba username is different from the local username.

-R *resolve_order*
  Sets the resolve order of the name servers. This option is similar to the resolve order configuration option and can take any of the four parameters lmhosts, host, wins, and bcast, in any order. If more than one is specified, the argument is specified as a space-separated list.

-s *username*
  Causes *smbpasswd* not to prompt for passwords from */dev/tty*, but instead to read the old and new passwords from the standard input. This is useful when calling *smbpasswd* from a script.

-S
  Queries the domain controller of the domain, as specified by the workgroup parameter in the Samba configuration file, and retrieves the domain's SID. This will then be used as the SID for the local system. A specific PDC can be selected by combining this option with the -r option, and its domain's SID will be used. This option is for migrating domain accounts from a Windows NT primary domain controller to a Samba PDC.

-U *username[%password]*
  Changes the password for *username* on the remote system. This is to handle instances in which the remote username and local username are different. This option requires that -r also be used. Often used with -j to provide the username of the administrative user on the primary domain controller for adding computer accounts.

smbsh

The *smbsh* program allows SMB shares to be accessed from a Unix system. When *smbsh* is run, an extra directory tree called */smb* becomes available to dynamically linked shell commands. The first level of directories under */smb* represent available workgroups, the next level of subdirectories represent the SMB servers in each workgroup, and the third level of subdirectories represent the disk and printer shares of each server.

Samba must be compiled with the --with-smbwrappers option to enable *smbsh*.

Options

-d *debug_level*
  Sets the debug (sometimes called logging) level. The level can range from 0, the default, to 10. Debug level 0 logs only the most important messages; level 1 is normal; levels 3 and above are primarily for debugging and slow *smbsh* considerably.

-l *filename*
  Sets the name of the logging file. By default, messages are sent to *stderr*.

-L *directory*
  Specifies the location of *smbsh*'s shared libraries, overriding the compiled-in default.

-P *prefix*
  Sets the name of the root directory to use for the SMB filesystem. The default is */smb*.

-R *resolve_order*

Sets the resolve order of the name servers. This option is similar to the `resolve order` configuration option and can take any of the four parameters lmhosts, host, wins, and bcast, in any order. If more than one is specified, the argument is specified as a space-separated list.

-U *username*

Provides the username, and optionally the password, for authenticating the connection to the SMB server. The password can be supplied using the *username%password* format. If either or both the username and password are not provided, *smbsh* will prompt interactively for them.

-W *workgroup*

Specifies the NetBIOS workgroup or domain to which the client will connect. This overrides the workgroup parameter in the Samba configuration file and is sometimes necessary to connect to some servers.

smbspool

The *smbspool* program provides a CUPS-compatible interface to Samba printing by providing a way to send a print job to an SMB printer using the command-line format specified by CUPS printers. Although *smbspool* is designed to work best with CUPS printers, it can be used to send print jobs to non-CUPS Samba printers as well.

Command synopsis

    smbspool *job user title copies options filename*

The arguments for *smbspool*, as shown here, are those used in the CUPS printing system. However, some of the arguments are currently ignored because they don't correspond to the Samba printing system. These arguments must be supplied in the command and can be filled in with "dummy" values.

The *job* argument refers to the job number and is currently ignored. The *user* argument is the name of the user who submitted the print job and is also ignored. The *title* argument is the name of the print job and must be supplied. It is used as the name of the remote print file. The *copies* argument is the number of copies that will be printed. This number is used only if the (optional) *filename* argument is supplied. Otherwise, only one copy is printed. The *options* argument, for specifying printing options, is ignored. The *filename* argument is used for specifying the name of the file to be printed. If it is not provided, the standard input will be used.

The printer that the job is to be sent to is specified in the DEVICE_URI environment variable. The format for the printer name is a device Universal Resource Indicator, which can be in any of the following formats:

smb://server/printer
smb://workgroup/server/printer
smb://username:password@server/printer
smb://username:password@workgroup/server/printer

smbstatus

This program lists the current connections on a Samba server.

Options

-b

Causes *smbstatus* to produce brief output. This includes the version of Samba and auditing information about the users that are connected to the server.

-d

Gives verbose output, which includes a list of services, a list of locked files, and memory usage statistics. This is the default.

-L

Prints only the list of current file locks.

-p

Prints only a list of *smbd* process IDs.

-P

Prints only the contents of the profiling memory area. Requires that Samba has been compiled with the profiling option.

-S

Prints only a list of shares and their connections.

-s *filename*
Specifies the Samba configuration file to use when processing this command.

-u *username*
Limits the report to the activity of a single user.

smbtar

The *smbtar* program is a shell-script wrapper around *smbclient* for doing tar-format archiving operations. It is functionally very similar to the Unix *tar* program.

Command synopsis

    smbtar [options]

Options

-a

Resets (clears) the archive attribute on files after they are backed up. The default is to leave the archive attribute unchanged.

-b *blocksize*
Sets block size, in units of 512 bytes, for reading or writing the archive file. Defaults to 20, which results in a block size of 10240 bytes.

-d *directory*
Changes the working directory on the remote system to *directory* before starting the restore or backup operation.

-i

Specifies incremental mode; files are backed up only if they have the DOS archive attribute set. The archive attribute is reset (cleared) after each file is read.

-l *log_level*

Sets the logging level. This corresponds to the -d option of *smbclient* and other Samba programs.

-N *filename*

Backs up only files newer than *filename*. For incremental backups.

-p *password*

Specifies the password to use to access a share. An alternative to using the *username%password* format with the -u option.

-r

Restores files to the share from the tar file.

-s *server*

Specifies the SMB server. See also the -x option.

-t *filename*

Specifies the file or Unix device to use as the archiving medium. The default is *tar.out* or the value of the TAPE environment variable, if it has been set.

-u *username*

Specifies the user account to use when connecting to the share. You can specify the password as well, in the format *username%password*. The username defaults to the user's Unix username.

-v

Operates in verbose mode, printing error messages and additional information that can be used in debugging and monitoring. Backup and restore operations will list each file as it is processed.

-x *share*

States the name of the share on the server to which to connect. The default is backup. See also the -s option.

-X *file_list*

Tells *smbtar* to exclude the specified files from the backup or restore operation.

---

smbumount

The *smbumount* command exists to allow an ordinary (nonsuperuser) user to unmount a smbfs filesystem, which the user had previously mounted using *smbmount*.

Command synopsis

```
smbumount mount_point
```

For ordinary users to issue the command, *smbumount* must be made suid root.

testparm

The *testparm* program checks a Samba configuration file for obvious errors.

Command synopsis

```
testparm [options] [filename] [hostname IP_addr]
```

If the configuration file is not provided using the *filename* argument, then it defaults to */usr/local/samba/lib/smb.conf*. If the hostname and an IP address of a system are included, an extra check is made to ensure that the system is allowed to connect to each service defined in the configuration file. This is done by comparing the hostname and IP address to the definitions of the hosts allow and hosts deny parameters.

Options

-h

Prints usage information for the program.

-L *server_name*

Sets the %L configuration variable to the specified server name.

-s

Disables the default behavior of prompting for the Enter key to be pressed before printing the list of configuration options for the server.

testprns

This is a very simple program that checks to see if a specified printer name exists in the system printer capabilities (printcap) file.

Command synopsis

```
testprns printername [printcapname]
```

If *printcapname* isn't specified, Samba attempts to use the one specified in the Samba configuration file with the printcap name parameter. If none is specified there, Samba will try */etc/printcap*.

wbinfo

This program retrieves and prints information from the *winbindd* daemon, which must be running for *wbinfo* to function.

Command synopsis

```
wbinfo [options]
```

Options

-u

Prints all usernames that have been mapped from the Windows NT domain to Unix users. Users in all trusted domains are also listed.

-g

Prints all group names that have been mapped from the Windows NT domain to Unix groups. Groups in all trusted domains are also reported.

-h *NetBIOS_name*

Queries the WINS server and prints the IP address of the specified system.

-n *name*

Prints the SID corresponding to the name specified. The argument can be specified as *DOMAIN/name* (or by using a character other than the slash, as defined by the winbind separator character) to specify both the domain and the name. If the domain and separator are omitted, the value of the workgroup parameter in the Samba configuration file is used as the name of the domain.

-s *SID*

Prints the name mapped to a SID, which is specified in the format S-1-*N*-*N*-*D*-*D*-*D*-*R*.

-U *UID*

Prints the SID mapped to a Unix UID, if one exists in the current domain.

-G *gid*

Prints the SID mapped to a Unix group ID, if one exists in the current domain.

-S *SID*

Prints the Unix UID that winbind has mapped to the specified SID, if one exists.

-Y *SID*

Prints the Unix group ID that winbind has mapped to the specified SID, if one exists.

-t

Tests to see that the workstation trust account for the Samba server is valid.

-m

Prints a list of Windows NT domains trusted by the Windows server. This does not include the PDC's domain.

-r *username*

Prints the list of Unix group IDs to which the user belongs. This works only if the user's account is maintained on a domain controller.

-a *username%password*

Checks to see if a user can authenticate through *winbindd* using the specified username and password.

-A *username%password*

Saves the username and password used by *winbindd* to the domain controller. For use when operating in a Windows 2000 domain.

Downloading Samba with CVS

In Chapter 2 we showed you how to download the latest stable version of Samba published by the Samba developers. For most purposes (including virtually all production servers) this procedure will meet your needs. However, sometimes you might want to run a version of Samba that includes the latest bug fixes and features, maybe for research and testing purposes, or just to see what the Samba developers have been up to lately.

The Samba team keeps the latest updates of the Samba source code in a Concurrent Versions System (CVS) repository. CVS is a freely available configuration management tool and is distributed under the GNU General Public License. You can download the latest copy from *http://www.cvshome.com/*. The Samba team describes various ways to access its CVS repository at *http://www.samba.org/samba/cvs.html*.

 Although the CVS code contains the latest features, it also contains the latest bugs and sometimes won't even compile properly! If you prefer a less "bleeding edge" release, try looking in the *alpha* and *pre* directories on the Samba FTP server. The *alpha* directory contains alpha releases, and the *pre* directory contains (usually more stable) prerelease versions. (See Chapter 2 for information on downloading via FTP.) Alpha releases might be a little behind the latest CVS code, but are less buggy and usually compile properly on the more common Unix versions.

One of the nicest things about CVS is its ability to handle remote logins. This means that people across the globe on the Internet can download and update various source files for any project that uses a CVS repository. Such is the case with Samba. Once you have CVS installed on your system, you must first log in to the Samba source server with the following command:

```
$ cvs -d :pserver:cvs@pserver.samba.org:/cvsroot login
```

When you are prompted for a password, enter cvs. You are connected to the CVS server at pserver.samba.org. Once you are connected, you can download the latest source tree with the following command:[*]

```
$ cvs -z5 -d :pserver:pserver@pserver.samba.org:/cvsroot co samba
```

This downloads the entire Samba distribution (file by file) into a directory called *samba*, created in your current directory. The *samba* directory has the same structure as the Samba source distribution described in Chapter 2, except that it has additional directories named *CVS* throughout the source tree. These directories are used by CVS to store information about each file in the source tree and how to update them. After the download is completed, you can follow the instructions in Chapter 2 to configure, compile, and install your new Samba release.

The Samba developers typically update the Samba source code one or more times per day. Whenever you want to catch up to the latest changes, simply *cd* to the *samba* directory and run the following command:

```
$ cvs update -d -P
```

Each time you do this, you will need to reconfigure, recompile, and reinstall to update your installation as we showed you in Chapter 2.

---

[*] The -z option causes the transfer to be made in GNU gzip compressed format and requires the *gzip* program to be installed on your system to work. If you do not have *gzip*, omit the -z option.

Configure Options

As we explained in Chapter 2, the *configure* program is run before the Samba source code is compiled to fit the compilation process to the local architecture. At this stage, it is possible to specify options to customize Samba's behavior further and include or exclude features. This is an example of specifying configure options:

```
# ./configure --with-smbmount --with-configdir=/etc/samba --with-manpages-langs=ja
```

This example configures the Samba installation to support mounting SMB filesystems, look for the Samba configuration file in */etc/samba* (instead of the default location of */usr/local/samba/lib*), and install Japanese-language manual pages. We have picked these three configure options because they illustrate the usage of the three types of options that are included up to Samba 3.0. The `--with-smbmount` option is a Boolean option, which can take a value of yes or no. All the Boolean options are set to no by default, and it is only necessary to provide the option to turn it on. If you want to be more explicit, you can specify `--with-smbmount=yes`. To turn an option off explicitly, you can also specify `--without-`*feature* rather than `--with-`*feature*`=no`.

In the case of the other two options we have shown, an argument must be supplied after the equals (=) sign. Some of the options are used to specify the directories that Samba uses for various purposes. Only one option is in the last group, where something other than a directory is specified as an option argument.

The supported configure options vary from release to release. For example, between Samba 2.2.x and Samba 3.0, many options were dropped, and a few were added. To get a list of the configure options for your release, use the following command:

```
# ./configure --help
```

Table E-1 lists Samba's configure options.

Table E-1. Configuration options

Configuration option	Description
`--with-acl-support`	Support Windows NT/2000/XP ACLs
`--with-afs`	Support the Andrew Filesystem (AFS)

Table E-1. Configuration options (continued)

Configuration option	Description
--with-automount	Support the NFS automounter
--with-codepagedir=*dir*	Location of codepage files
--with-configdir=*dir*	Location of configuration files
--with-dce-dfs	Support DCE/DFS
--with-fhs	Use FHS-compliant locations of files
--with-included-popt	Use Samba's *popt( )*
--with-krb4=base-*dir*	Support Kerberos 4
--with-krb5=base-*dir*	Support Kerberos 5 (Microsoft ADS)
--with-ldapsam	Support LDAP SAM
--with-libiconv=*directory*	Specify *iconv* library
--with-libsmbclient	Build *smbclient* library
--with-lockdir=*directory*	Location of lock files
--with-logfilebase=*directory*	Location of log files
--with-manpages-langs=*language*	Specify language for manual pages
--with-msdfs	Support Microsoft Dfs
--with-nisplus-home	Support NIS+ home directories
--with-nisplussam	Support NIS+ SAM
--with-pam	Support PAM restrictions
--with-pam_smbpass	Build *pam_smbpass.so* PAM module
--with-piddir=*directory*	Location of PID files
--with-privatedir=*directory*	Location of *smbpasswd* file
--with-profiling-data	Support gathering of profiling information
--with-quotas	Support disk quotas
--with-readline=*directory*	Specify readline library
--with-sendfile-support	Support *sendfile( )* system call
--with-smbmount	Support *smbmount* and smbfs
--with-smbwrapper	Build *smbwrapper* library for *smbsh* support
--with-spinlocks	Use spinlocks instead of fcntl locks
--with-ssl	Support SSL
--with-sslinc=*directory*	Location of SSL include files
--with-ssllib=*directory*	Location of SSL libraries
--with-swatdir=*directory*	Location of SWAT files
--with-syslog	Support syslog message logging
--with-tdbsam	Support TDB database files for SAM
--with-utmp	Support utmp file accounting
--with-winbind	Build winbind

`--with-acl-support`

Includes support for Windows NT/2000/XP access control lists (ACLs). For this to work, you need to have POSIX ACL support in the host operating system. See Chapter 8 for details.

`--with-afs`

Includes support for the Andrew Filesystem (AFS), for authenticating users who are accessing files through AFS.

`--with-automount`

Includes support for the automounter, a feature often used in conjunction with NFS, to mount NFS shares automatically at the first attempt to access them. You might wish to enable this feature if any of the directories shared by your Samba server are (or include) NFS-mounted directories.

`--with-codepagedir=directory`

Specifies the directory in which to put codepage files for internationalization support. See the "Internationalization" section earlier in this chapter for more information on this feature. By default, this directory is */usr/local/samba/lib/codepages*.

`--with-configdir=directory`

Specifies the directory in which Samba keeps its configuration file, usually called *smb.conf*. By default, this is */usr/local/samba/lib*.

`--with-dce-dfs`

Includes support for the Distributed Computing Environment Distributed Filesystem (DCE/DFS). This is a distributed filesystem included in some Unix variants and is not the same as Microsoft's Distributed Filesystem (Dfs).

`--with-fhs`

Adheres to the Filesystem Hierarchy Standard when locating files. For details, see *http://www.pathname.com/fhs*.

`--with-included-popt`

Includes Samba's own support for parsing command-line options, instead of using the local system's *popt( )* C-library function.

`--with-krb4=base-dir`

Includes support for Kerberos Version 4.0, specifying the base directory of the Kerberos distribution. Kerberos is an authentication protocol developed at MIT that uses private-key cryptography to provide strong security between nodes. This version is not the same as Microsoft's adaptation of Kerberos in Active Directory, which is the preferred version for use with Samba. This option exists only in versions of Samba earlier than 3.0.

`--with-krb5=base-dir`

Includes support for Kerberos Version 5.0, specifying the base directory of the Kerberos distribution. This version of Kerberos is compatible with the Kerberos authentication in Microsoft's Active Directory used in Windows 2000 and Windows XP.

--with-ldapsam

Includes support for using LDAP instead of the *smbpasswd* file for maintaining Samba's equivalent to the Windows NT SAM database. This option is necessary to use the parameters ldap admin dn, ldap filter, ldap port, ldap server, ldap ssl, and ldap suffix in the Samba configuration file. It is necessary to specify --with-ldapsam only in Samba versions prior to 3.0.

--with-libiconv=*directory*

Specifies a location for *iconv()* support. The *iconv()* function exists in the C library to perform conversion between different character sets. This option allows Samba's default method of determining the location of the *iconv()* library to be overridden. Ordinarily, the configuration process checks for support in the C library on the system and, if not found, uses code included in the Samba source tree. Using --with-libiconv, it is possible to specify explicitly where the support is located. The include files are assumed to be in *directory/include*, and library files are assumed to be in *directory/lib*. This option is new in Samba 3.0.

--with-libsmbclient

Allows applications outside the Samba suite to access Samba's features. When --with-libsmbclient is specified, the library is built during the compilation process.

--with-lockdir=*directory*

Specifies the directory in which Samba keeps lock files. By default this directory is */usr/local/samba/var/locks*.

--with-logfilebase=*directory*

Specifies the directory in which Samba keeps log files for the *smbd*, *nmbd*, and *winbindd* daemons. This defaults to */usr/local/samba/var*.

--with-manpages-langs=*language*

Starting with Samba 3.0, Samba's manual pages are available in different languages. The default is en for English, and the language can be specified as ja for Japanese or pl for Polish.

--with-msdfs

Includes support for Microsoft Distributed Filesystem (Dfs). See Chapter 8 for more information on this feature. Specifying this option is necessary only in Samba versions prior to 3.0.

--with-nisplus-home

Includes support for locating the NIS+ server that is serving a particular user's home directory and telling the client to connect to it. Use --with-automount along with this option.

--with-nisplussam

Includes support for integrating NIS+ into Samba's equivalent of the Windows NT password database.

`--with-pam`

When this configure option is specified and the parameter obey pam restrictions in the Samba configuration file is set to yes, obeys PAM's configuration regarding account and session management. When encrypted passwords are in use, Samba uses the *smbpasswd* file for authentication, bypassing the PAM subsystem. Therefore, this option works only when encrypt passwords is set to no.

`--with-pam_smbpass`

When this option is specified, the compilation process builds a PAM module called *pam_smbpass.so* and places it in the *source/bin* directory. This module allows applications outside of the Samba suite to authenticate users with Samba's *smbpasswd* file. For more information, see the *README* file in the *source/pam_smbpass* directory of the Samba distribution and the file *PAM-Authentication-And-Samba.html* in the *docs/html* directory.

`--with-piddir=directory`

Specifies the directory in which Samba keeps files such as browse lists, WINS data, and PID files for keeping track of the process IDs of the Samba daemons. The default is */usr/local/samba/var/locks*.

`--with-privatedir=directory`

Specifies the directory in which Samba keeps the *smbpasswd*, *secrets.tdb,* and related files for authentication. The default is */usr/local/samba/private*.

`--with-profiling-data`

Includes support for analyzing the execution time of Samba's internal code. This is normally used only by the Samba developers.

`--with-quotas`

Includes disk-quota support. This is classified as an experimental option by the Samba developers.

`--with-readline=directory`

Specifies a location for *readline()* support. The *readline()* function exists in the C library to accept a line of input from an interactive user and provide support for editing and history. Samba uses these functions in *smbclient* and *rpcclient*.

This option allows Samba's default method of determining the location of the readline() library to be overridden. Ordinarily, the configuration process checks for support in the C library on the system and, if not found, uses code included in the Samba source tree. Using `--with-readline`, it is possible to specify the directory explicitly in which the library containing *readline()* is located.

`--with-sendfile-support`

Checks to see if the Samba host operating system supports the *sendfile()* system call, which speeds up file transfers by copying data directly to and from kernel buffers, avoiding the overhead of copying to and from buffers in user space. If the operating system has the *sendfile()* system call, support is included in Samba for the use sendfile configuration file option. This is an experimental option included in Samba 2.2.5 and later versions.

--with-smbmount

Must be specified if you want to mount SMB shares in your Unix filesystem using the smbfs filesystem and the *smbmount* command, as discussed in Chapter 5. Currently, this works only with Linux.

--with-smbwrapper

To use *smbsh* to access SMB shares from Unix (as discussed in Chapter 5), use this option to include the *smbwrapper* library.

--with-spinlocks

Uses spin locks instead of the normal method of file locking that uses the *fcntl()* C-library function. Using this option results in a Samba installation that consumes much more CPU time on the host system. Use it only when absolutely necessary.

--with-ssl

Includes support for running Samba with SSL encryption. This little-used feature was dropped for Samba 3.0. It still works with Samba 2.2.x and before, but a better method is to use a virtual private network (VPN).

--with-sslinc=*directory*

Specifies the location of the SSL include files. */usr/local/ssl/include* is the default location. This option exists in versions prior to Samba 3.0.

--with-ssllib=*directory*

Specifies the location of the SSL libraries. The default location is */usr/local/ssl/lib*. This option exists in versions prior to Samba 3.0.

--with-swatdir=*directory*

Specifies where to install the files for SWAT. */usr/local/samba/swat* is the default location.

--with-syslog

Includes support for syslog error logging. This option must be specified for the Samba configuration file parameters syslog and syslog only to work. This option is widely supported, but might not work correctly on all Samba host systems.

--with-tdbsam

Includes support for keeping Samba's equivalent of the Windows NT SAM in a *.tdb* database file rather than in the *smbpasswd* file. This is an experimental feature.

--with-utmp

Includes support for user accounting in the system's *utmp* file. It is necessary for the utmp and utmp directory Samba configuration file options to work. This option is widely supported, but might not work correctly on all Samba host systems.

`--with-winbind`

Includes winbind support in Samba. Instead of defaulting to `no`, as with other boolean options, `--with-winbind` is automatically set to yes on systems that support winbind functionality. The only time you would need to specify this option is to turn it off, like this:

```
# configure --without-winbind
```

This excludes winbind functionality from Samba even when the local operating system can support it. For more information on winbind, see Chapter 9.

Running Samba on Mac OS X Server

Mac OS X Server is an Apple operating-system product based on Mac OS X, with the addition of administrative tools and server software. One area in which it differs from Mac OS X is in the configuration of Samba-based services. In this appendix, we'll tell you how to set up SMB file and printer shares, enable client user access, and monitor activity. Our specific focus is on Mac OS X Server 10.2.

Setup Procedures

The first thing to note is that the procedure described in Chapter 2 using System Preferences to enable Samba does not apply to Mac OS X Server. Unlike Mac OS X, the Sharing pane of System Preferences does not include an option to turn on Windows File Sharing. Instead, there is a set of applications to configure, activate, and monitor services: Workgroup Manager, Server Settings, Server Status, and Open Directory Assistant, all located in the directory */Applications/Utilities*.

> In addition to being installed with Mac OS X Server, these and other administrative applications are included on a separate installation CD-ROM sold with the operating system. They can be used to manage Mac OS X Server systems remotely from any Mac OS X machine.
>
> For more information, refer to the *Mac OS X Server Administrator's Guide*, included as a PDF file in the */Library/Documentation/MacOSXServer* directory, and also downloadable from Apple Computer's web site at *http://www.apple.com/server/*.

Briefly, the procedure for setting up SMB file and printer shares is as follows:

1. Designate share points in Workgroup Manager for file sharing.

2. Set up print queues in Server Settings for printer sharing, and activate Printer Service.

3. Configure and activate Windows Services in Server Settings.

4. Activate Password Server and enable SMB authentication in Open Directory Assistant.

5. Enable Password Server authentication for user accounts in Workgroup Manager.

6. Monitor file and print services with Server Status.

Sharing Files

The first step to enable SMB file sharing is to designate one or more *share points*. Share points are folders that form the root of shared volumes for any of the protocols supported by Mac OS X Server: Apple Filesharing Protocol (AFP), Network Filesystem (NFS), File Transfer Protocol (FTP), and SMB.

To designate a share point, launch Workgroup Manager. You will be prompted for the local or remote server's hostname or IP address, as well as for a username and password; this process is required by all the Mac OS X Server administrative applications. Once Workgroup Manager is open, click the Sharing button in the toolbar. The list on the left, under the Share Points tab, displays currently defined share points. To add a new one, click the All tab, and navigate to the folder you want to share.

On the right, under the General tab, check the box labeled Share this item and its contents, change the ownership and permissions if desired, then click the Save button. Next, under the Protocols tab, select Windows File Settings from the pop-up menu, and ensure that the box labeled Share this item using SMB is checked. At this point, you can also decide whether to allow guest access to the share, change the name of the share displayed to SMB clients, or set permissions for files and folders created by SMB clients. Click the Save button when you're finished making changes. See Figure F-1.

Sharing Printers

Printer shares are set up differently. First, launch Server Settings; under the File & Print tab, select Print, then Configure Print Service.... Check the box labeled Automatically share new queues for Windows printing. Next, click the Print icon again and then Show Print Monitor. Make sure the printers you want to share are listed. Printers directly attached to the server should have queues created automatically, but remote printers you wish to reshare must be added by clicking New Queue and discovering or specifying the printers. When you're finished, click Save, select the Print icon one more time, and select Start Print Service. See Figure F-2.

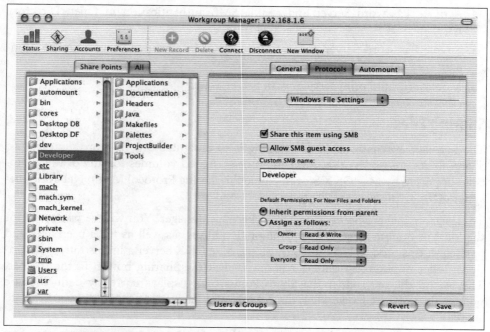

Figure F-1. Workgroup Manager: Share Points and Windows File Settings

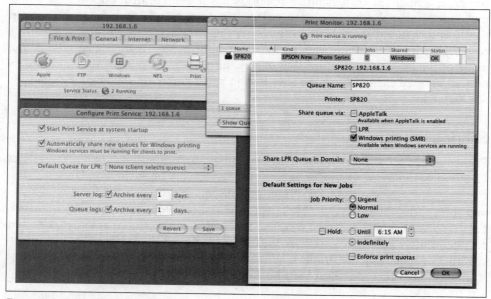

Figure F-2. Server Settings: Print Service

Server Settings will make local printers available for sharing only if they're PostScript compatible. Unfortunately, many printers, including consumer-grade USB inkjet printers, aren't. If you want to make one of these printers available to SMB clients, you can still add the share to */etc/smb.conf* yourself with a text editor. See "Rolling Your Own" later in this chapter for instructions and caveats related to making manual changes to *smb.conf*.

Configuring and Activating Services

At this point, neither the file shares nor the printer shares are available to SMB clients. To activate them, click the Windows icon in Server Settings, and click Configure Windows Services.... Under the General tab, you can set the server's NetBIOS hostname, the workgroup or Windows NT domain in which the server resides, and the description that gets displayed in a browse list. You can also specify the code page for an alternate character set. Finally, you can enable boot-time startup of Samba. See Figure F-3.

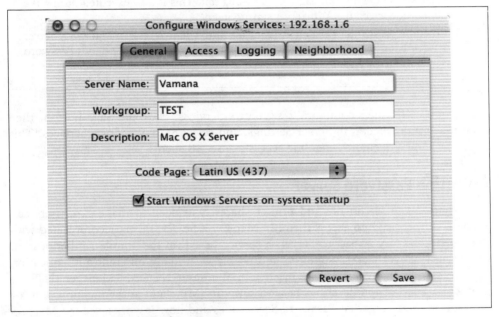

Figure F-3. Server Settings: Windows Services

The Windows Services Access tab offers options to enable guest access and limit the number of simultaneous client connections; under the Logging tab, you can specify the verbosity of your logging. With options under the Neighborhood tab, you can configure your machine as a WINS client or server or have it provide browser services locally or across subnets.

Password Server

Password Server is a feature introduced with Mac OS X Server 10.2. In prior versions of Mac OS X Server, Windows authentication was handled with Authentication Manager, which stored a user's Windows password in the `tim_password` property of the user's NetInfo record. This can still be done in Version 10.2, although it's strongly discouraged because the encrypted password is visible to other users with access to the NetInfo domain and can potentially be decrypted.

If you need to use Authentication Manager, use the following procedure to enable it:

1. On every machine hosting a domain that will bind into the NetInfo hierarchy, execute the command `tim -init -auto` *tag* for each domain, where *tag* is the name of the domain's database.

2. When prompted, provide a password to be used as the encryption key for the domain. This key is used to decrypt the Windows passwords and is stored in an encrypted file readable only by root, */var/db/netinfo/.tag.tim*.

3. Set `AUTHSERVER=-YES-` in */etc/hostconfig*.

4. Start Authentication Manager by invoking *tim*. This is also executed during the boot sequence by the AuthServer startup item.

5. Reset the password of each user requiring SMB client access. In Mac OS X Server 10.2 or later, make sure the user is set up for Basic authentication, not Password Server authentication.

When you've finished configuring Windows Services, click the Save button, then click the Windows icon in Server Settings, and select Start Windows Services. This starts the Samba daemons, enabling access from SMB clients.

Activating Password Server

Now that you've set up file and printer shares, you need to make sure users can properly authenticate to access them. In Mac OS X Server, this is accomplished with the Open Directory Password Server, a service based on the Simple Authentication and Security Layer (SASL) standard and usable with many different authentication protocols, including the LAN Manager and Windows NT LAN Manager (NTLM) protocols. This section describes how to support SMB client authentication, but for more information on what Password Server does and how it works, see the Mac OS X Server Administrator's Guide.

To enable Password Server or merely check its settings, start the Open Directory Assistant. Unless you wish to change any of the settings, just click the right arrow button in the lower-right corner of the window until you get to the first Security step. At this point, activate Password Server by selecting the option marked Password and authentication information will be provided to other systems. The next step displays the main administrative account, and the one after that gives you a choice of authentication protocols to enable (see Figure F-4). Make sure that SMB-NT is checked, and check SMB-Lan Manager if you have Windows 95/98/Me or older clients. The final step saves the Password Server configuration and prompts you to reboot.

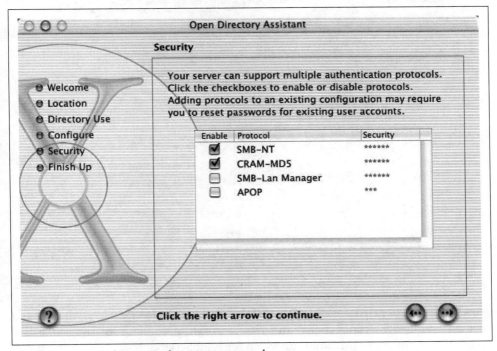

Figure F-4. Password Server authentication protocols

Enabling Password Server

To enable the use of Password Server for a user account, launch Workgroup Manager, and click the Accounts button in the toolbar. Under the Users tab on the far left (with the silhouette of a single person), select the account, and under the Advanced tab on the right, select Password Server for the User Password Type (see Figure F-5). You are prompted to enter a new user password to be stored in the Password Server database. After saving the account configuration, the user can authenticate and access shares from an SMB client.

Monitoring Services

Once you've got everything working, you'll want to keep an eye on things. The Server Status application gives you views into the various services provided by Mac OS X Server. For Windows Services, you can see the current state of the service,

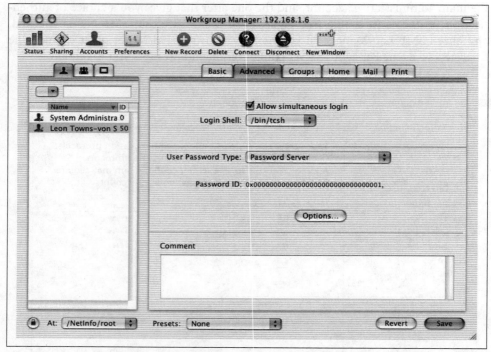

Figure F-5. Workgroup Manager: Enabling Password Server authentication

browse the logs (located in the directory */Library/Logs/WindowsServices*), display and terminate individual connections, and view a graph of connections over time (see Figure F-6). Similar information is provided for Print Service.

Configuration Details

Underneath the GUI, a lot of activity takes place to offer Windows Services. In the non-Server version of Mac OS X, selecting Windows File Sharing sets the SMBSERVER parameter in */etc/hostconfig* and triggers the Samba startup item. In Mac OS X Server, under normal circumstances the Samba startup item and the SMBSERVER parameter are never used.

Instead, a process named *sambadmind* generates */etc/smb.conf* from the configuration specified in Server Settings and Workgroup Manager and handles starting and restarting the Samba daemons as necessary. The *sambadmind* process is in turn monitored by *watchdog*, which keeps an eye on certain processes and restarts those which fail. The *watchdog* utility is configured in */etc/watchdog.conf*, a file similar to a System V *inittab*, which specifies how the services under *watchdog*'s purview are to be treated. For example, the line for *sambadmind* looks like this:

```
sambadmin:respawn:/usr/sbin/sambadmind -d    # SMB Admin daemon
```

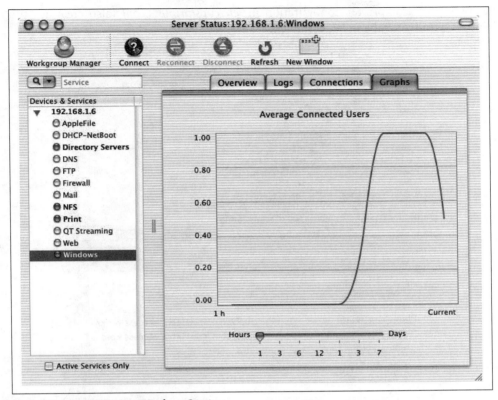

Figure F-6. Server Status: Windows Services

Using a *watchdog*-monitored process such as *sambadmind* to start the Samba daemons, instead of a one-time execution of a startup item, results in more reliable service. In Mac OS X Server, if a Samba daemon dies unexpectedly, it is quickly restarted. (Examples of other services monitored by *watchdog* are Password Server, Print Service, and the Server Settings daemon that allows remote management.)

There's another wrinkle in Mac OS X Server: the Samba configuration settings are not written directly to */etc/smb.conf*, as they are in the non-Server version of Mac OS X. Instead, they're stored in the server's local Open Directory domain,[*] from which *sambadmind* retrieves them and regenerates *smb.conf*. For example, the Samba global parameters are stored in */config/SMBServer* (see Figure F-7). Share point information is also kept in Open Directory, under */config/SharePoints*, while CUPS takes

---

[*] In versions of Mac OS X prior to 10.2, Open Directory domains were called NetInfo domains. NetInfo Manager (located in */Applications/Utilities*) provides a graphical interface to view and modify the contents of Open Directory databases. For more information, see the *Mac OS X Server Administrator's Guide*, as well as *Understanding and Using NetInfo*, downloadable from the Mac OS X Server resources web page at *http://www.apple.com/server/resources.html*.

responsibility for printer configuration in */etc/cups/printers.conf* (also creating stub entries used by Samba in */etc/printcap*).

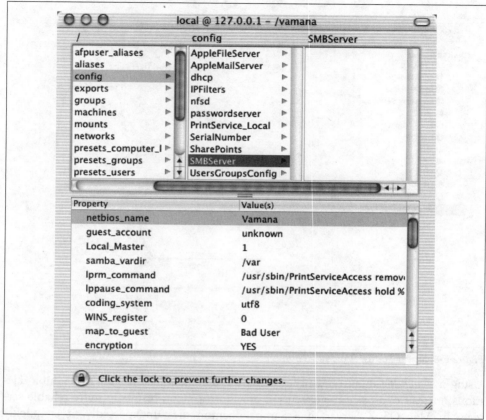

Figure F-7. NetInfo Manager: SMBServer properties

Table F-1 summarizes the association of Windows Services settings in the Server Settings application, properties stored in Open Directory, and parameters in */etc/smb.conf*.

Table F-1. Samba configuration settings in Mac OS X Server

Server Settings graphical element in Windows Services	Open Directory property in */config/ SMBServer*	Samba global parameter in */etc/smb.conf*
General → Server Name	netbios_name	netbios name
General → Workgroup	workgroup	workgroup
General → Description	description	server string
General → Code Page	code_page	client code page
General → Start Windows Services on system startup	auto_start	N/A

Table F-1. Samba configuration settings in Mac OS X Server (continued)

Server Settings graphical element in Windows Services	Open Directory property in */config/SMBServer*	Samba global parameter in */etc/smb.conf*
Access → Allow Guest Access	`guest_access`, `map_to_guest`	`map to guest`
N/A	`guest_account`	`guest account`
Access → Maximum client connections	`max_connections`	`max smbd processes`
Logging → Detail Level	`logging`	`log level`
Neighborhood → WINS Registration → Off	`WINS_enabled`, `WINS_register`	`wins support`
Neighborhood → WINS Registration → Enable WINS server	`WINS_enabled`	`wins support`
Neighborhood → WINS Registration → Register with WINS server	`WINS_register`, `WINS_address`	`wins server`
Neighborhood → Workgroup/Domain Services → Master Browser	`Local_Master`	`local master`
Neighborhood → Workgroup/Domain Services → Domain Master Browser	`Domain_Master`	`domain master`
Print → Start Print Service	`printing`	N/A
N/A	`lprm_command`	`lprm command`
N/A	`lppause_command`	`lppause command`
N/A	`lpresume_command`	`lpresume command`
N/A	`printer_admin`	`printer admin`
N/A	`encryption`	`encrypt passwords`
N/A	`coding_system`	`coding system`
N/A	`log_dir`	N/A
N/A	`smb_log`	`log file`
N/A	`nmb_log`	N/A
N/A	`samba_sbindir`	N/A
N/A	`samba_bindir`	N/A
N/A	`samba_libdir`	N/A
N/A	`samba_lockdir`	N/A
N/A	`samba_vardir`	N/A
N/A	`stop_time`	N/A

Rolling Your Own

When making manual changes to the Samba configuration file, take care to block changes initiated from graphical applications by invoking this command:

```
# chflags uchg /etc/smb.conf
```

From that point on, the GUI will be useful only for starting, stopping, and monitoring the service—not for configuring it.

If you install your own version of Samba, you can still manage it from Server Settings by changing some of the Open Directory properties in /config/SMBServer.

To do this, open NetInfo Manager and modify the samba_sbindir and samba_bindir properties to match the location of your Samba installation. Optionally, you can modify samba_libdir, samba_vardir, and samba_lockdir. Assuming a default Samba installation, you can also change these at the command line with the following commands:

```
# nicl . -create /config/SMBServer samba_sbindir /usr/local/samba/bin
# nicl . -create /config/SMBServer samba_bindir /usr/local/samba/bin
# nicl . -create /config/SMBServer samba_libdir /usr/local/samba/lib
# nicl . -create /config/SMBServer samba_vardir /usr/local/samba/var
# nicl . -create /config/SMBServer samba_lockdir /usr/local/samba/var/locks
```

You can check your settings with this command:

```
# nicl . -read /config/SMBServer
```

In Server Settings, select Stop Windows Services, then run this command:

```
# killall sambadmind
```

The *watchdog* utility restarts *sambadmind* within seconds. Finally, go back to Server Settings, and select Start Windows Services.

If you don't modify Open Directory properties to match your active Samba installation (because you wish to manage your configuration another way), be sure never to activate Windows Services from the Server Settings application, or you'll wind up with two sets of Samba daemons running concurrently.

GNU Free Documentation License

GNU Free Documentation License

Version 1.2, November 2002

Copyright © 2000, 2001, 2002 Free Software Foundation, Inc.

59 Temple Place, Suite 330, Boston, MA 02111-1307 USA

Everyone is permitted to copy and distribute verbatim copies of this license document, but changing it is not allowed.

0. PREAMBLE

The purpose of this License is to make a manual, textbook, or other functional and useful document "free" in the sense of freedom: to assure everyone the effective freedom to copy and redistribute it, with or without modifying it, either commercially or noncommercially. Secondarily, this License preserves for the author and publisher a way to get credit for their work, while not being considered responsible for modifications made by others.

This License is a kind of "copyleft", which means that derivative works of the document must themselves be free in the same sense. It complements the GNU General Public License, which is a copyleft license designed for free software.

We have designed this License in order to use it for manuals for free software, because free software needs free documentation: a free program should come with manuals providing the same freedoms that the software does. But this License is not limited to software manuals; it can be used for any textual work, regardless of subject matter or whether it is published as a printed book. We recommend this License principally for works whose purpose is instruction or reference.

1. APPLICABILITY AND DEFINITIONS

This License applies to any manual or other work, in any medium, that contains a notice placed by the copyright holder saying it can be distributed under the terms of this License. Such a notice grants a world-wide, royalty-free license, unlimited in duration, to use that work under the conditions stated herein. The "Document", below, refers to any such manual or work. Any member of the public is a licensee, and is addressed as "you". You accept the license if you copy, modify or distribute the work in a way requiring permission under copyright law.

A "Modified Version" of the Document means any work containing the Document or a portion of it, either copied verbatim, or with modifications and/or translated into another language.

A "Secondary Section" is a named appendix or a front-matter section of the Document that deals exclusively with the relationship of the publishers or authors of the Document to the Document's overall subject (or to related matters) and contains nothing that could fall directly within that overall subject. (Thus, if the Document is in part a textbook of mathematics, a Secondary Section may not explain any mathematics.) The relationship could be a matter of historical connection with the subject or with related matters, or of legal, commercial, philosophical, ethical or political position regarding them.

The "Invariant Sections" are certain Secondary Sections whose titles are designated, as being those of Invariant Sections, in the notice that says that the Document is released under this License. If a section does not fit the above definition of Secondary then it is not allowed to be designated as Invariant. The Document may contain zero Invariant Sections. If the Document does not identify any Invariant Sections then there are none.

The "Cover Texts" are certain short passages of text that are listed, as Front-Cover Texts or Back-Cover Texts, in the notice that says that the Document is released under this License. A Front-Cover Text may be at most 5 words, and a Back-Cover Text may be at most 25 words.

A "Transparent" copy of the Document means a machine-readable copy, represented in a format whose specification is available to the general public, that is suitable for revising the document straightforwardly with generic text editors or (for images composed of pixels) generic paint programs or (for drawings) some widely available drawing editor, and that is suitable for input to text formatters or for automatic translation to a variety of formats suitable for input to text formatters. A copy made in an otherwise Transparent file format whose markup, or absence of markup, has been arranged to thwart or discourage subsequent modification by readers is not Transparent. An image format is not Transparent if used for any substantial amount of text. A copy that is not "Transparent" is called "Opaque".

Examples of suitable formats for Transparent copies include plain ASCII without markup, TEXinfo input format, LATEX input format, SGML or XML using a publicly available DTD, and standard-conforming simple HTML, PostScript or PDF designed for human modification. Examples of transparent image formats include PNG, XCF and JPG. Opaque formats include proprietary formats that can be read and edited only by proprietary word processors, SGML or XML for which the DTD and/or processing tools are not generally available, and the machine-generated HTML, PostScript or PDF produced by some word processors for output purposes only.

The "Title Page" means, for a printed book, the title page itself, plus such following pages as are needed to hold, legibly, the material this License requires to appear in the title page. For works in formats which do not have any title page as such, "Title Page" means the text near the most prominent appearance of the work's title, preceding the beginning of the body of the text.

A section "Entitled XYZ" means a named subunit of the Document whose title either is precisely XYZ or contains XYZ in parentheses following text that translates XYZ in another language. (Here XYZ stands for a specific section name mentioned below, such as "Acknowledgments", "Dedications", "Endorsements", or "History".) To "Preserve the Title" of such a section when you modify the Document means that it remains a section "Entitled XYZ" according to this definition.

The Document may include Warranty Disclaimers next to the notice which states that this License applies to the Document. These Warranty Disclaimers are considered to be included by reference in this License, but only as regards disclaiming warranties: any other implication that these Warranty Disclaimers may have is void and has no effect on the meaning of this License.

2. VERBATIM COPYING

You may copy and distribute the Document in any medium, either commercially or noncommercially, provided that this License, the copyright notices, and the license notice saying this License applies to the Document are reproduced in all copies, and that you add no other conditions whatsoever to those of this License. You may not use technical measures to obstruct or control the reading or further copying of the copies you make or distribute. However, you may accept compensation in exchange for copies. If you distribute a large enough number of copies you must also follow the conditions in section 3.

You may also lend copies, under the same conditions stated above, and you may publicly display copies.

3. COPYING IN QUANTITY

If you publish printed copies (or copies in media that commonly have printed covers) of the Document, numbering more than 100, and the Document's license notice requires Cover Texts, you must enclose the copies in covers that carry, clearly and legibly, all these Cover Texts: Front-Cover Texts on the front cover, and Back-Cover Texts on the back cover. Both covers must also clearly and legibly identify you as the publisher of these copies. The front cover must present the full title with all words of the title equally prominent and visible. You may add other material on the covers in addition. Copying with changes limited to the covers, as long as they preserve the title of the Document and satisfy these conditions, can be treated as verbatim copying in other respects.

If the required texts for either cover are too voluminous to fit legibly, you should put the first ones listed (as many as fit reasonably) on the actual cover, and continue the rest onto adjacent pages.

If you publish or distribute Opaque copies of the Document numbering more than 100, you must either include a machine-readable Transparent copy along with each Opaque copy, or state in or with each Opaque copy a computer-network location from which the general network-using public has access to download using public-standard network protocols a complete Transparent copy of the Document, free of added material. If you use the latter option, you must take reasonably prudent steps, when you begin distribution of Opaque copies in quantity, to ensure that this Transparent copy will remain thus accessible at the stated location until at least one year after the last time you distribute an Opaque copy (directly or through your agents or retailers) of that edition to the public.

It is requested, but not required, that you contact the authors of the Document well before redistributing any large number of copies, to give them a chance to provide you with an updated version of the Document.

4. MODIFICATIONS

You may copy and distribute a Modified Version of the Document under the conditions of sections 2 and 3 above, provided that you release the Modified Version under precisely this License, with the Modified Version filling the role of the Document, thus licensing distribution and modification of the Modified Version to whoever possesses a copy of it. In addition, you must do these things in the Modified Version:

1. Use in the Title Page (and on the covers, if any) a title distinct from that of the Document, and from those of previous versions (which should, if there were any, be listed in the History section of the Document). You may use the same title as a previous version if the original publisher of that version gives permission.

2. List on the Title Page, as authors, one or more persons or entities responsible for authorship of the modifications in the Modified Version, together with at least

five of the principal authors of the Document (all of its principal authors, if it has fewer than five), unless they release you from this requirement.

3. State on the Title page the name of the publisher of the Modified Version, as the publisher.

4. Preserve all the copyright notices of the Document.

5. Add an appropriate copyright notice for your modifications adjacent to the other copyright notices.

6. Include, immediately after the copyright notices, a license notice giving the public permission to use the Modified Version under the terms of this License, in the form shown in the Addendum below.

7. Preserve in that license notice the full lists of Invariant Sections and required Cover Texts given in the Document's license notice.

8. Include an unaltered copy of this License.

9. Preserve the section Entitled "History", Preserve its Title, and add to it an item stating at least the title, year, new authors, and publisher of the Modified Version as given on the Title Page. If there is no section Entitled "History" in the Document, create one stating the title, year, authors, and publisher of the Document as given on its Title Page, then add an item describing the Modified Version as stated in the previous sentence.

10. Preserve the network location, if any, given in the Document for public access to a Transparent copy of the Document, and likewise the network locations given in the Document for previous versions it was based on. These may be placed in the "History" section. You may omit a network location for a work that was published at least four years before the Document itself, or if the original publisher of the version it refers to gives permission.

11. For any section Entitled "Acknowledgments" or "Dedications", Preserve the Title of the section, and preserve in the section all the substance and tone of each of the contributor acknowledgments and/or dedications given therein.

12. Preserve all the Invariant Sections of the Document, unaltered in their text and in their titles. Section numbers or the equivalent are not considered part of the section titles.

13. Delete any section Entitled "Endorsements". Such a section may not be included in the Modified Version.

14. Do not retitle any existing section to be Entitled "Endorsements" or to conflict in title with any Invariant Section.

15. Preserve any Warranty Disclaimers.

   If the Modified Version includes new front-matter sections or appendices that qualify as Secondary Sections and contain no material copied from the Document, you may at your option designate some or all of these sections as invariant. To do this, add their titles to the list of Invariant Sections in the Modified

Version's license notice. These titles must be distinct from any other section titles.

You may add a section Entitled "Endorsements", provided it contains nothing but endorsements of your Modified Version by various parties—for example, statements of peer review or that the text has been approved by an organization as the authoritative definition of a standard.

You may add a passage of up to five words as a Front-Cover Text, and a passage of up to 25 words as a Back-Cover Text, to the end of the list of Cover Texts in the Modified Version. Only one passage of Front-Cover Text and one of Back-Cover Text may be added by (or through arrangements made by) any one entity. If the Document already includes a cover text for the same cover, previously added by you or by arrangement made by the same entity you are acting on behalf of, you may not add another; but you may replace the old one, on explicit permission from the previous publisher that added the old one.

The author(s) and publisher(s) of the Document do not by this License give permission to use their names for publicity for or to assert or imply endorsement of any Modified Version.

5. COMBINING DOCUMENTS

You may combine the Document with other documents released under this License, under the terms defined in section 4 above for modified versions, provided that you include in the combination all of the Invariant Sections of all of the original documents, unmodified, and list them all as Invariant Sections of your combined work in its license notice, and that you preserve all their Warranty Disclaimers.

The combined work need only contain one copy of this License, and multiple identical Invariant Sections may be replaced with a single copy. If there are multiple Invariant Sections with the same name but different contents, make the title of each such section unique by adding at the end of it, in parentheses, the name of the original author or publisher of that section if known, or else a unique number. Make the same adjustment to the section titles in the list of Invariant Sections in the license notice of the combined work.

In the combination, you must combine any sections Entitled "History" in the various original documents, forming one section Entitled "History"; likewise combine any sections Entitled "Acknowledgements", and any sections Entitled "Dedications". You must delete all sections Entitled "Endorsements".

6. COLLECTIONS OF DOCUMENTS

You may make a collection consisting of the Document and other documents released under this License, and replace the individual copies of this License in the various documents with a single copy that is included in the collection, provided that you follow the rules of this License for verbatim copying of each of the documents in all other respects.

You may extract a single document from such a collection, and distribute it individually under this License, provided you insert a copy of this License into the extracted document, and follow this License in all other respects regarding verbatim copying of that document.

7. AGGREGATION WITH INDEPENDENT WORKS

A compilation of the Document or its derivatives with other separate and independent documents or works, in or on a volume of a storage or distribution medium, is called an "aggregate" if the copyright resulting from the compilation is not used to limit the legal rights of the compilation's users beyond what the individual works permit. When the Document is included as an aggregate, this License does not apply to the other works in the aggregate which are not themselves derivative works of the Document.

If the Cover Text requirement of section 3 is applicable to these copies of the Document, then if the Document is less than one half of the entire aggregate, the Document's Cover Texts may be placed on covers that bracket the Document within the aggregate, or the electronic equivalent of covers if the Document is in electronic form. Otherwise they must appear on printed covers that bracket the whole aggregate.

8. TRANSLATION

Translation is considered a kind of modification, so you may distribute translations of the Document under the terms of section 4. Replacing Invariant Sections with translations requires special permission from their copyright holders, but you may include translations of some or all Invariant Sections in addition to the original versions of these Invariant Sections. You may include a translation of this License, and all the license notices in the Document, and any Warranty Disclaimers, provided that you also include the original English version of this License and the original versions of those notices and disclaimers. In case of a disagreement between the translation and the original version of this License or a notice or disclaimer, the original version will prevail.

If a section in the Document is Entitled "Acknowledgements", "Dedications", or "History", the requirement (section 4) to Preserve its Title (section 1) will typically require changing the actual title.

9. TERMINATION

You may not copy, modify, sublicense, or distribute the Document except as expressly provided for under this License. Any other attempt to copy, modify, sublicense or distribute the Document is void, and will automatically terminate your rights under this License. However, parties who have received copies, or rights, from you under this License will not have their licenses terminated so long as such parties remain in full compliance.

10. FUTURE REVISIONS OF THIS LICENSE

The Free Software Foundation may publish new, revised versions of the GNU Free Documentation License from time to time. Such new versions will be similar in spirit to the present version, but may differ in detail to address new problems or concerns. See *http://www.gnu.org/copyleft/*.

Each version of the License is given a distinguishing version number. If the Document specifies that a particular numbered version of this License "or any later version" applies to it, you have the option of following the terms and conditions either of that specified version or of any later version that has been published (not as a draft) by the Free Software Foundation. If the Document does not specify a version number of this License, you may choose any version ever published (not as a draft) by the Free Software Foundation.

Index

Symbols

__MSBROWSE__ resource entry, 16, 229
. (period)
    NetBIOS names and, 14
    (see also dot files)
%$ variable, 192

Numbers

127.0.0.1 (localhost), 73
    bind interfaces only option, 208

A

%a variable, 143, 192
    variable substitution, 191
abort shutdown script option (smb.conf
        file), 401
Access Control Entries (ACEs), 31, 253
Access Control Lists (see ACLs)
access control options, 287–288
access, controlling (see ACLs; controlling
        access to shares)
accounts (see computer accounts, adding;
        users)
ACLs, 30
    configuration options, 260–262
    inheriting, 416
    installing Samba with support for, 495
    mapping to Unix permissions, 426
    POSIX.1e, 259
    support in Samba 2.2, 37
    Unix, 259
    versus Unix file permissions, 31
    Windows NT/2000/XP, 165, 253–262

Active Directory
    Samba 2.2, 34, 121
    Samba 3.0, 34
    server, specifying, 402
    time synchronization and, 340
adapters, 69
add machine script option (smb.conf
        file), 402
add printer command option (smb.conf
        file), 401
add share command option (smb.conf
        file), 402
add user script option (smb.conf file), 159,
        402
admin users option (smb.conf file), 285, 287,
        402
admin users (see root accounts)
administrator (see domain administrator)
ads server option (smb.conf file), 402
AFS (Andrew Filesystem), installing Samba
        with support for, 495
Albitz, Paul, 383
algorithmic rid base option (smb.conf
        file), 402
allow hosts option (smb.conf file), 403
allow trusted domains option (smb.conf
        file), 403
analogX Atomic TimeSync, 340
announce as option (smb.conf file), 234, 403
announce version option (smb.conf
        file), 235, 403
anonymous
    restricting access, 434
    (see also guest access)

We'd like to hear your suggestions for improving our indexes. Send email to *index@oreilly.com*.

/etc/passwd file, creating entries manually, 127
/etc/printcap.local file, 330
/etc/resolv.conf file, 73, 220
Ethereal (SMB sniffer), 20, 361
exec option (smb.conf file), 412
executable file permission bit, 248
ext2/ext3 filesystem, 37

F

fake directory create times option (smb.conf file), 342, 412
fake oplocks option (smb.conf file), 273, 412
FAQs, Samba, 391
fault tree, troubleshooting Samba, 362–391
file locking (see locks and oplocks)
file permissions
    executable bit, 248
    on MS-DOS and Unix, 245–253
    options, 250–253
    setting in Windows NT/2000/XP, 165
    setting maximum allowable, 406
    Unix permission bits summary, 247
    Unix permissions versus ACLs, 31
    versus ACLs, 31
file transfer using smbclient, 170
filenames
    conventions, 262
        (see also name mangling)
    representing and resolving in Samba, 264
Filesystem Hierarchy Standard, 495
filesystem options, 243–245
findsmb program, 40, 455
firewall configuration, 60
fmask option (sbmount), 176
follow symlinks option (smb.conf file), 242, 243, 412
force create mode option (smb.conf file), 251, 412
force directory mode option (smb.conf file), 251, 413
force directory security mode option (smb.conf file), 262, 413
force group option (smb.conf file), 249, 251, 413
force security mode option (smb.conf file), 261, 413
force unknown acl user option (smb.conf file), 413
force user option (smb.conf file), 249, 251, 413
Frisch, Æleen, 325

fstab file, warning about editing, 177
fstype option (smb.conf file), 350, 413

G

%G variable, 192
%g variable, 192
gcc binaries, 44
get command, 170
getwd cache option (smb.conf file), 243, 414
[global] section (smb.conf file), 193
GNU configure script (see configure script)
GNU Free Documentation License, 511–518
Google, 392
group ID (GID), 31
group option (smb.conf file), 414
grouppol.inf file, 153
groups
    additional information, 16
    overriding a user's normal group membership, 413
    setting a group share in smb.conf file, 283
    system group file, 283
    (see also workgroups; SMB, groups)
guest access, 286
guest account option (smb.conf file), 286, 288, 414
guest ok option (smb.conf file), 286, 414
guest only option (smb.conf file), 288, 414

H

%H variable, 192, 283
%h variable, 192
hide dot files option (smb.conf file), 240, 244, 414
hide files option (smb.conf file), 241, 244, 414
hide local users option (smb.conf file), 415
hide unreadable option (smb.conf file), 415
hiding files, 240–242
h-node (NetBios node type), 13
home directory, setting, 420
homedir map option (smb.conf file), 281, 415
[homes] share (smb.conf file), 125, 194, 233, 284
    peculiarities with, 284
host msdfs option (smb.conf file), 280, 415
hostname, defending, 12
hosts allow option (smb.conf file), 204–207, 415

About the Authors

Jay Ts is a system administrator and programmer with many years of experience working with several versions of Unix and other operating systems. Nowadays he works as an independent consultant out of his home in Sedona, Arizona. When he is not busy reading the Samba mailing lists and learning about new computer technology, Jay might be analyzing stock market behavior, meditating, playing around in his recording studio, or hiking in the wilderness near his home.

Robert Eckstein enjoys dabbling with just about anything related to computers. From rendering to electronic commerce to compiler construction to fuzzy logic, most of his friends agree that Robert spends far too much time in front of a computer screen. At O'Reilly, Robert works mostly on Java books (notably *Java Swing*, Second Edition) and is also responsible for the *XML Pocket Reference*, Second Edition, and *Webmaster in a Nutshell*, Second Edition. In his spare time, he has been known to provide online coverage for popular conferences. He also writes articles for *Java-World* magazine. Robert holds bachelor's degrees in computer science and communications from Trinity University. In the past, he has worked for the USAA insurance company and, more recently, has spent four years with Motorola's cellular software division. He now lives in Austin, Texas, with his newlywed wife, Michelle. They hope to adopt a talking puppy soon.

David Collier-Brown is a consulting systems integrator, currently working for the performance and engineering group at Sun Opcom in Toronto. In his spare time, he reads assiduously, keeps score for his wife's baseball team, and, in the two weeks of the local summer, sails from Toronto's outer harbor.

Colophon

Our look is the result of reader comments, our own experimentation, and feedback from distribution channels. Distinctive covers complement our distinctive approach to technical topics, breathing personality and life into potentially dry subjects.

The animal on the cover of *Using Samba*, Second Edition, is an African ground hornbill (*Bucorvus cafer*). This type of bird is one of 50 hornbill species. The African ground hornbill is a medium- to large-size bird characterized by a bright red waddle under a very long beak, dark-colored body and wings, long eyelashes, and short legs. Like all hornbills, it has a casque, a large but lightweight growth on the top of its beak, which grows more folds as the bird ages. It is the only ground-dwelling species of hornbill, though it is able to fly when necessary. It lives in the grasslands of Southern and Eastern Africa and nests in the foliage of dense trees, not in nest holes in the ground as other hornbills do. Its diet includes mostly fruit, as well as large insects and small mammals. The African ground hornbill is considered to be sacred by many Africans, and as such, this bird is part of many legends and superstitions.

Darren Kelly was the production editor, Jeffrey Holcomb was the copyeditor, and Audrey Doyle was the proofreader for *Using Samba*, Second Edition. Linley Dolby, Colleen Gorman, and Claire Cloutier provided quality control. Reg Aubry, Phil Dangler, Genevieve d'Entremont, and Judy Hoer provided production support. Julie Hawks wrote the index.

Edie Freedman designed the cover of this book. The cover image is a 19th-century engraving from the Dover Pictorial Archive. Emma Colby produced the cover layout with QuarkXPress 4.1 using Adobe's ITC Garamond font.

David Futato designed the interior layout. This book was converted by Mike Sierra to FrameMaker 5.5.6 with a format conversion tool created by Erik Ray, Jason McIntosh, Neil Walls, and Mike Sierra that uses Perl and XML technologies. The text font is Linotype Birka; the heading font is Adobe Myriad Condensed; and the code font is LucasFont's TheSans Mono Condensed. The illustrations that appear in the book were produced by Robert Romano and Jessamyn Read using Macromedia FreeHand 9 and Adobe Photoshop 6. The tip and warning icons were drawn by Christopher Bing. This colophon was written by Nicole Arigo.

Other Titles Available from O'Reilly

Linux

Linux in a Nutshell, 4th Edition

By Ellen Siever, Stephen Figgins
& Aaron Weber
4th Edition June 2003 (est.)
800 pages (est.), ISBN 0-596-00482-6

Linux in a Nutshell features many new commands that appear in major distributions, along with boot parameters, common configuration issues for the GNOME and KDE desktops, and the RPM and Debian package managers. New topics for the fourth edition incorporate GRUB (the bootloader used in new versions of Red Hat), vim (a popular enhancement to the vi editor), and configuration options for the Postfix mail server.

Running Linux, 4th Edition

By Matt Welsh, Matthias Kalle
Dalheimer, Terry Dawson
& Lar Kaufman
4th Edition December 2002
692 pages, ISBN 0-596-00272-6

After six years, this classic is still recommended by knowledgeable Linux users over any other guide. Everything you need for understanding, installing, and using the Linux operating system is explained in detail. In the new fourth edition, *Running Linux* delves deeper into installation, configuring the windowing system, system administration, and networking. Several new topics about laptops, cameras and scanners, sound and multimedia, ADSL, the GNOME desktop, MySQL, PHP, and configuring an NFS server are included.

The Root of All Evil

By Illiad
1st Edition August 2001
144 pages, ISBN 0-596-00193-2

It's back to Columbia Internet, "the friendliest, hardest-working, and most neurotic little Internet Service Provider in the world," for our third installment from the hit online comic, *User Friendly*. The cast: hardcore techies, self-absorbed sales staff, well-meaning execs, and assorted almost-humans. The background: too little office space, warring operating systems, and eternally clueless customers.

Practical PostgreSQL

By Command Prompt, Inc
1st Edition January 2002
636 pages, ISBN 1-56592-846-6

Practical PostgreSQL is a fast-paced, business-oriented guide to installing, config-uring, and running Post-greSQL. Readers will find all the basics here, such as how to create databases and objects, such as tables, within those databases. Or they can go straight to advanced topics like inheritance, replication, user management, and backup and recovery. The book also introduces the PL/pgSQL procedural language. Finally, a complete PostgreSQL command reference makes "looking it up" easy.

Learning Red Hat Linux, 3rd Edition

By Bill McCarty
3rd Edition March 2003
336 pages, ISBN 0-596-00469-9

The third edition of *Learning Red Hat Linux* guides you through the process of installing and running Red Hat Linux on your PC. Written in a friendly, easy-to-understand style, this book contains all you need to get started, including the complete Red Hat 8.0 distribution on CDs. With new tutorials covering OpenOffice Tools and the desktop, this book is excellent for first-time Linux users who want to install the operating system on a new PC or convert an existing system to Linux.

Peer-to-Peer: Harnessing the Power of Disruptive Technologies

Edited by Andy Oram
1st Edition March 2001
448 pages, ISBN 0-596-00110-X

This book presents the goals that drive the developers of the best-known peer-to-peer systems, the problems they've faced, and the technical solutions they've found. The contributors are leading developers of well-known peer-to-peer systems, such as Gnutella, Freenet, Jabber, Popular Power, SETI@Home, Red Rover, Publius, Free Haven, Groove Networks, and Reputation Technologies. Topics include metadata, performance, trust, resource allocation, reputation, security, and gateways between systems.

O'REILLY®

To order: 800-998-9938 • *order@oreilly.com* • *www.oreilly.com*
Online editions of most O'Reilly titles are available by subscription at *safari.oreilly.com*
Also available at most retail and online bookstores.

Other Titles Available from O'Reilly

Unix System Administration

Essential System Administration, 3rd Edition

By Æleen Frisch
3rd Edition August 2002
1176 pages, ISBN 0-596-00343-9

This is the definitive practical guide for Unix system administration, covering all the fundamental and essential tasks required to run such divergent Unix systems as Solaris, Linux, AIX, IRIX, BSD and more. Beginners and experienced administrators alike will quickly be able to apply its principles and advice to solve everyday problems.

Essential System Administration Pocket Reference

By Æleen Frisch
1st Edition November 2002
144 pages, ISBN 0-596-00449-4

This pocket reference brings together all the important Unix and Linux system administration information in a single compact volume. Not only are all of the important administrative commands covered, but this reference also includes the locations and formats of important configuration files (including both general system databases like the password and group files as well as the configuration files for major subsystems like DNS, DHCP and sendmail).

Managing NFS and NIS, 2nd Edition

By Hal Stern, Mike Eisler &
Ricardo Labiaga
2nd Edition July 2001
510 pages, 1-56592-510-6

This long-awaited new edition of a classic, now updated for NFS Version 3 and based on Solaris 8, shows how to set up and manage a network filesystem installation. *Managing NFS and NIS* is the only practical book devoted entirely to NFS and the distributed database NIS; it's a "must-have" for anyone interested in Unix networking.

The Perl CD Bookshelf, Version 3.0

By O'Reilly & Associates, Inc.
Version 3.0 September 2002
768 pages, Features CD-ROM
ISBN 0-596-00389-7

We've updated this best selling product with the electronic versions of 7 popular Perl books. Included are the second edition of *Perl in a Nutshell* (paperback version included), the third editions of *Learning Perl* and *Programming Perl*, the *Perl Cookbook*, and 3 new titles: *Perl & XML, Perl & LWP*, and *Mastering Perl/Tk*. Formatted in HTML, *The Perl CD Bookshelf*, Version 3.0, can be accessed with any web browser and includes a master index for the entire library.

Programming with Qt, 2nd Edition

By Matthias Kalle Dalheimer
2nd Edition January 2002
520 pages, ISBN 0-596-00064-2

Take full advantage of Qt, the powerful, easy-to-use, cross-platform GUI toolkit. Completely updated for Qt Version 3.0, Programming Qt guides you through the steps of writing your first Qt application. It's also a reference to the what, how, and why of every GUI element in Qt. And it covers advanced topics like 2D transformations, drag-and-drop, and custom image file filters.

Unix Backup & Recovery

By W. Curtis Preston
1st Edition November 1999
734 pages, Includes CD-ROM
ISBN 1-56592-642-0

This guide provides a complete overview of all facets of Unix backup and recovery and offers practical, affordable backup and recovery solutions for environments of all sizes and budgets. It explains everything from freely available backup systems to large-scale commercial utilities.

O'REILLY®

To order: 800-998-9938 • *order@oreilly.com* • *www.oreilly.com*
Online editions of most O'Reilly titles are available by subscription at *safari.oreilly.com*
Also available at most retail and online bookstores.

How to stay in touch with O'Reilly

1. Visit our award-winning web site

http://www.oreilly.com/

★ "Top 100 Sites on the Web"—PC Magazine
★ CIO Magazine's Web Business 50 Awards

Our web site contains a library of comprehensive product information (including book excerpts and tables of contents), downloadable software, background articles, interviews with technology leaders, links to relevant sites, book cover art, and more. File us in your bookmarks or favorites!

2. Join our email mailing lists

Sign up to get email announcements of new books and conferences, special offers, and O'Reilly Network technology newsletters at:

http://elists.oreilly.com

It's easy to customize your free elists subscription so you'll get exactly the O'Reilly news you want.

3. Get examples from our books

To find example files for a book, go to:

http://www.oreilly.com/catalog

select the book, and follow the "Examples" link.

4. Work with us

Check out our web site for current employment opportunities:

http://jobs.oreilly.com/

5. Register your book

Register your book at:

http://register.oreilly.com

6. Contact us

O'Reilly & Associates, Inc.
1005 Gravenstein Hwy North
Sebastopol, CA 95472 USA
TEL: 707-827-7000 or 800-998-9938
     (6am to 5pm PST)
FAX: 707-829-0104

order@oreilly.com
For answers to problems regarding your order or our products. To place a book order online visit:

http://www.oreilly.com/order_new/

catalog@oreilly.com
To request a copy of our latest catalog.

booktech@oreilly.com
For book content technical questions or corrections.

corporate@oreilly.com
For educational, library, government, and corporate sales.

proposals@oreilly.com
To submit new book proposals to our editors and product managers.

international@oreilly.com
For information about our international distributors or translation queries. For a list of our distributors outside of North America check out:

http://international.oreilly.com/distributors.html

adoption@oreilly.com
For information about academic use of O'Reilly books, visit:

http://academic.oreilly.com

O'REILLY®

To order: 800-998-9938 • *order@oreilly.com* • *www.oreilly.com*
Online editions of most O'Reilly titles are available by subscription at *safari.oreilly.com*
Also available at most retail and online bookstores.